The Handbook of
SOCIAL WELFARE MANAGEMENT

The Handbook of
SOCIAL WELFARE MANAGEMENT

Edited by
Rino J. Patti

Sage Publications, Inc.
International Educational and Professional Publisher
Thousand Oaks ▪ London ▪ New Delhi

For information:

Sage Publications, Inc.
2455 Teller Road
Thousand Oaks, California 91320
E-mail: order@sagepub.com

Sage Publications Ltd.
6 Bonhill Street
London EC2A 4PU
United Kingdom

Sage Publications India Pvt. Ltd.
M-32 Market
Greater Kailash I
New Delhi 110 048 India

Printed in the United States of America

Library of Congress Cataloging-in-Publication Data

This book is printed on acid-free paper.

Main entry under title:

The handbook of social welfare management / edited by Rino J. Patti.
      p. cm.
Includes bibliographical references and index.
  ISBN 0-7619-1470-6 (cl.: alk. paper) — ISBN 0-7919-1471-4 (pbk.: alk. paper)
  1. Social work administration. 2. Social welfare—Management. 3. Public welfare—Management. I. Patti, Rino J. II. Title.
  HV41 .H325 2000
  361'.0068—dc21   99-050748

00 01 02 03 04 05 06 7 6 5 4 3 2 1

Acquisition Editor:	Nancy S. Hale
Production Editor:	Elly Korn
Editorial Assistant:	Cindy Bear
Typesetter:	Danielle Delahunty
Indexer:	Virgil Diodato
Cover Designer:	Candice Harman

Contents

Preface   ix

**Part I. What Is Social Welfare Management?
Mapping the Field of Practice**   1

  1. The Landscape of Social Welfare Management   3
     Rino J. Patti

  2. Social Work and Social Welfare Administration:
     A Historical Perspective   27
     David M. Austin

  3. The Environmental Context of Social Welfare Administration   55
     Lawrence L. Martin

  4. Administrative Ethics   69
     Frederic G. Reamer

Part II. Understanding Social Welfare Organizations   87

  5. Social Welfare Administration and Organizational Theory   89
     Yeheskel Hasenfeld

6. Structural and Fiscal Characteristics of Social Service Agencies 113
   Margaret Gibelman

7. Agency-Environment Relations: Understanding Task Environments 133
   Hillel Schmid

8. Organizational Structure and Performance 155
   David F. Gillespie

9. Motivating Work Performance in Social Services 169
   Diane Vinokur-Kaplan and Daniel Bogin

10. Organizational Climate and Culture 195
    Charles Glisson

11. The Individual in the Organization: The Impact
    of Human Service Workers' Attributes on Job Response 219
    Gary F. Koeske and Randi Koeske

**Part III. Dimensions of Social Welfare Management:
Issues, Functions, and Tasks**   **243**

12. What Managers Do and Why They Do It 247
    David Menefee

13. Managing for Service Outcomes: The Critical Role of Information 267
    John Poertner

14. Interorganizational Collaboration in the Task Environment 283
    Catherine Foster Alter

15. The Manager as Leader 303
    David Bargal

16. Managing Information for Decision Making 321
    Dick Schoech

17. Managing the Planning Process 341
    Michael J. Austin and Jeffrey R. Solomon

18. Manager as Resource Developer 361
    Philip McCallion

19. Financial Management 377
    Mark Ezell

20. Managing Personnel   395
    Peter J. Pecora and Michael Wagner

21. Managing for Diversity and Empowerment in Social Services   425
    Alfreda P. Iglehart

22. Initiating and Implementing Change   445
    Felice Davidson Perlmutter

Part IV. Managing in Fields of Service: Issues and Challenges   459

23. Points of Tension: Mental Health Administration
    in a Managed Care Environment   461
    Barbara J. Friesen

24. Services for Families and Children:
    The Changing Context and New Challenges   481
    Marie Weil

25. Health Care and Social Work: Dilemmas and Opportunities   511
    Andrew Weissman and Gary Rosenberg

26. Aging   521
    Kathleen H. Wilber

Author Index   535

Subject Index   554

About the Authors   572

Preface

The invitation to edit a handbook on social welfare management came as I was leaving a 9-year tenure as Dean of the School of Social Work at the University of Southern California. In the transition back to the academic life, I looked forward to resuming my work on the relationships between management practice, organizational processes, and consumer outcomes in the human services, a subject that had been a central preoccupation for much of my academic career. When this opportunity presented itself, however, I quickly took up the challenge, because it seemed to me that this was a propitious time to attempt a broad and integrated treatment of social welfare management, one that would seek to pull together the developing but still scattered scholarship on this subject that has emerged over the last two decades. Moreover, it seemed to me that the scholarship on organizations had not been used to inform the general practice literature and that neither of these was adequately reflected in management writing in particular fields of service. This project seemed a wonderful opportunity to facilitate a convergence between these scholarly domains.

Since the 1970s, scholarship and education in social welfare management have developed rapidly along three related fronts. In public policy, increased attention to the organization and management of social welfare came in the wake of growing social disorganization and massive public investments in social interventions to address these problems. The need for policy makers to know more about how to implement policy and make it work in a burgeoning social welfare system intersected naturally with increased attention to management development, because managers are key players in the administration of social policy. In social work, where a significant portion of the profession has always been concerned with the administration of social services, that decade marked the beginning of serious efforts to construct a theoretical and empirical basis for the practice and to systematically prepare social workers for careers in this arena. In the years since the 1970s, largely because of the growing interest in social program intervention and the growing role of voluntary agencies in the delivery of public policy, a broad interdisciplinary interest in nonprofit organizations has also developed (Drucker, 1990; Herman, 1994), including focuses on their missions, distinctive characteristics, management, and interaction with the public sector. Much of this work has involved nonprofit social welfare organizations and their management.

Despite the rich and varied scholarship that emerged from this broad interest in social welfare management, there have been few efforts to assemble an integrated state-of-the-art assessment of administration in the field of social welfare. Indeed, since the publication of Slavin's (1985) ambitious two-volume edited book on management practice, there have been no books of similar scope. An excellent volume by Herman on nonprofit leadership and management was published in 1994, but this was devoted to management in all fields of nonprofit activity and not specifically to social welfare in both public and private sectors, which is the central concern of this book. Since Slavin's book, there have been significant textbook contributions to leadership and technology in social welfare management (Edwards, Yankey, Alpeter, 1998; Gummer, 1990; Gummer & McCallion, 1995) and some important insights into the nature and dynamics of human service organizations (Austin, 1988; Hasenfeld, 1992). Each of these has necessarily focused on aspects of management or organization and not on the relationships between them.

This volume draws on and seeks to integrate these important contributions but also attempts to paint on a larger canvas. With the benefit of space and the expertise of scholars and practitioners whose work has touched virtually every corner of the social welfare management landscape, we have had the luxury of exploring this field of practice in historical and institutional contexts, assembling the latest theory and research on human service organizations and how it might inform the design and operation of social agencies, critically examining the broad array of roles and functions that social welfare managers perform, and addressing management issues and challenges that occur in several fields such as mental health, health, family and children's services, and services to the aged. In presenting this multidimensional treatment of social welfare management, the Handbook critically examines the current state of knowledge about organizations and best management practices and raises important questions that will challenge future practitioners and scholars in the field.

The Handbook is organized in four major sections. Section 1 contains four chapters that seek to define the boundaries of social welfare management, its historical development as a practice and a field of inquiry, the social and economic conditions in society that are likely to shape this practice in the new millennium, and key ethical issues confronting practitioners. As a whole, this section is about past and future forces that shape the values and priorities of managers in the social welfare sector. Section 2 presents several perspectives on the behavior of human service organizations, with a particular emphasis on the relationships between organizational conditions and processes and effectiveness. In these chapters, human service organizations are analyzed from several perspectives, including interaction with their environments, their structures and climates, their interpersonal processes, and the characteristics of individual employees. Many of these chapters have parallel chapters regarding various management functions in Section 3, and these can be read profitably as companion pieces. Section 3, the longest in the Handbook, is concerned with application or the ways in which managers perform the many roles and functions that are essential to their jobs. These chapters aim to provide concrete guidance on how to accomplish important facets of managers' responsibility and how doing so makes social agencies more effective. Finally, in Section 4, chapter authors review demographic, policy, and technology trends occurring in several fields of social and health services that will provide the strategic context for management in the decades ahead. Here, the authors do not dwell on the particulars of management but rather explore what changes in the policy, funding, and structure of service systems will mean for how managers must strategically position their agencies to deal with new threats and opportunities.

The editor of a book like this relies essentially on the talents of others, the authors who generously contribute their time and scholarship to an enterprise for which they receive little extrinsic reward. I have enjoyed and benefitted enormously from my interactions with these most able and prolific scholars, and I feel a special pride in what they have here brought to the professional and academic communities. Jim Nageotte, until recently at Sage, provided the original idea for the Handbook series, of which this is one volume, and was wonderfully supportive and encouraging throughout the project. Heidi Van Middlesworth at Sage provided gentle but persistent reminders about deadlines and deliverables and saw to it that the rough product made its way toward a finished form. Finally, with age, one is ever more mindful of how powerfully early experiences shape later life. In this spirit, I dedicate this book to Ro and Jo, who provided safe harbor and inspiration in turbulent times.

Rino J. Patti

REFERENCES

Austin, D. (1988). *The political economy of human service programs.* Greenwich CT: JAI Press.

Drucker, P. F. (1990). *Managing nonprofit organizations: Practices and principles.* New York: Harper Collins.

Edwards, R. L., Yankey, J. A., & Altpeter, M. A. (1998). *Skills for effective management of nonprofit organizations.* Washington, DC: NASW.

Gummer, B. (1990). *The politics of social administration: Managing organizational politics in social agencies.* Englewood Cliffs, NJ: Prentice Hall.

Gummer, B., & McCallion, P. (Eds.). (1995). *Total quality management in the social services.* Albany, NY: Rockefeller College, University at Albany, State University of New York.

Hasenfeld, Y. (1992). The nature of human service organizations. In Y. Hasenfeld (Ed.), *Human services as complex organizations* (pp. 3-23). Newbury Park, CA: Sage Publications.

Herman, R. D. (Ed.). (1994). *The Jossey-Bass handbook of non profit leadership.* San Francisco: Jossey-Bass.

Slavin, S. (Ed.). (1985). *Social administration: The management of the social services.* New York: Haworth Press.

PART I

What Is Social Welfare Management? Mapping the Field of Practice

This introductory section provides the reader with a broad view of the landscape of social welfare administration in historical, contemporary, and future dimensions. The intent is to offer a conceptual map of this field of practice, including its purposes, the forces that have and will continue to shape management practice, and the ethical boundaries within which administration is practiced.

Chapter 1 discusses the parameters of social welfare management and its distinctive characteristics as a variant of management. Included here is a discussion of the terms *administration* and *management* and their relationship to social welfare. The chapter argues that although social welfare management draws o50n general management for much of its conceptual and technological foundation, it differs from management in other fields in a number of ways. The reader may wish to read this chapter along with Chapter 12, by David Menefee, which also lays out the distinctive elements of social welfare management.

Chapter 2, by David Austin, provides a detailed analysis of the emergence of administration in the context of social welfare institutions over the last two centuries. Austin shows that ideas about how to manage emerged in the crucible of day-to-day practice in voluntary, nonprofit, and public sectors and were later refined and rationalized as management theory was formalized. The often ambivalent relationship between the profession of social work and social welfare management is also discussed.

Lawrence L. Martin's chapter on the future of social welfare management seeks to identify current and prospective trends in society that will shape how management is practiced. After examining major demographic, political, and economic changes, Martin postulates the likely directions of management practice in the near future and their implications for social welfare.

The decisions and practices of social welfare managers have always been fraught with ethical dilemmas and promise to be more so in the future. In Chapter 4, Frederic G. Reamer discusses common ethical issues, suggests some strategies for addressing them, and proposes ways in which administrators can minimize ethical problems.

CHAPTER ONE

The Landscape of Social Welfare Management

RINO J. PATTI

Management, or what managers do or cause to happen, is critical to the development, implementation, and effectiveness of social welfare services. People may argue about the precise nature of the manager's contribution to these objectives, or how managers can best achieve them, but there is little question that managers are central players in the social welfare enterprise. For better and sometimes for worse, managers matter. Because they play such a central role in this large and important institutional sector, it is crucial that we understand what management is and is not, what managers do, how and why they do it, and with what consequences. This Handbook is intended to provide a broad and critical examination of these questions.

The purpose of this chapter is to identify the landscape of management practice in social welfare (what we shall also call human services). We will discuss the terminology used to describe social welfare management, ways in which it varies from management in other sectors, and selected issues that affect how this practice is carried out and with what consequences for consumers. Although managers in social welfare come from a variety of professions, and several disciplinary perspectives now inform the practice, we shall be primarily concerned with the role of social workers in this field. Social workers remain the primary source of management personnel in social welfare, so the quality and preparedness of this professional group is a key concern.

MANAGEMENT AND ADMINISTRATION: USAGE AND IDEOLOGY

In this Handbook, the terms *management* and *administration* are used interchangeably. Efforts have been made to distinguish the two (Patti, 1983), but these distinctions have not been widely adopted. Historically, in social work and in the nonprofit social agency field, the term administration has enjoyed wider use than management because the latter suggested a practice oriented to control and profit, which was anathema in social welfare at the time. Indeed, until the 1980s, most books and *Encyclopedia of Social Work* titles on this subject used the term administration (Atwater, 1940; Spencer, 1959; Street, 1931; Trecker, 1977) to describe practice in social agencies, public and private.

In the late 1970s and early 1980s, the usage became more mixed. For example, in the 1980s and early 1990s, a number of widely used texts on administration used this designation (Patti, 1983; Perlmutter & Slavin, 1980; Rapp & Poertner, 1992), but many others employed *management* (Christian & Hannah, 1983; Crow & Odewahn, 1987; Keys & Ginsberg, 1988; Weiner, 1982). In the 1990s, management has become the preferred term to describe the practice in social welfare. Most recent books on the subject have management in the title (Brody, 1993; Edwards, Yankey, & Altpeter, 1998; Weinbach, 1998), and *management* is increasingly used by social workers to describe what they do, for example, the National Network of Social Work Managers.

Was this simply an arbitrary change in language or did it reflect something about the evolution of underlying belief systems? One can only speculate, but it appears that the change may have reflected two interrelated processes.

During the 1970s, the size and scope of the social welfare enterprise experienced major growth, and with it, a growing interest on the part of policymakers in how to improve the performance of these organizations and make them more accountable. As policymakers and agency leaders sought to address these issues, they naturally looked to the experience of business, both here and abroad (for example, in Japan) to inform their efforts. Strategies and technologies such as management by objectives, Total Quality Management, cost accounting, marketing, and strategic planning became part of the language, if not always the practice of social agencies. Although scholars and practitioners in social welfare have cautioned against the indiscriminate adoption of such technology without careful attention to its impact (Gregiore, Rapp, & Poertner, 1995; Patti, 1975), the pace of dissemination appears to have quickened. As these ways of thinking about the operation of social agencies became normalized, it is not surprising that social agency administrators would begin to think of themselves as managers, sharing many of the same tools and challenges as their counterparts in the for-profit sector.

The process of technology dissemination was facilitated when management theorists such as Peter Drucker (1990) and Richard Cyert (1975) began to turn their attention to the nonprofit "service" institution, and other business scholars adapted technologies to social welfare (Anthony & Young, 1994; Kotler, 1982). Although they recognized essential differences between for-profit and nonprofit organizations and cautioned against "running the nonprofit like a business," Drucker and others were nonetheless instrumental in showing how tools developed in the business sector could be usefully adapted to nonprofit organizations. The association of business management with bottom-line, command and control organizations was largely a thing of the past by the 1990s.

Whether the term used is management or administration, the word is applied in several ways. Management/administration is often employed to describe the particular person or persons high in the organization's hierarchy whose policies and decisions constitute a leadership regime, as in the phrase, "the management of this agency is fiscally conservative, or dynamic, or visionary."

Management/administration is also used to address the totality of processes and functions that are performed throughout the organization to accomplish its goals. In this sense, the administration of the agency is characterized as a "system of coordinated and cooperative effort" that extends beyond the responsibilities of managers to include all those who have a stake in the performance of the agency (Stein, 1970; Weinbach, 1998). This concept of management stresses the notion of collective responsibility, "wherein each person (i.e., role), every functional entity in the agency, plays a vital part in the administrative process" (Patti, 1983, p. 25).

Finally, management/administration refers to a set of roles and tasks that are largely the province of people in middle and upper levels of organizations. In this meaning, the manager or administrator engages in a purposeful method of practice that is aimed at helping the organization to develop a mission, acquire resources, and use them productively in the interest of meeting the needs of consumers and other important stakeholders. Note the use of the word *helping*, which implies that managers seldom accomplish these things unilaterally. Their core function is to lead, to catalyze action, to create circumstances that enable other people, primar-ily professional service providers, to perform their best.

Adjectives used with the terms management/administration also reflect implicit biases. Four terms are commonly used: *human services, social, social welfare,* and *social work.* Although there is a great deal of overlap and sometimes fuzziness about the conceptual boundaries of these definitions, it is possible to identify some differences.

Human services refers to a wide spectrum of organizations in the health, mental health, and education and social services fields that are presumed to share certain fundamental similarities. Although the settings in which these services are delivered vary widely, they are thought to share a number of similar characteristics that collectively distinguish them from other types of organizations. These include the heavy reliance on third-party financing, the goal of changing clients, the use of technologies that are not highly determinate, and reliance on the judgment and discretion of front-line professional personnel. (See Austin, 1988; Demone & Harshbarger, 1974; Hasenfeld, 1992b.) In this formulation, the issues confronting managers in these settings are sufficiently similar to justify a generic model of management (Austin, 1994). The words *human services* have come into wide usage in recent years. A number of public agencies have been renamed to reflect their more encompassing (and, we can hope, more integrated) mission and perhaps to distance the agencies themselves from the unfavorable connotation attached to the words *social* and *welfare.* Many recent texts on management have also adopted this terminology (Brody, 1993; Crow & Odewahn, 1987; Martin, 1993; Weiner, 1982), yet, it is not always clear whether such books intend to speak to management in

the wide array of agencies that the terms encompass.

Social welfare or *social* management/admin-
istration typically refers to management that is
shaped by the objectives, technologies, and professional cultures found in organizations that
deliver personal or social services. This approach has largely focused on public and nonprofit delivery systems for social services provided outside the marketplace (Patti, 1983;
Perlmutter & Slavin, 1980; Rapp & Poertner,
1992; Skidmore, 1990). Like the broader human services arena, social welfare organizations
have political, economic, governance, and cultural characteristics that differentiate them
from organizations in other fields. However,
unlike organizations in the health and education fields, those in social welfare tend to have
somewhat less supportive environments,
weaker technologies, and greater reliance on
uncredentialed personnel. Moreover, because
social workers and the social work profession
are the dominant source of person power in social welfare and are, arguably, a major source
of intellectual and philosophical orientation,
the profession and the sector tend to share
many assumptions and cultural norms. These
attributes and processes in social welfare organizations shape the management praxis and
differentiate it, we would argue, from both the
other human service fields and from the for-
profit sector.

Social work administration/management suggests that social work professionals have a particular knowledge, value, and skill base that enhances their ability to lead. Among the
attributes social workers are thought to bring to
management work are ethical commitments
and values having to do with social justice and
the primacy of client interests, an understand-

ing of human behavior, interpersonal skills, and
knowledge and experience with delivery technologies and the kinds of supports necessary to
deliver them effectively. The knowledge, skills,
and values of social work suffuse the practice of
management and presumably shape the behavior and decision making of the professional social worker (Skidmore, 1990; Weinbach, 1998).
Years ago, Schwartz (1970) characterized this
view as follows: "that in the administration of
social welfare, the knowledge, skills, and attitudes of social work are more important than
the knowledge and skills of general administrative method" (p. 25). This position justified the
teaching of administration as one of the social
work methods, on a par with casework, group
work, and community organizations (Spencer,
1959), opening the way for social work schools
to become seriously involved in training people
for this practice. Although many believe that social workers bring a distinctive perspective to
management, it is still not clear whether managers trained as social workers perform differently
or, if differences can be discerned, whether these
contribute in some way to the performance of
organizations.

The conceptual boundaries of this Handbook draw largely from the *social welfare* parameters discussed above, but one will find authors using these terms and others to describe
the sector and the management that takes place
in it.

ESSENTIAL CHARACTERISTICS OF SOCIAL WELFARE ADMINISTRATION

Is social welfare management a distinctive form
of management? This question has been the
subject of some dispute in the past. Some have

argued that the most essential elements of the management craft are enduring and transferable, adaptable across sectors. Knowledge of the substantive nature of a field—its policies, technologies, and professional culture—is considered at best an increment to basic management principles and processes, usually understood to mean business administration (Rapp & Poertner, 1992; Rimer, 1987; Thompson, 1970). This position enjoys some currency for several reasons.

At the center of a triumphant capitalistic system is the for-profit corporation (Gummer, 1997; Martin, Chapter 3, this volume). It has become emblematic of the success of societies and has conferred on those countries that are successful a great deal of power in global affairs. In the United States, clearly the most powerful economy in the world, theories of business management and economics are considered essential to the effective operation of the corporation, and although practicing managers may criticize the academy for producing graduates with too much or too little of certain skills and values (Gummer, 1997), such graduates are still eagerly sought. To the extent that business school graduates are valued by corporations and corporations are considered the flower of American society, it is no surprise that society associates business education and private sector management experience with success. The frequent movement of business executives into high-level positions with public agencies speaks to the belief that a successful business manager can provide effective leadership (perhaps the best leadership) in any setting.

The legitimacy of business administration is further strengthened by an academic enterprise that consists of hundreds of graduate programs, thousands of faculty, and hundreds of journals.

The growing popularity of books on management celebrates the success and insights produced by practitioners in the business enterprise and promises solutions to the problems facing all types of organizations. Business administration is the dominant paradigm against which all others are compared (Gummer, 1997).

Even though specialized academic programs in social work and nonprofit management have produced a generation of people specifically trained for this sector, people trained in business management technologies and perspectives may still be considered the most effective managers for social welfare organizations. Findings from a survey of social agency executives indicates that more than one half believed that skills acquired in general management degrees, for example, public and business administration, were better preparation for top-level management positions in social agencies, whereas only 14% considered the MSW the preferred degree (Hoefer, 1993).

An alternative view based on an extensive review of social welfare organization and administration over the last 40 years argues that social welfare management is a distinctive variant of general management. Although there are core generic elements in management wherever it is practiced, this position maintains that that effective management in social welfare requires a theory and praxis tailored to the distinctive needs and characteristics of the organization in this domain (Austin, 1988, 1994; Harshbarger, 1974; Hasenfeld, 1992b; Patti, 1983; Schwartz, 1970; Weiner, 1982). Some have questioned whether the characteristics of these organizations are so different from those in other sectors (Rimer, 1987). There are differences in emphasis and language in many of these analyses, but there is a substantial convergence of scholarly opinion around the functions and tasks that collectively compose this unique praxis and its relationship to certain preferred organizational outcomes.

In setting forth elements of a social welfare management paradigm, it is important to recognize that we are referring to the functions and tasks carried out by managers at several levels, that is, executive, mid-management, and supervisory. It is the coordinated execution of these functions, rather than the behavior of one person, for example, the executive, that produces organizational excellence, although responsibility for particular functions may fall more heavily at one or another level. In what follows, it is important to remember that the functions and tasks are the responsibility of managers at all levels, acting in some purposefully collective fashion to achieve organizational goals.

These elements of the management paradigm are presented as propositions, because there is much yet to learn about the exact nature of the relationships between management and organizational performance. Taken together, these tasks and functions mark off the boundaries of management in this field and suggest the increments to basic management skills that are necessary for successful performance. Stated differently, if a manager performed all the basic functions of management—for example, planning, organizing, staffing, controlling—and did not particularize them to the needs of social welfare settings as discussed below, it is unlikely that the agency could be successful, judged by almost any set of criteria. The propositions are both descriptive, in that they describe what is expected of managers in these environments, and prescriptive, in that they suggest what must

be done to produce good organizational outcomes.

1. Social welfare managers are routinely confronted with moral dilemmas that require ethically defensible decisions. (See Reamer, Chapter 4, this volume.)

Although guided by public policy and institutional ideologies (Hasenfeld, 1992b), managers must address a host of difficult moral choices. These range from the most macro-level (e.g., whether to focus agency resources on the most needy and frail populations or on those with less urgent needs but perhaps greater potential for rehabilitation) to program- and service-level decisions (e.g., whether to deprive parents of their parental rights, whether to return people with disabilities to their families or send them for care in a nursing home, whether to deprive a mentally ill person of the right to refuse treatment). These and similarly difficult decisions are pervasive in the human services and can have profound implications for the welfare of individuals, families, and communities. Human service administrators are directly or indirectly involved in making such choices (Austin, 1994; Hasenfeld, 1992b; Patti, 1983) or defending those made by subordinates. For this reason, their values and ethics are constantly being brought into play in decision making.

Administrative decisions in social welfare often involve values that are contested by important agency stakeholders. They frequently pose ethical dilemmas where two or more important and equally compelling values are at issue. Moreover, resolutions often entail trade-offs, that is, sacrificing or subordinating one value to achieve another. In this decision environment, managers are pressed to make reasoned choices that are based on explicitly ethical criteria. Opportunistic, self-serving, or inconsistent decisional patterns reflect a lack of ethical grounding and create a morally ambiguous climate in the organization in which normative guidelines are not clear. In an important sense, managers model probity and ethical reasoning for the entire organization and, in so doing, create a normative climate for decision making at every level. This is critical because the social welfare organization conducts a wide range of transactions with consumers, collaborators, and supporters; long-term success depends in great measure on a sense of mutual trust and fairness (Austin, 1994; Lewis, 1985).

2. Management practice in the human services requires attention to mediating, reconciling, and influencing the preferences and expectations of external constituencies. (See Schmid, Chapter 7, this volume.)

Social welfare organizations rely on a variety of groups for the resources needed to develop, maintain, and improve agency programs. Managers rely on the support and cooperation of several constituencies to do the work of the organization and are seldom in a position to act unilaterally on key issues (Gummer, 1990, p. 53). Clients or consumers are the "raw material" that agencies work with to achieve the goals for which the agency is funded. Legislatures, government agencies, federated funding agencies, donors, and foundations provide funds needed to sustain agency operations. Boards and legislators provide authorization and policy direction, which frame the parame-

ters of service delivery. Accrediting bodies review and legitimate the agency against some criteria of quality. Under the best of circumstances, these groups have similar expectations for the focal organization, but this is seldom the case. It thus falls to the administrator to accommodate the needs and interests of these groups, while at the same time achieving sufficient congruence among them to avoid exposing the agency to conflicting expectations that will fragment and diffuse its resources.

One source of divergent expectations grows out of the fact that those who consume services pay little of the cost for providing them. Financing is typically provided by third parties such as government, foundations, endowments, and insurance. David Austin (1994) points out that the types of outcomes sought by consumers and funders are often different. The former will seek services that provide them a personal or "private good," whereas the latter will typically expect a community benefit or so-called "public good." A government agency that funds mental health services may be quite intent on minimizing hospitalization rates and see this as an indicator of agency performance, whereas consumers—let us say, relatives of people who are seriously mentally ill—will be more concerned with using whatever type of program is needed, including hospitalization, to manage symptoms and ensure their safety. The problem is complicated if, as is often true, the organization uses personal service technologies that depend centrally on achieving agreement between service provider and consumer regarding treatment goals and means. Social welfare managers are thus confronted with trying to meet the needs of both groups, imposing the public good definition of outcomes on the consumer, or persuading the funder that the public interests are served by producing personal goods. A failure to achieve some symmetry of expectations is likely to create problems for the organization because staff will face conflicting demands and/or resources will be diffused to meet multiple and incompatible objectives. The major task of managers, then, is to mediate these differences.

3. Social welfare managers advocate for stigmatized, disvalued groups to mobilize public sentiment and resources.

Perhaps to an even greater extent than managers in other human services fields, those who oversee personal social services must often work to change stereotypes about the disfavored groups they serve and/or public priorities regarding the needs of such groups. Child welfare administrators may need to convince state or county legislators that abusive parents are worth rehabilitating; mental health managers will work with local government officials to make the case that the homeless mentally ill are not content with their way of life and will respond to outreach services; directors of delinquency prevention programs will work to persuade the public that gang members have aspirations other than crime and can be helped to choose a different lifestyle if provided with opportunities; managers of teenage pregnancy prevention programs will seek to persuade community leaders that their clients are not having babies to qualify for welfare.

The common theme in all these situations is that the consumers of these programs are morally stigmatized. As such, they are perceived to be unworthy of assistance and/or deserving of punishment. There are at least three reasons why social welfare managers must become involved in advocacy for these consumers. First, the purpose of the social welfare agency is to change people or their social circumstances. The agency cannot acquire the resources and cooperation it needs to succeed in that mission if community leaders do not believe in the potential of morally disfavored people or see the relationship between their fate and broader community interests. Second, providers of services to such consumer groups will receive little recognition or respect, because no matter how skilled or challenging their work is perceived to be, the objects of the service are not considered deserving. The aura of disfavor tends to undermine staff morale over time, contributing to turnover, burnout, and other performance problems. Finally, an agency's claim to public resources rests, in part, on the perception that what its employees do contributes in some way to the quality of life in the community. If perceptions of morally disfavored groups cannot be changed so that they are seen as a potential asset to the community, or at least less of a threat, then the agency's success will have little meaning to the community.

4. Social welfare managers collaborate with other agencies to mobilize and focus resources on a common clientele to achieve the benefits of an enlarged pool of specialists and improved cooperation. (See Alter, Chapter 14, this volume.)

Because the care and change of human beings is typically produced cooperatively by networks of agencies, human service management requires the development and maintenance of interagency collaborations. To a very large extent, the outcomes achieved with the consumers of an agency are dependent on the complementary or supportive services provided by other agencies in the service-delivery system. In some sense, it can be argued that desirable impacts with many consumer groups can only be achieved when agencies collaborate in a purposeful way. Although collaboration has long been desirable as a strategy to fill service gaps, improve access, and achieve economies, recent developments have made it essential to agency success.

Over the last two decades, several demographic and social policy developments have produced a very different kind of clientele for social agencies. One development is the growing disparity of wealth abetted by economic and tax policies that have favored upper-income groups. In this context, the rate of poverty, most notably among children, has slowly but steadily risen. Concurrently, there was rapid growth in the number of older people, with their attendant health and social problems; a marked increase in the number of mentally ill and developmentally disabled people in need of community services; and an influx of immigrants, many with traumatic backgrounds. Taken together, these trends converged to produce a broad segment of the population dependent on publicly supported social services.

Concurrently, there was a parallel development in social policy. During the 1970s and 1980s, the demand for services grew faster than the ability of publicly supported programs to accommodate it, in part because there was neither the resources or the public will to fund expanded services. Funding for social welfare declined in means-tested and discretionary programs aimed at the poor and near-poor

(Salamon, 1998, pp. 139-140). To deal with the growing lag between need and resources, policymakers at federal and state levels increasingly turned to rationing strategies, which focused resources on the most needy and troubled while excluding those with less urgent or less threatening needs.

The net effect of these interacting population and policy changes was to dramatically increase the number of multiproblem, frail, highly needy people in the social services. Overwhelmed with the complexity of these needs, at a time when resources were not increasing, policymakers and social agency managers became aware that single-agency and/or single-profession solutions would not be sufficiently robust to address the problems they confronted. Thus emerged a keen interest in collaborative solutions that would not only provide economies in operation but also yield more comprehensive and integrated program strategies. Social agency managers, who once saw the promotion of their agency's interests as the highest calling, began to see that these interests and those of consumers would best be served through collaborative service arrangements.

Collaboration is now built into the fabric of policy making. Where once public, private, and proprietary sectors were reasonably distinct, we have evolved what Salamon (1998) refers to as third-party government, in which government relies on for-profit and nonprofit entities to carry out public policy. This reliance on "third party governance" is now so ubiquitous that virtually all areas of social policy are implemented using a complex set of intersector mechanisms. Social welfare managers, whether in a public, nonprofit, or for-profit organization, must be able to work effectively at these collaborative intersections.

5. Social welfare managers articulate values and goals that inspire the moral commitment of supporters, staff, and volunteers.

Social welfare managers, perhaps more than managers in other sectors, must be able to mobilize organizational members around values and purposes that are personally meaningful to them (Brody, 1993; Patti, Poertner, & Rapp, 1988). Supporters, professionals, and others tend to be drawn to this kind of work because they feel deeply about the need to change the world in some way, whether it be to protect the vulnerable from perpetrators, ensure the rights of the disenfranchised, or preserve and strengthen families. Social agencies are, among other things, places where professionals seek to realize these values.

Although we know that the performance of social workers and other professionals employed in social welfare organizations is shaped by a number of factors, ranging from their own personality characteristics (see Koeske & Koeske, Chapter 11, this volume; Vinokur-Kaplan & Bogin, Chapter 9, this volume) to organizational climate, culture, and structure (see Gillespie, Chapter 8, this volume; Glisson, Chapter 10, this volume; Vinokur-Kaplan & Bogin, Chapter 9, this volume), one of the most important sources of motivation is their belief in the work, purposes, and mission of the organization. Etzioni's (1964) classic formulation of the types of power used in organizations to elicit involvement of members posited that human service organizations primarily used moral power to obtain the normative involvement of their employees. In social welfare organiza-

tions, service providers are the instruments of service. The quality of this service depends to a great extent on the personal resources of the providers and their willingness to use these in transactions with clients. It seems clear that if service providers are committed to the purposes of the agency, they will be more inclined to expend personal resources on behalf of consumers.

The normative involvement of staff also serves organizational purposes. In organizations that have difficult-to-specify goals, that use service technologies with variable and uncertain impact, and that rely on the judgment and discretion of front-line staff, the normative involvement of employees is a major source of coherence and reliability. Lacking the ability to observe and directly monitor the behavior of staff, agencies depend on the staff's commitments to agency goals and values to ensure performance.

6. Social welfare managers seek measures of organizational performance that are responsive to standards of accountability imposed by funding and policy bodies, while attempting to reconcile these with available resources, the unpredictable efficacy of service technologies, and the preferences of service providers and consumers.

While the definition and measurement of organizational performance remains a complex undertaking, it is clear that policy and funding bodies are increasingly proactive in specifying desired consumer outcomes in return for the support provided (Martin & Kettner, 1996). Unlike the for-profit sector, nonprofit organizations have no universally acceptable indicators of performance, nor are there standards that apply across various fields of service. Outcomes will look different in service programs in mental health, child welfare, aging, and so on. Nevertheless, agencies are being pressed to define and account for performance outcomes. In child welfare, such performance criteria as preserving families with at-risk children, placing children in permanent living arrangements, and reducing the rates of repeated child abuse and neglect have become essential to measuring success. In mental health, the maintenance and adjustment of the seriously mentally ill in the community is an increasingly prevalent standard. In income assistance programs, the reduction of welfare dependency and participation in the work force are now a matter of national policy. In addition to program-specific standards, there are broader policy and funding arrangements such as managed care and the Government Performance and Results Act of 1993, which will require social welfare agencies in the nonprofit and public sectors to develop and account for increasingly refined standards of performance (Martin & Kettner, 1996, pp. 11-14).

These developments have and will make the definition and measurement of performance an integral part of the social welfare manager's responsibility. This, in turn, has other implications. If funding (reimbursement) is tied to the achievement of service outcomes, then, the ability to determine the resources and processes that must be applied to achieve these outcomes will become increasingly important. Specifying service technologies, selecting and training personnel who can implement these services (see Pecora & Wagner, Chapter 20, this volume), and developing management information systems to track how service efforts are related to outcomes (See Poertner, Chapter 13, this volume; Schoech, Chapter 16, this volume): All will become imperative in this service environ-

ment. To the extent that funding is tied to outcomes, the ability of managers to determine the cost of services is vital to the financial viability of agencies.

Although all of these developments are now well under way in social services (although not as far along as in health care and education), implementation is not without its problems and dilemmas. Consumers, as mentioned earlier, come to the service experience with their own goals and ways of assessing the quality and effectiveness of service (Anspach, 1990). As outcomes and the means for achieving them are increasingly predetermined rather than mutually defined in service transactions, it may become difficult to elicit the kinds of involvement and cooperation from consumers that are necessary to meet performance standards. Indeed, such a scenario raises the specter of consumer disempowerment, which is antithetical to the collaborative production of desired service outcomes (Hasenfeld, 1992c). Alternately, the practice of "creaming" may become more attractive as agencies look for consumers who fit best with the service technologies that are thought to be the most effective. The quintessential challenge for social welfare managers will be to develop service technologies that allow for the exercise of consumer choice and influence in the context of more and more specific performance expectations.

7. Social welfare managers seek to develop supportive and empowering processes in the agency to build commitment and ownership and to maintain a climate conducive to psychological and physical health.

We have already referred to the importance of agency values in attracting and engaging staff and others in the work of the agency. But sustaining a high level of commitment also requires that managers be centrally concerned with the development and maintenance of personnel because they are the instruments through which services are provided. Service transaction typically requires the use of personal qualities and behaviors (e.g., judgment, empathy, disclosure, modeling) in interaction with consumers who are troubled, oppressed, confused, and sometimes very difficult (Austin, 1994). To be at their best, professional staff and volunteers must sustain high levels of personal commitment. This can be enervating, and to the extent that support and stress management strategies are not effective, a number of untoward effects such as emotional withdrawal, depersonalization of consumers, and emotional problems can occur. Throughout this volume, there are chapters devoted to the strategies and techniques through which this is accomplished. (See Glisson, Chapter 10, this volume; Iglehart, Chapter 21, this volume; Pecora & Wagner, Chapter 20, this volume; Vinokur-Kaplan & Bogin, Chapter 9, this volume.) Suffice it to say here that social welfare managers must attend to creating conditions that promote satisfaction and motivation, lest the service-delivery capacities of the agency become degraded.

8. Social welfare managers must maintain some control of their programs, even while they can't be in control of them.

The nature of service technologies is such that they involve largely private transactions between providers and consumers. Moreover, the interactions between staff and clients are typically dynamic exchanges that require ad hoc adjustments and novel solutions. In short, although service interventions are guided by service-delivery protocols, supervision, and training, there are inescapable and probably desirable elements of discretion and judgment required if workers and clients are to find a way of making progress toward the consumer's goals. Professionals value this exercise of judgment, and professional cultures reinforce the norm of autonomy in the context of certain norms.

Lacking independent means for collecting information about services and outcome, social welfare managers are dependent on staff to provide it. Typical command-and-control accountability mechanisms are unlikely to produce reliable information, especially if service providers believe that the information is going to be used to evaluate performance. On the other hand, if information is seen as a means to learn about and improve performance, if it is used to facilitate the development of staff and better serve consumers, there are reasons for professionals to participate. Among other things, this kind of posture requires staff participation in the design of information systems and the use of information to provide feedback to staff. (See Poertner, Chapter 13, this volume; Schoech, Chapter 16, this volume.) Such systems seem to work best in structures of decentralized authority.

Social welfare managers at all levels must be accountable for their units. Superiors and external entities require information to confirm compliance and often demand that managers make changes if performance is below expectations. Yet, it seems that social welfare managers are more likely to acquire information and to use it to make changes when this is done in the context of a learning culture (see Gillespie, Chapter 8, this volume), which emphasizes professional development and organizational improvements geared to providing better service to consumers.

9. Because consumers of human services are active participants in the service experience and are largely responsible for the changes that are sought, social welfare managers must attend to how they can be directly engaged in the choice of means and outcomes of service delivery.

In recent years, it has come to be recognized that consumers of social services are vital partners in the creation of change. They are co-producers of change. Changes in behavior, attitudes, skills, and even environmental conditions require the active participation of consumers. Although this is now conventional wisdom, there remain significant forces in organizational and professional practice that work to maintain the power of service providers and perpetuate their dependence (Hasenfeld, 1992c). These forces are counteracted in governance procedures, in the promotion of cultural norms that normalize consumers and recognize their strengths and capacities (Rapp & Poertner, 1992), and in the delivery of service technologies that allow for consumer choice and influence (Gutiérrez, 1992; see also Iglehart, Chapter 21, this volume). Social service consumers are often disempowered in their lives, lacking the political and bureaucratic skills necessary to assert their claims. This, and the fact that most organizations draw their legitimacy and funding from people other than clients, makes it tempting for managers and providers to disregard or neglect the interests and the contribution of consumers to the service process. Man-

agers play a vital role in seeing that this does not happen, that clients are related to as partners.

These nine characteristics explain much of what is distinctive about management in the social welfare sector. To some extent, these functions and tasks are found in other fields of human service and in the for-profit sector. Taken together, however, they appear to be more pivotal to the success of social welfare management than they are in other fields.

SOCIAL WORKERS IN SOCIAL WELFARE MANAGEMENT

Despite the development of education for social welfare management in social schools over the last three decades, most social workers in management are trained originally as direct service practitioners and, with experience in the ranks, promoted into administrative positions. This pattern of selection reflects the persistence of the long-held view in social work that direct practice is a necessary if not sufficient basis for management practice (Patti, 1983). Many have argued that this pattern of professional preparation for management does not produce the most capable administrators (Patti, Diedrick, Olson, & Crowell, 1979; Rimer, 1987; Sarri, 1973). Despite this contention, there is no direct empirical evidence to suggest that this career profile is more or less desirable. There are some indications that people who move from direct practice to management perceive themselves unprepared for their responsibilities (Patti et al., 1979), but whether they are more or less effective than people with specialized management training and under what circumstances is still unclear.

There is some indirect evidence to suggest that social workers may not be faring well in the management job market. First, there seems a general perception among informed observers that people from business, public administration, and other fields are taking an ever larger percentage of middle- and upper-level management positions or are at least more favorably perceived as a source of management talent (Gummer, 1987; Keys & Capaiuolo, 1987). Social workers, it is said, are not prepared to use the technologies that are essential to modern agency management and may not be socialized to the culture of management, which requires making difficult trade-offs in the context of scarcity (Gummer, 1987).

Membership surveys by the National Association of Social Workers (NASW) seem to indicate that the percentage of members working in supervisory and management positions has declined over the years. In the late 1960s, as many as 50% of all social workers were reported to be involved in management (Stamm, 1969). A study comparing the jobs held by NASW members in 1981 and 1985 found that 38.1% and 45.1% respectively were in management or supervisory jobs (Chess, Norlin, & Jayaratne, 1987). A 1988 membership survey recorded 24.1% of the membership in management and supervision as a primary job function (Gibelman & Schervish, 1993, p. 90), whereas the most recent data from NASW indicates that only 22.3% of those responding to a 1991 membership survey reported doing supervision (6.1%) or management (16.2%) in their primary function. These studies are not entirely comparable because they employ different sampling and data collection methods and varying definitions. The most recent data may also underreport the number of social workers involved in adminis-

tration and supervision (p. 13). The number of management jobs in social agencies may actually be declining in light of budget constraints and the tendency in some sectors, for example, health, to reduce the number of supervisory and middle management jobs. These data are far from definitive, but if they reflect a real trend, then we should be asking why and learning more about the criteria that organizations are using to select and promote managers. Again, the research is sparse, but there are a few studies that may suggest some answers.

Keys and Capaiuolo's (1987) interviews with past and current county and state public welfare administrators in two states in the late 1980s found a widely shared view that social workers are not adequately prepared for public welfare administration. Some respondents in this study felt that social workers were no longer considered the most appropriate profession to provide leadership in this field. This finding apparently contrasted with a survey nearly a decade earlier, also using public welfare administrators as respondents, which found that for upper-level management positions in public welfare, social workers with specialized management training were preferred over those with MBAs (Patti & Rauch, 1978). Hoefer's (1993, pp. 8-11) survey of a heterogeneous sample of human service agency administrators in one large urban area found that respondents favored those with public administration, business, other types of degrees and no degrees over social workers trained in management for middle-level management positions (73% to 27%). For top-level executive positions, social workers were considered less desirable than competitors with other or no degree by an even larger percentage of respondents (86% to 14%). For executive-level positions, those with either MBAs or MPAs were perceived to be more qualified than those with MSWs. Those skill areas in which social workers were considered lacking included decision making, oral communication, written communication, and professionalism; interestingly, these are interpersonal and cognitive skills rather than technical ones.

In the end, the most important question is whether it makes a difference that fewer social workers are providing leadership in social agencies. Clearly, it makes a difference to social workers who aspire to these jobs and to the profession whose presence in the leadership ranks is a barometer of professional influence in its domain. Does it mean that social agencies led by others will be less oriented to clients, less ethical in their decisions, less effective in delivering services, less productive and innovative? At this point, we only speculate about these matters, but the profession's claim to leadership in this sector may ultimately rest on the answers.

THE PREPARATION OF SOCIAL WORKERS FOR MANAGEMENT

Given the nature of social welfare management and the fact that social workers continue to be a major source of person power for this practice, it is important to examine how well or poorly the profession is preparing people for these responsibilities. This analysis is hampered by the lack of research on the educational and experiential characteristics of managers in social welfare and more by the paucity of comparative information about how people with different profiles perform in this capacity. For example, with a few exceptions (Patti et al., 1979;

Perlmutter, 1990; Scurfield, 1981), there has been little systematic attention to the careers of clinicians turned managers, their performance as managers and leaders, and the factors that hinder or promote their effectiveness. Even less attention has been given to comparing different options for postgraduate education, for example, general degrees in macro practice versus degrees specifically in administration. A number of prior analyses have argued that it is not possible to adequately prepare students for this practice with the current content and structure of management education in schools of social work (Faherty, 1987; Raymond, Teare, et al., 1996; Rimer, 1987). However, at this point, it is not possible to offer more than a speculative commentary on this question. One hopes there will be more inquiry into this and related questions.

Over the last two decades or so, the trend in graduate social work education has been to combine the teaching of administration, community organization, and policy practice into single curricular concentrations. This approach is based on the argument that practitioners in all these modalities draw on similar sets of skills (Jansson, 1987). But for the most part, this curriculum design seems to have been propelled more by enrollment demographics and available faculty expertise than by a systematic analysis of the needs of practitioners. Most schools simply cannot justify the maintenance of separate curricula for community organization, administration, and policy practice because student enrollments are too small. In addition, because macro curricula were relatively late in developing, they have often been shaped by the preferences and professional histories of faculty whose interests and expertise developed during the 1960s and 1970s.

A national survey of macro educational programs in graduate schools of social work, conducted in the early 1990s (McNutt, 1995), found that 70% of the programs offered a combination of methods (e.g., administration, community organization, policy practice) rather than a single method. Slightly more than 20% offered a free-standing curriculum on administration. Moreover, a majority of the macro programs were 1-year specialties. These concentrations provided an average of nearly eight courses (with a standard deviation of 6.29) taught by an average of five faculty members (standard deviation of 2.67). Although administration-related content dominated most of these curricula, the range, depth, and quality of the content varied substantially. Personnel management and financial management were especially uneven. Recent data from the Council on Social Work Education (CSWE, 1996) reveal that curricula continue to include several modalities of macro practice, often in combination with direct practice and/or problem areas.

How much management education is enough for proficient management practice? What subjects and academic experiences best prepare for the demands of practice? These descriptive data do not provide answers to these questions. As in many other areas, education is only one of a number of factors in interaction (e.g., personal qualities and aptitudes, quality of mentoring and role models, work experience, opportunities for upward mobility) that ultimately determine how successful a manager will be. Nevertheless, on the face of it, uneven and superficial exposure to core management material would seem to be a definite liability. Even in those programs that are able to offer an array of relevant courses, such courses are typically concentrated in 1 year of study, which may

not be sufficient time to become socialized to this practice arena.

The quality or perceived quality of education is probably most instrumental in initially positioning graduates for management careers. If graduate education has not instilled ways of thinking about organizational issues and managerial strategies for addressing them, if it has not socialized graduates to the expectations of managers, if it has not imparted technical skills and language, then potential employers are not likely to perceive graduates as credible candidates for management jobs. Such perceptions may influence the level of initial appointment, estimates of professional promise, and subsequent career development opportunities in the agency.

In contrast to this pessimistic scenario, there is some evidence to suggest that a graduate program that specializes in education for management can produce graduates who will fare well in the job market. Martin, Pines, and Healy (1999) reported findings of a study of 113 social work administration graduates from a school of social work that provides 32 hours of management instruction. Findings on graduates over a 15-year period indicate that 70% were employed in middle- and upper-level management jobs. Most perceived their preparation as adequate to good in most management skills, and a large majority were satisfied with their careers. The data in this study are based on self-report and do not provide any direct evidence of proficiency or effectiveness in role. Nonetheless, the findings suggest that a program focused on preparation for management can produce managers who are "employable in significant managerial positions and who have confidence in their preparedness for managerial work" (Martin et al., 1999, p. 90).

Although the quality of education for social welfare management is of concern, the paucity of graduates trained in this modality also poses a problem. In the last decade, the number of students in all macro education concentrations (including those who combine community organization, policy practice, and administration with direct practice and/or social problems or fields) is typically less than 15% of all students enrolled in social work master's degree programs, or about 2,000 to 3,000 per year. The number of students specializing only in management education is much smaller, typically about 3% of graduate enrollment. Clearly, the number of social workers with specialized educational preparation in social welfare management is not (and has not been) sufficient to meet the demands for administrators in the field. This leaves the job market to those trained in other professions or to social workers whose education and training is in direct service.

STRATEGIC CHOICES FOR SOCIAL WORK

At this writing, it does not seem that social work education is serving the management needs of social welfare very well. To be sure, there are centers of excellence that produce competent management prospects, and certainly, there are individual social workers who are exemplary administrators. But neither social work education nor professional associations, foundations, or governments have taken the leadership in developing a far-reaching strategy for addressing how social work can best meet needs for management personnel in social welfare.

So what of the future? Several options deserve continuing investigation. They are not necessarily mutually exclusive, although some nest better than others.

The most obvious choice is to continue on the current path. Schools would continue to offer a broad approach to macro education. Macro concentrations would continue to attract a relatively small proportion of students and provide a broad foundation of knowledge and skill, which serves as a platform for several career paths, including, for a significant minority of students, direct practice. The management job market in social welfare is sufficiently large and diverse to absorb a significant number of the graduates of these programs. Graduates from these types of programs may have more flexible access to a wider variety of macro practice positions.

Another approach would be to reinvigorate the dual degree options that showed promise in the early 1970s and 1980s. These early efforts aimed to build the capabilities of social work management curricula by developing joint programs with schools of business and public administration. Then, schools of social work seemed to abandon the strategy. Joint programs remain at several institutions, but it does not appear that they attract many students. This strategy must overcome the inertial forces that impede interdisciplinary collaboration on campuses, the opportunity costs for academic units involved, and the disincentives for students that arise from the additional costs and time needed to acquire degrees.

A third strategy would be for schools to focus their resources more narrowly on the teaching of administration. Such a strategy would have the advantages of building critical masses of faculty and students, which would allow for more coverage of more content that is essential to management practice. It would enable schools to market their programs more effectively, projecting to potential students a broad array of opportunities for influencing how services are delivered in career paths that offer status and relatively good remuneration. By projecting a less ambiguous image of macro practice, schools might attract students whose career interests are in social welfare management but who choose other management-degree programs because they are not clear about the credibility of management education in social work.

Some will argue that this strategy would deny opportunities for students who are interested in planning and organizing and policy practice careers, but the number of jobs in these fields is quite small compared to those in management (Gibelman & Schervish, 1993). In any case, some schools with sufficient numbers of students to justify multiple separate tracks would continue to offer these specialties. Other schools might choose to focus on community organizing or policy practice because of local demand and/or the configuration of their faculties. But for the most part, if the schools are going to support the management needs of the social welfare sector, they need to concentrate their resources.

Focusing resources on management education will trouble some who believe that administrators need the perspectives and skills provided by policy practice and community organization. It is certainly true that aspects of the knowledge and skills in these practice fields should be an important part of the manager's repertoire. But there is no reason that management concentrations couldn't be defined (and indeed sometimes are) to include those elements of policy practice, planning, and organizing that we know are essential to the effective management practice. But integrating these

into a curriculum that is framed by a management paradigm and takes that practice as its primary referent is different than training students in several different practice paradigms in the hope that they will later integrate these in management practice.

A fourth option would be to align social work management education more closely with the emerging field of nonprofit management. Although there are some ties between social work and the nonprofit management field, the latter has developed without much intellectual or professional input from social work and increasingly looks like a professional competitor in the social welfare job market. Largely in response to the dramatic growth of organizations in the nonprofit sector following World War II, universities began to develop management programs to serve this market. Broadly conceived to serve nonprofits in health, education, culture and arts, religion, and the social services, nonprofit management is based on the idea that organizations in the independent sector share common characteristics (e.g., general missions, tax status, governance, legal foundations, resource acquisition and marketing needs, etc.) that require specialized knowledge, skills, and values (Drucker, 1990). The rationale for this emerging field, it should be noted, is similar in many respects to the arguments that have been made for a distinctive field of social welfare management.

A 1995 survey to determine the nature and prevalence of nonprofit management programs in American universities found 76 graduate-degree programs with a concentration in nonprofit management (Wish & Mirabella, 1998). In addition, 43 universities offered one or two graduate courses in this area, and 47 provided noncredit, continuing education, or undergraduate programs. Comparative data from 1992 and 1995 surveys indicate the number of graduate programs with a concentration in nonprofit management had grown from 32 to 76. One must assume that the number in 1995 was larger than reported, because the survey, which went to 1,000 colleges and universities, received only a 25% response. In addition to the educational programs, nonprofit management shows other signs of institutional maturity. Several scholarly journals focus on the interests of nonprofit organizations and their management, there are several university-based research centers (e.g., at Yale and Harvard), and several professional and scholarly groups provide a forum for the exchange of ideas (O'Neill & Fletcher, 1998).

There would seem to be several advantages to effecting a closer educational collaboration with the nonprofit management field. Of all the management disciplines, it is based on philosophical premises and organizational and policy realities that also inform social work management education and scholarship. It is an interdisciplinary field of endeavor with ties to several disciplines, including public administration and business, yet, is not "owned" by either. Interdisciplinary collaboration is normative in this field, and those drawn to it are likely to be interested in cross-professional endeavors. Social work education can make a significant contribution to the expansion of the nonprofit management movement by associating its educational and scholarly resources with this field, while at the same time drawing on the growing body of scholarship and educational resources that are produced there. Indeed, a recent text in management produced by social work educators is aimed at the general field of nonprofit organizations (Edwards et al., 1998). On some

campuses, social work schools could take the leadership in developing nonprofit management programs, as was done at the School of Applied Social Sciences at Case Western Reserve University. Finally, the foundation community seems to have a significant interest in the development of this field and has provided significant support in recent years (O'Neill & Fletcher, 1998). In sum, developing or joining collaborations in the nonprofit management field offers attractive advantages to social work management education.

Barring a significant growth in the number of students who opt for macro practice concentrations in schools of social work, which seems unlikely in the foreseeable future, there is little likelihood that schools will be able to expand courses and allocate more faculty to social welfare management. The most viable alternatives appear to be focusing faculty resources in more specialized curricula and/or seeking alliances with the emerging field of nonprofit management. The demands of this practice grow more complex, and the competition for jobs is likely to increase. If social work is to continue as a major source of management person power for this sector, it would behoove schools and professional associations to rethink the current approach to educating for this practice.

MANAGEMENT THEORY: WHERE TO FROM HERE?

A generation of scholarship in social welfare administration has gone a long way toward identifying the fundamental nature of human service organizations and their environments (Austin, 1988; Hasenfeld, 1992b; Schmid, Chapter 7, this volume); the roles, tasks, and activities performed by managers in these contexts to acquire and manage resources (Bargal, Chapter 15, this volume; Menefee, Chapter 12, this volume); and the conditions and processes that are associated with worker satisfaction and performance (Glisson, Chapter 10, this volume; Koeske & Koeske, Chapter 11, this volume; Vinokur-Kaplan & Bogin, Chapter 9, this volume).

Several normative theories have been formulated or adapted to describe the relationships between managerial behavior and organizational performance (see Hasenfeld, Chapter 5, this volume). Human relations theory has shaped fundamental assumptions regarding the development of human resources (Vinokur-Kaplan & Bogin, Chapter 9, this volume); systems theory has provided a framework for understanding the relationship of the organization to its environment and the need for managers to attend to the internal alignment of subsystems (Gillespie, Chapter 8, this volume; Glisson, 1985; Miringoff, 1980). Political and institutional theories have advanced our understanding of competition and conflict in the acquisition and allocation of resources and the processes through which human service agencies gain legitimacy (Gummer, 1990; Hasenfeld, 1992a).

In recent years, Quinn's (1988) competing values theory, extended and adapted to social welfare by Edwards and Austin (Edwards et al., 1998), has been proposed as an overarching framework. The competing values framework suggests that managers are effective when they give integrated and balanced attention to four organizational imperatives: internal stability, the development and maintenance of human resources, adaptation to opportunities and threats in the environment, and the productivity and efficiency of the organizations in achieving the organization's goals. Total quality management (TQM) has also enjoyed some favor in social welfare administration in recent years (Gummer & McCallion, 1995; Martin, 1993). Although adapted from the business sector, it proposes a coherent and specific model of management that is oriented to the satisfaction of consumer needs and is therefore quite consonant with the purposes of social welfare organization.

Notwithstanding this body of scholarship, social welfare management lacks a widely accepted theory of practice (Au, 1996). In part, this is due to the lack of agreement about the fundamental purposes of social welfare organizations. More specifically, there remains a lack of consensus about the relationship between managerial behavior and the several purposes of such organizations. Clearly, managers must ensure the survival and legitimacy of their organizations. They must see to the social and psychological needs of organizational members. They must acquire resources from an environment with diverse expectations for performance. They must attend to the developing structures and decision processes that support the technologies employed. Managers must attend to sustaining productivity and quality in service delivery. And they must see that service outcomes are achieved.

These and other purposes are indisputably essential to organizational survival and performance. In the long term, however, as I have argued elsewhere (Patti, 1985; Patti et al., 1988), all of these goals should be considered instrumental or intermediate purposes, essential but not sufficient to achieving the basic mission of the organization, which is to change people's lives and social circumstances. It is true that managerial strategies and behaviors necessary to achieve these multiple purposes can sometimes work at cross-purposes with the achievement of service effectiveness. Moreover, there are occasions when service-effectiveness goals may have to receive lower priority while other goals are realized. The central question for a theory of social welfare management is how the manager achieves acceptable levels of performance in all the instrumental purposes and then mobilizes these achievements in the interest of service outcomes.

The service effectiveness criterion is widely (although not universally) embraced in the literature (Martin & Kettner, 1996), but there remain problems in defining what this is and how to measure it, concerns about whose conception of effectiveness should guide agency action, and apprehension about whether service effectiveness is widely achievable in a context of uneven support and indeterminate technologies. Some are troubled that effectiveness is a normative criterion that is proposed for but is often not the central object of management or agency behavior, suggesting that it is not a practical or realistic standard to use in judging administrative action. Aside from the fact that agencies will increasingly be assessed against some definition of effectiveness, a theory of professional practice should seek to promote best outcomes. The determination of these outcomes is always an exercise in judgment, informed by values and by good information, ultimately negotiated between stakeholders. We know a good deal about the management of social welfare organizations. It remains for us to test current and developing models of practice to determine which ones can produce the best outcomes for consumers of service.

REFERENCES

Anspach, R. R. (1990). Everyday methods for assessing organizational effectiveness. *Social Problems 38*(1), 1-19.

Anthony, R. N., & Young, D. W. (1994). *Management control in nonprofit organizations.* Burr Ridge, IL: Irwin.

Atwater, P. (1940). *Problems of administration in social work.* Minneapolis: University of Minnesota Press.

Au, C. (1996). Rethinking organizational effectiveness: Theoretical and methodological issues in the study of social welfare organizations. *Administration in Social Work, 20*(4), 1-21.

Austin, D. (1988). *The political economy of human service programs.* Greenwich, CT: JAI Press.

Austin, D. (1994). *The human service organization: A distinctive administrative setting.* Unpublished manuscript, Austin, TX.

Brody, R. (1993). *Effectively managing human service organizations.* Newbury Park, CA: Sage.

Chess, W. A., Norlin, J. M., & Jayaratne, S. D. (1987). Social work administration: Alive, happy, and prospering. *Administration in Social Work, 11*(2), 67-77.

Christian, W. P., & Hannah, G. T. (1983). *Effective management in human services.* Englewood Cliffs, NJ: Prentice Hall.

Council on Social Work Education (CSWE). (1996). *Statistics on social work education in the U.S., 1995.* Washington, DC: Author.

Crow, R. T., & Odewahn, C. A. (1987). *Management of the human services.* Englewood Cliffs, NJ: Prentice Hall.

Cyert, R. M. (1975). *The management of nonprofit organizations.* Lexington, MA: D. C. Heath.

Demone, H. W., & Harshbarger, D. (1974). *A handbook of human service organizations.* New York: Behavioral Publications.

Drucker, P. F. (1990). *Managing nonprofit organizations: Practices and principles.* New York: HarperCollins.

Edwards, R. L., Yankey, J. A., & Altpeter, M. A. (1998). *Skills for effective management of nonprofit organizations.* Washington, DC: NASW Press.

Etzioni, A. (1964). *Modern organizations.* Englewood Cliffs, NJ: Prentice Hall.

Faherty, V. E. (1987). The battle of the Ms: The MBA, MPA, MPH, and MSW. *Administration in Social Work, 11*(2), 3-43.

Gibelman, M., & Schervish, P. H. (1993). *Who are we? The social work labor force as reflected in the NASW membership.* Washington, DC: NASW Press.

Glisson, C. A. (1985). A contingency model of social welfare administration. In S. Slavin (Ed.), *Introduction to human services management* (pp. 95-109). New York: Haworth.

Gregiore, T., Rapp, C., & Poertner, J. (1995). The new management: Assessing the fit of total quality management and social agencies. In B. Gummer & P. McCallion (Eds.), *Total quality management in the social services* (pp. 3-32). Albany: State University of New York at Albany.

Gummer, B. (1987). Are administrators social workers? The politics of interprofessional rivalry. *Administration in Social Work, 11*(2), 19-31.

Gummer, B. (1990). *The politics of social administration: Managing organizational politics in social agencies.* Englewood Cliffs, NJ: Prentice Hall.

Gummer, B. (1997). Public versus business administration: Are they still alike in unimportant ways? *Administration in Social Work, 21*(2), 81-98.

Gummer, B., & McCallion, P. (Eds.). (1995). *Total quality management in the social services.* Albany: State University of New York at Albany.

Gutiérrez, L. M. (1992). Empowering ethnic minorities in the twenty-first century: The role of human service organizations. In Y. Hasenfeld (Ed.), *Human services as complex organizations* (pp. 320-338). Newbury Park, CA: Sage.

Harshbarger, D. (1974). The human service organization. In H. W. Demone & D. Harshbarger (Eds.), *Handbook of human service organizations* (pp. 22-37). New York: Behavioral Publications.

Hasenfeld, Y. (Ed.). (1992a). *Human services as complex organizations.* Newbury Park, CA: Sage.

Hasenfeld, Y. (1992b). The nature of human service organizations. In Y. Hasenfeld (Ed.), *Human services as complex organizations* (pp. 2-23). Newbury Park, CA: Sage.

Hasenfeld, Y. (1992c). Power in social work practice. In Y. Hasenfeld (Ed.), *Human services as complex organizations* (pp. 259-275). Newbury Park, CA: Sage.

Hoefer, R. (1993). A matter of degree: Job skills for human service administrators. *Administration in Social Work, 17*(3), 1-20.

Jansson, B. S. (1987). From sibling rivalry to pooled knowledge and shared curriculum: Relations among community organization, administration, planning, and policy. *Administration in Social Work, 11*(2), 5-18.

Keys, P. R., & Capaiuolo, A. (1987). Rebuilding the relationship between social work and public welfare administration. *Administration in Social Work, 11*(1), 47-58.

Keys, P. R., & Ginsberg, L. H. (Eds.). (1988). *New management in the human services.* Silver Spring, MD: NASW Press.

Kotler, P. (1982). *Marketing for nonprofit organizations.* Englewood Cliffs, NJ: Prentice Hall.

Lewis, H. (1985). Management in the nonprofit social service organization. In S. Slavin (Ed.), *An introduction to human services management* (pp. 6-13). New York: Haworth.

Martin, L. L. (1993). *Total quality management in human service organization.* Newbury Park, CA: Sage.

Martin, L. L., & Kettner, P. M. (1996). *Measuring performance on human service programs.* Newbury Park, CA: Sage.

Martin, M. E., Pines, B. A., & Healy, L. M. (1999). Mining our strengths: Curriculum approaches for social work management. *Journal of Teaching in Social Work, 18*(1/2), 73-97.

McNutt, J. G. (1995). The macro practice curriculum in graduate social work education: Results of a national study. *Administration in Social Work, 19*(3), 59-74.

Miringoff, M. (1980). *Management in social welfare.* New York: Macmillan.

O'Neill, M., & Fletcher, K. (Eds.). (1998). *Nonprofit management education.* Westport, CT: Praeger.

Patti, R. J. (1975). The new scientific management: Systems management for social welfare. *Public Welfare, 33*(2), 23-31.

Patti, R. J. (1983). *Social welfare administration: Managing social programs in a developmental context.* Englewood Cliffs, NJ: Prentice Hall.

Patti, R. J. (1985). In search of purpose for social welfare administration. *Administration in Social Work, 9*(3), 1-14.

Patti, R. J., Diedrick, E., Olson, E., & Crowell, J. (1979). From direct service to administration: A study of social workers' transitions from clinical to management roles. *Administration in Social Work, 3*(2), 131-151.

Patti, R., Poertner, J., & Rapp, C. A. (Eds.). (1988). *Managing for service effectiveness in social welfare organizations.* New York: Haworth.

Patti, R., & Rauch, R. (1978, December). Social work administration graduates in the job market: An analysis of managers' hiring preferences. *Social Service Review,* pp. 567-583.

Perlmutter, F. (1990). *Changing hats.* Silver Spring, MD: NASW Press.

Perlmutter, F. D., & Slavin, S. (1980). *Leadership in social administration*. Philadelphia: Temple University Press.

Quinn, R. E. (1988). *Beyond rational management: Mastering the paradoxes and competing demands of high perfromance*. San Francisco: Jossey-Bass.

Rapp, C. A., & Poertner, J. (1992). *Social administration: A client-centered approach*. New York: Longman.

Raymond, G. T., Teare, R. J., et al. (1996). Do management tasks differ by field of practice? *Administration in Social Work, 20*(1), 17-30.

Rimer, E. (1987). Social administration education: Reconceptualizing the conflict between MPA, MBA, and MPH programs. *Administration in Social Work, 11*(2), 45-55.

Salamon, L. M. (1998). Nonprofit management education: A field whose time has passed? In M. O'Neill & K. Fletcher (Eds.), *Nonprofit management education* (pp. 137-145). Westport, CT: Praeger.

Sarri, R. C. (1973). *Effective social work intervention in administrative and planning roles: Implications for education*. Washington, DC: Council on Social Work Education.

Schwartz, E. E. (1970). Some views of the study of social welfare administration. In H. A. Schatz (Ed.), *Social work administration: A resource book*. New York: Council on Social Work Education.

Scurfield, R. (1981). Clinician to administrator: Difficult role transition. *Social Work, 26*, 47-60.

Skidmore, R. (1990). *Social work administration*. Englewood Cliffs, NJ: Prentice Hall.

Spencer, S. (1959). *The administration method in social work education* (Vol. 3). New York: Council on Social Work Education.

Stamm, A. J. (1969). NASW membership: Characteristics, deployment, and salaries. *Personnel Information, 12*.

Stein, H. (1970). Social work administration. In H. A. Schatz (Ed.), *Social work administration: A resource book*. New York: Council on Social Work Education.

Street, E. (1931). *Social work administration*. New York: Harper.

Thompson, J. D. (1970). Pittsburg Committee Report on the common and uncommon elements in administration. In H. A. Schatz (Ed.), *Social work administration: A resource book*. New York: Council on Social Work Education.

Trecker, H. B. (1977). *Social work administration: Principles and practices*. New York: Association Press.

Weinbach, R. W. (1998). *The social worker as manager*. Boston: Allyn & Bacon.

Weiner, M. E. (1982). *Human services management*. Homewood, IL: Dorsey.

Wish, N. B., & Mirabella, R. M. (1998). Nonprofit management education: Course offerings and practices in university-based programs. In M. O'Neill & K. Fletcher (Eds.), *Nonprofit management education* (pp. 13-22). Westport, CT: Praeger.

Social Work and Social Welfare Administration: A Historical Perspective

DAVID M. AUSTIN

The development of social welfare administration in the United States has followed a pattern that is distinctive, indeed unique, among national societies, with the possible exception of Canada. The development of social welfare administration in the United States has been shaped by four forces: the development of the "limited liability stock corporation" as the model for business organizations; the development of voluntary, nonprofit, charitable corporations during the last half of the 19th century; the development of professional training programs in social work and of social work as an organized profession beginning in the early 20th century; and the creation of a nationwide public social welfare sector beginning in the 1930s. This historical examination of social welfare administration will deal with all four of these forces, but with particular attention to the interface between the development of social work professional education and social welfare administration.

BEGINNINGS

Early settlements in what would become the United States incorporated English social welfare patterns in which the local community carried the responsibility for meeting the needs of those who could not maintain themselves (Leiby, 1978). However, in many of the settlements, the local community involved forms of governance in which there was a high degree of overlap, either formally or in terms of the individuals involved, between religious organization and civil government, whether among the Protestant New Englanders or the Quakers in Maryland and Pennsylvania, or those communities in which the Church of England was the dominant religious organization. The concern for people who needed help reflected both the community concerns of civil government and the "charity" missions of religious organizations and religious congregations.

The early growth of seaport cities was followed by an increase in the number of individual church organizations, primarily representing the various strains of Protestant theology coming out of Europe. When the Constitution established the principle of separation of civil government from religious organization, churches were free to develop their own patterns of charitable activities, activities that often included religious proselytizing. One outgrowth of this was the organization of charitable activities within individual churches under "lay" leadership, rather than under the leadership of the pastor or minister, particularly in the congregation-governed Protestant denominations. A second outgrowth was the city missions supported by Protestant churches and established in crowded, central-city, slum neighborhoods (Leiby, 1978).

The years following the 1860s Civil War brought dramatic changes in the United States, particularly in the Northeast and Midwest, the center of industrial development, urbanization, and large-scale immigration from Europe. The Civil War period resulted in a rapid expansion of industrial production in these regions. Factories, rather than the farmlands of the Midwest, became the employment centers for the majority of new immigrants. New arrivals crowded into cities. This resulted in a variety of social problems and public health problems, as well as creating a fear among wealthy families of the possibility of social unrest growing out of the revolutionary ideas of Karl Marx and Friedrich Engels, ideas that had been set loose in Europe as a response to the social and economic changes arising out of the Industrial Revolution (Lens, 1966).

One of the responses of wealthy businessmen and civic leaders in cities such as New York, Boston, Philadelphia, and Chicago was to support what became an alternative social welfare system, largely separate from the democratic, but boss-controlled, governance structures of these cities. This private, philanthropic social welfare system, which had its beginnings in the charity activities of churches, was an alternative to the expansion of public poor-relief programs, which were part of municipal and county governments in the larger cities (Lubove, 1965).

In part, this private philanthropic initiative reflected the unwillingness of the newly emerging, entrepreneurial business leaders to support a system of public taxes and public services that they did not control. This became particularly problematic as the new immigrants became voters, and political "ward bosses" became the centers of political control in the large cities. The existence of widespread corruption and graft in city government (Bruno, 1957, pp. 91-95; Leiby, 1978), which also reached into state government, reinforced the reluctance of wealthy businessmen to pay taxes to support a system of public social welfare services.

The diversity of the voluntary charitable and philanthropic organizations that emerged reflected the diverse, and often competitive pattern of religious organizations. The support for voluntary charity was reinforced by the philosophy that charity should be based on a personal connection between the person providing assistance and the person receiving assistance (Lowell, 1884). Without such a personal connection, it was argued, financial assistance to individuals would lead to "pauperism," that is, chronic dependency, which would be perpetuated into the next generation (Lubove, 1965).

The public sector services that were recognized by wealthy civic leaders were custodial institutions at the state level for groups of people viewed as needing special attention—people with mental illness, people who were mentally retarded, orphaned children, people who were blind or deaf, and criminals (Leiby, 1978). In the period following the Civil War, a number of state governments established unpaid state boards of charity, consisting of recognized civic leaders, to oversee the management of these institutions.

A meeting of members from several state boards of charities was held in 1874 in conjunction with a meeting of the American Social Science Association (Bruno, 1957). By 1879, a separate organization, the National Conference of Charities and Correction, was established. The National Conference, which met annually, also included civic leaders from the emerging private, nonprofit, philanthropic social welfare organizations in the cities (Broadhurst, 1971). These organizations included both those based in individual churches and religious denominations, and nonsectarian organizations, which were not affiliated with any one religious organization, although they broadly reflected Protestant traditions and theology (Marty, 1980).

The early, religiously based, social welfare organizations were organized largely as "charitable associations" with limited attention to any form of legal status—given the separation of church and state, which kept governments from intruding into the activities of individual churches or denominations. However, in the latter part of the 19th century, the "limited liability stock corporation," which made it possible for a large number of individuals to invest funds in a business without exposing themselves to the risk of individual responsibility for the debts of the firm if it went bankrupt—in comparison to the traditional business partnership—became a widely recognized form of business organization.

In turn, the nonprofit "corporation" became the preferred form that business leaders used for the organization of the philanthropic and civic activities they supported financially, in particular, the larger charity organizations, which had begun to employ a staff of investigators or agents who were responsible for investigating the need for assistance and determining the "worthiness" of individual families (Lubove, 1965). The wealthy civic leaders who agreed to serve as trustees, or as members of a board of directors, for a private, philanthropic nonprofit corporation could thus exercise control over the operations of the organization without incurring legal liability for debts or other obligations that might be incurred by the organization. One of the objectives of the business leaders who served as members of the boards of directors of the Charity Organization Societies that were established in many of the larger cities was to bring concepts of administrative efficiency from the world of business into the administration of charity (Lubove, 1965).

THE EMERGENCE OF THE VOLUNTARY SOCIAL WELFARE SECTOR

During the last half of the 19th century, there was a rapid development of this private, non-profit, philanthropic sector, particularly in the cities. In addition to charity agencies, this included higher education, museums, orchestras, public health programs, hospitals, and youth-serving organizations such as the YMCA and YWCA. These nongovernmental public service institutions became central elements in the pattern of "welfare capitalism" that became the pragmatic alternative in the United States to the choices posed by economic theorists between laissez-faire capitalism and European socialism.

In these philanthropic corporations, the most important leadership position was that of the chairman of the board of trustees or board of directors. The chairman, almost always male, was usually a wealthy businessman who was also one of the largest contributors to the support of the organization. The chairman often held this position for many years, in reality functioning as a volunteer chief executive officer (CEO), being actively involved in the running of the organization, including most, or all, personnel decisions. For example, Civil War General James Barnett served as the president of the Cleveland Associated Charities from 1884 to 1907 (Waite, 1960). Board committees in the charity agencies were involved in making decisions about the handling of individual case situations, and wives of board members were often active service volunteers in the form of "friendly visitors" (Leiby, 1978). The employed

staff, in addition to a "general secretary" consisted largely of investigators or agents.

Exceptions to this board-dominated pattern of organization were social welfare organizations that were initially created and run by a single individual with a social reform mission. This was particularly characteristic of the first generation of settlement houses, in which the "head-worker" was the person in charge, and the board of directors was essentially a fund-raising support body (Carson, 1992). Jane Addams is the most widely recognized among the original headworkers, but every large city had one or more "neighborhood settlements." However, the relationship between the board and the new headworker often became similar to that in other voluntary nonprofit service agencies when the original founder of the settlement retired or died, and the board of directors had the responsibility for selecting a new headworker.

During the last quarter of the 19th century, two important efforts were made to improve the efficiency and effectiveness of private charity administration. Under the leadership of influential businessmen, Charity Organization Societies (COSs) were established in many cities in an effort to establish some degree of order and coordination among the numerous charitable organizations, all of whom were seeking contributions from wealthy families and business leaders (Bruno, 1957; Leiby, 1978). During this same period, the leaders of the private charity movement made systematic efforts to eliminate public poor-relief programs (Kaplan, 1978). The second effort, to improve the effectiveness of voluntary charity organizations, involved the development of training programs for charity investigators, or agents who, by the end of the century, were being identified as "social workers."

A new source of organizational leadership for COS organizations and other voluntary social welfare agencies began to develop as colleges and universities established academic social science programs (Broadhurst, 1971). Particularly important was the development of the first Ph.D. program in social science at Johns Hopkins University. A number of men who graduated from this program became general secretaries or executives of philanthropic organizations, as did men who took undergraduate courses in social ethics at Harvard and other private universities.

The first widely recognized university-educated philanthropic administrator was Amos Warner (1894), who was appointed as general secretary of the Baltimore Charity Organization Society in 1887 while still a doctoral student at Johns Hopkins. Following completion of his doctoral studies, he was appointed to be the superintendent of charities for the District of Columbia. The most influential of the university-trained charity executives was Edward T. Devine, a graduate of the Wharton School of Business at the University of Pennsylvania, who was appointed as general secretary of the New York COS at the age of 29. In that position, he would have a leading role in the early development of professional education for social workers.

In 1893, Mary Richmond, who had been employed initially as an assistant treasurer at the Baltimore COS, was selected by its board, which included President Gilman of Johns Hopkins, to be general secretary following Amos Warner. From the beginning of her appointment as general secretary, Mary Richmond became recognized as a leader in the development of systematic charity, or "scientific philanthropy," as it became known in the 1890s. She

had become general secretary at the beginning of a national economic depression that affected not only Baltimore but most industrial cities. Voluntary charity organizations expanded their work, employing as investigators, in many cases, young women who had recently graduated from one of the new women's colleges. Richmond was particularly concerned with the need for systematic training of these new charity workers (Richmond, 1899).

At the center of the Richmond model of training for new staff members, most of whom had no personal experience with poverty or with the immigrant neighborhoods of big cities, was the importance of carrying out a systematic "social diagnosis" of each household situation (Richmond, 1917). This included an analysis not only of the problems and resources of the individual family but also of the potential sources of family, church, and neighborhood assistance that might be mobilized in support of a particular family.

At the 1897 National Conference, Mary Richmond made a speech calling for the establishment of a national social work training center (Richmond, 1897). In 1898, Edward Devine at the New York COS initiated the New York Summer School of Applied Philanthropy, which, by 1910, had become a 2-year graduate program of professional training in social work (Meier, 1954). By the early 1920s, there was a national association of schools of social work, as well as four national associations of professional social workers.

From 1900 to 1909, Richmond served as the general secretary of the Society for Organizing Charity in Philadelphia. She was, in many ways, the first woman to be a career social welfare administrator. She was dependent on her salary for economic support, rather than being supported by a husband or family wealth, sources of economic support available to a number of other women in social welfare leadership positions.

During her 9 years in Philadelphia, Mary Richmond was a nationally recognized writer and speaker about the administration of charity agencies (Pittman-Munke, 1985). She also served as the editor of a national newsletter for such organizations. Among the concerns in her writings and speeches were the respective responsibilities of the philanthropic charity organization executive and the board of directors, a subject that was an important part of her experience in Philadelphia. In 1909, Richmond was invited to join the staff of the newly created Russell Sage Foundation. In her role as the director of the Charity Organization Department at the foundation, she served until 1928 as a national consultant to charity organizations across the United States (Glenn, Brandt, & Andrews, 1947).

THE 1920S

The 1920s brought important changes in the pattern of administration in private nonprofit social welfare organizations. There were more individuals with technical/professional education in social work and with professional experience in nonprofit social welfare agencies. Some of them, primarily men, were recruited by the boards of directors to serve as administrators. James F. Jackson, who served as general secretary of the Cleveland Associated Charities from 1904 to 1927, was one example. A graduate of Carleton College, he served as general secretary of the St. Paul Associated Charities and as secretary of the Minnesota State Board of Charities, and he spent a year at the New

York COS before coming to Cleveland. Members of the board of the Cleveland Associated Charities "were impressed, too, by the breadth of his knowledge and experience and by the down-to-earth practicality that accompanied his enthusiasm and vision" (Waite, 1960, p. 76).

The new social agency executives, like Jackson, often brought their own ideas about the most effective way to organize social work services. To implement these ideas, it was essential to clarify the relationship between the responsibilities of the executive and those of the board of directors. Out of this period came the assertion, primarily supported by agency executives, that the function of the board of directors was to establish policy, whereas the function of the executive was to have full responsibility for the day-to-day operations of the service agency, including the hiring of other personnel (Kirschner, 1986).

As Francis McLean (1927), a national consultant on the staff of the Russell Sage Foundation, stated, "In the actual case work of the [charity organization] society, a board will be extremely chary of interfering" (cited in Lubove, 1965, p. 163). Along with a redefinition of the roles of the board and the executive came such rationalizing ideas as rotating board memberships, board nominating committees, limited terms for board officers, and annual elections of board officers, all intended, in part, to reduce the level of control often exercised by long-term board members. For example, from the 1920s on, 4 years was the longest that any individual served as president of the Cleveland Associated Charities/Family Service Association, in comparison to the 23 years served by General Barnett (Waite, 1960).

There was no systematic training in the 1920s for tasks of administration in either schools of social work or in social science departments, although there were recommendations that social work education should include such training. James Hagerty (1931), who carried out a study of social work education in the 1920s, asserted that the "most important task they [schools] should be engaged in" was "the education of the leaders, the organizers, and the administrators—in short, the executives in social work administration" (p. 99). On-the-job experience in a voluntary social welfare agency, including staff supervision, was the primary qualification for appointment as an agency executive. The Milford Conference Report in 1929, representing a national effort to define the nature of social work, included administration as a fundamental technique of social work, but the report included detailed recommendations for training only for casework and did not specify what administrators should know and be able to do (Patti, 1983).

As Arthur Dunham (1939) stated, "Administration was not ordinarily distinguished from direct practice, nor thought of as a separate function" (p. 16). The major responsibilities of the nonprofit executive were internal, overseeing the work of staff members who combined various amounts of formal educational preparation and professional experience. The members of the board of directors carried the general responsibility for acting on program policy issues brought to it by the executive, raising the funds for the service organization, and overseeing the budget.

The new role for the service agency executive was strengthened by the development of federated community fund-raising campaigns, which began in the second decade of the 20th century and expanded dramatically during the period of World War I. Business leaders supported the concept of a once-a-year fund-raising campaign, the Community Chest, to replace a continuous, year-long process of individual appeals from each community agency (Cutlip, 1965). In most cities, the organization of the Community Chest was followed by the organization of a "council of social agencies" as a structure through which the service agencies could participate in the process of setting a goal for the annual fund-raising campaign and in carrying out community "surveys" to document the need for greater financial support.

In these developments, the agency executive became the primary agency representative and spokesperson, although the president of the board of directors was also often involved. Social service executives also had a leading role in the creation of the national associations that emerged in such fields as child welfare and charity/family service, associations that began to be a major source of consultation assistance for communities organizing new social service agencies.

Some of the earliest training materials dealing specifically with the administration of nonprofit social welfare organizations, other than the materials that came from the Charity Organization Department of the Russell Sage Foundation (Glenn et al., 1947), were developed within the YMCA, which was the largest of the national youth-serving organizations. The national YMCA was essentially a national federation of local organizations, each of which had its own board of directors, raised its own funds, and developed a program that was responsive to local interests. Educational programs for training YMCA personnel to establish consistent standards of work throughout the organization were established at George Williams College in Chicago and Springfield College in

Massachusetts. Financial support as well as employment opportunities for young adult members of the YMCA came from the business leaders who served on the YMCA boards of directors. The model for the YMCA general secretary was the application of business-like management methods in an expanding organization (Johns, 1954).

THE EMERGENCE OF A
PUBLIC SOCIAL WELFARE SECTOR

Local public poor-relief programs, which began to be called "public welfare," expanded during the first decades of the 20th century, particularly in periods of economic crisis and high unemployment, such as the late 1920s (Breckinridge, 1927). However, the National Conference of Social Work, as the National Conference of Charities and Corrections had been retitled in 1918, gave little attention to the organization and management of these public welfare programs.

> During the period of surprising prosperity (1922-1929) that followed the depression [1921], when, however, the number of the unemployed was actually rising in every large city in the country, and when both public and private resources for assistance to the unemployed and their families was strained to the utmost, the current Proceedings [of the National Conference of Social Work] was silent. (Bruno, 1957, pp. 297-298)

Tax-supported welfare programs continued to be regarded with suspicion by business leaders, as well as by leaders in the private philanthropy sector, including President Herbert Hoover.

However, during the first quarter of the 20th century, there were also efforts to promote the establishment of a governmental system of social insurances. This effort was influenced by the development of national systems of old age pensions for industrial workers in Germany in the 1880s and in England in the 1890s. Academic economists from the United States who had studied in Germany during the last part of the 19th century provided leadership for the American Social Security Association (Rubinow, 1913).

Governor Robert La Follette of Wisconsin, together with Professor John Commons, an economist who had moved from Johns Hopkins to the University of Wisconsin, developed the proposal for the first state-level social insurance program—workmen's compensation—which was approved by the Wisconsin state legislature in 1911. During the 1920s, a number of states began to establish old age and blind pension programs and mothers pensions, as well as workmen's compensation programs (Chambers, 1963). States and counties had also begun to establish local public child welfare programs to take care of abused and neglected children, particularly in rural and small-town communities that had no private social service organizations (Bremner, 1974, p. 616).

The 1930s brought dramatic changes in the structure of social welfare in the United States. Faced with dramatic unemployment soon after his inauguration in 1929, Herbert Hoover turned to the Community Chest and the private charity/family service agencies to serve as the ultimate "safety-net" (Bruno, 1957). However, the economic devastation was too extensive and too prolonged (Lens, 1969). The pressure for more far-reaching action came both from social reform advocates, including settlement house leaders and other social workers, and from business leaders, who were threatened by social protest and a rapidly growing and increasingly militant union movement (Lens, 1966).

State governments, responding to the demands from cities for help in providing assistance to unemployed workers and their families, rapidly exhausted their financial resources. Under President Franklin D. Roosevelt, temporary programs of emergency assistance were initiated followed by the appointment of a Committee on Economic Security to develop longer-term solutions to the problems of unemployment and household poverty. At issue were the choices to be made between a system of governmentally funded pensions or contributory social insurance; between federal administration or state administration; and between a standardized, impersonal, rule-regulated bureaucratic pattern of administration or an individualized social service program, including both financial assistance and casework counseling.

In the Social Security Act of 1935, the United States established a diverse public social welfare system that included both employer/employee, contributory, social insurance programs and government-financed, means-tested public assistance programs, both federal-administered and state-administered systems and both impersonal, rule-regulated programs and individualized social service programs. The policy extremes included in the Social Security Act were represented by the contributory, federally administered, impersonal, social insurance program for retired workers 65 and older and the general revenue-funded, federally regulated-state administered, individualized, Aid to Dependent Children (ADC, later Aid to Families With Dependent Children [AFDC]) program. The ADC program was included primarily at the insistence of the social work leadership, in particular Grace and Edith Abbott, Julia

Lathrop, and Sophrenisba Breckinridge, who were identified with Hull House, the establishment of the Children's Bureau in 1912, and the creation of the School of Social Service Administration at the University of Chicago (Gordon, 1994).

Whereas the retirement insurance program and the state-administered unemployment insurance programs were developed within a bureaucratic public administration framework, the ADC (and Aid to Blind and Aid to Aged and later Aid to the Disabled) public assistance programs led to the creation of a nationwide system of public social welfare administration at the state and county level, with a mixture of bureaucratic and professional social work characteristics. The basic characteristics of these public welfare programs were largely determined by Harry Hopkins, a social worker who was also one of Franklin Roosevelt's closest advisers (Kurzman, 1974).

Key elements in the new public welfare programs, as set forth by Hopkins, were that to ensure universal coverage, the programs were to be administered through a single state agency and within the state by state and county governments, not through grants to local nonprofit charity organizations. The workers in these governmental agencies were also to be protected through civil service regulations to keep the employment of public welfare workers and the granting of financial assistance from being used for political purposes (Leighninger, 1987).

Although some cities and states had established public welfare departments during the 1920s (Breckinridge, 1927; Bruno, 1957), the expansion of such departments came with the Federal Emergency Relief Administration in the early 1930s under Roosevelt and Hopkins. It made funds available to the states for emergency assistance. In many instances, states and counties turned to existing voluntary charity organizations for experienced workers, many of whom became supervisors and administrators in the new public welfare agencies (Waite, 1960). However, over time, the new public welfare agencies turned to the field of public administration for guidance in establishment of administrative procedures, rather than to social work, which was centered on casework practice (Street, 1940).

By the end of the 1930s, the focus of state/county public welfare programs had shifted from emergency assistance for unemployed workers and their families to the administration of the ADC, Aid to the Blind, and Aid to the Aged federal/state programs. Its social work supporters initially conceived of the ADC program as an expanded version of the private charity/family service agency, with both individualized "social casework" counseling, as well as financial assistance based on the development of individualized family budgets (Gordon, 1994).

The Social Security Act (Title V, part 3) also provided federal grants-in-aid to support "child welfare" programs in rural counties (Bremner, 1974, p. 615). In many states, these child welfare programs were modeled after the private, nonprofit "child protection" agencies that existed in larger urban areas. A small number of professionally educated social workers were employed, sometimes one person for an entire county, or combination of counties. A model of professional leadership and professional mentoring developed among the public child welfare workers in many states (Bremner, 1974, p. 618). Prior experience "in the field" was assumed to be a requirement for appointment to administrative leadership positions.

Within less than a decade, there were two social welfare sectors. One sector included the relatively small, voluntary, nonprofit service organizations with staffs of professional workers and professionally experienced executives, as well as the public child welfare service organized around a similar professionalized model. The other sector included the larger state or county public welfare offices, often administering multimillion-dollar "entitlement" programs, identified as being part of social work but with only a few individuals, at the most, with any type of specialized training in either social work or administration.

The organizational separation of public social welfare from the private voluntary version of social welfare was symbolized by the organization in 1931 of the American Public Welfare Association by public welfare administrators. This action came, in part, as a reaction to the limited attention that had been given to the unemployment crisis and to the administration of public welfare programs by the National Conference of Social Work. But it also reflected the need of state administrators for their own channel of communication with federal officials and lawmakers.

This dual, parallel, but largely separated private and public structure of welfare capitalism in the United States continued from the late 1930s until the 1970s and 1980s, when the creation of quasi-governmental nonprofit service organizations and the use of purchase-of-service contracts between governmental organizations and private nonprofit organizations began to blur the distinctions between these two sectors. This process culminated in the 1990s with the large-scale privatization of governmental social service programs.

By the end of the 1930s, there were also two models of social welfare administration—administration in the private nonprofit sector and administration in the public welfare sector. Nationally, the headquarters of the private non-profit social welfare sector was in New York City; the headquarters of the public social welfare sector was in Washington, D.C. The private nonprofit model of administration assumed that professional education and direct service experience were significant criteria for appointment to an administrative position. There was also a general assumption that such administrative positions were in small and medium-size organizations. The executive was directly involved with personnel administration and probably personally acquainted with all of the professional staff, if not with every member of the support staff. Moreover, a central element in the role of the nonprofit administrator was the working relationship with members of the volunteer board of directors and, through them, with well-to-do supporters of the organization and with business leaders in the community. The board members, in turn, were largely responsible for overseeing the organizational budget and providing for the financial support of the organization.

In the public administration/public welfare model of administration, individuals with and without direct service experience were appointed to positions of responsibility for the management of large-scale programs with bureaucratic, standardized procedures, both for the implementation of the service programs and for internal personnel and fiscal procedures. Among the credentials that were often relevant for such appointments, as in other positions in public administration following World War II,

was prior experience as a military officer, with military veterans being given preference in civil service selection procedures.

RECENT DEVELOPMENTS IN PUBLIC AND PRIVATE SOCIAL WELFARE ADMINISTRATION

During the 1960s, there were dramatic increases in the public social welfare sector. Public child welfare programs, with federal funding under the Social Security Act, were expanded to cover urban areas as well as rural counties with statewide administrative structures. In 1962, federal funding for social work counseling services was added to the redesignated AFDC program. The AFDC program also grew dramatically, as the industrial recession of the late 1950s rippled through urban areas. The increased numbers of unemployed men became reflected in an increase in the number of family breakups and desertions and, in turn, the number of single-parent households in central-city neighborhoods who were receiving AFDC payments. In large cities, many of these households resided in large, high-rise, public housing projects, which served to isolate them from access to most employment opportunities.

The establishment of the War on Poverty by President Lyndon Johnson resulted in the creation of government-sponsored nonprofit "community action" agencies, agencies that often drew on the cadre of experienced social work administrators from the nonprofit sector for executive leadership. By the late 1960s, the development of community mental health center programs, many of which were organized as governmental nonprofit organizations, also drew social workers into positions of administrative leadership.

During the 1970s and 1980s, a large number of new, nonprofit, community-based, or "alternative" service organizations were created in cities. These organizations were responsive to newly identified needs—violence against women, homelessness, services for de-institutionalized mental health patients, and, later, services for HIV-AIDS patients. They were also generally "anti-establishment," anti-bureaucratic, and hostile to standard forms of hierarchical administrative practice. Distinctions between employed staff and volunteers were blurred, and collective decision making substituted for formal lines of authority (Perlmutter, 1988; Powell, 1986).

Through the 1970s, there was an assumption that growth would continue in the public social welfare sector. AFDC programs had grown dramatically during the 1960s, although at the beginning of the 1970s, there was a federally mandated separation between the tasks of eligibility determination and supportive social work services. This ultimately resulted in the disappearance of individualized social work counseling services for AFDC households. The passage of Title XX of the Social Security Act in the early 1970s provided funding for a variety of "hard" social services for AFDC parents, including day care and family planning, intended to replace "soft" social work counseling services. Food Stamps went from a small demonstration program to a nationwide, universal program of financial assistance. The consolidation of Aid to the Blind, Aid to Aged, and Aid to the Disabled in the federally administered Supplementary Security Income (SSI) program in 1972 removed these programs from state public welfare management, converting them into a single, federally administered rule-regulated program with a public administration, bureaucratic administrative structure.

The expansion of the number and scope of categorical federal social welfare programs brought increased attention to the preparation of social welfare managers and to the necessity of coordination among specialized programs. Federal funding was provided for the development of management training programs in a small number of schools of social work. The American Public Welfare Association received funds for a national program of in-service training for managers in public social service organizations. Federally funded demonstration programs in service coordination at state and local levels contributed to the identification of "case management" as an important part of service provision, particularly for multiproblem family situations and for individuals with chronic illness conditions, such as severe and persistent mental illness. The concept of case management was, in reality, very similar to the concept of "district case conferences" dealing with individual impoverished households, which had been one of the initiatives of the COSs 100 years earlier.

The 1980s brought a sharp reversal in the expansion of the public social welfare structure (Perlmutter, 1984). There were cutbacks in the level of federal support for social welfare programs, including community action and urban renewal; federal categorical programs, such as support for community mental health centers, were converted into federal block grants; and there were proposals for the contracting out or privatization of publicly funded programs (Kamerman & Kahn, 1989). Professional qualifications in social work were not viewed as useful for administrative positions in public social welfare programs, as financial management and technical skills in program evaluation and cost-effectiveness analysis, using computer-produced data, began to receive increased attention.

By the end of the 1980s, the establishment of the JOBS program began the transformation of AFDC from what had initially been an individualized social casework, household-support program primarily for widows to an employment-oriented, bureaucratically administered program primarily for unmarried, separated, and divorced mothers. This transformation was completed with the 1996 passage of the Personal Responsibility and Work Opportunity Reconciliation Act (PRWORA), including the Temporary Assistance to Needy Families (TANF) legislation. This legislation also shifted the responsibility for program administration from state public welfare/human service agencies to state employment services, or "workforce commissions."

The 1980s brought renewed interest in the role of voluntary nonprofit service organizations as direct service providers, as an alternative to the expansion of public sector service organizations. The use of government-sponsored nonprofit corporations, for example, for the organization of community mental health centers, also served to limit the direct control by state and local governments over publicly funded social welfare services. By the end of the 1980s, it was apparent that privatization contracts with public funding bodies, rather than charitable contributions, had become the major source of funding for many established nonprofit service organizations and even for some of the newer, community-based, alternative organizations (Salamon, 1989). However, reductions in the total amount of public funding

available also led to increased attention being given to "cut-back management" in both governmental programs and nonprofit organizations (Edwards, Lebold, & Yankey, 1998) and to increased financial pressures on traditional nonprofit organizations (Kettner & Martin, 1996). Some nonprofit service organizations began to place increased emphasis on earnings from user fees and from ancillary, profit-making activities (Weisbrod, 1998).

During this period, the pattern of funding through the United Way began to change from the earlier budget-balancing approach, in which the United Way funds were the major source of funding for many private nonprofit service agencies, to a more specifically targeted and contract mode under which the proportion of United Way funds in any single agency's budget was substantially reduced (Brillant, 1990). Provisions for donors to designate which agency their contributions should go to, including agencies that were not members of the United Way, reduced the importance of the United Way budget review and allocation process in shaping the development of the private nonprofit service sector.

This development also increased the importance of financial entrepreneurship for executives in private nonprofit service organizations (Young, 1991). The shift toward an administrative focus on financial management and entrepreneurial initiative raised new questions about the conceptual connections between training for social work administration and the rest of the professional education program in social work.

The privatization movement meant that public social welfare administrators, including the administrators of public child welfare services and public mental health services, were increasingly involved in the processes of contract management. Responsibilities for the day-to-day operation of such programs shrank as public programs were declassified, deprofessionalized, and privatized, with reductions in the number of directly employed government service providers. The development of contract proposals for governmental funding bodies and for foundations, and the preparation of the reports called for under such contracts, became a major function of nonprofit administrators (Green, 1998). The detailed responsibility for maintaining the flow of agency funding was now fully on the shoulders of the agency executive (Grønbjerg, 1993; Kramer, 1985), although boards of directors often took on an expanded fund-raising responsibility, in part because many of the funding contracts did not cover the full costs of providing services and did not provide support for core administrative costs of organizational maintenance.

The 1990s brought an acceleration of these changes in both public and private social welfare. The commercialization of health care and mental health care services began with private employer health insurance contracts, but it was then extended to government-funded mental health services and Medicaid-funded medical services. The process of privatization was also extended in many states to include publicly funded child welfare services of many types. The additional complexities in funding arrangements, particularly for obtaining government funds, contributed to a process of merger and consolidation among traditional nonprofit social service and health organizations (Singer & Yankey, 1991; Wernet & Jones, 1992; Yankey, Wester, & Campbell, 1998), as well as to an increased emphasis on the financial management responsibilities of nonprofit chief executive officers (Alperin, 1993; Strachan, 1998).

By the 1980s, there was also an expansion in employment opportunities for social work administrators in for-profit business firms, in particular in employee assistance programs and in for-profit service organizations, which provided specialized services through contracts with employee assistance programs (Akabas & Kurzman, 1982). The appearance of for-profit "managed care" and "managed behavioral health care" organizations in the 1990s also created some new management opportunities for social workers with professional experience in mental health services and health care services.

THEORIES OF ADMINISTRATION AND SOCIAL WELFARE ADMINISTRATION

The role of organizational theories in the development of social welfare administration is dealt with in greater detail in a later chapter (Hasenfeld, Chapter 5). However, the role of organizational theory has been affected by the diversity in the settings in which social welfare administration has been practiced during the past century. In the early decades of the 20th century, administration in the private nonprofit sector was viewed as essentially a facilitating function that supported the work of professional practitioners. It was generally assumed that the "mission" of the service organization as defined by the board of directors, representing the financial supporters of the organization, was compatible with the social service objectives of the professional staff.

The administrator provided the linkage between the board of directors and the professional staff, interpreting the perceptions of each group to the other with the objective of maintaining a harmonious operation. It was also assumed that services provided by the staff members of the organization were, in fact, beneficial for the service users and appreciated, so that there was an assumed consistency in objectives among contributors, board members, administrators, service staff, and users. The scope of the service program was defined by the level of contribution support, which was largely the responsibility of the board of directors.

Little attention was given to deconstructing the motives of board members, professional staff members, or service users. For example, the most visible and influential voluntary social service organizations, both at a local level and nationally, maintained service-eligibility patterns, prior to the 1960s, that were consistent with 100 years of racial segregation and discrimination. These service patterns were seldom questioned, avoiding an examination of the personal and community damage created by them (Morton, 1998). However, community-based or alternative social service programs created in the 1960s and 1970s attacked many of the underlying assumptions of the traditional nonprofit service organizations, claiming that both administrative structures and service patterns of traditional agencies reinforced institutional racism and sexism (Hyde, 1992). This contributed to a more careful examination of the diversity of interests represented by the various stakeholder constituencies of nonprofit social welfare organizations.

The development of the public social services introduced alternative conceptions of the role of social welfare administration. From the beginning, social work, as part of the reform movements of the early 20th century, rejected the well-established practice of governmental administration as the allocation of political spoils—jobs and service benefits—in return for votes. However, the official theory of public administration, originally set forth by Woodrow Wilson (1887/1978) as an alternative to the spoils system, emphasized the role of administrators as politically neutral implementers of the public policies established through the democratic political system, regardless of their personal judgments about the soundness, or the humaneness, of the policies adopted.

Public administrators were expected to be independent of the political system so that the administration of public services could proceed smoothly even after a shift from liberal to conservative control of the governing body, or vice versa. Such a concept, however, created tensions within social work, particularly in the 1960s, when social welfare administrators in southern states attempted to rationalize their role as social workers in carrying out racially discriminatory policies established by the existing governmental structure in their state. Similar tensions exist currently as public social welfare administrators are expected to implement legislated policies under the PRWORA of 1996 that exclude immigrant residents and ultimately can deny all forms of systematic financial assistance to children in the most poverty-stricken households.

Contemporary theories about organizational processes include those that emphasize the role of deterministic social processes, both within individual organizations and in the society at large, in shaping the events in individual organizations, contrasted with voluntaristic theories, which place more emphasis on the role of organizational leaders and other organizational participants in shaping the development of the individual organization. To a substantial degree, deterministic theories, including organizational ecology and institutional theory (Tucker, Baum, & Singh, 1992), have been generated by social scientists, who have focused on the generalities of social dynamics across a population of organizations. Voluntaristic leadership theories have been generated by researchers and theory builders in professional schools, such as business schools and schools of social work, or by consultants whose responsibility it is to prepare individual administrators to take responsibility for the performance of particular organizations. Leadership theories are more likely to be based on qualitative field studies and single-case studies than on quantitative studies of larger populations of organizations.

Writers such as Mary Parker Follett (Graham, 1995; Metcalf & Urwick, 1941) and, more recently, Mintzberg (1989), Sayles (1976), Peters and Waterman (1982), Quinn (1988), Drucker (1992), and Kanter (1997) focus on the interactive entrepreneurial leadership role of administrators in shaping organizational performance. Underlying these voluntaristic leadership approaches is an assumption that individual actors can, in fact, through individual initiatives be a dynamic and decisive factor in improving the effectiveness and efficiency of organizations.

These leadership perspectives have recently entered the social work administration literature primarily through the writings of Quinn, as interpreted by Edwards and Austin (1991; Edwards, Austin, & Altpeter, 1998). The organizational leadership assumptions, which have been reflected in social welfare administration textbooks, emphasize the entrepreneurial leadership behaviors of organizational administrators—initiating, controlling, interacting personally, and adapting—under conditions of unpredictable change and opportunity (Edwards & Yankey, 1991; Edwards, Yankey, & Altpeter, 1998).

SOCIAL WELFARE ADMINISTRATION AND THE ORGANIZED PROFESSION OF SOCIAL WORK

Social welfare administrators and social work faculty members teaching administration have always had a marginal connection with official organizational structures within the organized profession of social work and within social work education (Gummer, 1987). In the private nonprofit model of administration, many administrators identified with their field of practice—child welfare, family service, mental health, settlements, and community centers—rather than with administration as a practice method. In the public social services state, administrators and other public assistance managers often became individual members of the American Public Welfare Association (APWA). In the 1980s, state child welfare administrators established the National Association of Public Child Welfare Administrators as a subsection of APWA.

Administration in social work was the one area of social work practice that had not established a national social work association prior to the consolidation that led to the creation of

NASW in 1956. However, during the early years of NASW, when specialty sections were established for the pre-existing professional associations that had been merged into a single national association, a Council on Social Work Administration was created. However, it and the other specialty sections were, in turn, eliminated shortly after NASW became an established organization.

In 1985, The Network for Social Work Managers was organized, following a meeting of administrators at the NASW Professional Conference. The initial leadership came primarily from individuals involved in social welfare administration in national organizations and within the federal government. As of 1998, there were over 500 members in the Network. In 1994, the Network became the sponsor of the journal *Administration in Social Work,* and in 1998, the Academy of Certified Social Work Managers was created to establish a Certified Social Work Manager Program.

In 1987, faculty members teaching in the areas of administration and community organization created a specialized faculty organization, the Association for Community Organization and Social Administration (ACOSA), primarily because of the lack of attention to these areas of the curriculum in the Annual Program Meetings (APM) of the Council on Social Work Education (CSWE). ACOSA currently has some 400 members. After holding separate meetings prior to the APM for several years, ACOSA was recognized as a symposium-sponsoring organization within the APM program structure and has organized symposiums at each APM. However, these symposiums have been limited to social work faculty members; there is no interaction with practicing administrators. In 1994,

ACOSA became the sponsor of the journal *Community Practice in Social Work.*

THE SOCIAL WORK CURRICULUM AND EDUCATION FOR ADMINISTRATION

The selection of agency administrators from among individuals with professional casework education and professional experience persisted in private nonprofit "social service agencies" in the period following World War II. However, questions emerged about the role of social work education in the preparation of individuals for public social service administration. Individuals from a variety of backgrounds, including both social work and public administration, who were being employed as administrators in public social service programs came to schools of social work seeking training in administration. The place of training for social welfare administration in the professional curriculum was part of the larger set of issues involving the relation of professional social work education to the new system of public social services.

During the late 1920s and particularly in the 1930s, undergraduate social work degree programs were established, first within sociology departments and then as separate degree programs, in state universities and private colleges in the Midwest and Southwest, particularly in states where graduate social work education programs did not exist (Austin, 1998). The main purpose of these programs was to prepare men and women for positions in government public welfare agencies (Leighninger, 1987). This was in part a response to the human crisis of the Depression, but it was also based on an assumption that there would be a demand for college-educated social workers in state and county public welfare organizations.

These undergraduate social work programs, some of which also included an optional "fifth year" program of graduate studies leading to a master's degree, sought recognition from the American Association of Schools of Social Work (AASSW) as accredited social work education programs (Leighninger, 1987). The AASSW, which had established a requirement for 2 years of graduate studies as the basis of accreditation, refused to grant such recognition. An intense conflict developed, which ultimately led to a national study of social work/social welfare personnel training needs under the leadership of Ernest Hollis and Alice Taylor, who were federal leaders in education and social welfare (Hollis & Taylor, 1951).

One outcome of this study was the creation of a new governing body for social work education—the CSWE. There was also a reaffirmation of the basic structure of professional social work education—2 years of graduate study in a program affiliated with a college or university (Leighninger, 1987). Having confirmed that accreditation would be limited to graduate programs, there was a concern with the need to define more explicitly the nature of the professional curriculum.

In response to the concerns about preparing social workers for administrative positions in public welfare, the Hollis/Taylor (1951) study recommended that the social work education curriculum be broadened to give more attention to "administration, supervision, teaching, and research" (p. 397). However, the existing graduate, accredited, social work education programs, largely in private colleges and universities, were organized around the private nonprofit model of social work practice, with a central emphasis on teaching social casework. This model assumed that professional education should focus on the preparation of entry-level social caseworkers and that selection for administrative positions should be based on professional experience as a social caseworker rather than on formal training in administration (Spencer, 1959).

In 1952, following the Hollis/Taylor report, the new CSWE issued a curriculum policy statement declaring that information about organizations and administrative procedures was to be included for all students, but only schools with "adequate resources" would be able to offer a practice concentration in administration: "The educational objectives for administration in the Policy Statement are limited and timid" (Dinerman & Geismar, 1984, p. 11). This meant that the social work curriculum was to continue to focus on the preparation of entry-level direct service social caseworkers; the assumption remained that no social worker should be appointed to an administrative position without first having served as a professionally educated social caseworker.

CSWE followed the issuance of this curriculum policy statement by commissioning a national curriculum study, which was carried out under the leadership of Professor Warner Boehm of Rutgers University. The curriculum study recommended that administration be included in the graduate curriculum as one of five professional practice methods (Boehm, 1959). However, the curriculum policy statement issued by CSWE in 1962, following the failure of the CSWE to adopt major recommendations of the Boehm study, referred to administration only as an "enabling method," to be treated as an informational knowledge area for direct service practitioners (CSWE, 1962). A footnote was added: "Provision may be made by schools with adequate resources for a concentration in administration . . . for specially selected students" (p. 5).

Although the 1962 curriculum policy study had excluded administration as a core professional practice area in social work to be included in all curricula, a growing number of schools offered concentrations or specializations in administration and/or community organization, as forms of "macro" professional practice. This development was influenced, in part, by the establishment of the doctoral education program at the Florence Heller School for Advanced Studies in Social Welfare at Brandeis University in 1959. During the 1960s, this was the largest of the new social work doctoral programs. The Heller School curriculum was based on a macro-level social science approach to social welfare, with an emphasis on political science, policy analysis, and quantitative research. Many of the 1960s graduates from this program became deans and senior faculty members of graduate social work education programs in the 1970s and supported the development of macro practice concentrations.

As part of the effort to develop a larger cadre of trained administrators for the expanding public social welfare sector, short-term administration training programs were established for public social welfare managers in the 1970s. These programs were organized by schools of social work with funding through Title XX of the Social Security Act, which for a short period of time earmarked a portion of the funds available to each state specifically for public social services staff development training by schools of social work. There were also several federally funded curriculum development projects during the 1970s, often with an emphasis on interdisciplinary content and joint degree programs.

In the curriculum policy statements that CSWE issued in the decades following 1962, the issue of including or not including specific practice concentrations in the graduate professional curriculum was avoided by stating that graduate programs must include some form of "advanced practice" concentrations, and, in turn, provide justification for the particular concentrations that were included.

In the early 1970s, CSWE, with federal funding, carried out a national study of macro practice concentrations; it indicated that a substantial number of the graduate programs had concentrations in macro practice areas, including administration, but that only some 10% to 15% of the students in these schools selected such concentrations and that only 5% of all graduate social work students were enrolled in such concentrations (Kazmarski & Macarov, 1976). However, the growth in the number of schools of social work with macro practice concentrations leveled off in the 1980s. Recent reports indicate little change since then. In 1998, CSWE reported that some 14% of the more than 34,000 students enrolled in MSW-degree programs selected macro practice concentrations, including administration, planning, and community organization (CSWE, 1998).

A 1991 study of macro concentration curricula included information from 44 graduate schools of social work, out of 59 schools that had identified themselves in 1988 as having a macro practice concentration (McNutt, 1995). These curricula included various combinations of administration, community organization, and policy practice. McNutt notes,

The data suggested that the stress is on interpersonal/interactional skills (such as communication and participatory management). While there is a core of agreement over which areas must be covered, several technical areas (financial management and personnel management) are either ignored or treated in a superficial manner. (p. 71)

Professional literature pointed out that many beginning social workers would be supervisors and administrators after a few years of direct practice experience (Patti, 1983) and that, therefore, graduate students should have more content in these areas. But this did not significantly change curricula or the curriculum choices made by students. The emphasis among faculties, and among students, the largest group of which came from undergraduate programs in psychology, continued to be primarily on the development of the knowledge base and skills perceived as being required for initial employment as a direct service or clinical practitioner. Students choosing a concentration in administration were more likely to be those individuals who already had work experience in social service settings. This pattern has continued. For example, a survey of the graduates from the 1995-1996 academic year at the University of Michigan School of Social Work indicated that 12% were in macro-practice positions, whereas 82% were in some form of clinical practice or clinical case management (School of Social Work, 1998).

The separation between preparation for clinical or direct practice professional service and preparation for administration is reflected in recent changes in the examination content of the Advanced Practice (for nonclinical experienced practitioners) licensing examination administered through the AASSWB. A November 1996 report states that in a 1996 revised form

of the Advanced Practice examination, the content on direct practice issues was decreased from 32% to 17%, while there were increases in content on diversity (2% to 5%), communication (3% to 7%), and ethics (3% to 8%), with the addition of a new content area of "Social Work Interface With Other Systems" at 7% (AASSWB, 1996).

Increased attention to the role of nonprofit service organizations, beginning in the 1980s with privatization and the expansion of governmental contracts with nonprofit organizations, has been followed by the development of new graduate academic programs dealing with nonprofit management. In March 1997, 76 colleges and universities were offering graduate degree programs in the management of nonprofit organizations, including three or more courses (Wish & Mirabella, 1998). Among these programs, 47% were affiliated with schools of public administration/public policy, 14% were affiliated with schools of social work, and 8% were affiliated with schools of business management (Wish & Mirabella, 1998). Michael O'Neill of the Institute for Nonprofit Organization Management at the University of San Francisco has stated that these programs include some 1,000 students a year ("The Nonprofit Sector," 1998). These nonprofit management education programs attend not only to health and social service programs but to the entire range of nonprofit organizations, including museums, symphony orchestras, private colleges and universities, foundations, and so on.

Central to these nonprofit management education programs, and largely missing from management education programs in schools of social work, is curriculum content dealing explicitly with economics, fund-raising, public finance, and fiscal management. Similar findings were reported by Rimer (1987) in comparing administration concentrations in social work with MPA, MBA, and MPH programs.

ADMINISTRATIVE PRACTICE IN THE SOCIAL WORK LITERATURE

Mary Parker Follett, a graduate of Radcliffe College with a year of study in England, became a settlement house social worker at the Roxbury Neighborhood House in Boston in 1900, and she worked there for many years (Metcalf & Urwick 1941). Originally recognized as the initiator of the proposal adopted by the Boston School Board for using neighborhood schools in Boston as community development centers with adult education and community leadership training, Follett was appointed by the governor of Massachusetts to serve as a public member of the state arbitration board that dealt with labor-management conflicts. Through an increasing involvement in positions of public leadership dealing with business leaders during the 1920s and early 1930s, she became recognized as an international expert on business management (Graham, 1995; Metcalf & Urwick, 1941). In 1924, and in several years following, she was invited to speak to the annual conference of the Bureau of Personnel Management in New York City. Later, she was invited to speak at the National Institute of Industrial Psychology in England.

The writings of Mary Parker Follett were critical of the then-popular engineering version of scientific management, which emphasized a rational, machine-like organization of production with a hierarchical, command-and-control model of administration, like that of a military organization. Her writings on management emphasized the importance of the science of psychology rather than the science of engineering (Follett, 1924). She wrote about the human relationships involved in organizational management, including the role of power, constructive conflict, leadership, and coordination, as well as about the individual in the group and in society. She wrote that conflict is an opportunity to understand, rather than to defeat, an opponent; that management is not exclusive to business; that management is a functional process, rather than a series of technical competencies; and that businesses and other administrative organizations are primarily social organizations (Kanter, 1995, pp. 4-8; Metcalf & Urwick, 1941). These concepts were largely ignored from the 1930s until they were rediscovered in the 1990s by writers on business management, including Rosabeth Moss Kanter (1995) of the Harvard Business School and Peter Drucker (1995) and by writers in social work including Weiner (1990) and Selber and Austin (1996) in "Mary Parker Follett: Epilogue to or Return of a Social Work Management Pioneer?"

Alternative models of social welfare administration have been reflected in the social work textbooks dealing with administration. In the 1950s, a series of textbooks appeared that were based on the private nonprofit organization model, several of them written by authors with experience in the YMCA, published through Association Press (Johns, 1954; Street, 1948; Tead, 1945; Trecker, 1961). In 1970, CSWE published *Social Work Administration: A Resource Book,* edited by Harry A. Schatz, a long-time nonprofit organization executive.

By the late 1970s, an increasing number of introductory textbooks dealt with social work administration, more than 30 such textbooks having been published since 1978. These textbooks, which are most heavily used in the single required course on organizational administration that is taken by most social work students, generally reflect a rational, structured, prescriptive approach to training for administrative tasks, which are assumed to be primarily tasks that deal with internal organizational processes (Austin, 1995). One exception is Burton Gummer's (1990) book, *The Politics of Social Administration: Managing Organizational Politics in Social Agencies*. Most of the textbook material is nonspecific as to government or private nonprofit auspice or as to the type of service program to be administered.

Little attention is given in these textbooks to the involvement of the service organization with external constituencies or to the political and economic dynamics of the larger society that may affect the relation of such constituencies to the service organization. Although many of the administrative positions in social welfare since the 1930s have been in the public sector, these textbooks give little attention to the role of political decision making or to the relation of the public administrator to legislative bodies and elected officials.

Most of these textbooks also give limited attention to the role of professional social workers or other professional specialists as members of the organizational service staff; to the dynamics of dealing with gender and ethnic diversity among service users, direct service staff members, and members of the administrative staff; to collaboration with a private nonprofit board of directors drawn largely from the business community; or to fund-raising. Only *Women Managers in Human Services* by Karen

Haynes (1989) explicitly addresses gender issues in administrative practice.

However, the publication of *The Management of Nonprofit Organizations* (McLaughlin, 1986) and *Skills for Effective Management of Nonprofit Organizations* (Edwards, Yankey, et al., 1998), and the initiation of the journal *Nonprofit Management & Leadership* in 1991 does reflect an increasing awareness of the growing importance of specialized training for the administration of nonprofit organizations within the total social welfare/human services system of the United States.

A LOOK TO THE FUTURE

Each decade of the 20th century has brought unanticipated and often dramatic changes in social welfare. Any effort to anticipate the events at the beginning of the 21st century is speculative at best. Among the issues that will continue to generate demands for a wide variety of social welfare services are longer lifespans; cultural diversity and the assimilation of newcomers into the society of the United States; realignments of the position of women; changes in the structure of the family and discontinuities in the growing-up experiences of children and adolescents; the management of chronic illness conditions, including mental illness, through medications; the combination of economic opportunity and economic turmoil resulting from the globalization of the economy; the impact of new technologies; and the persistence of economic inequality.

There may be a wide diversity of societal responses to those demands. However, some general trends appear likely to affect social welfare administration in the United States during the next several decades. The public social welfare sector will probably move in two directions. One direction involves the growth of the governmental social insurance sector, in major part as a result of the impact of the baby-boomer generation on programs serving older adults, including Social Security and Medicare. SSI will also continue to function as a major economic support system for individuals with severe disabilities, thus continuing to provide a community-based alternative to state-administered custodial institutions. Senior administrative positions in these social insurance programs are likely to be filled by people with public administration/public policy training rather than by people with social work education, given a continuing absence of content on political science, public finance, and financial management in the social work curriculum.

The second direction of future development in the public sector will be a continuation of privatization, that is, of a separation between the public authority that is the government-funding and regulatory body and private nonprofit, government nonprofit, and for-profit service providers that are the actual producers of services supported by government funds. This pattern will expand across mental health, public health, child welfare, and family assistance. Again, it is likely that many of the administrators in the government-funding organizations or authorities will have backgrounds in public administration or in business administration. This process of privatization will mean that many of the professionalized or specialized social service, health, and mental health programs actually providing services to individuals, families, and communities with funding from gov-

ernment appropriations will be operated by a combination of nonprofit and for-profit human service organizations. The nonprofit service providers will include a variety of semigovernmental nonprofit corporations, which will continue to be created as a result of governmental initiatives, as community mental health centers were created. These public nonprofits will be independently incorporated, draw funding from multiple sources, and have a governing board of directors appointed by external sources, rather than having a self-selecting and self-perpetuating board, as is generally characteristic of traditional private nonprofit organizations. All of these service-provider organizations will serve a broader cross-section of the population than either traditional nonprofit charitable organizations or traditional government entitlement programs.

The process of mergers and consolidations among established nonprofit service organizations will continue as purchase-of-service contracts become the major form of funding (Kettner & Martin, 1996; Singer & Yankey, 1991). But new service organizations will still be created by groups of individuals with strong interests in particular types of specialized services that larger organizations fail to provide (Bess, 1998). These new organizations will generally be able to find "start-up" sources of funding with the continued expansion of financial resources in the economy of the United States and modest tax levels. Moreover, new organizations with high visibility may be in an advantageous position as donor-choice patterns expand in community-wide fund-raising. An increase is likely in nonprofit community development organizations that are involved in long-range developmental strategies, including economic development, and in the operation of service programs in specific neighborhoods or communities.

Administrative leadership in all of the different types of nonprofit service organizations will require both community organization political skills and an understanding of both public finance and marketplace economics, in addition to general management skills. As the nonprofit sector expands, advocacy organizations of many types and service organization trade associations will increase, at both state and federal levels; these may attract individuals with a background in social welfare administration.

Administrators in this elaborated nonprofit sector are likely to be drawn from social work, specialized nonprofit management programs, and MBA programs. Nonprofit management programs and MBA programs will provide more technical preparation in financial management, financial planning, and fund-raising, all of which will become increasingly important. Social work training can provide students with substantive background in critical professional skill characteristics of service programs, service delivery networks, and the characteristics of service users; it may provide more content on interpersonal processes in administration. Social work education programs may also continue to be viewed as more supportive of students who are women, who are from diverse ethnic backgrounds, who are people with disabilities, or who have strong personal commitments to social justice issues.

However, the role of social work education in preparing individuals for positions in social welfare administration is likely to be affected by broader curriculum developments. Increased emphasis on the role of nonprofit organizations, rather than government agencies, as the providers of direct services, either through direct funding or through contracts, may reinforce a curriculum concept that all MSW graduates, regardless of prior experience, should begin their professional careers at a generalist direct-service level. This includes an assumption that direct-service experience should be the primary criterion for selection for supervisory or administrative positions.

Moves toward making "advanced clinical generalist" the dominant model of concentration specialization at the graduate level is likely to have a significant impact on the place in the curriculum of specialized training for positions in administration. In this case it is likely that many, if not most, graduates from schools of social work will increasingly follow a career line toward private, or contract, advanced professional practice, rather than a career of organizational supervision or administration. An alternative may be that a limited number of social work education programs will develop major concentrations in macro practice, including both administration and community organization/community development, with expanded curriculum content on public policy, economic analysis, and financial management.

Many of the women who, in the future, may consider enrolling in administration concentrations in schools of social work will be aware of the diversity of career opportunities now available to women in business management and entrepreneurial business development, and they may be looking for similar opportunities in social welfare. Mid-management positions in large, bureaucratic governmental social welfare organizations may have limited appeal, particularly because in the future, there is likely to be less assurance of permanent, long-term employment in such organizations, as well as limited opportunity for personal initiative and professional autonomy.

There will be an increase in social welfare administrative positions in the for-profit sector. This includes in-house employee assistance programs in a wide variety of for-profit corporations, as well as for-profit contract employee assistance programs. As the required level of background knowledge and technical skill increases in many industries, it will become increasingly important to provide support services and treatment services for personnel, who are often both difficult and expensive to replace. There will also be a variety of administrative opportunities in managed health care and managed behavioral health care, for which social work training and social work experience may be relevant. However, for the immediate future, these administrative career paths in health care are likely to be highly individual and often very unpredictable, rather than representing a substantive field of social work administrative practice.

Social welfare provisions in the 21st century are likely to be very different from those that were dominant during the 20th century. This includes the transformation of government social welfare programs, the expansion and diversification of the nonprofit sector ("The Nonprofit Sector," 1998), and the growth of the for-profit sector in social welfare. All together, the scope of social welfare programs of all types will expand, with an increase in the number and variety of administrative leadership positions. This may create new opportunities for social work practitioners and for schools of social work. However, this is also likely to bring continuing increases in other types of specialized training for social welfare administrators, including nonprofit management programs, and increased attention to the social welfare/human services sector in MBA programs.

REFERENCES

Akabas, S. H., & Kurzman, P. A. (1982). *Work, workers and work organizations: A view from social work.* Englewood Cliffs, NJ: Prentice Hall.

Alperin, D. E. (1993). Family service agencies: Responding to need in the 1980s. *Social Work, 38*(5), 597-602.

American Association of State Social Work Boards. (1996). *Social work job analysis in support of the American Association of State Social Work Boards examination program—Final report.* Culpeper, VA: Author.

Austin, D. M. (1995). Management in social work. In *Encylopedia of social work* (19th ed.). Washington, DC: NASW Press.

Austin, D. M. (1998). The institutional development of social work education: The first 100 years—and beyond. *Journal of Social Work Education, 33*(3), 573-586.

Bess, G. (1998). A first-stage organizational life cycle study of six emerging nonprofit organizations in Los Angeles. *Administration in Social Work, 22*(4), 35-52.

Boehm, W. (1959). *Objectives for the social work curriculum of the future: Vol. 1.* New York: Council on Social Work Education.

Breckinridge, S. (1927). *Public welfare administration.* Chicago: University of Chicago Press.

Bremner, R. H. (Ed.). (1974). *Children and youth in America: A documentary history: Vol. III. 1933-1973.* Cambridge, MA: Harvard University Press.

Brillant, E. L. (1990). *The United Way: Dilemmas of organized charity.* New York: Columbia University Press.

Broadhurst, B. P. (1971). Social thought, social practice, and social work education: Sanborn, Ely, Warner, Richmond (Doctoral dissertation, Columbia University, 1971). *Dissertation Abstracts International, 32*(9), 5342A.

Bruno, F. J. (1957). *Trends in social work 1874-1956: A history based on the proceedings of the National Conference of Social Work* (2nd ed.). New York: Columbia University Press.

Carson, M. J. (1992). *Settlement folks: Social thought in the American Settlement Movement.* Chicago: University of Chicago Press.

Chambers, C. A. (1963). *Seedtime of reform: American social service and social action, 1918-1933.* Minneapolis: University of Minnesota Press.

Council on Social Work Education. (1962). *Official statement of curriculum policy for the master's degree program in graduate professional schools of social work.* New York: Author.

Council on Social Work Education. (1998). *Statistics on social work education in the United States: 1997.* Alexandria, VA: Author.

Cutlip, S. M. (1965). *Fund raising in the United States: Its role in American philanthropy.* New Brunswick, NJ: Rutgers University Press.

Dinerman, M., & Geismar, L. L. (Eds.). (1984). *A quarter-century of social work education.* Washington, DC: NASW Press.

Drucker, P. F. (1992). *Managing the nonprofit organization: Principles and practices.* New York: HarperCollins.

Drucker, P. F. (1995). Introduction. In P. Graham (Ed.), *Mary Parker Follett: Prophet of management: A celebration of writings from the 1920s.* Boston: Harvard Business School Press.

Dunham, A. (1939). The administration of social agencies. In *Social work yearbook* (Vol. 16). New York: Russell Sage Foundation.

Edwards, R. L., & Austin, D. M. (1991). Managing effectively in an environment of competing values. In R. L. Edwards & J. A. Yankey (Eds.), *Skills for effective human services management.* Washington, DC: NASW Press.

Edwards, R. L., Austin, D. M., & Altpeter, M. A. (1998). Managing effectively in an environment of competing values. In R. L. Edwards, J. A. Yankey, & M. A. Altpeter (Eds.), *Skills for effective management of nonprofit organizations.* Washington, DC: NASW Press.

Edwards, R. L., Lebold, D. A., & Yankey, J. A. (1998). Managing organizational decline. In R. L. Edwards, J. A. Yankey, & M. A. Altpeter (Eds.), *Skills for effective management of nonprofit organizations.* Washington, DC: NASW Press.

Edwards, R. L., & Yankey, J. A. (Eds.). (1991). *Skills for effective human services management.* Washington, DC: NASW Press.

Edwards, R. L., Yankey, J. A., & Altpeter, M. A. (Eds.). (1998). *Skills for effective management of nonprofit organizations.* Washington, DC: NASW Press.

Follett, M. P. (1924). *Creative experience.* New York: Longmans, Green.

Glenn, J. M., Brandt, L., & Andrews, F. E. (1947). *Russell Sage Foundation 1907-1946.* New York: Russell Sage Foundation.

Gordon, L. (1994). *Pitied but not entitled: Single mothers and the history of welfare.* Cambridge, MA: Harvard University Press.

Graham, P. (Ed.). (1995). *Mary Parker Follett: Prophet of management: A celebration of writings from the 1920s.* Boston: Harvard Business School Press.

Green, R. K. (1998). Maximizing the use of performance contracts. In R. L. Edwards, J. A. Yankey, & M. A. Altpeter (Eds.), *Skills for effective management of nonprofit organizations.* Washington, DC: NASW Press.

Grønbjerg, K. A. (1993). *Understanding nonprofit funding: Managing revenues in social services and community development organizations.* San Francisco: Jossey-Bass.

Gummer, B. (1987). Are administrators social workers? The politics of intraprofessional rivalry. *Administration in Social Work, 11*(2), 19-32.

Gummer, B. (1990). *The politics of social administration: Managing organizational politics in social agencies.* Englewood Cliffs, NJ: Prentice Hall.

Hagerty, J. E. (1931). *The training of social workers.* New York: McGraw-Hill.

Haynes, K. S. (1989). *Women managers in human services.* New York: Springer.

Hollis, E. V., & Taylor, A. L. (1951). *Social work education in the U.S.* New York: Columbia University Press.

Hyde, C. (1992). The ideational system of social movement agencies: An examination of feminist health centers. In Y. Hasenfeld (Ed.), *Human services as complex organizations* (pp. 121-144). Newbury Park, CA: Sage.

Johns, R. (1954). *Executive responsibility.* New York: Association Press.

Kamerman, S. B., & Kahn, A. J. (1989). *Privatization and the welfare state.* Princeton, NJ: Princeton University Press.

Kanter, R. M. (1995). Preface. In P. Graham (Ed.), *Mary Parker Follett: Prophet of management: A celebration of writings from the 1920s* (pp. 4-8). Boston: Harvard Business School Press.

Kanter, R. M. (1997). *Frontiers of management.* Boston: Harvard Business School Press.

Kaplan, B. J. (1978). Reformers and charity: The abolition of public outdoor relief in New York City, 1870-1898. *Social Service Review, 52*(2), 202-210.

Kazmarski, K., & Macarov, D. (1976). *Administration in the social work curriculum.* New York: CSWE.

Kettner, P. M., & Martin, L. L. (1996). The impact of declining resources and purchase of service contracting on private, nonprofit agencies. *Administration in Social Work, 20*(3), 21-38.

Kirschner, D. S. (1986). *The paradox of professionalism: Reform and public service in urban America, 1900-1940.* Westport, CT: Greenwood.

Kramer, R. M. (1985). The future of the voluntary agency in a mixed economy. *Journal of Applied Behavioral Science, 21*(4), 377-392.

Kurzman, P. (1974). *Harry Hopkins and the New Deal.* Fairlawn, NJ: Burdick.

Leiby, J. (1978). *A history of social welfare and social work in the United States.* New York: Columbia University Press.

Leighninger, L. (1987). *Social work: Search for identity.* New York: Greenwood.

Lens, S. (1966). *Radicalism in the United States.* New York: Thomas Y. Crowell.

Lens, S. (1969). *Poverty: America's enduring paradox: A history of the richest nation's unwon war.* New York: Thomas Y. Crowell.

Lowell, J. S. (1884). *Public relief and private charity.* New York: G. P. Putnam's Sons.

Lubove, R. (1962). *The Progressives and the slums: Tenement house reform in New York City, 1890-1917.* Pittsburgh, PA: University of Pittsburgh Press.

Lubove, R. (1965) *The professional altruist: The emergence of social work as a career, 1890-1930.* Cambridge, MA: Harvard University Press.

Marty, M. E. (1980). Social services: Godly and godless. *Social Service Review, 54*(4), 463-481.

McLaughlin, C. P. (1986). *The management of nonprofit organizations.* New York: John Wiley.

McLean, F. H. (1927). *The family society: Joint responsibilities of board, staff, and membership.* New York: American Association for Organizing Social Work.

McNutt, J. G. (1995). The macro practice curriculum in graduate social work education: Results of a national study. *Administration in Social Work, 19*(3), 59-74.

Meier, E. (1954). *A history of the New York school of social work.* New York: Columbia University Press.

Metcalf, H. C., & Urwick, L. F. (Eds.). (1941). *Dynamic administration: The collected papers of Mary Parker Follett.* Bath: Management Publications Trust.

Mintzberg, H. (1989). *Mintzberg on management: Inside of the strange world of organizations.* New York: Free Press.

Morton, M. J. (1998). Cleveland's child welfare system and the "American dilemma," 1941-1964. *Social Service Review, 72*(1), 112-136.

The nonprofit sector: Love or money. (1998, November 14). *The Economist, 349,* 68, 73.

Patti, R. (1983). *Social welfare administration: Managing social programs in a developmental context.* Englewood Cliffs, NJ: Prentice Hall.

Perlmutter, F. D. (1984). *Human services at risk.* Lexington, MA: Lexington Books.

Perlmutter, F. D. (1988). Administering alternative social programs. In P. R. Keyes & L. H. Ginsberg (Eds.), *New management in human services.* Silver Spring, MD: NASW Press.

Peters, T. J., & Waterman, R. H. (1982). *In search of excellence.* New York: Warner.

Pittman-Munke, P. (1985). *Mary Richmond and the wider social movement, Philadelphia 1900-1909.* Doctoral dissertation, University of Texas at Austin.

Powell, D. M. (1986). Managing organizational problems in alternative service organizations. *Administration in Social Work, 10,* 57-70.

Quinn, R. E. (1988). *Beyond rational management: Mastering the paradoxes and competing demands of high performance.* San Francisco: Jossey-Bass.

Richmond, M. E. (1897). The need of a training school in applied philanthrophy. *Proceedings of the National Conference of Charities and Correction, 1897.* Boston: George H. Ellis.

Richmond, M. E. (1899). *Friendly visiting among the poor: A handbook for charity workers.* New York: Macmillan.

Richmond, M. E. (1917). *Social diagnosis.* New York: Russell Sage Foundation.

Rimer, E. (1987). Social administration education: Reconceptualizing the conflict with MPA, MBA, and MPH programs. *Administration in Social Work, 11*(2), 45-55.

Rubinow, I. M. (1913). *Social insurance.* New York: Henry Holt.

Salamon, L. M. (1989). The changing partnership between the voluntary sector and the welfare state. In V. Hodgkinson & R. K. Lyman (Eds.), *The future of the nonprofit sector: Challenges, changes, and policy considerations* (pp. 41-60). San Francisco: Jossey-Bass.

Sayles, L. (1976). *Leadership: What effective managers do and how they do it.* New York: McGraw-Hill.

Schatz, H. A. (1970). *Social work administration: A resource book.* New York: CSWE.

School of Social Work, University of Michigan. (1998). News from the office of student and multicultural affairs. *Ongoing, 14.*

Selber, K., & Austin, D. M. (1996). Mary Parker Follett: Epilogue to or return of a social work management pioneer? *Administration in Social Work, 21*(1), 1-15.

Singer, M., & Yankey, J. (1991). Organizational metamorphosis: A study of eighteen nonprofit mergers, acquisitions, and consolidations. *Nonprofit Management & Leadership, 1*(4), 357-370.

Spencer, S. (1959). *The administration method in social work education: Vol. 3. A report of the curriculum study.* New York: CSWE.

Strachan, J. L. (1998). Understanding nonprofit financial management. In R. L. Edwards, J. A. Yankey, & M. A. Altpeter (Eds.), *Skills for effective management of nonprofit organizations.* Washington, DC: NASW Press.

Street, E. (1940). *The public welfare administration.* New York: McGraw-Hill.

Street, E. (1948). *A handbook for social agency administration*. New York: Harper.

Tead, O. (1945). *Democratic administration*. New York: Association Press.

Trecker, H. B. (1961). *New understandings of administration*. New York: Association Press.

Tucker, D. J., Baum, J. A. C., & Singh, J. V. (1992). The institutional ecology of human service organizations. In Y. Hasenfeld (Ed.), *Human services as complex organizations*. Newbury Park, CA: Sage.

Waite, F. T. (1960). *A warm friend for the spirit*. Cleveland, OH: Family Service Association.

Warner, A. G. (1894). *American charities: A study in philanthropy and economics*. New York: Thomas Y. Crowell.

Weiner, M. E. (1990). *Human services management: Analysis and applications* (2nd ed.). Belmont, CA: Wadsworth.

Weisbrod, B. A. (Ed.). (1998). *To profit or not to profit: The commercial transformation of the nonprofit sector*. New York: Cambridge University Press.

Wernet, S. P., & Jones, S. A. (1992). Merger and acquisition activity between nonprofit, social service organizations: A case study. *Nonprofit and Voluntary Sector Quarterly, 21*(4), 367-380.

Wilson, W. (1978). The study of administration. In J. M. Shafritz & A. C. Hyde (Eds.), *Classics of public administration*. Oak Park, IL: Moore. (Original work published 1887)

Wish, N. B., & Mirabella, R. M. (1998). Curricular variations in nonprofit management graduate programs. *Nonprofit Management & Leadership, 6*(1), 99-109.

Yankey, J. A., Wester, B., & Campbell, D. (1998). Managing mergers and consolidations. In R. L. Edwards, J. A. Yankey, & M. A. Altpeter (Eds.), *Skills for effective management of nonprofit organizations*. Washington, DC: NASW Press.

Young, D. R. (1991). Developing entrepreneurial leadership. In R. L. Edwards & J. A. Yankey (Eds.), *Skills for effective human services management*. Washington, DC: NASW Press.

CHAPTER THREE

The Environmental Context of Social Welfare Administration

LAWRENCE L. MARTIN

Strategic planning teaches us that the practice of social welfare administration is influenced by the external environment (Bryson, 1995). Major economic, political, social, and technological factors in the external environment can play an important role in shaping, and in some instances may largely determine, how social welfare administration is both conceptualized and practiced. As we enter the new millennium, it seems appropriate to pause and consider how the external environment may influence the future practice of social welfare administration.

This chapter identifies and discusses a select number of major environmental factors that the author believes will largely define the context of social welfare administration in the coming years. Several major administrative trends flow-

ing from the major environmental forces are also identified and discussed.

An undertaking of this nature is fraught with difficulties, and certain disclaimers must be articulated at the outset. Any attempt to deal with a topic of this magnitude in one chapter of a book can only be accomplished by resort to brevity and simplicity. As in the conduct of any strategic planning exercise, realism and not idealism must guide the endeavor. The frame of reference for this discussion is social welfare administration in the public sector, although implications for social welfare administration in the nonprofit sector are also drawn. In researching this topic, an attempt was made to consult a broad literature. However, readers are cautioned that the major environmental factors and administrative trends identified here represent one perspective on the future of social welfare administration, not the only perspective. Finally, as the ancient Greek philosopher Heraclitus (circa 500 BCE) was fond of saying: "Things change."

Environmental forces and administrative trends that appear overwhelming today can be slowed, neutralized, and even reversed by unforeseen events tomorrow.

MAJOR ENVIRONMENTAL FORCES

From the universe of political, economic, social, and technological factors that will help to define the context of social welfare administration in the coming years, the following appear particularly relevant: the collapse of communism, the global economy, the change in national political power, the devolution of social welfare policy, the "graying" of America, the rediscovery of community, the accountability movement, and advances in information technology.

The Collapse of Communism

For the better part of the last 100 years, an experiment was conducted between two competing economic ideologies: capitalism and Marxism in its various incarnations. Empirically, capitalism has proven to be superior. Today, capitalism and the free market reign supreme, with no new ideological challenger on the horizon (Elliott, 1998).

The collapse of communism, or if one prefers the triumph of capitalism, has resulted in a worldwide re-evaluation of the merits of centrally planned economies. Former hard-line Marxist countries such as China and Cuba, as well as democratic socialist countries such as Great Britain, France, and Sweden, are all moving their economies more toward capitalism and the free market (e.g., Echikson, 1998a). The pervasiveness and acceptance of capitalism and the free market in the United States today are extraordinary. For example, in 1960, only about 10% of American households owned stock or mutual funds; today, the figure is more than 50% and rising (Piskora, 1998, p. 27). By definition, the majority of Americans are capitalists.

The collapse of communism may be the most important of the environmental factors that will help to define the future practice of social welfare administration. The collapse of communism means that capitalism and the free market are under less social and political pressure to apologize for, let alone correct, their shortcomings, such as job dislocations and greater income inequalities. In addition, governments today, both here and abroad, are placing more emphasis on private-sector and free-market solutions to economic and social problems and less emphasis on public-sector and bureaucratic solutions (i.e., solutions requiring growth in the physical size of government). Competition, the hallmark of capitalism and the free market, is increasingly viewed as a preferred public policy tool.

The collapse of communism, the predilection for private-sector and market solutions, and the public policy preference for competition have resulted in more for-profit business firms becoming involved in the provision of social welfare-type services including child-support enforcement, welfare-to-work programs, and others (Garland, 1997, p. 134). Large American aerospace corporations (e.g., Lockheed-Martin) are also moving into the arena of social welfare as they continue to search for new markets to replace lost defense contracts (Wayne, 1998). The example of Lockheed-Martin represents a particularly interesting phenomenon. A consequence of continued decreases in federal spending on national defense may well be the increased intrusion of defense and aerospace corporations into the social welfare sector.

All of the above creates a paradox for social welfare administration (Edwards, Cooke, & Reid, 1996). Social welfare has traditionally been viewed as comprising those activities that lie outside the arena of capitalism and the free market (Karger & Stoesz, 1998). The practice of social welfare administration in the future may be largely concerned with attempting to find creative ways of resolving this paradox by blending traditional social welfare values with competitive free-market administrative mechanisms.

The Global Economy

Economic globalization continues to accelerate. No longer do U.S. states, cities, and communities control their own economic destinies; these are increasingly determined by multinational corporations and international banks, which can whisk capital, businesses, and jobs from location to location at the touch of a computer. As Thurow (1998) notes, the global economy "simultaneously permits, encourages, and forces companies to move their activities to the lowest-cost locations" (p. 25). As the member nations of the European Union have already come to discover, global economic competition does not favor nations with generous welfare benefits because of the taxes necessary to finance them (Kuttner, 1998, p. 24). Consequently, global economic competition will

likely restrict, restructure, and perhaps reduce the social welfare systems of most industrialized nations, including the United States (Echikson, 1998b, p. 106).

Because of the global economy, the United States continues to lose blue-collar manufacturing jobs to developing countries, which have absolute advantages in terms of lower labor costs, less favorable working conditions, and fewer environmental, social, and political constraints. Blue-collar manufacturing workers constituted some 40% of the U.S. labor market in the 1950s; this proportion declined to some 20% in the 1990s, and it is expected to decline still further, to about 10% by the year 2010 (Drucker, 1995, pp. 221-222; Echikson, 1998b, p. 106). The continuing loss of blue-collar manufacturing jobs means that a historically important path of upward mobility for lower-skilled and less educated U.S. workers is also being lost. At the same time, the U.S. labor market continues to bifurcate into higher-paying information and technology jobs and lower-paying service jobs. African Americans will be one of the groups hit hardest by these changes (Drucker, 1995).

In the global economy, flexibility, competitiveness, quality, and productivity are said to be essential survival skills (Dobyns & Crawford-Mason, 1991; Drucker, 1992; Fisher & Karger, 1997). The global economy has taught American consumers the value of quality products and services (Dobyns & Crawford-Mason, 1991). U.S. citizen consumers now expect quality in their government services (Cohen & Brand, 1993) as well as their social welfare services (Gummer & McCallion, 1995; Gunther & Hawkins, 1996; Martin, 1993).

Increased productivity has always been a key component of U.S. economic growth and a major determinant of the country's basic level of economic prosperity. Economic growth in the future will be less dependent on the productivity of the manufacturing sector and more dependent on the productivity of the high-tech and service sectors (including social welfare services). As Peter Drucker (1992) has observed, the major economic challenge of the future will be increasing the productivity of technical, computer, and knowledge workers (including social welfare professionals).

Future challenges for social welfare administration brought about by the global economy will include finding creative ways (in collaboration with schools, colleges, and businesses) to increase the educational, knowledge, and skill levels of U.S. workers and to provide quality social welfare products and services. In the latter case, "doing more with less" will continue to be the mantra of social welfare administration (Gore, 1996).

National Political Power

National political power in the United States continues to migrate from the Northeast to the South and West. The South and West regions of the United States are different from the Northeast region in terms of political culture and basic orientation toward politics, government, the private sector, and social welfare (Elazar, 1972). Of the 10 historically most liberal states, 5 are located in the Northeast (New York, Massachusetts, New Jersey, Connecticut, and Pennsylvania), whereas 9 of the 10 historically most conservative states are located in the South and West (Mississippi, Arkansas, South Carolina, Arizona, Alabama, Tennessee, Nevada, Georgia, and South Carolina; Kligman & Lammers, 1984, p. 602).

As a result of the geographical shift, national political power is becoming increasingly less liberal and increasingly more conservative. As evidence, one has only to consider the composition of the U.S. House of Representatives. The House is reapportioned every 10 years following the decennial census. For the last four decades, the Northeast has lost representation, whereas the South and West have gained. Over the same period, the once-solid Democratic South has increasingly become the solid Republican South ("South's Embrace," 1998). Because of the geographical shift and the increasing conservative flavor of national political power, the Republican party became in 1994 the dominant party in the House of Representatives for the first time in nearly half a century.

Neither the direction nor the flavor of national political power shows any sign of changing in the foreseeable future. According to the Bureau of the Census, the fastest-growing regions of the United States between now and the year 2025 will be the West, followed closely by the South ("The Booming West," 1997, p. A16).

In terms of social welfare administration, the geographical shift and the increasing conservatism of national political power can be expected to give added impetus to control of the size, scope, and cost of government; the predilection for private-sector and free-market solutions to economic and social problems; and the preference for state, local, and community control over public policy in general and social welfare policy in particular.

The Devolution of Social Welfare Policy

Social welfare policy is becoming less national and less uniform and more decentralized, or devolved, and more diverse. Uniform national social welfare policies and priorities once determined in Washington are increasingly giving way to diverse social welfare policies and priorities determined in state capitals, city halls, and county seats. At exactly the same time that states, cities, and counties are experiencing an increasing loss of control over their economic futures due to the global economy, they are simultaneously being asked to assume greater responsibility for social problems and social welfare. As this observation suggests, the major external forces that will affect social welfare administration in the future are not necessarily complementary.

Although the devolution of social welfare policy from the national level to the state and local government levels is due, at least in part, to the geographical shift in national political power, it is also a reflection of a worldwide phenomenon that has been ongoing for some time (Naisbitt, 1982). The speed of the shift in the United States, however, has increased significantly in recent years. A prime example of the devolution of social welfare policy is of course The Personal Responsibility & Work Opportunity Act of 1996, which transformed a national child welfare *entitlement* program into a decentralized state discretionary *benefit* program.

In some states, such as the bellwether states of California and Florida, social welfare policy is being further devolved to the local government level (cities and counties) and in some instances to the community level (Austin, 1998; Martin, 1999). An expectation exists that the 11 states with county-based welfare systems (Alabama, California, Colorado, Georgia, Minnesota, New York, North Carolina, Ohio, South Carolina, Virginia, and Wisconsin) will

further devolve social welfare policy down to the county level (Martin, 1999).

A by-product of the devolution of social welfare policy will be a changing labor market for social welfare administrators. Employment opportunities for social welfare administrators will continue to decline at the federal level. Total federal government employment peaked in the early 1990s and has declined steadily ever since (U.S. General Accounting Office [GAO], 1998). Fortunately, employment opportunities for social welfare administrators will continue to increase at the state government, local government, and community levels. Despite all the rhetoric about "downsizing" and "rightsizing," employment at the state and local government levels continues to increase (Walters, 1998).

The practice of social welfare administration in a devolved policy environment will be more diverse. Policy diversity may well become a social welfare norm. Policy diversity will obviously lead to greater differences among states, cities, counties, and communities in terms of social welfare priorities and administrative practices.

The "Graying" of America

The face of America continues to change, but change in the future will be less an issue of ethnicity and gender and more an issue of age. The last several decades saw tremendous changes in terms of the ethnic and gender composition of the U.S. labor force, the workforces of social welfare agencies, and the client populations served. But as Gummer (1998) has observed, these demographic shifts have largely run their course. The next big demographic challenge will be dealing with an increasingly older population.

The post-World War II "baby boom" generation is now entering its 50s. As Buford (1998) notes, the baby boom generation is the master trend: the one that "will continue to dominate both the economy and the social climate well past the first third of the twenty-first century" (p. 39). Because of the baby boom generation, older Americans (those over age 65) in the future will represent an increasingly larger proportion of the U.S. population, the U.S. labor market, and the client population of many social welfare agencies. Between 2000 and 2010, the over-65 population is expected to increase by 17% to some 40 million people. Between 2010 and 2030, the over-65 population is expected to increase by 75% to some 70 million people (National Aging Information Center, 1996).

Prolonging the working lives of older Americans, as well as providing them with co-production (i.e., situations where service recipients also participate in service delivery) and more traditional volunteer opportunities, will become increasingly important for all social welfare administrators, not just those whose field of practice is aging. The cost to society and government of providing pensions, social security, health care, long-term care, and other social and supportive services to the increasing numbers of older Americans will be staggering. If there are to be sufficient funds left over to address other social problems and other target groups, all social welfare administrators in the coming years will necessarily have to concern themselves with the older American population.

Extending the work life of older Americans and providing co-production and other volunteer opportunities will help reduce fiscal pressures on retirement systems and health systems while simultaneously helping to reduce the costs of social welfare programs (The Urban Institute, 1998). Providing work, co-production, and volunteer opportunities for older Americans may require significant "out-of-the-box" thinking on the part of social welfare administrators in terms of how jobs are conceptualized and structured and how social welfare services are planned and delivered.

The Rediscovery of Community

Society appears to be rediscovering the virtues and benefits of community. Communities can be geographical in nature, or they can be groups of individuals that have a common cultural identity or shared interest (Fisher & Karger, 1997). Many reasons exist for the rediscovery of community, but clearly three, important ones are the decline in public funding for social welfare, the reassessment of the role of social welfare professionals, and the rebirth of spirituality.

The decline in public funding for social welfare has led to an increased focus on community and nonpublic approaches to addressing social problems. However, it would be a mistake to assume that the rediscovery of community is due only to this influence. Equally important is the increasing realization that social welfare professionals do not lie at the heart of helping systems, but rather that care and support are provided by families, churches, schools, clubs, and other types of organizations and groups (Adams & Nelson, 1997, p. 69). As one observer of the contemporary social welfare scene has commented, the pendulum is swinging back to communities and groups as models of primary care, prevention, and natural support (Meenaghan, 1998, p. 1).

Along with the rediscovery of community has come the realization that communities are something more than merely collections of social problems and pathologies, but that they comprise human, family, and social capital that can be used in a self-help fashion to improve the lives of citizens (Kingsley, McNeely, & Gibson, 1997). As part of the rediscovery of community, state, city, and county governments are increasingly relying on community groups to provide foster care, health care, counseling, and other social welfare services on a neighborhood basis (Chen, 1998, p. B4). Welfare reform itself places a heavy reliance on community collaboration in efforts to move social welfare clients to independent living status.

The rediscovery of community is also being aided by the rebirth of spirituality. The United States, like most of the rest of Western civilization, is experiencing a rebirth of spirituality due at least in part to the "millennium pull." A similar rebirth of spirituality was recorded leading up to the end of the first millennium (circa 1000 BCE; Naisbitt & Aburdene, 1990). In many geographical communities, faith-based groups constitute an important component of social capital and are becoming increasingly involved in social change initiatives and the actual delivery of social welfare services ("The New Holy War," 1998). Faith-based groups also rely heavily on volunteers for the delivery of social welfare and other community services and thus provide co-production and volunteer opportunities for older Americans (Printz, 1998).

The rediscovery of community means that social welfare administrators will be increasingly called on to demonstrate their community-organizing and community-development skills (Weil, 1996). Assisting in the development and nurturing of collaborative community initiatives will become an increasingly important activity for many social welfare agencies. Social welfare administrators will also have to understand their new supporting role in community-focused support systems. A phrase that may well capture this new orientation is the "social welfare society."

The Accountability Movement

Social welfare administration in the future will become increasing concerned with demonstrating and documenting the performance (outputs, quality, and outcomes) of social welfare programs, including a primary focus on the achievement of client outcomes. The continued push for greater performance accountability will come from a variety of sources, including government, managed care, and private foundations.

The performance measurement movement, which began in earnest during the 1990s, has become codified in federal law, The Government Performance & Results Act, and in the statutes, policies, and administrative procedures of virtually all 50 states (Melkers & Willoughby, 1998). Managed care, an umbrella term for a variety of approaches to controlling service delivery costs while maintaining a defined level of quality (National Association of Social Workers [NASW], 1997), has become an integral part of the accountability movement in the areas of health and mental health. Managed care is also spreading to social welfare services such as child day care, residential care, adoption services, and others (GAO, 1997b, p. 10). Private foundations are also becoming increasingly concerned with performance accountability (outputs, quality, and outcomes) and continue to attach more requirements to their funding (Gurwitt, 1998).

Although the performance-accountability movement is concerned with government in general, its effects may be felt most strongly in the area of social welfare, due in large measure to the maturation of social welfare. Social welfare today is big business. Estimates of combined government (federal, state, and local) spending on human service programs today is in excess of $200 billion annually (Melia, 1997, p. 2). Federal expenditures for health and social welfare today rival those of national defense (GAO, 1997a, p. 1).

Because of the accountability movement and the size of social welfare in terms of the proportion of government budgetary outlays, the language of performance will become an essential part of the vocabulary of social welfare administration in the future.

Advances in Information Technology

The increasing availability and application of information technology will continue to affect social welfare and social welfare administration in a variety of ways, including how clients access services, how social welfare professionals perform their functions, and how clients and social welfare professionals interact.

If information is power, then information technology has the potential to both "democratize" social welfare (Linder, 1998, p. 20) and to empower clients. Because of information technology, citizens are increasingly able to learn about social welfare services and agencies via Internet access made available in homes, agencies, libraries, service centers, schools, and other outlets. In the not too distant future, social welfare clients will be able to apply for fi-

nancial assistance and services over the Internet, have eligibility determination and certification conducted electronically, have assistance benefits automatically deposited to their bank accounts via electronic transfer, access cash through automated teller machines (ATMs), and make purchases with debit cards (Peyrot, Harris, Fenzel, & Burbridge, 1997; Poulos, 1998, p. 50; Technology Assessment Board, 1993). Homebound clients will be able to reach out and touch the world and other homebound people via the Internet, and we will most likely see the advent of "virtual friendly visiting."

Information systems will become the "spinal columns" of social welfare administration (Newcombe, 1998). Information technology will enable social welfare professionals to conduct client interviews, case planning, counseling, home visits, and monitoring and evaluation activities via cell phone, e-mail, fax, video conferencing, and the Internet. Integrated community-wide information systems and databases will provide social welfare administrators will real-time needs assessment, resource availability, and client-outcome data for planning, marketing, and evaluation purposes (Hile, 1998; Krepcho, Marks, Garnett, Snell, & Olson, 1998). Information technology will also significantly decrease the lag time in social welfare technology sharing. New ideas, new programs, and new lessons learned by social welfare agencies in one region of the country will be instantaneously shared with social welfare agencies in other regions.

A corollary to the increased use of information technology in social welfare will be the increased partnering between social welfare agencies and private-sector businesses. For at least the foreseeable future, government in general and social welfare agencies (both public and private) in particular will be unable to offer competitive salaries for computer and information technology professionals, compared to private-sector businesses (Swope, 1998, p. 37). The maintenance of increasingly sophisticated information technology systems in government and nonprofit social welfare agencies, as well as the delivery of electronic benefits and other information technology-intensive services, will increasingly be accomplished by contractual and partnering relationships with private business firms. Already, a number of southern states contract with banks to operate their electronic benefit systems for cash assistance and food stamp recipients (Florida Department of Children and Families, 1996).

MAJOR ADMINISTRATIVE TRENDS

In the coming years, we can expect the major environmental forces identified above to result in numerous changes in how social welfare administration is practiced. Although many of these changes were identified, or at least hinted at, in the preceding discussion, it is useful to consider them as a whole. In thinking about these trends, it may be useful to conceptualize them as movement away from some existing administrative practices and toward new administrative practices that are more in keeping with the identified major environmental forces. In the future, social welfare administration will involve

1. More competitive behaviors. Traditionally, the relationship between social welfare agencies has been described as more cooperative than competitive. This description is becoming less accurate. Weinbach (1998, p. 37) suggests that in reality, most human service agencies today are already competing with each other for funding, programs, and clients. Competition will take many forms, including competition for new sources of revenue (government contracts, foundation grants, development of new products and services, and others). Competition will also take the form of more coordination and collaboration between social welfare agencies (e.g., Harbert, Finnegan, & Tyler, 1998). One benefit of all this interagency cooperation and collaboration will be the increased competitiveness and cost-efficiency of the participating agencies.

2. More privatization. Given the conservative and anti-government environment, social welfare administrators may have little choice but to consider more use of privatization techniques such as contracts, grants, vouchers, coproduction, volunteers, and others (Karger & Stoesz, 1998, p. 209). Privatization may in fact be a "super-optimum" social welfare policy (Nagel, 1997) because it restricts the physical size of government (thus appealing to conservatives), while simultaneously enabling government to continue providing social welfare services (thus appealing to liberals). Contracting will most likely continue in its position as the privatization technique of choice. Some predictions suggest that by the year 2010, as much as 80% of all public human services funding may be contracted (Lauffer, 1997, p. 74). An increasing proportion of these contracts are likely to be of the performance type (Martin, in press).

3. More restructuring. Because of more competition, more privatization, and more use of information technology, public and nonprofit social welfare agencies in the future will increasingly alter their organizational structures. Many social welfare agencies will downsize; some will get larger, and most will specialize. Social welfare agencies will become leaner. Information technology will enable social welfare administrators to increase their span of management control. As Drucker (1995) points out, organizing around information and information technologies—what today we call *re-engineering* (Hammer, 1996; Hammer & Champy, 1993)—generally means fewer management levels and fewer middle managers in an organization.

Numerous new and creative alliances and collaborations involving social welfare agencies will take place. The distinction between the public and private social welfare sectors will continue to blur. And at least some blurring will occur between the nonprofit social welfare sector and the for-profit business sector, as nonprofits forge partnerships with for-profits and as for-profits acquire (buy out) nonprofits (Guard, 1998).

4. *More marketing.* Social welfare administrators will discover that traditional social planning and needs-assessment techniques are insufficient by themselves to ensure the future survival of their programs and agencies. Such issues as who pays and how services can best be packaged and promoted to be optimally attractive to clients and funding sources will become increasingly important. For guidance in such matters, social welfare administrators will necessarily have to resort to greater use of marketing techniques (e.g., Herron, 1997).

5. *More entrepreneurial management.* In the decentralized and devolved social welfare policy world characterized by fewer categorical federal grant programs and more block grants, social welfare administration will necessarily have to become more entrepreneurial. The basic nature of social welfare administration will likely change from a focus on implementation to a focus on entrepreneurialism. Being expert in implementing a particular federal or state social welfare program will become less important, whereas being creative and entrepreneurial in the development of new policies, programs, collaborations, and funding streams to address social problems will become more important.

6. *More quality management.* The traditional approach to ensuring quality in social welfare services has been the quality assurance approach (i.e., professionals determine quality) (Evers, Haverines, Leeichsenring, & Wistow, 1997; Martin, 1993). Placing more emphasis on quality management will necessarily entail making more use of quality teams and soliciting client feedback through client satisfaction surveys and other techniques.

7. *More emphasis on results.* In the future, social welfare administration will be less concerned with processes and more concerned with outputs and outcomes (e.g., Mullen & Magnabosco, 1997). This change will require a major adjustment for many social welfare professionals—particularly social workers—whose education, training, and work experience over the years has stressed process. The practice of social welfare administration will increasingly entail performance measurement, performance budgeting, and performance contracting (Martin, 1997, 2000; Martin & Kettner, 1996).

8. *More strategic planning.* It seems likely that most social welfare agencies and administrators will need to develop some type of systematic approach to the ongoing assessment and evaluation of environmental forces and their potential client, program, and agency impacts. Although marketing techniques can pro-

vide some insights in this area, a more likely conceptual frame of reference is strategic planning, with its focus on environmental opportunities and threats.

9. *More advocacy.* Given the conservative flavor of national politics and the graying of America, aggressive advocacy for social welfare in general and for groups other than the aging will be particularly important in the future. The needs of vulnerable populations such as children, the mentally ill, people with disabilities, and others will necessarily have to be constantly articulated and fought for at the national, state, and local government levels.

10. *More emphasis on clients.* Too often in the past, the focus of social welfare administration has been on the needs of agencies and programs. With more competition for clients and funding and more emphasis on performance accountability, quality management, marketing, strategic planning, and advocacy, the hope is that clients will be returned to their rightful place as the true focus of social welfare administration.

CONCLUSION

Some social welfare administrators reading this chapter will view the major environmental factors and administrative trends identified herein as threats; others will see them as opportunities. As we learn from strategic planning, environmental threats and opportunities are really just two sides of the same coin. Whether one views these major environmental forces and administrative trends as threats or opportunities, if the discussion causes readers to pause and take stock of the future, then the purpose of this writing will have been achieved.

One prognostication about social welfare administration in the third millennium can be made with absolute 100% assurance: The future will be different from the past.

REFERENCES

Adams, P., & Nelson, K. (1997). Reclaiming community: An integrative approach to human services. *Administration in Social Work, 21*(3/4), 67-81.

Austin, M. (1998). Services integration: Introduction. *Administration in Social Work, 21*(3/4), 1-7.

The booming west. (1997, September 3). *New York Times,* p. A16.

Bryson, J. M. (1995). *Strategic planning for public & nonprofit organizations.* San Francisco: Jossey-Bass.

Buford, B. (1998). How boomers, churches, and entrepreneurs can transform society. In F. Hesselbein et al. (Eds.), *The community of the future* (pp. 35-46). San Francisco: Jossey-Bass.

Chen, B. (1998, June 3). Nationwide emphasis on neighborhoods. *New York Times,* p. B4.

Cohen, S., & Brand, R. (1993). *Total quality management in government.* San Francisco: Jossey-Bass.

Dobyns, L., & Crawford-Mason, C. (1991). *Quality or else.* Boston: Houton Mifflin.

Drucker, P. F. (1992). *Managing for the future.* New York: Truman/Talley Books.

Drucker, P. (1995). *Managing in a time of great change.* New York: Truman Talley Books.

Echikson, W. (1998a, June 28). A quiet revolution. *Business Week,* pp. 46 and 48.

Echikson, W. (1998b, April 27). Workplace earthquake? *Business Week,* p. 106.

Edwards, R., Cooke, P., & Reid, N. (1996). Social work management in an era of diminishing federal responsibility. *Social Work, 41*(5), 468-479.

Elazar, D. J. (1972). *American federalism: The view from the states.* New York: Thomas Y. Cromwell.

Elliott, M. (1998, May 4). The romance of the marketplace. *Newsweek,* p. 37.

Evers, A., Haverines, R., Leeichsenring, K., & Wistow, G. (Eds.). (1997). *Developing quality in personal social services: Concepts, cases, and comments.* Brookfield, VT: Ashgate.

Fisher, R., & Karger, H. J. (1997). *Social work and community in a private world: Getting out in public.* New York: Longman.

Florida Department of Children and Families. (1996, January 5). *Children and Families Department signs contract with CitiBank to deliver public assistance benefits electronically* [News release]. Tallahassee, FL: Author.

Garland, S. B. (1997, May 19). A rich new business called poverty. *Business Week,* pp. 132-134.

Gore, A. (1996). *Reinventing's next steps: Governing in a balanced budget world.* Washington, DC: Government Printing Office.

Guard, M. (1998, June 17). *At-risk and special needs populations: An industry overview.* Presentation at the conference, Non-profits and for-profits: Reassessing the social service market place, sponsored by The Pew Charitable Trusts, Philadelphia, PA.

Gummer, B. (1998). Current perspectives on diversity in the workforce: How diverse is diverse? *Administration in Social Work, 22*(1), 83-100.

Gummer, B., & McCallion, P. (1995). *Total quality management in the social services.* Albany: State University of New York Press.

Gunther, J., & Hawkins, F. (1996). *Total quality management in human service organizations.* New York: Springer.

Gurwitt, R. (1998, April). With strings attached. *Governing, 11,* 18-22.

Hammer, M. (1996). *Beyond reengineering.* New York: HarperBusiness.

Hammer, M., & Champy, J. (1993). *Reengineering the corporation.* New York: Harper Business.

Harbert, A., Finnegan, D., & Tyler, N. (1998). Collaboration: A study of a children's initiative. *Administration in Social Work, 21*(3/4), 83-107.

Herron, D. (1997). *Marketing nonprofit programs and services.* San Francisco: Jossey-Bass.

Hile, M. (1998). The history and functions of the target cities management information systems: An introduction to the special issue. *Computers in Human Services, 14*(3/4), 1-7.

Karger, H. J., & Stoesz, D. (1998). *American social welfare policy.* New York: Longman.

Kingsley, G., McNeely, J., & Gibson, J. (1997). *Community building: Coming of age.* Washington, DC: The Urban Institute.

Kligman, D., & Lammers, W. (1984). The "general policy liberalism" factor in American state politics. *American Journal of Political Science, 28,* 598-610.

Krepcho, M., Marks, B., Garnett, D., Snell, L., & Olson, L. (1998). Dallas target cities safety network management information system. *Computers in Human Services, 14*(3/4), 29-49.

Kuttner, R. (1998, June 22). Left-of-center capitalists, unite. *Business Week,* p. 24.

Lauffer, A. (1997). *Grants, etc.* Newbury Park, CA: Sage.

Linder, B. (1998, February). To put the vision in place. *Government Technology, 11,* 18-21, 29.

Martin, L. L. (1993). *Total quality management in human service organizations.* Newbury Park, CA: Sage.

Martin, L. L. (1997). Outcome budgeting: A new entrepreneurial approach to budgeting. *Journal of Public Budgeting, Accounting & Financial Management, 9*(1), 108-126.

Martin, L. L. (1999). Administration and management of state human service agencies. In J. Gargan (Ed.), *Handbook of state administration* (pp. 461-482). New York: Marcel-Dekker.

Martin, L. L. (in press). Performance contracting: A comparative analysis of selected state practices. *Administration in Social Work.*

Martin, L. L., & Kettner, P. M. (1996). *Measuring the performance of human service programs.* Newbury Park, CA: Sage.

Meenaghan, T. (1998). Your social work career in the 21st century. *Currents, 15*(6), 1 and 10.

Melia, R. (1997). *Public profits from private contracts: A case study in human services.* Boston: The Pioneer Institute for Public Policy Research.

Melkers, J., & Willoughby, K. (1998). The state of the states: Performance budgeting requirements in 47 out of 50 states. *Public Administration Review, 58,* 66-73.

Mullen, E., & Magnabosco, J. L. (Eds.). (1997). *Outcomes measurement in the human services.* Washington, DC: NASW Press.

Nagel, S. (1997). *Super-optimum solutions and win-win policy.* Westport, CT: Quorum Books.

Naisbitt, J. (1982). *Megatrends.* New York: Warner.

Naisbitt, J., & Aburdene, P. (1990). *Megatrends 2000.* New York: William Morrow.

National Aging Information Center (NAIC). (1996). *Aging into the 21st century.* Washington, DC: U.S. Department of Health & Human Services, Administration on Aging. Available: http://pr.aoa.dhhs.gov/aoa/stats/aging21 (May 27, 1998)

National Association of Social Workers (NASW). (1997). *Preparing social workers for a managed care environment* (monograph). Washington, DC: Author.

Newcombe, T. (1998, May). Beacon puts state's welfare reform out front. *Government Technology, 11,* 46-47.

The new holy war. (1998, July 1). *Newsweek,* pp. 26-28.

Peyrot, M., Harris, W., Fenzel, L., & Burbridge, J. (1997). Welfare plastic: The transformation of public assistance in the electronic age. *Journal of Sociology and Social Welfare, 24,* 127-133.

Piskora, B. (1998, April 10). Average Americans are stocking up. *New York Post,* p. 27.

Poulos, C. (1998, May). The big sky country's welfare reform solution. *Government Technology, 11,* 50.

Printz, T. (1998). *Faith-based service providers in the nation's capital: Can they do more?* Washington, DC: The Urban Institute. Available: http://www.urban.org/periodcl/cnp/cnp_2.htm (May 28, 1998)

South's embrace of G.O.P. is near a turning point. (1998, March 16). *New York Times,* p. A12.

Swope, C. (1998, June). The high-tech brain drain. *Governing, 11,* 37-38.

Technology Assessment Board (TAB) of the 103rd Congress. (1993). *Making government work: Electronic delivery of federal services.* Washington, DC: Government Printing Office.

Thurow, L. (1998). Economic community and social investment. In F. Hesselbein et al. (Eds.), *The community of the future* (pp. 19-26). San Francisco: Jossey-Bass.

The Urban Institute. (1998). *Policy challenges posed by the aging of America.* Washington, DC: Author.

U.S. General Accounting Office (GAO). (1997a). *Department of Health & Human Services: Management challenges and opportunities.* Washington, DC: Author.

U.S. General Accounting Office (GAO). (1997b). *Social services privatization: Expansion poses challenges in ensuring accountability for results* (GAO/HEHS-98-6). Washington, DC: Author.

U.S. General Accounting Office (GAO). (1998). *Federal downsizing: Agency officials' views on maintaining performance during downsizing at selected agencies* (GAO/GGD-98-75). Washington, DC: Author.

Walters, J. (1998, February). Did somebody say downsizing? *Governing, 11,* 17-20.

Wayne, L. (1998, February 27). The shrinking military complex. *New York Times,* p. D1.

Weil, M. (1996). Community building: Building community practice. *Social Work, 41*(5), 481-499.

Weinbach, R. W. (1998). *The social worker as manager.* Boston: Allyn & Bacon.

CHAPTER FOUR

Administrative Ethics

FREDERIC G. REAMER

Knowledge germane to social welfare administration has burgeoned in recent years. As the discussions in this book demonstrate, to perform their duties competently, contemporary professionals must have a firm grasp of a wide range of substantive domains, including the political and economic dimensions of social welfare administration, leadership issues, theories and models of administrative practice, agency governance and climate, employee relations and supervision, management strategies, and agency-environment relations.

But this substantive knowledge, by itself, will not suffice. Administrators must also appreciate how each of these phenomena is fraught with ethical issues, that is, issues that raise questions about matters of right and wrong and administrators' moral duties and obligations. It is one thing for administrators to understand the technical nuances involved in formulating an annual budget; it is yet another for administrators to understand the ethical choices they must make if a budget shortfall requires programmatic cutbacks or employee layoffs. It is one thing for administrators to understand theories and models of personnel management; it is yet another for them to cultivate knowledge and skills that will enable them to handle an ethical crisis involving a program director who has been falsifying data in his quarterly reports. It is one thing for administrators to learn about marketing strategies to help promote an agency's services; it is yet another for administrators to critically examine the morality of the agency's mission and to understand the ethical choices involved in the use of subtly deceptive advertising. As Wright and McConkie (1988) note,

> To begin, the *significance* of organizational ethics is a major point of agreement. We work, study,

pray, play, travel, and sometimes eat and sleep in organizations. Organizations amplify the impact of administrators in all our lives. Decisions with ethical implications are especially magnified. . . . Administrative ethics are the formal and informal restraints that give legitimacy to the actions of an administrator. (p. 5)

To function competently, social welfare administrators must have a solid command of three key knowledge areas: (a) ethical issues and dilemmas in administration; (b) ethical analysis, moral reasoning, and decision-making strategies; and (c) ethical risk management—strategies to prevent ethics complaints and lawsuits from being filed against agency staff and organizations themselves.

Before embarking on a systematic review of issues germane to these three substantive areas, we must begin with a brief exploration of the context in which knowledge about administrative ethics has evolved: the nature of professional ethics generally and, more specifically, ethical issues in administration and in social work. Each of these areas has its own unique intellectual roots, although they are certainly intertwined.

THE EVOLUTION OF PROFESSIONAL, ADMINISTRATIVE, AND SOCIAL WORK ETHICS

The broad phenomenon now dubbed professional ethics began in earnest in the late 1960s and early 1970s (Callahan & Bok, 1980; Reamer & Abramson, 1982). This occurred for several reasons, including widespread recognition of ethical issues involved in the medical and health care fields (now known as bioethical issues) related to, for example, end-of-life deci-

sions, abortion, genetic engineering, dialysis, and organ transplantation; the influence of the 1960s' preoccupation with various rights concepts (e.g., civil rights, welfare rights, consumers' rights, prisoners' rights, patients' rights), increased awareness of ethical issues involved in public life (fueled significantly by the Watergate crisis), and increased litigation against professionals involving ethical issues (e.g., confidentiality breaches, incompetent care, sexual misconduct).

The emergence of the bioethics field foreshadowed a flurry of intellectual activity in other professions. Especially during the mid-to-late 1970s and early 1980s, a relatively small cadre of scholars and practitioners in fields as diverse as journalism, the law, engineering, nursing, dentistry, business and management, law enforcement, the military, and the various mental health professions (psychiatry, psychology, social work, and counseling) began exploring ethical issues faced by professionals. Since this period, the literature on professional ethics in each of these fields has burgeoned, as have educational and conference offerings. Many health care, social service, and business organizations, for example, now retain ethics consultants, sponsor ethics education and ethics committees, and conduct ethics "grand rounds." Many professions have completely rewritten and upgraded their ethics codes and require their members to obtain ethics-related continuing education.

This is not to say that none of the professions paid attention to ethical issues prior to the 1970s. Certainly, throughout their respective histories, various professions have engaged in earnest exploration and debate related to a number of values-related issues. However, the 1970s and early 1980s marked a sea change in professions' approach to ethics. It was during this period that professionals began their earnest attempt to draw on concepts and theoretical frameworks based in moral philosophy and ethics—and theology, to a lesser extent—in an effort to think systematically and comprehensively about ethical issues that practitioners face (Bayles, 1981; Rosenthal & Shehadi, 1988).

Developments in the fields of administration, management, and social work parallel this trend (Bowman & Menzel, 1998). According to Wright and McConkie (1988), the earliest discussions of administrative ethics can be summarized as "organizational ethics of God's order" and concerned matters related to the "divine right of rulers" (p. 4). This emphasis on the ethical character of rulers influenced the framers of the Declaration of Independence and the Constitution, leading to widespread belief that "governance must be based on ethical character of individual governors" (Wright & McConkie, 1988, p. 4).

However, the growing popularity of the scientific method in the late 19th and early 20th centuries, as well as the influence of Social Darwinism, led to a shift away from a preoccupation with the virtues and morality of rulers, governors, and administrators and toward an emphasis on the more secular values of administrative efficiency, power, strength, and effectiveness.

> The Ethics of God's Order eventually changed in tandem with societal changes brought about by the acceptance of the science of the period, wherein the value questions of organizational life became answerable by the scientific method. . . . The Protestant Ethic was replaced with a utilitarian precursor to social Darwinism. . . . From the pseudoscience of social Darwinism, the ethical trail leads to the empiricism of both the administrative and behavioral sciences. This occurred in the late 1800s and early 1900s. The acceptance of the scientific method led to either the abandonment of traditional values or at best their relegation to an insignificant position in management thought. We lost the societal view posited by the "Ethics of God's Order" as well as the concern for the individual pursued by the Founders. These were replaced with an ultimate value of impersonal efficiency. (Wright & McConkie, 1988, p. 5)

Over time, administration scholars and practitioners grew increasingly frustrated with the field's narrow focus on efficiency, particularly given the diverse values-related issues swirling around the 1960s and hard questions pertaining to the social and moral responsibility of organizations. In the social welfare field, in particular, widespread evidence that some agencies—especially public welfare agencies—were unethical, coercive, intrusive, capricious, discriminatory, racist, negligent, and self-serving in their granting of benefits and delivery of services stimulated considerable concern about organizational morality and a new brand of ethical activism. As Patti (personal communication) notes, "as organizational legitimacy was challenged, and activated constituencies demanded redress, ethical dilemmas began to emerge because choices now led to potentially untoward consequences. Prior to that time, social agencies were often seen as inherently moral, ethical agents. Ethical consideration hardly concerned those who were felt to be custodians of community morality."

The formal emergence of the public administration field was critical in the development of administration ethics. In the late 19th and early 20th centuries, Woodrow Wilson and Frank Goodnow helped pave an intellectual path that later stimulated the earnest exploration of ethical issues in administration. Both Wilson and Goodnow argued for a science of administration in which civil servants neither made policy nor struggled with its morality. Following World War II, however, many scholars actively rejected the idea of value-free or morally neutral public administration. Over time, this inclination to introduce moral and ethical content into organizational life led to the creation of specialized concepts, knowledge, and frameworks in the fields of administration and business (Bowman, 1991; Wright & McConkie, 1988).

During roughly the same time span, the social work field experienced its own maturation with respect to ethical issues, both in general and with respect to issues of administration. Focus during the late 19th century on morality issues rooted in religious beliefs and traditions—related especially to the morality of the "pauper"—eventually shifted toward more secular concerns with practitioners' ethics (Reamer, 1983, 1987b). Until the late 1970s and early 1980s, social workers focused primarily on the profession's core values and ethical issues pertaining to clients' rights to confidentiality and self-determination (Levy, 1976). As was the case in other professions, in the early 1980s, a relatively small group of social work scholars embarked on an ambitious attempt to explore ethical issues in depth; draw on relevant concepts, principles, and theories from moral philosophy; and develop conceptually based models to help social workers address ethical issues that arise in practice (Loewenberg & Dolgoff, 1982; Reamer, 1982; Rhodes, 1986). This paradigm shift in social workers' approach to ethics has led to a burgeoning literature on the subject and more assertive efforts to educate and train social work students and practitioners about ethical issues in the profession. The proliferation of intellectual activity in this area culminated in the 1996 ratification of a new National Association of Social Workers (NASW) Code of Ethics, which represents a remarkable departure from the association's two earlier codes with respect to the breadth and depth of its content (NASW, 1996; Reamer, 1995a, 1998a).

In light of this history, a comprehensive typology of ethical issues in administration should be informed by the recent expansion of knowledge related to the broad field of applied and professional ethics and, more specifically, the more specialized fields of administration and social work. As summarized above, this typology should address three major topics: (a) ethical issues and dilemmas in administration; (b) ethical analysis, moral reasoning, and decision-making strategies; and (c) ethical risk management, including strategies to prevent ethics complaints and lawsuits filed against agency staff and organizations themselves.

ETHICAL DILEMMAS IN ADMINISTRATION

Ethical dilemmas occur when administrators face conflicting ethical obligations and duties. For example, administrators who face budget cutbacks may have to make exceedingly difficult decisions about how to allocate scarce or limited resources in a way that minimizes harm to vulnerable clients—what philosophers refer to as issues of *distributive justice*. In such situations, administrators may find it impossible to meet the simultaneous needs of all clients (Andrews, 1989; Joseph, 1983; Levy, 1982; Reamer, 1997; Ritchie, 1988); programs or services for some clients may have to be sacrificed to meet the needs of the agency's most vulnerable clients (ethical triage). Or, administrators may have to decide whether to disclose confidential information, without a client's consent, to protect a third party who has been threatened by the client. That is, administrators are caught between their obligation to protect the client's right to confidentiality and protect a third party from harm. Using terminology introduced by the moral philosopher W. D. Ross (1930), administrators sometimes have to choose between competing or conflicting *prima facie duties* and select an *actual duty,* that is, the duty that takes precedence. As Cooper (1990) notes,

> Confronting conflicting responsibilities is the most typical way public administrators experience ethical dilemmas. We may feel torn between two sets of expectation or inclination, neither of which is without significant costs. "Damned if you do, damned if you don't" is a common way of expressing this feeling of being caught between incompatible alternatives. Frequently we do not identify this dilemma as an ethical issue, only as a practical problem. However, at base these situations involve ordering our values and principles, consciously or otherwise. They are, therefore, problems of ethics, as well as practical problems. (p. 83)

Ethical issues and dilemmas faced by administrators tend to fall into three broad categories. First, there are ethical dilemmas that arise out of administrators' oversight of subordinates' or employees' efforts to deliver services to individuals, families, and small groups. These are most likely to occur in agencies or organizations that provide direct services, such as family service agencies, community mental health centers, child welfare programs, community action pro-

grams, and programs for people with disabilities. Examples include ethical dilemmas involving confidentiality (e.g., disclosing confidential information without clients' consent to protect third parties or to comply with statutes, regulations, or court orders), boundary issues (e.g., accepting clients' invitations to attend significant life-cycle events, such as graduations, weddings, religious ceremonies; accepting gifts from clients; entering into friendships with former clients; bartering for services or making fee adjustments to accommodate clients' special circumstances), and professional paternalism (e.g., placing limits on clients who are engaging in self-destructive or high-risk behaviors or activities, interfering with clients' right to self-determination).

Second, administrators face ethical dilemmas involving program design, administrative policy, organizational design, management decisions, and program development. These more macro issues concern the ethical dimensions of formal policy and procedures, regulations, and statutes (Cooper, 1990; Guy, 1990; Jackall, 1989; Levy, 1982; Pops, 1991; Ritchie, 1988; Snoeyenbos, Almeder, & Humber, 1983). As Guy (1990) concludes,

> Some of the most common ethical dilemmas emanate from hierarchical relationships that produce a clash between administrative routines and professional, personal, or democratic values. . . . Day-to-day decisions highlight the fact that even apparently routine decisions about budgeting and financial issues, personnel procedures, marketing strategies, supervisory styles, and reporting functions involve ethical issues and consequences. (p. xvi)

Commonly occurring issues in social service organizations involve complying with contracts, policies, regulations, and statutes (e.g., policies, regulations, or statutes that compromise or violate clients' rights or professional standards, such as personnel policies that discriminate against women or people with disabilities; unfair intake criteria; regulations that require the invasive collection of private information from clients or employees; or insurance regulations that limit services made available to vulnerable clients); program design and goals (e.g., selection of criteria to determine what clientele is served, what services will be offered, and what goals will shape the agency's operation, for example, whether the agency will challenge new managed care policies, serve high-cost "multi-problem" clients as opposed to "creaming" or "skimming" low-cost clients, aim to generate a profit or break even, and maintain unprofitable but important services); allocation of scarce or limited resources (e.g., being diligent stewards of agency resources, developing criteria and procedures to distribute resources—such as agency funds, personnel, shelter beds—in a fair and equitable manner, for example, whether to base allocation decisions on need, affirmative action principles, principles of equality); deceptive or fraudulent practices (e.g., embezzling agency funds, exaggerating program statistics or client information to enhance future funding or obtain insurance reimbursement for critically important programs and services, using false or inaccurate advertising to market an agency's program and attract clients, exaggerating a program's effectiveness to attract financial support); and personnel issues (e.g., exploiting or harassing employees, conducting fair performance evaluations, deciding whether to hire staff based entirely on merit or to factor in affirmative action considerations, deciding

whether to terminate staff who are not sufficiently competent).

Third, administrators sometimes face ethical dilemmas involving relationships among agency staff or colleagues. Typically, these involve instances where administrators become aware of organizational scandals or staff or colleagues who have engaged in unethical behavior, and they must decide on an appropriate course of action, for example, whether to notify the board of directors or contact the media about organizational wrongdoing or to report an unethical colleague to administrative superiors, a professional association, or licensing board—a form of whistle-blowing (Barry, 1986; Bok, 1980; Cooper, 1990; Levy, 1982). Comparable dilemmas can arise when administrators are concerned about employees' level of competence or impairment.

ETHICAL DECISION MAKING

Prior to the emergence of applied and professional ethics in the 1970s, two principal frameworks had evolved in the administration field for approaching ethical decision making: the *bureaucratic ethos* and the *democratic ethos* (Fleishman & Payne, 1980; Pugh, 1991). The bureaucratic ethos—rooted in the Weberian model of bureaucracy, the Wilsonian distinction between politics and administration, Taylor's theory of scientific management, and the classic theoretical perspectives of Goodnow and Willoughby—entails making ethical decisions with a keen eye toward their implications for organizational efficiency, efficacy, expertise, loyalty, and accountability. The democratic ethos, in contrast, emphasizes the critical importance of concepts such as regime values (i.e., core values expressed in documents such as the U.S. Constitution: personal liberty, property, equality), citizenship, public interest, and social equity.

Perhaps the most significant by-product of the dramatic growth of the applied and professional ethics field has been the development of newer conceptual models to facilitate moral reasoning and assist practitioners who face difficult ethical dilemmas and decisions (Hosmer, 1991; Jennings, 1991; Stewart & Sprinthall, 1991). As noted above, since the early 1980s, a number of philosophers and scholars in various professions have developed frameworks to facilitate ethical decision making. Although the frameworks vary somewhat, their formats are similar. Typically, the frameworks include a series of steps that professionals can follow as they navigate difficult ethical dilemmas. The frameworks are not designed to suggest that difficult ethical dilemmas can be reduced to simple algorithms or that following the outline of steps guarantees clear, straightforward, unequivocal solutions to complex problems. Rather, the frameworks are designed to alert professionals to relevant ethical concepts and issues that should be incorporated into their decision making and to enhance the likelihood that these decisions will be made systematically and thoughtfully (Guy, 1990; Loewenberg & Dolgoff, 1996; Reamer, 1995b, 1998b, 1999).

These various decision-making frameworks typically incorporate a number of key elements for professionals to consider.

Conflicting values and duties. An inherent feature of ethical dilemmas is conflicting values and duties. The concept of value is difficult to define. It derives from the Latin *valere,* meaning "to be strong, to prevail, or to be of worth" (Meinert, 1980, p. 5). Values also refer to "the desirable end states which act as a guide to human endeavor or the most general statements of legitimate ends which guide social action" and "normative standards by which human beings are influenced in their choice among the alternative courses of action which they perceive" (Rescher, 1969, p. 2).

Scholars of administration have developed several different conceptualizations of core values that ought to guide administrators' ethical decisions. For example, in her essay on the moral foundations of administration, Denhardt (1991) focuses on the central role of three core concepts: honor, benevolence, and justice. Honor, according to Denhardt, is

> adherence to the highest standards of responsibility, integrity, and principle. . . . Honor denotes a quality of character in which the individual exhibits a high sense of duty, pursuing good deeds as ends in themselves, not because of any benefit or recognition that might be accrued because of the deeds. (pp. 102-103)

Benevolence involves

> [the] disposition to do good and to promote the welfare of others. . . . Based on the Latin words *bene* (well) and *volens* (wishing), benevolence implies not only *actions* that promote good and the welfare of others but also *motivation* to pursue those ends. (p. 104)

And justice, writes Denhardt, "signifies fairness and regard for the rights of others. The rights of others include, most fundamentally, respect for the dignity and worth of each individual" (p. 106). Justice further involves "a commitment to developing and preserving rights for individuals that will ensure that their dignity and worth will not be violated by others in the society" (p. 106).

In a more detailed typology, Gellerman, Frankel, and Ladenson (1990) examine emerging consensus in the organization and human systems development field concerning core values and divide them, and related professional duties, into five categories:

1. responsibility to ourselves (e.g., acting with integrity and authenticity, striving for self-knowledge and personal growth, asserting individual interests in ways that are fair and equitable)
2. responsibility for professional development and competence (e.g., accepting responsibility for the consequences of our acts, developing and maintaining individual competence and establishing cooperative relations with other professionals, recognizing our own needs and desires and dealing with them responsibly in the performance of our professional roles)
3. responsibility to clients and significant others (e.g., serving the long-term well-being of our client systems and their stakeholders; conducting ourselves honestly, responsibly, and with appropriate openness; establishing mutual agreement on a fair contract)
4. responsibility to the profession (e.g., contributing to the continuing professional development of other practitioners and the profession as a whole; promoting the sharing of professional knowledge and skill; working with other professionals in ways that exemplify what the profession stands for)
5. social responsibility (e.g., acting with sensitivity to the consequences of our recommendations for our client systems and the larger systems within which they function, acting with awareness of our cultural filters and with sensitivity to multinational and multicultural

differences and their implications, and promoting justice and serving the well-being of others)

Another prominent typology of core values in administration is more philosophically oriented (Solomon, 1992, pp. 145-190). Solomon argues that organizational life and administrators' actions should be grounded in six core values associated with Aristotle's writings, such as the *Nichomachean Ethics* and *Politics:*

1. community: "We are, first of all, members of organized groups, with shared histories and established practices governing everything from eating and working to worshiping." (Solomon, 1992, p. 146)
2. excellence: "It is a word of great significance and indicates a sense of mission, a commitment beyond profit potential and the bottom line. It is a word that suggests 'doing well' but also 'doing good.'" (Solomon, 1992, p. 153)
3. membership: "The idea that an employee or executive develops his or her personal identity largely through the organizations in which he or she spends most of adult waking life." (Solomon, 1992, p. 161)
4. integrity: "Integrity is essentially *moral courage,* the will and willingness to do what one knows one ought to do." (Solomon, 1992, p. 168)
5. judgment: "Aristotle thought that it was 'good judgment' or *phronesis* that was of the greatest importance in ethics." (Solomon, 1992, p. 174)
6. holism: "The ultimate aim of the Aristotelian approach to business is to cultivate whole human beings, not jungle fighters, efficiency automatons, or 'good soldiers.' . . . But one of the problems of traditional business thinking is our tendency to isolate our business or professional roles from the rest of our lives." (Solomon, 1992, p. 180)

Considered as a group, Solomon claims, these virtues provide the moral foundation that is essential in the organizational or corporate world: "Together, they form an integrative structure in which the individual, the corporation, and the community, self-interest and the public good, the personal and the professional, business and virtues all work together instead of against one another" (p. 145).

Along with typologies of values formulated by students of administration, social welfare administrators also need to be mindful of comparable frameworks in the social work field. Over the years, several scholars and professional groups have developed typologies of core values in social work (see, e.g., Bartlett, 1970; Biestek, 1957; Gordon, 1965; NASW, 1982; Plant, 1970; Pumphrey, 1959; Teicher, 1967; Timms, 1983; Vigilante, 1974). The NASW Code of Ethics Revision Committee, which drafted the 1996 NASW Code of Ethics (chaired by this author), conducted a thorough review of various typologies of social work values and generated a list of six core values that are now formally incorporated in the code and pertain to social welfare administration: service ("Social workers' primary goal is to help people in need and to address social problems"), social justice ("Social workers challenge social injustice"), dignity and worth of the person ("Social workers respect the inherent dignity and worth of the person"), importance of human relationships ("Social workers recognize the central importance of human relationships"), integrity ("Social workers behave in a trustworthy manner"), and competence ("Social workers practice within their areas of competence and develop and enhance their professional expertise").

It is important for social welfare administrators to grasp the core values that constitute the foundation of administrative and social welfare or social work ethics. After all, ethical dilemmas emerge when such values, and the professional duties that stem from them, conflict.

Moral and ethical theory. A key ingredient in all decision-making frameworks is the use of moral and ethical theory to analyze ethical dilemmas. Although moral and ethical theory can be traced back to the Socratic, Platonic, and Aristotelian eras, the deliberate application of such theory to ethical dilemmas faced by professionals began in earnest only in the mid-1970s. During this period, a group of philosophers interested in the real-life ethical dilemmas facing contemporary professionals, and a small group of professionals with a keen interest in ethics, began to explore the ways in which classic moral and ethical theory could be used to help professionals think through and assess complex ethical challenges (Reamer, 1993b). This was not a passing intellectual fad; since this period, both philosophers and professionals have continued to apply moral and ethical theory to their analysis of ethical dilemmas.

Nearly all of these scholarly efforts include the application of relevant theories of normative ethics and, to a lesser degree, meta-ethics (Beauchamp, 1982; Frankena, 1973; Reamer, 1989, 1990). Meta-ethics, as the prefix implies, involves efforts to answer relatively abstract questions such as What do we mean by terms such as justice, equality, right and wrong, and good and bad? How can we operationalize such concepts? What criteria should we use to determine whether various ethical theories and principles are valid? Not surprisingly, serious meta-ethical discussions tend to concern moral philosophers; few professionals care to devote significant attention to these abstruse, albeit important questions (Gortner, 1991).

Rather, those interested in the practical problems of ethics focus their attention on normative ethics. Normative ethics involves the application of ethical theories, principles, and guidelines to actual ethical dilemmas. This is the most pragmatic side of the ethics field, comparable to the application of theories of administration to actual challenges faced by agency administrators and the application of clinical intervention theories by clinical social workers.

Theories of normative ethics are typically divided into two groups: *deontological* and *teleological* (also known as *consequentialist*). Deontological theories (from the Greek *deontos,* of the obligatory), which have their principal origins in the works of the 18th-century German philosopher, Immanuel Kant, claim that certain actions or behaviors are inherently right or wrong, or good or bad. For example, an agency administrator who is tempted to exaggerate or falsify intake statistics to ensure future funding would be constrained by a deontological theory that asserts that people have an inherent obligation to "tell the truth" and "never lie or promote falsehoods." Similarly, an agency administrator would be obligated to honor a contract entered into with another party, even if doing so might seriously jeopardize the agency's finances and future stability—promises must be kept. Or, an administrator who plans to lay off employees would have an inherent obligation to be honest with staff in response to their direct questions about job security.

In contrast, teleological theories (from the Greek *teleios,* brought to its end or purpose)

promote a completely different way of thinking about ethical dilemmas. From this perspective, individuals faced with an ethical dilemma should measure the moral rightness of their actions based on the moral goodness of the consequences (hence, the term consequentialism). According to teleologists, to act primarily out of a sense of obligation or some concept of what is inherently right or wrong is to act naively and to engage in rule worship (Smart, 1971), rule-governed thinking (Solomon, 1992), or authoritative obedience (Jennings, 1991). That is, when faced with an ethical dilemma, administrators should carefully examine the potential outcomes, weigh their relative merits and demerits, and act in a manner that produces the most favorable consequences.

Of course, how one defines *favorable* is critical, and this has been a much debated issue. In this respect, there are two major schools of teleological thought. *Ethical egoism* is a form of teleology that claims that one ought to act in a way that produces the greatest good for one's self—a self-centered, selfish perspective. Thus, egotistical administrators would "resolve" ethical dilemmas in ways that protect their job security, enhance their income or public image, generate agency profit, avoid embarrassment, and so on. Clearly, only the most brazen, unconscionable administrator would argue that teleological egoism ought, as a matter of principle, to guide ethical decisions. Ethical egoism may be more common, and even acceptable, in the business world, where profit and career advancement—as opposed to "doing good"—are valued as legitimate ends in and of themselves and, hence, foster a different ethical culture and set of moral norms.

More common is the teleological perspective of *utilitarianism,* which favors actions that promote the greatest good for the greatest number (Solomon, 1992). According to this point of view, as originally formulated by the English philosophers Jeremy Bentham (in the 18th century) and John Stuart Mill (in the 19th century), when faced with conflicting values or ethical duties, one should engage in a calculus to determine which set of consequences will produce the greatest good. For example, if an administrator is struggling with a decision about whether to hire a person with a physical disability for a staff position, consistent with affirmative action principles, rather than a more competent applicant who does not have a disability, the administrator would, according to utilitarianism, assess which outcome is more likely to produce the greatest good (in terms of job performance, benefits to clients, agency revenue, and so forth). The administrator's "inherent obligation" to comply with affirmative action regulations (consistent with a deontological perspective) would not be a compelling consideration. Or, if an administrator were struggling to decide how to allocate limited agency funds among competing agency-sponsored programs, the administrator would be concerned only about which funding pattern would produce the greatest good (however defined); the administrator would not be concerned about basic or fundamental principles of fairness or distributive justice. Administrators who are guided primarily by their aim to promote the greatest aggregate good, regardless of how the outcome is distributed, would act in accord with what is called *good-aggregative utilitarianism*. Administrators who are guided primarily by their aim to produce the greatest good for the greatest number (that is, to spread the good outcomes around as much as possible) would act in accord with *locus-aggregative utilitarianism* (Gewirth,

1978). As one might imagine, many social welfare administrators implement some form of utilitarian thinking, even though they may not use the formal labels in doing so. This is evident in prominent discussions of the importance of efficiency in social welfare administration, that is, producing maximum benefits for consumers (clients) with the least cost (Patti, Rapp, & Poertner, 1988; Pruger & Miller, 1991; Rapp & Poertner, 1992).

One of the most useful distinctions in ethical theory is between *act* and *rule utilitarianism* (Gorovitz, 1971). According to act utilitarianism, the rightness of an action is determined by the goodness of its consequences in that individual case or set of circumstances. In contrast, rule utilitarianism requires one to anticipate the net and long-run consequences that will result if one generalizes from the immediate case or circumstances and acts accordingly in all similar situations. For instance, imagine an administrator who faces an ethical decision about whether to falsify information in a report submitted to an accreditation agency. The administrator might try to justify this deception on act utilitarian grounds, arguing that in this one instance, the falsification of information is ethically permissible because it is the only way to assure accreditation for an agency that provides critically important services to a vulnerable population. However, from a rule utilitarian perspective, one might argue that this act of deception would establish a harmful and dangerous precedent; that is, if this practice were generalized, we would face large numbers of agencies that would be granted accreditation based on false information, an unacceptable outcome that could have devastating consequences for the social welfare field and the general public. It would be difficult to promote a general practice that would permit all agency administrators to use their discretion as to whether or not their data summaries should be falsified when applying for accreditation.

The distinctions between deontological and teleological perspectives reflect the contrasting schools of thought that have evolved in the administration field with respect to ethical issues: the bureaucratic ethos and democratic ethos. As noted above, the bureaucratic ethos tends to focus on ends or consequences (e.g., efficacy, expertise, accountability), whereas the democratic ethos emphasizes sacred or inherent values and obligations, such as core regime values, citizenship, public interest, and social equity. As Pugh (1991) observes,

> Bureaucratic ethos is teleological, employs instrumental rationality, and is predicated on the values of capitalism and a market society. Democratic ethos, in contrast, is deontological, is based on substantive rationality, and emanates from classical values of the state and higher law. (p. 26)

Jennings (1991) is particularly astute in his assertions about the relevance of these contrasting perspectives to administrative ethics:

> Applied ethics offers an alternative to the ethical frame of authoritative obedience, a frame that presents a different image of public administration's public purpose and professional vocation. With its emphasis on the structure and logic of moral reasoning—the derivation of justified decisions and courses of action from covering ethical principles applied to specific factual situations—applied ethics goes beyond the restricted notions of efficiency and instrumental rationality offered by ethics as authoritative obedience. In this way it reempowers public officials as responsible moral agents charged with the pursuit of principled ends and not solely the devising of efficient means and

> aims to provide sufficient moral guidance for the exercise of power by professional experts and political elites. (p. 74)

As noted earlier, ethical theories do not guarantee clean, unambiguous, simple solutions to complex ethical dilemmas. Rather, they can help administrators organize and shape their thinking and examine the arguments for and against different courses of action (much the way competing theories of administration or clinical intervention can help professionals think through the pros and cons of different strategies).

Ethics consultation. Another by-product of the maturing applied and professional ethics field has been the speciality of ethics consultation. Ethics consultation takes several forms. First, many agencies have developed their own ethics committees whose function is to help staff and clients examine ethical dilemmas that were not resolved through other mechanisms (e.g., supervision, administrative meetings). The phenomenon of ethics committees (often called institutional ethics committees) first emerged in 1976, when the New Jersey Supreme Court ruled that Karen Ann Quinlan's family and physicians should consult an ethics committee in their efforts to decide whether to remove her from life-support technology (although a number of hospitals have had something resembling ethics committees since at least the 1920s). The court based its ruling on an important article by a pediatrician that appeared in the *Baylor Law Review* in 1975, in which the author advocated the use of ethics committees in cases in which health care professionals face difficult ethical choices (Teel, 1975). Since then, many non-health care agencies have established ethics committees to serve similar functions (Fletcher, 1986; Fletcher, Quist, & Jonsen, 1989; La Puma & Schiedermayer, 1991; Reamer, 1987a; Skeel & Self, 1989).

Ethics committees ordinarily include representatives from various disciplines and professions, such as social work, the clergy, nursing, allied health, and agency administration. In large organizations, ethics committees sometimes include a professional ethicist, someone who is knowledgeable about the ethics literature and various ethical decision-making protocols and strategies. Some ethics committees include an organization's attorney, although this is controversial in light of attorneys' professional duty to offer advice intended to protect their clients; some critics believe that attorneys' unique role is inconsistent with the mission of an ethics committee to provide impartial consultation (to the extent true impartiality in ethics is possible).

Agency-based ethics committees usually serve several functions. They provide case consultation to those who request it and nonbinding advice. Issues might include the agency's handling of sensitive confidential information, informed consent criteria, whistle-blowing matters, program design, and controversial decisions to terminate programs or services in the face of budget cuts. Case consultation may occur to provide help in the midst of a compelling ethical dilemma (concurrent case consultation), to review the controversial handling of a recent matter (retrospective case consultation), or to think through how ethical dilemmas that might arise in the future, perhaps based on the experiences of other agencies, will be handled (prospective case consultation).

Ethics committees can also organize and sponsor staff training on relevant ethical issues, and they may critically examine, modify, or draft agency policies that address ethical issues.

In addition, on occasion, administrators may want to draw on the expertise of formally trained ethics consultants. These are individuals, often affiliated with academic institutions, who have developed expertise—in the form of familiarity with ethics literature, concepts, and decision-making strategies—that may be helpful to administrators facing difficult ethical choices.

Administrators should also familiarize themselves with relevant ethics-related policies, regulations, statutes, and codes of ethics. Many agencies have internally generated policies or regulations that are germane to ethical dilemmas (e.g., informed consent, confidentiality, boundary issues, conflict of interest policies). Furthermore, state and federal statutes may include important guidelines (for example, concerning disclosure of confidential information pertaining to school records, drug abuse treatment, and sexually transmitted diseases and concerning minors' right to obtain mental health treatment without parental or guardian consent).

Contemporary codes of ethics can also be a useful resource. Unlike older versions, many current codes are conceptually rich and sophisticated tools that alert professionals to key ethical issues and provide practical guidance concerning common ethical concerns (Kultgen, 1982). Although codes of ethics cannot possibly provide one-stop shopping for the resolution of complex ethical dilemmas, comprehensive codes can provide a framework to help practitioners organize their thinking.

A compelling example is the current NASW Code of Ethics, ratified in 1996. In contrast to the two earlier versions of the NASW code (ratified in 1960 and 1979), the 1996 code contains a detailed overview of a wide range of ethical issues germane to social welfare administration. Examples include new and expanded content on informed consent and confidentiality guidelines; cultural competence and social diversity; conflicts of interest; dual and multiple relationships; sexual harassment; termination of services; interdisciplinary collaboration; consultation and referral for services; practitioner impairment, incompetence, and unethical conduct; staff supervision and consultation; continuing education and staff development; performance evaluation; record-keeping and documentation; billing; resource allocation; commitments to employers; labor-management disputes; discrimination; dishonesty, fraud, deception, and misrepresentation; client solicitation; social and political action; and research and evaluation (NASW, 1996; Reamer, 1998a).

ETHICS RISK MANAGEMENT

One of the practical reasons for social welfare administrators to become more familiar with ethical guidelines and literature, and to educate staff about professional ethics, is to prevent ethics complaints and lawsuits that allege some kind of ethical lapse, negligence, or misconduct (Besharov, 1985; Houston-Vega, Nuehring, & Daguio, 1997; Reamer, 1993a, 1994). This is particularly important in light of general increases in the numbers of complaints and lawsuits filed against human service professionals in recent years (Austin, Moline, & Williams, 1990).

A significant component of ethics risk management is education about key legal concepts. Administrators should become familiar with concepts such as liability, malpractice, negligence, standards of care, misfeasance, malfeasance, nonfeasance, acts of commission and omission, assumption of risk, vicarious liability (or *respondeat superior*), joint liability, strict liability, comparative negligence, and abandonment (Austin et al., 1990; Reamer, 1994). More specifically, administrators should be familiar with major risk areas involving possible ethical mistakes, ethical decisions, and ethical misconduct. Potential risks involve administrators' relationships with staff (e.g., hiring and firing decisions, sexual harassment, performance evaluations, staff supervision, employee impairment) and clients (e.g., the limitations of clients' right to confidentiality, use of high-risk and nontraditional treatment strategies and interventions, boundary issues [including dual and multiple relationships with clients], sexual harassment, conflicts of interest, informed consent, defamation of character, consultation and referral, documentation, and termination of social services). Administrators should be especially careful to keep current with research and evaluation results pertaining to their programmatic responsibilities, particularly in light of ethical standards that require social workers to "critically examine and keep current with emerging knowledge relevant to social work and fully use evaluation and research evidence in their professional practice" (NASW, 1996, p. 25).

In recent years, social welfare administrators, along with other professionals, have increased their understanding of the critical role of professional ethics. Surrounding the programmatic, supervisory, personnel, and fiscal challenges facing administrators is a wide range of complex ethical issues. Some ethical issues are fairly straightforward; others, however, are dauntingly complex.

In light of current knowledge, it behooves administrators to become familiar with the panoply of ethical issues and dilemmas that permeate organizations and with the conceptual tools that have evolved as the applied and professional ethics field has matured. Administrators should also be familiar with practical strategies designed to prevent ethics complaints and lawsuits involving ethical issues.

But administrative ethics is about more than ethical decision making and risk management. It is also about such "big picture" issues as the moral aims of social welfare, the ends we seek to achieve, and the morality of the means we use to pursue our goals. These deliberations entail issues of moral judgment: "the capacity to discriminate among available courses of action on the basis of an interpretive understanding of shared values embedded in an ongoing institutional practice and in a broader form of communal life" (Jennings, 1991, p. 68).

Administrators face a never-ending series of complex duties. Their ethical responsibilities—which necessarily involve decisions about moral duty and obligation—constitute the core of their professional mission. Administrators' task is to cultivate both the internal and external controls and compass that are essential for ethical practice. As Cooper (1990) concludes, "as administrators define the boundaries and content of their responsibility in resolving specific ethical dilemmas, both great and small,

they create for themselves an 'ethical identity.'" (p. 6).

REFERENCES

Andrews, K. R. (1989). *Ethics in practice: Managing the moral corporation.* Boston: Harvard Business School Press.

Austin, K. M., Moline, M. E., & Williams, G. T. (1990). *Confronting malpractice: Legal and ethical dilemmas in psychotherapy.* Newbury Park, CA: Sage.

Barry, V. (1986). *Moral issues in business* (3rd ed.). Belmont, CA: Wadsworth.

Bartlett, H. M. (1970). *The common base of social work practice.* New York: Columbia University Press.

Bayles, M. D. (1981). *Professional ethics.* Belmont, CA: Wadsworth.

Beauchamp, T. L. (1982). *Philosophical ethics: An introduction to moral philosophy.* New York: McGraw-Hill.

Besharov, D. S. (1985). *The vulnerable social worker.* Silver Spring, MD: National Association of Social Workers.

Biestek, F. P. (1957). *The casework relationship.* Chicago: Loyola University Press.

Bok, S. (1980). Whistleblowing and professional responsibilities. In D. Callahan & S. Bok (Eds.), *Ethics teaching in higher education* (pp. 277-295). New York: Plenum.

Bowman, J. S. (Ed.). (1991). *Ethical frontiers in public management.* San Francisco: Jossey-Bass.

Bowman, J. S., & Menzel, D. C. (Eds.). (1998). *Teaching ethics and values in public administration programs.* Albany: State University of New York Press.

Callahan, D., & Bok, S. (Eds.). (1980). *Ethics teaching in higher education.* New York: Plenum.

Cooper, T. L. (1990). *The responsible administrator.* San Francisco: Jossey-Bass.

Denhardt, K. G. (1991). Unearthing the moral foundations of public administration: Honor, benevolence, and justice. In J. S. Bowman (Ed.), *Ethical frontiers in public management* (pp. 91-113). San Francisco: Jossey-Bass.

Fleishman, J. L., & Payne, B. L. (1980). *Ethical dilemmas and the education of policymakers.* Hastings-on-Hudson, NY: The Hastings Center.

Fletcher, J. (1986). The goals of ethics consultation. *Biolaw, 2,* 36-47.

Fletcher, J. C., Quist, N., & Jonsen, A. R. (1989). *Ethics consultation in health care.* Ann Arbor, MI: Health Administration Press.

Frankena, W. K. (1973). *Ethics* (2nd ed.). Englewood Cliffs, NJ: Prentice Hall.

Gellerman, W., Frankel, M. S., & Ladenson, R. F. (1990). *Values and ethics in organization and human systems development.* San Francisco: Jossey-Bass.

Gewirth, A. (1978). *Reason and morality.* Chicago: University of Chicago Press.

Gordon, W. E. (1965). Knowledge and value: Their distinction and relationship in clarifying social work practice. *Social Work, 10,* 32-39.

Gorovitz, S. (Ed.). (1971). *Mill: Utilitarianism.* Indianapolis, IN: Bobbs-Merrill.

Gortner, H. F. (1991). How public managers view their environment: Balancing organizational demands, political realities, and personal values. In J. S. Bowman (Ed.), *Ethical frontiers in public management* (pp. 34-63). San Francisco: Jossey-Bass.

Guy, M. E. (1990). *Ethical decision making in everyday work situations.* New York: Quorum Books.

Hosmer, L. T. (1991). *The ethics of management* (2nd ed.). Homewood, IL: Irwin.

Houston-Vega, M., Nuehring, E. M., & Daguio, D. (1997). *Prudent practice: A guide for managing malpractice risk.* Washington, DC: NASW Press.

Jackall, R. (1989). Moral mazes: Bureaucracy and managerial work. In K. R. Andrews (Ed.), *Ethics in practice: Managing the moral corporation* (pp. 167-184). Boston: Harvard Business School Press.

Jennings, B. (1991). Taking ethics seriously in administrative life: Constitutionalism, ethical reasoning, and moral judgment. In J. S. Bowman (Ed.), *Ethical frontiers in public management* (pp. 64-87). San Francisco: Jossey-Bass.

Joseph, M. V. (1983). The ethics of organizations: Shifting values and ethical dilemmas. *Administration in Social Work, 7,* 47-57.

Kultgen, J. (1982). The ideological use of professional codes. *Business and Professional Ethics Journal, 1,* 53-69.

La Puma, J., & Schiedermayer, D. L. (1991). Ethics consultation: Skills, roles, and training. *Annals of Internal Medicine, 114,* 155-160.

Levy, C. S. (1976). *Social work ethics.* New York: Human Sciences Press.

Levy, C. S. (1982). *Guide to ethical decisions and actions for social service administrators.* New York: Haworth.

Loewenberg, F., & Dolgoff, R. (1982). *Ethical decisions for social work practice.* Itasca, IL: F. E. Peacock.

Loewenberg, F., & Dolgoff, R. (1996). *Ethical decisions for social work practice* (4th ed.). Itasca, IL: F. E. Peacock.

Meinert, R. G. (1980). Values in social work called dysfunctional myth. *Journal of Social Welfare, 6,* 5-16.

National Association of Social Workers. (1982). *Standards for the classification of social work practice.* Silver Spring, MD: Author.

National Association of Social Workers. (1996). *NASW code of ethics.* Washington, DC: Author.

Patti, R., Rapp, C. A., & Poertner, J. (Eds.). (1988). *Managing for service effectiveness in social welfare organizations.* New York: Haworth.

Plant, R. (1970). *Social and moral theory in casework.* London: Routledge & Kegan Paul.

Pops, G. M. (1991). Improving ethical decision making using the concept of justice. In J. S. Bowman (Ed.), *Ethical frontiers in public management* (pp. 261-285). San Francisco: Jossey-Bass.

Pruger, R., & Miller, L. (Eds.). (1991). *Efficiency and the social services.* New York: Haworth.

Pugh, D. L. (1991). The origins of ethical frameworks in public administration. In J. S. Bowman (Ed.), *Ethical frontiers in public management* (pp. 9-33). San Francisco: Jossey-Bass.

Pumphrey, M. W. (1959). *The teaching of values and ethics in social work* (Vol. 13). New York: Council on Social Work Education.

Rapp, C. A., & Poertner, J. (1992). *Social administration: A client-centered approach.* New York: Longman.

Reamer, F. G. (1982). *Ethical dilemmas in social service.* New York: Columbia University Press.

Reamer, F. G. (1983). Ethical dilemmas in social work practice. *Social Work, 28,* 31-35.

Reamer, F. G. (1987a). Ethics committees in social work. *Social Work, 32,* 188-192.

Reamer, F. G. (1987b). Values and ethics. In A. Minahan (Ed.-in-Chief), *Encyclopedia of social work* (18th ed., Vol. 2, pp. 801-809). Silver Spring, MD: NASW Press.

Reamer, F. G. (1989). Toward ethical practice: The relevance of ethical theory. *Social Thought, 15,* 67-78.

Reamer, F. G. (1990). *Ethical dilemmas in social service* (2nd ed.). New York: Columbia University Press.

Reamer, F. G. (1993a). Liability issues in social work administration. *Administration in Social Work, 17,* 11-25.

Reamer, F. G. (1993b). *The philosophical foundations of social work.* New York: Columbia University Press.

Reamer, F. G. (1994). *Social work malpractice and liability.* New York: Columbia University Press.

Reamer, F. G. (1995a). *Social work values and ethics.* New York: Columbia University Press.

Reamer, F. G. (1995b). Social work values and ethics. In R. L. Edwards (Ed.-in-Chief), *Encyclopedia of social work* (19th ed., Vol. 1, pp. 893-902). Washington, DC: NASW Press.

Reamer, F. G. (1997). Managing ethics under managed care. *Families in Society, 78,* 96-101.

Reamer, F. G. (1998a). *Ethical standards in social work: A critical review of the NASW Code of Ethics.* Washington, DC: NASW Press.

Reamer, F. G. (1998b). Social work. In R. Chadwick (Ed.-in-Chief), *Encyclopedia of applied ethics* (Vol. 4, pp. 169-180). San Diego: Academic Press.

Reamer, F. G. (1999). *Social work values and ethics* (2nd ed.). New York: Columbia University Press.

Reamer, F. G., & Abramson, M. (1982). *The teaching of social work ethics.* Hastings-on-Hudson, NY: The Hastings Center.

Rescher, N. (1969). *Introduction to value theory.* Englewood Cliffs, NJ: Prentice Hall.

Rhodes, M. L. (1986). *Ethical dilemmas in social work practice.* London: Routledge & Kegan Paul.

Ritchie, J. B. (1988). Organizational ethics: Paradox and paradigm. In N. D. Wright (Ed.), *Papers on the ethics of administration* (pp. 159-184). Provo, UT: Brigham Young University.

Rosenthal, D. M., & Shehadi, F. (Eds.). (1988). *Applied ethics and ethical theory.* Salt Lake City: University of Utah Press.

Ross, W. D. (1930). *The right and the good.* Oxford, UK: Clarendon.

Skeel, J. D., & Self, D. J. (1989). An analysis of ethics consultation in the clinical setting. *Theoretical Medicine, 10,* 289-299.

Smart, J. J. C. (1971). Extreme and restricted utilitarianism. In S. Gorovitz (Ed.), *Mill: Utilitarianism* (pp. 195-203). Indianapolis, IN: Bobbs-Merrill.

Snoeyenbos, M., Almeder, R., & Humber, J. (Eds.). (1983). *Business ethics: Corporate values and society.* Buffalo, NY: Prometheus Books.

Solomon, R. C. (1992). *Ethics and excellence: Cooperation and integrity in business.* New York: Oxford University Press.

Stewart, D. W., & Sprinthall, N. A. (1991). Strengthening ethical judgment in public administration. In J. S. Bowman (Ed.), *Ethical frontiers in public management* (pp. 243-260). San Francisco: Jossey-Bass.

Teel, K. (1975). The physician's dilemma: A doctor's view: What the law should be. *Baylor Law Review, 27,* 6-9.

Teicher, M. (1967). *Values in social work: A reexamination.* New York: NASW Press.

Timms, N. (1983). *Social work values: An enquiry.* London: Routledge & Kegan Paul.

Vigilante, J. L. (1974). Between values and science: Education for the profession; or, is proof truth? *Journal of Education for Social Work, 10,* 107-115.

Wright, N. D., & McConkie, S. S. (1988). Introduction. In N. D. Wright (Ed.), *Papers on the ethics of administration* (pp. 1-18). Provo, UT: Brigham Young University.

PART II

Understanding Social
Welfare Organizations

The seven chapters in this section are concerned with exploring organizational conditions and processes that contribute to the performance of social service agencies. Together, they will provide a condensed but critical overview of theory and research on environmental, structural, interpersonal, and individual factors that influence the performance of social agencies. The chapters were constructed with a view to helping managers develop grounding in organizational theory and how it can be applied to understanding issues and problems they commonly encounter.

Chapter 5 by Hasenfeld offers a broad-based analysis of extant organizational theories and their relationship to administrative practice. It provides a critical assessment of the utility of several major theories and shows how they variously contribute to understanding critical issues in social welfare organizations. Hasenfeld argues that social welfare administration can strengthen its intellectual theoretical foundations by looking more seriously at organizational theory.

Gibelman's Chapter 6 speaks to the fundamental characteristics of social welfare agencies, including the several kinds of auspices under which social service agencies operate, and how different ways of organizing and financing services shape their purposes. Especially important is the discussion about the convergence and interdependence of public and private sector organizations and what this may portend for the future.

In Chapter 7, Schmid examines how agencies interact with other organizations and institutions to acquire the resources they need to achieve their purposes. The author analyzes these issues through the prism of political-economic and institutional theories, showing how these two patterns of interaction influence the goals and programs of the social agency. This chapter complements the discussion on collaboration found in Chapter 14.

In Chapter 8, Gillespie provides a critical analysis of positional and relational theories of organizational structure and suggests that although each accounts for some of the variance in organizational performance, they are in the end too static to adequately explain organizational behavior. Instead, he proposes that structure be viewed from the systems dynamic perspective, which focuses on multiple causal loops and includes both formal and informal structures and processes.

Because social workers are the instruments as well as the providers of service, it is critical that we understand how organizational environments can be managed to motivate their performance. In Chapter 9, Vinokur-Kaplan and Bogin focus at the level of interpersonal and group processes, presenting several theories that offer explanations for how and why workers are motivated to perform. This discussion provides a context in which they critically analyze a range of empirical studies that seek to explain satisfaction and burnout among social workers.

In Chapter 10, Glisson addresses organizational culture and climate as determinants of worker performance. Although they are often treated as though they were the same thing, Glisson conceptually distinguishes culture from climate and demonstrates, based on his own research and other studies, that both exert powerful influences on the performance of human service workers and ultimately the outcomes of clients they serve. Both chapters 9 and 10 should be read in conjunction with Bargal's chapter on leadership (Chapter 15).

Much research on organizations in social welfare has assumed that the primary causal factors are in the work environment. In a far-reaching analysis of theory and research, Koeske and Koeske argue in Chapter 11 that the relationship between individual attributes and organizational conditions is more interactive than unidirectional. Their review suggests that the psychological and social attributes of workers also make significant contributions to performance.

CHAPTER FIVE

Social Welfare Administration and Organizational Theory

YEHESKEL HASENFELD

Despite the maturing of social welfare administration as a field, a recent review of 13 major texts published between 1980 and 1992 found that their theoretical, let alone empirical, grounding was tenuous (Au, 1994). The predominant theoretical framework, when present, was based on either a rational or a resource dependency approach, and there was a "lack of empirical support for the main arguments and propositions presented in the major texts" (Au, 1994, p. 44). If we are to have a theory-based practice that can be verifiable, it must emanate from an empirically grounded organizational theory. In this chapter, I examine the use of organizational theory and research in developing models of social welfare administration. By necessity, the analysis is confined mostly to the United States.[1]

It may be argued that the management of human service organizations is not appreciably different from the management of other organizations (e.g., Drucker, 1990). Indeed, with the increasing commercialization of the human services, as well as the blurring distinctions among public and private nonprofit or for-profit organizations (Salamon, 1995; Weisbrod, 1998), there is greater pressure on human service organizations to adopt management practices and principles that have been developed for business organizations and have stood the test of the competitive marketplace (e.g., Total Quality Management). Still, management strategies that gain widespread acceptance may not deliver on their promises because they lack a strong grounding in organizational theory and research. The management field, including social welfare administration, is very susceptible to fads and fashions that, under critical theoretical and empirical analysis, are revealed to be of limited merit (Mintzberg, 1996). Most important, a seemingly appropriate management tool for business organizations may not work for human service organizations. To guard against such pitfalls, social welfare administration practices must first and foremost recognize the unique attributes of their organizations. Second, they must be anchored in organizational theories that take into account these attributes. Third, they must be empirically verifiable.

What sets human service organizations apart from many other organizations is a combination of attributes emanating from the fundamental fact that they work on people to transform them (Hasenfeld, 1992). As a result, human service organizations engage in moral work, upholding and reinforcing moral values about "desirable" human behavior and the "good" society. Therefore, human service organizations are embedded in an institutional environment from which they derive their legitimacy and license to work on people. It is also from the institutional environment that human service organizations must obtain their service technologies, technologies that are inherently indeterminate and fraught with ambiguities. Moreover, the success of these technologies depends greatly on the reactivity of the clients. That is, clients present various contingencies and constraints that affect the trajectory of the service delivery process, making it uncertain. And the clients' degree of compliance is critical to the effectiveness of the technology. Hence, a dominant feature of human service organizations is the centrality of client-staff relations in determining service outcomes. Finally, the definition and measurement of service effectiveness

is equally indeterminate, ambiguous, and multidimensional. Other types of organizations may exhibit one or more of these attributes, but it is the combination and interaction of all of them that makes human service organizations distinctive.

One can readily see how in such an organizational context, social welfare administration is exceedingly complex. It has to cope with a turbulent environment, grapple with service design and management issues that are highly value-laden, address the lack of clear and unambiguous end states, and manage staff and clients who cannot be readily controlled. Moreover, although there is a consensus that the primary aim of social welfare administration is to promote service effectiveness (e.g., Abels & Murphy, 1981; Patti, 1987; Rapp & Poertner, 1992), the definition of service effectiveness typically is a contested terrain that greatly affects administrative strategies and choices.

ORGANIZATIONAL THEORY AND ADMINISTRATIVE PRACTICE

To address these challenges, social welfare administration looks for practice principles. These, in turn, implicitly or explicitly are guided by the choice of an underlying organizational theory that offers a rationale for these principles. The choice is often dictated by the key administrative tasks the theory attempts to explain. Table 5.1 identifies major administrative tasks and the relevant organizational theories that address them. It is important to keep in mind that several theories may address the same task by offering very different perspectives, conceptualizations, and possible solutions.

TABLE 5.1 Administrative Tasks and Organizational Theories

Administrative Task	Organizational Theory
Goal attainment	Rational-legal, scientific management
Management of people	Human relations, feminist perspective
Proficiency and efficiency	Contingency
Adaptation and mobilization of resources	Political economy
Founding and survival	Population ecology
Institutionalization	New-Institutionalism
Integration and social cohesion	Culture, sense-making
Knowledge, power, and control	Neo-Marxist, postmodern, structuration
Social change	Critical theory, radical feminism

GOAL ATTAINMENT

The rational approach views the organization as an efficient machine to attain specific goals (Morgan, 1997). The model assumes that once the goals are specified, an efficient service technology can be chosen to meet them. Such a technology can be implemented through an internal division of labor where roles and authority relations are clearly specified and formalized. The organizational structure is rational because it can be shown that the service technology and its attendant division of labor ensure the most efficient way to attain the organizational goals. This engineering approach has its roots in Taylor's scientific management and what has been labeled *Fordism* after Henry Ford's innovations in mass production (Zuboff, 1998). In addition, the organizational structure is legal (Weber, 1924/1968) because the division of labor and exercise of authority are based on legally accepted normative rules (e.g., professional expertise, administrative law).

Kettner, Moroney, and Martin (1990) exemplify this approach in their "effectiveness-based" approach to social welfare administration. As they state,

Effectiveness-based program planning involves taking a program through a series of steps designed to produce a clear understanding of the problem to be addressed, to measure client problem type and severity at entry, to provide a relevant intervention, to measure client problem type and severity at exit. (p. 15)

Similarly, Lewis, Lewis, and Soufleé (1991) picture human service management as a rational process. It includes (a) setting goals, objectives, and strategies; (b) organizing, identifying, and arranging the work needed to carry out the plans; (c) mobilizing the people to make the program work; (d) planning the use of financial resources to reach the goals; (e) supervising to enhance the skills and motivation of the service providers; and (f) evaluating the accomplishments of the program. Again, the purpose of management is to produce a highly efficient and effective service delivery system that is governed by norms of rationality.

Although the rational model of organizations is predominant in social welfare administration, it has been shown to be theoretically weak and empirically untenable (for a review, see Scott, 1998). The organization is conceptualized as a closed system with little attention to the broader social system in which it is embedded. Decision making is based on an economic model of organizational behavior that lacks empirical validity (Pfeffer, 1997). Structure is devoid of the processes of sense-making and interpretative interactions by organizational actors (Weick, 1995). One can also readily see how a rational model fails to take into account the unique attributes of human service organizations. In particular, the theory falters in the face of multiple and conflicting goals and the existence of indeterminate service technologies. Critics have also argued that the rational model has provided the ideological and intellectual justification for the concentration of power in large organizations and the hierarchical authority of a managerial class (Reed, 1996). Hence, questions arise regarding the compatibility of the rational model with social work values and ethics.

MANAGEMENT OF PEOPLE

The rational approach assumes an economic model of human behavior. Such a model cannot adequately explain the complex interdependencies, social ties, and forms of cooperation that exist among members of the organization. The human relations perspective, in contrast, assumes that behavior is embedded in a web of social relations. How members relate to each other within and without the organization will influence their motivation, patterns of work, productivity, and self-identity. Therefore, when there is consonance between the needs of the individual and the needs of the organization, both will flourish (Argyris, 1964). According to the human relations perspective, such consonance is attained when the workers find meaning and satisfaction in their work, when they actively participate in the management of the organization, and when leadership is person-oriented.

The human relations approach has produced a rich body of theory, research, and management practices. Contemporary theorizing and research within this perspective have focused on four major interrelated areas: (a) job satisfaction, (b) human resource practices management, (c) trust, and (d) leadership. Job satisfaction has been shown to be correlated with such job-related attributes as relations with supervisors, work conditions, pay and promotion opportunities, job security, coworkers' attitudes, and personal growth (for a review, see Jayaratne, 1993; for an extended discussion, see Chapter 12, this volume). Related studies have explored the idea of person-environment fit, especially between individual predispositions and job requirements (Chatman, 1989). The relationship between human resource practices and performance, including participatory management, has been the focus of many studies (Pfeffer, 1997). Factors such as decentralization, participation, teamwork, job enrichment, autonomy and flexibility, high-level training, and performance-based rewards have been correlated with organizational performance. Similarly, trust is viewed as a key to cooperative relations and teamwork within the organization (Creed & Miles, 1996). Leadership skills are viewed as vital to organizational success. Hart and Quinn (1993) showed that high performance organizations have executives with high levels of "behavioral complexity," playing four critical roles: vision setter, motivator, analyzer, and task master.

The appeal of the human relations perspective to the human services is obvious, considering the centrality of worker-client relations. Trust, values, emotions, and feelings are critical to these relations, and they are assumed to be influenced by how workers feel about their work, how their self-actualization needs are being met, and how the internal environment facilitates their work. Indeed, considerable research from the human relations perspective has been done in the human services. The concept of burnout and much of the research on that topic are attributable to human service workers (Maslach & Schaufeli, 1993). Role conflict and lack of support from colleagues and supervisors were found to be the main determinants of burnout. Participatory management, often recast in the human services as the empowerment of workers, has been shown to contribute to organizational effectiveness (Whiddon & Martin, 1989). Guterman and Bargal (1996) noted a relationship between the sense of empowerment that social workers feel and their perceptions of service outcomes. Glisson and Hemmelgarn (1998) found, in the case of children's services, that the success of caseworkers in improving the psychosocial functioning of the children was related to "higher levels of job satisfaction, fairness, role clarity, cooperation, and personalization" (p. 416). Leadership in the social services is also seen as important in empowering the workers. Keller and Dansereau (1995) proposed that when superiors empower subordinates, subordinates reciprocate by performing in accordance with the preferences of the supervisors. Glisson (1989) showed that the more workers perceive their leaders to have power and matu-

rity, the greater their commitment to the organization.

Despite the extensive research, the application of human relations theory and research to social welfare administration has been uneven (e.g., Abels & Murphy, 1981). As we have seen, participatory management and staff empowerment are taken to be important administrative practices. Similarly, the role of leaders in articulating a vision and a nurturing culture for the agency is viewed as a central administrative function (e.g., Pearlmutter, 1998; Weil, 1988). But only Skidmore (1995) articulates a model of administration that fully embraces the human relations perspective. Indeed, he begins his book with the following introduction:

> Administration in social work is changing from a pyramid to a circle. No longer does one person at the top have absolute power to dictate and control agency policies and practices. Such power is being shared more and more with staff and clients.... In many agencies, in varying patterns, administrators, staff, and clients are working cooperatively together to make decisions and deliver agency services. (p. 1)

Skidmore proposes three guiding principles that are consonant with the human relations perspective: acceptance of leaders and staff, democratic involvement in formulation of agency policies and procedures, and open communication. Accordingly, the social work administrator is described as accepting, caring, creating, democratizing, trusting, approving, maintaining personal equilibrium and balance, planning, organizing, setting priorities, delegating, interacting with the community, making decisions, facilitating, communicating, timing, building, and motivating. Teamwork and motivation strategies are central to his model.

There is something surreal about such a model, being so removed from the complex and difficult realities of human service work. This is not surprising because the human relations perspective tends to view the organization in isolation from its environment, thus diminishing the importance of external factors in shaping organizational dynamics. It assumes that both the organization and its people are highly malleable and that changes in how people behave will have great impact on organizational performance. Yet, the empirical evidence is quite weak. For example, in the case of leadership, studies have been able to show modest impact, at best, on organizational performance (Pfeffer, 1997). In addition, the human relations perspective presents an image of the effective organization that is presumed to be applicable to most situations. Again, it does so by neutralizing much of the impact of the external environment. It is difficult to see, for example, how in public welfare agencies, characterized as street-level bureaucracies (Lipsky, 1980), human relations strategies can have but limited effects (Weatherley, 1983). This is not to imply that strategies to reduce job stress, empower workers, and provide charismatic leaders are not valuable. Moreover, service technologies that require teamwork, close communication, cooperation, and coordination among staff could indeed benefit from human relations strategies. However, if the strategies are applied to make workers "feel better" under very trying circumstances, thus deflecting attention from important organizational barriers to effective service delivery, then they are counterproductive. Therefore, the applicability of human relations must be assessed within the organizational and broader context in which they are to be undertaken. Otherwise, their application might have the opposite effect, resulting in frustration and cynicism. Yet, little consideration of these factors is built into proposed human relations practices for social welfare administration.

PROFICIENCY AND EFFICIENCY

Contingency theory attempts to overcome some of the limitations of the rational approach by embracing an open systems perspective and discarding the normative structure inherent in the rational model. Instead, structure is made variable and contingent on the characteristics of the organization's environment, including environmental heterogeneity and stability, technological certainty, organizational size, and power (Mintzberg, 1979). Organizational effectiveness and efficiency are assumed to be a function of the fit between the contingency and the internal structure. Therefore, as the environment becomes more heterogeneous and unstable, the internal structure shifts from a centralized bureaucracy to a decentralized and organic structure (e.g., flexible, informal). Similarly, as the task becomes more variable and the knowledge more uncertain, the structure will move from a simple bureaucracy to a professional mode (Perrow, 1967). In the same vein, increase in size leads to greater internal differentiation and specialization by function, a finding that has been widely replicated (Donaldson, 1996). Finally, Mintzberg (1979, p. 288) proposed that as the external control of the organization increases, there is more internal centralization and formalization. A burgeoning field of organizational design has emerged showing how strategic choices regarding markets, clients, and products influence the internal design of the organization (e.g., Galbraith & Kazanjian, 1986).

Although contingency theory has produced an impressive body of studies, including management practice principles, it has lost much of its luster (Pfeffer, 1997). In part, the empirical research, especially on the relationship between technology and structure, has failed to provide a convincing verification of the theory (Glisson, 1992; Schoonhoven, 1981). In addition, the theory is quite complex, and there is considerable difficulty in clearly defining and operationalizing all its variables.

Little attention has been given to contingency theory in social welfare administration, despite the importance of designing structures that can achieve optimal service effectiveness. This is even more ironic because some important research testing the contingency model has been done on human services. A series of empirical studies by Glisson and colleagues (Glisson, 1978; Glisson & Durick, 1988; Glisson & Martin, 1980) is particularly noteworthy. In a groundbreaking study, Glisson (1978) showed that, in the human services, structure determines how workers will implement the technology. That is, if the structure is centralized and formalized, the workers will treat the clients in a uniform and routine manner (see also Glisson, 1992). In a later study, Glisson and Martin (1980) found that productivity and efficiency were highly correlated with a centralized authority structure. Hence, the dilemma facing human service administrators: focusing on productivity and efficiency at the expense of staff and client satisfaction. In a study of addiction treatment programs, Savage (1988) identified four different technologies, which she classified as limited, specialized, individualized, and encompassing. She showed how internal structures varied by technology and how the scope of the technology was greater (i.e., individual-

ized and encompassing) as service effectiveness increased. More recent work by D'Aunno and colleagues (D'Aunno, Sutton, & Price, 1991) examined the effects of hybrid structures as mental health agencies diversified into drug treatment.

Yet, despite such research, Patti (1983) is among the few who refer to contingency theory when discussing the development of an organizational structure to implement a program. Weiss (1989) incorporates findings from contingency theory in explicating management strategies to structure the organizations. Weinbach (1990) offers several alternative structures and a list of factors to consider in selecting an appropriate model, but he makes only an opaque reference to contingency theory and research. The glaring disparity between the research and the resultant administration practice principles is reflective of the state of the art of the field. It may also be due to an ideological aversion to theories that recognize the functionality of bureaucratic structures under certain technological and environmental contingencies.

ADAPTATION AND MOBILIZATION OF RESOURCES

A political economy perspective recognizes the importance of environmental contingencies but rejects the rational model implicit in contingency theory. Rather, it views the organization as a collectivity that has multiple and complex goals, paramount among them, survival and adaptation to the environment. Moreover, internal processes and structures also reflect diverse and possibly conflicting interests and relations. As a result, the organization in operation is quite different from its official or formal design (Perrow, 1986). As articulated by Wamsley and

Zald (1976), the capacity of the organization to survive *and* to provide services depends on its ability to mobilize power, legitimacy, and economic resources (e.g., money, personnel, clients). To obtain these resources, the organization must interact with elements in its task environment that control them. The ensuing process of negotiation and its outcome will reflect the degree of organizational dependency on the resources controlled by each element (Pfeffer & Salancik, 1978). The greater the resource dependency of the organization on an element in the environment (e.g., governmental funding agency, regulatory organization, professional association, providers, or clients), the greater the ability of the element to influence organizational policies and practices. Therefore, many organizational practices, such as the service delivery system, will reflect the constraints and contingencies imposed by those who control needed resources (Cress & Snow, 1996).

The internal dynamics of the organization will also reflect the power relations of different interest groups and individuals within the organization. Some of these groups (e.g., professional staff, executive cadre) derive their power from relations with important external organizations; others possess personal attributes, control internal resources (e.g., information and expertise), or carry out important functions (e.g., manage the budget) that are not easily substituted (Lachman, 1989). The emerging power relations shape the internal structure and the resource allocation rules. These, in turn, reinforce the power relations (Astley & Sachdeva, 1984; Pfeffer, 1992).

Disturbances in the external and internal political economies will result in changes within the organization. The power of external groups may rise or fall as the environment changes, altering the power relations between the organization and its task environment. These, in turn, will affect the operative goals and the service delivery system. Similarly, the need for different internal resources or functions to meet new environmental challenges or the rise of new alliances will modify internal power relations and, with them, structure and processes (Pfeffer, 1992).

The political economy perspective has served as a platform for extensive research on human service organizations, beginning with Zald's pioneering study of the YMCA (Zald & Denton, 1963). More recent research looked at innovations in community mental health centers (Sheinfeld Gorin & Weirich, 1995) and the implementation of welfare-to-work programs (Handler & Hasenfeld, 1991). In addition, the perspective has been applied to analyze organizational issues including the dynamic relations between human service organizations and their task environment (e.g., Benson, 1975; Hasenfeld & Cheung, 1985), the position of women in social welfare agencies (Martin & Chernesky, 1989), and the relations between nonprofit organizations and government (e.g., Gronbjerg, 1993; Kramer & Grossman, 1987). One can readily see the appeal of the political economy perspective to social welfare administration. The relatively high dependence of human service organizations on their external environment for legitimacy and resources makes them particularly susceptible to external influences. Hence, concerns with survival and adaptation must be balanced with the goal of service effectiveness (e.g., Brodkin, 1997; Hyde, 1992). Moreover, having to respond to multiple external and internal constituencies with conflicting interests is also a common experience for most administrators. Internally, agency administrators typically have to balance among the interests and claims for resources of different program components, each with its own constituent staff and clients. This is particularly the case in multiprofessional organizations.

Gummer (1990) presents the most systematic application of political economy theory to social welfare administration. It is also a model of how the field can be enriched by a thoughtful articulation between organizational theory and administrative practices. Paying close attention to the distinct issues facing social service agencies—scarcity of resources, multiple goals, uncertain technologies—Gummer proposes that their solutions can best be addressed from a political economy perspective. Handling budgetary constraints effectively through strategic planning requires several power resources, such as centralized authority, continuity of top management, rapid and accurate feedback, budget flexibility, and incentives to conserve resources. Recognizing that program implementation is a political process, Gummer argues that effective implementation requires administrators to assume several broad roles: policy advocate, negotiator of organizational linkages, and manager of worker discretion (p. 107). To mobilize power and use it to influence organizational processes, administrators must employ various political strategies, ranging from controlling agendas to building network relations and managing impressions. Because administrators rarely have sufficient power to impose their will on other actors, they must negotiate and bargain, and Gummer enunciates a number of strategies and tactics for successful negotiations (pp. 153-183). Undoubtedly, use of power to achieve administrative objectives raises many ethical issues, but as Gummer points out, it is

not the use of power that is at stake, but rather the ends for which power is used: that is, the extent to which it benefits the clients.

The political economy perspective has its limitations. First, it understates the importance of values and cultural norms in the survival of the organization, an issue addressed by the new institutionalism. This is a particularly critical issue for human service organizations because they engage in moral work. Moreover, by emphasizing survival and adaptation, less attention is given to the desired outcomes that the organization is expected to attain. Second, the unit of analysis remains the single organization. Yet, administrative practices must pay attention to industry-wide or sectoral patterns and the dynamics that shape their organizational forms (Scott, 1985). Because organizations are embedded in industries and are part of a population of similar organizations, their survival is influenced by the extent to which their organizational features are consonant with those characterizing the industry or population. For example, because community mental health agencies are constituent elements of the mental health sector, they acquire structural and operative features that are systemic to that sector (Scott & Meyer, 1983). As members of a population consisting of community mental health agencies, the characteristics and dynamics affecting the entire population impact their survival (Tucker, Baum, & Singh, 1992).

FOUNDING AND SURVIVAL

The ecological perspective addresses this central issue. The unit of analysis is a population of organizations, defined as a set of organizations engaged in similar activities and with similar patterns of resource utilization (Baum, 1996, p. 77). The ecological approach wants to explain the conditions that generate (or inhibit) diversity of organizations and change over time. Using the metaphor of evolutionary biology, Hannan and Freeman (1989) state that "current diversity of organizational forms reflects the cumulative effect of a long history of variation and selection, including the consequences of founding processes, mortality processes, and merger processes" (p. 20). Over time, successful variations are retained as surviving organizations come to be characterized by them. Rates of organizational founding and failure are explained by two interrelated ecological processes, labeled *population dynamics* and *density dependence* (Baum, 1996). Population dynamics posits that prior organizational founding signals the existence of opportunities in the environment that stimulate new founding. However, as new organizations enter the field, competition increases, thus discouraging new founding. Similarly, prior failures release resources that also stimulate new founding, but further failures signal a hostile environment discouraging founding. Density dependence (i.e., the number of organizations in the population) proposes that an initial increase in density signals institutional legitimacy (e.g., favorable governmental policies) for such organizations, which enables them to secure resources. However, as density rises, competition over the resources increases, leading to higher rates of failure and discouraging further founding.

The ecological processes are not the only determinants of organizational founding and failure. Technological developments influence the importance of various resources, creating new opportunities while rendering the competencies of existing organizations obsolete (Tushman &

Anderson, 1986). Institutional developments such as changing government policies and funding will also affect rates of founding and failure (Tucker, et al., 1992). Similarly, linkages to community and public institutions provide resources and legitimacy that reduce failure rates (Baum & Oliver, 1991). Finally, demographic characteristics—age and size—also affect rates of failure. Older and larger organizations are less likely to fail.

The ecological perspective has produced a substantial body of research, including important studies on human service organizations. It also has implications for administrative practices. It demonstrates how environmental forces set considerable limits on the success of administrative practices. It proposes that individual managers are constrained by existing organizational forms, scarcity of resources, and forces at the population level that cannot be readily understood by each manager (Hannan & Freeman, 1989, pp. 42-43). Especially for the administration of human service organizations, there is a dual message. First, although administrators can make a difference in improving the agency's chances to survive and be effective, their capacity to do so is highly constrained. This is an unwelcome message to both theorists and practitioners of social welfare administration. Second, macro-level strategies that affect an entire population of agencies are more important for their overall survival and effectiveness. These strategies include influencing governmental policies, coalescing and lobbying to alter funding patterns, and developing extensive institutional linkages that increase the legitimacy of the organizations. One can readily understand, for example, that to rescue urban child protection agencies from the almost chronic crisis they encounter depends much less

on the behavior of any single administrator than on macro changes in the social, economic, and political environment in which these agencies are embedded. Unfortunately, in the current state of theorizing in social welfare administration, little attention has been given to this message.

One of the chief limitations of the ecological perspective, especially concerning human service organizations, is its failure to fully acknowledge and incorporate the importance of these macro-level strategies. In particular, the theory understates the role that organizations play, individually and collectively, in constructing the environment in which they operate. Although at any given point in time, the environment is taken as given, from a historical perspective, one can see how organizations, acting as industries, influence the policies, flows of resources, and the very processes of selection and retention of certain organizational forms. This can be gleaned, for example, from the history of the evolution of the medical or mental health "industry" (Grob, 1991; Starr, 1982). In a related way, the theory fails to address the processes by which organizations mobilize legitimacy that is so vital to their survival (Zucker, 1989). The new institutional perspective addresses some of these issues (Scott, 1995).

INSTITUTIONALIZATION

The underlying premise of the new institutional perspective is that the survival of organizations depends on the degree to which their structures reflect and reinforce institutional rules. Institutional rules include (a) regulative rules and laws, (b) normative rules (i.e., values and expectations), and (c) cognitive rules (i.e., categories

and typifications) shared by the community of organizations (Scott, 1995). In contrast to political economy with its emphasis on resources, the new institutionalism gives primary emphasis to legitimacy and the dominant role of cultural institutions (regulative, normative, and cognitive) in the survival of organizations. It proposes that the more organizations adhere to the rules of these institutions—by embedding the rules in their structures—the greater will be their legitimacy and chances of survival.

Meyer and Rowan (1977) also make an important distinction between technical and institutional organizations. Technical organizations have highly specified production systems designed to produce explicitly defined outputs. Institutional organizations have neither explicit output goals nor concrete technologies to attain them. Therefore, human services are institutional organizations par excellence. Their success depends less on using effective service technologies than on designing structures that conform to dominant institutional rules. Consequently, structure is only loosely coupled with the technology. Schools, for example, must employ only certified teachers, adhere to sanctioned curricula and textbooks, and establish approved graduation requirements. Yet, these actions have little to do with the educational technology teachers are likely to use in the classroom (Meyer & Rowan, 1983). In other words, many of the activities of human service organizations involve the production of myths and ceremonies whose function is to uphold institutional rules. These will take precedence over actual service performance because they are more important to the survival of the organization. Indeed, the organization may survive despite objective failure (Meyer & Zucker, 1989). A key difficulty with the new institutionalism is its failure to explain how institutional rules come about (Zucker, 1988). Tolbert and Zucker (1996) proposed that the organizations themselves are not passive in conforming to institutional rules but are actually active in shaping the institutionalization process itself.

The new institutionalism is a powerful framework for the analysis of human service organizations precisely because it focuses on the critical relations between these organizations and cultural institutions, the values and norms these organizations are expected to promote (i.e., institutional rules), and the way institutional rules affect their internal structures. And yet, theorizing in social welfare administration has by and large failed to capitalize on the rich insights and research from this framework. An important exception is an article by Martin (1980), who uses the new institutional perspective to outline the role of administrators in finding a balance between adhering to dominant cultural values and responding to the needs of other constituents, especially clients. Neugeboren (1991) briefly mentions the importance of managing the institutional system and the role of boards in linking the agency to legitimizing institutions.

Rapp and Poertner (1992) make the moral entrepreneurship of social service agencies the centerpiece of their administrative approach, an approach that is highly compatible with new institutionalism. Yet, they fail to use it to anchor and buttress their model. By advocating for a client-centered management, they articulate four guiding principles: (a) venerating the people called clients, (b) creating and maintaining the focus on clients and client outcomes, (c) developing a healthy disrespect for the impossible, and (d) continuing to learn more effective ways to help people. Nonetheless, most of the administrative practices they enunciate have little bearing on these principles, especially in laying out strategies to implement them. Had they based their model on new institutionalism, they could have formulated administrative practices, supported by theory and research, on how to institutionalize these laudatory principles.

INTEGRATION AND SOCIAL COHESION

The new institutionalism points to the importance of organizational culture and sense-making as major forces in shaping organizational structure and processes. Organizational culture ensures consonance with dominant institutional rules. But it also provides an internal integrative mechanism by having a common interpretative schema. It enables members of the organization to make sense of their work and to construct a common understanding of their internal and external environment (Weick, 1995). Trice and Beyer (1993) distinguish between the substance of culture—shared emotionally charged belief systems (i.e., ideologies)—and cultural forms: observable entities, including actions, through which members of a culture express, affirm, and communicate the substance of the culture to one another. Similarly, Weick's (1995) concept of sense-making provides members of the organization with a frame that consists of (a) ideologies that combine beliefs about cause-effect relations, preferences for certain outcomes, and expectations of appropriate behavior; (b) vocabulary that provides premise control, especially when the technology is nonroutine; (c) paradigms—standard operating procedures, shared definitions of the environment, and agreed-upon systems of power and authority; (d) vocabularies of coping—theories of action to guide behavior; (e) tradition; and (f) stories that describe how difficult situations were handled, providing sequencing and facilitating diagnosis. As stated by Weick (1995),

> Sensemaking is an effort to tie beliefs and actions more closely together as when arguments lead to consensus on action, clarified expectations pave the way for confirming actions, committed actions uncover acceptable justifications for their occurrence, or bold actions simplify the world and make it clearer what is going on and what it means. (p. 135)

Therefore, sense-making is most often retrospective.

Organizations also have subcultures. Trice and Beyer (1993) suggest that organizational subcultures consist of distinctive clusters of ideologies, cultural forms, and practices exhibited by identifiable groups. Occupational subcultures are most common, and they have powerful socialization functions.

For human service organizations, the concept of culture extends beyond shared assumptions and beliefs. It also incorporates moral assumptions about the clients as well as practice ideologies of how to work with them that are embedded in the service technology. Both have important consequences for how service delivery systems will be organized (Hasenfeld, in press). Moreover, the notion of occupational subcultures, each with their own distinct moral conceptions and practice ideologies, is important in understanding how services are organized to accommodate them (Strauss, Fargerhaugh, Suczek, & Wiener, 1985). Hence, viewing the agency as a multicultural system is par-

ticularly apt in understanding many of its structural and operational features.

Organizational culture has become a rhetoric and an all-embracing concept in management theory, preoccupied with social controls and performance (Czarniawska-Joerges, 1992, pp. 168-170). There is a burgeoning field of management literature on the competitive advantages of fostering a "strong" organizational culture (e.g., Cameron & Quinn, 1996; Peters & Waterman, 1982). Such a culture is said to inculcate a sense of vision and mission that is deeply felt by all members, a commitment to organizational values that guide personal behavior, and self-fulfillment derived from identification and participation in the organization. Management experts have also argued that a strong culture is correlated with high performance (e.g., Deal & Kennedy, 1982), although the empirical evidence is inconclusive (Pfeffer, 1997, p. 122).

The assumption that organizational culture can be a unifying and integrating force has been challenged by numerous ethnographic studies (for a review, see Martin & Frost, 1996). The theme of these studies is of cultural inconsistencies—organizations are beset by value conflicts, disjunctures between norms and actual behavior, and frail consensus. This theme is taken up again when I discuss postmodernist approaches to organizations. The idea of cultural ambiguity should not come as a surprise to social work. Meyerson (1992) showed that one cannot appreciate the professional culture of social work without paying close attention to the many value ambiguities, multiple goals, indeterminate technology, and uncertainty of results that characterize the field. In this context, it is not clear how much organizational culture can be "managed."

When culture is addressed in social welfare administration (which is not frequently), the integrative perspective on organizational culture prevails. (Later, we will see that the feminist perspective also addresses culture, but from a very different angle.) Rapp and Poertner (1992) argue that in a client-centered approach, the organizational culture should promote organizational learning, especially through the use of information on client services and outcomes. They are mindful that staff encounter many contingencies and constraints that must be taken into account in how an information system is designed, what data are collected, and how they are used and interpreted. Brody (1993) accepts the premise that productivity is greatly influenced by culture and that "effective managers play a significant role in influencing the culture by the messages they communicate and, more important, through their own behavior" (p. 21). For Brody, the essence of culture is a set of values. The first is job ownership, which is promoted by "instilling in staff a sense of higher purpose, emotional bonding, trust, stakeholder involvement, and pride in their work" (p. 25). The second value is the primacy of consumers, which can be maintained through a good feedback system from the consumers. The third value is quality of work, which is strengthened through various quality control mechanisms. Few would object to these values and the lofty strategies to attain them, and that is precisely the difficulty with the approach. There is exceedingly limited verifiable knowledge on how to change organizational culture and little recognition that it is a complex, difficult, and multifaceted process (Trice & Beyer, 1993). Because culture emerges out of dialectic processes in which members attempt to make sense of their external and internal environments, changing it requires addressing these institutional, political, and economic environments (see, e.g., Snyder, 1995).

KNOWLEDGE, POWER, AND CONTROL

The notion that culture is a major source of social control in the organization; that it objectifies the values, norms, and knowledge of those in power; and that it perpetuates patterns of dominance is a central theme in the postmodern conception of organizations. As Cooper and Burrell (1988) put it,

> The key to understanding the discourse of postmodernism is the concept of *difference:* a form of self-reference in which terms contain their own opposite and thus refuse any *singular* grasp of their meanings. . . . At the very centre of discourse, therefore, the human agent is faced with a condition of irreducible indeterminacy. (p. 98)

Deconstruction, therefore, is a process of showing "how artificial are the ordinary, taken-for-granted structures of our social world" (Cooper & Burrell, 1988, p. 99). Postmodernism questions the assumption of individual rationality (Gergen & Thatchenkery, 1996). It argues that what is assumed to be rational is a cultural construction that gives preference to certain culturally defined discourses over others (e.g., masculine or Anglo-centric over feminist or Afro-centric). It also contends that what passes as empirical knowledge is in fact socially constructed because language itself is value-laden, and "meaning is not universal and fixed, but precarious, fragmented and local" (Alvesson & Deetz, 1996, p. 208). Finally, language acquires meaning through its use in action. "To 'tell the truth,' on this account, is not to furnish an accurate picture of 'what actually happened' but to participate in a set of social conventions" (Gergen & Thatchenkery, 1996, p. 361). Consequently, power is embedded in how knowledge is produced. "Power resides in the discursive formation itself—the combination of a set of linguistic distinctions, ways of reasoning and material practices that together organize social institutions and produce particular forms of subjects" (Alvesson & Deetz, 1996, p. 209).

Postmodernism has important implications for organizational theory and research. It makes problematic the very concept of organization and its constituent elements such as structure, technology, division of labor, staff, and clients. A postmodernist approach is to examine how such concepts come into being and how they acquire their self-reifying qualities (Chia, 1995). The emphasis is on micro-processes of actions, interactions, and emergence of local patterns of relations. Studying the processes of organizing, the researcher is concerned with how certain interaction patterns become stabilized, dominant, and self-reproduced. The focus is on the heterogeneous material, the multiple identities, and the ongoing struggles and resistance that are inherent in organizing processes. Put differently, what we take for granted as organization, staff, and client are actually reflective of these dynamic and ever-changing micro-processes. When we objectify the organization, we not only ignore these processes, but we fail to recognize the struggles, meanings, and identities that have been silenced. Moreover, the language we use to describe organizational properties and processes is actually a form of social control because of its self-reifying qualities. Thus, for example, a feminist analysis critiques the concept of gender as political, of organizational hierarchy as oppressive, and of "bounded rationality" as devaluing emotional experiences (Mumby & Putnam, 1992). Some have argued that even theories and research about organizations, once deconstructed, can be shown to objectify bureaucratic organizations and justify their power (Cooper, 1989).

The postmodernist perspective can offer important insights about human service organizations. The moral work and the maintenance of cultural symbols—the essence of these organizations—typically become objectified and acquire a taken-for-granted quality in the service technologies and staff-client relations. Only when deconstructed, can we study the dynamics of how they have become dominant, how they exclude alternative conceptions, and how they control the very language used by professionals. Indeed, professional knowledge and language can be seen as powerful tools of social control, or what Foucault (1977) sees as a disciplinary mode of domination. Schram (1995), for example, showed how food shelves [distributors], unable to accommodate the flood of people asking for food, embraced prevailing definitions of dependency. As he put it,

> Food shelf personnel must invoke discursive practices that enable them to shift responsibility for hunger back onto the poor themselves. Imputing deficiencies to the poor allows food shelf staff the room to justify the regulations of clients' behavior and the rationing of food and to maintain a sense of control over their own operation. (p. 64)

The result is that the food shelves adopt the dominant moral assumptions of blaming the victim.

The postmodern approach asks us to deconstruct the prevailing models of social welfare administration and their underlying assumptions. Such an exercise may uncover discursive practices that maintain and reinforce patterns of domination and control over staff and clients while excluding alternative perspectives. Having done so, however, postmodernism fails to offer the foundations on which to build a theory of organizations, let alone a model for social welfare administration. Structuration theory tries to overcome this serious deficiency.

The idea that there is a reciprocal relationship between human agency and social structure is developed by Giddens's (1984) structuration theory. It is based on the notion of "the *duality of structure,* which relates to the *fundamentally recursive character of social life, and expresses the mutual dependence of structure and agency*" (Cassell, 1993, p. 122). In other words, social structure both enables and constrains human agents whose actions produce and reproduce the structure. Human agents are viewed as capable of reflexive action, of being knowledgeable about the conditions and consequences of what they do in their daily lives (Giddens, 1984, p. 281). In particular, agents are not only able to observe and understand what they are doing, but they can also adjust their observation rules. For example, workers who know that their decisions about their clients are affected by their own moral beliefs can modify such decisions. When agents do so, they can effect change in the social structure. Structure is conceptualized as recursively organized rules and resources that agents draw on and reconstitute in their daily activities. Therefore, "structure has no existence independent of the knowledge that agents have about what they do in their day-to-day activity" (Giddens, 1984,

p. 26). As a result, "the structural properties of social systems are both the medium and outcome of the practices they recursively organize" (p. 25). This implies that structure is not something external to human agents but is both enabled by them and constrains them. An important element of the theory is the idea of modalities—interpretative schemes that include meaning, normative elements, and power—that agents draw on in the reproduction of social interactions that also reconstitute their structural properties. Again, these schemes sanction certain modes of social practices, but they also enable the change of such practices.

Structuration theory has been incorporated into organizational analysis in numerous ways. Orlikowski (1992) showed how technology can be conceptualized as being both a social construction by members of the organization and, once constructed, a reified and objectified structure that constrains their behavior. Sarason (1995) showed how it could be used to understand organizational change. More recently, Sandfort (1997) used the theory to explain how welfare workers, constrained by the administrative policies they find difficult to accept, develop their own interpretive schemes, which enable them to continue to work in a difficult environment. These schemes, in turn, affect and alter the structure of their work, in ways that may not have been intended by the policies.

Structuration theory can provide an important analytic approach to understand human service organizations. It draws attention to how workers, in their daily activities, reproduce and reify organizational assumptions and conceptions about the clients, as well as how they change them. It pays close attention to the interpretative schemes that workers use because these determine how clients are morally constructed, how actions are justified, and how they become reproduced in the structural properties of the agency. At the same time, the theory also provides important insights into the processes of organizational change, especially in the capacity of the workers to be knowledgeable and reflexive about the rules they use; it explains how reflexive action can bring about change in organizational structure. Therefore, it has the potential to both understand and inform social welfare administration practices.

SOCIAL CHANGE

Critical theorists echo the postmodernist critique of organizations as repressive systems. Marxist theory, from which critical theory has sprung, views the organization as an instrument of the capitalist class. The very structure of the organization—hierarchy, division of labor—aims to strip from workers any discretion or control over the means of their work, to prevent the workers from organizing as collectivities, and to shift power to the managerial class (e.g., Braverman, 1974; Edward, 1979). Alienation and inequity are, therefore, viewed as endemic to all organizations. Human service organizations, embedded in a capitalist economy, also exhibit these attributes (Clegg & Dunkerley, 1980). According to Marxist theory, these organizations also assume a special role in a capitalist economy. They serve as buffers between the capitalist and the working classes. The benefits and services they provide are designed to maintain a compliant and complacent working class while defining and isolating as deviants those who might challenge the capitalist system (e.g., Galper, 1975; Piven & Cloward, 1971; Quadagno, 1988).

Critical theory revises the Marxist perspective by viewing patterns of domination and oppression to extend beyond class and to be inherent in the very project of modernism. Modernism, embracing science and technical rationality, only produces new forms of domination, inauthentic social relations, and technocratic consciousness. As a result, according to Habermas (1971), moral and reflexive social interactions have been displaced. The domination of technical and instrumental reasoning is reproduced because those subjugated by it actively accept its hegemony (Alvesson & Deetz, 1996). According to Alvesson and Deetz (1996),

> The central goal of critical theory in organizational studies has been to create societies and workplaces which are free from domination, where all members have equal opportunity to contribute to the production of systems which meet human needs and lead to the progressive development of all. (p. 198)

Thus, unlike those following other theoretical approaches, critical theorists are quite explicit about the purpose of their research: to achieve social change by turning the organizations from instruments of domination to authentic, dialogic communities (Handler, 1990). Such communities are characterized by communicative rationality, that is, viewpoints are freely exchanged and accepted on the basis of the strength of the argument rather than on the basis of power, status, and ideology.

The main strategy of critical theory, not unlike postmodernism, it to critique the underlying ideologies that legitimate our social institutions, showing how they maintain and reinforce patterns of domination, including those based on gender and ethnicity, and foster distorted and inauthentic communication patterns that repress emancipation and justice. Looking at the organization, Alvesson and Deetz (1996, p. 198) suggest that critical analysis focuses on four major themes showing that (a) organizational forms need not be accepted as the natural order of things, (b) management interests are not universal, (c) the emphasis on technical rationality represses understanding and mutual determination of the desired ends, and (d) the organizational culture fosters the hegemony of dominant groups. In studies of management practices, Alvesson and Willmott (1996) tried to show how strategic management, for example, is actually a form of domination because strategic discourse and the decision-making process are controlled by the managerial elite, thus legitimizing its hegemony. Similarly, a critical analysis of information systems is likely to show how they control patterns of communication and stifle reflexive thinking.

The usefulness of critical analysis of human services and administrative practices lies in its ideology critique. Ideologies play a dominant role in creating the moral construction of the clients, in defining the desired ends, in shaping the service technologies, and in socializing and controlling the staff. Administrative practices inherently reinforce these ideologies. As Handler (1990) demonstrated, a legal-bureaucratic ideology fosters hierarchy, domination, and distrust between staff and clients. In contrast, an ideology of dialogism based on autonomy, shared decision making, and equality promotes trust and staff-client relations that empower both. Although such ideology is an exception in the organization of human services, it does occur, and it is predicated on three conditions: (a) professional norms that embrace dialogism, (b) a service technology in which success requires shared decision making with clients, and (c) reciprocal financial incentives for both staff and clients to cooperate.

If the aim of social welfare administration is to improve and protect the well-being of clients, it must critically examine its own ideologies. With the exception of the feminist critique, discussed below, administrative practices have not been subject to such analysis. A critique might show that the preoccupation of social welfare administration with technical rationality—such as Total Quality Management, strategic planning, and performance measurement systems—reinforces the domination of powerful interest groups that control the agency's resources. It will show that such practices prevent an open, authentic, and reflexive discourse about the goals of the agency by all its constituents, including workers and clients. Such a critique can also point to administrative practices that can foster a more dialogic and, therefore, client-oriented organization.

The feminist critique, rooted in critical theory, is particularly important to social welfare administration because much of the work in the human services is gendered. Women constitute the majority of human service workers, and yet, men are more likely to assume the key administrative positions. There are, of course, several feminist approaches to explain and remedy gender inequality in organizations, and each offers a different perspective on the organization itself (for a review, see Calas & Smircich, 1996). Liberal feminism, for example, does not challenge mainstream conceptions of organizations, but it acknowledges that inequality is a result of stereotypes and discriminatory practices that block job and advancement opportunities. The remedies are legal-rational, such as antidiscrimination and sexual harassment policies, equal worth pay, gender-free performance appraisals, and unbiased promotion criteria (e.g., Kanter, 1977; Powell, 1992; Reskin & Hartmann, 1986).

In contrast, radical feminism, building on the notion of gender domination and repression, has a distinctive conception of the organization and offers an alternative organizational form. As a result, it has attracted particular attention in social welfare administration. Acker (1990) proposed that organizations are inherently gendered. They reproduce male domination through (a) divisions along gender lines, (b) construction of symbols and images that explain and reinforce these divisions, (c) interaction between men and women including patterns of dominance, (d) production of gendered components of personal identity, and (e) expression in ongoing social structure. In other words, gendered organizations subordinate women via structural arrangements and power relations that give primacy to male dominance while suppressing feminist values. These values are "egalitarianism rather than hierarchy, cooperation rather than competition, nurturance rather than rugged individualism, peace rather than conflict" (Taylor, 1983, p. 445).

Radical feminism is committed to the development of alternative organizations imbued with feminist values that "focus on the primacy of interpersonal relations; empowerment and personal development of members; building of self-esteem; the promotion of enhanced knowledge, skills, and political awareness; personal autonomy; and the politics of gender" (Martin, 1990, p. 192). The most important characteristics of these alternative organizations are (a) participatory decision making, (b) systems of rotating leadership, (c) flexible and interactive job designs, (d) equitable distribution of in-

come, and (e) interpersonal and political accountability (Koen, 1984, cited in Calas & Smircich, 1996). A number of such alternative organizations have emerged in the human services, ranging from feminist health centers (Hyde, 1992; Schwartz, Gottesman, & Perlmutter, 1988) to rape crisis centers (Martin, DiNitto, Byington, & Maxwell, 1992) and schools (Rothschild & Whitt, 1986). They have demonstrated that human service organizations can be designed to be nonhierarchical and egalitarian, where social controls are noncoercive and rewards are intrinsic and where relations among workers and between workers and clients are nurturing, caring, and based on mutual responsibility and accountability (Iannello, 1992; Rothschild & Whitt, 1986). Nonetheless, such organizations remain the exception in the human services because of serious external and internal obstacles (Hyde, 1992).

On the basis of research on such feminist organizations, Hyde (1989) enunciated a feminist model of social welfare administration. It is based on several principles: (a) the centrality of women's values, lives, and relationships; (b) consciousness-raising—linking the personal and the political; (c) the reconceptualization of power from zero-sum to "infinite, unifying, enabling, facilitating, and democratizing" (p. 155); (d) democratized processes and structures; and (e) commitment to eliminating patriarchal society. Hyde recognizes the numerous obstacles in implementing such a practice. As social movement organizations trying to survive in a generally hostile environment, feminist organizations inevitably experience internal and external pressures to assume the characteristics of mainstream organizations. The demand for high commitment often results in the professionalization of the leadership and the rise of an unacknowledged elite. Maintaining balance between social action and the provision of services is difficult, especially when the organization depends on external resources. Therefore, the success of such organizations is always precarious. Still, the incorporation of feminist theory and research into social welfare administration would profoundly enrich the field, in particular by examining how and under what conditions alternative practices, more in tune with social work values, can be implemented. Such a project still awaits the field.

CONCLUSION

Although social welfare administration is maturing as a field of practice, its intellectual foundations remain shaky. On the one hand, models of practice are often rationalized on the basis of organizational theories that have questionable validity, especially when applied to human service organizations. On the other hand, important theoretical developments and empirical research that could inform social welfare administration remain neglected. With a few important exceptions, when models of practice refer to organizational theories, the use of such theories to inform practice principles is superficial and uncritical. Equally serious is the tendency to emulate popular management models that lack empirical validity or sensitivity to the attributes of human service organizations. For the field to flourish, it must be grounded in theory and research. It need not embrace any particular theoretical orientation. To paraphrase Weick (1995), over time, administrators will act as if they are feminist, rationalist, political economist, or radicalist. Therefore, social welfare administration should embrace and adapt orga-

nizational theories that most effectively address its particular administrative issues within the social welfare context. In doing so, however, it needs to study and assess the implementation and consequences of such practices. With such accumulated knowledge, social welfare administration will enrich and be enriched by organizational theories and research while finding and maintaining its own distinct voice.

NOTE

1. I do not attempt a comprehensive review of all books on social work administration. Rather, I have selected books that illustrate key trends in the theoretical development of the field.

REFERENCES

Abels, P., & Murphy, M. J. (1981). *Administration in the human services*. Engelwood Cliffs, NJ: Prentice Hall.

Acker, J. (1990). Hierarchies, jobs, bodies: A theory of gendered organizations. *Gender & Society, 4,* 139-158.

Alvesson, M., & Deetz, S. (1996). Critical theory and postmodernism approaches to organizational studies. In S. Clegg, C. Hardy, & W. Nord (Eds.), *Handbook of organization studies* (pp. 191-217). London: Sage.

Alvesson, M., & Willmott, H. (1996). *Making sense of mnagement*. London: Sage.

Argyris, C. (1964). *Integrating the individual and the organization*. New York: John Wiley.

Astley, W. G., & Sachdeva, P. S. (1984). Structural sources of intraorganizational power: A theoretical synthesis. *Academy of Management Review, 9,* 104-113.

Au, C.-F. (1994). The status of theory and knowledge development in social welfare administration. *Administration in Social Work, 18,* 27-58.

Baum, J. A. C. (1996). Organizational ecology. In S. R. Clegg, C. Hardy, & W. R. Nord (Eds.), *Handbook of organization studies* (pp. 77-114). London: Sage.

Baum, J. A., & Oliver, C. (1991). Institutional linkages and organizational mortality. *Administrative Science Quarterly, 36,* 187-218.

Benson, J. K. (1975). The interorganizational network as a political economy. *Administrative Science Quarterly, 20,* 229-249.

Braverman, H. (1974). *Labor and monopoly capital: The degradation of work in the twentieth century.* New York: Monthly Review Press.

Brodkin, E. Z. (1997). Inside the welfare contract: Discretion and accountability in state welfare administration. *Social Service Review, 71,* 1-33.

Brody, R. (1993). *Effectively managing human service organizations.* Newbury Park, CA: Sage.

Calas, M. B., & Smircich, L. (1996). From "the woman's" point of view: Feminist approaches to organizational studies. In S. R. Clegg, C. Hardy, & W. R. Nord (Eds.), *Handbook of organizational studies* (pp. 218-257). London: Sage.

Cameron, K. S., & Quinn, R. E. (1996). *Diagnosing and changing organizational culture.* San Francisco: Jossey-Bass.

Cassell, P. (Ed.). (1993). *The Giddens reader.* Stanford, CA: Stanford University Press.

Chatman, J. A. (1989). Managing people and organizations: Selection and socialization in public accounting firms. *Administrative Science Quarterly, 36,* 459-484.

Chia, R. (1995). From modern to postmodern organizational analysis. *Organization Studies, 16,* 580-604.

Clegg, S., & Dunkerley, D. (1980). *Organization, class, and control.* London: Routledge & Kegan Paul.

Cooper, R. (1989). Modernism, post modernism, and organizational analysis 3: The contribution of Jacques Derrida. *Organization Studies, 10,* 479-502.

Cooper, R., & Burrell, G. (1988). Modernism, postmodernism and organizational analysis: An introduction. *Organization Studies, 9,* 91-112.

Creed, W. E., & Miles, R. E. (1996). Trust in organizations: A conceptual framework. In R. M. Kramer & T. R. Tyler (Eds.), *Trust in organizations* (pp. 16-38). Thousand Oaks, CA: Sage.

Cress, D., & Snow, D. A. (1996). Mobilizing at the margins: Resources, benefactors, and the viability of homeless social movement organizations. *American Sociological Review, 61,* 1089-1109.

Czarniawska-Joerges, B. (1992). *Exploring complex organizations: A cultural perspective.* Newbury Park, CA: Sage.

D'Aunno, T., Sutton, R., & Price, R. (1991). Isomorphism and external support in conflicting institutional environments: A study of drug abuse treatment units. *Academy of Management Journal, 34,* 636-661.

Deal, T., & Kennedy, A. (1982). *Corporate cultures: The rites and rituals of corporate life.* Reading, MA: Addison-Wesley.

Donaldson, L. (1996). *For positivist organization theory: Proving the hard core.* London: Sage.

Drucker, P. (1990). *Managing the non-profit organization.* New York, HarperCollins.

Edward, R. (1979). *Contested terrain: The transformation of the workplace in the twentieth century.* New York: Basic Books.

Foucault, M. (1977). *Discipline and punish: The birth of the prison.* New York: Pantheon.

Galbraith, J. R., & Kazanjian, R. K. (1986). *Strategy implementation.* St. Paul, MN: West.

Galper, J. H. (1975). *The politics of social services.* Englewood Cliffs, NJ: Prentice Hall.

Gergen, K. J., & Thatchenkery, T. J. (1996). Organization science as social construction: Postmodern potentials. *Journal of Applied Behavioral Science, 32,* 356-377.

Giddens, A. (1984). *The constitution of society: Outline of the theory of structuration.* Berkeley: University of California Press.

Glisson, C. A. (1978). Dependence of technological routinization on structural variables in human service organizations. *Administrative Science Quarterly, 23,* 383-395.

Glisson, C. (1989). The effect of leadership on workers in human service organizations. *Administration in Social Work, 13,* 99-116.

Glisson, C. (1992). Structure and technology in human service organizations. In Y. Hasenfeld (Ed.), *Human services as complex organizations* (pp. 184-204). Newbury Park, CA: Sage.

Glisson, C., & Durick, M. (1988). Predictors of job satisfaction and organizational commitment in human service organizations. *Administrative Science Quarterly, 33,* 61-81.

Glisson, C., & Hemmelgarn, A. (1998). The effects of organizational climate and interorganizational coordination on the quality and outcomes of children's service systems. *Child Abuse & Neglect, 22,* 401-421.

Glisson, C. A., & Martin, P. Y. (1980). Productivity and efficiency in human service organizations as related to structure, size, and age. *Academy of Management Journal, 23,* 21-37.

Grob, G. N. (1991). *From asylum to community: Mental health policy in modern America.* Princeton, NJ: Princeton University Press.

Gronbjerg, K. A. (1993). *Understanding nonprofit funding: Managing revenues in social services and community development organizations.* San Francisco: Jossey-Bass.

Gummer, B. (1990). *The politics of social administration: Managing politics in social agencies.* Englewood Cliffs, NJ: Prentice Hall.

Guterman, N. B., & Bargal, D. (1996). Social workers' perceptions of their power and service outcomes. *Administration in Social Work, 20,* 1-20.

Habermas, J. (1971). *Toward a rational society: Student protest, science, and politics.* London: Heinemann.

Handler, J. F. (1990). *Law and the search for community.* Philadelphia: University of Pennsylvania Press.

Handler, J. F., & Hasenfeld, Y. (1991). *The moral construction of poverty.* Newbury Park, CA: Sage.

Hannan, M. T., & Freeman, J. (1989). *Organizational ecology.* Cambridge, MA: Harvard University Press.

Hart, S. L., & Quinn, R. E. (1993). Roles executives play: CEOs, behavioral complexity, and firm performance. *Human Relations, 46,* 543-574.

Hasenfeld, Y. (1992). The nature of human service organizations. In Y. Hasenfeld (Ed.), *Human services as complex organizations* (pp. 3-23). Newbury Park, CA: Sage.

Hasenfeld, Y. (in press). Organizational forms as moral practices: The case of welfare departments. *Social Service Review.*

Hasenfeld, Y., & Cheung, P. (1985). The juvenile court as a people-processing organization: A political economy perspective. *American Journal of Sociology, 90,* 801-824.

Hyde, C. (1989). A feminist model for macro-practice: Promises and problems. *Administration in Social Work, 13,* 145-181.

Hyde, C. (1992). The ideational system of social movement agencies: An examination of feminist health centers. In Y. Hasenfeld (Ed.), *Human services as formal organizations* (pp. 121-144). Newbury Park, CA: Sage.

Iannello, K. P. (1992). *Decisions without hierarchy.* New York: Routledge.

Jayaratne, S. (1993). The antecedents, consequences, and correlates of job satisfaction. In R. T. Golembiewski (Ed.), *Handbook of organizational behavior* (pp. 111-140). New York: Marcel Dekker.

Kanter, R. M. (1977). *Men and women of the corporation.* New York: Basic Books.

Keller, T., & Dansereau, F. (1995). Leadership and empowerment: A social exchange perspective. *Human Relations, 48,* 127-146.

Kettner, P. M., Moroney, R. M., & Martin, L. L. (1990). *Designing and managing programs: An effectiveness-based approach.* Newbury Park, CA: Sage.

Kramer, R., & Grossman, B. (1987). Contracting for social services: Process management and resource dependencies. *Social Service Review, 61,* 32-55.

Lachman, R. (1989). Power from what? Reexamination of its relationships with structural conditions. *Administrative Science Quarterly, 34,* 231-251.

Lewis, J. A., Lewis, M. D., & Soufiée, F. (1991). *Management of human service programs.* Pacific Grove, CA: Brooks/Cole.

Lipsky, M. (1980). *Street-level bureaucracy.* New York: Russell Sage Foundation.

Martin, J., & Frost, P. (1996). The organizational culture war games: A struggle for intellectual dominance. In S. R. Clegg, C. Hardy, & W. D. Nord (Eds.), *Handbook of organizational studies* (pp. 599-621). London: Sage.

Martin, P. Y. (1980). Multiple constituencies, dominant societal values, and the human service administrator: Implications for service delivery. *Administration in Social Work, 4,* 15-27.

Martin, P. Y. (1990). Rethinking feminist organizations. *Gender & Society, 4,* 182-206.

Martin, P. Y., & Chernesky, R. H. (1989). Women's prospects for leadership in social welfare: A political economy perspective. *Administration in Social Work, 13,* 117-143.

Martin, P. Y., DiNitto, D., Byington, D., & Maxwell, M. S. (1992). Organizational and community transformation: The case of a rape crisis center. *Administration in Social Work, 16,* 123-145.

Maslach, C., & Schaufeli, W. B. (1993). Historical and conceptual development of burnout. In W. Schaufeli, C. Maslach, & T. Marek (Eds.), *Professional burnout: Recent developments in theory and research* (pp. 1-18). Washington, DC: Taylor & Francis.

Meyer, J. W., & Rowan, B. (1977). Institutionalized organizations: Formal structure as myth and ceremony. *American Journal of Sociology, 83,* 340-363.

Meyer, J. W., & Rowan, B. (1983). The structure of educational organizations. In J. W. S. Meyer & W. R. Scott (Eds.), *Organizational environments: Ritual and rationality* (pp. 71-98). Beverly Hills, CA: Sage.

Meyer, M., & Zucker, L. (1989). *Permanently failing organizations.* Newbury Park, CA: Sage.

Meyerson, D. (1992). "Normal" ambiguity? A glimpse on an occupational culture. In P. Frost, L. Moore, M. Louis, C. Lundberg, & J. Martin (Eds.), *Reframing organizational culture* (pp. 131-144). Newbury Park, CA: Sage.

Mintzberg, H. (1979). *The structuring of organizations.* Englewood Cliffs, NJ: Prentice Hall.

Mintzberg, H. (1996). Musings on management. *Harvard Business Review, 74,* 61-67.

Morgan, G. (1997). *Images of organization.* Thousand Oaks, CA: Sage.

Mumby, D. K., & Putnam, L. L. (1992). The politics of emotion: A feminist reading of bounded rationality. *Academy of Management Review, 17,* 465-486.

Neugeboren, B. (1991). *Organization, policy, and practice in the human services.* Binghamton, NY: Haworth.

Orlikowski, W. J. (1992). The duality of technology: Rethinking the concept of technology in organizations. *Organization Science, 3,* 398-427.

Patti, R. (1983). *Social welfare administration: Managing social programs in a developmental context.* Englewood Cliffs, NJ: Prentice Hall.

Patti, R. J. (1987). Managing for service effectiveness in social welfare: Toward a performance model. *Administration in Social Work, 11,* 7-22.

Pearlmutter, S. (1998). Self-efficacy and organizational change leadership. *Administration in Social Work, 22,* 23-38.

Perrow, C. (1967). A framework for the comparative analysis of organizations. *American Sociological Review, 32,* 194-208.

Perrow, C. (1986). *Complex organizations: A critical essay* (3rd ed.). New York: Random House.

Peters, T. J., & Waterman, J. R. H. (1982). *In search of excellence.* New York: Harper & Row.

Pfeffer, J. (1992). *Managing with power: Politics and influence in organizations.* Boston: Harvard Business School Press.

Pfeffer, J. (1997). *New directions for organizational theory: Problems and prospects.* New York: Oxford University Press.

Pfeffer, J., & Salancik, G. R. (1978). *The external control of organizations: A resource dependence perspective.* New York: Harper & Row.

Piven, F. F., & Cloward, R. (1971). *Regulating the poor: The functions of public welfare.* New York: Random House.

Powell, G. N. (1992). *Women and men in management.* Newbury Park, CA: Sage.

Quadagno, J. (1988). *The transformation of old age security.* Chicago: University of Chicago Press.

Rapp, C. A., & Poertner, J. (1992). *Social administration: A client-centered approach.* White Plains, NY: Longman.

Reed, M. (1996). Organizational theorizing: A historically contested terrain. In S. R. Clegg, C. Hardy, & W. R. Nord (Eds.), *Handbook of organization studies* (pp. 31-56). London: Sage.

Reskin, B. F., & Hartmann, H. I. (1986). *Women's work, men's work: Sex segregation on the job.* Washington, DC: National Academy Press.

Rothschild, J., & Whitt, A. J. (1986). *The cooperative workplace.* Cambridge, UK: Cambridge University Press.

Salamon, L. M. (1995). *Partners in public service.* Baltimore, MD: The Johns Hopkins University Press.

Sandfort, J. R. (1997). *The structuring of front-line work: Conditions within local welfare and welfare-to-work organizations in Michigan.* Paper presented at the annual conference of the Association for Public Policy Analysis and Management, Washington, DC.

Sarason, Y. (1995). A model of organizational transformation: The incorporation of organizational identity into a structuration theory framework. *Academy of Management Journal* (Best Papers Proceedings 1995), 47-51.

Savage, A. (1988). Maximizing effectiveness through technological complexity. In R. J. Patti, J. Poertner, & C. A. Rapp (Eds.), *Managing for service effectiveness in social welfare organizations* (pp. 127-143). New York: Haworth.

Schoonhoven, C. B. (1981). Problems with contingency theory: Testing assumptions hidden within the language of contingency "theory." *Administrative Science Quarterly, 26,* 349-377.

Schram, S. F. (1995). *Words of welfare.* Minneapolis: University of Minnesota Press.

Schwartz, A. Y., Gottesman, E. W., & Perlmutter, F. D. (1988). Blackwell: A case study in feminist administration. *Administration in Social Work, 12,* 5-15.

Scott, R. (1985). Systems within systems. *American Behavioral Scientist, 28,* 601-618.

Scott, R. W., & Meyer, J. W. (1983). The organization of environments: Network, cultural, and historical elements. In J. W. S. Meyer & W. R. Scott (Eds.), *Organizational environments: Ritual and rationality* (pp. 129-154). Beverly Hills, CA: Sage.

Scott, W. R. (1995). *Institutions and organizations.* Thousand Oaks, CA: Sage.

Scott, W. R. (1998). *Organizations: Rational, natural, and open systems.* Upper Saddle River, NJ: Prentice Hall.

Sheinfeld Gorin, S. N., & Weirich, T. W. (1995). Innovation use: Performance assessment in a community mental health center. *Human Relations, 48,* 1427-1453.

Skidmore, R. A. (1995). *Social work administration: Dynamic management and human relationships.* Boston: Allyn & Bacon.

Snyder, N. M. (1995). Organizational culture and management capacity in a social welfare organization: A case study of Kansas. *Public Administration Quarterly, 19,* 243-264.

Starr, P. (1982). *The social transformation of American medicine.* New York: Basic Books.

Strauss, A., Fargerhaugh, S., Suczek, B., & Wiener, C. (1985). *Social organization of medical work.* Chicago: University of Chicago Press.

Taylor, V. (1983). The future of feminism in the 1980s: A social movement analysis. In L. Richardson & V. Taylor (Eds.), *Feminist frontiers: Rethinking sex, gender, and society.* Reading, MA: Addison-Wesley.

Tolbert, P. S., & Zucker, L. G. (1996). The institutionalization of institutional theory. In S. R. Clegg, C. Hardy,

& W. R. Nord (Eds.), *Handbook of organization studies* (pp. 175-190). London: Sage.

Trice, H. M., & Beyer, J. M. (1993). *The cultures of work organizations.* Englewood Cliffs, NJ: Prentice Hall.

Tucker, D., Baum, J., & Singh, J. (1992). The institutional ecology of human service organizations. In Y. Hasenfeld (Ed.), *Human services as complex organizations* (pp. 47-72). Newbury Park, CA: Sage.

Tushman, M. L., & Anderson, P. (1986). Technological discontinuities and organizational environments. *Administrative Science Quarterly, 31,* 436-465.

Wamsley, G. L., & Zald, M. N. (1976). *The political economy of public organizations.* Bloomington: Indiana University Press.

Weatherley, R. (1983). Participatory management in public welfare. *Administration in Social Work, 7,* 39-50.

Weber, M. (1968). *Economy and society: An interpretive sociology.* New York: Bedminister. (Original work published 1924)

Weick, K. E. (1995). *Sensemaking in organizations.* Thousand Oaks, CA: Sage.

Weil, M. (1988). Creating an alternative work culture in a public service setting. *Administration in Social Work, 12,* 69-82.

Weinbach, R. W. (1990). *The social worker as manager: Theory and practice.* White Plains, NY: Longman.

Weisbrod, B. A. (Ed.). (1998). *To profit or not to profit: The commercial transformation of the nonprofit sector.* New York: Cambridge University Press.

Weiss, R. M. (1989). Organizational structure in human service agencies. In L. E. Miller (Ed.), *Managing human service organizations* (pp. 21-38). New York: Quorum.

Whiddon, B., & Martin, P. Y. (1989). Organizational democracy and work quality in a state welfare agency. *Social Science Quarterly, 70,* 667-686.

Zald, M. N., & Denton, P. (1963). From evangelism to general service: The transformation of the YMCA. *Administrative Science Quarterly, 8,* 214-234.

Zuboff, S. (1998). *In the age of the smart machine.* New York: Basic Books.

Zucker, L. (1988). Where do institutional patterns come from? Organizations as actors in social systems. In L. Zucker (Ed.), *Institutional patterns and organizations* (pp. 23-52). Cambridge, MA: Ballinger.

Zucker, L. G. (1989). Combining institutional theory and population ecology: No legitimacy, no history. *American Sociological Review, 54,* 542-545.

CHAPTER SIX

Structural and Fiscal Characteristics of Social Service Agencies

MARGARET GIBELMAN

This chapter examines structure as a necessary and important aspect of organizational functioning and a variable in determining whether the goals of the organization are achieved. The structure of an organization is predicated, in part, on organization type (i.e., public, nonprofit, for-profit) and, in turn, the type of organization is interdependent with the financial basis of operations.

Beginning with an overview of the different types of organizations, this chapter then explores organizational mission and authority as these affect and interrelate with structural and financial considerations. Since the structure of the organization also determines its governance

pattern, different governance arrangements are detailed, including issues related to the delegation of specified roles to management and the creation of substructures to carry out the organization's work. Patterns of financing in different types of human service organizations are then identified within the context of an increasing trend toward "boundary blurring," in which the different types of organizations are eligible and compete for the same funding sources. Thus, it is maintained that the current fiscal environment in which all human service organizations function has led to the creation of hybrid organizations in which the distinctive characteristics traditionally ascribed to each organizational type are now accurate in degree rather than kind. Such boundary blurring is considered within the context of the increasing societal and political preference to de-bureaucratize and de-federalize human services and the consequent growth in purchase of service arrangements.

Organizational structure has been defined as "the formal arrangement of people and functions necessary to achieve desired results" (Page, 1988, p. 46). Hall (1982) sees structure as the "formal positional distribution and role relations of persons in a human service organization" (p. 53). Skidmore (1990) further defines structure as the "actual arrangements and levels of an organization in regard to power, authority, responsibilities, and mechanisms for carrying out its [organizational] functions and practices" (p. 97).

Human service organizations, the vehicle through which most human services are provided, are viewed as those organizations that assist in the growth and development of individuals and families (Wellford & Gallagher, 1988). The services offered by human service organizations are, typically, "uniquely intimate and personal in nature" (Wellford & Gallagher, 1988, p. 49). These organizations may be public (governmental) at the federal, state, or local level; proprietary (for-profit); or nonprofit.

No sector has a monopoly on the provision of a particular type of service. However, the nearly 40% of social workers who are members of the National Association of Social Workers (NASW) deliver services through not-for-profit organizations, both sectarian and nonsectarian (Gibelman & Schervish, 1997). (It should be noted that the NASW database, although it represents only about 33% of all social workers in the United States, is the only source of detailed

aggregate information on the nature and breadth of social work employment.) Another perspective on the professional representation within the different types of organizations can be discerned from data collected through the 1990 Census of Population and Housing. Under the occupational category of "social worker," the total number of employees is 537,450, of whom 58,890 work in the for-profit sector, 146,600 in the not-for-profit sector, and 331,960 in government (as cited in Hodgkinson & Weitzman, 1996, p. 148). The census data tap individuals who hold the titled position of social worker, with an unknown proportion holding a professional degree at the BSW or MSW level. These different data sources (NASW and the census) thus have an overlapping but nevertheless distinct population base.

TYPES OF ORGANIZATIONS

The aegis under which social services are delivered is known as the *auspice* of practice. Lowenstein (1964) referred to auspice as that which

> differentiates between the private [for-profit] provision of a service and the provision of that service by an organization set up by the community at large, either through government or voluntary association, with accountability for, and control over, the service resting with the community at large. Such control and accountability are in contrast to the private control of the contractual relationship mutually exercised by a private practitioner and his client. (p. 4)

The practice of social work has traditionally been carried out in organizational settings. Throughout the history of American social welfare, these settings have basically been of two types: public and private. Public agencies are generally associated with bureaucracies, such as large public assistance or child welfare agencies. Social workers who work for the government typically fall under civil service rules and regulations.

The private sector includes both not-for-profit and for-profit agencies. Within the not-for-profit sector, there are two types of agencies: sectarian and nonsectarian. Sectarian agencies are those that have their origins under the auspices of or operate with the financial support of religious organizations, or that are oriented toward providing services primarily to members of a specific religious group. Examples include Catholic Charities USA and its affiliates across the country, Jewish social agencies, Lutheran Social Services, and the Methodist Board of Child Care (Barker, 1995).

Nonprofit organizations, based on philanthropic support of the arts, education, and human services, have a uniquely American flavor. This voluntary sector is much more developed in the United States than it is in other Western democracies. It is only in recent years that we have seen a substantial expansion of this organizational type in such countries as Britain, France, and the Netherlands, and then with substantial guidance and practical help from U.S. counterparts (Eisenberg, 1990).

Public agencies may be at the federal, state, or local level. For example, the network of Veterans Administration hospitals is under federal auspices, even though the hospitals themselves are based in communities across the country. Public child welfare and aging services are typically under the jurisdiction of state agencies, although a sizable proportion of the budget for services comes from the federal government. Each state has substantial leeway in how it organizes its service delivery system; thus, there is no one "structural format" that applies to all states. The state, through its legislature, is the operating authority for public agencies (Page, 1988).

Nonprofit social welfare agencies may be under a national rubric, such as the affiliates of the Child Welfare League of America or Alliance for Children and Families, but they are also located within communities and attempt to be responsive to community needs within the parameters set by their national standard-setting organizations.

The National Taxonomy of Exempt Entities (National Center for Charitable Statistics, 1993) considers not-for-profit organizations in the human services to be

> organizations or programs that promote or provide a broad range of social or human services to individuals or families, even though specific programs operated within those agencies may be classified elsewhere, i.e., American Red Cross, YM, YWCAs, YM, YWHAs, etc.; family service agencies, including shelters and aftercare programs for victims of domestic violence; organizations that provide direct social services to children and adolescents (e.g., adoption and foster care services, child day care, etc.); personal social services for individuals (e.g., credit-counseling, personal enrichment, self-help services, travelers' aid, etc.); residential, custodial care facilities and services for individuals unable to live independently due to developmental disabilities, age, or physical infirmity; and programs that promote general independent functioning/living of individuals (e.g., retarded citizens associations; guide dog services for the disabled; etc.). (p. 93)

Nonprofit human service organizations are based in local communities and are governed by volunteers. Sources of revenue to carry out their programs come from a variety of sources:

contributions, donations, grants, purchase of service, and fees for service. Most of the traditional social service and social change organizations are not-for-profit. A not-for-profit agency is accountable to its board of directors, which sets overall policy. The bylaws of the agency explicate which clients are to be served, what problems are the focus of the agency's attention, and what methods are to be used in providing services (Barker, 1995).

In recent years, for-profit organizations have increasingly entered into the human service enterprise, particularly in such settings as nursing homes, home health, residential treatment centers, and **adult and child day care**. Although these organizations employ social workers and other mental health professionals, for-profits are owned and operated like any other business (Morales & Sheafor, 1992). Many such businesses, in fact, are part of super-corporations, such as Psychiatric Institute, which owns and operates in- and outpatient psychiatric facilities across the country, and nursing home chains such as Beverly Enterprises. The entrance of for-profits as providers of human services can largely be explained by changes in federal funding regulations in the late 1960s, which began to allow for-profit organizations to apply for and receive contract funds (Gibelman, 1998). Furthermore, such changes in federal regulations reflect a growing preference for things private (a phenomenon known as privatization), based on the largely unproven premise that the free market and heightened competition will increase efficiency and reduce costs.

Gibelman and Schervish (1997) found that the vocabulary used by social workers to describe their profession and their practice is by no means standard. For example, NASW members were not found to distinguish accurately between private not-for-profit and private for-profit auspices. Despite this lack of common nomenclature, organizational structure has a significant effect on how services are delivered. No sector has a monopoly on the provision of a particular type of service. Social services are thus delivered under a variety of auspices. Complicating these organizational arrangements is that each auspice is characterized by different types of practice settings. For example, social services are delivered through private practice (for-profit or not-for-profit), institutions, hospitals, school systems, clinics or centers (public, for-profit, and not-for-profit), and correctional facilities (typically public, but increasingly run by for-profit corporations). The range of practice settings in which social services are carried out is broad, and agencies may specialize in providing select types of services to certain populations who may have a particular type of problem (Gibelman, 1995b; Morales & Sheafor, 1992). Such classifications include mental health, health, family and children's services, aging, schools, and substance abuse.

Although there are similarities among all human service organizations (particularly in relation to their people-serving activities), auspice does affect how the work of the organization is carried out. Such differences include financial and legal bases, service focus, clients served (e.g., fee-for-service versus means-tested), operating philosophies, governing structures, and the technologies employed. As discussed below, however, there is a substantial amount of overlap in the characteristics of all human service organizations, largely the by-product of boundary blurring brought about by public financing of many privately delivered human services.

TABLE 6.1 Operating Authority of Human Service Organizations

Type of Organization	Operating Authority
Not-for-profit	Incorporation in the state or locality in which it operates, with a charter, constitution, and bylaws; and Has its own governing body; and/or Is organized as an identified organization of a religious body with legal status or is an identified organization of another legal entity that is recognized under the laws of the jurisdiction
Public	Authorized and established by statute; or Is a subunit of a public organization with which a clear administrative relationship exists
Proprietary (for-profit)	Organized as a legal entity as a corporation, partnership, sole proprietorship, or association; and Has a charter, partnership agreement, or articles of association and a constitution and bylaws

SOURCE: Adapted from Council on Accreditation of Services to Families and Children, Inc. (1997).

MISSION AND OPERATING AUTHORITY

The different purposes for which the organization is established and the nature of its operating authority are evidenced in the way in which the organization conducts its business (see Table 6.1).

Organizational Mission

The mission of the organization refers to why the organization exists and what it seeks to accomplish. In the case of a nonprofit (voluntary) agency, the devising of the mission is part of the responsibilities of the board of directors. It is usually contained within a mission statement, which is not a static document. Most boards periodically re-examine the mission to determine whether it needs to be re-affirmed, updated, or revised (Axelrod, 1994). Salamon

(1994) sees a mission orientation as the fundamental distinguishing characteristic of nonprofit organizations: "Where for-profit organizations acquire their organizational raison d'être fundamentally from the pursuit of profit, nonprofit organizations get theirs from the pursuit of a mission, a purpose that binds the agency's personnel, supporters, and beneficiaries together in common purpose" (p. 95).

The mission of a public agency is codified in statute and may be delineated more specifically in association with other documents authorizing the organization to operate as a subunit of another legal entity and materials describing the larger entity's legal status. In this later group would be "mega" public agencies, such as departments of human services that include subunits such as child welfare, mental health, and mental retardation/developmental disabilities. Public social welfare agencies are typically associated with the "pure" type of bureaucratic form described by Max Weber (1922/1994). Such organizations are characterized by their size, hierarchy, and division of labor, centralization of decision making, long-term career tenure on the job, codified rules and procedures, and longevity and durability.

That structures are not static can be observed in one of the notable features of bureaucracy: reorganization. In New York City, the Administration for Children's Services was, many years ago, known as the Bureau of Child Welfare. It was not simply a change in name. This same city agency has gone back and forth between a highly centralized structure and a highly decentralized, community-based structure. These ebbs and flows in structure have been part and parcel of philosophical changes in how the goals and objectives of the organization can best be carried out. For example, a community-based, decentralized structure is predicated on a model of service delivery that emphases proximity and accessibility for consumers.

Structural change may also be promoted by changes in federal or state legislation. For example, during the 1960s, the separation of income maintenance and social services established in the Social Security Amendments of 1962 led to the creation of two service-delivery structures in public assistance agencies where there had been one. The complexity of structural arrangements has also been affected by the increase in the number of clients served and the expanded range of services offered to meet client needs. Technology has also made decentralized structures possible, with heightened coordination through the use of computers.

The mission of the for-profit organization is quite straightforward. As with any entrepreneurial business, the purpose or reason for being is to make a profit (Weinbach, 1994). Even though the commodity offered—services—serves a public interest, the product can be conceptualized as no different than the manufacturing of widgets or canned fruit. The bottom line of profit rather than service raises serious concerns among human service professionals. As Hasenfeld (1984) states,

> There is . . . concern that the commercialization of human services will inevitably substitute the profit motive for quality care and concern for the client's welfare. Organizations may select treatment technologies and establish service modalities that enhance their profitability but are not necessarily the most appropriate for or most responsive to the service needs of the population. Moreover, professional autonomy over practice may be seriously eroded as professional decisions become subject to corporate control. (p. 526)

Such concerns have also been echoed in the press. A *Boston Globe* headline questioned, "Schoolchildren as commodities?" in an article about a for-profit company that manages charter schools (Ackerman, 1998, p. C1).

Human Service Organizations as Businesses

Although distinctions between businesses and human service organizations have been noted (see, e.g., Weinbach, 1994), such differences are rapidly dissipating as human service organizations adapt to their environment by incorporating the practices of business to survive and prosper. In fact, social workers have been faulted for not having business savvy; such accusations have been particularly strong during periods of fiscal cutbacks of human services and, more recently, with the rapid spread of managed care as the structure through which health and human services are delivered (Brown, 1994; Gibelman & Demone, 1990).

The accuracy of classifying human service organizations as a form of business enterprise may depend on the specific organization or organizational type; the differences within types of human service organizations may be as or more substantial than differences based on product or service (Weinbach, 1994). Nonprofits can and should make a profit; the issue is how the profit is used. (In business, the profit is shared among owners and/or stockholders; in nonprofits, the profit is put back into programs of service to improve or expand them.) Social service programs that have no source of fiscal support are often cut back or eliminated. Corporate America, on the other hand, has moved toward a more humanistic operating mode by initiating employee assistance programs and human resource units within their structures. As discussed below, one of the most profound phenomena affecting the organizational structure of human service agencies is that of boundary blurring.

GOVERNANCE

How the business of the organization is carried out is affected by its operating authority. Each organization has a governing body responsible for setting its policies, defining its services, guiding its development, and ensuring its accountability to the defined community it serves. In a nonprofit organization, this governance function resides with a board of directors; in the case of a for-profit agency, such as one that is owner-operated, one person (a designated or managing partner or the owner/president) acts as the governing body and assumes responsibility for the operation of the organization and its services.

The authority of the governing body is set forth in sections of the articles of incorporation, constitution, or bylaws. The leadership function is exercised through different means, depending on the operating authority. The corporation's constitution and bylaws, the partnership agreement, or the organization's written operational procedures (in those instances when the agency functions as a subunit of an organized legal entity)

- describe the organizational structure, size, and responsibilities of the governing body and/or of the advisory board, as appropriate
- establish the mechanisms for selection, rotation, and duration of membership and for election of officers
- set the minimum number of formal meetings of the full board
- set the quorum for these meetings
- specify to what body, such as its executive committee, interim authority is delegated by the governing body and/or advisory board (Council on Accreditation [COA], 1997, p. 16)

Effective governance, however, is not guaranteed by its structure. For example, board involvement and attendance can vary significantly, affecting the process and outcome of governance. Clarity about procedures may be lacking, and/or the structure may not follow the prescriptions listed in the articles of incorporation. More often than not, the implementation process is inadequate, rather than the prescribed structure and process. For example, members of the governing body and/or advisory board may not be formally oriented to the organization's goals, objectives, structure, and methods of operation, or they may lack sufficient familiarity with agency programs and services. Scheduled orientation for the governing body, including site visits to the agency and a comprehensive board manual, help to provide governing members with the information they need to carry out their function effectively. Orientation should be formal and include a review of organization and board goals, objectives, programs, methods, and finances (COA, 1997).

The organizational structure and size of the governing body and advisory board, if applicable, should be adequate to carry out appropriate responsibilities for adoption of policies, selection and evaluation of the chief executive officer, strategic planning, financial oversight, resource development, and community-organization relationships. Larger organizations are likely to carry out their work through a detailed committee or task group structure, whereas a small organization/board may not require an elaborate committee structure to accomplish these goals.

In voluntary, not-for-profit organizations, the board of directors is responsible for adopting the policies of the organization. The governing body that is effectively fulfilling its role will actively exercise its policy-setting prerogatives, periodically review policies, and address specific (new or revisited) policy matters on a frequent basis. Policy is viewed as the board's major means of providing a framework and guidance for the organization's overall direction. In public and some for-profit organizations, advisory boards typically have input into policy making, but such input may carry different degrees of influence depending on the specific situation, and recommendations may not

necessarily be binding on the organization's management.

Delegation of Operating Authority

The auspice or operating authority under which an organization functions influences how the day-to-day management is carried out. Most organizations, regardless of auspice, delegate the management of the organization to a chief executive officer (CEO). In the case of a for-profit organization, this CEO may be the owner or managing partner. Except when the organization is for-profit and owner-operated, it is the governing body or the designated authority acting for the governing body (in the case of a public organization) that has responsibility for appointing the CEO and delegating authority and responsibility for the organization's management and implementation of policy.

The CEO's job description will vary depending on organizational structure. Among the responsibilities typically delegated to the chief executive officer are

- planning and coordinating with the governing body and, where the organization is so constituted, its advisory board, the development of policies governing the organization's program of services
- attending all meetings of the governing body and/or voluntary board and their standing and ad hoc committees and task forces, with the possible exception of those held for the purpose of reviewing the executive's performance, status, or compensation (COA, 1997)

In addition, the CEO is delegated authority for ensuring that the organization's personnel management is in accord with written organizational policy. In practice, it is not unusual for there to be some confusion as to the respective roles of the board and the CEO. This is because governance is more a shared function than classical organizational theory suggests. For example, it is appropriate for the CEO to identify policy needs and make recommendations to the board. On the other hand, the board has some jurisdiction over the responsibilities of the CEO, such as the development of policy to guide the organization's management in personnel matters.

No matter what the operating authority of the organization, the CEO is held accountable for organizational performance. A major means of holding the CEO accountable is through periodic reports to the governing body. The COA (1997), one of the major voluntary accrediting bodies for social service agencies, recommends that the CEO report to the governing body at least quarterly about program operations and compliance with organizational goals, the financial status of the organization, funding issues and alternatives, and longer term financial planning. It is the job of the governing body to evaluate the CEO's performance based on written performance criteria and objectives.

When the owner/operator of a proprietary organization fulfills the functions of leadership and management, an advisory board may provide input to the owner/governing body. However, the extent to which such mechanisms are formalized and provide systematic and ongoing input is likely to vary substantially, depending on the style of management and preferences of the owner. The likelihood that decision-making authority will be centralized in one individual or a small group of individuals is greater in for-profit and public organizations than in non-profits. The board of directors holds clear decision-making authority in nonprofit organizations, whereas other organizational types have fewer legal and traditional restrictions to centralization of authority. Centralization is typically accompanied by a high degree of formalization, characteristic of the public agency, in which prescribed procedures detail how work is to be accomplished, and a division of labor is established that assigns responsibility for task completion (Glisson, 1985).

Substructures

The legal or operating authority of a human service organization, in combination with its mission and pattern of governance, provides its structural and overarching parameters. Organizations, once created, seek to establish systems to carry out their work and, furthermore, to ensure their own survival and growth. This self-protective aspect of organizations encourages the development of substructures, both formal and informal, that affect how and how well the work of the organization is carried out.

An organizational chart is one of the commonly used ways of describing the structure of an organization and includes its lines of authority, relationships, and substructures (which may be called departments, units, or divisions). Such charts, however, do not show the informal structures, which often have a profound impact on how the organization functions.

Formal substructures include personnel and their relationship to one another, appointed and elected committees, and board-administration-staff arrangements. Although staff interactions are included as a component of the formal substructure, an informal system operates, as well. Formal staff interactions generally refer to those prescribed in the organization's policies and procedures. The informal substructures refer to arrangements and operations that are separate from and outside of the codified, regular, and planned structure of the agency (Skidmore, 1990), particularly in regard to communication systems. Glisson (1985) describes such informal arrangements under the rubric of a "psychosocial subsystem," involving the psychological and social relationship factors that affect the behavior of personnel and, consequently, the performance of the entire organization (p. 97). The human relations model of organizations, concerned with the environment in which work is carried out, has sought to explain organizational behavior in terms of "human factors" such as personalities, motivation, job satisfaction, anxiety, attitudes, and interpersonal interactions (see, e.g., Argyris, 1957; Bennis, 1967; Bolman & Deal, 1997; Likert, 1967).

Another substructure can be found in vertical and horizontal dimensions. The classic bureaucratic organization illustrates a vertical structure, with a hierarchy of personnel from top to bottom. Horizontal arrangements concern a particular level within the structure that goes sideways (Skidmore, 1990). Horizontal arrangements reflect the division of tasks within an organization according to specialized knowledge and skills; they can also reflect distinct programs, such as foster care, day care, family counseling, and adoption offered under the umbrella of one organization (Page, 1988).

In general, smaller organizations, typical of the community-based nonprofit, will show characteristics of horizontal structure, with an emphasis on teams, working groups, and open communication. Although there is clear assign-

ment of the leadership function, decision making, it is claimed, is more democratic and takes into account the input of personnel and key players as appropriate through, for example, strategic planning and evaluation of services (Oster, 1995). Kramer (1981) sees nonprofits as "open systems" in regard to their use of volunteers, their involvement with the community in the identification of service needs, and the board structure, which tends to be large relative to for-profit boards and more diversified in terms of composition. However, Kramer also argues that decision making is still concentrated in the hands of a relatively small group. Research is needed to determine the extent to which the various arenas of input into organizational planning and decision making actually function in the open system manner desired and perceived by some, or whether open versus closed characterizations are a matter of degree as represented by a continuum. When horizontal arrangements predominate, the need for coordination between divisions of the organization is accentuated.

Size has been viewed as an important determinant of the overall structure of an organization and the nature and breadth of its substructures. Large public bureaucracies, for example, are characterized by centralization of decision making and formalization of work procedures through guidelines and a clear division of labor to allocate responsibility for the organization's work (Glisson, 1985). This type of subsystem is described best in the classic rational models of organizations such as those of Weber (1922/1994) and Taylor (1916/1996).

The range of potential subsystems is great. Geography, for example, may require multiservice sites to provide accessibility for clients. These satellite service centers constitute a decentralized subsystem to control the local implementation of programs and services. Public human service agencies are often structured on a county-by-county basis, with varying degrees of control from the umbrella state organization. Page (1988) refers to these arrangements as "spatial dispersion" (p. 54). The size of the organization, the number of clients served, and the range of programs it offers are also important variables in determining the need for and nature of subsystems.

Professionals and Organizational Structure

The influence of the professionals who are employed within organizations is another factor in understanding organizational structure and functioning; professionals, in fact, constitute a subsystem and culture within most organizations. Meyer and Rowan (1983) propose that each profession attempts to realize its values and norms in regard to the configuration of human service organizations. Similarly, in their view, professionals will also, to varying degrees, ignore, circumvent, or possibly challenge organizational structures that conflict with professional beliefs and domain. The professionals employed within human service organizations are thus in a position to influence organizational structure and behavior (Page, 1988).

As human service organizations proliferated in the 1960s in size, type, and scope of activity, scholars began to focus on the conflicts or points of congruence between professionals and bureaucracies (see, e.g., Etzioni, 1969; Freidson, 1974; Scott, 1966). By virtue of their training and ability to perform specialized tasks autonomously, professionals could, understandably, have different priorities and work styles than those of the employing organization.

In ideal form, the employee would identify with and have unconditional loyalty to the organization, with a high level of acceptance of the goals and activities of the organization and consistent values and norms (Scott, 1966). However, professional ethos is a potent influence and conflict can often occur.

One means of addressing the conflict is to create informal systems, as discussed above, that may circumvent and override formal processes. The extent to which the professional culture, in the form of a subsystem, develops and persists depends on the degree of accommodation between professional norms and values and organizational demands. As noted by Hasenfeld and English (1974), "The critical issue is the extent to which professional norms and values will determine organizational structure and service delivery patterns, or the extent to which organizational demands and exigencies will influence professional practice" (p. 414).

It is not uncommon to hear social workers voice dissatisfaction with their employing organization. Typical career development patterns show that social workers tend to switch jobs several times, particularly in the earlier days of their practice (Gibelman, 1995b). Such patterns are probably based in the conflict between what practitioners learn in their professional education and their experience on the job. Professionally trained practitioners in the public sector tend to express the highest level of dissatisfaction; this is not a surprise, because in this arena, the classic division of labor, hierarchy of authority, and procedural specifications are most characteristic (see, e.g., Ginsberg, 1983). Nonprofits are often the employing agency of choice because of the more professional atmosphere and greater level of participation in decision making.

TABLE 6.2 Sources of Funding by Type of Organization

Organizational Type	Primary Source of Funding
Public	Government (legislative) allocations
	Occasional private funds for special purposes (such as Fannie Mae support for computerization)
Nonprofit	Direct contributions (bequests, donations)
	Fee-for-services
	Government grants and contracts
	Foundations
	Campaigns (e.g., United Way, Combined Federal Campaign)
	Medicaid/Medicare
For-profit	Fee-for-services
	Government grants and contracts
	Medicaid/Medicare

FINANCING

Historically, the three sectors have been identified with different and noncompeting financial bases. The public sector, of course, has its financial base in public allocations, which, in turn, come from tax dollars. This is as true today as it was at the time of the nation's founding. The nonprofit sector receives a large proportion of its financing from charitable contributions, including monies earmarked to specific types of organizations through the United Way of America and other combined campaigns. For-profit organizations are associated with fee-for-service financing, in which individuals or groups pay for the services rendered according to fees established by the organization based on what the market will bear. However, these historic patterns have changed dramatically in recent years.

Nonprofit organizations have, since the very beginning of public financing of social services, been the recipient of government funds to implement specific programs of service. Historical examples include early arrangements for the provision of public relief, in which the rudimentary system of outdoor relief administered by some local authorities was augmented by a system of contracting out and a related practice of auctioning off the aged, poor, or orphaned to private individuals for care (Gibelman & Demone, 1989). Traditionally, state and local governments have chosen to meet part of their responsibilities by financing the provision of care and services by local, nongovernmental organizations. The relationship between nonprofits and governments thus has a long history, the nature of which has varied over time depending on changing conceptions of the role and functions of each sector.

As illustrated in Table 6.2, there is substantial overlap in the funding base of nonprofits and for-profits, although the relative weight for each funding source differs substantially. For example, fees for service constitute a larger proportion of revenues for for-profits than for nonprofits, examples of which include nursing homes and day care centers.

In 1992, private contributions constituted 18% of the total funds received by nonprofit agencies (24,456 organizations qualify as tax exempt under 501[c][3] of the tax code, including those providing health, education, social, legal, and cultural programs and services), down from 26% in 1977. Funds received from government represented 27% of total revenues in 1977 and 31% in 1992. Private payments, including dues, fees, and charges, represented 39% of revenues, up from 38% in 1977 (Hodgkinson & Weitzman, 1996). Between 1977 and 1996, more than half of the growth in revenue for nonprofit organizations came from fees and other earned income (Moore, 1998). Comparable data for the for-profit sector are not available.

With the shift in funding patterns, for-profit and nonprofit organizations are increasingly competing for the same pools of money. At the same time, the growth in contracting has diminished the people-serving functions of most public agencies, while increasing the proportionate share of the service market held by the private sector. As discussed below, these shifts have had pronounced and long-term affects on organizational structure, mission, and operations.

THE REALITY OF BOUNDARY BLURRING

Despite distinct attributes in the operating authority, mission, patterns of governance, and mode of operation of each sector, public and private organizations are becoming more alike and represent a continuum rather than pure types. This hybrid model is largely the result of funding patterns, as the functions performed by organizations increasingly overlap and/or duplicate each other (Gibelman & Demone, 1989). Similar types of organizations, such as those offering home health care, may be under different auspices. Community mental health agencies similarly vary. The range of organizational types is illustrated in Table 6.3.

Nongovernment Preferences

Since the mid-1970s, the concept and practice of privatization has been widespread in all sectors of the economy, including human services. Privatization refers to the divesting of government responsibility for the funding and provision of products or services (Gibelman, 1998). Within the human services, privatization in its purest form is unlikely, because government maintains a substantial role in the financing of services. However, one of the prevailing themes of the last two decades has been that of promoting linkages between the public and private sector and, in so doing, to shift heretofore public functions and responsibilities to the private sector (Gibelman, 1998). The political ideology favoring the reduction of the size and power of government is centered not only on anti-government sentiment and intolerance of abuses of the public trust, but also on the belief that the private sector can do a better job (Gibelman, 1998; Morin, 1995; Passell, 1998). In its present form, such divestiture has been termed "reinventing government" by the Clinton administration. Its goal is to reduce the federal bureaucracy by 12% or more (Barr, 1993; Clinton, 1993; Ingraham, Thompson, & Sanders, 1995). New and revised structural forms for state and local agencies have been an

TABLE 6.3 Types of Health and Human Service Organizations: Boundary Blurring

Public	Quasi-Public	Quasi-Private	Private
Classic bureaucratic agencies with civil service personnel	Quangos[a]	Privately owned and operated	Privately owned and operated
Legal mandates	Almost exclusive reliance on public funds	Governed by board of directors	Governed by board of directors or advisory board
Tax supported	Missions consistent with public purposes	Missions may not be consistent with public purposes	Mission established by charter
Public authority	Includes Legal Aid agencies, earlier Office of Economic Opportunity agencies using private charters, and regional health planning	Use private charters but now receive a high proportion of funds from public sources, for example, nursing homes, visiting nurse or homemaker service	Could operate effectively without any public support but may engage in contracting
Can delegate some responsibilities through contracts	May be for-profit or not-for-profit	May be for-profit or not-for-profit	Usually for-profit but may have not-for-profit subsidiary, or vice versa

SOURCE: Adapted from Gibelman and Demone (1989).

a. "Quangos" is a term that began to emerge in the 1980s in the press and in articles concerning contracting relationships. It refers to the creation and rise of quasi-public organizations as part of the contracted human services system, with some of the attributes of nonprofit organizations, but with a greater degree of dependence on public funds. In fact, some nonprofits have been created solely because of the availability of government funds for earmarked purposes. For a related discussion, see Demone and Gibelman (1989).

inevitable consequence as federal programs shrank and program management was delegated to the states (Glisson, 1985; Page, 1988).

It is important to note that some of the negative structural features of public agencies led to the desire to seek alternative means of delivering services (see, e.g., Weiss, 1989). The rigidity of bureaucratic rules as these affected clients, the anti-professionalism associated with the public sector, and the slow, cumbersome, user-unfriendly systems were epitomized in a service delivery system that was unpopular with social workers, clients, politicians, and the public at large.

Purchase of Service

In light of the concurrent movements to decentralize decision making and service delivery, to de-bureaucratize and de-federalize and, in the affirmative, to privatize human services, among other enterprises, purchasing services from the private sector is a favored means of delivering social services. In recent years, it has been estimated that over 50% of the services offered by nonprofit human service agencies are financed by government through grants and contracts (Gibelman, 1998), resulting in upward of $15 billion a year in government financing of nonprofit services (Smith & Lipsky, 1993). Adding to this is the billions of dollars annually spent on health and human services through Medicaid and Medicare, in which consumers are given the responsibility of selecting their own provider of choice.

The old adage "he who pays the piper calls the tune" is an apt description of the end result of these contracting arrangements. On the positive side, nonprofits have, as a condition of government funding, had to develop new management competencies, including negotiating skills and financial accountability systems. Nonprofit agencies have been able to introduce new programs and services, and in some cases, voluntary agencies have come into being as a direct result of the availability of public funds to finance particular types of services, such as assistance to victims of crime (Smith, 1989). The negative by-products of these public-private relationships, however, are formidable. Questions about the autonomy of nonprofits have increasingly been raised (Gibelman, 1995a), as these contracted agencies must modify their service delivery systems to align with public program priorities and as the public sector becomes more vigilant in its accountability requirements. The consequences of contracting have been seen as so pervasive that nonprofits have been accused of becoming agents of the state (Goldstein, 1993). The key factor in this transformation has been the growing reliance of nonprofits on contract funds, making them resource-dependent on government. (For an extensive discussion of actual and perceived effects of this resource-dependence, see Kramer, 1994.)

The 1967 amendments to the Social Security Act, for the first time, authorized states to purchase services from nonprofit or proprietary

agencies. Initially, government was looking for service providers, and nonprofits were in a positive negotiating position. As these arrangements mushroomed, the public sector began to impose its own bureaucratic rules and regulations on its contracted providers, focused not only on the outcomes of such services but also on the process in which programs and services were carried out (Gibelman, 1998). Both profit and nonprofit agencies contracting to do business with government have thus, themselves, taken on some of the bureaucratic features typically associated with the public sector.

Purchase-of-service arrangements have also led nonprofits down the road of goal displacement. As nonprofits sought to take advantage of existing or new public funds, they initiated some programs that may not have been on target or consistent with their mission. The end result has been a dilemma: To what extent should organizational maintenance and growth needs take precedence over organizational mission (Gibelman, 1998)? Such questions are less pertinent to for-profit organizations engaged in contracting, because their mission is defined as profitability.

Besides their relationship with government through contracts, nonprofits are also the beneficiary of public policy on their behalf. For example, nonprofits benefit from government largesse in regard to special postage rates that are federally subsidized. (However, a 1993 law changed the way that Congress subsidizes the U.S. Postal Service for delivering nonprofit mail; federal subsidies are gradually being phased out; Hall, 1998.) The Internal Revenue Service sets interest rates (typically below market rates) for computing charitable deductions for trusts, gift annuities, charitable lead trusts, and some other deferred gifts (Billitteri &

Stehle, 1998). And, of course, taxpayers benefit from their ability to claim tax deductions for charitable giving in cash and kind. There is increased pressure on Congress to pass new tax incentives to encourage charitable giving, particularly at a time in which nonprofit organizations are seen as key players in solving the country's problems ("Panel on Civic Renewal," 1998). Such positive impacts of public policy further highlight the interdependence between the sectors.

For-profits, too, continue to extend their boundaries as the human services are now fair game for private enterprise. Despite authorization to contract with for-profits dating back to the 1960s, the closer relationship between government and nonprofits favored purchase of service from the nonprofit sector. However, lawmakers continued to look for service-delivery options as intractable social problems remained just that—intractable. A viable option was to open the door to businesses to compete for government contracts for a larger array of social service programs, with the hope that new alternatives might be found, and increased competition would lead to better cost-efficiency (Moore, 1998).

In 1996, Connecticut became the first state to retain a private company, Maximus, Inc., of McLean, Virginia, to manage its entire program of child care benefits and services for families on welfare and the working poor (Rabinovitz, 1997). A year later, the company was at risk of losing the $12.8 million contract because the system it was hired to fix had become more rather than less problem plagued. Such an outcome is not a surprise, nor unique to for-profits. A primary rationale for using purchase-of-service ar-

rangements is their ability to implement new programs quickly and effectively (Gibelman, 1998). However, what constitutes rapid response time on the part of the government agency paying the bill may be perceived as unreasonable and unrealistic by the contracted party. Nevertheless, in this instance, Connecticut remains committed to privatization of its welfare system, whether it be with the current company or another for-profit.

The special arenas of nonprofit programs are thus dissipating as a direct result of public policy choices. The 1996 welfare reform law furthered the competition among the sectors by allowing for-profits to bid against nonprofits and state and local public agencies for billions of dollars in job-training contracts. For-profits were also allowed to compete for about $3 billion a year in contract funds to run foster care programs (Moore, 1998). Even privatization of Head Start is being considered by Congress, with the first step taken by the Senate in July 1998 to approve legislation that would allow for-profits to apply for funds heretofore restricted to nonprofits and government agencies (Moore, 1998).

As we look toward the future, we are likely to see increased competition between not-for-profit and for-profit organizations, as well as the continued decline in the direct-service role of the public sector. Indeed, one of the hallmarks of the last decade has been the proliferation of for-profit companies offering services previously provided primarily by nonprofit and government organizations, including, most recently, the field of job training (Moore, 1998). Such competition had already been experienced by nonprofit hospitals, many of which were taken over by for-profit chains or were forced to merge or restructure their operations to continue on a fiscally sound basis (Moore, 1998). Conversion of organizations from one type to another—profit to nonprofit or non-profit to profit—is also having the effect of dissipating the traditional distinctions among and between the sectors. Such conversions have been notable in the health field, not only in hospitals and nursing homes but also in the health maintenance industry. Such conversions from nonprofit to for-profit, investor-owned entities have raised concerns about the focus on profitability and the potential for inappropriate, aggressive marketing and pricing strategies to achieve financial gain. The fallout is expected in regard to a potential decline in the quality of care (Langwell, 1990).

Boundary blurring between the sectors continues to be a pervasive phenomenon, and government has inserted itself even more to ensure that nonprofits maintain their unique charitable focus. A current example of such government oversight can be seen in Section 4958 of the Internal Revenue Code, enacted as an amendment on July 30, 1996. Known as the Taxpayer Bill of Rights 2, Public Law 104-168 (110 Stat. 1452), this amendment seeks to control "excessive" pay of nonprofit executives. Excess benefits are subject to tax and penalties and are defined as "any transaction in which an economic benefit provided by an applicable tax-exempt organization to, or for the use of, any disqualified person exceeds the value of consideration received by the organization in exchange for the benefit" (Internal Revenue Service, 1998). The independence of the independent sector is further diminished to the ex-tent that government can now decide on the limits of nonprofit executive pay.

CONCLUSION

All organizations have formal structures through which to carry out their work and achieve the purposes for which they were created. Within the human services, typologies have been developed on the basis of the operating authority under which such organizations were created and their mission established. However, it may well be that the traditional classifications of human service organizations are more accurate in theory than in practice. In light of the pervasive blurring of boundaries between "pure" types of organizations—public, nonprofit, and for-profit—we have witnessed, and continue to observe, the creation of hybrid human service agencies. As the public sector has transferred direct service responsibility to the private sector, the competition between the for-profit and not-for-profit sectors has increased. Questions are being raised about whether nonprofit groups have sufficiently prepared themselves for the aggressive level of competition from for-profits (Moore, 1998). If the answer proves to be in the negative, nonprofits could be out of the running.

Complicating the picture is the increased congressional scrutiny of the preferred tax status nonprofits receive. Policymakers are examining whether and to what extent the programs run by tax-exempt organizations differ from those run by for-profit companies. Indeed, such an examination appears warranted in light of the boundary blurring that has primarily resulted from large-scale government contracting. The desire on the part of government to establish alternative service-delivery structures, using the expertise of the private sector has, ironically, threatened the distinctive character of the private sector.

Modifications in formal and informal structural relationships have resulted from the complex mosaic of funding patterns and the ongoing preference to shrink the government system in favor of the private sector. Whereas in earlier days, nonprofits were in the favored and sometimes exclusive position of providing government-funded services through contracts, the market is now open, and the distinctive attributes of each type of agency continue to fade. Those concerned with the structure of human service organizations—administrators, practitioners, consumers, and scholars—need to be ever vigilant in monitoring the impact of funding patterns on organizational structure and modifying conceptions of organizational types and functions on the basis of the new realities.

REFERENCES

Ackerman, J. (1998, January 25). Schoolchildren as commodities? For-profits seek to revive education. *Boston Globe*, p. C1.

Argyris, C. (1957). The individual and organization: Some problems of mutual adjustment. *Administrative Science Quarterly, 2*, 1-24.

Axelrod, N. R. (1994). Board leadership and board development. In R. D. Herman & Associates (Eds.), *The Jossey-Bass handbook of nonprofit leadership and management* (pp. 119-136). San Francisco: Jossey-Bass.

Barker, R. (1995). *Social work dictionary* (3rd ed.). Washington, DC: NASW Press.

Barr, S. (1993, September 5). Gore report targets 252,000 federal jobs. *Washington Post*, pp. A1, A18.

Bennis, W. (1967). Organizations of the future. *Personnel Administration, 30*, 6-19.

Billitteri, T. J., & Stehle, V. (1998, July 16). Charities breathe easier after court decision on gift annuities; model law delayed. *Chronicle of Philanthropy*, p. 40.

Bolman, L. E., & Deal, T. E. (1997). *Reframing organizations* (2nd ed.). San Francisco: Jossey-Bass.

Brown, F. (1994). Resisting the pull of the health insurance tarbaby: An organizational model for surviving managed care. *Clinical Social Work Journal, 22*, 59-71.

Clinton, W. (1993). *A vision of change for America*. Washington, DC: Government Printing Office.

Council on Accreditation of Services for Families and Children. (1997). *Behavioral health care standards: United States edition*. New York: Author.

Demone, H. W., Jr., & Gibelman, M. (Eds.). (1989). *Services for sale: Purchasing health and human services*. New Brunswick, NJ: Rutgers University Press.

Eisenberg, P. (1990, July 10). Europe's nascent non-profits turn to America. *Chronicle of Philanthropy*, p. 35.

Etzioni, A. (Ed.). (1969). *The semi-professions and their organization*. New York: Free Press.

Freidson, E. (1974). Dominant professions, bureaucracy, and client services. In Y. Hasenfeld & R. A. English (Eds.), *Human service organizations* (pp. 428-447). Ann Arbor: University of Michigan Press.

Gibelman, M. (1995a). Purchasing social services. In R. L. Edwards (Ed.-in-Chief), *Encyclopedia of social work* (19th ed., pp. 1998-2007). Washington, DC: NASW Press.

Gibelman, M. (1995b). *What social workers do*. Washington, DC: NASW Press.

Gibelman, M. (1998). Theory, practice, and experience in the purchase of services. In M. Gibelman & H. W. Demone, Jr. (Eds.), *The privatization of human services: Policy and practice issues* (Vol. 1, pp. 1-51). New York: Springer.

Gibelman, M., & Demone, H. R., Jr. (1989). The evolving contract state. In H. W. Demone, Jr., & M. Gibelman (Eds.), *Services for sale: Purchasing health and human services* (pp. 17-57). New Brunswick, NJ: Rutgers University Press.

Gibelman, M., & Demone, H. W., Jr. (1990). Negotiating: A tool for inter-organizational coordination. *Administration in Social Work, 14*(4), 29-42.

Gibelman, M., & Schervish, P. (1997). *Who we are: A second look*. Washington, DC: NASW Press.

Ginsberg, L. (1983). *The practice of social work in public welfare*. New York: Free Press.

Glisson, C. A. (1985). A contingency model of social welfare administration. In S. Slavin (Ed.), *An introduction to human services management* (2nd ed., Vol. 1, pp. 95-109). New York: Haworth.

Goldstein, H. (1993, July 13). Government contracts are emasculating boards and turning charities into agents of the state. *Chronicle of Philanthropy,* p. 41.

Hall, H. (1998, July 16). Non-profit groups gird for double-digit increases in postage rates. *Chronicle of Philanthropy,* p. 39.

Hall, R. H. (1982). *Organizations: Structure and process* (3rd ed.). Englewood Cliffs, NJ: Prentice Hall.

Hasenfeld, Y. (1983). *Human service organizations.* Englewood Cliffs, NJ: Prentice Hall.

Hasenfeld, Y. (1984). The changing context of human service administration. *Social Work, 29*(6), 522-529.

Hasenfeld, Y., & English, R. A. (1974). *Human service organizations.* Ann Arbor: University of Michigan Press.

Hodgkinson, V. A., & Weitzman, M. S. (1996). *Nonprofit almanac, 1996-1997: Dimensions of the independent sector.* San Francisco: Jossey-Bass.

Ingraham, P. W., Thompson, J. R., & Sanders, R. P. (Eds.). (1995). *Transforming government.* San Francisco: Jossey-Bass.

Internal Revenue Service. (1998, August). *Text of proposed I.R.S. rules on excess compensation,* 26 CRF Parts 53 and 301. Available: http://philanthrop.com/update.dir/ regstext.htm

Katz, D., & Kahn, R. L. (1978). *The social psychology of organizations* (2nd ed.). New York: John Wiley.

Kramer, R. M. (1981). *Voluntary agencies in the welfare state.* Berkeley: University of California Press.

Kramer, R. M. (1994). Voluntary agencies and the contract culture: "Dream or nightmare?" *Social Service Review, 68*(1), 33-60.

Langwell, K. M. (1990). Structure and performance of health maintenance organizations: A review. *Health Care Financing Review, 12,* 1-26.

Likert, R. (1967). *The human organization.* New York: McGraw-Hill.

Lowenstein, S. (1964). *Private practice in social casework.* New York: Columbia University Press.

Meyer, J. W., & Rowan, B. (1983). Institutionalized organizations: Formal structure as myth and ceremony. In J. W. Meyer & W. R. Scott (Eds.), *Organizational environments.* Beverly Hills, CA: Sage.

Moore, J. (1998, August 13). A corporate challenge for charities. *Chronicle of Philanthropy,* p. 1, 34-36.

Morales, A. T., & Sheafor, B. R. (1992). *Social work: A profession of many faces* (6th ed.). Needham Heights, MA: Allyn & Bacon.

Morin, R. (1995, October 11). A united opinion: Government doesn't go a good job. *Washington Post,* p. A12.

National Center for Charitable Statistics and The Foundation Center. (1993). *The national taxonomy of exempt entities* (rev. ed.). Washington, DC: Independent Sector.

Oster, S. M. (1995). *Strategic management for nonprofit organizations: Theory and cases.* New York: Oxford University Press.

Page, W. J. (1988). Organizational structure and service delivery arrangements in human services. In J. Rabin & M. B. Steinhauer (Eds.), *Handbook on human services administration* (pp. 45-75). New York: Marcel Dekker.

Panel on civic renewal adds another voice to calls for tax incentives to promote giving. (1998, July 16). *Chronicle of Philanthropy,* p. 51.

Passell, P. (1998, January 5). Doing the American-opposition-to-big-government 2-step. *New York Times,* p. D10.

Rabinovitz, J. (1997, October 24). Company hits snags running welfare plan. *New York Times,* p. A25.

Salamon, L. M. (1994). The nonprofit sector and the evolution of the American welfare state. In R. D. Herman & Associates (Eds.), *The Jossey-Bass handbook of nonprofit leadership and management* (pp. 83-116). San Francisco: Jossey-Bass.

Scott, R. W. (1966). Professionals in bureaucracies—areas of conflict. In H. M. Vollmer & D. L. Mills (Eds.), *Professionalization* (pp. 264-275). Englewood Cliffs, NJ: Prentice Hall.

Skidmore, R. A. (1990). *Social work administration* (2nd ed.). Englewood Cliffs, NJ: Prentice Hall.

Smith, S. R. (1989). Federal funding, nonprofit agencies, and victim services. In H. W. Demone, Jr., & M. Gibelman (Eds.), *Services for sale: Purchasing health and human services* (pp. 215-227). New Brunswick, NJ: Rutgers University Press.

Smith, S. R., & Lipsky, M. (1993). *Nonprofits for hire: The welfare state in the age of contracting.* Cambridge, MA: Harvard University Press.

Taylor, F. W. (1996). The principles of scientific management. In J. M. Shafritz & J. S. Ott (Eds.), *Classics of organization theory* (4th ed., pp. 66-79). New York: Harcourt Brace. (Original work published 1916)

Weber, M. (1994). Bureaucracy. In F. Fischer & C. Sirianni (Eds.), *Critical studies in organization and bureaucracy* (2nd ed., pp. 4-19). Philadelphia: Temple University Press. (Original work published 1922)

Weinbach, R. W. (1994). *The social worker as manager: Theory and practice* (2nd ed.). Boston: Allyn & Bacon.

Weiss, R. M. (1989). Organizational structure in human service agencies. In L. E. Miller (Ed.), *Managing human service organizations* (pp. 21-38). New York: Quorum Books.

Wellford, W. H., & Gallagher, J. G. (1988). *Unfair competition: The challenge to charitable exemption.* Washington, DC: The National Assembly of National Voluntary Health and Social Welfare Organizations.

CHAPTER SEVEN

Agency-Environment Relations: Understanding Task Environments

HILLEL SCHMID

This chapter presents the main theoretical approaches that describe and analyze the relations between organizations and their environments. The first part provides a definition of organizational environment and a typology of environments, followed by a presentation of the main theoretical approaches: organization adaptation theories, ecological theory, and institutional theory. The discussion highlights the unique contribution of each theory toward understanding organization-environment relations, as well as the connections between the theories. In addition, the chapter deals with strategies of adaptation to changing environments. The concluding section discusses the relationships that emerge between characteristics of the environment and strategies, structure of organizations, and internal processes,

mainly in human service and social welfare organizations.

ORGANIZATIONAL ENVIRONMENTS: DEFINITION

Organizational environment has been defined as all external conditions that actually or potentially affect the organization (Hawley, 1968), or as conditions and constraints outside of the organization that affect its functioning. The environment includes individuals, groups, and organizations, as well as state and institutional systems. It encompasses social, economic, cultural, political, religious, technological, military, legal, demographic, geographic, ecological, and physical elements representing ethics, beliefs, and behavior norms that influence the goals and functioning of the organization (Lammers & Hickson, 1979).

One major approach to describing organization-environment relations emphasizes the difference between the objective environment and the subjective or perceived environment, which is the product of the actor's perceptions of environmental conditions and individual attributes (Duncan, 1972; Starbuck, 1976; Weick, 1979). According to this approach, organizations respond to what they perceive, and unnoticed events do not affect them (Leifer & Huber, 1977; Miles, Snow, & Pfeffer, 1974; Yasai-Ardekani, 1986). Organizations may, however, perceive the same environmental attributes differently. "The same environment one organization perceives as unpredictable, complex, and evanescent, another organization might see as static and easily understood" (Starbuck, 1976, p. 1080). Indeed, Miles et al.'s (1974) study of publishing companies revealed that top managers in some organizations perceived no changes or uncertainties in their environments, whereas managers at the same level in other organizations perceived continuous changes and considerable uncertainty (Yasai-Ardekani, 1986).

However, organizations not only perceive and interpret their environment, they also create and influence it. In this connection, it is assumed that "if one defines situations as real, their outcomes are real" (Thomas, 1928). Weick (1976) uses the term *enactment* to emphasize the more active role played by individuals and organizational participants in defining the environments they confront. According to Weick (1976), "the concept of an enacted environment is not synonymous with the concept of a perceived environment." Rather, the label enactment "is meant to emphasize [that] managers construct, rearrange, single out, and demolish many objective features of their surroundings" (p. 164). The process of enacting is one in which "the subject partly interacts with and constitutes the object" (p. 165). The organization does more than observe and interpret: It modifies and directly influences the state of its environment through its own actions (Scott, 1992) and "through information and the creation of meaning" (Kreps, 1987, p. 116).

Within the environment, the organization defines its domain. The domain identifies the points at which the organization is dependent on inputs from the environment (Thompson, 1967, p. 27). It consists of the claims it makes with respect to products or services provided, the technology employed, population served, and services rendered (Hardy, 1994; Levine & White, 1961). In defining its domain, the organization has to create a unique identity that differentiates it from other organizations. The organization must determine its added value, in addition to developing its distinctive competence in terms of human, material, and technological relative advantages. To the extent that the organization succeeds in defining its unique identity and distinctive competence, it will be able to change power-dependence relations with its environment and ensure a steady flow of resources.

The organization also defines its boundaries through negotiations and bargaining with elements in the task environment. There is no need for formal, rigid definitions of these boundaries. Rather, the organization should be attentive to developments and changes in its environment and should recognize the boundaries of other organizations there. In the case of human, social, community, and voluntary organizations, the boundaries cannot be so rigid that they obstruct mutual influence and accessibility to clients. Clients must be able to voice their opinions, particularly in community service organizations, which expect their clients to be partners in designing and implementing service programs (Hasenfeld & Schmid, 1989).

Given this situation, it has been argued that "the establishment of a domain cannot be an arbitrary, unilateral action. Only if the organization's claims to domain are recognized by those who can provide the necessary support, by the task environment, can a domain be operational" (Thompson, 1967, p. 28). This is the *domain consensus,* which Thompson defines as "a set of expectations both for members of an organization and for others with whom they interact about what the organization will and will not do" (p. 26).

Legitimation of the organization's domain is expressed formally and informally. Specifically, legitimation means acquiring social support and approval from actors in the surrounding environment, which ensures the organization's right to survive. Such approval and support position the organization in the environment and enable it to acquire resources. Once the organization receives legitimation, it is also possible to deflect questions regarding its right to provide specific resources or products. From the formal perspective, the organization requires accreditation and licensing by the formal authorities and establishment (government, municipal, local, and others). At the same time, it should be noted that in the early stages of their existence, organizations require resources that ensure their survival, even before they receive formal legitimation. On the informal level, legitimation is provided by clients who consume the products and/or services offered by the organization. In so doing, they confirm the need for its

existence and largely influence its ability to function independently. The greater the extent of legitimacy, the stronger the position of the organization in its environment and the greater its ability to make elements in the environment more dependent on its services. Legitimation derives from relations that the organization develops with actors in the external environment. Thus, for example, Baum and Oliver (1991) found that day care centers and nursery schools that have established linkages to organizations such as community centers and municipal authorities showed a survival advantage over those without such linkages. This advantage increased significantly with the intensity of competition.

TYPOLOGY OF ENVIRONMENTS: GENERAL AND TASK ENVIRONMENTS

Classic organizational literature distinguishes between general environments and task environments (Dill, 1958; Evan, 1966; Hasenfeld, 1983), as well as between milieus and niches (Kurke & Ulrich, 1988).

Milieu refers to the general environment, which consists of conditions external to the organization. The focal organization has little or no control over many of the external conditions, such as technological change, culture, labor markets, demography, climate, volatility, rates of change, munificence, grain, and uncertainty. *Niche* refers to the task environment, which consists of actors external to the organization with whom the focal organization transacts directly and whom the focal organization can influence.

This distinction between the two environments was made in the 1960s and 1970s, in an attempt to describe changes and trends in the general environment that affect the organization but are not felt directly or immediately. Specifically, task environment referred specifically to the environment in which organizations negotiate to exchange inputs for outputs. In the 1990s, however, when modern technology and rapid changes have turned the world into a small village, there is no longer a need for a formal distinction between the task and general environments. It is difficult to view the task environment as a filter of constraints and effects in the general environment, because these effects derive from both environments and are almost equally relevant to the organization's activities as well as to its strategic, structural, and organizational behavior. It can therefore be argued that the environment is characterized by several factors and distinctions (e.g., economic, social, cultural, political, technological, and sociodemographic) that actually or potentially affect the organization, its policies, espoused goals, and operative goals.

National economy has an immediate impact on the economic stability of organizations. Decisions related to monetary or fiscal changes have implications for the decisions and behavior of organizations, whereas economic prosperity and recession affect decision making and allocation of resources in these organizations. Under conditions of full employment, excess demand or insufficient demand affect the organization's strategic activity, as well as its ability to raise funds and hire staff.

Social tension, gaps, or inequality between groups in society affect the way organizations organize themselves to render services. Cultural values, attitudes, and prevailing beliefs have an effect and are reflected in processes within the organization. Political elements rep-resented by interest groups affect the policies and goals of the organization as well as allocation of resources for various service programs. Moreover, new legislation or revisions to existing legislation affect the existence of organizations (Edelman & Suchman, 1997). Thus, for example, the National Health Insurance Law in Israel has led to the collapse of voluntary organizations that dealt for years with collection of fees and financing of medical services that were not provided by official state institutions. Similarly, changes in adoption laws have enabled voluntary and for-profit organizations to enter a domain formerly under the exclusive control of state institutions. Advanced information technology systems have also affected management of organizations, division of labor, relations with clients, and provision of services. Clearly, the demographic composition of the environment also affects the nature of services provided, as well as the organization's very survival. Furthermore, religiosity affects the organization's goals and operation; that is, the stronger the religious elements in the environment, the more the organization gears its service programs to the unique characteristics of those clients. In addition, the organization is often required to recruit staff with specific personal characteristics, who understand the needs of the clients and are able to communicate with them effectively.

On a more immediate level, organizations maintain relations with key elements in their environment that are consistent with the more narrowly construed goals of the organization: (a) clients of the organization; (b) suppliers of resources, raw materials, work, capital, and equipment; (c) competitors for markets and resources; (d) formal and state organizations as well as institutions that are responsible for legislation and establishment of regulations and by-laws pertaining directly to the organization's activity; and (e) providers of complementary services (Hasenfeld, 1983; Mintzberg, 1979).

The task environment provides the organization with the legitimacy and resources it requires for its continued activity. The official authorities in charge of legislation and licensing grant legitimacy and also have the power to enforce, control, and evaluate the organization's activities. The task environment includes all actual and potential clients of the organization. In this connection, it should be noted that organizations cannot rely solely on existing clients but must expand their activities and reach a broad potential population. Moreover, not every organization develops all of the services required by its clients. Thus, some organizations rely on complementary services from other organizations, whether they are part of the organization or whether they are hired by the organization for these purposes. For example, specialized services such as family counseling can be provided to social agencies that lack the professional and human infrastructure to offer them.

The task environment also includes organizations that compete for scarce resources. Organizations that succeed in controlling more resources dominate larger segments of the environment and cause others to become dependent on their resources.

CHARACTERISTICS OF THE TASK ENVIRONMENT

Task environments can be characterized according to various criteria and dimensions. Possible classifications are based on the degree of uncertainty, the extent to which resources are concentrated, and the rate and intensity of changes in the environment, as well as stability and availability of resources. According to this perspective, several types of criteria for classifying environments can be distinguished (Emery & Trist, 1965; Hasenfeld, 1983; Mintzberg, 1979):

- *Placidity versus turbulence*—determines the dynamics of the environment in terms of changing goals, values, and extent to which the organization has knowledge of environmental characteristics.
- *Homogeneity versus heterogeneity*—homogeneity is defined as the extent to which there is similarity between organizations as opposed to heterogeneity, which highlights differences.
- *Richness versus paucity*—determined on the basis of the existence and accessibility of resources required by the organization.
- *Stability versus instability*—determined according to the level and rate of changes in the environment.
- *Organized versus unorganized*—determined according to the presence of mobilized individuals, groups, coalitions, and organizations representing the interests of clients, consumers, and residents.
- *Certainty versus uncertainty*—determines the extent of information available to the organization in its relations with the environment. This criterion reflects the gap between potential information existing in the environment and information controlled by the organization. The larger the gap, the greater the uncertainty of organization-environment relations.

To adapt to its environment, the organization must learn and recognize the inherent opportunities and threats. The more turbulent, dynamic, uncertain, and unpredictable the environment, the more difficult it is for the organization to learn about its characteristic behavior. At the same time, turbulent, rapidly changing environments stimulate learning and enhance the ability of the organization to provide innovative, spontaneous solutions to acute needs. Stable, placid, simple, and certain environments, in contrast, do not stimulate organizational activity, even though they are conducive to learning and better knowledge of the organization. The technology adopted in these settings is standard, solutions are routine, responses are slow, and employees' development is limited to some extent (Schmid, 1986, 1992).

THEORETICAL APPROACHES TOWARD UNDERSTANDING RELATIONS BETWEEN THE ORGANIZATION AND TASK ENVIRONMENT

This section will discuss the main theoretical approaches toward understanding the relations between the organization and the task environment: (a) organization adaptation theories, (b) ecological theories, and (c) institutional theory.

Organization Adaptation Theories

These theories are based on the concept of adaptation, which is defined as the process of evolutionary change by which the organization provides a better and better solution to the problem, and the end result is the state of being adapted (Lewontin, 1978). A state of adaptation, in a biological sense, describes a state of survival for an organism. Analogously, a state of adaptation for an organization is one in which it can survive in the conditions of its environment (Chakravarthy, 1982). It involves sensing and understanding both internal and external envi-

ronments, as well as taking action to achieve a fit between the two.

In this process, the organization may be forced to alter part of its identity or distinctive characteristics, because adaptation to the complexities of the environment also demands changes in goals, objectives, service technologies, and operating procedures. Therefore, in the adaptation process, the organization should also develop what Motamedi (1977) called "copability," that is *coping* and *ability,* which means the internal ability of an organization to maintain its identity and overcome the problem of change. The essence of copability is the ability of a system to converse its integrity and distinct characteristics, or "to hold one's own" (Motamedi, 1977). To ensure organizational effectiveness, it is necessary to combine adaptability and copability, which preserves the organization's self-identity as well as its ability to adapt to changes in the environment.

Adaptation can also be described as a learning process. Organizations learn their environment, and the better they do this, the more effectively they can adapt themselves and ensure their survival (Hedberg, 1981; Herriot, Levinthal, & March, 1984; Levinthal & March, 1981; March, 1981a, 1981b; Nelson & Winter, 1982). As in every learning process, the stimulus-response paradigm is applied. Accordingly, organizations react to stimuli from their external environment and respond after filtering, coding, and processing the information that flows into them. By receiving and decoding stimuli, organizations learn the strengths and weaknesses of other organizations in the environment, which are actual or potential competitors or partners. Organizations not only respond to stimuli but also scan their environment to identify needs for which they have developed solutions. By scanning and gathering information, organizations discover new environmental spaces for expansion of their domain.

The main theoretical approaches attesting to this active process of adaptation between the organization and its environment are contingency theory, political-economy theory, and resource dependence theory.

Contingency theory provides an important paradigm for analyzing organizational structure. According to this theory, there is no single organizational structure that is effective for all organizations (Donaldson, 1996a, 1996b). Rather, organizational structures have to be matched with the contextual demands of contingency factors, that is, size, environment, and technology. According to this theory, organizations that fit the contextual features of their environment are more likely to have higher performance levels as well as better chances of survival than those that do not (Lawrence & Lorsch, 1967; Thompson, 1967). Because structural contingency theory emphasizes the organization's adaptation to its environment, it is considered part of adaptation theory.

Burns and Stalker (1961) were among the first scholars to develop this approach. In a study of the electronics industry in Britain, they distinguished between mechanistic and organic structures. A mechanistic structure is one characterized by a clear hierarchy and division of tasks, formal systems of communication and coordination, and formal reporting procedures. This organizational structure develops primarily in organizations operating in stable, certain environments characterized by gradual change and easy access to information. In contrast, organic structures are characterized by a low level of formality, lack of a clear hierarchy, and informal flow of communication, which is not chan-

neled through the lines of hierarchy and command. This kind of structure fits organizations operating in rapidly changing environments characterized by high uncertainty.

At about the same time, another British researcher examined the relationship between organizational structure and contingency factors in manufacturing organizations (Woodward, 1958, 1965). Those studies, however, revealed no relationship between the structure and size of these organizations, and the author argues that operations technology is the key correlate of organizational structure. Specifically, Woodward (1965) found that organizations with simple, manual production technology tend to be informal and organic, whereas those with complex technology based on mass production (e.g., automobile assembly plants) tend to be formal and mechanistic. Woodward's (1965) conclusions also indicate that organizations with a growing volume of work that becomes increasingly complex tend to integrate organic elements, such as task groups, which are based on principles that deviate from the strict mechanistic patterns characterizing the overall structure of the organization. Integration of these elements also contributes toward higher performance.

In a similar vein, Lawrence and Lorsch (1967) proposed a theory based on their study of three types of industries in the United States: containers, processed foods, and plastic. According to Lawrence and Lorsch (1967), the level and rate of changes in the external environment affect the extent of differentiation and integration in the organization itself. In environments characterized by rapid change and heterogeneous needs and demands, organizations are required to develop a high level of differentiation. Such differentiation is reflected, for example, in numerous organizational units that focus on development of knowledge, ideas, and research. These units scan and map the environment in an attempt to reduce uncertainty in the organization. Under these circumstances, the organization also requires a higher level of integration to tighten the connection between organizational units and enhance effectiveness. The balance between differentiation and integration is the only way to ensure that the organization will be able to adapt itself to contingency factors originating in the external environment.

In line with this approach, Thompson (1967) argued that the environment affects organizations, which structure themselves to respond to the differential needs of the environment. Similarly, Perrow (1986) argued that knowledge technology is a contingency of organizational structure. According to this perspective, the clearer and more specific the interpretations of the knowledge, and the fewer exceptions to the rules, the greater the tendency of the organization to adopt a hierarchical, centralized structure.

Critics of this approach have questioned the relevance of contingency theory to analysis of interrelations between characteristics of the external environment and organizational strategies (Miller & Friesen, 1980; Mintzberg, 1979; Pennings, 1992). Moreover, it has been argued that the contingency approach focuses on a few environmental variables and often ignores essential intervening variables, particularly those relating to strategic choice (Child, 1972; Pfeffer & Salancik, 1978). According to this argument, there is a mutual relationship between organizations and their environment. Specifically, not only does the environment influence organizations and their structure, but organizations influence their environment and try to change it.

This is especially true of large organizations, which have a strong influence on the development of their environment and on creation of new areas of activity. Critics of this approach also emphasize the strong bias toward cross-sectional analysis rather than longitudinal studies of organizations (Benson, 1975), as well as the proclivity to draw sample-wide conclusions about relationships among variables, even when the sample includes diverse types of organizations (Miller, 1979). In addition, contingency theorists have characterized the external environment in objective terms, totally disregarding subjective perceptions of the environment that might influence organizational activities.

Regarding the relevance of this theory to human and social welfare organizations, it should be mentioned that very few empirical studies have been conducted on this topic. In one of the studies, relationships between environmental characteristics, organizational strategy, and organizational structure were found in three types of human service organizations: youth organizations, community service organizations, and home care organizations (Schmid, 1992).

The second approach is the political-economy theory (Wamseley & Zald, 1976; Zald, 1970), which recognizes that to survive and produce services, the organization must garner two fundamental types of resources: (a) legitimacy and power (i.e., political) and (b) production resources (i.e., economic). The underlying premise of this approach is the organization's dependence on resources controlled by agents and interest groups in the external environment. The greater the organization's dependence on these resources, the stronger the influence of external interest groups on processes within the organization.

A further derivative of this approach is resource dependence theory, which provides a general conceptual framework that applies ideas from social exchange theory (Blau, 1964; Emerson, 1962). This framework explains interorganizational dependencies created by the need of all organizations to acquire scarce resources. Resource dependence theory (Aldrich & Pfeffer, 1976; Pfeffer & Salancik, 1978) proposes that organizations often become dependent on their environments for resources that are critical to their survival, which generates uncertainty. According to Pfeffer and Salancik (1978), "the underlying premise of the external perspective on organizations is that organizational activities and outcomes are accounted for by the context in which the organization is embedded" (p. 39). Moreover, exchange of resources with the task environment enables the organization to acquire the various resources it needs to survive. In this process, organizational directors must manage their environment at least well as they manage their organizations to ensure an adequate resource supply. In this respect, managing the environment may be even more important than managing the organization itself (Aldrich & Pfeffer, 1976). The organization must change its power-dependence relations with the environment and direct activities toward (a) reducing dependence on the external environment as much as possible by controlling necessary resources and (b) increasing dependence of agents in the environment on the distinctive services and/or products of the organization. By adopting this approach, the organization can attain more discretion and achieve a relative advantage in acquiring necessary resources (Mizruchi & Galaskiewicz, 1993). In this process, the organization develops strategies for reducing its dependence on the environment based on cooperation, as well as on strategies of competition and disruption (see the section in this chapter dealing with "Strategies of Adaptation to the Task Environment").

Notwithstanding the contribution of resource dependence theory toward understanding power-dependence relations between organizations and their environments, it does not sufficiently stress environmental constraints on strategic choice (Child, 1972; Galaskiewicz, 1985; Whittington, 1989). For example, organizations and directors do not accept the environment as a constraint that unilaterally influences their behavior, which imposes goals on them and chooses their domain. Although this approach recognizes the impact of environmental constraints such as formal restrictions on organizational behavior (Edelman & Suchman, 1997), it tends to ignore other forms of institutional restriction such as the material environment (Reitan, 1998, p. 296). Regarding the relevance of this theory to human service organizations, the main drawback is that it ignores other important factors that may affect organization-environment interaction, such as ideologies, values, behavior norms, and the commitments they evoke.

Ecological Theories

These theories derive from the Darwinian and genetic schools, which argue that genetic variations can be traced to processes of mutation and natural selection, expressed as "survival of the fittest." This approach has been adopted in studies of organization-environment relations and is known as the population ecology theory (Baum, 1996; Baum & Singh, 1994a; Hannan & Freeman, 1977, 1984; Pfeffer, 1995; Singh & Lumsden, 1990). Unlike the adaptation theories, which focused on individual organizations, the basic unit of analysis is a population of organizations, that is, all organizations that share the following characteristics: (a) common dependence on resources controlled by the environment, (b) similar organizational structure, (c) organizational features that remain relatively stable over time (Hannan & Freeman, 1977), and (d) a similar extent of homogeneity in terms of vulnerability to external constraints (Hannan & Carroll, 1992).

The key concept of this theory is the existence of a niche. Based on Hutchinson's (1957) biological definition, Hannan and Freeman (1977) state that a niche is an "an area in constraint space (the space whose dimensions are levels of resources, etc.) in which the (species) population outcompetes all other local (species) populations" (p. 947). The ecological niche, therefore, is resource space that determines the carrying capacity, limiting the number of organizations able to operate in the niche (Baum & Singh, 1994b, 1994c). Two dimensions may characterize niches: breadth and depth. Breadth indicates the extent to which organizations attract resources from many actors in a niche, whereas depth indicates the extent to which the focal organization is dependent on the other organizations.

In the process of natural selection, organizations that survive within the ecological niche are those that possess the unique characteristics required by the environment. The environment selects the most appropriate organizations, while the individual organizations have relatively little influence (Aldrich, 1979). In contrast to theories of adaptation, this approach views organizations as passive and as accepting environmental constraints. Directors and members of the organization cannot influence ecological processes through their decisions and activities, because they are controlled by deterministic process.

Critics of this theoretical approach argue that biological development models are inappropriate for social organizations (Young, 1988), mainly on the grounds that they lack a clear concept of the environment. According to Perrow (1986), for example, the ecological model tends to be mystic and disregards power relations, conflicts, disturbances, and power struggles among interest groups in the organization. The theory recognizes the considerable power of the environment and its deterministic processes, but it fails to acknowledge the ability of organizations to alter their environments. This approach contradicts the theory of dependence on political, economic, and institutional resources. Aldrich (1979), for example, recognizes the key role of the state and its ideologies in shaping the environment, particularly in human service, social service, and community organizations. Thus, political and economic elements have a particularly strong impact on the establishment, survival, and dissolution of organizations (Tucker, 1994; Tucker, Baum, & Singh, 1992).

In line with this approach, it is argued that social and human service organizations do not disappear easily. Instead, they change their strategies or target populations. For example, in the process of de-institutionalization, mental health institutions have sent clients out into the community and received new target populations. This reflects a new cycle of dissolution, life, and renewal in organizations. Thus, as long as there is a social interest or human need that

TABLE 7.1 Resource Dependence and Population Ecology Theories: A Comparative Analysis

Focus of Interest	Population Ecology	Resource Dependence
Level and unit of analysis	Populations of organizations	Individual organizations
Time perspective	Long-range	Short-range, incremental
Conceptualizing the environment	Focus on exogenous environments	Focus on exogenous environments as well as changes within the organization
Organizational life cycle	Focus on organizational birth and death	Ignores organizational birth and death
Rationale of approach	Less normative, emphasis on randomness	More normative, emphasis on deliberate action
The organization	Not concerned with events in the organization itself	Concerned with the organization, its decisions and actions
Power and influence of environments	Environments are powerful and determine the organization's survival	Organizations determine their own survival through effective adaptation
Organization's strategic behavior	Reactive	Proactive

requires a response, social service organizations tend to survive.

At the same time, it is clear that the risk of dissolution or death in these organizations can be traced to two causes—ecological and institutional. These contexts change rapidly, whereas organizations find it difficult to adapt themselves at the same pace. The process of adaptation entails modifications in the organization's ideology, strategies, structure, internal processes, and management of human resources. All of this requires a major organizational effort as well as investment of time and resources that are not always at the organization's disposal. Failure to adapt rapidly and reorganize systems creates a gap that threatens the organization's survival.

In addition, attempts to apply this model toward selection of organizations and organiza-tion-environment relations have not provided clear explanations of the natural selection process. Nor do they explain why some organizations survive while others dissolve. Moreover, this approach assumes that organizations have no influence on shaping the environment and behave according to the power of the "invisible hand"; that is, their behavior is reactive and passive. In reality, however, organizations actively scan, learn, and influence their environment (Child, 1972; Child & Kieser, 1981). Similarly, decisions made by organizational directors are not arbitrary but derive from planned activities aimed at attaining the goals of the organization and at mobilizing support from the task environment (Pennings, 1981).

In Table 7.1, a comparative analysis of the resource dependence and population ecology theories sums up the differences between them

(Scott, 1992). First, differences were found in the levels and units of analysis. Population ecology theory focuses primarily on populations of organizations rather than on specific organizational settings (Baum & Oliver, 1992).

Second, the theories differ in terms of their time perspectives. Population ecology theory is based on a long-range perspective, whereas resource dependence theory is short-range. Specifically, the population ecology theory focuses on the organizational life cycle, which requires comprehensive longitudinal analysis. In contrast, examination of the adaptation of individual organizations is often incremental and continues for short, specified periods.

Third, there are several differences between the two approaches with regard to conceptualization of the environment, even though they also share some perspectives in common. Both theories emphasize the critical importance of environmental characteristics in terms of abundance and scarcity of resources. Moreover, both emphasize the dimensions of certainty and uncertainty. Nonetheless, ecological theories focus on exogenous environments, although these environments can change over time. According to resource dependence theory, however, environments not only change but also reflect the actions taken by the organization to manage problems of interdependence (Pfeffer, 1982).

Fourth, population ecology theory deals with processes of organizational birth and death that are not addressed at all by resource dependence theory (Tucker, Singh, & Meinhard, 1990).

Fifth, there are differences regarding the extent of rationalism underlying each of the approaches. The orientation of the population ecology approach is less normative than that of the resource-dependence theory, and it places more emphasis on randomness as opposed to deliberate action.

Sixth, population ecology theory is less concerned with events and processes within the organization than it is with long-term trends and changes in the population of organizations.

Seventh, according to population ecology theory, the organizational environment plays an extremely powerful role and determines whether or not the organization will survive. In contrast, resource dependence theory argues that the organization determines its own destiny in the ongoing struggle with its environment and with other organizations in that environment. The ability of organizations to survive can be attributed to continuous improvements and appropriate strategic choices, which enable effective adaptation and ensure the organization's survival.

Eighth, according to the population ecology approach, the organization is characterized by passive behavior; that is, it reacts to events in the external environment that force it to adopt a structure that fits the environmental constraints. However, according to the resource dependence theory, organizations play an active role in their relationship with the external environment and constantly attempt to change their dependency relations with the agents that control resources and power. In this context, the organization seeks new domains of activity while enhancing its independence and making other agents dependent on it.

Institutional Theory

Institutional theory asserts that organizations are driven to incorporate the practices and procedures defined by prevailing rationalized and institutionalized concepts of organizational operations. Organizations that succeed in doing so increase their legitimacy and, consequently, their prospects for survival, irrespective of the immediate efficacy of the required practices and procedures.

Institutional theorists (DiMaggio & Powell, 1983; Meyer & Rowan, 1977, 1983; Tolbert & Zucker, 1996; Zucker, 1988) suggest that changes in the formal structure of organizations are often introduced to make organizations more aligned with the changing institutional environment of "rationalized myths" (Meyer & Rowan, 1977, p. 346).

Organizations that conform to the requirements and expectations of the institutional environment gain the legitimacy and resources needed to survive and grow, even if they do not intend to realize the rationalized myths (Meyer & Rowan, 1983). This process results in institutional isomorphism, which means developing identical processes, increasing similarity, and copied organizational forms (D'Aunno, Sutton, & Price, 1991). This, in turn, generates increased bureaucratization, formalism, and standardization in the organizations themselves (Meyer, Scott, Strang, & Creighton, 1988).

In the case of human service organizations, legitimacy and social support are derived less from the distinctive products (services) they offer than from adopting a system of social values accepted in the society and community. These organizations support their espoused goals on the basis of accepted ideologies (Perrow, 1986; Zald, 1970).

Critics of this approach argue that it is deterministic and that institutional agencies such as the government largely determine the destiny of organizations. This is especially true of human service organizations, which are highly dependent on resources controlled by the external environment. It is also argued that the institutional approach ignores internal organizational elements, which have the ability to make choices and decisions. These elements influence the destiny of organizations and constantly aspire toward achieving the organization's goals. Moreover, it is argued that this theory ignores changes and conflicts in the institutional environment (Reitan, 1998) and that it tends to be mystical, introverted, and distrustful (Lowndes, 1996).

Comparative analysis of the various theoretical approaches toward organization-environment relationships reveals the unique contribution of each one. Contingency theory emphasizes the internal and external factors that influence the process of adapting and structuring the organization, as well as attainment of organizational effectiveness. Resource dependence theory emphasizes the proactive role of the organization in scanning and mapping the external environment for opportunities and risks. According to this approach, the organization does not accept the environment as a constraint. Rather, it makes a consistent effort to change dependence relations with the environment. In contrast, the population ecology theory emphasizes the impact of the environment on the organization's survival. According to this theory, organizations cannot keep up with the rapid changes in the environment, which generate crises in the organizations themselves that may end in their death. Finally, institutional theory emphasizes the mythical aspects of the environment, which organizations adopt as a condition for adaptation and survival. Specifically, it focuses on the power of the institutional environment and ignores the ability of organizations to cope with or change environmental constraints.

Each theoretical approach makes a separate contribution, and the relationships among them are also noteworthy. It has been argued, for example, that the relationship between ecological and institutional theories is complementary and that they should be synthesized into a single explanatory framework (Baum, 1996; Hannan & Carroll, 1992; Hannan & Freeman, 1989; Zucker, 1989). Others conceive of institutional theory as contextual to ecological theory and argue that the relationship between them is not only complementary but also hierarchical (Tucker et al., 1992).

The attempt to integrate these theories indicates that the institutional elements in the organization's ecological niche have a considerable impact on its continued existence. Thus, for example, it is argued that the government can enact legislation and amendments that influence organizational behavior and determine whether or not organizations survive (Barnett & Carroll, 1993; Baum, 1996; Baum & Oliver, 1991; Freeman & Lomi, 1994; Schmid & Hasenfeld, 1993; Singh, Tucker, & Meinhard, 1991).

Integration of resource dependence and institutional theories reveals another perspective, particularly with respect to human service organizations (Edelman, 1992; Scott, 1994; Sutton, Dobbin, Meyer, & Scott, 1994). These organizations lack their own resources and are dependent on the external environment to provide for their needs. Thus, they tend to accept the norms, values, and social and national myths as a condition for attaining legitimation. By adopting behavior that conforms with the standards of the government agencies, these organizations ensure a steady flow of resources.

STRATEGIES OF ADAPTATION TO THE TASK ENVIRONMENT

Competition versus cooperation: In the process of reducing dependence on external resources controlled by agents in the task environment, the organization adopts several strategies, some of which are competitive and some of which are cooperative (Gidron & Hasenfeld, 1994; Hasenfeld, 1983; Huxham & Vangen, 1996; Kanter, 1990; Oster, 1995; Schmid, 1995; Thompson, 1967; Thompson & McEwen, 1958; Waddock, 1989; Yankey, 1991; York & Zychlinski, 1996).

Competition is a pattern of rivalry between two or more organizations that compete for scarce resources, for their share of the environment, for influence, and for support from clients.

Bargaining is a type of negotiation that leads to agreements for exchange of products or resources between two or more organizations. In some cases, organizations negotiate for the domains and territory in which they operate. In this process, organizations are subject to supervision and control by other organizations, so that they cannot operate arbitrarily or unilaterally to further their own interests without considering the other parties.

Co-optation is a strategy of bringing in new members and absorbing them into the organization and its leadership. In this way, the organization neutralizes threats and pressures, for example, from community representatives who join the organization and acquire personal power that threatens the activities of the organization as well as its management and dominant coalition.

Coalition is a pattern of cooperation between two or more organizations seeking to achieve a common goal, namely attainment of resources. These organizations adapt themselves to changing conditions but are subject to numerous restrictions that limit their autonomy; that is, they cannot set policies arbitrarily and unilaterally without considering their partners in the coalition.

Other related strategies are *exerting authority and power.* For example, in certain situations, organizations with power and control over resources dictate the conditions and behavior they desire from the other party. According to Benson (1975), this strategy is authoritative in the sense that the party dictating the conditions uses its power to determine the other party's activities without necessarily providing encouragement or rewards. The ability to use this strategy is measured by the extent to which the party dictating the conditions is able to exercise control and impose the conditions on the other party if necessary. Government agencies that control resources and have the power to make decisions about various programs often use this strategy vis-à-vis welfare agencies contracted by the government to provide services. In this case, the government may also finance the services and impose its policies and standards on the contractors, in addition to imposing services programs on clients. In certain cases, the financing agent even intervenes in internal organizational processes related to the professional criteria employees must meet, the number of job positions, and supervision and control within the organization itself.

Another strategy is *disruption,* in which one party breaks rules and violates codes of fairness, thus preventing the other party from attaining its goals. In this way, one party threatens the other and prevents it in various ways from attaining the legitimacy and resources it needs for its activities. Strategies of disruption are chosen by organizations under certain conditions:

1. The organization strives at all costs to enter the arena of service provision, and the other organizations prevent it from doing so.
2. The organization is powerless vis-à-vis the elements operating in the task environment, which ignore its demands and needs.
3. The organization has little to lose in the struggle with its competitors and uses any means at its disposal to prevail.
4. An ideological conflict exists between the organization and external agents in the environment. Thus, for example, following the enactment of the Long-Term Care Insurance Law in Israel, nonprofit organizations attempted to prevent private, for-profit organizations from entering the domain of home-care service provision. In this effort, they tried to persuade the government to refrain from allocating resources to those organizations.

Organizations adopting this strategy must prepare themselves for a counterattack from the other party (either the competitor or the government), which may threaten their existence or at least withhold resources.

Generalism versus specialism: The strategy of generalism encompasses a wide array of activities aimed at incorporating a diverse range of relations with environmental elements for optimal utilization of existing and potential resources. Organizations adopting this strategy offer a variety of products, services, and programs. Specialism, in contrast, entails concentration of activities within a relatively narrow range of the environmental domain, as well as development of distinctive competence and attainment of a relative advantage regarding products and/or services exported by the organization to its environment (Brittain & Freeman, 1980).

Complementary to the issue of generalism versus specialism is that of the "first movers" (R) versus the "slow movers" (K) strategies. According to Brittain and Freeman's (1980) definition, "pure R strategists are organizations that move quickly to exploit resources as they first become available . . . they trade on speed of expansion" (p. 311). Operationally, the R strategy is associated with being the first to market, so as to optimize one's chances for extensive resource exploitation. K strategists, in contrast, seek to gain a competitive advantage through efficiency of operations. In essence, they trade off expansion opportunities for more certain control of resources in established domains.

The activities of organizations are often determined by a combination of the two pairs of strategies (Brittain & Freeman, 1980), so that in effect there are four possible paths of adaptation. Whereas R specialists exploit available resources rapidly within a relatively narrow domain, R generalists exploit resources rapidly within a broad range of domains. Similarly, K specialists emphasize efficiency of operations within a narrow domain, whereas K generalists emphasize efficiency over a broad range of domains. Research has revealed that focusing organizational efforts in one direction (i.e., specialism) provides the advantage of gaining a lead and concentrating expertise in a confined market segment. Moreover, this strategic approach allows for more efficient use of limited resources and enhances the organization's ability to respond quickly to the changing needs

of clients, thus creating environmental dependence on the organization in its area of specialization (Romanelli, 1987). Generalism requires complex handling of diverse branches, whereas concentration on a single product or service is considered risky. According to this approach, specialization makes the organization more vulnerable to technological, economic, demographic, and other changes. In addition, there is a danger of total extinction as substitute products or services penetrate the organization's domain.

RELATIONSHIPS BETWEEN TASK ENVIRONMENT CHARACTERISTICS AND THE STRATEGY AND STRUCTURE OF THE ORGANIZATION

Relationships with the task environment affect processes occurring within the organization itself. Organizations in environments where change is slow have little difficulty collecting information. Organizational strategies are long-range, whereas tactics are derived from those strategies and adapted to the moderate changes. However, organizations operating in unstable environments characterized by extensive change encounter difficulty in the process of scanning and gathering information. The process of formulating strategic policies is complex, tactics change frequently, and operational programs are short-term.

The type of environment, its characteristics, and rate of change affect organizational strategy from other points of view (Butler & Wilson, 1990). Organizations operating in dynamic, changing environments with abundant resources must adopt completely different strategies than those operating in stable environments with limited resources. In these contexts, organizations can adopt proactive or reactive strategies (Miles & Snow, 1978). In the first case, the organization not only responds to the needs of the environment but also seeks to influence and change it. In contrast, organizations adopting a reactive strategy are directed and oriented by agents in the task environment and encounter difficulty implementing changes or influencing resource allocation.

The environment also affects organizational structure. For example, the structure is affected in different ways by turbulent and uncertain environments compared to placid, homogeneous, and stable environments (Lawrence & Lorsch, 1967). Organizations operating in a turbulent environment, characterized by high demand for their product and a high level of change, tend to develop decentralized structures based on the principle of loosely coupling (Weick, 1976). According to this principle, subsystems in the organization can provide solutions to needs that arise, without depending on the other units. They preserve their unique identity as well as their independence, while maintaining loose relations with other units in the organization. This structure enables the organization to develop mechanisms for sensing, scanning, and absorbing stimuli from the environment without being hampered by formal, bureaucratic systems. The ability of these organizations to survive and the extent to which the units are adapted is determined by the dynamics that prevail in the environment. If the stability of one organizational unit is undermined, the overall system is not affected. In this organizational setting, costs of coordination and communication are relatively low. In placid, stable environments characterized by a slow rate of change, the organizational structure tends to be rela-

tively centralized, mechanistic, and formal. Work procedures are standard, and the mechanisms of coordination and control are relatively simple (Freeman, 1973; Pfeffer & Leblibei, 1973; Schmid, 1992; Thompson, 1967).

Finally, it should be noted that the extent of stability and instability in environments affects the organization's strategies (Schmid & Hasenfeld, 1993). Thus, for example, a study of for-profit and nonprofit organizations providing home care services revealed that, in environments with a high level of stability, voluntary nonprofit organizations chose a strategy of specialism owing to their established relationship with the government and offered their clients relatively few service programs. In contrast, for-profit organizations had less established relations with the government and chose a strategy of generalism, which was expressed in a large number of programs. In so doing, the for-profits spread the risks involved in raising funds required for programs. As the for-profit organizations increased their share in the market of home-care service provision, the share allotted to voluntary nonprofits declined. Concurrently, the environment of voluntary nonprofits became unstable and uncertain. Thus, they began to adopt the generalist strategy and enter new domains of activity, including establishment of satellite organizations to assist with mobilizing resources (Schmid, 1998).

SUMMARY

This chapter presented the main theories and concepts pertaining to organization-environment relations and discussed the contribution of these theories toward understanding how organizations adapt to rapid changes in their task environment. Ecological theory argues that deterministic processes affect the organization's survival. Advocates of this approach contend that the dynamics characterizing the external environment are much more rapid and powerful than the ability of organizations to adapt to changes. In this context, adaptation is construed as adopting an appropriate strategy, adapting structure and procedures, training staff to cope with internal changes caused by the transition from one structural pattern to another, changing service technologies, and establishing new relations with elements that provide legitimacy and resources. The gap between the rapid changes in the external environment and the ability of organizations to adapt their activity at various levels can generate a profound crisis and even threaten their survival.

Adaptation theory, in contrast, argues that the organization learns its environments and reacts to events, in addition to initiating activities and changes as well as influencing the task environment. According to this approach, social service organizations do not accept environmental constraints as given and unchangeable. Rather, the organizations and their directors have a choice of making their own decisions, setting and even changing priorities, allocating resources for various activities, and influencing elements in the environment, particularly their clientele. The process of learning environments is continuous and dynamic. It is a daily experience that involves scanning and mapping the environment, as well as identifying needs, threats, and opportunities inherent in the environment. Organizations that fail to learn their environments may find themselves in an inferior position vis-à-vis other organizations, which take over their functions, particularly in

the era of increasing competition between human service and social welfare organizations.

Learning the environment and interpreting events is largely subjective and depends on the way the environment is construed by directors and members of the organization. This chapter places special emphasis on the distinction between the objective and subjective or perceived environment. This distinction suggests that different possible strategies derive from the organization's perception of the environment. Environments can be characterized in terms of economic, social, technological, and other indicators (e.g., rates of growth in the economy, unemployment rates, cost of living indices, the level of social tension between different population sectors, inequality in distribution of income, rates of change, and technological innovations). Nonetheless, it is the subjective interpretations of these measures that play a decisive role as organizations adopt strategies in an effort to adapt to the external environment. The adaptation process itself is not limited to immediate elements in the task environment but also refers to major developments that have turned the world into a village. In the "global village," political changes generate economic changes, and decisions to introduce technological changes affect the functioning and structure of organizations. Similarly, economic and political crises in one part of the world affect other regions, because the economies of different countries are interconnected. However, organizations do not always have a chance to follow international events without being directly involved or affected by them. Therefore, organizations must develop sensors and mechanisms for observation in an attempt to obtain information that may be critical in determining their fate and their ability to cope effectively with crises and changes.

REFERENCES

Aldrich, H. E. (1979). *Organizations and environments.* Englewood Cliffs, NJ: Prentice Hall.

Aldrich, H. E., & Pfeffer, J. (1976). Environments of organizations. *Annual Review of Sociology, 11,* 79-105.

Barnett, W. P., & Carroll, G. R. (1993). How institutional constraints affected the organization of early American telephony. *Journal of Law, Economics, and Organization, 9,* 98-126.

Baum, J. A. C. (1996). Organizational ecology. In S. R. Clegg, C. Hardy, & W. R. Nord (Eds.), *Handbook of organization studies* (pp. 77-114). Thousand Oaks, CA: Sage.

Baum, J. A. C., & Oliver, C. (1991). Institutional linkages and organizational mortality. *Administrative Science Quarterly, 36,* 187-218.

Baum, J. A. C., & Oliver, C. (1992). Institutional embeddedness and the dynamics of organizational populations. *American Sociological Review, 57,* 540-559.

Baum, J. A. C., & Singh, J. V. (1994a). *Evolutionary dynamics of organizations.* New York: Oxford University Press.

Baum, J. A. C., & Singh, J. V. (1994b). Organizational niches and the dynamics of organizational founding. *Organization Science, 5,* 483-501.

Baum, J. A. C., & Singh, J. V. (1994c). Organizational niches and the dynamics of organizational mortality. *American Journal of Sociology, 100,* 346-380.

Benson, J. K. (1975). The interlocking network as a political economy. *Administrative Science Quarterly, 20*(2), 229-249.

Blau, P. M. (1964). *Exchange and power in social life.* New York: John Wiley.

Brittain, J. W., & Freeman, J. H. (1980). Organizational proliferation and density dependent selection. In J. R. Kimberly & R. H. Miles (Eds.), *The organizational life cycle* (pp. 291-338). San Francisco: Jossey-Bass.

Burns, T., & Stalker, G. M. (1961). *The management of innovation.* Chicago: Quadrangle.

Butler, R. J., & Wilson, D. C. (1990). *Managing voluntary and nonprofit organizations: Strategy and structure.* London & New York: Routledge.

Chakravarthy, B. S. (1982). Adaptation: A promising metaphor for strategic management. *Academy of Management Review, 7*(1), 35-44.

Child, J. (1972). Organizational structure, environment, and performance: The role of strategic choice. *Sociology, 6,* 1-22.

Child, J., & Kieser, A. (1981). Development of organizations over time. In P. C. Nystrom & W. H. Starbuck (Eds.), *Handbook of organizational design* (Vol. 2, pp. 28-64). London: Oxford University Press.

D'Aunno, T., Sutton, R., & Price, R. (1991). Isomorphism and external support in conflicting institutional environments: A study of drug abuse treatment units. *Academy of Management Journal, 34,* 636-661.

Dill, W. R. (1958). Environment as an influence on managerial autonomy. *Administrative Science Quarterly, 2,* 409-443.

DiMaggio, P. D., & Powell, W. (1983). The iron cage revisited: Institutional isomorphism and collective rationality in organizational fields. *American Sociological Review, 48,* 147-160.

Donaldson, L. (1996a). *For positivist organization theory: Proving the hard core.* London: Sage.

Donaldson, L. (1996b). The normal science of structural contingency theory. In S. R. Clegg, C. Hardy, & W. R. Nord (Eds.), *Handbook of organization studies* (pp. 57-76). Thousand Oaks, CA: Sage.

Duncan, R. B. (1972). Characteristics of organizational environment and perceived environmental uncertainty. *Administrative Science Quarterly, 17,* 313-327.

Edelman, B. L., & Suchman, M. C. (1997). The legal environments of organizations. *Annual Review of Sociology, 23,* 479-515.

Edelman, L. (1992). Legal ambiguity and symbolic structures: Organizational mediation of civil rights law. *American Journal of Sociology, 97,* 1531-1576.

Emerson, P. M. (1962). Power dependence relations. *American Sociological Review, 26,* 31-41.

Emery, F. E., & Trist, E. L. (1965). The causal texture of organizational environments. *Human Relations, 18,* 21-32.

Evan, W. M. (1966). The organization-set: Toward a theory of interorganizational relations. In J. D. Thompson (Ed.), *Approaches to organization design* (pp. 174-191). Pittsburgh, PA: University of Pittsburgh Press.

Freeman, J. H. (1973). Environment, technology, and the administrative intensity of manufacturing. *American Sociological Review, 38*(6), 750-763.

Freeman, J. H., & Lomi, A. (1994). Resource partitioning and founding of a banking cooperative in Italy. In J. A. C. Baum & J. V. Singh (Eds.), *Evolutionary dynamics of organizations* (pp. 269-293). New York: Oxford University Press.

Galaskiewicz, Y. (1985). Interorganizational relations. *Annual Review of Sociology, 82,* 929-964.

Gidron, B., & Hasenfeld, Y. (1994). Human service organizations and self-help groups: Can they collaborate? *Nonprofit Management and Leadership, 5*(2), 159-172.

Hannan, M. T., & Carroll, G. R. (1992). *Dynamics of organizational populations: Density, competition, and legitimation.* New York: Oxford University Press.

Hannan, M. T., & Freeman, J. (1977). The population ecology of organizations. *American Journal of Sociology, 82,* 929-964.

Hannan, M. T., & Freeman, J. (1984). Structural inertia and organizational change. *American Sociological Review, 49,* 149-164.

Hannan, M. T., & Freeman, J. (1989). *Organizational ecology.* Cambridge, MA: Harvard University Press.

Hardy, C. (1994). Understanding interorganizational domains: The case of refugee systems. *Journal of Applied Behavioral Science, 30*(3), 278-296.

Hasenfeld, Y. (1983). *Human service organizations.* Englewood Cliffs, NJ: Prentice Hall.

Hasenfeld, Y. (1992). *Human services as complex organizations.* Newbury Park, CA: Sage.

Hasenfeld, Y., & Schmid, H. (1989). The community center as a human service organization. *Nonprofit and Voluntary Sector Quarterly, 18*(1), 47-61.

Hawley, A. (1968). Human ecology. In D. L. Sills (Ed.), *International encyclopedia of social sciences.* New York: Macmillan.

Hedberg, B. (1981). How organizations learn and unlearn. In P. C. Nystrom & W. H. Starbuck (Eds.), *Handbook of organizational design* (pp. 3-27). London: Oxford University Press.

Herriot, S. R., Levinthal, D., & March, J. G. (1984). Learning from experience in organizations. *American Economic Review: Papers and Proceedings, 75,* 298-302.

Hutchinson, G. E. (1957). Concluding remarks. *Cold Spring Harbor Symposium on Quantitative Biology, 22,* 415-427.

Huxham, C., & Vangen, S. (1996). Managing interorganizational relationships. In S. P. Osborne (Ed.), *Managing in the voluntary sector* (pp. 202-216). London: International Thomson Business Press.

Kanter, R. M. (1990). When giants learn cooperative strategies. *Planning Review, 18*(1), 15-25.

Kreps, G. L. (1987). *Organizational communication: Theory and practice.* New York: Longman.

Kurke, L. B., & Ulrich, D. (1988). *When do theories of environmental selection and organizational adaptation best apply?* Paper presented at the Academy of Management Conference, Anaheim, CA.

Lammers, C. J., & Hickson, D. J. (1979). A cross-national and cross-institutional typology of organizations. In C. J. Lammers & D. J. Hickson (Eds.), *Organizations alike and unlike.* London: Routledge & Kegan Paul.

Lawrence, P. R., & Lorsch, J. W. (1967). *Organization and environment: Managing differentiation and integration.* Boston: Harvard University, Graduate School of Business Administration.

Leifer, R., & Huber, G. P. (1977). Relations among perceived environmental uncertainty, organizational structure, and boundary spanning behavior. *Administrative Science Quarterly, 22,* 235-247.

Levine, S., & White, P. E. (1961). Exchange as a conceptual framework for the study of interorganizational relationships. *Administrative Science Quarterly, 5,* 583-601.

Levinthal, D., & March, J. G. (1981). A model of adaptive organizational search. *Journal of Economic Behavior and Organization, 2,* 307-333.

Lewontin, R. C. (1978). Adaptation. *Scientific American, 239,* 212-230.

Lowndes, V. (1996). Varieties of new institutionalism: A critical appraisal. *Public Administration, 74,* 181-197.

March, J. G. (1981a). Decisions in organizations and theories of choice. In A. H. Van de ven & W. F. Joyce (Eds.), *Perspectives on organization design and behavior* (pp. 205-244). New York: John Wiley.

March, J. G. (1981b). Footnotes to organizational change. *Administrative Science Quarterly, 26,* 563-577.

Meyer, J. W., & Rowan, B. (1977). Institutionalized organizations: Formal structure as myth and ceremony. *American Journal of Sociology, 83,* 340-363.

Meyer, J. W., & Rowan, B. (1983). The structure of educational organization. In J. W. Meyer & W. R. Scott (Eds.), *Organizational environments: Ritual and rationality* (pp. 71-98). Beverly Hills, CA: Sage.

Meyer, J. W., Scott, W. R., Strang, D., & Creighton, A. (1988). Bureaucratization without centralization: Changes in the organizational system of U.S. public education, 1940-1980. In L. Zucker (Ed.), *Institutional patterns and organizations* (pp. 139-168). Cambridge, MA: Ballinger.

Miles, R., & Snow, C. (1978). *Organizational strategy, structure, and process.* New York: McGraw-Hill.

Miles, R. E., Snow, C. C., & Pfeffer, J. (1974). Organization-environment: Concepts and issues. *Industrial Relations, 13,* 244-264.

Miller, D. (1979). Strategy, structure, and environment: Context influences on bivariate associations. *Journal of Management Studies, 16,* 294-316.

Miller, D., & Friesen, P. (1980). Archetypes of organizational transition. *Administrative Science Quarterly, 25,* 268-299.

Mintzberg, H. (1979). *The structuring of organizations.* Englewood Cliffs, NJ: Prentice Hall.

Mizruchi, M. S., & Galaskiewicz, J. (1993). Networks of interorganizational relations. *Sociological Methods and Research, 22,* 46-70.

Motamedi, K. K. (1977). Adaptability and copability: A study of social systems, their environment, and survival. *Group and Organization Studies, 2*(4), 480-490.

Nelson, R. R., & Winter, S. G. (1982). *An evolutionary theory of economic change.* Cambridge, MA: Belknap Press of Harvard University.

Oster, S. M. (1995). *Strategic management for nonprofit organizations.* New York: Oxford University Press.

Pennings, J. (1981). Strategically interdependent organizations. In P. C. Nystrom & W. H. Starbuck (Eds.), *Handbook of organizational design* (Vol. 2, pp. 28-64). London: Oxford University Press.

Pennings, J. (1992). Structural contingency theory: A reappraisal. *Research in Organization Behavior, 14,* 267-309.

Perrow, C. (1986). *Complex organizations: A critical essay* (3rd ed.). New York: Random House.

Pfeffer, J. (1982). *Organizations and organization theory.* Marshfield, MA: Pitman.

Pfeffer, J. (1995). Mortality, reproducibility, and the persistence of styles of theory. *Organization Science, 6*(6), 681-686.

Pfeffer, J., & Leblibei, H. (1973). The effect of competition on some dimensions of organizational structure. *Social Forces, 52*(2), 268-279.

Pfeffer, J., & Salancik, G. R. (1978). *The external control of organizations.* New York: Harper & Row.

Powell, W. W., & DiMaggio, P. J. (Eds.). (1991). *The new institutionalism in organizational analysis.* Chicago: University of Chicago Press.

Reitan, T. C. (1998). Theories of interorganizational relations in the human services. *Social Service Review, 72*(3), 285-309.

Romanelli, E. (1987). *Contexts and strategies of organization creation: Patterns in performance.* Paper presented at the Annual Meeting of the Academy of Management.

Schmid, H. (1986). Managing the environment: Strategies for executives in human service organizations. *Human Systems Management, 6,* 307-315.

Schmid, H. (1992). Strategic and structural change in human service organizations: The role of the environment. *Administration in Social Work, 16*(3-4), 167-186.

Schmid, H. (1995). Merging nonprofit organizations: Analysis of a case study. *Nonprofit Management and Leadership, 5*(4), 377-391.

Schmid, H. (1998). *Israeli Long-Term Care Insurance Law: Impact on nonprofit and for-profit organizations.* Paper presented at the 20th anniversary of the Centre for Voluntary Organisation, London School of Economics & Political Science.

Schmid, H., & Hasenfeld, Y. (1993). Organizational dilemmas in the provision of home care services. *Social Service Review, 67*(1), 40-54.

Scott, W. R. (1992). *Organizations, rational, natural, and open systems.* Englewood Cliffs, NJ: Prentice Hall.

Scott, W. R. (1994). Institutional analysis: Variance and process theory approaches. In W. R. Scott & J. W. Meyer (Eds.), *Institutional environments and organizations: Structural complexity and individualism* (pp. 81-99). Thousand Oaks, CA: Sage.

Singh, J. V., & Lumsden, C. J. (1990). Theory and research in organizational ecology. *Annual Review of Sociology, 16,* 161-195.

Singh, J. V., Tucker, D. J., & Meinhard, A. G. (1991). Institutional change and ecological dynamics. In W. W. Powell & P. J. DiMaggio (Eds.), *The new institutionalism in organizational analysis* (pp. 390-422). Chicago: University of Chicago Press.

Starbuck, W. H. (1976). Organizations and their environments. In M. Dunnette (Ed.), *Handbook of organizational and industrial psychology* (pp. 1069-1123). Chicago: Rand McNally.

Sutton, J., Dobbin, F., Meyer, J., & Scott, W. R. (1994). The legislation of the workplace. *American Journal of Sociology, 99,* 944-971.

Thomas, W. I. (1928). *The child in America.* New York: Alfred Knopf.

Thompson, J. D. (1967). *Organization in action.* New York: McGraw-Hill.

Thompson, J. D., & McEwen, W. J. (1958). Organizational goals and environment: Goal setting as an interaction process. *American Sociological Review, 23*(1), 23-30.

Tolbert, P. M., & Zucker, L. G. (1996). The institutionalization of institutional theory. In S. R. Clegg, C. Hardy, & W. R. Nord (Eds.), *Handbook of organization studies* (pp. 175-190). Thousand Oaks, CA: Sage.

Tucker, D. J. (1994). Progress and problems in population ecology. In J. A. C. Baum & J. V. Singh (Eds.), *Evolutionary dynamics of organizations* (pp. 327-336). New York: Oxford University Press.

Tucker, D. J., Baum, J. A. C., & Singh, J. V. (1992). The institutional ecology of human service organizations. In Y. Hasenfeld (Ed.), *Human services as complex organizations* (pp. 47-72). Newbury Park, CA: Sage.

Tucker, D. J., Singh, J. V., & Meinhard, A. G. (1990). Organization form, population dynamics, and institutional change: The founding patterns of voluntary organizations. *Academy of Management Journal, 33,* 151-178.

Waddock, A. (1989). Understanding social partnership: An evolutionary model of partnership organizations. *Administration and Society, 21,* 78-100.

Wamseley, G. L., & Zald, M. N. (1976). *The political economy of public organizations.* Lexington, MA: Heath.

Weick, K. E. (1979). *The social psychology of organizations* (2nd ed.). New York: Addison-Weseley.

Whittington, R. (1989). *Corporate strategies in recession and recovery: Social structure and strategic choice.* London: Unwin Hyman.

Woodward, J. (1958). *Management and technology.* London: Her Majesty's Stationery Office.

Woodward, J. (1965). *Industrial organization: Theory and practice.* London: Oxford University Press.

Yankey, J. A. (1991). *Mergers, acquisitions, and consolidations in the nonprofit sector: Trends, processes, and lessons.* Paper presented at the Research Conference on Nonprofit Organizations in a Market Economy, Cleveland, OH.

Yasai-Ardekani, M. (1986). Structural adaptations to environments. *Academy of Management Review, 11*(1), 9-21.

York, A., & Zychlinski, E. (1996). Competing nonprofit organizations also collaborate. *Nonprofit Management and Leadership, 7*(1), 15-27.

Young, R. C. (1988). Is population ecology a useful paradigm for the study of organizations? *American Journal of Sociology, 94*(1), 1-24.

Zald, M. N. (1970). Political economy: A framework of comparative analysis. In M. N. Zald (Ed.), *Power in organizations* (pp. 221-261). Nashville, TN: The Vanderbilt University Press.

Zucker, L. G. (1988). Where do institutional patterns come from? Organizations as actors in social systems. In L. Zucker (Ed.), *Institutional patterns and organizations* (pp. 23-52). Cambridge, MA: Ballinger.

Zucker, L. G. (1989). Combining institutional theory and population ecology: No legitimacy, no history. *American Sociological Review, 54,* 542-545.

CHAPTER EIGHT

Organizational Structure and Performance

DAVID F. GILLESPIE

Organizational structure affects performance (Ketchen et al., 1997; Pfeffer, 1991). The structures of an agency reflect the division of work into tasks to be performed and the coordination of these tasks to accomplish goals (Mintzberg, 1979). Because performance indicates how well goals are being met, there is an inextricable interdependence of structures and performance. Our current understanding of this relationship, driven largely by mechanical metaphors and linear thinking, is based on coefficients of overall organizational structure with measures of performance. These static images have presented structure as being an overarching constraint designed to control behav-

ior. Although there is truth to this claim, the picture remains incomplete.

Today, ideas about organizational structure and its relationship to performance are evolving from static to dynamic thinking, from independent influences of one variable on another to interdependent systems, and from correlation to operational thinking. This evolution can be summarized in three phases: the earliest positional view of structure, followed by the more recent relational view, and the most recent system dynamics view. In considering the relationship between structure and performance, I emphasize system dynamics because it is the most promising but least understood of these ap-

AUTHOR'S NOTE: I want to express my appreciation to Rino Patti and Karen Joseph Robards for their insightful, helpful comments and suggestions, which increased the clarity of this chapter.

proaches and because it has yet to appear in the social work literature. The system dynamics approach is introduced and illustrated following a brief summary of the positional and relational approaches.

Although ideas of structure have been evolving, the conceptualization of performance has remained relatively stable. Even though preferences for particular measures have changed from time to time, performance consistently describes how the output of a process conforms to requirements, expectations, or goals and indicates how well an individual, task group, or organizational process is working. The criteria most often associated with performance include counts (productivity), costs (efficiency), or client improvement (effectiveness). Administrators set targets for performance and then measure degrees of conformity to those targets. These measurements provide a way of evaluating performance and can serve as a basis for learning how to make improvements. Because the performance of individuals almost always depends on the process of which they are a part (Deming, 1986), the nature of this process is a potentially powerful leverage point to improve performance.

Although the various approaches to structure each assume a causal relationship between structure and performance, the specific nature of this relationship is quite different in each case. The differences between these approaches lead to radically different images of organizational structure, with correspondingly different implications for altering structure to improve performance. The following sections summarize each approach—positional, relational, and system dynamics—giving primary characteristics, key indicators, and strengths and weaknesses.

POSITIONAL APPROACH

The classical view of organizational structure is rooted in the work of Weber (1922/1947), Parsons (1951), and Homans (1958). In their view, structure is the pattern of relations among positions in the organization (or in the group, community, or society). Associated with each position is a set of roles that the people occupying the positions are expected to perform. These roles comprise the designated behaviors and obligatory relations incumbent on the people in the positions. In an organization, the positions and their roles are formally defined and exist independently of the individuals who fill them. The individuals who assume these positions are seen as transients who move from position to position. Individuals are viewed as less permanent than the positions themselves. Taken as a collective, the positions and attached roles constitute the relatively stable and enduring structure of the organization, often reflected in an organizational chart. James and Jones (1976) define structure as "the enduring characteristics of an organization reflected by the distribution of units and positions within an organization and their systematic relationships to each other" (p. 76). From this view of structure, roles and positions are seen as largely determining who talks to whom, who does what, and who supervises whom.

The key indicators of structure derived from the positional approach include configuration (size, span of control), complexity (vertical, horizontal, geographical differentiation), formalization, and centralization. Although there is disagreement with respect to the conceptual and empirical definition of organizational size (Gillespie & Mileti, 1976; Kimberly, 1976), it most often refers to the total number of full-time and some percentage of part-time employees (Blau & Schoenherr, 1971). Span of control is the number of subordinates reporting directly to a superior (Healey, 1956). Complexity is the number of hierarchical levels, divisions or occupational roles, and geographic locations (Blau & Schoenherr, 1971). Formalization is the number of written policies and procedures (Hage & Aiken, 1969). Centralization is the extent to which decision-making power is held by a few central decision makers or decentralized through the broader organization (Hall, 1982, pp. 114-115). Each indicator contributes to our understanding of structure.

Despite an explicit emphasis on predicting performance, tests of the relationship between distinct structural configurations and performance have been disappointing (Barney & Hoskisson, 1990; Ketchen, Thomas, & Snow, 1993; Meyer, 1991). Roughly equal numbers of studies have yielded null results versus positive results (McGee & Thomas, 1986; Thomas & Venkatraman, 1988). Ketchen et al.'s (1997) meta-analysis of 40 studies found that overall structural configuration accounted for about 8% of the variance in performance. The percentage of variance explained increased when broad definitions of configuration were used, when organizations from a single industry were examined, and when longitudinal designs were used. Organizational structure does affect performance, but the effect is weaker than postulated in theories.

The positional view of structure captures an important aspect of organizations. Organizations do have designated positions that people fill, and the roles attached to these positions specify, enable, and constrain the behavior of incumbents. This formal structure is useful in clarifying relationships and responsibilities for smoother operations and coordination. On the other hand, network analysts argue that this view of structure is overly simplistic and incomplete (Burt, 1976; Coleman, 1973). Specifically, the positional approach has been criticized for its inability to take into account the active part individuals play in creating and shaping organizational structure.

RELATIONAL APPROACH

Structural theorists in the network tradition focus primarily on the role of human action in forging linkages and thereby enacting structure. Instead of the prescribed roles and hierarchical relations, these theorists argue that much of what is meaningful about structure lies in the emergent interactions between people. In this view, the actual structure of relations in organizations may or may not coincide with its formal structure. Individuals almost always interact in ways that are not dictated by their positions. For example, a highly competent executive secretary may have more power than the organizational role indicates. Network analysts conceive of the relationships among people in a system as worthy of study in their own right. The relational approach became increasingly popular among organizational theorists during the late 1970s and early 1980s (Brass, 1984; Roberts & O'Reilly, 1978; Tichy, 1981). However, most of this work concentrated on interorganizational networks. There is very little empirical work on configurations of organizational network structure and performance (Krackhardt & Brass, 1994).

Size, density, distance, and components are some key indicators of structure derived from the relational view. Size is the number of actors linked to the network (Marsden, 1990). Density is the proportion of possible links in a network to those that actually exist (Tolsdorf, 1976). Distance is the maximum number of links required to connect actors that have relations (Burt, 1991). There are two kinds of groupings of organizational members. Cliques comprise members who interact and share relationships with others in the same group (Burt, 1987). Examples include standing committees, task forces, and work groups. Structural equivalence describes members who have similar types of relations to other actors in the network (Borgatti & Everett, 1992). Middle-level administrators often represent a structural equivalent group in that they have similar relations to their superiors and subordinates, even though they do not necessarily relate to each other. Together, these indicators describe network structure.

The main distinction between the positional and relational approaches is that the relational approach focuses on actual interaction whereas the positional approach focuses on the role prescriptions associated with positions. The positional view approaches structure as top down, formal, and relatively static. The emphasis is on designing structures that produce efficient and effective performance. The relational approach sees structure as bottom-up, formal and informal, mostly individually motivated, and more dynamic. The emphasis is on finding structures that build morale and support innovation or growth. Whereas relational theory is rooted in systems theory (Buckley, 1967) and assumes a dynamic structure, the studies of networks are mostly based on cross-sectional data and therefore present a static picture.

Both the positional and relational approaches seek to predict performance from structural factors. In the positional approach, structural variables act independently and causality runs one way. For example, the span of control is expected to influence subordinate performance. In the relational approach, structural variables emerge from the interaction between actors, which assumes two-way causality. For instance, the size of an actor's network may positively affect performance in cases where coordination with others is the goal (Gillespie, Colignon, Banerjee, Murty, & Rogge, 1993, p. 90). However, studies of relational structure are based on point estimates at some period of time, such as the frequency of contacts or average distance between actors, and these yield a network snapshot of the relations among actors. This allows the weighting of such factors to be fixed, and it keeps the causal mechanism implicit, represented only by the sign of the coefficients. For these reasons, the promise of the relational approach has failed to be realized.

SYSTEM DYNAMICS APPROACH

In contrast to the positional and relational approaches, system dynamics assumes that each variable is linked in a circular process to both performance and to some of the other variables. These circular processes form feedback loops. This shift from one-way to circular causality and from independent factors to interdependent relations is profound. Instead of viewing organizational performance as an outcome resulting from a set of static, stimulus-response relations, it is viewed as an ongoing, interdependent, self-sustaining, dynamic process. Rather than trying to predict outcomes at a given point in time, this focus seeks to understand the structure of relations that is driving the levels of performance over time.

System dynamics originated in the work of Forrester (1961, 1971, 1975). In system dynamics, the emphasis shifts from the local spatial and temporal perspective of an independent variable affecting a dependent variable to a web of ongoing interdependencies. The focus is less on the particular variables of structure and more on the rising and falling patterns of relationships among those variables. For example, the positive relationship between size and number of clients is just one small piece of the staffing picture. If increasing size makes it possible to help more clients, then increasing the number of clients adds pressure to bring about further increases in size, which will eventually affect performance (Forrester, 1971). This pattern of circular or two-way causation holds for most of the relationships that compose the dynamics of performance.

The key indicators of dynamic structure are reflected in the distribution of critical variables over time, feedback loops, and delays in the effects of one variable on another. At the simplest level, behavior-over-time (BOT) graphs—sometimes called reference modes—are trend lines or distributions of variables over time. By plotting the behavior over time of two or more variables on the same graph, we are able to see dynamic relationships. Although people are able to understand the structure of relationships (the form or pattern apparent in the way variables are interrelated) that make a system work, they are not very good at understanding how the dynamics (changing patterns of interrelationships) operate (Richmond & Peterson, 1996). This limitation results from our mental models, which tend to emphasize attributes, direct cause and effect, and linear extrapolations. Seeing the world this way, as Senge (1990) points out, leads us to "miss critical feedback relationships,

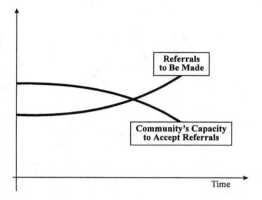

Figure 8.1. Behavior-Over-Time Graph

misjudge time delays, and often focus on variables that are visible or salient, not necessarily high leverage" (p. 203).

Figure 8.1 shows the behavior over time of a hypothetical community's capacity to accept referrals and the number of clients screened for referral by an agency. The graph shows that, until recently, the community's capacity to accept referrals was stable and slightly larger than the number of referrals made. This meant that there was minimal delay between making referrals and actually connecting clients with services. However, when the community's capacity declined, the ability of the agency to make timely referrals was constrained, and this created a backlog of clients ready to be referred. Because the agency was committed to making referrals within 48 hours, the backlog represented an agency performance problem. The pattern of this problem is best represented by events happening over time.

The concept of feedback also describes dynamic structure. Feedback is a term from general systems theory that refers to information about performance being sent back to affect subsequent performance. The feedback loop is

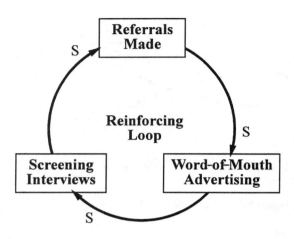

Figure 8.2. Causal Loop Diagram of a Reinforcing Feedback Loop

NOTE: S = same direction (positive relationship: more = more, less = less).

mouth advertising, which feeds back to further increase screening interviews. Or, decreasing the number of screening interviews leads to a decrease in referrals, which could lead to negative word-of-mouth advertising and thus feed back to further decrease screening interviews. The S symbol next to the arrow indicates that the two variables move in the same direction: increase-increase or decrease-decrease. Reinforcing feedback loops are the engines of organizational growth and decline. The presence of reinforcing loops is commonly referred to as virtuous or vicious cycles, bandwagon effects, or snowball effects.

There is a ceiling or limit to every growth curve, and there is a floor or bottom to every decline. These limits define the second basic type of feedback, balancing or stabilizing loops. Figure 8.3 is a CLD showing the structure of a

the most basic structural feature in organizations. Every decision occurs within a feedback loop (Forrester, 1971, p. 4). Feedback loops can be identified with causal loop diagrams (CLDs), which are graphs that show how the relationships among variables influence each other to reinforce or constrain performance. CLDs make explicit our understanding of the structure underlying performance, provide visual representation to help communicate this understanding to others, and capture key aspects of complex systems in a succinct form.

There are two types of feedback loops: reinforcing and balancing. Figure 8.2 is a CLD representing a reinforcing or amplifying feedback process. It shows that increasing the number of screening interviews leads to an increase in referrals made; assuming satisfied clients, the increase in referrals leads to positive word-of-

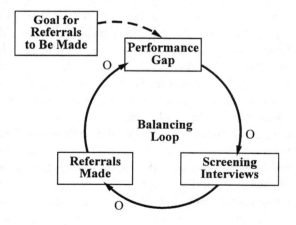

Figure 8.3. Causal Loop Diagram of a Balancing Feedback Loop

NOTE: O = opposite direction (negative relationship: more = less, less = more). Dashed line = relationship governed by a constant.

balancing feedback process. The goal defines the target behavior; in this hypothetical example, the desired number of referrals to be made. The difference between the target number of referrals and actual number of referrals yields a gap, which is a measure of performance. The closer the actual number of referrals is to the goal, the smaller the gap (i.e., the better the performance). An increase in the gap (i.e., a decrease in performance) suggests a need to increase the number of screening interviews. An increase in screening interviews leads to an increase in the referrals made. More referrals reduce the gap (i.e., improve the performance).

Balancing feedback loops operate whenever there is goal-seeking behavior. The process works to close the gap between a goal and the actual condition. The smaller the gap, the better the performance. The goal can be an explicit target, such as increasing by 10% the number of clients served, or it can be implicit, such as competing with colleagues to win recognition. Balancing loops are more difficult to identify than reinforcing loops, partly because the increases and decreases average out to a steady performance and produce straight-line BOT graphs, which make it seem that there is no change.

A third key feature of dynamic systems is the delay in the time it takes for the information about performance to circle around and affect subsequent performance. These delays may result from the lags in time it takes for one variable to affect another or because the performance variable is embedded in a web of relations in which the feedback effect transpires through a chain of several other variables. It is extremely rare in organizational systems for performance to reach a stated goal and maintain that level continuously. Delayed effects in feedback loops are one reason for this rarity.

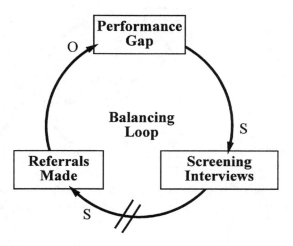

Figure 8.4. Causal Loop Diagram of a Balancing Feedback Loop With Delay

NOTE: S = same direction (positive relationship: more = more, less = less). O = opposite direction (negative relationship: more = less, less = more). // = delayed effect.

Figure 8.4 extends the goal-seeking balanced feedback loop to show a delay between screening applications and referrals made in the feedback loop. Delays tend to create under- and overadjustment around the goal. This is because delays make it difficult to judge that performance levels have reached their targets; when the target is reached, it is impossible to stop the process abruptly, which leads to an oscillating pattern of behavior over time, over- and undershooting the goal. Delays are both pervasive and frequently misjudged in organizational systems. Although there is some amount of delay in every feedback loop, this is rarely considered by either practitioners or theoreticians. Yet, as Senge (1990, p. 89) points out, reducing delays is one of the highest leverage points for improving performance. For example, knowing the trend lines for the number

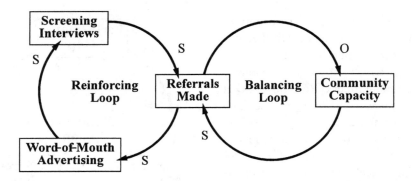

Figure 8.5. Causal Loop Diagram of Combined Reinforcing and Balancing Feedback Loops

NOTE: S = same direction (positive relationship: more = more, less = less). O = opposite direction (negative relationship: more = less, less = more).

of clients, the number of employees, and the number of clients that each worker can optimally serve allows administrators to manage the gap between the number of staff needed to provide optimal service and the number of staff currently employed.

Every organizational performance trend line is driven by some combination of reinforcing and balancing feedback loops. Like delays, combining loops complicates performance patterns. The webs of reinforcing and balancing feedback loops that make up our organizations can create counterintuitive behaviors that challenge social service administrators. The identification of feedback loops can illustrate how actions reinforce or counteract each other (Senge, 1990). Figure 8.5 shows how the reinforcing loop between screening interviews and referrals is constrained by a balancing loop between referrals made and the community's capacity to accept referrals. As referrals are made, the positive word-of-mouth advertising brings more potential clients to be screened, which leads to more referrals being made. The growing number of referrals eventually reaches a limit. In this

case, the limit is governed by the community's capacity to accept referrals. As the number of referrals goes up, community capacity is reduced. As community capacity is reduced, fewer referrals are made. If an administrator were interested in agency growth, it would be apparent from this structure that the leverage lies in expanding the community's capacity to handle referrals. Thus, models of the structure underlying performance patterns provide administrators with the ability to discover interrelationships rather than getting distracted by particular links in linear cause-effect chains. This discovery provides the opportunity to focus on recurring patterns and to work *on* the system instead of *in* the system; to be designers rather than merely operators.

Certain basic systemic structures, called *archetypes* (Senge, 1990), have been found in many kinds of organizations under many different circumstances. The structure shown in Figure 8.5 is called the Limits to Growth or Limits to Success archetype (Senge et al., 1999). Because social service agencies operate in response to the effects of complex interrelationships rather than simpler linear cause and effect chains, it sometimes happens that these interrelationships operate at a point where small changes in the organization result in a large effect that seems out of proportion to the cause. For example, most successful organizational change efforts have started from a small project prototype (Schrage, 1999). A better understanding of nonproportional interrelationships in organizations is needed for effective decision making and policy analysis (Forrester, 1975).

Social service agencies are complex systems that evolve over time and require simplification to manage. O'Toole (1993) suggests that "before an executive can usefully simplify, though, she must fully understand the complexities involved" (p. 5). Wheatley (1992) states that "when we give up myopic attention to details and stand far enough away to observe the movement of the total system, we develop a new appreciation for what is required to manage a complex system" (p. 110). Using system dynamic modeling helps us to simplify our understanding.

CREATING A STRUCTURAL THEORY OF PERFORMANCE

To illustrate how BOT graphs and CLDs can be used to create a system dynamic theory of performance, I will present the hypothetical case of Human Services Referral, Inc. (HSR). HSR has carved out a niche by screening people who are experiencing problems and referring them to the appropriate community agencies. Screening interviews take about 2 hours, referrals are made within 1 or 2 days, and confirmation of client contracts with the agency are generally received within a week. To avoid having clients turned away or put on waiting lists, HSR checks weekly on community capacity to accept referrals. HSR has experienced relatively steady growth over the past 2 years.

During the last 6 months, however, the agency had seen wild fluctuations in the community's capacity to accept referrals. At first, the administrators assumed that this signaled increasing competition in the community due to a new agency making referrals. They were concerned about sustaining their growth and hoped that by gaining a deeper understanding of the structural issues involved, they might discover some decisions or policies they could take to affect the problem.

The HSR administrators began by drawing a BOT graph. On a BOT line graph, the horizontal axis is always the variable of time and the vertical axis is the reference mode or behavior to be tracked. When there is more than one reference mode, as shown above with the example in Figure 8.1, it is important to distinguish and label the trend lines because they often cross, which complicates accurate interpretation. Although it is advisable to use as much detail as warranted by the data, the most important information in BOT graphs is the general trend and patterns of covariation.

Figure 8.6 is the HSR graph of community capacity. It shows an expanding oscillation pattern, with the amplitude expanding for the last 6 months. As described above, the oscillation pattern results from a balancing loop structure. This happens because the net change in the number of referrals that can be accepted by the community shifts back and forth over time, from positive to negative and negative to positive, as it first overshoots and then undershoots the target goal. Because the oscillation pattern suggests a balancing process with delays

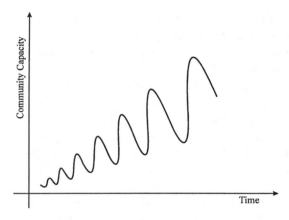

Figure 8.6. Behavior-Over-Time of Community Capacity

(Roberts, Anderson, Deal, Garet, & Shaffer, 1983), administrators spent the next few weeks gathering data and talking to peers at the agencies they sent referrals to explore what might be causing the oscillations in capacity.

Based on this information, the administrators drew a CLD. Because CLDs show causal relationships and feedback loops within a system, all variables in a CLD must be able to increase or decrease. The key to identifying feedback loops is to focus on one reference mode or variable and identify the relationships that are causing it to change for the period of time being considered (Richardson & Pugh, 1981). Delays, indicated with a break in the arrow or slashes across the arrow, should be included when there is a significant amount of time before the effect of one variable has an impact on another. Kim (1992) reports a set of guidelines for constructing CLDs.

As shown Figure 8.7, the backlog of screened applications at HSR increased as a complex function of the decrease in community capacity.

This happened because the processing of screening applications required special training, and only certain staff had received this training. When the community's capacity to accept referrals dropped below the typical number of screening applications processed by HSR each week, fewer referrals could be made, which in turn increased the performance gap to the point that a backlog began to accumulate, and thus the time to make referrals took longer. Of course, the agencies that HSR sent referrals had their own client referral processes as well. Therefore, when the time it took HSR to make a referral increased, the other agencies intensified efforts around their own referral sources and also turned to HSR's competitor, which brought about a decline in the number of people to screen.

Each time the backlog hit a critical level, HSR administrators responded by adding staff on a temporary basis. The added staff, combined with a decrease in the number of people to screen, enabled the agency to work off the backlog, and the referral time would return to the original 1- or 2-day goal. However, it took several weeks for the community agencies that HSR dealt with to learn of the improved referral time and shift their effort to depend again on HSR for clients. Therefore, the community's capacity to receive HSR referrals oscillated as a function of the agency's internal efforts to match the number of people screened with the human service capacity in the community.

The CLD helped the administrators to see how their internal effort was affecting the referral stream and thus their performance. Although they had previously assumed that periodic downturns in community capacity were the result of competitive pressures or cyclical trends in the community, their structural assess-

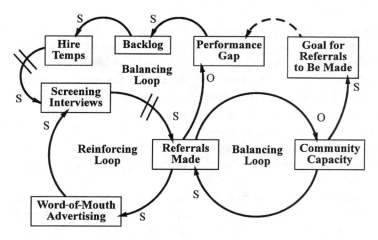

Figure 8.7. Causal Loop Diagram of Feedback Loops With Delays

S = same direction (positive relationship: more = more, less = less). O = opposite direction (negative relationship: more = less, less = more). // = delayed effect. Dashed line = relationship governed by a constant.

ment suggested that their internal policies could be making the situation worse. With a better understanding of how the number of trained interviewers affected community capacity, the administrators instituted a flexible workforce policy to cross-train staff. All employees were trained to conduct the screening interviews and recommend referrals. This added flexibility to the agency's screening capability, making it possible to respond more quickly to fluctuations in community capacity and reduce the fluctuations in the backlog of clients to be screened.

UNDERSTANDING PERFORMANCE AS A FUNCTION OF DYNAMIC STRUCTURE

In today's human service organizations, performance trends are rarely as simple as those illustrated above. Periods of growth punctuated by periodic downturns are usually the result of many reinforcing and balancing processes occurring simultaneously. These webs of shifting dynamics cannot be adequately understood through cross-sectional correlation of variables. The BOT graphs and CLDs are useful tools that provide a good starting point for developing a deeper structural understanding of problems. As we dig deeper into the structures of our organizations and the behaviors they produce, additional loops representing additional relationships are added until there is an accurate account of the situation under study.

The strength of any particular feedback or "closed-loop structure" in a system will rise and fall over time. A closed-loop structure depicts the variables and relationships that cause the pattern of behavior observed. Certain loops will dominate for awhile; then other loops will take over. After another period of time, the first loop might be re-energized, or a third loop might assume dominance. Therefore, addressing a problem of poor performance in complex situations cannot be a one-time effort, or a search for the "most important" factor, nor for the individual to blame. It is essential to consider the ongoing, interdependent relations whose strengths vary over time, partly in response to changes that are being made, intentionally or unintentionally, and partly as a result of the ongoing dynamics (i.e., feedback, delays) inherent in the system structure. As we develop insight into the structures of behavior that are creating the observed performance, we are able to see beyond symptoms to design policies and take actions that alter the source of a problem. The great potential of this system dynamics approach comes from its focus on the level of systemic structure, where the greatest leverage lies for solving problems.

BOT graphs and CLDs are developed through computer simulation of actual conditions (Richardson & Pugh, 1981). The word *simulation* originally meant to imitate. A simulation model may be a physical replica, a mental conception, a set of mathematical equations, a computer model, or some combination of these (Roberts et al., 1983). Dynamic simulation models map the relationships that are important to a performance problem and then use computers to simulate the interaction of those variables over time. The equations, which represent the variables' performances, are constantly recomputed as time changes, producing BOT graphs that show behavior and the effects of changes in the variables. Simulation is the most powerful tool for investigating the structure that drives performance (Forrester, 1971). Richardson (1991) describes how "the use of digital simulation to trace through time the behavior of a dynamic system makes it easy to incorporate nonlinearities" (p. 155). Only re-

cently has the technology caught up with the theory (Richmond & Peterson, 1996). Simulation now combines both the power of systems theory and the emerging science of complexity in the form of computer models to be used as an administrative tool by the practitioner.

SUMMARY AND CONCLUSION

Although the positional, relational, and system dynamics approaches all view organizational structure as a key determinant of performance, the differences between these approaches, summarized in Table 8.1, lead to radically different conceptions of structure and very different implications for intervention. The positional approach is prescriptive in the sense that it uses the organizationally prescribed positions and roles, whereas both the relational and system dynamics approaches are descriptive. The positional and relational approaches are static compared to system dynamics. System dynamics integrates the positional top-down view and formal organizational aspects with the relational bottom-up view and the individually motivated informal relations. Positional theorists and practitioners see structural variables as being created by administrators and directly causing performance; causality is one-way. Relational theorists and practitioners see structural variables as partly created by administrators and partly emerging from individually motivated patterns of interaction, which then cause performance; causality is two-way and direct. System dynamics theorists see structure as partly created by administrators and partly emerging from patterns of interaction that form feedback loops to cause performance; causality is two-way, direct and indirect.

TABLE 8.1 Summary Characteristics of the Positional, Relational, and System Dynamics Approaches

Positional	Relational	System Dynamics
Prescriptive	Descriptive	Descriptive
Static	Static	Dynamic
Top-down	Bottom-up	Up and down
Formal positions	Informal individual relations	Formal and informal relationships
One-way direct causality	Two-way direct causality	Two-way direct and indirect causality

Using system dynamics as a theoretical foundation, social service administrators can observe and better understand the web of interrelationships found in organizations and, as a result, increase their competence in locating, designing, and instituting high-leverage change measures. To use the new conceptual and methodological tools of system dynamics, we need to educate ourselves about its theory and practice and apply this theory to the most persistent problems faced by social service administrators. The development of system dynamic models and experimentation through computer simulation of performance problems can help improve our understanding of complex dynamics and ultimately improve performance.

REFERENCES

Barney, J. B., & Hoskisson, R. E. (1990). Strategic groups: Untested assertions and research propositions. *Managerial and Decision Economics, 11,* 187-198.

Blau, P. M., & Schoenherr, R. A. (1971). *The structure of organizations.* New York: Basic Books.

Borgatti, S. P., & Everett, M. G. (1992). Notions of position in social network analysis. In P. V. Marsden (Ed.), *Sociological methodology 1992* (pp. 1-35). Washington, DC: American Sociological Association.

Brass, D. J. (1984). Being in the right place: A structural analysis of individual influence in an organization. *Administrative Science Quarterly, 29,* 518-539.

Buckley, W. (1967). *Sociology and modern systems theory.* Englewood Cliffs, NJ: Prentice Hall.

Burt, R. S. (1976). Positions in networks. *Social Forces, 55,* 93-122.

Burt, R. S. (1987). Social contagion and innovation: Cohesion versus structural equivalence. *American Journal of Sociology, 92,* 1287-1335.

Burt, R. S. (1991). *STRUCTURE: Reference Manual* (Version 4.2). New York: Columbia University, Research Center in Structural Analysis.

Coleman, J. (1973). *The mathematics of collective action.* Chicago: Aldine.

Deming, W. E. (1986). *Out of the crisis.* Cambridge, MA: MIT Center for Advanced Engineering Study.

Forrester, J. W. (1961). *Industrial dynamics.* Cambridge, MA: MIT Press.

Forrester, J. W. (1971). *Principles of systems.* New York: Wright-Allen Press.

Forrester, J. W. (1975). *Collected papers of Jay W. Forrester.* Cambridge, MA: MIT Press.

Gillespie, D. F., Colignon, R. A., Banerjee, M. M., Murty, S. A., & Rogge, M. (1993). *Partnerships for community preparedness* (Monograph No. 53). Boulder, CO: Institute of Behavioral Science.

Gillespie, D. F., & Mileti, D. S. (1976). A refined model of differentiation in organizations. *Sociology and Social Research, 61,* 263-278.

Hage, J., & Aiken, M. (1969). Routine technology, social structure, and organizational goals. *Administrative Science Quarterly, 14,* 366-376.

Hall, R. H. (1982). *Organizations.* Englewood Cliffs, NJ: Prentice Hall.

Healey, J. H. (1956, September). Coordination and control of executive functions. *Personnel, 33,* 106-117.

Homans, G. (1958). Social behavior as exchange. *American Journal of Sociology, 62,* 597-606.

James, L., & Jones, A. (1976). Organizational structure: A review of structural dimensions and their relationships with individual attitudes and behavior. *Organizational Behavior and Human Performance, 16,* 74-113.

Ketchen, D. J., Combs, J. G., Russell, C. J., Shook, C., Dean, M. A., Runge, J., Lohrke, F. T., Naumann, S. E., Haptonstahl, D. E., Baker, R., Beckstein, B. A., Handler, C., Honig, H., & Lamoureux, S. (1997). Organizational configurations and performance: A meta-analysis. *Academy of Management Journal, 40*(1), 223-240.

Ketchen, D. J., Thomas, J. B., & Snow, C. C. (1993). Organizational configurations and performance: A comparison of theoretical approaches. *Academy of Management Journal, 36*(6), 1278-1313.

Kim, D. H. (1992). Guidelines for drawing causal loop diagrams. *The Systems Thinker, 3*(1), 7-8.

Kimberly, J. R. (1976). Organizational size and the structuralist perspective: A review, critique, and proposal. *Administrative Science Quarterly, 21,* 571-597.

Krackhardt, D., & Brass, D. J. (1994). Intraorganizational networks: The micro side. In S. Wasserman & G. Joseph (Eds.), *Advances in social network analysis* (pp. 207-229). Thousand Oaks, CA: Sage.

Marsden, P. V. (1990). Network data and measurement. *Annual Review of Sociology, 16,* 435-463.

McGee, J., & Thomas, H. (1986). Strategic groups: Theory, research, and taxonomy. *Strategic Management Journal, 7,* 141-160.

Meyer, A. D. (1991). What is strategy's distinctive competence? *Journal of Management, 17,* 821-833.

Mintzberg, H. (1979). *The structuring of organizations.* Englewood Cliffs, NJ: Prentice Hall.

O'Toole, J. (1993). *The executive's compass: Business and the good society.* New York: Oxford University Press.

Parsons, T. (1951). *The social system.* New York: Free Press.

Pfeffer, J. (1991). Organization theory and structural perspectives on management. *Journal of Management, 17,* 789-803.

Richardson, G. P. (1991). *Feedback thought in social science and systems theory.* Philadelphia: University of Pennsylvania Press.

Richardson, G. P., & Pugh, A. L., III. (1981). *Introduction to system dynamics modeling with DYNAMO.* Cambridge, MA: MIT Press.

Richmond, B., & Peterson, S. (1996). *An introduction to systems thinking.* Hanover, NH: High Performance Systems.

Roberts, K. H., & O'Reilly, C. A. (1978). Organizations as communications structures: An empirical approach. *Human Communication Research, 4,* 283-293.

Roberts, N., Anderson, D., Deal, R., Garet, M., & Shaffer, W. (1983). *Introduction to computer simulation: A system dynamics modeling approach.* New York: Addison-Wesley.

Schrage, M. (1999, May). The proto project. *Fast Company, 24,* 138-144.

Senge, P. M. (1990). *The fifth discipline.* New York: Currency Doubleday.

Senge, P. M., Kleiner, A., Roberts, C., Ross, R., Roth, R., & Smith, B. (1999). *The dance of change.* New York: Currency Doubleday.

Thomas, H., & Venkatraman, N. (1988). Research in strategic groups: Progress and prognosis. *Journal of Management Studies, 25,* 537-555.

Tichy, N. M. (1981). Networks in organizations. In P. Nystrom & W. Starbuck (Eds.), *Handbook of organizational design* (Vol. 2, pp. 225-249). New York: Oxford University Press.

Tolsdorf, C. C. (1976). Social networks, support, and coping: An exploratory study. *Family Process, 15,* 407-417.

Weber, M. (1947). *The theory of social and economic organization.* New York: Free Press. (Original work published 1922)

Wheatley, M. J. (1992). *Leadership and the new science: Learning about organization from an orderly universe.* San Francisco: Berrett-Koehler.

CHAPTER NINE

Motivating Work Performance in Social Services

DIANE VINOKUR-KAPLAN
DANIEL BOGIN

Despite the adoption of sophisticated electronic technologies in today's workplace, managers throughout the American economy need to understand that, in the long run, their most valuable resource is their personnel, including their frontline employees (see Gummer, 1995). This perspective is particularly germane to the labor-intensive social services workplace, in which social service managers and policymakers have sometimes overlooked workers' needs. The staff's resulting demoralization or departure negatively influence the agency's effectiveness and realization of its mis-

sion. The current environment in which many social services find themselves is especially competitive (Kearns, 1996; Kramer, 1994; Ryan, 1999; Salamon, 1994), and any costs accrued by poor employee selection, performance, or retention are particularly acute. Thus, in a workplace with an increased use of "temps," freelancers, and part-time workers, work performance, motivation, professional burnout, turnover, and retention are significant concerns of social service managers (Jayaratne & Chess, 1984; Kahn, personal communication, May 12, 1999; Soderfeldt, Solderfeldt, & Warg,

AUTHORS' NOTE: The authors thank Professors Robert L. Kahn (The University of Michigan), Rino Patti (University of Southern California), and Robert A. Roe (Tilberg University, The Netherlands) for their comments and help with this chapter.

1995; Vinokur-Kaplan, 1995a; Vinokur-Kaplan, Jayaratne, & Chess, 1994).

Such managers' efforts to improve human service workers' performance must be conducted while upholding professional ethics. For example, professional social work managers are obliged to attend to practitioners' morale and job satisfaction, in keeping with the NASW (1996) Code of Ethics concern for treating colleagues with respect. This code also admonishes managers to learn about and appreciate each practitioner's true nature, rather than prejudging the worker's capability based on such social signals as language, gender, and financial status (Calas & Smircich, 1996). It proscribes managers from unethical and illegal exploitation or harassment of workers.

This chapter seeks to provide readers with a concise orientation to a voluminous topic that has been addressed with many different approaches and emphases by psychologists and other social scientists. In a recent review on matching motivational strategies with organizational contexts, Mitchell (1997) points out that the major motivational variables currently being studied empirically include dispositions, needs, goals, expectancies, self-efficacy, fairness, rewards, social influence, and job design. Yet despite this wide array of theories, he urges that "no one theory is best, and we must therefore strive to match our motivational interventions with our resources, and the demands and constraints of the situation" (p. 57).

To establish a common focus, we first present a contemporary approach to defining and addressing work performance. Second, we note the need to link individual goals and needs with organizational goals to enhance work performance. We then provide a schema to categorize various theoretical perspectives on motivation

from social science theory and research, which also can be applied in developing programs to enhance workers' performance. Thereafter, we highlight the paucity of studies on human service work performance and possible contributors to this situation. Then, we review social work research to extract workplace conditions that are empirically and positively related to proxy measures of human service work performance, such as job satisfaction and job retention. We conclude with recommendations for further studies to recognize and improve motivation and work performance in human services. Space does not allow for a full, empirically based critique of each theory mentioned, but for such recent reviews, the reader is referred to Dunnette and Hough (1990), Kanfer and Heggestad (1997), Kluger and DeNisi (1996, 1998), Mitchell (1997), Roe (1999), and Stajkovic and Luthans (1998).

DEFINING AND MEASURING WORK PERFORMANCE AND ITS ENHANCEMENT

Although we urge social service administrators to continually develop their skills to enhance their employees' motivation and performance, we also recognize that defining and conceptualizing performance in the workplace is a major challenge in itself. Several recent social science reviews have further elaborated the general approach to assessing the parameters and content of work performance. For instance, Roe (1999) limits his review on work performance to literature focusing on "the performance of people carrying out tasks with the purpose of some kind of economic exchange, [who are] typically employees of firms or public organizations" (p. 232). He further distinguishes between two interlinked definitions, or components, of work performance. One focuses on *process:* "Performance is the process by which people (individually or collectively) try to achieve a given work goal." The other interlinking definition focuses on *outcome:* "Performance is the congruence between the work goal and the outcome of the process by which people (individually or collectively) try to achieve that work goal" (p. 234).

To illustrate, let us assume that a social worker is placed in a bounded work environment (a social welfare agency), which is, in turn, embedded in a multidimensional context (e.g., social, legal, political, geographic). The work environment confronts the social worker with a goal (e.g., protect children from further family violence, finalize adoptions, or assess a community's most pressing needs). The environment evokes a regulated transformation process (e.g., intensive case management, family counseling, strategic planning) that results in a particular desired outcome (Roe, 1999, p. 234), (e.g., family's children developing and healthy, abandoned children successfully adopted, new community agenda set). Thus, both work process and work outcome reflect important aspects of work performance.

Arvey and Murphy's (1998) review of the work performance evaluation literature beginning in 1993 also summarizes three recent trends regarding how work performance must be approached. These trends point to important elements to include when designing interventions to enhance social service workers' performance.

1. The conception of work performance should be viewed as multifactorial in nature, and more than just the execution of simple, specific tasks (Arvey & Murphy, 1998). For example, Borman and Brush (1993) used published and unpublished studies to capture the complexity of managerial performance. They ultimately identified 18 factors, containing many complex tasks that should be considered in evaluating management performance (including planning and organizing, training, coaching, developing subordinates, and technical proficiency; Arvey & Murphy, 1998, pp. 145-146).

2. Definitions of job performance are becoming less precise, reflecting the more interchangeable, dynamic nature of work at the end of the 20th century. "Researchers are recognizing that job performance . . . involves a wider array of important organizational activities" (Arvey & Murphy, 1998, p. 141). This change reflects a departure from the earlier behavioristic/objective orientation of industrial/organizational psychology, "which emphasized on-task performance as the only important performance domain" (Arvey & Murphy, 1998, p. 148). The broader, contemporary approaches focus "on the personal competencies required to perform various work roles and jobs rather than a narrow review of specific tasks and duties inherent in fixed jobs and work roles" (Arvey & Murphy, 1998, p. 146).

For example, Borman and Motowidlo (1993) expand the parameters of job performance in their work on personnel selection and management. Their emerging taxonomy of managerial performance requirements that should be evaluated goes beyond an assessment of *task performance* (the proficiency with which incumbents perform core technical activities that are important to their jobs). It also includes *contextual performance,* namely, "extra task proficiency that contributes more to the organizational, social, and psychological environment to help accomplish organizational goals" (Arvey & Murphy, 1998, pp. 146-147). Specifically, contextual performance includes

> persisting with enthusiasm and extra effort, volunteering to carry out duties not formally part of one's job, and endorsing and supporting organizational objectives. . . . Such contextual behaviors serve to facilitate communications, lubricate social communications, and reduce tension and/or disruptive emotional responses, and are viewed as important and contributing to organizational goals. (Arvey & Murphy, 1998, p. 147)

Further empirical research by Motowidlo and Van Scotter (1994), using supervisory ratings of over 400 Air Force mechanics, demonstrated that both task and contextual performance factors contribute independently to overall performance. Moreover, research generally suggests that cognitive abilities might be more relevant for predicting task performance, whereas personality variables might be more critical for predicting contextual performance (Arvey & Murphy, 1998, p. 148).

3. *Much has been learned about the measurement of job performance in terms of the validity of this construct, rating accuracy and rating error, individual versus group evaluation, and issues of rating fairness and bias* (see Arvey & Murphy, 1998, pp. 148-159). Recently, there is substantial interest in so-called "360-degree" performance measures that incorporate evaluations from a number of different rater perspectives: supervisor, peer, subordinate, self, and even customers. These are used for feedback and/or personnel decisions (Arvey & Murphy, 1998, p. 154).

Furthermore, such authors as Roe (1999) have helped us to better conceptualize the various types of personal energy that individuals use to perform work and how they regulate their energies. He notes that "performance always implies some (goal-directed) activity of people, and therefore implies the utilization of their cognitive, physical, and energetic resources" (p. 236). Performing tasks and producing outcomes, whether evaluated as good or bad, "has an impact on people's knowledge, skills, motivation, and self-image . . . it also evokes workload and emotions, and produces fatigue—in extreme cases also stress or burnout" (p. 236).

Thus, when a worker is confronted with a task (or perhaps a role) to perform, there are five self-regulating processes that the work performance evokes and that the worker assesses and modulates. Managers must consider this array of worker's self-regulation mechanisms if high work performance is to be initiated and maintained. To help distinguish these different types of regulation, we have added illustrations of the internal processes or "self-talk" in which individuals might engage when regulating their energies:

1. *Action regulation:* The person decides whether or not to initiate an action in accordance to a self-generated cognitive representation of the goal. (Should I or shouldn't I pursue this particular task, as I understand it?)

2. *Energetic regulation:* The person self-regulates the amount of psychic and related energy (perception, thinking, and motor control) to allocate to the action, including how much effort to put forth. (How much personal energy should I use to pursue this task?)

3. *Emotional regulation:* The person's own emotions and their regulation will affect his or her performance. (How am I feeling about doing this task?)

4. *Vitality regulation:* The person's long-term mental and physical health both affects and is

affected by performance. (Am I really up to doing this task? How is my mental and physical health being affected by this task?)

5. *Self-image regulation:* The person's performance is a by-product of the regulation of his or her self-image. (When I think about myself, is doing this task well or poorly congruent with my self-image?)

In sum, the conception, definition, and measurement approaches to work performance have gone much beyond the limited task-specific, directed approach parodied by Charlie Chaplin in the film *Modern Times.* Today, a much broader, dynamic, outcome-and-process approach is used. Much greater attention is also paid to the cognitive and self-regulation processes within workers, as well as the impact of their various actions on the broader work environment.

LINKING INDIVIDUAL AND ORGANIZATIONAL GOALS IN SOCIAL SERVICES

To enhance human service workers' performance successfully, organizational theorists have specifically recommended blending the organization's performance goals with the worker's own personal and career goals (see Weiner, 1990). The human service organization's performance goals include greater effectiveness of services, increased productivity, expanded acquisition of resources, increased staff morale, and greater staff efficiency. The human service worker's personal and career goals may include extrinsic and intrinsic rewards from work; more effective impact on clients; challenging, growth-enhancing work; and greater autonomy and self-determination in shaping

work (cf. Weiner, 1990, p. 328). This meshing is often referred to as the *motivational fit* of an individual and a job, and "reflects the continuous and reciprocal influence of personal characteristics and situational factors" (Kanfer & Heggestad, 1997, p. 1).

In designing such motivational fit for human service professionals, managers must first recognize the demands required by the wide variety and complexity of roles and tasks undertaken by human service workers in their offices and during their frequent visits to clients' homes, communities, and other settings. Moreover, human service workers focus on intense human relationships characterized by problems and suffering, as well as issues of vulnerability, dependency, and resistance (Brill, 1995). Further challenges in their positions are frequent interdependence with other professionals and interdisciplinary teams (Vinokur-Kaplan, 1995a, 1995b; Vinokur-Kaplan et al., 1994) and considerable uncertainty and ambiguity regarding the nature and long-term effectiveness of their interventions. In addition, public support of social work as a profession has wavered, possibly abetted by some negative portrayals in public media.

Furthermore, contemporary human service workers themselves manifest personal values and needs reflecting late 20th-century social trends. As noted by Seymour Sarason (1990) in a chapter on the changing attitudes and motivations of U.S. workers, there has been a "breakdown since World War II of the traditional separation among the work, personal-family, and educational domains of life" (Fishman & Cherniss, 1990, p. 205), and people have been stimulated "to think about themselves, their work, and their careers in new ways which are more integrated with the rest of their lives"

(Fishman & Cherniss, 1990, p. 205). These changing attitudes have resulted in new expectations from workers about such personally relevant benefits as day care for children and infirm family members, maternity and parental leave, and wellness and employee assistance programs. Even though social workers have often been at the forefront of advocating for such rights, many social work agencies still lag behind in addressing these growing expectations of their own employees.

Other general social trends affect the future generation of social work professionals. For instance, in the future, potential recruits for the profession may not have the same commitments and altruistic inclinations that characterized past generations (Mirvis, 1992). Moreover, there are expanding employment and financial opportunities, especially for women (Preston, 1990), who historically and currently represent the great majority of frontline social workers. Although these more equal opportunities are obviously to be lauded, job recruitment, satisfaction, and retention will continue to be serious issues facing professional social work in the future. Thus, in light of such challenges, and as with any other profession, it is important to address the question: How can the motivation of today's and tomorrow's social work practitioners to perform in the workplace be maintained and enhanced throughout their careers?[1]

OVERVIEW OF THEORETICAL APPROACHES FOR MOTIVATING WORK PERFORMANCE

Reviews of theoretical approaches to work performance motivation typically present a chronological overview. Often, they first note Tay-

lor's scientific management, followed by behaviorist, human relations, and expectancy theories later in the 20th century. Such an approach has limited success because the diverse approaches to motivation were often overlapping in time rather than sequential (Kahn, personal communication, May 12, 1999). Thus, for the purposes of this chapter, we find it more useful to aggregate various theories according to the different source of motivation or lens through which it is seen—individual (psychological), social (social psychological), and environmental (organizational/sociological). If we imagine managers sitting in their offices wondering how best to motivate their workers, we ask, Where could they look for answers? There are three ways they could easily frame the question of what has influence on workers' motivation and subsequent performance: Is it particular personality traits of workers? Is it their interaction with others? Or is it the structure or culture of their work within the agency's system of activities that affects their performance?

We choose this approach to worker motivation and performance for two reasons. First, this multiple lens can help managers to choose among the various types of interventions available to enhance their workers' performance and evaluate its appropriateness for their own workplace. For example, theories differ in their emphasis on rationality versus emotionality as an influence on workers' motivation and in their focus on attending to the external social world versus maximizing personal pleasure (see Ronen, 1994, p. 242). Second, this approach helps prevent managers from mis-attributing all lapses in their workers' performance strictly to workers' personality traits, an approach that historically dominated personnel selection. In the traditions of both social work and continuous quality improvement, we also approach a human problem from multiple levels to avoid blaming the victim (see Arches, 1991). Although ultimately, the intervention will influence the individual worker, we believe that it is also important to appreciate the model's particular emphases and the entire context in which action is taken.[2]

A summary of the main points of each theory is presented in Table 9.1. *Individually focused approaches* highlight addressing individuals and their own particular needs as they conceive of them. An important implication for managers is to use care in selection of both personnel and rewards as means to enhance work performance. Next, interactionally focused approaches highlight social interaction between focal workers and others in their environment. An important implication for managers is to attend to workers' own perceptions, appraisals, and comparison of themselves to others. Finally, environmentally or structurally focused approaches highlight enhancing workers' motivation through organizational changes in the environments in which they work. An important implication for managers is not to approach the work environment as static and irrevocable; rather, it should be seen as a dynamic setting with the potential to change workers' roles, assignments, evaluations, and interrelationships to enhance the organization's achievement of its mission.

Individually/Focused Approaches to Worker Motivation

Reinforcement Theory

This approach reflects a behaviorist orientation to motivation and examines how different types of reinforcements (positive reinforcement, negative reinforcement, extinction, and punishment) modify workers' job performances. Some of the classical works in reinforcement theory include Hull (1943) and Skinner (1938). Extensive research has been done using this approach, especially with regard to the schedule and contingencies of rewards. In its simplest version, the linkage between the organization's performance goals and the worker's personal and career goals would focus on making receipt of personally valued outcomes, such as a salary increase, directly contingent on work performance, such as improved productivity. Namely, workers are encouraged to work to a defined standard to receive a positive benefit (or avoid a punishment). This reward (or avoidance of punishment), in turn, reinforces their motivation to work hard at their jobs, in anticipation of another reward.

Such an approach may be especially appropriate for performance based on piecework efforts—for instance, the more files social workers close in a prescribed period of time, thereby meeting the organization's goal of efficiency, the greater their bonus pay might be. The limitation of such an approach is that workers adopt behaviors that generate immediate rewards for them, which may ignore other, more long-term goals of the agency, such as service effectiveness. Moreover, because much of the work done by social workers is not piecework, more comprehensive theories may be more applicable to enhancing social workers' performance.

Expectancy Theory

This perspective is more elaborate than reinforcement theory, and it adds a more cognitive

TABLE 9.1 Summary of Various Approaches to Motivation

Theory Type and Major Contributors	Theory's Main Perspective	Mechanism/Aspect of Motivation Emphasized	Associated Work Design Principles
Individually focused approaches			
Reinforcement Theory Hull (1943) Skinner (1938)	Theory focuses on stimulus-response associations. Examines how a history of past benefits or punishments modifies job performance.	Work performance improves when contingent on a certain reward or punishment.	Make valued personal outcomes (i.e., a salary increase or promotion) contingent on work performance (i.e., improved productivity or efficiency).
Expectancy Theory Tolman (1959) Vroom (1964)	People are motivated to work when they expect it will lead to personal gain.	Motivation results from three types of cognitive inputs (expectancy, instrumentality, and valence); it ascends when all three inputs are high.	All three types of cognititve inputs must be addressed to successfully motivate worker performance.
Hierarchy of Needs Maslow (1954)	Maslow argues that human needs can be understood in terms of a hierarchy of five types of needs. A need that is lower on the hierarchy is stronger and must be satisfied prior to the person ascending to a higher level.	Three needs, known as deficiency needs, must be met if an individual is to remain a healthy person. The gratification of the next two needs, known as growth needs, are responsible for helping individuals grow to their fullest potential.	Awareness of a worker's hierarchy of needs informs managers about forces driving worker motivation. Thus managers can redesign job tasks to be more harmonious with workers tiered needs.
Existence-Relatedness Needs Theory Alderfer (1972)	Like Maslow, Alderfer believes that individuals are driven by a desire to satisfy needs.	Unlike Maslow, Alderfer suggests that there are only three types of needs and that they are not activated in any specific order. The three needs are existence needs, relatedness needs, and growth needs.	Alderfer is aligned with Maslow in believing that satisfying human needs is an important aspect of motivating job performance.
Job Satisfaction/ Dissatisfaction Two-Factor Theory Herzberg, Mausner, & Snyderman (1959)	Job satisfaction and job dissatisfaction depend on two different and separate sets of factors. Factors that cause satisfaction are distinct from those that cause dissatisfaction.	Positive aspects of a job (e.g., recognition) are termed satisfiers, and these are found to be motivating. The removal of negative aspects of a job (e.g., poor working conditions) are termed dissatisfiers, and their removal is said to be nonmotivating.	People will only work harder for nonhygienic measures. A manager needs to distinguish between motivating and hygienic measures in the design of job tasks.
Personality Traits & Motivational Skills Theories For reviews, see Kanfer (1990); Kanfer & Heggestad, (1997)	In the classic industrial/ organizational psychology view, motivation is seen as a personality characteristic (or set of characteristics)	Non-ability individual differences in traits to relate to work behavior and job performance (e.g., achievement, anxiety).	Earlier, selection of persons with the desired traits for the job was emphasized; recent approaches also emphasize individual's self-regulating motivational skills.

TABLE 9.1 Continued

Theory Type and Major Contributors	Theory's Main Perspective	Mechanism/Aspect of Motivation Emphasized	Associated Work Design Principles
Interactionally focused approaches			
Equity Theory Adams (1965)	Workers are motivated to maintain fair, or "equitable," relationships among themselves. Effort and effectiveness are criteria for division of rewards.	Workers compare the ratio of their own outcomes (benefits, rewards) and inputs (ability, effort) to the ratio of other workers' outcomes and inputs. When workers perceive their position relative to others as being unfair, they will be motivated to correct for the inequity.	Two options can resolve inequitable states. Either a behavioral response is elicited in which a worker strives to augment inputs and outcomes, or the worker instead adopts a psychological response, choosing to think about the circumstance in a changed light.
Attribution Theories Heider (1958) Jones & Davis (1965) Kelley (1967, 1971, 1972, 1973)	When individuals observe their own or another's behavior, they try to establish whether it is a result of internal or external forces. When an action is internally caused, it is said to be under the personal control of the actor. When an action is externally caused, it is said to be a result of the person's environment.	Motivation is a result of either intrinsic or extrinsic sources. An intrinsically motivated individual performs an activity for the sole reason of performing the activity itself. An extrinsically motivated person undertakes an activity with the aim of receiving an expected reward.	If a worker decides to perform an activity solely as a result of environmental forces, then constant incentives, pressure, and surveillance will be required to keep the worker performing. If a worker performs an activity out of personal forces, then he or she will require little or no external influence.
Social Learning Theory Miller & Dollard (1941) Bandura (1971)	The human capacity to learn through observation (termed modeling) allows workers to develop successful patterns of behavior without having to resort to trial and error.	Workers are self-motivated to aspire to the performance level of comparable individuals whom they view as models.	Social learning relies on individual's self-regulatory, observational learning. By observing coworkers, individuals develop attitudes toward the organization, the job as a whole, and specific job aspects.
Structurally focused approaches			
Quality of Working Life Deci (1975) Hackman & Oldham (1980)	Workers can be intrinsically motivated. Suggests that jobs can be made more satisfying through a system emphasizing more worker participation.	Worker's motivation, satisfaction, and quality of performance increase when the following job dimensions are present: skill variety, task identity, task significance, and feedback.	Workers should be given more autonomy in doing their jobs. Performance targets are set by management and how these targets are achieved is left to workers.

(continued)

TABLE 9.1 *Continued*

Theory Type and Major Contributors	Theory's Main Perspective	Mechanism/Aspect of Motivation Emphasized	Associated Work Design Principles
Theory Y McGregor (1960)	Under appropriate management conditions, the average worker is capable of showing self-direction, responsibility, and initiative.	Increased worker influence, self-direction, and self-control will influence workers toward improving productivity and efficiency, and, as a by-product, motivation will be positively affected.	Management should create conditions that allow the worker's untapped productive tendencies to emerge and foster an environment in which all members may contribute to the limits of their ability.
Total (Continuous) Quality Management (Deming) See Walton (1986) Martin (1993)	Approaches the total system of production of goods or services and seeks to ensure and inspire quality throughout the organization.	Invokes participation of all employees in a common purpose of delivering quality; seeks documented root causes of most important, solvable problems in the organization rather than immediate blaming of workers.	Strategies include teams, training, "driving out fear," breaking down barriers between departments, elimination of quotas, program of education and self-improvement.

cast to motivation. Its roots are found in Kurt Lewin's (1938) field theory of behavior, and it was initially presented in the work of Tolman (1959) and further developed by Vroom (1964). Expectancy theory contends that people are motivated to work when they expect it will lead to personal gain. Thus, if workers perceive high productivity as a likely path leading to the attainment of distinct goals, they will tend to be high producers.

Specifically, this theory specifies how workers' needs develop by outlining motivation as the result of three different types of cognitive inputs:

1. *Expectancy:* the worker's estimate of the probability that a goal will be achieved (e.g., the worker's estimate that he or she can close 20 files in 1 week)

2. *Instrumentality:* the worker's feeling that rewards are indeed linked to one's performance and that he or she has the ability to obtain the reward

3. *Valence:* the degree of value the worker attaches to a reward (e.g., the amount of value that the worker attaches to obtaining a financial bonus)

This theory poses that higher levels of worker motivation will result when all three inputs are high. If, however, any one of the components is zero, then the overall level of motivation will be zero; workers' motivation will be very low if they feel that either (a) no amount of effort will lead to their prescribed achievement or (b) even if they do the work, it will not reliably lead to the desired rewards, or (c) the type of incentive or reward being offered is not of value to them.

Needs Theories

Various theorists have tried to specify the types of human needs that motivate workers and require satisfaction. The psychologist Abraham Maslow (1954) put forth perhaps the most famous taxonomy of needs. Therein, he proposed that human needs could be best understood in terms of a hierarchy of five types of needs, with higher level needs coming to the fore only after lower-level needs have been met. The hierarchy of needs includes, from lowest to highest: (a) physiological needs at the level of basic survival (e.g., food), (b) safety needs (e.g., a secure job), (c) social needs (e.g., friends), (d) ego needs (e.g., recognition), and (e) self-actualization needs (e.g., becoming the person you know you are capable of becoming) (Dessler, 1991, pp. 323-324). The first three needs, which Maslow names *deficiency needs,* must be met if an individual is to remain healthy. The two higher needs, known as *growth needs,* are responsible for helping individuals grow to their fullest potential. Once the lower needs have been met, according to Maslow, the human being is increasingly motivated to satisfy higher needs.

Previous approaches to motivating workers were oriented toward the use of economic rewards and the giving or withholding of job security, thereby recognizing only the lower-order needs (cf. Lewis, Lewis, & Souflée, 1991, p. 201). Thus, a major contribution of the hierarchy of needs theory was that it conceptually broadened the spectrum of human motivation to include more social and existential concerns about which managers would need to be concerned in enhancing their workers' motivation and performance.

In another vein, Jahoda (1982) further applied Maslow's theory to the unemployed, using the enlarged palette of human motivations, including higher levels. She theorized that their psychological distress is rooted in implicit, as opposed to explicit, functions of work. These include structuring time, providing a sense of purpose, and establishing personal status and identity. This perspective suggests the importance of managers satisfying workers' social status and identity needs when individuals disengage from work. Whether employees leave due to downsizing or retirement, managers must try to address their various needs, lest workers' frustration lead to poor mental or physical health, or in extreme cases, to violence (Price & Vinokur, 1995).

Other authors have also focused on need satisfaction as the driver of performance but have offered different conceptualizations. For example, Alderfer (1972) suggests that there are only three types of needs—existence, relatedness, and growth needs—and that they are not activated in any specific order. Another needs-based approach was put forth in Herzberg, Mausner, and Snyderman's (1959) motivator-hygiene theory and echoed in the goal-setting approach of Locke (1984). Herzberg proposed that workers have a lower level and a higher level set of needs and that the best way to motivate them is to offer to satisfy the higher level needs. The lower level needs, when unrequited, lead to job dissatisfaction. They are satisfied by hygiene factors and include better working conditions, salary, and supervision. Herzberg contends that these lower-level needs are easily satisfied; however, meeting more of them does not lead to greater job satisfaction. Rather, it is the higher level needs, such as achievement, self-

esteem, and recognition, which are never entirely satisfied but which lead to job satisfaction,
and they can be addressed through *motivator
factors* or *job content.*

Thus, according to Herzberg, the best way to
motivate employees is to build intrinsic rewards,
such as challenge and opportunities for achievement, into their jobs through job enrichment.
These motivators are designed into the job by
making it more interesting and challenging,
thereby increasing the opportunities for experiencing a feeling of responsibility, achievement,
growth, and recognition by doing the job well
(cf. Dessler, 1991, p. 326). Characteristics of
enriched jobs include new learning, more per-
sonalized scheduling, unique experiences, and
control over resources (Dessler, pp. 327-328).

Such job enrichment is costly, in terms of
training time, and may not be attractive to all
workers. However, it seems particularly relevant to professionals such as social workers,
who have already made a formal investment
and commitment to a particular, challenging
profession.

More recently, Ronen (1994) has extracted
an underlying structure of employees' work values using cross-cultural data, incorporating the
taxonomies of Maslow, Alderfer, and Herzberg.
These underlying dimensions of work values
are individualism versus collectivism cross-tab-
ulated with materialism versus nonmaterialism
(p. 263).

In a separate effort to integrate different theoretical perspectives, expectancy theory and
needs theory also have been combined in later
research (Lawler, 1973; Staw, 1977) because
this approach "allows better predictors about
the conditions that affect the cognition of outcomes likely to be valued and the factors that affect those values" (Ronen, 1994, p. 243).

Personality Traits and Motivational Skills Theories

Personality traits represent the oldest scientific perspective on motivation, and it predomi-
nated in early personnel selection efforts, for
example, to find measures of character and
temperament that were validly related to sales
performance (Kanfer & Heggestad, 1997, p. 2).
During the past decade, renewed interest in
personality has arisen from conceptual and empirical advances in the study of relationships between motivationally relevant personality traits
(such as achievement and anxiety), motivationally relevant personality skills (such as emotion control and motivation control), and job
performance (see Kanfer & Heggestad, 1997,
pp. 12-14). Of particular interest to social work
managers may be greater delineation of individual motivational skills, which are more malleable." Whereas motivationally relevant traits are
seen as "relatively stable and enduring individual differences in personality," motivationally
relevant skills are conceptualized as "individual
differences in specific self-regulatory patterns
of activity during goal striving . . . [such skills]
involve cognition, affect, and behavior" (Kanfer
& Heggestad, 1997, p. 10). Both the enduring
personality traits and the conditions in the task
environment influence these motivational skills.
So although a trait such as anxiety may be taken
as permanently present, the skills a worker can
use to self-regulate energies may be changeable
or learnable. Thus, such skills are important in
the workplace, because they may influence how
workers differentially react in light of pressures, frustrations, and boredom.

Kuhl (1985) originally put forth two such
self-regulation strategies. First, emotion control self-regulation serves "to protect on-task

attention and effort from distracting emotional states." It countervails against "experiencing excessive worry about performance, low self-efficacy, and lack of task persistence" (Kanfer & Heggestad, 1997, pp. 40-41). This self-regulation process occurs especially when learning new or novel tasks (as illustrated by constructive self-talk used in cognitive therapy). Second, motivation control self-regulation, according to Kuhl (1985), "explicitly aims at strengthening of the current intention's motivational basis" (quoted in Kanfer & Heggestad, 1997, p. 41). This skill is especially pertinent in situations when motivation begins to wane and additional incentives are needed to sustain task effort and persistence. Examples of motivational control skills include self-initiated goal setting, creating imaginary and contrived consequences for performance outcomes, and other practices that maintain high levels of attention and effort toward task performance" (Kanfer & Heggestad, 1997, p. 41).

Interactionally Focused Approaches to Worker Motivation

Several more sociopsychological approaches to motivation have looked not only at the internal needs of individuals, but also at the way workers' perception or interaction with others influences that motivation. These approaches also suggest various social interventions to enhance various workers' performance over time in the workplace (e.g., mentoring, training and education, and cognitive reframing).

Social Learning and Self-Efficacy Theories

Social learning theory emphasized the importance of modeling in the performance of tasks, as put forth in the classic works of Miller and Dollard (1941) and Bandura (1971). Individuals learn through observation to develop patterns of behavior without having to resort to trial and error. Workers are self-motivated to aspire to the level of comparable individuals, whom they view as models. Thus, by observing coworkers, individuals develop attitudes toward the organization, the job as a whole, and specific job aspects. The broad implications of this perspective for social work management require administrators not only to look at one individual's behavior, but also to take into consideration how coworkers, mentors, and influential others affect workers' self-perception and performance.

Bandura's original work has evolved to emphasize the importance of self-efficacy as a central cognitive factor determining behavior, including performance. "Perceived self-efficacy refers to beliefs in one's capabilities to organize and execute the course of action required to produce given attainments" (Bandura, 1997, p. 3) and "bears similarities to self-confidence" (Roe, 1999, p. 255). The wide array of events over which personal influence is exercised vary, and "influence may entail regulating one's own motivation, thought processes, affective states, and actions, or it may involve changing environmental conditions, depending on what one seeks to manage" (Bandura, 1997, p. 3).

Self-efficacy determines whether an individual's coping behavior will be initiated, how much task-related effort will be expended, and how long that effort will be sustained despite disconfirming evidence (Bandura, 1986). "Individuals who perceive themselves as highly efficacious activate enough effort, if well executed, to produce successful outcomes, whereas those who perceive low self-efficacy are likely to stop their efforts prematurely and fail on the task" (Bandura, 1986, 1997) (Stajkovic & Luthans, 1998, p. 240).

A recent meta-analytic review on self-efficacy by Stajkovic and Luthans (1998) found two noteworthy findings. First, overall, self-efficacy was found to be positively and strongly related to work-related performances. Second, the relationship between self-efficacy and work-related performance is moderated by task complexity (objectively measured) and locus of performance (whether real or simulated) (cf. pp. 255, 243).

Attribution and Equity Theories

Attribution theories, as developed by such social psychologists as Heider (1958), Jones and Davis (1965), and Kelley (1967, 1971, 1972, 1973), propose that when individuals observe their own or another's behavior, they try to establish whether it is a result of internal or external forces. When an action is deemed internally caused, it is said to be under the personal control of the actor. When an action is deemed externally caused, it is said to be a result of the person's environment. (Such determinations indeed surface in everyday life in the attribution of responsibility for all kinds of acts and performance, including accidents and crimes.) Motivation is also seen as a result of either internal or external forces. An internally motivated individual performs an activity for its own sake. An externally motivated person undertakes an activity with the aim of receiving an expected reward. If workers perform an activity as a result of external forces, then constant incentives, pressure, and surveillance will be required to keep them performing. If workers

perform an activity out of internal forces, then they will require little or no external influence. (These internal forces are reminiscent of Herzberg's motivators and Maslow's growth needs.) This approach again broadens the perspective on workers' performance and on the ways that their reflections and their attribution of the causation of performance by themselves or others (such as their clients, coworkers, and supervisors) may be influenced.

The equity theory of motivation, developed first by Adams (1965), assumes that people have a strong need to balance their abilities and efforts (or inputs) with the rewards they receive (outcomes) and that workers are motivated to maintain fair or equitable relationships among themselves. If a person perceives an inequity, a tension or drive will develop in the person's mind and she or he will be motivated to reduce or eliminate the tension and perceived inequity. In other words, when workers perceive their level of reward relative to others as being unfair, they will be motivated to correct the perceived inequity.

The inequity can be resolve through one of two responses: (a) a behavioral response, in which the worker strives to augment inputs and outcomes; or (b) a psychological response, in which the worker thinks about the circumstances in a changed light and may re-evaluate whether such behavior is attributable to internal or external causes. Exactly how workers go about reducing the perceived inequity is further influenced by whether they are paid on a piece-rate basis (by the piece) or on a straight salary basis. If workers are paid a salary, as most social workers are, and if they feel underpaid, then both their work quality or quantity should decrease. If, however, workers receive a salary and feel overpaid, then their work quality or quantity should increase, because such effort will help reduce perceived inequity between their high salary and their low quality or quantity of work (cf. Dessler, 1991, p. 329).

Environmentally Focused Approaches to Work Motivation

This final group of approaches broadens the scope of the context of work motivation and performance. Herein, we look at approaches that do not so much emphasize a particular individual's needs, personal traits, or the influence of others on their perceptions and performance. Rather, this perspective embraces the impact of overall quality of life in the workplace and how the environment must be restructured to enhance workers' performance.

Quality of Working Life and Job Redesign

In the second half of the 20th century, work motivation theorists have urged that more attention be given to creating supportive work conditions and environments that allow the worker's untapped productive tendencies to emerge. For example, the quality of work life approaches (e.g., Deci, 1975; Hackman & Oldham, 1980) argue that workers can be intrinsically motivated when their jobs are made more satisfying through a more participatory system. In particular, it proposes that motivation, satisfaction, and quality of performance all increase when the following job dimensions are present: skill variety, task identity, task significance, and feedback. They also suggest that although management sets performance targets, workers should have more autonomy in choosing the means to achieve them.

Recent work on these various job dimensions has illustrated that they in themselves are complex concepts needing greater specification. For example, recent meta-analytic research on feedback interventions to improve performance has shown that feedback, a familiar mantra of effective supervision, is actually a double-edged sword: In some cases, it actually diminishes performance (Kluger & DeNisi, 1996, 1998). One of the practical implications these authors recommend is to use feedback intervention only in combination with a goal-setting intervention, which has been found to augment the feedback intervention's effects on performance. They note further that "employees who wish to have more feedback than they are receiving often suffer from the absence of clear goals" (1998, p. 71).

Total (Continuous) Quality Management

Another approach to systemically alter the relationships and processes in the workplace to enhance overall performance is found in the various schools of Total Quality Management (TQM), as proposed by Deming, Juran, Crosby, Feigenbaum, and others (Martin, 1993, Chapter 2; Walton, 1986). Therein, such core work practices as customer focus, an organization-wide commitment to continuous improvement, and teamwork are purported to lead to both quality performance (less re-work, more satisfaction of customers' or clients' legitimate requirements) and such "work-related outcomes as [workers'] satisfaction, communication, and [more positive] perceptions of the work environment" (Morrow, 1997, p. 363; also see Dean & Bowen, 1994). In particular, Deming decried punitive, inspection-ridden, worker-blaming American management practices; he urged instead that management "drive out fear" and "remove barriers to pride of workmanship" (see Walton, 1986, Chapters 12 and 16). He estimated that "workers are responsible for only 15% of the problems, the system for the other 85%. The system is the responsibility of management" (Walton, 1986, p. 94). Although originally applied to mostly industrial settings, TQM has recently been fruitfully applied in human services (see Gummer & McCallion, 1995).

RECENT RESEARCH RELEVANT TO MOTIVATING WORK PERFORMANCE IN SOCIAL SERVICES

We next summarize recent research published in the 1990s pertinent to motivating work performance in social services. We have found relatively few studies that explicitly observe and measure the work performance of human service workers. This underrepresentation is noteworthy compared to the wide literature on workers' performance in industrial and other settings, as well as more extensive literature on some related topics in the human service workplace, such as burnout.

We speculate that several contributing factors could help explain this lack of work performance research. First, although social work is considered a profession, it is also seen by some as "a calling." Therefore, social workers' motivation could be powered by devotion to values of altruism or social justice; thus, their motivation is purportedly intrinsic and self-actualizing, and their work performance is assumed to be adequately good. Second, the variety, subtlety, and unpredictability of tasks and roles that social workers perform are not as easy to define and measure as the more concrete and determi-

nate technologies found in business and industrial settings. Third, social work's long-standing emphasis (until recently) on process, as compared to outcome, did not mesh well with the seemingly harsh, scrutinizing dimensions of work performance. Finally, it also may be that the work of human service workers is not publicly described or acknowledged, as frequently happens with the performance of human nurturing, educational, and care-giving efforts. Thus, perhaps not much attention or value has been given to the important but invisible work that social workers perform and the positive outcomes they help render.

Therefore, we have broadened our search and found a number of published studies in the social work management literature related to motivation and work performance. However, often, motivation is not primarily or directly measured but rather inferred from scales or subscales measuring morale, burnout, mental health, or well-being. Similarly, work performance is often not independently measured; assessment relies more on such proxy measures as workers' self-reports of their sense of job challenge or personal effectiveness, their stated intentions to leave the job, or as a possible proxy measure, their job satisfaction. So we must remember that in most cases discussed, first, the dependent variable actually measures how well workers think they are performing, rather than how well they are actually performing their work; and second, the independent variables measure their job-related attitudes or other characteristics, which are usually related to— but not identical with—work motivation.

Moreover, these researchers have often struggled with issues of defining social workers and other human service providers (some studies include other helping professions as well).

They have also encountered issues of sampling and small sample sizes, response bias, and especially the difficult issues of inferring causality (for example, does high motivation cause job satisfaction, or does job satisfaction cause high motivation?). Admittedly, these issues of causality perplex work performance researchers in related fields as well (cf. Roe, 1999). Thus, our review is more descriptive and mainly focuses on variables that systematically vary together, rather than on proving or disproving causal models.

Despite its limitations and challenges, the literature we reviewed has provided three advances. First, some fairly consistent findings regarding particular conditions for work performance seem especially salient to professional social workers. (This literature also builds on earlier research, especially including the various national surveys of NASW workers by Jayaratne, Chess, and their colleagues, including David Himle, Tony Tripodi, Mary Lou Davis-Sacks, and Kristine Siefert; the stress, coping, and social support literatures; and the pervasive influence of the Maslach-Pines burnout scale.) However, preferences for particular working conditions may vary according to the types of positions that social workers hold (such as clinical, supervisory, and administrative; cf. Poulin, 1995). Second, various theoretical models are applied to investigate the human service workplace (e.g., personality traits or perspectives, stress and coping, social support, and organizational culture). Third, a range of primary and secondary survey methodologies are used, including cross-sectional (e.g., Jayaratne & Chess, 1985), longitudinal (e.g., Poulin, 1994), and comparative (e.g., Chess, Norlin, & Jayaratne, 1987; Vinokur-Kaplan, 1996; Vinokur-Kaplan et al., 1994), as well as

case studies (see Gummer & McCallion, 1995). We again use the three-pronged division of individual, interpersonal, and social structural contexts previously presented to categorize major theories of motivation. Although we acknowledge that some issues overlap (especially with regard to categorizing studies of autonomy and control in the workplace), we use this schema heuristically to condense a diverse literature and to integrate this social work research within a larger context of work performance studies.

Individually/Trait-Focused Social Service Studies

Several researchers have focused on particular individual traits or characteristics that would especially enhance the effectiveness or job continuity of human service providers. For example, Koeske and Kirk (1995b) studied optimism among experienced case managers with challenging mental health clients. A further longitudinal investigation of these intensive case managers (Koeske & Kirk, 1995a) "explored which, if any, personal stable attributes or sociopsychological characteristics measured at the time the workers were hired predict subsequent perceptions and morale" (p. 18). The authors found that "the better adjusted the worker was at the start of the job, the better the later work outcomes" (pp. 23-24).

Job Satisfaction and Dissatisfaction Studies

A limited number of studies reflect the influence of the previously discussed theories of motivation and job satisfaction. For example, following Herzberg's approach, Vinokur-Kaplan (1991) probed a variety of hygienic and motivational factors contributing to job satisfaction and retention among human service personnel. In a study of new child welfare practitioners, a stepwise regression predicting 43% of the variance in job satisfaction revealed the five strongest predictors to be dissatisfying salary, dissatisfying working conditions, satisfying and dissatisfying feelings of accomplishment, and other dissatisfying factors (see p. 86).

Other studies of social workers have tried to use job satisfaction as a way to gather and compare attitudes possibly related to motivation and job performance as expressed in different social service settings (e.g., Jayaratne & Chess, 1985), positions (Jayaratne, Davis-Sacks, & Chess, 1991), and periods of time (Chess et al., 1987; Vinokur-Kaplan, 1996).

Another study of job satisfaction and retention of NASW members compared those employed in public and nonprofit agencies, as well as in private practice (Vinokur-Kaplan et al., 1994). The authors found a variety of demographic workplace conditions (i.e., job security) and workplace motivators (e.g., autonomy, promotion opportunities) accounting for 37% to 40% of the variance in job satisfaction and 14% to 23% of the variance in intention to seek another job.

Although such studies have been noteworthy in giving voice to social workers' attitudes toward their jobs, they have been notably limited by the following methodological issues: (a) lack of true longitudinal studies of representative samples that could better distinguish cause and effect, (b) self-reports not accompanied by other independently obtained measures (e.g., supervisors, significant others, or agency performance data), and (c) the inadequately studied relationship between social workers' own personal levels of job satisfaction (or their intention to stay on the job) and their actual work performance.

INTERACTIONALLY FOCUSED SOCIAL SERVICE STUDIES

Self-Efficacy and Sense of Control

Using prior research on self-efficacy by Bandura (1997, Chapter 10) and others, researchers have focused on the personal sense of control that human service workers feel in their positions and how it influences their attitudes and intended behaviors. For example, Guterman and Jayaratne (1994) studied the role of work stress and sense of personal control in child welfare direct practitioners' assessment of their own service effectiveness. (Control referred to "workers' abilities to manage and influence events in the work environment, particularly in the face of stressful situations" [p. 100]). They found "a significant relationship between worker control and workers' professional effectiveness assessment" (p. 99).

Other related studies have looked further at Bandura's self-efficacy model and focused on the relative importance of personal competence (mastery in knowledge and skills, or efficacy expectation) and personal control or autonomy (ability to perform those actions in a given context or environment, or outcome expectancy). Among social workers in private practice and public agency settings, Jayaratne, Vinokur-Kaplan, and Chess (1995) found that "autonomy appears to be a more important and consistent predictor than competence in explaining job satisfaction and burnout for workers in both settings" (p. 47).

These findings dovetail with those of other researchers in which job autonomy and a sense of personal control over jobs have been found to be consistently correlated with job satisfaction (see Poulin, 1994, p. 22). Indeed, in a longitudinal study of social workers' job satisfaction, Poulin (1994) found that "increased job autonomy is associated with increased job satisfaction . . . [and] the strongest organizational predictor of [positive] job satisfaction change was satisfaction with professional development opportunities" (Poulin, 1994, p. 35).

Worker participation in agency decision making has also been promoted as a means to encourage motivation and commitment to organizational decisions. Yet, studies by Ramsdell (1994) and others of staff participation in organizational decision making at family planning organizations reported "relatively low levels of actual influence in administrative decision making by workers, despite previous studies that workers, supervisors, and administrators view workers as capable of significantly greater contributions in this area" (p. 69).

Social Support and Other Social Psychological Theories of Motivation

In light of the stressful, demanding situations and the emotional distress experienced in most social work positions, several researchers have also investigated the direct and buffering effects of varying types and degrees of social support on job satisfaction, burnout, and health (Jayaratne, Tripodi, & Chess, 1983). Given the complexity of the interpersonal relationships involved (work and family-related) and the various types of social support that can be measured (emotional, informational, instrumental, tangible, esteem), it is not surprising that there are sometimes conflicting results. Generally, findings favor a negative relationship between social support and perceived stress and strain. However, there are mixed results regarding the buffering effect of social support in moderating the effects of stress on strain (e.g., poor mental health). For example, Jayaratne et al. (1983) found no evidence to support the buffering hypothesis, whereas Koeske and Koeske (1989) reported that social support was directly related to job satisfaction and buffered the effect of work demands on burnout.

Recent studies have also examined the effects of negative social support (often called social undermining or social conflict) on workplace attitudes and other indicators of wellness. For example, Gant et al. (1993) investigated the respective effects of both social support and social undermining on African American social workers' perceptions of coworker and supervisor relationships and those workers' psychological well-being.

The negative impact of others on social workers' particular activities was also noted by Jayaratne, Vinokur-Kaplan, Nagda, and Chess (1995) in studies of violence in the workplace. They point out the particularly corrosive effect on social workers' sense of personal accomplishment and mental health that results from experiencing verbal abuse or sexual harassment by clients in the workplace.

This more recent attention to negative social contact for social workers is important, because Gant et al.'s (1993) study and others (e.g., Vinokur & van Ryn, 1993) have found negative social interactions (social undermining) to be more potent in influencing such outcomes as psychological well-being than positive social support. Overall, these studies have been helpful in examining social workers' attitudes, job satisfaction, and planned retention, as well as their complex interdynamics with other factors in the workplace. However, like most other studies we have reviewed, these do not have additional, external measures of the actual work performance of these respondents.

Finally, we did not locate studies of the motivational forces of attribution and equity vis-à-vis professional social work. However, the latter may develop in the future, especially given the growing percentage of U.S. social workers who belong to unions and current trends of increased and successful labor organizing among professionals (Tambor, 1995).

ENVIRONMENTALLY FOCUSED SOCIAL SERVICE STUDIES

Several recent studies of human service organizations have sought to include the influence of the ambience of the organization on workers' performance, or variables related to performance. A major step in this direction was Glisson and Durick's (1988) study of predictors of both job satisfaction (a response to the experience of specific job tasks) and organizational commitment (an affective response to beliefs about the organization) in 22 human service organizations. Specifically, organizational commitment, as described by Mowday, Porter, and Steers (1982), captures "a strong belief in the organization's goals and values, a willingness to exert considerable effort on behalf of the organization, and a strong desire to remain a member of the organization" (cited in Glisson & Durick, 1988, p. 64). The study found,

> Job satisfaction and organizational commitment are each affected by a unique hierarchy of predictors . . . two job characteristics, skills variety and role ambiguity, are the best predictors of job satisfaction, while two organization characteristics, leadership and the organization's age, are the best predictors of commitment. (Glisson & Durick, 1988, p. 61)

Other job task and organizational predictors of job satisfaction include satisfaction with supervision and adequacy of organizational resources (cf. Poulin, 1994, pp. 22-23).

Glisson has expanded research on organizational effects in a carefully designed study of the effects of organizational climate and interorganizational coordination on the quality and outcomes of children's service systems (Glisson & Hemmelgarn, 1998). Organizational climate "provide[s] an appraisal of the degree to which employees view their work environment as beneficial versus detrimental to their own well-being and the success of their work" (Glisson & Hemmelgarn, 1998, p. 411). The study used a quasi-experimental, longitudinal design, collecting both quantitative and qualitative data from 32 public children's services offices, using multiple respondents (including caseworkers). "[Its] most important finding is that improvements in psychosocial functioning are significantly greater for children served by offices with more positive climates" (p. 415). The authors' findings "suggest that agencies with higher levels of job satisfaction, fairness, role clarity, cooperation, and personalization, and lower levels of role overload, conflict, and emotional exhaustion are more likely to support caseworkers' efforts . . . that lead to success" (p. 416).

The findings show that organizational climate (including low conflict, cooperation, role clarity, and personalization) is the primary predictor of positive service outcomes (the children's improved psychosocial functioning) and a significant predictor of service quality (Glisson & Hemmelgarn, 1998, p. 401). (Service quality was an index based on measures of comprehensiveness and continuity of services, as well as availability and responsiveness of workers.)

Interestingly, these findings also reflect the principles proposed by the Total Quality Management (TQM) approach to the work environment. Other specific social service applications of the TQM approach can be found in a recent volume of case examples edited by Gummer and McCallion (1995) and a brief textbook by Martin (1993).

SUMMARY AND CONCLUSIONS

This chapter has sought to provide a review of contemporary social science theories regarding motivating work performance, using it as a guide to organize and understand the recent social work management literature on work performance in the human service workplace. It has highlighted several recent developments from which the following conclusions are drawn.

First, Roe's (1999) emphasis on work performance containing both process and outcome needs to be acknowledged and well-integrated into performance enhancement programs, if recipients are to receive quality services. Moreover, the several levels of analysis and the variety of theories of motivation and work performance require managers to address these concepts with a multifaceted approach. Not only do the particular personality and characteristics of workers as individuals need to be addressed, but the social and organizational environments of the workplace must also be examined.

Second, the conceptualization of the individual worker must also be multifaceted. Past research helped to articulate the variety of work-ers' needs. More recent research on how an individual approaches or continues a task has adopted the more cognitive approach of contemporary psychology, highlighting the several self-regulating systems and the internal information processing involved.

Third, in addition to further elaborating these dimensions, recent reviews of work performance also underline the need to look at the even broader scope of influences on performance. These general performance conditions "influence the activity of any task incumbent, regardless of personal abilities, personality traits, or other characteristics" (Roe, 1999, p. 258). They include additional conditions that we have not addressed here but that warrant research in the human service workplace, such as the conditions of sleep (quality and deprivation), working hours, length of workday, work pauses, schedules, and shift work (e.g., see Sparks, Cooper, Fried, & Shirom, 1997), as well as the effects of being observed by audiences and through personal or electronic monitoring.

Fourth, rather than providing one, sure-fire prescription for motivating work performance in human services, we underline the variety of possible levels and points of intervention.

Fifth, and finally, we wish to take a step back and ask, Why motivate human service work performance? For what? It is essential that social work managers focus on the organizational missions and humane social and societal purposes that workers are being motivated to achieve. Recent research from the social work management literature emphasizes that better outcomes for clients, workers, and organizations are achieved in positive organizational environments in which social workers can practice their profession with autonomy, respect, and collegiality. Trying to establish and maintain such an environment in an era of deprofessionalization, "contract-ization," and industrialization of social work and human services (Bernstein, 1991; Fabricant, 1985; Fabricant & Burghardt, 1992) can be challenging, if not daunting. We hope that greater education and public appreciation of humanity's shared fate and the crucial roles human service workers play in encouraging compassionate care and beneficial relationships in society will provide the inspiration, support, and resources to continue motivating and enhancing work performance in these important social work efforts.

NOTES

1. In that vein, given the historic and continuing role of professional social workers in providing human services, this chapter will focus on paid professional social workers working in social service agencies or host institutions (e.g., hospitals); it will not directly address issues of motivation of volunteers.

2. There is also a rich literature on group performance and group motivation, which is especially important in light of new management theories that emphasize teams and empowered groups. Due to limitations of space, we pose our discussion in terms of motivating the performance of an individual, but many of these points may also be relevant to groups.

REFERENCES

Adams, J. (1965). Inequity in social exchange. In L. Berkowitz (Ed.), *Advances in experimental social psychology* (2nd ed., pp. 267-299). New York: Academic Press.

Alderfer, C. P. (1972). *Existence, relatedness, and growth: Human needs in organizational settings.* New York: Free Press.

Arches, J. (1991). Social structure, burnout, and job satisfaction. *Social Work, 36*(3), 202-206.

Arvey, R. D., & Murphy, K. R. (1998). Performance evaluation in work settings. *Annual Review of Psychology, 49,* 141-168.

Bandura, A. (1971). *Social learning theory.* New York: General Learning Press.

Bandura, A. (1986). *Social foundations of thought and action: A social cognitive theory.* Englewood Cliffs, NJ: Prentice Hall.

Bandura, A. (1997). *Self-efficacy: The exercise of control.* New York: W. H. Freeman.

Bernstein, S. R. (1991). *Managing contracted services in the nonprofit agency: Administrative, ethical, and political issues.* Philadelphia: Temple University Press.

Borman, W. C., & Brush, D. H. (1993). More progress toward a taxonomy of managerial performance requirements. *Human Performance, 6*(1), 1-21.

Borman, W. C., & Motowidlo, S. J. (1993). Expanding the criterion domain to include elements of contextual performance. In N. Schmitt, W. C. Borman, et al. (Eds.), *Personnel selection in orgaizations* (pp. 71-98). San Francisco: Jossey-Bass.

Brill, N. I. (1995). *Working with people: the helping process.* White Plains, NY: Longman.

Calas, M. B., & Smircich, L. (1996). From "the woman's" point of view: Feminist approaches to organization studies. In S. R. Clegg (Ed.), *Handbook of organization studies* (pp. 218-257). London: Sage.

Chess, W. A., Norlin, J. M., & Jayaratne, S. D. (1987). Social work administration 1981-1985: Alive, happy, and prospering. *Administration in Social Work, 11*(2), 67-77.

Dean, J. W., & Bowen, D. E. (1994). Management theory and total quality: Improving research and practice through theory development. *Academy of Management Review, 19,* 392-418.

Deci, E. L. (1975). *Intrinsic motivation.* New York: Plenum.

Dessler, G. (1991). *Personnel/human resource management* (5th ed.). Englewood Cliffs, NJ: Prentice Hall.

Dunnette, M. D., & Hough, L. (Eds.). (1990). *Handbook of industrial and organizational psychology* (2nd ed.). Palo Alto, CA: Consulting Psychologists Press.

Fabricant, M. B. (1985). The industrialization of social work practice. *Social Work, 30*(5), 389-395.

Fabricant, M. B., & Burghardt, S. (1992). *The welfare state crisis and the transformation of social service work.* Armonk, NY: M. E. Sharpe.

Fishman, D. B., & Cherniss, C. (1990). Emerging managerial themes for the 1990s: Interdependencies and synergies among individual, organizational, and societal well-being. In D. B. Fishman & C. Cherniss (Eds.), *The human side of corporate competitiveness* (pp. 203-213). Newbury Park, CA: Sage.

Gant, L. M., Nagda, B., Brabson, H. V., Jayaratne, S., Chess, W. A., & Singh, A. K. (1993). Effects of undermining and social suport upon workers: Perceptions of coworker and supervisor relationships and psychological well-being. *Social Work, 38*(2), 158-165.

Glisson, C., & Durick, M. (1988). Predictors of job satisfaction and organizational commitment in human service organizations. *Administrative Science Quarterly, 33*(1), 61-81.

Glisson, C., & Hemmelgarn, A. (1998). The effects of organizational climate and interorganizational coordination on the quality and outcomes of children's service systems. *Child Abuse & Neglect, 22*(5), 401-421.

Gummer, B. (1995). American managers discover secret weapon—their employees! Developing human capacities in organizations, using the Japanese management approach. *Administration in Social Work, 19*, 93-110.

Gummer, B., & McCallion, P. (Eds.). (1995). *Total quality management in the social services: Theory and practice* (Resource guide and publication series on management and supervision). Albany, NY: Professional Development Program of Rockefeller College.

Guterman, N. B., & Jayaratne, S. (1994). Responsibility at risk: Perceptions of stress, control, and professional effectiveness in child welfare direct practitioners. *Journal of Social Service Research, 20*(1/2), 99-120.

Hackman, J. R., & Oldham, G. R. (1980). *Work redesign.* Reading, MA: Addison-Wesley.

Heider, F. (1958). *The psychology of interpersonal relations.* New York: John Wiley.

Herzberg, F., Mausner, B., & Snyderman, B. (1959). *The motivation to work* (2nd ed.). New York: John Wiley.

Hull, C. L. (1943). *Principles of behavior: An introduction to behavior theory.* New York: D. Appleton-Century.

Jahoda, M. (1982). *Employment and unemployment: A social-psychological analysis* (Psychology of social issues No. 1). Cambridge, UK: Cambridge University Press.

Jayaratne, S., & Chess, W. A. (1984). Job satisfaction, burnout, and turnover: A national study. *Social Work, 29*(5), 448-453.

Jayaratne, S., & Chess, W. A. (1985). Factors associated with job satisfaction and turnover among child welfare workers. In A. Hartman & J. Laird (Eds.), *A handbook of child welfare: Context, knowledge, and practice* (pp. 760-766). New York: Collier Macmillan.

Jayaratne, S., Davis-Sacks, M. L., & Chess, W. A. (1991). Private practice may be good for your health and well-being. *Social Work, 36*(3), 224-229.

Jayaratne, S., Tripodi, T., & Chess, W. A. (1983). Perceptions of emotional support, stress, and strain by male and female social workers. *Social Work Research & Abstracts, 19*(2), 19-27.

Jayaratne, S., Vinokur-Kaplan, D., & Chess, W. A. (1995). The importance of personal control: A comparison of social workers in private practice and public agency settings. *Journal of Applied Social Sciences, 19,* 47-59.

Jayaratne, S., Vinokur-Kaplan, D., Nagda, B. A., & Chess, W. A. (1995). A national study on violence and harassment of social workers by clients. *Journal of Applied Social Sciences, 20*(1), 1-14.

Jones, E. E., & Davis, K. E. (1965). From acts to dispositions: The attribution process in person perception. In L. Berkowitz (Ed.), *Advances in experimental social psychology* (2nd ed.). New York: Academic Press.

Kanfer, R., & Heggestad, E. C. (1997). Motivational traits and skills: A person-centered approach to work motivation. *Research in Organizational Behavior, 19,* 1-56.

Kearns, K. P. (1996). *Managing for accountability: Preserving the public trust in public and nonprofit organizations.* San Francisco: Jossey-Bass.

Kelley, H. H. (1967). Attribution theory in social psychology. In D. Levine (Ed.), *Nebraska symposium on motivation* (15th ed.). Lincoln: University of Nebraska.

Kelley, H. H. (1971). *Attribution in social interaction.* New York: General Learning Press.

Kelley, H. H. (1972). Attribution in social interaction. In E. E. Jones, D. E. Kanouse, H. H. Kelley, R. E. Nisbett, S. Valins, & B. Weiner (Eds.), *Attribution: Perceiving the causes of behavior.* New York: General Learning Press.

Kelley, H. H. (1973). The processes of causal attribution. *American Psychologist, 28,* 107-128.

Kluger, A. N., & De Nisi, A. (1996). The effects of feedback interventions on performance: Historical review, a meta-analysis, and a preliminary feedback intervention theory. *Psychological Bulletin, 119,* 276-299.

Kluger, A. N., & De Nisi, A. (1998). Feedback interventions: Toward the understanding of a double-edged sword. *Current Directions in Psychological Science, 7*(3), 67-72.

Koeske, G. F., & Kirk, S. A. (1995a). The effect of characteristics of human service workers on subsequent morale and turnover. *Administration in Social Work, 19*(1), 15-31.

Koeske, G. F., & Kirk, S. A. (1995b). The fate of optimism: A longitudinal study of case managers' hopefulness and subsequent morale. *Research on Social Work Practice, 5*(1), 47-61.

Koeske, G. F., & Koeske, R. D. (1989). Construct validity of the Maslach burnout inventory: A critical review and reconceptualization. *Journal of Applied Behavioral Science, 25*(25), 131-144.

Kramer, R. M. (1994). Voluntary agencies and the contract culture: "Dream or nightmare?" *Social Service Review, 68*(1), 33-60.

Kuhl, J. (1985). Volitional mediators of cognition-behavior consistency: Self-regulatory processes and action vs. state orientation. In J. Kuhl & J. Beckmann (Eds.), *Action control: From cognition to behavior* (pp. 101-128). New York: Springer-Verlag.

Lawler, E. E. (1973). *Motivation in work organizations.* Monterey, CA: Brooks/Cole.

Lewin, K. (1938). *The conceptual representation and the measurement of psychological forces* (Contributions to psychological theory No. 4). Durham, NC: Duke University Press.

Lewis, J. A., Lewis, M. D., & Soufleé, F., Jr. (1991). *Management of human service programs* (2nd ed.). Pacific Grove, CA: Brooks/Cole.

Locke, E. (1984). Job satisfaction. In M. Gruneberg & T. Wall (Eds.), *Social psychology and organizational behavior* (pp. 93-117). Chichester, UK: John Wiley.

Martin, L. L. (1993). *Total quality management in human service organizations* (Sage human services guides No. 67). Newbury Park, CA: Sage.

Maslow, A. (1954). *Motivation and personality.* New York: Harper & Row.

McGregor, D. (1960). *The human side of enterprise.* New York: McGraw Hill.

Miller, N. E., & Dollard, J. (1941). *Social learning and imitation.* New Haven, CT: Yale University Press.

Mirvis, P. H. (1992). The quality of employment in the nonprofit sector: An update of employee attitudes in nonprofits versus business and government. *Nonprofit Management and Leadership, 3*(1), 23-41.

Mitchell, T. R. (1997). Matching motivational strategies with organizational contexts. *Research in Organizational Behavior, 19,* 57-149.

Morrow, P. C. (1997). The measurement of total quality management principles and work-related outcomes. *Journal of Organizational Behavior, 18,* 363-376.

Motowidlo, S. J., & Van Scotter, J. R. (1994). Evidence that task performance should be distinguished from contextual performance. *Journal of Applied Psychology, 79*(4), 475-480.

Mowday, R., Porter, L., & Steers, R. (1982). *Organizational linkages: The psychology of commitment, absenteeism, and turnover.* New York: Academic Press.

National Association of Social Workers. (1996). *Code of ethics.* Washington, DC: Author.

Poulin, J. E. (1994). Job task and organizational predictors of social worker job satisfaction change: A panel study. *Administration in Social Work, 18*(1), 21-38.

Poulin, J. E. (1995). Job satisfaction of social work supervisors and administrators. *Administration in Social Work, 19*(4), 35-49.

Preston, A. E. (1990). Changing labor market patterns in the nonprofit and for-profit sectors: Implications for nonprofit management. *Nonprofit Management and Leadership, 1*(1), 15-28.

Price, R. H., & Vinokur, A. D. (1995). Supporting career transitions in time of organizational downsizing: The Michigan JOBS Program. In M. London (Ed.), *Employees, careers, and job creation: Developing growth-oriented human resource strategies and programs.* San Francisco: Jossey-Bass.

Ramsdell, P. S. (1994). Staff participation in organizational decision-making: An empirical study. *Administration in Social Work, 18*(4), 51-71.

Roe, R. A. (1999). Work performance: A multiple regulation perspective. *International Review of Industrial and Organizational Psychology, 14.*

Ronen, S. (1994). An underlying structure of motivational need taxonomies: A cross-cultural confirmation. In M. D. Dunnette & L. M. Hough (Eds.), *Handbook of industrial and organizational psychology* (Vol. 4). Palo Alto, CA: Consulting Psychologists Press.

Ryan, W. P. (1999, January-February). The new landscape for nonprofits. *Harvard Business Review,* 127-136.

Salamon, L. M. (1994). Marketization of social services. In R. D. Herman & associates (Eds.), *Jossey-Bass handbook of nonprofit leadership and management.* San Francisco: Jossey-Bass.

Sarason, S. B. (1990). New attitudes and motivations in workers: Growing interdependence among the work, personal-family, and educational spheres of life. In D. B. Fishman & C. Cherniss (Eds.), *The human side of corporate competitiveness* (pp. 51-66). Newbury Park, CA: Sage.

Skinner, B. F. (1938). *The behavior of organisms: an experimental analysis.* New York: D. Appleton-Century.

Soderfeldt, M., Soderfeldt, B., & Warg, L.-E. (1995). Burnout in social work: Review of the literature. *Social Work, 40,* 638-646.

Sparks, K., Cooper, C., Fried, Y., & Shirom, A. (1997). The effects of hours of work on health: A meta-analytic review. *Journal of Occupational and Organizational Psychology, 70*(4), 391-408.

Stajkovic, A. D., & Luthans, F. (1998). Self-efficacy and work-related performance: A meta-analysis. *Psychological Bulletin, 124*(2), 240-261.

Staw, B. M. (1977). Motivation in organization: Toward synthesis and redirection. In B. M. Staw & G. R. Salancik (Eds.), *New directions in organizational behavior.* Chicago: St. Clair Press.

Tambor, M. (1995). Unions. *Encyclopedia of social work* (Vol. 3, pp. 2418-2426). Washington, DC: NASW Press.

Tolman, E. C. (1959). Principles of purposive behavior. In S. Koch (Ed.), *Psychology: A study of a science* (Vol. 2). New York: McGraw-Hill.

Vinokur, A. D., & van Ryn, M. (1993). Social support and undermining in close relationships: Their independent effects on the mental health of unemployed persons. *Journal of Personality & Social Psychology, 65*(2), 350-359.

Vinokur-Kaplan, D. (1991). Job satisfaction among social workers in public and voluntary child welfare agencies. *Child Welfare, 70*(1), 81-91.

Vinokur-Kaplan, D. (1995a). Enhancing the effectiveness of interdisciplinary mental health treatment teams. *Administration and Policy in Mental Health, 21*(6), 525-530.

Vinokur-Kaplan, D. (1995b). Social workers' adoption of quality management in a multi-disciplinary host setting. In B. Gummer & P. McCallion (Eds.), *Total quality management in the social services: Theory and practice* (pp. 231-256). Albany, NY: Professional Development Program of Rockefeller College.

Vinokur-Kaplan, D. (1996). Workplace attitudes, experiences, and job satisfaction of social work administrators in nonprofit and public agencies: 1981 & 1989. *Nonprofit and Voluntary Sector Quarterly, 25*(1), 89-109.

Vinokur-Kaplan, D., Jayaratne, S., & Chess, W. A. (1994). Job satisfaction and retention of social workers in public agencies, non-profit agencies, and private practice: The impact of workplace conditions and motivators. *Administration in Social Work, 18*(3), 93-121.

Vroom, V. H. (1964). *Work and motivation.* New York: John Wiley.

Walton, M. (1986). *The Deming management method.* New York: Perigee.

Weiner, M. E. (1990). *Human services management: Analysis and applications* (2nd ed.). Belmont, CA: Wadsworth.

CHAPTER TEN

Organizational Climate and Culture

CHARLES GLISSON

UNDERSTANDING ORGANIZATIONAL CLIMATE AND CULTURE

What Is Organizational Climate and Culture?

Organizational climate and culture are popular constructs that receive a great deal of attention in both the trade and academic press. Researchers and practitioners alike are attracted to the potential that climate and culture offer for understanding the work environments of organizations. Organizational climate has a longer history in the research literature, but organizational culture is more frequently mentioned in trade texts on organizations and currently receives as much or more attention than climate in the academic literature. Of particular interest to both researchers and practitioners are the ways that climate and culture contribute to or detract from individual performance and organizational effectiveness.

The general notion that climate and culture describe critical, palpable dimensions of organizational life that members experience as a consequence of that membership is widely accepted. Moreover, the concepts of climate and culture have generated interest in the power of organizations to influence and affect the behavior, attitudes, and health of members. Some especially influential books have gained popularity in both the research and practice worlds by developing conceptual links between organizational culture and effectiveness. Of these, Peters

AUTHOR'S NOTE: The research reported in this chapter was supported by NIMH grants R01-MH56563 and R24-MH53623.

and Waterman's (1982) *In Search of Excellence* was one of the first and most successful and can be credited for spawning much of the current interest in organizational culture. Their emphasis on norms and values in the workplace (culture) as the key predictors of organizational success attracted the attention of numerous writers and fueled the organizational development efforts of several *Fortune 500* businesses. The publication of *In Search of Excellence* occurred at a time when it was generally believed that American businesses were competing unsuccessfully in the increasingly globalized market. By giving case examples of some of America's most successful businesses, Peters and Waterman offered the promise of improving American competitiveness in the global marketplace and inspired a nationwide infatuation with culture as the key to success.

A decade later, Osborne and Gaebler's (1992) *Reinventing Government* extended the work of Peters and Waterman to the public sector by describing the importance of culture to the performance of government agencies. After visiting and assessing a number of government agencies and programs, Osborne and Gaebler identified several key dimensions of culture that are characteristic of successful public organizations. They emphasized the importance of workplace cultures that value results over process, emphasize mission over bureaucratic rules, and promote worker autonomy and discretion rather than control. A number of federal agencies and several state governments have attempted to adopt these guidelines.

More recently, Schorr's (1997) *Common Purpose* built directly on Osborne and Gaebler's work by explaining the roles that organizational culture can play in revitalizing the nation's public child and family service systems. Her focus on transforming the bureaucracies that manage these services so that caseworkers are freed to focus on results and are less hampered by red tape and other bureaucratic barriers directly links organizational culture to social service outcomes. Her book and the previous two provide many real world examples of how culture and climate (although the latter term is rarely used in these three texts) contribute to organizational performance. Recent research findings support the observations made in the case studies reported in these books and adds to the evidence that culture and climate are critical to organizational performance (Brown & Leigh, 1996; Denison & Mishra, 1995; Glisson & Hemmelgarn, 1998; Gordon & DiTomaso, 1992; Petty, Beadles, Lowery, Chapman, & Connell, 1995; Zamanou & Glaser, 1994).

The challenge for both researchers and practitioners, however, is to understand these intuitively appealing constructs in a way that clearly defines them, distinguishes them from other organizational characteristics, and establishes convincing links to performance and outcome criteria. The constructs, although extremely popular, continue to be used inconsistently by researchers as well as practitioners. They are applied in ways that confuse them with related organizational characteristics such as structure, technology, and leadership and with individual worker characteristics such as job satisfaction, motivation, and commitment (Verbeke, Volgering, & Hessels, 1998).

Definitions of climate. Today, organizational climate is widely defined in terms of employees' perceptions of their work environment (Schneider, 1990). The distinction between *psychologi-*

cal and *organizational* climate developed by Larry James and colleagues drives much of the current theoretical and empirical work concerning climate (James & James, 1989; James, James, & Ashe, 1990; James & Jones, 1974; James & Sells, 1981). Psychological climate is an employee's perception of the psychological impact of the work environment on his or her own personal well-being. Brown and Leigh (1996) operationalize a positive psychological climate in terms of psychological safety and meaningfulness. They emphasize that positive climates are those in which workers perceive that their work environment poses no threat to their personal self-image or career and provides a return on their investment of personal energy.

All work environments create psychological climates, but organizational climates are created by shared psychological climates. In other words, the psychological climate of a work environment is a worker's perception of how the work environment is negatively or positively affecting him or her. So it is an employee's perception of the work environment and not the environment itself that is most important. An organizational climate exists to the extent that employees agree on their perceptions. When employees in a particular work environment agree on their perceptions of their work environment, their shared perceptions can be aggregated to describe the organization's climate (Jones & James, 1979; Joyce & Slocum, 1984). Dimensions of climate included in widely used instruments are workers' perceptions of work environment support, conflict, challenge, depersonalization, equity, opportunity, stress, ambiguity, task significance, and emotional exhaustion.

Definitions of culture. Definitions of organizational culture have depended to a great extent on definitions of societal culture, which emerged from anthropological research. Definitions commonly used in the organizational literature emphasize that culture includes the shared values, beliefs, and behavioral norms in an organization (Ouchi, 1981; Swartz & Jordan, 1980; Van Maanen & Schein, 1979). But there is much more disagreement surrounding definitions of culture than climate, and there is overlap in definitions of the two constructs that blurs the boundaries that separate them. Larry James and colleagues distinguish climate from culture by emphasizing that culture is a property of the social system (the norms and values that drive behavior in the system), as compared to climate, which they describe as a property of the individuals (their perceptions) within that system (James et al., 1990; James & McIntyre, 1996).

There are other related definitions of culture that emphasize different properties and characteristics. Rousseau (1990) describes culture as the social process by which members share their values, beliefs, and norms. Schein (1992) defines culture as the shared assumptions that are taught to new members but restricts this socialization process to perceptions, thinking, and feelings, specifically excluding behavior. Jelinek, Smircich, and Hirsch (1983), in their introduction to a special issue of *Administrative Science Quarterly* devoted to culture, describe culture as both product and process, the shaper of human interaction and the outcome of it.

Common to most definitions of culture are the values and norms that drive behavior in an organization. However, there is disagreement about whether culture is a property of the individual or the social system, whether it includes perceptions as well as behavior, and whether it is social process, social structure, or both. Elements that are included in many instruments used to measure culture include risk taking, results orientation, collaboration, innovation, adaptability, perfectionism, competitiveness, and integrity (Rousseau, 1990). But other elements of culture that are included in measurement instruments, such as cooperation or fairness, overlap with many elements that are included in measures of climate, creating confusion about the differences and similarities between climate and culture.

Similarities and differences between climate and culture. Although many questions remain unresolved, culture and climate continue to be popular constructs in both the practice and research literatures. Yet, the question of what differentiates culture from climate, or what unites them, has not been adequately answered (Denison, 1996). A review of the history of the terms in the research literature as well as of recent findings about their links with other variables provides insight into their similarities and differences, but more work remains to be done to fully understand their value to organizational performance.

This chapter defines organizational climate as a property of the individual (perception) that is shared by other individuals in the same work environment. That is, organizational climate is the shared perceptions that employees have of the psychological impact that their work environment has on those who work there. In contrast, culture is defined as a property of the collective social system. It comprises the norms and values of that social system that drive the way things are done in the organization. These norms include how employees interact, how

they approach their work, and what work behaviors are emphasized in the organization through rewards and sanctions. Thus, culture describes the social context of the work environment, and climate describes the psychological impact of the work environment. Culture captures patterns of social interaction, and climate captures the personal meaning that individual workers give to those interactions.

It would be misleading to imply that there is widespread agreement on the distinction being made here between climate and culture. Both climate and culture have been described in the literature at one time or the other as properties of the organization and as properties of the individual. For example, there is still no consensus "as to whether culture exists only in the evaluations people make of a social context . . . or whether culture is an attribute of an organization in the same sense that structure and technology are organizational attributes" (Jones, 1983, p. 454). However, as described in the next section, a review of the history of the development of the two constructs offers support for the distinction made here. The key to understanding the distinction is found in the roles that perception and behavior play in climate and culture, respectively.

Culture depends on the norms of the organization as a social system. It is the way things are done in the organization and what is deemed to be most important in the organization. Although we may measure it by asking individuals in an organization to describe activities and interactions, we would be asking them to describe what happens in the organization. As a result, culture is defined as a property of the collective social system. If workers agree that a particular norm characterizes their organization, we conclude that it is a part of that organization's culture. Here, we could use a measure of interrater agreement among respondents to assess whether we are indeed tapping a cultural dimension that is characteristic of the organization. If there is disagreement among the respondents about a certain norm, then we would conclude that that norm is not characteristic of the organization's culture.

In contrast, when we define organizational climate as shared perceptions, we are not using the term *shared* to refer to interrater reliability in measuring the construct. The construct we are measuring is an individual property similar to asking whether respondents experience the temperature of a room as hot, comfortable, or cold. If most respondents feel hot, but others feel comfortable, we don't challenge the accuracy of the perceptions of those who feel comfortable. Those who are comfortable are merely experiencing the temperature of the room differently from those who feel hot. So even if we characterize the temperature of the room as hot for most respondents, we could still conclude that others do truly feel comfortable because the characteristic we are assessing remains a property of the individual. It is in this sense that climate remains a property of the individual, whether there is agreement or disagreement among the respondents' perceptions of the work environment.

An individual's perception of the impact of working in a particular organizational environment is a property of the individual, even if all of the individuals in that particular organization agree (or disagree) on that particular perception. Although the perceptions on which they agree make up the organization's climate, the perceptions are the evaluations each individual makes about working in that particular environment (James & McIntyre, 1996).

The History of Culture and Climate as Organizational Constructs

Organizational climate in the fifties, sixties, and seventies. Although climate and culture are now often mentioned in tandem (Barker, 1994; Hoy, 1990; Rentsch, 1990; Schneider, 1990; Schneider, Gunnarson, & Niles-Jolly, 1994; Verbeke et al., 1998), their individual histories within the organizational literature are quite distinct (Denison, 1996; Reichers & Schneider, 1990). Climate has a significantly longer history. Articles as far back as the fifties identify organizational climate as a key factor in worker performance (Argyris, 1958; Fleishman, 1953). Early work emphasized the roles of leadership and group dynamics in the development of work-group climate. This coincided with the surge of academic interest in leadership and groups that developed following World War II. Scholarly work on organizational climate began to mature during the sixties, when key texts were published that focused specifically on climate (Litwin & Stringer, 1968; Tagiuri & Litwin, 1968). Empirical research on climate flourished during the seventies, with numerous articles appearing in many different journals (e.g., Hellriegel & Slocum, 1974; James, Hater, Gent, & Bruni, 1978; James & Jones, 1974; Payne & Mansfield, 1973; Schneider, 1972; Schneider & Bartlett, 1970). A number of scales for measuring climate were developed and refined during this time, and linkages with an array of antecedents and consequences of climate were explored (Hellriegel & Slocum, 1974).

The emergence of organizational culture in the seventies. Although the notion that organizations are social systems with varying norms is found in such early classics as Gouldner (1954) and Selznick (1949), the concept of *organizational culture* did not appear in the organizational literature until the late seventies (Handy, 1976; Pettigrew, 1979). Borrowing heavily from anthropology as well as sociology, the early approach to studying culture can be contrasted sharply with the psychological focus of the climate studies. As a result of its academic roots, a decidedly qualitative focus to studying organizational culture was taken in early work, which continues to influence much of the current literature on culture.

Although relatively late in its beginning, the interest in organizational culture expanded quickly. During the eighties, several texts on culture emerged, which emphasized the importance of culture to the performance of business and industrial organizations (Deal & Kennedy, 1982; Frost, Moore, Louis, Lundberg, & Martin, 1985; Ott, 1989; Sathe, 1985; Schein, 1992). These texts and the large number of articles on culture that appeared in the eighties in a variety of journals served to place culture in a position of prominence in the organizational literature equal to or surpassing that of climate (Ouchi & Wilkins, 1985).

The evolution of culture and climate in the nineties. During the nineties, the constructs of culture and climate began to appear in print together, and their similarities and differences began to be discussed. Schneider (1990) devoted an entire text to this issue, and articles in a variety of disciplines examined both constructs simultaneously (Barker, 1994; Hoy, 1990; Johnson & McIntyre, 1998; Rentsch, 1990; Schneider et al., 1994; Verbeke et al., 1998).

As the two constructs were increasingly discussed and examined together, it became clear that theorists and researchers were not in agreement about several important issues. Perhaps the most important issue is simply whether climate and culture are actually distinct concepts or are merely two views of the same concept (Ouchi & Wilkins, 1985). Although not resolved, if culture and climate are defined as they have been described above, the two are distinct. That is, the norms that guide work in an organization can be distinguished from the perceptions that individual workers have of the psychological impact of their work environment.

A second issue, if it is assumed that climate and culture are distinct concepts, concerns the relationship between the two. Does one affect the other, is there a reciprocal effect, or are the two associated by their respective relationships with a common third variable? Although there are undoubtedly common variables that affect norms and affect workers' perceptions, it is likely that the concepts affect each other in a number of ways. Workers' perceptions of the impact that their work environment has on them are most certainly affected by the norms that drive behavior in that environment (Schneider et al., 1994). For example, if a hospital emphasizes billable hours and profitable procedures at the expense of individualized care, health care providers may perceive their work environment as depersonalized and as having a negative psychological impact on their own well-being.

It is also possible that workers' perceptions of their work environment affect behavioral norms in the organization. For example, if most child protection workers in a state agency perceive that they are not supported by their administration, common norms for defensive practice in that agency may develop. Supervisors and case managers might then emphasize extensive written documentation and routinized, by-the-book protocols to be able to defend their actions as based on required procedure if a decision or action is challenged by the court or a client advocate.

A third issue concerns whether culture can be quantitatively assessed in an organization in the way that climate has traditionally been assessed (Cooke & Rousseau, 1988; Ouchi & Wilkins, 1985). This issue is rooted in the respective histories of the two concepts and has originated with some theorists, who have criticized quantitative approaches as inappropriate for assessing culture (Deal, 1986; Schein, 1986). The qualitative versus quantitative methods debate is familiar to many social scientists, but in this case, qualitative methodologists argue that each organization has a unique, complex culture that can only be understood by extensive observation and dialogue with its members. Moreover, it is argued that the information gathered in that dialogue cannot be quantified but only described in qualitative terms. Others argue that both methods can be used and, in fact, complement each other (Denison & Mishra, 1995; Hofstede, Neuijen, Ohayv, & Sanders, 1990; Rousseau, 1990). For example, in a study of the cultures of hospital emergency rooms, the results of extensive, open-ended interviews were used to compare emergency room cultures qualitatively. The results were then used to develop questionnaires that became the basis of quantitative comparisons of the emergency room cultures, which confirmed the qualitative observations (Hemmelgarn, Glisson, & Dukes, in press).

Why Are Culture and Climate Important to Social Services?

The success of human service organizations generally depends on the relationships and interactions between service providers and service recipients. Whether the organizations provide social, medical, educational, or other human services, these relationships and interactions are central to the quality and outcomes of the service. Culture and climate are important to human services because the nature and tone of these relationships and interactions are molded by and reflect the organizational culture and climate in which they occur (Blau, 1960; Hoy, 1990; Johnson & McIntyre, 1998; Rentsch, 1990).

The role of service system norms and values in social services. The norms that drive service-provider behavior and communicate what is valued in organizations and the shared perceptions that influence service-provider attitudes create a social and psychological context that shapes the tone, content, and objectives of the service (O'Reilly & Chatman, 1996; Perkins, Shaw, & Sutton, 1990). Interestingly, one of the early classic studies of work-group norms and employee perceptions was conducted in a state social welfare agency (Blau, 1960). This study provided the first evidence of the connections between the norms and values of a social service organization, the perceptions of work-group members, and the quality and outcomes of service. Although progress in understanding the connections in greater detail has been disappointingly slow in the decades that followed, more recent studies have added to the evidence that they exist.

In the study of emergency rooms mentioned previously, the organizational cultures were found to prescribe significant differences in the way emergency rooms provide emotional support to the families of children with serious medical emergencies (Hemmelgarn et al., in press). In some emergency rooms, parents and children are rarely separated from each other, health care providers are careful to respond fully to the concerns and questions raised by parents, and it is common for physicians and nurses to comfort parents during the most serious pediatric cases. These are important components of family-centered care, which has been linked to effective pediatric health care, but the study shows that the extent to which they are practiced varies as a function of the culture of the emergency room in which the physician, nurse, or social worker is working.

The emergency room research provides evidence that the nature and tone of physicians', nurses', and social workers' interactions with pediatric patients and parents are determined by their organization's culture rather than by their profession, training, or experience. In some emergency rooms, providing support to the families of children who are seriously injured or ill is valued and is the norm. In other emergency rooms, it is neither valued nor the norm, so it does not occur regardless of the training or experience of the individual health care provider.

In addition to molding the nature and tone of interactions between service provider and service recipient, organizational culture can affect technical aspects of service. For example, the service and custodial decisions made by case managers about children placed in state custody have been found to be dictated more by organizational norms than by the actual needs of the children (Glisson, 1996; Martin, Peters, & Glisson, 1998). In these studies, case managers ignored the results of standardized needs assessments and instead followed the organization's established norms for referring children to placements and mental health services, regardless of actual need. For example, it was the norm for males to be placed in more restrictive placements than females, even when matched on age, reason for custody, and problem behavior.

We have known for decades that workers in many human service organizations operate within "well-worn paths" that routinize service delivery in a way that prevents individualized care (Glisson, 1978). These well-worn paths constitute sets of behavioral norms for an organization. Well-worn paths are created because organizations generally value certainty and predictability, whereas they discourage innovation and unique approaches to work. As will be discussed below, formal and informal, tangible and intangible rewards and sanctions exert pressure on workers to behave in ways that conform to these norms, independently of the actual needs of those who are being served.

The role of service provider perceptions in social services. Brown and Leigh (1996) emphasize that it is employees' perceptions of their work environment rather than the environment itself that mediate employee attitudes and behavior. Perceptions are particularly important in social services because of the nature of the helping relationships that are central to the work. Social service relationships consist of human interactions that are focused on enhancing human functioning. As a result, the attitudes and perceptions that service providers carry into these interactions can dramatically influence the nature and tone of the interactions

(Schneider, White, & Paul, 1998). If a work environment is nonsupportive, impersonal, and stressful, employees' interactions with those who receive their services will reflect the lack of support, impersonality, and stress that the employees perceive in their work environment. Whether the employees are teachers, nurses, social workers, psychologists, or bank tellers, employees' perceptions of the impact of their work environment influence how they interact with those they serve in that environment (Schneider et al., 1998).

Much of the work in many social service organizations also requires that social workers interact with others outside their organization. Many times, this includes advocacy on behalf of individual clients, information seeking, or service coordination activities. Particularly in public social services, effectiveness in completing these types of tasks requires a great deal of personal and extended effort on the part of individual workers. In addition to knowledge and skill, tenacity and innovation can be critical to solving unexpected problems or navigating complex barriers to services. It is more likely that social workers will be tenacious and innovative in the face of unexpected problems or barriers if they perceive that their work environment treats them fairly and provides personal support for their effort. In short, if workers perceive that their organization stands behind them and can be counted on when the going gets tough, they are more likely to put the extra effort into the work that is required for success. In short, positive organizational climates complement and encourage the type of service efforts that lead to success (Glisson & Hemmelgarn, 1998).

A very close relationship has been found consistently between organizational climate and worker attitudes toward their job and organization (James & Tetrick, 1986; Johnson & McIntyre, 1998). Workers who perceive their organizational climate in positive terms report higher job satisfaction and greater commitment to their organization. As found in other types of organizations, research on social service organizations has shown that social workers' perceptions of their work environment affect both their job satisfaction and organizational commitment (Glisson & Durick, 1988).

How culture and climate link organizations to service outcomes. Culture and climate link organizations to outcomes through the behaviors, perceptions, and attitudes that are associated with employee performance (Denison & Mishra, 1995; Glisson & Hemmelgarn, 1998; Hoy, 1990; Joyce & Slocum, 1984; Petty et al., 1995; Schneider et al., 1994; Wilkins & Ouchi, 1983). Two issues are especially important to understanding how culture and climate affect social service outcomes. The first is that social services employ soft technologies, which are particularly vulnerable to the behavioral norms that make up an organization's culture. The second is that social service core technologies depend on human interaction and relationships, which are especially sensitive to the perceptions that service providers have of their work environment. Both culture and climate influence human interaction, and human interactions compose the core technologies of social service organizations (Denison, 1996).

The core technology of any organization includes the skills, activities, and materials that are required to produce the product or create the service for which the organization is remunerated. Some technologies are "harder" and some are "softer." Harder technologies include more concrete processes and materials that can be clearly specified in advance and have more predictable and determinant outcomes. The harder the technology, the more workers can rely on their knowledge of the raw materials and their skills for using those materials to successfully create the product or service. For example, the quality of stainless steel, the performance of a personal computer, or the beauty and durability of a house painting project is a direct function of the quality of the materials and the skill of those who use the materials to create the steel, build the computer, or paint the house. In contrast, softer technologies include fewer concrete processes, more variable raw material, and have less predictable and determinant outcomes. Even highly knowledgeable and skilled workers are not always successful in the use of soft technologies. Moreover, there is much more variability in the way experienced workers implement soft technologies than hard technologies. For example, skilled mental health professionals in the best equipped residential facilities treat drug addiction in distinctly varied ways, and all experience many failures. As another example, highly regarded oncologists treat specific malignancies in very different ways and have a high ratio of failures to successes in treatment.

Factors that make technologies harder or softer also make them more or less vulnerable to the cultures in which they are implemented. Soft technologies are molded to fit within existing organizational norms with few visible consequences. They can be molded by an organization because the best way to implement the technology is not widely agreed on, outcomes are unpredictable, and it is difficult to determine whether an organization is implementing the technology effectively. Hard technologies, on the other hand, are more resistant to organizational differences. For hard technologies, there are widely known and agreed on practices that consistently result in predictable outcomes, and it is therefore possible to determine whether an organization is implementing a hard technology correctly according to those practices.

We have known for some time that social service systems incorporate soft technologies that are vulnerable to the organizational context in which they are implemented (Glisson, 1978, 1992). Organizations that have identical missions and that provide similar services to the same target population can have core technologies that are implemented in very different ways. When organizational norms emphasize the importance of extensive paperwork, following bureaucratic rules, and obtaining prior approval for all decisions, social workers place more importance on following procedures and documenting their activities with a paper trail than on meeting the individual needs of their clients. When organizational norms place more emphasis on the importance of social workers' discretion and flexibility in addressing unique problems, social workers focus more on the individual needs of each client. In the former organizations, the core technology is highly routinized with work proceeding in an assembly line fashion. Social workers in these organizations perceive their clients as having similar problems and believe that they know what each client needs, even before learning about the characteristics of the individual case. In the latter organizations, the core technology is nonroutinized, and social workers describe their clients as having many unique problems that they cannot anticipate and that require individualized plans of care (Glisson, 1978, 1992).

Workers' perceptions of their work environment reflect a general appraisal of whether they view their work environment as beneficial or detrimental (James & James, 1989). This general appraisal determines their attitudes about their work and how they approach it (James & McIntyre, 1996). Workers' perceptions of their work environment, therefore, affect how they perform in that environment (Brown & Leigh, 1996; James, Demaree, Mulaik, & Ladd, 1992). Because human interaction and human relationships are central to successful social services, social workers' perceptions of their work environment are particularly important to that success.

A study of public children's services systems found that positive, less restrictive climates complement and encourage the type of service-provider activities that lead to improved outcomes (Glisson & Hemmelgarn, 1998). The success that social workers had in improving children's psychosocial functioning depended on their consideration of each child's unique needs, their responsiveness to unexpected problems, their tenacity in navigating complex bureaucratic and judicial hurdles, and their personal relationships with each child they served. Among agencies that provided the same service to the same target population, those in which caseworkers reported higher levels of work environment fairness, role clarity, cooperation, and personalization and lower levels of work environment conflict and stress provided higher quality service and achieved better outcomes.

WHY ORGANIZATIONS HAVE DIFFERENT CLIMATES AND CULTURES

We know that organizations that do the same work can have different cultures and climates. It is less clear why organizations develop different cultures and climates, how those cultures and climates are maintained over time, and what differences in culture and climate distinguish different types of organizations. If, in fact, certain cultures and climates lead to success as explained above, why do organizations not adopt those that are most effective? Herbert Simon's (1957) Nobel prize-winning work several decades ago explained that organizational decision making is not rational and not always in the long-term best interests of the organization. Rather than selecting the best alternative, many organizations tend to "satisfice," or adopt the first acceptable approach or solution that emerges. The first acceptable approach or solution usually addresses one or more relevant issues for the organization, but frequently, those that are addressed are merely the easiest or most accessible issues, not the most important ones. This is central to understanding why organizations have different cultures and climates.

As explained above, social service organizations incorporate core technologies that cannot guarantee success. Moreover, if they are successful, the success is difficult to document. Consider this reality for social service organizations when combined with their constituents' demands for accountability, efficiency, or responsiveness. For these organizations, the demand for accountability may create an emphasis on documenting the process of work, the demand for efficiency may create an emphasis on reducing the cost per person served, and the demand for responsiveness may result in an emphasis on increasing the number of people who receive the service (Glisson & Martin, 1980). Although these strategies may well address concerns raised by boards of directors, funders, legislators, or public interest groups, none of these strategies address effectiveness or outcomes. This is to say that the factors contributing to the development of an organization's culture or climate may be unrelated or at times detrimental to its effectiveness, while at the same time being central to its survival.

How Do Climate and Culture Develop in an Organization?

There are three groups of factors that contribute to the norms that define an organization's culture and to the perceptions that define its climate. These three groups of factors are individual differences among workers, the characteristics of the organization's external environment, and the design of the organization as a social system.

The contribution of individual differences to climate and culture. Individual workers have personal traits that can influence the norms and values that develop within an organization and the perceptions that they have of their work environment (James & McIntyre, 1996; Wiener, 1988; Wilkins & Ouchi, 1983). For example, if enough new workers are hired whose personality traits include high levels of achievement motivation, an organization's culture could develop new behavioral norms for achievement that did not previously exist. Other worker traits such as reliability, competitiveness, risk taking, or perfectionism could exert similar in-

fluences on culture. Such individual traits can redefine organizational norms as more and more employees are hired who share those traits. Administrators use selective hiring and firing as means of either maintaining existing norms or changing them (Wiener, 1988). Of course, to do so suggests that administrators have a sense of the traits they desire in their employees and are then able to identify workers or applicants who have the traits (James & McIntyre, 1996).

Climate can also be influenced by individual differences in workers' perceptions of the impact of their work environment. Research has documented that a certain portion of the variation in individual perceptions is consistent across work environments (Staw & Ross, 1985). That is, individuals who view their work environments more positively relative to other employees also tend to view former and future work environments more positively. Also, employees who view their work environments more negatively relative to other employees tend to view former and future work environments more negatively as well. In other words, if an employee perceives his or her work environment as less supportive and less fair than other employees in that organization, then in subsequent jobs, the employee is likely to perceive the new work environments as less supportive and less fair than other employees in those organizations (Arvey, Bouchard, Segal, & Abraham, 1989). If new employees are selected who share tendencies to perceive their work environments either more positively or more negatively, the organization's climate is affected by the perceptions that are shared by the new employees.

Importing climate and culture from the external environment. Organizations adopt ways of doing things that resemble other organizations in their external environment with which they compete or cooperate (Hannan & Freeman, 1977; Martin & Glisson, 1989; Pennings, 1980; Pennings & Gresov, 1986). The similarities among competing or cooperating organizations have been described as the result of certain practices ensuring survival in given environments, regional differences in management practices, or organizational mimicry (DiMaggio & Powell, 1983; Martin & Glisson, 1989; Weiss & Delbecq, 1987). Organizational mimicry occurs when the norms of one organization that is seen as more successful are adopted by another organization in an effort to emulate that success. For example, a mental health center may receive positive attention and attract new funding as the result of developing innovative ways of reaching previously underserved populations. As a result, the board of directors and chief executive officer of another mental health center may begin to promote similar innovative approaches to service among its own employees.

Another way culture is imported from the external environment is through the norms that workers have internalized as members of the society in which the organization is embedded (Martin & Glisson, 1989; Smircich, 1983). This is demonstrated by differences in interaction patterns, relationships with authority figures, openness in communication, and other characteristics of societal culture that determine how individuals relate to others (Hofstede et al., 1990). This explains why attempts to replicate certain Japanese models of management in the United States encountered barriers that had not been an issue in Japan.

Workers' perceptions of their work environments can also be affected by characteristics of their external environment that either offer additional options, provide new information, or create threats. Because workers' perceptions of their organizations are subjective appraisals, they can be influenced by the social, political, and economic realities in their organizations' external environments. For example, if the number of schools hiring social workers increases dramatically because of a newly recognized need by principals and school boards responding to increased school violence, then the recruitment of social workers with experience in schools becomes more competitive. As a result, social workers already working in schools may begin viewing their own work environments more critically as they begin to examine new job opportunities. Or, employees of a home-health care agency may begin to perceive their work environment more positively after their own agency survives decreases in federal and state funds that result in the demise of other agencies with which it has competed.

The impact of organizational design: structure, technology, and leadership. The structure, core technology, and leadership of a human service organization describe the patterns of interactions among practitioners, the nature of the interactions between practitioners and clients, and the administration's style of organizational governance, respectively. These interactions create behavioral norms that compose its culture and stimulate shared perceptions that compose its climate (Birleson, 1998; James & Tetrick, 1986; Pennings & Gresov, 1986; Rentsch, 1990; Schein, 1996).

Cultural dimensions affected by an organization's structure include such behavioral norms as flexibility, approval seeking, risk taking, and innovation. Hofstede and colleagues (1990) found that centralization, formalization, and specialization in structure were linked with a variety of cultural dimensions, particularly the extent to which workers were process oriented rather than results oriented. A highly centralized structure that restricts participation in decision making and maintains a narrow hierarchy of authority promotes approval seeking and reduces risk taking among employees. A highly formalized structure that carefully partitions labor and relies on strict procedural specifications places little value on flexibility or innovation.

Characteristics of an organization's core technology influence norms and values in the organization by workers generalizing behavior required by the core technology throughout the organization. For example, the careful attention to detail required in certain engineering core technologies has been found to influence the broader organizational culture, encouraging senior managers to give excessive attention to detail and control in nontechnology as well as technology matters (Barker, 1994; Schein, 1996). Changes in core technology such as those that accompany the introduction of computer systems can transform the cultures of human service organizations by changing the norms that govern and direct interactions among workers (Gundry, 1985).

The characteristics of the core technology can also affect climate dimensions such as employees' perceptions of personal accomplishment, role conflict, and depersonalization. If the core technology in a public child welfare system is a routinized, assembly line approach to service delivery that does not allow individualized attention to the needs of each child, social workers are likely to experience high levels of role conflict and depersonalization. On the other hand, if the core technology emphasizes individualized attention to the needs and well-being of each child, encouraging social workers to attend to unexpected problems in innovative ways, social workers may experience higher levels of personal accomplishment.

Organizational leaders can manipulate their organizations' cultures by implementing new structural and technological characteristics that determine how work is done in the organization. In fact, the manipulation (or maintenance) of culture is believed to be an essential function of leadership (Bryman, 1996; Peters & Waterman, 1982; Schein, 1992; Trice & Beyer, 1993). However, there is a difference of opinion between those who conclude that leaders manage meaning and values and those who argue that leaders dictate practices, not meaning. Hofstede and colleagues (1990) conclude that organizational founders and key leaders shape organizational cultures by creating shared practices in the organizations. Distinguishing between the values of the organizational leaders and the values of organizational members, they provide evidence that the leaders' values influence the members' practices without necessarily changing the members' values. This separation of members' values and practices underscores the difference between assessing common practices in an organization and assessing personal values (Hofstede, 1998). Rousseau (1990) and others have linked practices and values of organizational members in a direct way with the assumption that practices reflect deeply held values. But Hofstede et al. (1990) conclude that the values reflected in observed practices are more likely those of the leaders than of the members.

An organization's leadership has an important impact on workers' perceptions of fairness and support in their work environment. When leaders are considerate of their employees in their decisions, are open to communication from employees regarding policies and procedures, and recognize their employees' accomplishments, the employees are more likely to perceive their work environment as fair and supportive. Sheridan (1992) found that employees in firms emphasizing interpersonal relationships were much more committed to remaining with the firm. In social service organizations, good leadership has been identified as one of the few factors that contributes to both employee job satisfaction and commitment, each of which is highly correlated with positive organizational climate (Glisson & Durick, 1988; Glisson & Hemmelgarn, 1998).

How Are Climate and Culture Maintained in an Organization?

We know that culture and climate are stable characteristics of an organization that are maintained over time and gain considerable inertia as generations of workers come and go (Wiener, 1988). The mechanisms that explain the stability of the concepts are important to understanding the challenge of improving services by changing the behavior and perceptions of service providers. These mechanisms include the need for certainty, the need for power, and socialization.

The need for certainty. James Thompson has said that "organizations abhor uncertainty" (1967, p. 99). More accurately, perhaps, individuals in organizations abhor feeling uncertain about what they are doing and about how they fit within the organization. Most people want to be clear on what they should be doing in a

job, and they want to believe that what they are doing contributes to a meaningful goal. Culture contributes to certainty in an organization through shared norms and values (Louis, 1990; Trice & Beyer, 1993). Even when confronted with the uncertainty of a soft technology, a nonspecific mission, and unpredictable outcomes, organizations can create certainty through shared norms and values. This creation of certainty may have positive or negative repercussions for outcomes. Bureaucracies can create certainty through rites and ceremonies and by establishing norms that focus on process, routinization, regulations, and procedures that are unrelated to effectiveness (Trice & Beyer, 1984; Wiener, 1988).

This is not to say that norms and values only contribute to red tape and routinization. Shared norms and values can work in other ways to help create certainty in the face of confusion and challenge (Schein, 1992). Whether it is a combat team in battle, an emergency room team following a natural disaster, or a child protection unit determining whether a child should be immediately removed from a home, shared norms and values contribute to individuals feeling certain about decisions and actions. Even if the reality is that there is no one right decision or action, the perception of certainty is engendered by individuals in an organization sharing common ideas about the way they get things done.

The emergency room research described above found that norms varied significantly among hospitals about providing emotional support to families, but in each emergency room, the existing norms had what Schein (1992) describes as "survival value." That is, the demands on medical personnel in emergency rooms require strategies for adapting to the associated stress. The cultures that evolve in response to these demands serve important functions that are valued by the members and are resistant to change (Hemmelgarn et al., in press). Those who attempt to change the cultures of work groups find that even those members who are most vocal about the negative aspects of their work environment can be among the most resistant to change when their adaptive patterns of survival behavior are threatened.

The need for power. Whereas individuals in an organization may abhor uncertainty, most appear to be attracted to and influenced by power. Political-cultural analyses of organizations describe power as distributed both formally and informally through processes of conflict that lead to a negotiated order (Lucas, 1987). As a result of this negotiated order, individuals holding the same positions will not necessarily have the same power because of differences in experience, expertise, access to information, relationships in the organization, and membership in interest groups. These factors contribute to power structures that are built and maintained by the norms that drive behavior in the organization (O'Reilly & Chatman, 1996; Trice & Beyer, 1993). Therefore, many members in an organization have an investment in perpetuating existing norms because those are the basis of their power (Barker, 1994). When existing norms change, an opportunity for shifts in power structures occurs, and changes in norms are therefore resisted by those most invested in the existing power structures (Sherwood, 1988).

For this reason, when organizations are formally restructured, the opportunity for cultural change is presented. Many writers believe that efforts to make significant changes in organizational culture are much more likely to be successful when they coincide with major mergers, reorganizations, or new administrations. Related to the need for certainty described above, as well as to the dissolution of old power structures, members of organizations in the midst of major structural changes are thought to be much more receptive to new norms. On the other hand, the role of existing power structures also explains why large state service systems are so resistant to change. Although top officials may come and go with different governors or political administrations, most state bureaucracies maintain consistent structures over long periods of time in which existing cultures are firmly entrenched and rarely challenged.

Power also plays a role in the development of perceptions of work environments. Social information-processing theory explains that perceptions are influenced by social interactions (Salancik & Pfeffer, 1978). From this point of view, social interaction is used to create a mutually agreed on perception of the work environment by the members of that environment. Each member does not arrive at his or her perception of the work environment independently. Rather, the perception is arrived at through consensus building in the work group. So, if the workers' shared perception of a work environment is that it is not supportive of them, social information-processing theory would argue that the shared perception evolved through a process of social interaction (Louis, 1990; Salancik & Pfeffer, 1978). Moreover, the conclusions arrived at by those interactions may be less a result of any objective weighing of evidence and more a function of the composition of the interaction group (Rentsch, 1990). For example, the interactions are likely to be influenced by persuasive individuals with strongly held views. Informal power contributes to persuasiveness in social interactions, and the shared perceptions that develop from those interactions reflect the views of those with more informal power.

Transferring climate and culture to new employees. We have known for almost half a century that employees in social welfare agencies are socialized by the organizations in which they work. A number of decades ago, Blau (1960) documented that the attitudes and behavior of social workers in social welfare systems are affected by the norms, values, and perceptions typical of their work groups. Perhaps even more important was the finding that this occurred even when the group's norms, values, and perceptions were anti-client. Through social information processing as described above, the need for social support, rites and ceremonies, and the rewards and incentives provided by the organization, most new employees are socialized into the culture and climate of their work group or they resign (Carroll & Harrison, 1998; Chatman, 1991; Hebden, 1986; Louis, 1990; Schneider, 1987; Sheridan, 1992; Trice & Beyer, 1984). The need to reduce uncertainty is a primary motivation in the socialization process (Falcione & Wilson, 1988; Lester, 1986). However, not all new employees experience the same pressure to adopt the shared norms, values, and perceptions of their coworkers. For some, social acceptance is less important than for others, and their feeling of certainty about their new jobs is more a function of their individual competence and experience.

Employee selection, therefore, becomes an important issue in maintaining existing cultures and climates as new employees are hired (Chatman, 1991; Hofstede et al., 1990). Although socialization plays an important role in that process, more experienced, competent, or confident new hires may import as many norms, values, and perceptions as they adopt. As Hofstede et al. (1990) point out, employees can also use prescribed practices without internalizing the values implied by the practices. Personal values can be more deeply held and carried from organization to organization. As was discussed earlier, there is a cross-situational consistency in the perceptions that employees have of their work environment that will be imported as well. Finally, the fit between the traits and abilities that new employees bring to the job and the expectations of the job can affect the employees' perceptions of their new work environment and their subsequent performance (Chatman, 1991; James et al., 1992; O'Reilly, Chatman, & Caldwell, 1991).

Climate and Culture Differences Between Types of Organizations

Very little comparative research on organizational culture and climate has been conducted, but there is evidence that different cultures and climates are found in different types of organizations (DiMaggio & Powell, 1983; Gordon, 1991; Lucas, 1987). Some of these differences are related to the factors discussed above, whereas others are independent of them. These differences are a function of the missions of the organizations, the way they are funded, and the external environments in which they must survive (Gordon, 1991; Pennings & Gresov, 1986). Therefore, three major dimensions can be used as the basis of categorizing organizations according to type. These are human service versus non-human service, profit versus nonprofit, and public versus private organizations.

Human service versus non-human service organizations. For a number of years, human service organizations have been recognized as having distinct qualities (Hasenfeld & English, 1974). These qualities are primarily related to the mission of improving the functioning or well-being of human beings, as opposed to manufacturing, selling, investing, or the many other things that organizations do. This is important because it emphasizes that the raw material that is the focus of the work of human service organizations is human. Therefore, it has a mind of its own, is highly complex, is relatively unpredictable, and is very difficult to mold, process, change, or enhance. This contributes to many of the qualities of the core technology that were discussed above. It also contributes to norms, values, and perceptions of workers in the organization that are interwoven with the welfare of human beings (Hasenfeld, 1992). This is the most important distinction between the cultures and climates of human service and non-human service organizations. The impact of workers' successes or failures, the frustrations generated by organizational barriers to success, and the motivation to do the core work of the organization are all linked to the workers' need to help other human beings. As a result, the norms and values that drive behavior in human service organizations evolve in part as a function of their impact on the welfare of the human beings that are served.

There has been very little empirical research that directly compares the cultures and climates of human service organizations to those of other types of organizations. In one of the more recent of those comparisons, Solomon (1986)

found that non-service or production organizations in Israel were much more likely to use performance-based reward systems than were service organizations, whether they were profit or nonprofit organizations. This difference is perhaps due in part to the fact that quantifying and assessing production performance is a more straightforwardly obvious endeavor than quantifying and assessing service performance. But that does not provide either a complete or satisfactory explanation of the difference between human service and non-service organizations. Service can be quantified, assessed, and used as the basis of employee rewards, as most large law offices demonstrate daily. Therefore, the finding that the use of such systems for performance-based rewards is less common in human service organizations than in other types of organizations is undoubtedly linked to norms that distinguish the cultures of human service organizations from other types of organizations.

Profit versus nonprofit organizations. The majority of social welfare organizations are nonprofit organizations. It is difficult to overestimate the impact that this has on an organization's culture and climate. When the bottom-line criterion of success is profit, the values and norms that drive behavior in the organization cannot deviate far from increasing earnings and decreasing costs. However, earnings and costs are also a concern for many nonprofit organizations as they struggle to survive in the face of policy changes that threaten their income.

But in nonprofit organizations as compared to profit organizations, monetary incentives cannot play the same role in providing rewards and incentives. As one person phrased it who worked for 1 year in a nonprofit organization after making a fortune in the business world, "It was interesting, but the stakes were so small!" Managers of profit organizations have the power to create behavioral norms and mold employee perceptions with monetary rewards and incentives far beyond the power of nonprofit managers. Nonprofit managers can hope to hire or promote people who have the desired norms, values, and traits they would like to see in their workers, and sometimes, they can fire or demote those who do not. But they have limited power to dramatically alter behavior or perceptions with large monetary bonuses, profit-sharing plans, or the significant increases in salary that can be provided in profit organizations.

On the other hand, nonprofit organizations are freed from the negative aspects of the pressure for profit. As the competition increases or the stakes get larger, the danger is that the motivation behind profit organizations becomes tied increasingly to the stakes rather than the quality and outcomes of the work. This affects the underlying norms and values of the organization as well as employee perceptions of the organization. Peters and Waterman (1982) provide descriptive examples of business and industrial organizations that suffer because of managers who focus more on the bottom line and lose touch with the meaning and quality of the work of their organizations.

Public versus private organizations. Public organizations provide classic examples of bureaucratic red tape, unresponsive bureaucrats, and large expenditures of taxpayers' money on ineffective services. The comparison of public and private service organizations projects images of inefficiency versus efficiency, incompetence versus competence, and unresponsiveness versus responsiveness (Vestal, Fralicx, & Spreier, 1997). But Osborne and Gaebler (1992) point out that these stereotypes have developed largely as the result of the constraints placed on public organizations by the public, not by the employees. They explain that the public has been so concerned about making sure that everyone is served in exactly the same way and that each employee follows precise procedures that all discretion and entrepreneurial qualities are drained from public work. This is echoed by Schorr (1997), who describes the nation's social service bureaucracies: "We are so eager, as a body politic, to eliminate the possibility that public servants will do anything wrong that we make it virtually impossible for them to do anything right" (p. 65).

There is also evidence that the quality of social welfare services provided by private agencies is no better than, and in some instances worse than, the quality provided by public agencies that serve the same population in the same geographical region (Petr & Johnson, 1999). The differences, then, in the cultures of public versus private organizations may be rooted less in whether employees are public employees than in the origin and focus of the control of public organizations. Or more precisely, they may be rooted in the fact that managers of public organizations are penalized by the public more for mistakes than they are rewarded by the public for successes. These types of differences between public and private sector organizations are represented in Solomon's (1986) findings that there is a greater emphasis on performance-based rewards and efficiency in the private sector than in the public sector. In addition, she found much higher job satisfaction in the private sector and concluded there is a need for restructuring the reward systems of public sector organizations to improve public sector job performance and job satisfaction. Nevertheless, many public service organizations, such as the social welfare systems described by Schorr (1997), have cultures that focus more on process than results, are rule-driven rather than mission-driven, and lose sight of the well-being of those they serve in their emphasis on bureaucratic procedures and red tape.

SUMMARY

Organizational climate and culture are important to social welfare administration because they provide the critical links between organizational characteristics and service outcomes. Their attractiveness as organizational constructs is tied to the way they explain how work environments determine the effectiveness of service providers. No other organizational constructs capture in such a successful way the importance of an organization as a psychosocial system that determines how its members approach and carry out their work.

The behavioral norms and values that make up culture and the subjective perceptions that make up climate explain the social and psychological impact of the structural and technological features of organizations. Since the turn of the century, it has been known that organizational design characteristics such as centralization, formalization, specialization, coordination, and routinization can affect an organization's productivity, measured in terms of units produced or number served. By the latter part of this century, however, it was clear that these characteristics were not as tightly coupled to the quality of the product or the effectiveness of the service produced by an organization. Climate and culture provide the direct link to product quality and service effectiveness that

broadens our understanding of how work environments affect worker performance.

Climate and culture are critical to service effectiveness because work in human services in general, and in social welfare in particular, can be stressful, complex, unpredictable, and indeterminate. So, to be effective, in addition to having the requisite skills and knowledge for the work, social workers and other human service providers must be tenacious, innovative, responsive, cooperative, flexible, committed, and supportive. These qualities are required when social workers face bureaucratic hurdles, difficult clients, conflicting job demands, frequent failures, a critical public, and other barriers to their work. Although individual workers differ in their potential to exhibit these qualities, ensuring that workers exhibit as much of these qualities as possible requires a work environment that promotes and sustains tenacity, innovativeness, responsiveness, cooperation, flexibility, commitment, and support among its workers. These are promoted and sustained by the social and psychological impact of the work environment's climate and culture.

Although the association between climate and culture on the one hand and organizational effectiveness on the other is intuitively and conceptually appealing, much more empirical work is needed to identify the specific linking mechanisms that join climate and culture to service outcomes in social welfare organizations. There is a need for research that contributes to defining and differentiating climate and culture as distinct constructs, to understanding the way each affects the behavior and attitudes that lead to successful service outcomes, and perhaps most important, to demonstrate how effective climates and cultures can be created in actual service systems.

Adequately addressing these knowledge gaps is difficult, time consuming, and costly. It requires that true experimental designs be used to manipulate climate and culture in actual service systems and that improvements in client well-being be linked to differences in organizational climate and culture. This type of elaborate research has yet to be completed, but one of our current projects (No. R01-MH56563), funded by the National Institute of Mental Health, is designed to address these knowledge gaps. This 5-year research project includes child welfare offices in 30 counties and is the first to use a true experimental design to examine the consequences of climate and culture, including service outcomes operationalized as improvements in child well-being. The offices assigned to the treatment group will receive an extensive, 1-year organizational intervention designed to create work environments that generate tenacity, innovativeness, responsiveness, cooperation, flexibility, commitment, and support. A key to the success of the project will be the extent to which improvements can be created in the climates and cultures of the child welfare offices assigned to the treatment group.

The excitement and interest generated by popular texts on organizational climate and culture continue to fuel efforts to create positive work environments. Many of these efforts have been doomed by misunderstandings of the constructs, poor interventions, and a lack of investment in the change effort. As explained in this chapter, individual dispositions and traits among workers, pressures from the organization's external environment, the need for certainty among members of a work environment, and existing informal and formal power structures all play roles in maintaining existing climates and cultures. Nevertheless, over time, we witness evolutions in the climates and cultures of organizations in various private and public service sectors. Unfortunately, most of these changes occur without empirical documentation, and we are left with the type of anecdotal evidence that is characteristic of many popular texts. The challenge now is to submit these ideas to rigorous empirical examination to more fully explicate the ways in which climate and culture affect the quality and outcomes of social welfare services.

REFERENCES

Argyris, C. (1958). Some problems in conceptualizing organizational climate: A case study of a bank. *Administrative Science Quarterly, 2,* 501-520.

Arvey, R. D., Bouchard, T. J., Segal, N. L., & Abraham, L. M. (1989). Job satisfaction: Environmental and genetic components. *Journal of Applied Psychology, 74*(2), 187-192.

Barker, R. A. (1994). Relative utility of culture and climate analysis to an organizational change agent: An analysis of General Dynamics, Electronics Division. *The International Journal of Organizational Analysis, 2*(1), 68-87.

Birleson, P. (1998). Learning organisations: A suitable model for improving mental health services? *Australian and New Zealand Journal of Psychiatry, 32,* 214-222.

Blau, P. M. (1960). Structural effects. *American Sociological Review, 25,* 178-193.

Brown, S. P., & Leigh, T. W. (1996). A new look at psychological climate and its relationship to job involvement, effort, and performance. *Journal of Applied Psychology, 81*(4), 358-368.

Bryman, A. (1996). Leadership in organizations. In S. R. Glegg, C. Hardy, & W. R. Nord (Eds.), *Handbook of organization studies* (pp. 276-292). Thousand Oaks, CA: Sage.

Carroll, G. R., & Harrison, J. R. (1998). Organizational demography and culture: Insights from a formal model and simulation. *Administrative Science Quarterly, 43,* 637-667.

Chatman, J. A. (1991). Matching people and organizations: Selection and socialization in public accounting firms. *Administrative Science Quarterly, 36,* 459-484.

Cooke, R. A., & Rousseau, D. M. (1988). Behavioral norms and expectations. *Group & Organizational Studies, 13*(3), 245-273.

Deal, T. E. (1986). Deeper culture: Mucking, muddling, and metaphors. *Training and Development Journal, 40*(1), 32.

Deal, T. E., & Kennedy, A. A. (1982). *Corporate cultures: The rites and rituals of corporate life.* Reading, MA: Addison-Wesley.

Denison, D. R. (1996). What is the difference between organizational culture and organizational climate? A native's point of view on a decade of paradigm wars. *Academy of Management Review, 21*(3), 619-654.

Denison, D. R., & Mishra, A. K. (1995). Toward a theory of organizational culture and effectiveness. *Organizational Science, 6*(2), 204-223.

DiMaggio, P. J., & Powell, W. W. (1983). The iron cage revisited: Institutional isomorphism and collective rationality in organizational fields. *American Sociological Review, 48,* 147-160.

Falcione, R. L., & Wilson, C. E. (1988). Socialization processes in organizations. In G. M. Goldhaber & G. A. Barnett (Eds.), *Handbook of organizational communication.* Norwood, NJ: Ablex.

Fleishman, E. A. (1953). Leadership climate, human relations training, and supervisory behavior. *Personnel Psychology, 6,* 205-222.

Frost, P. J., Moore, L. F., Louis, M. R., Lundberg, C. C., & Martin, J. E. (1985). *Organizational culture.* Beverly Hills, CA: Sage.

Glisson, C. A. (1978). Dependence of technological routinization on structural variables in human service organizations. *Administrative Science Quarterly, 23*(3), 383-395.

Glisson, C. (1992). Technology and structure in human service organizations. In Y. Hasenfeld (Ed.), *Human services as complex organizations* (pp. 184-202). Beverly Hills, CA: Sage.

Glisson, C. (1996). Judicial and service decisions for children entering state custody: The limited role of mental health. *Social Service Review, 70*(2), 257-281.

Glisson, C., & Durick, M. (1988). Predictors of job satisfaction and organizational commitment in human service organizations. *Administrative Science Quarterly, 33*(1), 61-81.

Glisson, C., & Hemmelgarn, A. (1998). The effects of organizational climate and interorganizational coordination on the quality and outcomes of children's service systems. *Child Abuse and Neglect, 22*(5), 401-421.

Glisson, C. A., & Martin, P. Y. (1980). Productivity and efficiency in human service organizations as related to

structure, size, and age. *Academy of Management Journal, 23*(1), 21-37.

Gordon, G. G. (1991). Industry determinants of organizational culture. *Academy of Management Review, 16*(2), 396-415.

Gordon, G., & DiTomaso, N. (1992). Predicting corporate performance from organizational culture. *Journal of Management Studies, 29*(6), 783-798.

Gouldner, A. (1954). *Patterns of industrial bureaucracy.* New York: Free Press.

Gundry, L. (1985). Computer technology and organizational culture. *Computers and the Social Sciences, 1,* 163-166.

Handy, C. B. (1976). *Understanding organizations.* New York: Penguin.

Hannan, M. T., & Freeman, J. H. (1977). The population ecology of organizations. *American Journal of Sociology, 32,* 929-964.

Hasenfeld, Y. (1992). *Human services as complex organizations.* Newbury Park, CA: Sage.

Hasenfeld, Y., & English, R. A. (1974). *Human service organizations.* Ann Arbor: University of Michigan Press.

Hebden, J. E. (1986). Adopting an organization's culture: The socialization of graduate trainees. *Organizational Dynamics, 15*(1), 54-72.

Hellriegel, D., & Slocum, J. W. (1974). Organizational climate: Measures, research, and contingencies. *Academy of Management Journal, 17*(2), 255-280.

Hemmelgarn, A. L., Glisson, C., & Dukes, D. (in press). Emergency room culture and the emotional support component of Family-Centered Care. *Children's Health Care.*

Hofstede, G. (1998). Attitudes, values, and organizational culture: Disentangling the concepts. *Organization Studies, 19*(3), 477-492.

Hofstede, G., Neuijen, B., Ohayv, D. D., & Sanders, G. (1990). Measuring organizational cultures: A qualitative and quantitative study across twenty states. *Administrative Science Quarterly, 35,* 286-316.

Hoy, W. K. (1990). Organizational climate and culture: A conceptual analysis of the school workplace. *Journal of Educational and Psychological Consultation, 1*(2), 149-168.

James, L. R., Demaree, R. G., Mulaik, S. A., & Ladd, R. T. (1992). Validity generalization in the context of situational models. *Journal of Applied Psychology, 77,* 1-44.

James, L. R., Hater, J. J., Gent, M. J., & Bruni, J. R. (1978). Psychological climate: Implications from cognitive social learning theory and interactional psychology. *Personnel Psychology, 31*(4), 783-813.

James, L. A., & James, L. R. (1989). Integrating work environment perceptions: Explorations into the measurement of meaning. *Journal of Applied Psychology, 74,* 739-751.

James, L. R., James, L. A., & Ashe, D. K. (1990). The meaning of organizations: The role of cognition and values. In B. Schneider (Ed.), *Organizational climate and culture* (pp. 40-84). San Francisco: Jossey-Bass.

James, L. R., & Jones, A. P. (1974). Organizational climate: A review of theory and research. *Psychological Bulletin, 18,* 1096-1112.

James, L. R., & McIntyre, M. D. (1996). Perceptions of organizational climate. In K. R. Murphy (Ed.) *Individual differences and behavior in organizations* (pp. 416-450). San Francisco: Jossey-Bass.

James, L. R., & Sells, S. B. (1981). Psychological climate. In D. Magnusson (Ed.), *The situation: An interactional perspective.* Hillsdale, NJ: Lawrence Erlbaum.

James, L. R., & Tetrick, L. E. (1986). Confirmatory analytic tests of three casual models relating job perceptions to job satisfaction. *Journal of Applied Psychology, 71*(1), 77-82.

Jelinek, M., Smircich, L., & Hirsch, P. (1983). Introduction: A code of many colors. *Administrative Science Quarterly, 28,* 331-338.

Johnson, J. J., & McIntyre, C. L. (1998). Organizational culture and climate correlates of job satisfaction. *Psychological Reports, 82,* 843-850.

Jones, A. P., & James, L. R. (1979). Psychological climate: Dimensions and relationships of individual and aggregated work environment perceptions. *Organizational Behavior and Human Performance, 23,* 201-250.

Jones, G. R. (1983). Transaction costs, property rights, and organizational culture: An exchange perspective. *Administrative Science Quarterly, 28,* 454-467.

Joyce, W. F., & Slocum, J. W. (1984). Collective climate: Agreement as a basis for defining aggregate climates in organizations. *Academy of Management Journal, 24*(4), 721-742.

Lester, R. E. (1986). Organizational culture, uncertainty reduction, and the socialization of new organizational members. In S. Thomas (Ed.), *Communication and information science: Vol. 3. Studies in communication.* Norwood, NJ: Ablex.

Litwin, G. H., & Stringer, R. A. (1968). *Motivation and organizational climate.* Cambridge, MA: Harvard Business School.

Louis, M. R. (1990). Acculturation in the workplace: Newcomers as lay ethnographers. In B. Schneider (Ed.), *Organizational climate and culture.* San Francisco: Jossey-Bass.

Lucas, R. (1987). Political-cultural analysis of organizations. *Academy of Management Review, 12*(1), 144-156.

Martin, L. M., Peters, C. L., & Glisson, C. (1998). Factors affecting case management recommendations for children entering state custody. *Social Service Review, 72,* 521-544.

Martin, P., & Glisson, C. (1989). Social welfare organizations in three locales: Societal culture and context as predictors of perceived structure. *Organization Studies, 10*(3), 353-380.

O'Reilly, C. A., & Chatman, J. A. (1996). Culture as social control: Corporations, cults, and commitment. *Research in Organizational Behavior, 18,* 157-200.

O'Reilly, C. A., Chatman, J., & Caldwell, D. (1991). People and organizational culture: A profile comparison approach to assessing person-organization fit. *Academy of Management Journal, 34*(3), 487-516.

Osborne, D., & Gaebler, T. A. (1992). *Reinventing government.* Reading, MA: Addison-Wesley.

Ott, J. S. (1989). *The organizational culture perspective.* Belmont, CA: Dorsey Press.

Ouchi, W. G. (1981). *Theory Z.* Reading, MA: Addison-Wesley.

Ouchi, W. G., & Wilkins, A. L. (1985). Organizational culture. *Annual Review of Sociology, 11,* 457-483.

Payne, R. L., & Mansfield, R. (1973). Relationship of perceptions of organizational climate to organizational structure, context, and hierarchical position. *Administrative Science Quarterly, 18,* 515-526.

Pennings, J. M. (1980). Environmental influences on the creation process. In J. M. Kimberly & R. H. Miles (Eds.), *The organizational life cycle.* San Francisco: Jossey-Bass.

Pennings, J. M., & Gresov, C. G. (1986). Technoeconomic and structural correlates of organizational culture: An integrative framework. *Organization Studies, 7*(4), 317-334.

Perkins, A. L., Shaw, R. B., & Sutton, R. I. (1990). Summary: Human service teams. In J. R. Hackman (Ed.), *Groups that work (and those that don't)* (pp. 349-357). San Francisco: Jossey-Bass.

Peters, T., & Waterman, R. (1982). *In search of excellence: Lessons from America's best run corporations.* New York: Warner.

Petr, C. G., & Johnson, I. C. (1999). Privatization of foster care in Kansas: A cautionary tale. *Social Work, 44*(3), 263-267.

Pettigrew, A. (1979). On studying organizational cultures. *Administrative Science Quarterly, 24,* 570-581.

Petty, M. M., Beadles, N. A., Lowery, C. M., Chapman, D. F., & Connell, D. W. (1995). Relationships between organizational culture and organizational performance. *Psychological Reports, 76,* 483-492.

Reichers, A. E., & Schneider, B. (1990). Climate and culture: An evolution of constructs. In B. Schneider (Ed.), *Organizational climate and culture* (pp. 5-39). San Francisco: Jossey-Bass.

Rentsch, J. R. (1990). Climate and culture: Interaction and qualitative differences in organizational meanings. *Journal of Applied Psychology, 75*(6), 661-668.

Rousseau, D. M. (1990). Assessing organizational culture: The case for multiple methods. In B. Schneider (Ed.), *Organizational climate and culture* (pp. 153-192). San Francisco: Jossey-Bass.

Salancik, G. R., & Pfeffer, J. (1978). A social information processing approach to job attitudes and task design. *Administrative Science Quarterly, 23,* 224-254.

Sathe, V. (1985). *Culture and related corporate realities.* Homewood, IL: Irwin.

Schein, E. H. (1986). What you need to know about organizational culture. *Training and Development Journal, 40,* 30-33.

Schein, E. H. (1992). *Organizational culture and leadership.* San Francisco: Jossey-Bass.

Schein, E. H. (1996). Culture: The missing concept in organization studies. *Administrative Science Quarterly, 41,* 229-240.

Schneider, B. (1972). Organization climate: Individual preferences and organizational realities. *Journal of Applied Psychology, 56,* 211-217.

Schneider, B. (1987). The people make the place. *Personnel Psychology, 40,* 437-453.

Schneider, B. (1990). *Organizational climate and culture.* San Francisco: Jossey-Bass.

Schneider, B., & Bartlett, J. (1970). Individual differences and organizational climate II: Measurement of organizational climate by the multitract-multirater matrix. *Personnel Psychology, 23,* 491-512.

Schneider, B., Gunnarson, S. K., & Niles-Jolly, K. (1994). Creating the climate and culture of success. *Organizational Dynamics, 23*(1), 17-29.

Schneider, B., White, S. S., & Paul, M. C. (1998). Linking service climate and customer perceptions of service quality: Test of a causal model. *Journal of Applied Psychology, 83*(2), 150-163.

Schorr, L. B. (1997). *Common purpose.* New York: Doubleday.

Selznick, P. (1949). *TVA and the grass roots.* Los Angeles: University of California Press.

Sheridan, J. E. (1992). Organizational culture and employee retention. *Academy of Management Journal, 35*(5), 1036-1056.

Sherwood, J. J. (1988). Creating work cultures with competitive advantage. *Organizational Dynamics, 16*(3), 5-27.

Simon, H. A. (1957). *Models of man, social and rational.* New York: John Wiley.

Smircich, L. (1983). Concepts of culture and organizational analysis. *Administrative Science Quarterly, 28,* 339-358.

Solomon, E. E. (1986). Private and public sector managers: An empirical investigation of job characteristics and organizational climate. *Journal of Applied Psychology, 71*(2), 247-259.

Staw, B. M., & Ross, J. (1985). Stability in the midst of change: A dispositional approach to job attitudes. *Journal of Applied Psychology, 70*(3), 469-480.

Swartz, M., & Jordan, D. (1980). *Culture: An anthropological perspective.* New York: John Wiley.

Tagiuri, R., & Litwin, G. H. (1968). *Organizational climate: Explanation of a concept.* Boston: Division of Research, Harvard Graduate School of Business.

Thompson, J. D. (1967). *Organizations in action.* New York: McGraw-Hill.

Trice, H. M., & Beyer, J. M. (1984). Studying organizational cultures through rites and ceremonials. *Academy of Management Review, 9*(4), 653-669.

Trice, H., & Beyer, J. (1993). *The cultures of work organizations.* Englewood Cliffs, NJ: Prentice Hall.

Van Maanen, J., & Schein, E. H. (1979). Toward a theory of organizational socialization. In B. M. Staw & L. L. Cummings (Eds.), *Research in organizational behavior* (Vol. 1). Greenwich, CT: JAI Press.

Verbeke, W., Volgering, M., & Hessels, M. (1998). Exploring the conceptual expansion within the field of organizational behaviour: Organizational climate and organizational culture. *Journal of Management Studies, 35*(3), 303-329.

Vestal, K. W., Fralicx, R. D., & Spreier, S. W. (1997). Organizational culture: The critical link between strategy and results. *Hospital and Health Services Administration, 42*(3), 339-365.

Weiss, J., & Delbecq, A. (1987). High-technology cultures and management. *Group and Organization Studies, 12*(1), 39-54.

Wiener, Y. (1988). Forms of value systems: A focus on organizational effectiveness and cultural change and maintenance. *Academy of Management Review, 13*(4), 534-545.

Wilkins, H. L., & Ouchi, W. G. (1983). Efficient cultures: Exploring the relationship between culture and organizational performance. *Administrative Science Quarterly, 28,* 468-481.

Zamanou, S., & Glaser, S. R. (1994). Moving toward participation and involvement: Managing and measuring organizational culture. *Group & Organization Management, 19*(4), 475-502.

CHAPTER ELEVEN

The Individual in the Organization: The Impact of Human Service Workers' Attributes on Job Response

GARY F. KOESKE

RANDI KOESKE

Human service workers, like other workers, are affected by numerous external influences as they carry out their work roles. These include structural aspects of the organization, physical characteristics of the workplace, the political and economic context in which the agency or practice operates, and the network of social relationships and roles that their work setting and professional identity provide. But workers also bring various personal attributes to the work environment in which they work, and these may be understood as resources that affect the performance of their jobs or pathways through which various environmental factors exert their impacts. The purpose of this chapter is to examine the role played by these worker characteristics on the strains and satisfactions of human service work, as described in the available empirical literature.

The present chapter will deal only with what is known about *human service* workers as a group, not with what is known about workers in general. It will examine how various attributes of these human service workers influence or explain important work impacts, notably the strains, satisfactions, and longevity of work roles. Worker attributes will thus be conceptualized as part of a time-ordered pathway that leads from actual work environment to worker outcome. Within this pathway, we will consider whether worker attributes tend to account for strains and outcomes (i.e., act as predictors, intervening variables, or mediators) or whether they tend to interact with or buffer other impacts (i.e., act as moderator variables).

Our primary objective is to focus attention on those general and work-specific attributes of workers that affect their job response, understanding this response within a framework of stresses, strains, and outcomes (SSO). We will, thus, say little about (a) the overall levels of stress, strain, and negative outcome found among social service workers and (b) the pattern of findings that has resulted in the SSO framework's emergence as an overarching conceptual scheme for the field.

The first of these issues is difficult to assess, in any case, because different conceptual and operational definitions have been used for stress and for various outcomes (e.g., job satisfaction and turnover intentions). In contrast, the emotional exhaustion subscale of the Maslach Burnout Inventory, or MBI (Maslach & Jackson, 1984, 1986), has become a near standard for assessing strain, but it has yielded burnout scores ranging from quite low to quite high in different human service samples. Job satisfaction, the most frequently assessed outcome of stress and strain, has usually—but not always (see Glisson & Durick, 1988)—shown moderate to high levels. Because almost all reported research has involved currently employed workers, however, we may presume that available studies underestimate burnout and dissatisfaction, because those who are most exhausted and unhappy probably leave for jobs inside or outside the human services field.

The second issue has already received ample documentation. A large work-relevant litera-ture demonstrates linkages between stress and strain, as well as between strain and various outcomes (see reviews by Burke & Richardsen, 1996; Cordes & Dougherty, 1993; Cox, Kuk, & Leiter, 1993; Jayaratne & Chess, 1983; Lee & Ashforth, 1996; Leiter, 1991a, 1991b; Schwab, Jackson, & Shuler, 1986; Um & Harrison, 1998; Wright & Cropanzano, 1998). In Koeske and Koeske (1993), we present our own SSO model test. Given that the empirical validity of the general SSO model is well-documented across a number of different measures of stress and outcome, it seems preferable here to attend to the less-studied role of how personal attributes may operate within the overall SSO framework.

Our review of worker attributes will focus on the key job-response variables of burnout (strain) and job satisfaction (outcome), which together reflect the largest research emphasis in the field. Because one or both of these variables is usually measured, focusing on their role will provide a window on other job responses.

Within the available literature, burnout has usually been understood as a job response reflecting strain, which may be operationalized by reports of job-related emotional exhaustion. Associated with it are self-perceptions of personal failure arising from personal work efforts and negative attitudes toward those served (depersonalization or derogation of clients). Job satisfaction, on the other hand, has usually been understood as an outcome reflecting worker responses to particular job characteristics, stresses, or strains. It has typically been operationalized as an attitude or evaluative reaction toward the job and its various facets. Although it is sometimes measured globally by a single-item rating, most studies of job satisfaction have relied on one of several established and standardized multiple-item scale measures.

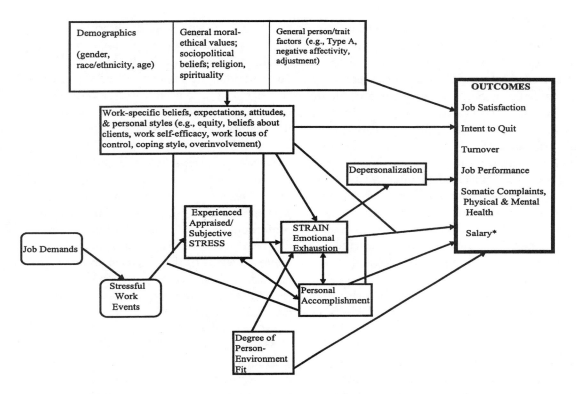

Figure 11.1. The Role of Personal Variables in the Stress-Strain-Outcome Process

*"Salary" used as dependent measure in some research. Moderated (buffering) effects shown with non-arrowed lines drawn to effect lines. Paths reflect presence of at least some empirical work or theory, not definitive, established relationships.

Figure 11.1 presents a heuristic model consistent with the Demands → Events → Stress → Strain → Outcomes path within which we believe burnout and job satisfaction may best be conceptualized. It is not intended as a comprehensive causal path model. No studies have simultaneously examined every one of the primary variables listed in Figure 11.1, of course, but the figure attempts to capture a common core of ideas around which many studies may be organized. In the figure, arrowed path lines indicate causal relationships and non-arrowed lines indicate the moderating or buffering of known causal relationships.

The model is heuristic—intended simply to clarify our review of variables and to reflect some of the ways in which worker attributes have been examined in recent theory and research. The model distinguishes between features of the concrete environment, characteristics of individuals, and clear-cut behavioral outcomes, and it further recognizes that individual characteristics may themselves be broken down into sets of experiences and attributes, some of which are more antecedent or more consequent than others. A variety of job responses are also listed in the figure and will be taken up at various points in the chapter review.

Organizing our review of research in the field around this heuristic model offers a useful way of proceeding and also helps clarify where additional work is needed. It lets us pinpoint where measurement or methodological issues currently complicate data interpretation. We must emphasize, however, that the focus of the heuristic model presented in Figure 11.1 is worker attributes, which form the particular concern of this chapter. Not every variable with demonstrable relevance to burnout and job satisfaction, or every distinction necessary to a full understanding of worker experiences, has been included in the model. Some key variables, such as social support (i.e., the use of external resources) have not been included explicitly in the model. Others, notably job demands and stressful work events, have been simplified into a single variable to permit elaboration of the many categories of worker attributes. This simplification is reflected in the figure by enclosing such environmental variables in boxes with rounded instead of square corners. Readers are referred to chapters elsewhere in this volume, which focus on these additional variables in some detail.

DEMOGRAPHIC VARIABLES AND JOB RESPONSE

We begin by summarizing the most frequently studied demographic influences on job response—namely, gender, race/ethnicity, and age. In this area, salary has often been treated as an outcome variable, because there has been much concern with possible discrimination in material rewards. We then examine how demographic variables relate to job satisfaction, burnout, and other job responses, considering available tests of a general causal model linking environmental and outcome variables through the intervening mechanisms of stress and strain.

Gender and race/ethnicity differences in salary. For decades, roughly three fourths of direct service providers in social work have been women. As is true in the related human service professions of nursing and education, a minority of management positions have been filled by women. Details of this situation and its sociopolitical implications are documented in Dressel (1992). Differences in work roles seem to produce and sustain a power and salary differential based on gender.

Marini and Fan (1997) showed that, at career entry, women earned 84 cents for every dollar earned by a man; Fortune and Hanks (1988) found that salary differentials (of nearly $1,000) emerged over time rather than at entry. Some, but not all, of this difference was attributable to men moving into (or staying in) administrative positions, although men tended to receive higher salaries, even when role and other relevant factors were controlled. Yamatani (1982) found that men achieve more substantial salary increases by changing jobs or being awarded promotions with greater salary improvement.

Larger-scale studies report similar results. Brownstein and Hardcastle's (1984) study of over 700 NASW members in administrative positions found significantly higher salaries paid to men than to women, even after controlling for years of experience. McNeely's (1992) study of over 2,000 human services employees in six county welfare departments replicated these salary differences: Euro-American males earned higher salaries than other gender-by-race subgroups, even after correcting for education, length of employment, and occupational rank. McNeely (1989a, 1989b, 1989c) also used his rich database to contrast salaries of Caucasian, Hispanic, and African American workers. Based on data obtained in the mid-1980s, Caucasian workers ($M = \$20,699$) earned significantly more than African American ($M = \$16,049$) or Hispanic ($M = \$17,249$) workers, even when tenure, education, and job rank were controlled.

We know of no comparable but more current data documenting gender and race differences in salaries among human service workers. Continued retrenchment in social services, licensing issues, managed care policies, and other human service and general societal changes may have acted in unknown ways to modify the past inequities reported.

Gender and job satisfaction. Despite the apparent salary differences between male and female workers, there is little evidence of a gender difference in general, extrinsic, or intrinsic job satisfaction (Glisson & Durick, 1988; Jayaratne & Chess, 1983; McNeely, 1992; Mottaz, 1987). Even satisfaction with salary did not differ between the sexes.

In a 1989 survey of nearly 900 NASW members, Vinokur-Kaplan, Jayaratne, and Chess (1994) reported a modest but significant correlation of gender and job satisfaction, with female workers indicating more satisfaction. McNeely (1984) also reported significantly higher intrinsic job satisfaction among female workers in one of six counties studied, although the gender difference disappeared when data were aggregated across all counties.

Many researchers of job satisfaction do not report tests for gender differences, and we might conclude from this that no significant or substantial differences have been found. This would lead to the tentative conclusion that if gender differences in job satisfaction exist at all, they are small and insubstantial. The absence of differences, or the possibility of slightly higher satisfaction among females, is surprising given the data suggesting promotion and salary discrimination against women. Research might be directed toward achieving a better understanding of this anomaly.

Although there is little evidence for a direct gender effect on job satisfaction, McNeely (1992) reports two aspects of the job that were significantly stronger predictors of job dissatisfaction for women: (a) a sense of not having sufficient opportunity to use one's abilities and (b) the perception of excessive pressure and performance expectations. The second difference was also reported by Jayaratne and Chess (1983). McNeely also found that, among young female workers, concerns about income and benefits eroded satisfaction. Explaining less of the satisfaction variance among women employees were factors such as having decisional authority, exercising judgment, and having entree to promotions.

The moderating influence of gender on the link between job characteristics and satisfaction is hard to explain. The lower importance to women of achieving decisional authority and promotion may be a motivational factor contributing to women's underrepresentation in managerial positions. Or, it may reflect resignation arising from a rational assessment that a "glass ceiling" impedes women's advancement.

Although resigned to such a reality, dissatisfied women might rightly feel that their abilities are being underused.

It does not seem that women seek less demanding or challenging jobs. For men and women alike, a challenging job, as opposed to a dull or monotonous one, was consistently the biggest predictor of job satisfaction (Jayaratne & Chess, 1983; McNeely, 1992). A highly speculative and tentative synthesis of these gender effects is that women are motivated by challenging job roles that use their abilities but are resigned to a current reality that limits their potential for advancement.

Race/ethnicity and job satisfaction. McNeely's (1992) comprehensive, multicounty study and review provide us most of what is known about the relevance of race/ethnicity to job satisfaction among human service employees. His results were complex. He found that apparent higher satisfaction among minority respondents dissolved when analyses controlled for the county in which the worker was employed, because counties often differed in racial composition and degree of service or budget retrenchment. African Americans were dissatisfied in work sites in which they felt racial discrimination in cutbacks and in settings that left them feeling disaffiliated from the organization or their informal work group.

More recently, Gant and colleagues (1993) found that "undermining" of African American workers by supervisors or coworkers resulted in substantial increases in their irritability, depression, anxiety, and depersonalization. Whereas African American workers did not differ from Caucasian workers in overall or intrinsic job satisfaction, when they *did* feel dissatisfied, it was usually due to perceived discrimination.

Although other racial/ethnic groups have been little studied, McNeely's (1992) research permits the following additional generalizations. Asian Americans experience racial discrimination due to not feeling they are equitably rewarded for their educational attainment or years of work service, yet they do not differ in job satisfaction from majority workers. And Hispanic workers are more generally and intrinsically satisfied than non-Hispanics, despite the tendency for newly employed Hispanic professionals to receive lower salaries.

Age and job satisfaction. Worker's age has been given modest attention as a predictor of job satisfaction. McNeely's (1988) multisite data compared three age groups of human service workers—those under 30, those 30 to 54, and those over 55—and found greater satisfaction among older workers. Because age is normally confounded with tenure in a job or profession, this difference may simply reflect greater attrition in the oldest group.

The linear effect of age ($r = .18$) was small in this study, and its effect apparently occurred through differences in perceived job dullness and use of abilities. Dullness was a particularly important predictor of job dissatisfaction for the oldest worker group, whereas use of abilities was a comparatively unimportant predictor. One of a number of explanations for the study's results is that the oldest workers' seniority enabled them to choose work tasks that were interesting and challenging, an interpretation favored by McNeely himself.

Vinokur-Kaplan et al. (1994) tested age effects in their NASW sample of nearly 900 workers. In a multiple regression analysis in which age was entered with both demographic variables and workplace conditions (e.g., pay, security, physical environment, job challenge, and promotional opportunities), age was significantly related to global job satisfaction (beta = .14, $p < .01$, simple $r = .16$), but only for those in nonprofit agencies. Job tenure was not significantly related to job satisfaction for any practice context.

In three other studies (Glisson & Durick, 1988; Jayaratne & Chess, 1984; Mottaz, 1987), no significant or substantial relationship between age and job satisfaction was found, except for a subgroup of child welfare workers in the 1984 study. For these workers, age was related to higher satisfaction (beta = .36) when it was entered into a regression analysis with nine other predictors. Only promotion opportunities proved substantially more predictive than age.

Several of the studies on age used linear statistical tests, which are not sensitive to the presence of a possible quadratic trend in satisfaction for the oldest workers (those in their last decade before retirement). Overall, little evidence has been found that age contributes meaningfully to job satisfaction. The weak relationship often found between age and job satisfaction indicates that older workers may be slightly more satisfied than younger ones.

Burnout and worker demographics. Although the burnout literature is vast, there has been little interest in relating burnout to demographic characteristics. Instead, burnout has typically been studied as an emotional strain on workers produced by job demands or situational stressors, or it has been examined as a variable that mediates between stress and job dissatisfaction, turnover, or other negative outcomes (cf. Figure 11.1). Gender, race, and age have usually not been conceptualized as predis-

posing stress factors, even in the earliest literature (Freudenberger, 1980; Paine, 1982; Pines & Aronson, with Kafry, 1981), nor have they been viewed as potent moderators of Stress → Strain → Outcomes relationships.

As mentioned above, overall levels of burnout are easier to compare than overall levels of job satisfaction, because burnout is more often assessed using a single standard measure (the MBI). The nearly exclusive tendency for studies of burnout and job satisfaction to sample only workers who are currently employed, however, may introduce a possible bias into efforts to link these two variables, because the most burned-out or dissatisfied workers may have already escaped to a more comfortable work environment. If job satisfaction is a longer-term outcome than burnout and depends on other conditions as well, then failure to ask people about their previous jobs or to track people through job changes over longer periods may obscure important interrelationships between burnout and job satisfaction.

Gender, age, and race/ethnicity have sometimes been found to relate differently to particular dimensions of burnout. Cordes and Dougherty's (1993) review of gender and emotional exhaustion burnout, for example, noted no consistent pattern, although in the largest study of human service professionals available (Maslach & Jackson, 1984), females reported significantly higher exhaustion. For the related dimension of depersonalization, males were consistently higher. Mor and Laliberte's (1984) study of hospice staff found significantly higher exhaustion burnout in females, but no gender differences for the other burnout dimensions. Two studies (Beck, 1987; Streepy, 1981) reported somewhat higher burnout scores for men but used overall scores that did not separate depersonalization from exhaustion. A consistent finding across these various sources and settings is that younger workers report higher emotional exhaustion and, often, higher depersonalization.

There is no comparative data on race and ethnicity, nor sufficient data on how these three demographic characteristics might moderate the relationship between burnout and its antecedents or consequences.

Demographics in relation to other job responses. Little is known about how demographic attributes relate to other job responses. As might be expected, higher turnover intentions have been reported for younger workers (Blankertz & Robinson, 1997; Ross, 1984), who also show higher burnout and less job satisfaction. Glisson and Durick (1988) also reported that younger workers have lower job commitment, regardless of their job experience.

There is no evidence that race or gender relates to turnover or job commitment. Nor is there sufficient data to suggest relationships between age, gender, or race/ethnicity and other job responses, such as job performance or physical and mental health. Even when significant relationships have been found for demographic variables, they are usually of small magnitude and account for considerably less than 10% of the total job response variance.

WORKER ATTRIBUTES AND THEIR RELATIONSHIP TO JOB RESPONSES

By far the most studied worker variables in the literature on human service workers have been burnout and attitude toward the job (i.e., job satisfaction). Much of the research on other variables has involved exploring their relationship to burnout or job satisfaction. Such variables have been conceptualized as aspects of burnout, as moderators of particular burnout or job satisfaction relationships, or as outcomes in their own right. In our heuristic model (Figure 11.1), such variables appear as either general or work-specific traits or as elements with close links to emotional exhaustion (strain). Because a number of such attributes have been studied empirically they are discussed below under various categories and subcategories.

Worker Beliefs, Expectations, and Attitudes

This section will consider beliefs, expectations, and attitudes with direct relevance to burnout, job satisfaction, or other job responses. It will not address larger religious, ethical, and sociopolitical beliefs, in part because there is little empirical research on their influence.

Burnout and equity belief. Adams's (1965) social exchange theory hypothesizes that personal investments that do not match received rewards cause distress because they are felt to be inequitable, tending to motivate changes in behavior or perception that restore equity. In a work context, inequity may occur when either the client or the organization is perceived as unresponsive or unappreciative. Perceptions of inequity may thus result in burnout and low morale or motivate equity-restoring responses such as depersonalization, turnover intention, or lowered organizational or professional identification.

Support for the effect of inequity beliefs on emotional exhaustion was found by van Dierendonck, Schaufeli, and Buunk (1996) in two Dutch samples of therapists working with forensic psychiatric patients and a mentally handicapped sample. Those perceiving greater inequity in relations with clients or the organization showed higher exhaustion scores. The research team found further support for the inequity → burnout prediction in a sample of student nurses. Both organization-relevant and patient-relevant inequity were related to burnout, but organizational commitment was impaired only by a lack of reciprocity at the patient/ interpersonal level (Schaufeli, van Dierendonck, & van Gorp, 1996). Finally, an experimental intervention designed to increase equity perceptions resulted in a significant reduction of emotional exhaustion and improved duration of absence from work (van Dierendonck, Schaufeli, & Buunk, 1998).

Attitudes toward and beliefs about clients. Negative beliefs about clients, usually measured with Maslach's depersonalization scale, have been reliably linked to emotional exhaustion (Leiter, 1991b; Leiter & Maslach, 1988), but not to a lower sense of success in working with clients (Cox et al., 1993). Depersonalization seems to follow from exhaustion, but it is unclear if it should be regarded as another outcome of exhaustion, like job dissatisfaction and turnover intention, or as an antecedent of these outcomes. In one model (Cordes & Dougherty, 1993), depersonalization was conceptualized as an outcome arising from, besides exhaustion, dehumanizing and nonsupportive work environments, and it was expected to result in similar negative outcomes.

Direct correlations of personal accomplishment with work stress and negative outcomes have generally been smaller and less reliable than those for client derogation (Burke &

Richardsen, 1996; Cox et al., 1993). One explanation for this is that accomplishment beliefs play a buffering role in the burnout process. Koeske and Koeske (1989), for example, found crisis intervention work was related to higher burnout only for counselors who were low in personal accomplishment. Cox et al. (1993), however, did not find accomplishment playing a buffering role.

Success/failure perceptions have also been difficult to locate within the temporal flow of the burnout experience. A sense of failure might precede and contribute to emotional exhaustion, or exhausted workers, as a result of becoming depleted, might achieve less success or interpret their efforts as less beneficial. Workers who are less satisfied with their jobs might invest themselves less and receive feedback that their clients were less benefitted. Although accomplishment beliefs would seem to play an important part in the helping process, their specific role is not yet understood and needs additional research attention.

Expectations of effectiveness. Favorable expectations at the inception of a new intensive case management role have been shown to be related to a later sense of personal accomplishment, as well as to a number of other positive work outcomes (Kirk & Koeske, 1995). This finding was neither trivial nor expected because some of the earliest research and theorizing on burnout regarded hopeful expectations about effectiveness with clients as probable risk factors for burnout (Cherniss, 1980; Edelwich & Brodsky, 1980; Maslach & Jackson, 1984). High expectations were regarded as unrealistic and naive in these early conceptualizations, that is, as examples of achievement expectations that would be unmet by an unresponsive reality, resulting in burnout and all of its deleterious consequences.

Available data have not generally supported these early theory-derived expectations. Jackson, Schwab, and Schuler (1986), for example, hypothesized that unmet expectations would have negative consequences but failed to find empirical support for their hypothesis. Kirk and Koeske (1995) were unable to find negative outcomes at even the highest measured levels of optimistic expectation. Instead, the positive relationship of initial hopefulness and favorable worker outcomes was essentially linear.

The notion that holding unrealistic expectations for clients might place helping professionals at risk remains appealing, despite the lack of empirical support. Understood in inequity terms, such reality-insensitive workers would feel unreciprocated for their efforts and experience burnout. Perhaps, highly optimistic workers actually are more effective with clients or tend to perceive themselves as more effective than less optimistic workers, however. If so, they would experience equity between investments and rewards and not feel burned out.

Self-efficacy, self-esteem, and perceptions of the workplace. Another way of understanding the effect of efficacy expectations among workers is to view them as part of a work-specific or general disposition reflecting self-efficacy or "learned optimism." It has been suggested (Seligman, 1990) that the latter may be an attribute capable of enhancing or protecting self-image, even when some accuracy of perception is sacrificed.

Understanding a work-specific or general disposition of self-efficacy or optimism as a protective factor in the burnout process might ex-plain available results. In a recent large-sample study of physicians, college graduates, and Israeli students (Judge, Locke, Durham, & Kluger, 1998), for example, a measure of generalized self-efficacy was found to relate consistently to job satisfaction, and this effect was observed, irrespective of actual job characteristics. Judge et al. concluded that self-perception variables, such as self-esteem and self-efficacy, might well act to influence workers' very interpretations of their work environment.

If this is so, the substantial body of research on work and organizational climate may require reinterpretation, because qualities like ambiguity, conflict, and autonomy of the workplace environment are typically self-rated and may thus reflect the rater's general disposition, not environmental "fact." Perhaps, workers with high self-efficacy perceive workplaces as more controllable, unambiguous, and encouraging of worker autonomy than do those with low self-efficacy.

Research linking self-esteem to job outcomes may be seen as offering further support for Judge et al.'s (1998) conclusions. Poulin (1995), for example, found that supervisors and administrators with high self-esteem had significantly higher job satisfaction, even after organizational, job task, and personal factors were controlled. But if positive self-evaluation "acts through" (i.e., influences) such variables as support, job autonomy, and stress/pressure, its impact could be much greater than the Poulin regression analysis suggests. In fact, support for this interpretation was obtained in a study by Guterman and Jayaratne (1994), who found that perceived autonomy was significantly related to lower reported role ambiguity ($r = -.48$, $p < .0001$), even after controlling for sociodemographic influences. Finally, Rabin and Zeller (1992) reported that measures of assertiveness in daily life and in the job setting were related to role clarity and job satisfaction in a sample of mental health workers. In all of these studies, a personality style linked to self-efficacy and control orientation seems to have affected how the work environment was interpreted and appreciated.

Workers who are high in optimism and self-efficacy can be expected to see themselves as more "in control" of client and personal outcomes. In fact, Bandura (1977) conceptualizes self-efficacy as the personal belief that one can exercise control in one's life. The relevance of self-efficacy and control has often been noted in research on burnout as well, with studies frequently showing benefits for workers' sense of internal or personal control. Cherniss (1993), for example, one of the most enduring and significant contributors to burnout theory and research, has conceptualized the origins and amelioration of burnout using the concept of professional self-efficacy, emphasizing the concept's centrality. He reviewed the importance of self-efficacy in the organizational, task, and interpersonal domains, and noted that beliefs about one's inefficacy in influencing the social and political forces affecting social agencies were "particularly pernicious," because organizational demands and constraints represent well-documented sources of job stress and worker burnout (p. 142).

Leiter (1991b) has also placed burnout within a self-efficacy framework, concluding,

> Work experience that undermines a sense of competence also undermines self-esteem. Burn-out can be seen, then, as an indication of the extent to which working in an organizational context has weakened an individual's sense of self-efficacy as defined by Bandura. (p. 549)

Leiter offers an elaboration of his process model of burnout in which competence in "skill building and effective coping" reduces emotional exhaustion and increases personal accomplishment. He also suggests that "autonomy and participative decision making" tend to foster accomplishment (p. 551). In Leiter's approach, burnout arises largely from organizational problems that leave workers "feeling harrassed, powerless, and frustrated" (p. 554). He encourages the use of interventions that develop worker autonomy and believes that organizations supporting such autonomy will generally provide better services.

Leiter's conclusions are echoed by recent findings of Wall, Jackson, Mullarkey, and Parker (1996) on the importance of perceived control and autonomy in the work environment. Their study found that high work demand resulted in increased depression and diminished job satisfaction *only* among workers who were low or very low in perceived control. Workers who felt that their jobs provided them at least moderate control were not significantly impaired by high work demands.

Research has failed, however, to find a buffering effect of worker control on the perceived work stress → perceived effectiveness relationship (Guterman & Jayaratne, 1994). In a study of the direct effect of perceived autonomy among social workers, Arches (1991) found that autonomy was the only variable among 27 predictors in a multiple regression analysis that could significantly predict both (lower) burnout and (higher) job satisfaction. Seventeen of

Arches's variables measured aspects of the organization and of the supports within it. No buffering effect of autonomy was found.

Internal locus of control. The concept of self-efficacy is reminiscent of internal (versus external) locus of control (Phares, 1973; Rotter, 1966), another psychological construct with a long track record. And both constructs are similar to the concepts of self-mastery, "origin-pawn," and effectance (cf. deCharms, 1968).

Of these, locus of control has the most extensive research tradition, in part because it spawned the much-used Internality-Externality (I-E) scale (Rotter, 1966). Although Rotter did not intend for his measure of "generalized expectancies toward internality and externality" to be cast as a personality or trait measure, it has nonetheless been adapted to this purpose. People scoring high in internality show a general tendency to assign responsibility to themselves for their successes or failures, rather than locating the causes of such outcomes in the social or physical environment or attributing them to chance. People holding beliefs in personal responsibility or internal control could also be characterized as possessing high self-efficacy and self-mastery.

Because Rotter's scale is general and trans-situational, it often has not yielded substantial validity coefficients when used to assess locus of control in specific situations, particularly in work-related research (Spector, 1988). Consequently, Koeske (Koeske & Kirk, 1995a) developed an internality-externality measure that could be used specifically with direct providers of counseling services. Internality on this Counselor Locus of Control (CLOC) scale results from endorsing statements such as, "When my clients show improvement I get satisfaction from knowing I had a lot to do with it" or "Failures and setbacks among clients can largely be prevented by effective therapeutic intervention," as well as from rejecting statements like, "Chance has more to do with a client's progress than anything the case manager does." Some of the CLOC items refer to success situations, and others to failure outcomes, so that a worker scoring high in internality both takes credit for successes and accepts blame for failures. The CLOC, therefore, is not simply another measure of perceived effectiveness or accomplishment.

Koeske and Kirk (1995a) found that internal beliefs on the CLOC scale were significantly related to personal accomplishment, intrinsic and organizational job satisfaction, psychological well-being, and perceived favorable outcomes for clients. In addition, these counselor control beliefs significantly moderated several relationships between measures of stress/strain and outcome. For example, increasing exhaustion/burnout resulted in diminished life satisfaction and increased intention to quit the job for external workers, but it did not have these deleterious consequences for internal workers. There was, thus, evidence that perceived control played a buffering role in the link between stress/strain and outcome, a result later echoed by Wall et al. (1996), who used different measures of the key constructs. Spector and O'Connell (1994) also found internal workers to be more satisfied with their jobs and to report less work anxiety, conflict, and role ambiguity, using their own measure of Work Locus of Control. The factor most strongly related to internality in their study was the perception that the work environment provided autonomy.

In fact, the evidence for the benefits of worker control beliefs, however measured, is quite consistent and impressive. Such benefits have been demonstrated in direct relationships with theoretically and practically relevant outcomes, even after a number of other predictors have been controlled. At least as impressive is evidence for the buffering role of control beliefs, because theoretically meaningful and expected moderator effects are often difficult to demonstrate in correlational research because statistical detection power may be quite low (cf. Aguinis & Stone-Romero, 1997; Koeske & Koeske, 1991).

Many important questions remain unanswered, however, and both conceptual clarity and measurement clarity are needed. How are the concepts of perceived effectiveness and perceived control to be differentiated? How are they related to each other and to other relevant concepts? What role do control beliefs, personal accomplishment, and unmet expectations play in a Demands → Stress → Strain → Outcome model?

Glass and McKnight (1996) suggest that perceptions of lack of control in one's job trigger burnout and depression, but only when career expectations are unmet. This model proposes a buffering role for personal accomplishment/failure and casts lack of control as a stressor. Many of these same variables have been studied by different researchers over the years, but there is no single guiding model that integrates the variables in a uniform manner. Our heuristic model (Figure 11.1) is an attempt to organize the variables reviewed in this chapter, but, as stated earlier, it is not presented as an all-encompassing causal path model intended for empirical evaluation. Research and theory in this area continue to suffer from the same pre-paradigmatic status found in behavioral research generally, a point we hope this chapter will clarify.

Common to research in the area is the frequent confounding of *worker* attributes with *workplace* characteristics. This confound arises whenever both variables are measured using self-reports. Self-reports not only share method variance but make it difficult to determine whether measures of the environment reflect job demands, stressful work events, subjective stress, or some type of general or work-specific trait within the worker. These various possibilities have been conceptually distinguished in our heuristic model (Figure 11.1).

Personal Styles and Strategies: Coping and Workplace Strain

Job stress and strain, like other life challenges, should motivate the worker to activate plans and strategies for coping (cf. Lazarus & Folkman, 1984; Lazarus & Launier, 1978; Leiter, 1991a). Because people differ in the ways they cope, coping style offers another type of personal attribute with potential relevance to work outcomes. Of greatest concern is the ability of particular coping strategies to effectively alleviate or control work-related stress, strain, and negative outcomes.

Early research attempted to describe and classify alternative coping strategies. Shinn and her associates (Shinn & Morch, 1983; Shinn, Rosario, Morch, & Chestnut, 1984), for example, recommended a taxonomy in which individual coping was differentiated from group/coworker and agency coping strategies. These latter strategies largely involve seeking and giving social support, or in our terms, using external resources, a variable that lies outside the heuristic model presented in Figure 11.1, which is focused on person variables.

Shinn's agency-based strategies for coping may overlap with Cherniss's (1993) recent concern about exercising personal efficacy at the organzational level, however. Shinn labels agency strategies as "higher-level" approaches. Her data suggest that these highly proactive or activist strategies may be effective, particularly in reducing alienation and job satisfaction. Neither somatic nor psychological symptoms were affected by their use, however.

Some research has focused on individual coping strategies, which have sometimes been classified as problem-focused or emotion-focused (Folkman, Schaefer, & Lazarus, 1979; Pearlin & Schooler, 1978). Other taxonomies and measures have separated out control-based coping, avoidant/denial/escapist coping, or other styles (e.g., Cohen & Williamson, 1991; Holahan & Moos, 1987). Although there is imperfect consistency and clarity in the use of these style labels, coping behaviors classified as problem-focused usually involve behavior directed toward the source of the environmental stress or strain. Such coping may thus involve exercising or attempting to exercise control over the environment. Emotion-focused strategies, on the other hand, usually involve attempts to modulate the internal environment of negative personal feelings.

Shinn and her collaborators interpreted their results on coping style as supportive of earlier research (Pearlin & Schooler, 1978; Pines & Aronson, with Kafry, 1981), which had found that individual coping strategies were ineffective. They did report small but significant improvements in job satisfaction, alienation, and psychological symptoms associated with the use of problem-focused coping. Additional support for the effectiveness of control-oriented coping is found in the work of Leiter (1991a), who re-

ported that the inclusion of coping measures in a LISREL model clearly improved the explanation of emotional exhaustion and personal accomplishment. Escape/avoidant coping was neutral with respect to exhaustion in his study but actually tended to slightly worsen accomplishment.

Koeske, Kirk, and Koeske (1993) were able to examine four-wave data on intensive case managers, permitting an evaluation of the effects of coping strategies measured at Wave 1 on subsequent worker outcomes (exhaustion, depersonalization, accomplishment, and job satisfaction). Most previous research on coping has been cross-sectional rather than longitudinal. Their results clearly demonstrated the utility of control coping as a buffer of job stress and strain: The more workers used control coping strategies, the less the stress and strain they experienced produced negative outcomes. Avoidant strategies did not prove to be effective buffers if they operated exclusive of control strategies, but they did prove helpful when used in conjunction with control-oriented strategies.

Coping strategies in the Koeske et al. study were measured using a 33-item scale developed by Moos, Cronkite, Billings, and Finney (1987), which was factor analyzed. Thirteen of the scale items loaded on a subscale they labeled Control Coping. Sample items include "Tried to find out more about the situation," "Made a plan of action and followed it," and "Considered several alternatives for handling the problem." Some of the scale items were emotion-relevant, but all involved trying to exercise some form of control over oneself or the situation.

Taken together, the research on coping meshes nicely with that on the important role played by control beliefs and self-efficacy, reviewed above.

Overinvolvement. A worker characteristic that may be focal to the helping transaction, but that has received remarkably little attention, is the tendency for helpers to become overinvolved with clients who require intensive services. In their review of the burnout literature, Burke and Richardsen (1996) noted that the earliest analysts and researchers in the area had reported burned-out workers to be "empathic, sensitive, dedicated, idealistic, and people-oriented, but also anxious, obsessional, over-enthusiastic, and susceptible to overidentification with others" (p. 105). This description reminds us that a worker's investment of time, energy, and self in the helping process may operate in either a positive or negative way.

Research in nursing and medicine that antedates the burnout construct used the notion of "detached concern" to describe an attribute held up as a professional ideal for competent medical personnel (e.g., Lief & Fox, 1963). Social workers and other helping professionals who fail to develop detached concern may be described as overinvolved with their clients. This is a quite different phenomenon from work overload, excessive job demands, or too-heavy caseloads, because overinvolvement is considered to be a risk factor for burnout, even among those with moderate caseloads and modest job demands. It arises only in the context of intensive relationships with clients, however.

There is no research describing the general personality attributes that might predispose workers to become overinvolved or over-identified with their clients. Koeske and Kelly (1995) assessed degree of overinvolvement with an eight-item scale that included such statements as "My clients have a great influence on my moods," "I feel I don't do enough to help my clients," and "I worry about my clients." In a sample of NASW members, overinvolvement was unrelated to workload, social support, job experience, gender, age, or salary. But it was significantly related to burnout ($r = .48$), global job satisfaction ($r = -.28$), and self-esteem ($r = .26$).

Consistent with the process model that Koeske and Kelly (1995) tested on two separate samples, burnout mediated the impact of overinvolvement on job satisfaction. Overinvolvement predicted higher burnout, resulting in less job satisfaction. When burnout was controlled, however, overinvolvement had no direct effect on job satisfaction, suggesting that overinvolved workers came to dislike their jobs *because* they were burned out.

Although the Koeske and Kelly (1995) study used a cross-sectional design, the temporal ordering of variables they tested is consistent with theory and with common sense. Their results also confirm Williams's (1989) study showing that nurses who were higher in empathy were also higher in emotional exhaustion. If constraints placed on the length of therapeutic transactions by managed care also reduce their intensity, overinvolvement may be less likely in the future than it was in the past. The same system factors that limit client contact, however, might well reduce a counselor's sense of control and perceived efficacy, resulting in a continued risk of burnout despite the alteration in the system factors.

General Person Variables

Workers' mental health and adjustment. In terms of the heuristic model proposed above (Figure 11.1), actual turnover, poor work performance, poor personal adjustment (general well-being, mental health, psychological and somatic symptoms), and poor physical health represent possible outcomes of environmental demands and the stress and strain that result from them (cf. Burke & Richardsen, 1996; Cordes & Dougherty, 1993). Of these outcomes, actual turnover and poor job performance have been infrequently studied, however, so that little is known about them. We also could not locate any study of physical health problems arising from burnout, job stress, or job dissatisfaction for an exclusively human service worker sample. Evidence that job stress, pressure, or strain exert health consequences has been found in studies using general and non-human service samples, however (Taylor, 1999).

Whereas some studies have addressed the mental health consequences of burnout, there is also reason to believe that poor pre-existing personal adjustment among newly hired workers may affect their risk of developing negative work outcomes over time. Using their four-wave panel study of newly hired intensive case managers, Koeske and Kirk (1995b) found, for example, that the general psychological well-being of workers at the time of their hiring was the most substantial and consistent predictor of a composite measure of worker outcomes occurring 3, 12, and 18 months later. Included in this composite were measures of job satisfaction, exhaustion, depersonalization, personal accomplishment, and job event stress (not subjective or perceived stress). In addition, better adjusted hirees later perceived greater improvement in their clients. Turnover intentions and actual turnover were, however, unrelated to initial worker adjustment. Further analyses showed that the predictive power of prehiring

adjustment held up, even after controlling for age, years of work experience, negative life events, salary, and socioeconomic status of origin. In the context of poorer morale and possibly poorer job performance, however, an absence of increased turnover need not represent a particularly salutary outcome.

Type A behavior pattern. Type A behavior pattern (e.g., Friedman & Rosenman, 1974; Glass, 1977; Matthews, 1982) involves a hard-driving, goal-directed approach to work. The Type A worker has a sense of exaggerated time urgency, meeting the description of the "anxious, obsessional, [and] overenthusiastic" helper characterized by Burke and Richardsen (1996) as burnout-prone. It is important for Type A individuals to exercise control in task situations, and they are more highly reactive when their control is threatened. They willingly work longer hours and are competitive, achievement-oriented, task- instead of self-focused, and impatient with others (cf. Taylor's summary, 1999).

Type A pattern has predicted job stress and burnout among medical professionals (Rees & Cooper, 1992). It was found to be a better predictor of job tension in a sample of women working in a social service agency than a host of competing job characteristics, which included variety, challenge, and autonomy (Abush & Burkhead, 1984). Spector and O'Connell (1994) found support for the idea that the impatience-irritability and achievement-striving aspects of Type A operated independently. They found only impatience-irritability associated with somatic symptoms, perceived job conflict, and job constraints in their sample. The achievement-striving dimension of Type A was linked exclusively to perceived work overload, less role ambiguity, and less role conflict.

Cardiac reactivity and health risks associated with Type A may result only from the impatience-irritability dimension of the behavior pattern (Benotsch, Christensen, & McKelvey, 1997; Dembroski, MacDougall, Williams, Haney, & Blumenthal, 1985). It is unknown if Type A workers (a) simply perceive their work settings differently, (b) select themselves or are selected into different environments, or (c) act in ways that generate greater tension and conflict.

Negative and positive affectivity. Negative affectivity (NA) has been conceptualized as a tendency to experience and report a variety of negative emotions across time and situations (Spector & O'Connell, 1994; Watson & Clark, 1984), whereas positive affectivity (PA) has been understood as a general disposition to view people and events in a positive way (George, 1989). NA would thus operate as a personal characteristic predisposing workers to negative work experiences, whereas PA would operate as a personal characteristic predisposing them to positive work experiences.

On the other hand, NA has sometimes been viewed as a methodological artifact in the job-stress literature (Brief, Burke, George, Robinson, & Webster, 1988; Spector & O'Connell, 1994). In this role, it might account for the frequent correlations between self-reports of negative job attitudes, negative characterizations of the workplace (e.g., ambiguous, conflictual, lacking in autonomy, characterized by heavy workload), and negative worker qualities (e.g., exhausted, unsuccessful, derogating of clients and coworkers, prone to somatic complaints).

Various NA measures have been used, including anxiety scale items. Iverson, Olekalns, and Erwin (1998) used the following three

items: "Minor setbacks sometimes irritate me too much," "Often I get irritated at little annoyances," and "There are days when I am 'on edge' all the time." NA may be a variable of some predictive importance, because there is evidence that affective dispositions measured in adolesence predict job attitudes decades later (see Spector & O'Connell, 1994).

Spector and O'Connell (1994) measured NA and other personality variables in a sample of senior college students who were asked 12 to 15 months later about their job reactions. NA did not predict perceptions of autonomy or workload, but it did relate to reports of constraints in the job, work anxiety, symptoms, and conflict. Iverson and his collaborators (1998) tested an elaborate path model: They entered NA and PA as variables prior to work task and support and used these in turn to predict job stress and the three burnout dimensions of exhaustion, depersonalization, and personal accomplishment. These burnout variables, in turn, affected the two outcomes of job satisfaction and absenteeism. NA and PA directly and significantly affected the work-task variables, the support variables, and exhaustion and depersonalization. They did not, however, fully account for the effect of work variables, which still significantly affected job stress and burnout, even with NA and PA controlled. Each burnout dimension related to job satisfaction, but only personal accomplishment directly reduced absenteeism.

This study is generally consistent with other studies on the role of NA and PA in relation to work variables (Munz, Huelsman, Konold, & McKinney, 1996; Williams, Gavin, & Williams, 1996). Each of these studies found that PA and NA had direct relationships to work variables, presumably acting as both a substantive personality variable and a source of methodological/

measurement contamination. Yet, the work-relevant variables nevertheless retained their predictable and meaningful interrelationships when NA and PA were controlled or entered into the model at an earlier step. PA tends to relate to positively toned variables (accomplishment), NA to negatively toned ones (depersonalization, exhaustion).

Although the substantive meaning of NA and PA are unclear (NA seems very similar to anxiety, and PA to life satisfaction), they may be useful to retain in models that test the interrelationship of work variables, because of their ability to capture method artifacts. Even if NA and PA tap very basic affective traits, as well as artifact, it may be best to remove their impact from the intercorrelations found among a set of work-specific stress, strain, and outcome measures. It is comforting that oft-reported and theory-based relationships have generally remained significant when NA and PA are controlled, although their size is sometimes reduced. Although there is some danger that "true variance" may be removed by controlling for NA and PA, with a resulting loss of power in model tests, this may be better than failing to identify spurious results. Interested researchers can consult the cited references for commonly used measures of PA and NA.

Work Characteristics, Person Attributes, and Person-Environment Interactions

The present chapter's focus on worker attributes should not be taken as a suggestion that actual workplace characteristics are unimportant for understanding worker outcomes. It is likely that organizational structures set limits within which personal characteristics operate. Because of this, work characteristics *may* be

more important or explain more variance than person attributes in particular studies.

Assuming the priority of work situations over worker traits and attributes should be tempered by three concerns, however. First, individuals can choose their environments and can work to change them. With respect to change efforts, Cherniss's (1993) work on organization-focused coping and the importance of self-efficacy should be studied carefully. Second, as noted above, a vast majority of studies on work characteristics have employed self-report measures, thereby measuring agency characteristics such as role ambiguity, role conflict, autonomy, workload, and job challenge only in terms of their perception by workers. Such perceptions cannot help but be filtered through the worker's inner world of traits, beliefs, expectations, and priorities, thereby raising questions about the conceptual independence of work environments and worker attributes, and sometimes complicating the task of interpreting and analyzing measures. Finally, our review indicates that attribute measures have shown considerable explanatory power in work-relevant research. They have generally succeeded in accounting for work outcomes even when work attributes, demographic variables, and methodological contaminants were controlled.

One effort to go beyond assigning importance to either the work situation or workers' traits is the person-environment fit perspective, which focuses instead on the compatibility between workers' attributes and the qualities of environment that they encounter. Understood by statistical analogy, the person-environment fit model seeks to assess the explanatory power attributable to the interaction of people with environments, examining how the degree of complementarity found between a particular worker's personality and a particular organization's structure relates to job responses.

Schneider (1983), for example, outlined an attraction-selection-attrition (ASA) framework, which proposes that individuals will be attracted to and take up employment in organizations that seem compatible and that organizations will hire workers whose personal attributes mesh well with those of the organization and its managers. Socialization into the job should further strengthen this match. If an incompatibility arises, however, turnover (attrition) will assure that the remaining workers tend to fit over time what might be termed the organization's personality profile.

Consistent with the ASA perspective, Ostroff and Rothausen (1997) showed significant fit between measures of organizational climate and personal orientation, especially (as predicted) for a sample of educators with longer tenure (versus those with less tenure). Additional support comes from a study of 13,000 managers in 142 organizations representing a cross-section of U.S. industries. In this study, Schneider, Smith, Taylor, and Fleenor (1998) found that organizations were relatively homogeneous with respect to the personality attributes of their managers. There was significantly more variability in managers' personalities between organizations than within them. The authors expressed some concern that such homogeneity might not be healthy for organizational creativity and productivity.

Little is known about person-environment fit in social service agencies, however, where the ASA model has not been tested. Finding significant fit between workers and agency environments might prove healthy for both. On the other hand, in older agencies, in which the ASA process has had a long time to work, homogeneity of managers and supervisors might breed a conservative and unresponsive approach to service delivery likely to result in burnout or job dissatisfaction.

CONCLUSIONS AND RECOMMENDATIONS

Our review of the various categories of variables summarized in Figure 11.1 indicates that trait variables generally account for larger and more theoretically grounded effects than do demographics, whereas general moralethical values, sociopolitical beliefs, and religion or spirituality have been little studied. Work-specific traits, expectations, and styles exhibit substantial impacts on the stress → strain → outcome sequence. Evidence for the effects of these attributes is usually apparent even after concrete job demands and organizational variables have been statistically controlled and shared method variance has been removed. The separate impact of environmental features need not be small, but it has often been hard to detect because of its tendency to be conceptually and operationally confounded with existing attribute variables. Interactions between people and environments may also make a separate contribution to work outcomes, as theories of person-environment fit and attraction-selection-attrition predict, but both of these have been little studied in the human services field. A few recommendations for research and practice may be offered on the basis of the present review.

1. Researchers studying the role of variables that are measured by self-report should control for response bias and general affectivity in a planned, formal way, perhaps

by including measures of negative and positive affectivity and entering them before other predictors in model tests.

2. *Work* characteristics should be conceptualized and measured in ways that disentangle them from *worker* attributes. This has been rarely done, Glisson's (1989) work being a prominent and commendable exception.

3. Workplace-relevant person attributes, such as locus of control and self-efficacy, are best conceptualized and measured in a work-specific manner. *Worker* locus of control and *worker* self-efficacy can be expected to have higher validity coefficients than their general facsimiles.

4. Understudied concepts, such as religiosity and spirituality, overinvolvement, optimism, moral and ethical values, and sociopolitical beliefs should receive greater attention and should be connected specifically to the variables examined here.

5. There has been an accumulation of data regarding the importance of internal control beliefs, self-efficacy, and control-oriented coping strategies that is consistent and persuasive. People responsible for developing workplace stress-reduction interventions should especially take note of these findings.

REFERENCES

Abush, R., & Burkhead, E. J. (1984). Job stress in midlife working women: Relationships among personality type, job characteristics, and job tension. *Journal of Counseling Psychology, 31*(1), 36-44.

Adams, J. S. (1965). Inequity in social exchange. In L. Berkowitz (Ed.), *Advances in experimental social psychology* (Vol. 2, pp. 267-299). New York: Academic Press.

Aguinis, H., & Stone-Romero, E. F. (1997). Methodological artifacts in moderated multiple regression and their effects on statistical power. *Journal of Applied Psychology, 82,* 192-206.

Arches, J. (1991). Social structure, burnout, and job satisfaction. *Social Work, 36,* 202-206.

Bandura, A. (1977). Self-efficacy: Toward a unifying theory of behavioral change. *Psychological Review, 84,* 191-215.

Beck, D. (1987, January). Counselor burnout in family service agencies. *Social Casework: The Journal of Contemporary Social Work,* pp. 3-15.

Benotsch, E. G., Christensen, A. J., & McKelvey, L. (1997). Hostility, social support, and ambulatory cardiovascular activity. *Journal of Behavioral Medicine, 20,* 163-182.

Blankertz, L. E., & Robinson, S. E. (1997). Turnover intentions of community mental health workers in psychosocial rehabilitation services. *Community Mental Health Journal, 33,* 517-529.

Brief, A. P., Burke, M. J., George, J. M., Robinson, B. S., & Webster, J. (1988). Should negative affectivity remain an unmeasured variable in the study of job stress? *Journal of Applied Psychology, 73,* 193-198.

Brownstein, C. D., & Hardcastle, D. A. (1984). The consistent variable: Gender and income differences of social work administrators. *California Sociologist, 7*(1), 69-81.

Burke, R. J., & Richardsen, A. M. (1996). Stress, burnout, and health. In C. Cooper (Ed.), *Handbook of stress, medicine, and health* (pp. 101-117). Boca Raton, FL: CRC Press.

Cherniss, C. (1980). *Staff burnout: Job stress in the human services.* Beverly Hills, CA: Sage.

Cherniss, C. (1993). Role of professional self-efficacy in the etiology and amelioration of burnout. In W. B. Schaeufli, C. Maslach, & T. Marek (Eds.), *Professional burnout: Recent developments in theory and research* (pp. 135-149). Washington, DC: Taylor & Francis.

Cohen, S., & Williamson, G. M. (1991). Stress and infectious disease in humans. *Psychological Bulletin, 109,* 310-357.

Cordes, C. L., & Dougherty, T. W. (1993). A review and an integration of research on job burnout. *Academy of Management Review, 18,* 621-656.

Cox, T., Kuk, G., & Leiter, M. P. (1993). Burnout, health, work stress, and organizational healthiness. In W. B. Schaeufli, C. Maslach, & T. Marek (Eds.), *Professional burnout: Recent developments in theory and research* (pp. 177-193). Washington, DC: Taylor & Francis.

deCharms, R. (1968). *Personal causation.* New York: Academic Press.

Dembroski, T. M., MacDougall, J. M., Williams, R. B., Haney, T. L., & Blumenthal, J. A. (1985). Components of type A, hostility, and anger-in: Relationship to angiographic findings. *Psychosomatic Medicine, 47,* 219-233.

Dressel, P. L. (1992). Patriarchy and social welfare work. In Y. Hasenfeld (Ed.), *Human services as complex organizations* (pp. 205-223). Newbury Park, CA: Sage.

Edelwich, J., & Brodsky, A. (1980). *Burn-out: Stages of disillusionment in the helping professions.* New York: Human Sciences Press.

Folkman, S., Schaefer, C., & Lazarus, R. S. (1979). Cognitive processes as mediators of stress and coping. In V. Hamilton & D. M. Warburton (Eds.), *Human stress and cognition: An information processing approach* (pp. 265-298). London: Wiley.

Fortune, A. E., & Hanks, L. L. (1988). Gender inequities in early social worker careers. *Social Work, 33,* 221-226.

Freudenberger, H. J. (1980). *Burn-out: The high cost of achievement.* Garden City, NY: Anchor Press.

Friedman, M., & Rosenman, R. H. (1974). *Type A behavior and your heart.* New York: Knopf.

Gant, L. M., Nagda, B. A., Brabson, H. V., Jayaratne, S., Chess, W. A., & Singh, A. (1993). Effects of social support and undermining on African American workers' perceptions of coworker and supervisor relationships and psychological well-being. *Social Work, 38*(2), 158-164.

George, J. (1989). Mood and absence. *Journal of Applied Psychology, 74,* 317-324.

Glass, D. C. (1977). *Behavior patterns, stress, and coronary disease.* Hillsdale, NJ: Lawrence Erlbaum.

Glass, D. C., & McKnight, J. D. (1996). Perceived control, depressive symptomatology, and professional burnout: A review of the evidence. *Psychology and Health, 11*(1), 23-48.

Glisson, C. (1989). The effect of leadership on workers in human service organizations. *Administration in Social Work, 13*(3/4), 99-116.

Glisson, C., & Durick, M. (1988). Predictors of job satisfaction and organizational commitment in human service organizations. *Administrative Quarterly, 33,* 61-81.

Guterman, N. B., & Jayaratne, S. (1994). "Responsibility at-risk": Perceptions of stress, control, and professional effectiveness in child welfare direct practitioners. *Journal of Social Service Research, 20,* 99-120.

Holahan, C. J., & Moos, R. H. (1987). Personal and contextual determinants of coping strategies. *Journal of Personality and Social Psychology, 52,* 947-955.

Iverson, R. D., Olekalns, M., & Erwin, P. J. (1998). *Journal of Vocational Behavior, 52,* 1-23.

Jackson, S. E., Schwab, R. L., & Schuler, R. S. (1986). Toward an understanding of the burnout phenomenon. *Journal of Applied Psychology, 71,* 630-640.

Jayaratne, S., & Chess, W. A. (1983). Job satisfaction and burnout in social work. In B. Faber (Ed.), *Stress and burnout in the human service profession* (pp. 129-141). New York: Pergamon.

Jayaratne, S., & Chess, W. A. (1984). Job satisfaction, burnout, and turnover: A national survey. *Social Work, 29,* 448-453.

Judge, T. A., Locke, E. A., Durham, C. C., & Kluger, A. N. (1998). Dispositional effects on job and life satisfaction: The role of core evaluations. *Journal of Applied Psychology, 83,* 17-34.

Kirk, S. A., & Koeske, G. F. (1995). The fate of optimism: A longitudinal study of case managers' hopefulness and subsequent morale. *Research on Social Work Practice, 5,* 47-61.

Koeske, G. F., & Kelly, T. (1995). The impact of overinvolvement on burnout and job satisfaction. *American Journal of Orthopsychiatry, 65*(2), 282-292.

Koeske, G. F., & Kirk, S. A. (1995a). Direct and buffering effects of internal locus of control among mental health professionals. *Journal of Social Service Research, 20,* 1-28.

Koeske, G. F., & Kirk, S. S. (1995b). The effect of characteristics of human service workers on subsequent morale and turnover. *Administration in Social Work, 19*(1), 15-31.

Koeske, G. F., Kirk, S. A., & Koeske, R. D. (1993). Coping with job stresses: Which strategies work best? *Journal of Occupational and Organizational Psychology, 66,* 119-135.

Koeske, G. F., & Koeske, R. D. (1989). Workload and burnout: Can social support and perceived accomplishment help? *Social Work, 34*(3), 475-489.

Koeske, G. F., & Koeske, R. D. (1991). Underestimation of social support buffering. *Journal of Applied Behavioral Science, 27,* 475-489.

Koeske, G. F., & Koeske, R. D. (1993). A preliminary test of a stress-strain-outcome model for reconceptualizing the burnout phenomenon. *Journal of Social Service Research, 17*(3/4), 107-135.

Lazarus, R. S., & Folkman, S. (1984). *Stress, appraisal, and coping.* New York: Springer.

Lazarus, R. S., & Launier, R. (1978). Stress-related transactions between person and environment. In L. A. Pervin & M. Lewis (Eds.), *Internal and external determinants of behavior* (pp. 287-327). New York: Plenum.

Lee, R. T., & Ashforth, B. E. (1996). A meta-analytic examination of the correlates of the three dimensions of job burnout. *Journal of Applied Psychology, 81,* 123-133.

Leiter, M. P. (1991a). Coping patterns as predictors of burnout: The function of control and escapist coping patterns. *Journal of Organizational Behavior, 12,* 123-144.

Leiter, M. (1991b). The dream denied: Professional burnout and the constraints of human service organizations. *Canadian Psychology, 32,* 547-555.

Leiter, M. P., & Maslach, C. (1988). The impact of interpersonal environment on burnout and organizational commitment. *Journal of Occupational Behavior, 9,* 297-308.

Lief, H. O., & Fox, R. (1963). Training for detached concern in medical students. In H. I. Lief, V. I. Lief, & N. R. Lief (Eds.), *The psychological basis of medical practice* (pp. 12-35). New York: Harper & Row.

Marini, M. M., & Fan, P. (1997). The gender gap in earning at career entry. *American Sociological Review, 62,* 588-604.

Maslach, C., & Jackson, S. E. (1984). Burnout in organizational settings. In S. Oskamp (Ed.), *Applied social psychology annual: Applications in organizational settings* (Vol. 5, pp. 133-153). Beverly Hills, CA: Sage.

Maslach, C., & Jackson, S. E. (1986). *Maslach Burnout Inventory manual* (2nd ed.). Palo Alto, CA: Consulting Psychologists Press.

Matthews, K. A. (1982). Psychological perspectives on the Type A behavior pattern. *Psychological Bulletin, 91,* 293-323.

McNeely, R. L. (1984). Occupation, gender, and work satisfaction in a comprehensive human services department. *Administration in Social Work, 8*(2), 35-47.

McNeely, R. L. (1988). Age and job satisfaction in human service employment. *The Gerontologist, 28,* 163-168.

McNeely, R. L. (1989a). Gender, job satisfaction, earnings, and other characteristics of human service workers during and after midlife. *Administration in Social Work, 13*(2), 99-116.

McNeely, R. L. (1989b, April). Job satisfaction and other characteristics among Hispanic-American human services workers. *Social Casework: The Journal of Contemporary Social Work,* pp. 237-242.

McNeely, R. L. (1989c). Race and job satisfaction in human service employment. *Administration in Social Work, 13*(1), 75-94.

McNeely, R. L. (1992). Job satisfaction in the public social services: Perspectives on structure, situational factors, gender, and ethnicity. In Y. Hasenfeld (Ed.), *Human services as complex organizations* (pp. 224-255). Newbury Park, CA: Sage.

Moos, R. H., Cronkite, R. C., Billings, A. G., & Finney, J. W. (1987). *Health and daily living form manual* (rev. ed.). Stanford, CA: Stanford University Press.

Mor, V., & Laliberte, L. (1984). Burnout among hospice staff. *Health and Social Work, 9,* 274-283.

Mottaz, C. J. (1987). An analysis of the relationship between work satisfaction and organizational commitment. *The Sociological Quarterly, 28,* 541-558.

Munz, D. C., Huelsman, T. J., Konold, T. R., & McKinney, J. J. (1996). Are there methodological and substantive roles for affectivity in Job Diagnostic Survey relationships? *Journal of Applied Psychology, 81,* 795-805.

Ostroff, C., & Rothausen, T. J. (1997). The moderating effect of tenure in person-environment fit: A field study in educational organizations. *Journal of Occupational and Organizational Psychology, 70,* 173-188.

Paine, W. S. (Ed.). (1982). *Job stress and burnout: Research, theory, and intervention perspectives.* Beverly Hills, CA: Sage.

Pearlin, L. I., & Schooler, C. (1978). The structure of coping. *Journal of Health and Social Behavior, 19,* 2-21.

Phares, E. J. (1973). *Locus of control: A personality determinant of behavior.* Morristown, NJ: General Learning Press.

Pines, A. M., & Aronson, E., with Kafry, D. (1981). *Burnout: From tedium to personal growth.* New York: Free Press.

Poulin, J. E. (1995). Job satisfaction of social work supervisors and administrators. *Administration in Social Work, 19*(4), 35-49.

Rabin, C., & Zeller, D. (1992). The role of assertiveness in clarifying roles and strengthening job satisfaction of social workers in multidisciplinary mental health settings. *The British Journal of Social Work, 22,* 17-32.

Rees, D., & Cooper, C. L. (1992). Occupational stress in health service workers in the UK. *Stress Medicine, 8,* 79-90.

Ross, A. I. (1984). A study of child care staff turnover. *Child Care Quarterly, 13*(3), 209-224.

Rotter, J. B. (1966). Generalized expectancies for internal versus external control of reinforcement. *Psychological Monographs, 80*(1, Whole No. 609).

Schaufeli, W. B., van Dierendonck, D., & van Gorp, K. (1996). Burnout and reciprocity: Towards a dual-level social exchange model. *Work and Stress, 10*(3), 225-237.

Schneider, B. (1983). An interactionist perspective on organizational effectiveness. In K. S. Cameron & D. S. Whetten (Eds.), *Organizational effectiveness: A comparison of multiple models* (pp. 27-54). San Diego, CA: Academic Press.

Schneider, B., Smith, D. B., Taylor, S., & Fleenor, J. (1998). Personality and organizations: A test of the homogeneity of personality hypothesis. *Journal of Applied Psychology, 83,* 462-470.

Schwab, R. L., Jackson, S. E., & Schuler, R. S. (1986). Educator burnout: Sources and consequences. *Educational Research Quarterly, 10,* 14-29.

Seligman, M. E. (1990). *Learned optimism.* New York: Knopf.

Shinn, M., & Morch, H. (1983). A tripartite model of coping with burnout. In B. Faber (Ed.), *Stress and burnout in the human service professions* (pp. 227-240). New York: Pergamon.

Shinn, M., Rosario, M., Morch, H., & Chestnut, D. E. (1984). Coping with job stress and burnout in the human services. *Journal of Personality and Social Psychology, 46,* 865-876.

Spector, P. E. (1988). Development of the Work Locus of Control Scale. *Journal of Occupational Psychology, 61,* 335-340.

Spector, P. E., & O'Connell, B. J. (1994). The contribution of personality traits, negative affectivity, locus of control, and Type A to the subsequent reports of job stressors and job strains. *Journal of Occupational and Organizational Psychology, 67,* 1-11.

Streepy, J. (1981). Direct-service providers and burnout. *Social Casework: The Journal of Contemporary Social Work, 26,* 352-361.

Taylor, S. E. (1999). *Health psychology* (4th ed.). Boston: McGraw-Hill.

Um, M., & Harrison, D. F. (1998). Role stressors, burnout, mediators, and job satisfaction: A stress-strain-outcome model and an empirical test. *Social Work Research, 22,* 100-115.

van Dierendonck, D., Schaufeli, W. B., & Buunk, B. P. (1996). Inequity among human service professionals: Measurement and relation to burnout. *Basic and Applied Social Psychology, 18*(4), 429-451.

van Dierendonck, D., Schaufeli, W. B., & Buunk, B. P. (1998). The evaluation of an individual burnout intervention program: The role of inequity and social support. *Journal of Applied Psychology, 83,* 392-407.

Vinokur-Kaplan, D., Jayaratne, S., & Chess, W. A. (1994). Job satisfaction and retention of workers in public agencies, nonprofit agencies, and private practice: The impact of workplace conditions and motivators. *Administration in Social Work, 18*(3), 93-121.

Wall, T. D., Jackson, P. R., Mullarkey, S., & Parker, S. K. (1996). The demands-control model of job strain: A more specific test. *Journal of Occupational and Organizational Psychology, 69,* 155-166.

Watson, D., & Clark, L. A. (1984). Negative affectivity: The disposition to experience aversive emotional states. *Psychological Bulletin, 96,* 465-490.

Williams, C. A. (1989). Empathy and burnout in male and female helping professionals. *Research in Nursing and Health, 12*(3), 169-178.

Williams, L. J., Gavin, M. B., & Williams, M. L. (1996). Measurement and nonmeasurement processes with negative affectivity and employee attitudes. *Journal of Applied Psychology, 81,* 88-101.

Wright, T. A., & Cropanzano, R. (1998). Emotional exhaustion as a predictor of job performance and voluntary turnover. *Journal of Applied Psychology, 83,* 486-493.

Yamatani, H. (1982). Gender and salary inequity: Statistical interaction effects. *Social Work Research & Abstracts, 18,* 24-27.

PART III

Dimensions of Social Welfare Management: Issues, Functions, and Tasks

The purpose of this section is to provide a broad view of roles and tasks enacted by managers in social agencies to enhance the performance of their organizations, the challenges posed by current conditions, and trends and emerging approaches to practice. In these chapters, authors review state-of-the-art practices, synthesize relevant theory and research that show the relationships between managerial behavior and agency performance, and suggest ways in which practice is likely to change in future years.

Chapter 12 provides an extensive overview of tasks and functions performed by managers of social agencies. Menefee reviews different approaches to conceptualizing and studying management behavior and analyzes recent studies on how managers allocate their time to an array of tasks and the priority and importance they attach to them.

In recent years, increasing attention has been given to the role that managers play in promoting and supporting more effective services to clients. In Chapter 13, Poertner defines the types of outcomes sought by social agencies and focuses on how managers use information through leadership, organizational design, and culture building to support and enable workers to provide effective services to consumers.

Chapter 14 by Alter focuses on how managers build collaborative relations with critical constituencies and resource providers. Special attention is devoted to what is known about the processes of collaborating with other agencies, managing resources in this context, and making the strategic choices that managers confront when they engage in collaborative efforts. This chapter can be read in conjunction with Chapter 7.

Leadership is thought by many to be the core of management. In Chapter 15, Bargal traces the development of leadership theory in the 20th century, including the emergence of feminist models of leadership in the last few decades. Two critical aspects of leadership in current management practice, transformational and transactional, will be addressed, with particular attention to how they are manifested in social welfare agencies.

In the context of increased demands for accountability and the need to learn from and refine their practices, social agencies are eagerly searching for ways to improve their information capabilities. In Chapter 16, Schoech focuses on the resources, skills, and strategies needed to manage information at a time when social agencies must have better information to deal with the challenges confronting them. A complementary view of how information is used in social agencies can be found in Chapter 13.

In Chapter 17, Austin and Solomon discuss the essential role of planning in the management of social service agencies. Both strategic planning and operational planning are reviewed, as are the processes needed to see that plans are actualized in practice.

In the face of scarcity and competition, managers give increasing attention to developing resources for their agencies. Too often, fund-raising and grant-writing are reactive processes that seek to deal with immediate needs. In Chapter 18, McCallion examines resource development in the context of long-term strategic thinking about the needs of the organization and the clientele it serves. Skills and processes necessary for successful fund-raising and grant-writing are addressed.

As agencies become more accountable for how they spend funds, it is increasingly important that managers understand the fundamentals of fiscal management. In Chapter 19, Ezell provides a framework for managing agency financial affairs that addresses the related tasks of budgeting, forecasting, and controlling revenues and expenditures. Chapters 18 and 19 can be profitably read in tandem.

Increasingly bound by regulatory and case law, personnel management has become a sensitive and complex aspect of the management function. In Chapter 20, Pecora and Wagner provide an analysis of affirmative action and equal opportunity provisions and discuss an array of personnel management functions including recruitment, training, performance assessment, and performance problems and termination. Readers may wish to read this chapter in conjunction with Chapter 9 by Vinokur-Kaplan and Bogin.

The increasing diversity of society and the struggle to empower groups that have previously not had a voice in political and organizational decision making are important issues confronting social welfare agencies. In Chapter 21, Iglehart addresses strategies managers can use to build culturally diverse and competent agencies that respond to the needs and interests of ethnic minority groups. Organizational and programmatic strategies that increase access and promote engagement with agency services are also discussed.

Nothing, it has been said, is more constant than change. Social agencies, like other organizations, must be nimble and proactive to avoid threats and seize opportunities in rapidly changing environments. In Chapter 22, Perlmutter discusses strategies and tactics that agency administrators have used to change agencies in ways that make them more responsive to the needs of their consumers.

CHAPTER TWELVE

What Managers Do and Why They Do It

DAVID MENEFEE

Imagine building the Great Society, launching the Civil Rights Movement, or implementing welfare reform without the leadership of social work managers. Huh? "Impossible!" you say? Correct, although very few of us credit social work managers with playing a major role in these change efforts. In fact, social work management is largely unrecognized as a significant force shaping the social programs of our time (Patti, 1985). Yet, social work managers do perform a vital role in developing, implementing, managing, and evaluating social programs (Austin, 1981; Christian & Hannah, 1983; Ginsberg & Keys, 1995; Hasenfeld, 1983; Lewis, Lewis, & Souflee, 1991; Patti, 1983; Skidmore, 1983; Slavin, 1978; Weiner, 1982). Perhaps, our ignorance regarding what these managers do and why they do it is a conse-

quence of our general lack of attention to them and their accomplishments.

This chapter defines social work management as a set of informed and competent management responses to environmental (internal and external) demands that continuously improve an agency's capacity to serve its customers. To set the stage for understanding what social work managers do and why they do it, this chapter describes today's social service environment and industry, reviewing the characteristics of social service organizations that make them unique. Within this context, we describe the full practice domain of social work management, noting the complexity and dynamic nature of the role. We also examine the research on variation in management practice based on management level, gender, education, agency auspice, and so on. Then, we take the reader to the edge of our understanding of the relationship between what managers do and agency outcomes. Finally, we provide guidance regarding priorities for future research and education in social work management.

THE MANAGEMENT ENVIRONMENT

It is commonplace today to hear social work managers describe their environment as turbulent (Hasenfeld, 1992); and, we know from Tucker, Baum, and Singh (1992) that this turbulence exists in both the ecological and institutional components. That is, the availability and distribution of tangible resources as well as the normative framework for legitimizing social services are changing rapidly and will continue to do so well into the next century. This author believes that these changes amount to nothing less than a paradigm shift in the expectations placed on social work managers for a greater and wider range of management skills and competencies (Menefee & Thompson, 1994).

Active forces in our environment are perpetrating these changes (Menefee, 1997). First, the industry is grappling with an overall decrease in the availability of resources while the demand for service increases. The gradual decline of funds from the federal government since the early 1980s exacerbates this imbalance between supply and demand. Second, social problems are becoming more complex and intractable, making them more difficult to remedy with current social service technologies. As the gap between the rich and poor continues to widen, these social problems will become more pronounced. Third, the emphasis on account-

ability for demonstrating the relationship between services and outcomes (both cost and quality) is increasing (see Chapter 3, this volume, for a fuller discussion). The ability to show cost-effectiveness of services will be critical to sustaining future funding. Fourth, advanced social and information technologies to address these forces have yet to be mobilized. It may already be too late to overcome the lag in technological acumen.

These forces have changed the nature of the industry over the past 30 years. There is heightened competition among social service organizations, both public and private, for limited resources. To survive, agency directors must know how to compete effectively for these limited resources. There is increased expectation that social workers should be innovative in the methods they use to help client systems resolve social problems. This requires social work managers to have exceptionally good skills in program innovation, planning, and development. There is greater emphasis on continuous reporting of cost and quality outcomes using objective performance measures. Social work managers will need to develop and maintain an ongoing performance monitoring system. Finally, there is every reason to expect that information technology is and will be an indispensable tool for more effective management. Social work managers will need to acquire and learn how to use these technologies to further the ecological and institutional position of the agency.

These forces and their effects permeate every aspect of social work management, from the formulation of strategy to the control of performance. We turn our focus now to a second major set of influences that affect what managers

TABLE 12.1 Proportion of the public-serving nonprofit sector represented by each of its subsectors and the percent of annual resources it consumed (in 1992)

Subsector	Percentage of Total Sector Represented	Percentage of Total Annual Resources Consumed
Arts	3	2
Health	10	61
Education	20	22
Social Services	45	12
Civic	22	3

do and why they do it, the unique nature of the nonprofit sector.

MANAGEMENT AND THE NONPROFIT SECTOR

As of 1993, there were about 1.5 million organizations in the nonprofit sector in the United States, with total industry expenditures exceeding $500 billion (Salamon, 1997). The industry consists of two broad subsectors, member serving and public serving. Public-serving organizations include health care, social services, educational institutions, civic organizations, and the arts. Table 12.1 shows the proportion represented by each subsector and relates this to the proportion of resources consumed by each (Salamon, 1997).

The nonprofit sector is perhaps the fastest-growing business sector in America today (Hall, 1994). Total expenditures of the public-serving sector in 1992 were about $392 billion, or 6.5% of the U.S. gross national product (Salamon, 1997).

Various forces threaten the current growth trend. They include (a) decreasing governmental financial support, (b) declining philanthropic and private donor giving, (c) increasing scrutiny and emphasis on accountability, (d) growing challenges to agency legitimacy, (e) increasing competition within the nonprofit sector and with the for-profit sector, and (f) rapid technological advancement (Menefee, 1997). Will social work managers be ready to face these challenges?

The answer to this question is found partially in the current state of practice knowledge available to social work managers. Despite the rapid growth of the nonprofit sector over the last 40 years, only recently has the industry gained recognition in its own right as a unique sector for which unique management tools and methods are needed (Drucker, 1990). Authors, educators, and practitioners in academic programs and specific types of service-delivery systems (health care, government, social services) have worked hard to inform the practice of management within their own disciplines. Unfortunately, this condition has not promoted an integration of management theory and practice in the nonprofit sector (Au, 1994); in fact, it probably contributed to the continued fragmentation of knowledge and skills across disciplinary lines. This condition, supported by the frequent borrowing of management technologies from business schools, has been the soil from which management practice in the nonprofit sector has grown. Now that the sector is being officially recognized as "the most distinguishing feature of American society" (Drucker, 1990), the next challenge is to arrive at a management model that best serves the unique needs of the industry. Let us now look at the unique nature of social service organizations within the non-profit sector.

MANAGEMENT AND SOCIAL SERVICE ORGANIZATIONS

Hasenfeld (1983; Chapter 5, this volume) tells us that social service organizations have unique characteristics that set them apart from the private, for-profit sector. These characteristics make social service organizations among the most difficult to manage (Drucker, 1990). Social services are in the business of restoring, maintaining, and/or enhancing the welfare of individuals, of changing people, a value-laden mission subject to a wide variety of interpretations, sometimes leading to a great deal of conflict among opposing interest groups. Social services also tend to have ambiguous and conflicting goals that are especially difficult to quantify and relate to the processes that serve them. It is difficult to know the effects that a particular social work technology has on client outcomes, especially when outcome measures are absent, unreliable, or invalid. It is also difficult to manage the work of social service agencies because the work actually takes place vis-à-vis the closed relationship between the client and his or her caseworker. Finally, social work management in these organizations is often not viewed by frontline workers as essential to the welfare of clients.

For all of these reasons, those related to the external environment as well as inadequate management technologies, social work managers often find themselves in a quandary about what to do, why they do it, and what difference it is likely to make. Considering the context in which social work managers practice, let us now review what they do and why they do it.

WHAT DO SOCIAL WORK MANAGERS DO AND WHY DO THEY DO IT?

Early Studies

To answer this question, Patti (1977) conducted one of the earliest and most definitive empirical studies of what social work managers do. He used interview data provided by 90 managers in social service agencies to identify and prioritize 13 activities according to the amount of time managers devoted to each during a typical workweek. Supervising, information processing, controlling, direct practice, planning, and coordinating where among the most time-consuming activities, whereas less time was spent in extracurricular activities, representing, evaluating, negotiating, budgeting, staffing, and supplying. Cashman (1978) found that social work managers spent the greater part of their time administering, communicating, planning, and implementing, whereas less time was spent in such activities as counseling, evaluating, and filling temporary assignments. In a similar study, Files (1981) identified and prioritized 14 management tasks according to the proportion of time devoted to them by each of 50 managers. She then organized these tasks under the eight management functions of supervising, planning, coordinating, negotiating, evaluating, investigating, staffing, and representing.

These early studies set the stage for many management publications over the last two decades. These publications address a wide variety of management competencies and skills, ranging from communication to evaluation. However, very few are empirical works; most are normative studies that prescribe what managers should do and why they should do it. Furthermore, because these studies of management activity use different conceptual and descriptive frameworks, it is difficult to comparatively analyze them. Therefore, to organize and better understand these works, we will use the management model generated in a recent empirical study that examined what managers do (Menefee & Thompson, 1994). The management model generated by this study will be used as section headings for organizing definitive works in the literature.

Manager as Communicator

Authors emphasize the importance of effective communication in organizations (Itzhaky, 1987; Netting & Williams, 1989; Wodarski & Palmer, 1985; Wolk, Way, & Bleeke, 1982). They hold management directly responsible for the effectiveness of communication, both within the organization and between the organization and its external stakeholders. The skills of communication include exchanging written and verbal information between the agency and its external stakeholders; writing reports, memos, newsletters, and instructional materials; making formal presentations to groups outside the agency; and keeping agency staff informed (Menefee & Thompson, 1994). New modes of communication such as facsimile, electronic mail, voice mail, Internet conferencing, and telecommuting are now common management practices.

Manager as Boundary Spanner

Establishing interorganizational relations, developing partnerships, and integrating service delivery systems are essential activities for agency survival (Harris & Salazar, 1989; Healy, 1991; Moore, 1992; Netting & Williams, 1989; O'Looney, 1994). Managers need to know how to network, collaborate with, and influence political figures, collateral service providers, government officials, funding sources, and other key people to establish and maintain support and funding for their agencies. Managers need to use these same skills with agency staff to enlist their support of the agency's ever-changing priorities. Some authors refer to this cluster of activities as boundary spanning (Menefee & Thompson, 1994), which involves managing relationships, networking, and influencing others. Managing relationships is the work a manager does to establish and maintain mutually beneficial and supportive relationships with internal and external stakeholders. When networking, managers create and nurture linkages between their agency and major stakeholders in the environment (Kenney, 1990). Finally, influencing is the work a manager does to engender support for a particular perspective or action through the appropriate use of personal or organizational resources.

Manager as Futurist-Innovator

There is an increased emphasis placed on the social work manager's ability to forecast trends in the external environment and develop alternative and innovative strategies for responding to these forces (Bixby, 1995; Damanpour & Evan, 1984; Patti, Poertner, & Rapp, 1987; Thompson & Kim, 1992). Recall that this is a time of great uncertainty and instability in the industry. These conditions require that social work managers identify and interpret emerging national, state, and local trends, that they anticipate the impact of these trends on their agency, and that they continuously realign their agency structures, processes, and conditions (Schwartz, Gottesman, & Perlmutter, 1988; Vogel & Patterson, 1986). Social work managers need to define and communicate the agency's vision, mission, and strategic goals (Arndt, 1996; Steiner, Gross, Ruffolo, & Murray, 1994; Webster & Wylie, 1988). In addition, managers need to build a structure and process for ensuring that the agency's strategic plans are realized (Menefee, 1997) and not simply retired on a shelf somewhere. This will demand that social work managers seek creative ways to structure and manage programs and services and identify ways to influence service quality. They have to translate strategic goals into action plans that spawn new programs and prepare staff for helping the agency accomplish these changes. In sum, agency directors and program managers must focus on "futuring" (Menefee & Thompson, 1994) while simultaneously maintaining the effectiveness of current programs and services. The process of futuring demands skill in "reading the environment" (Morgan, 1988), strategic planning (Bryson, 1988), and innovating (Keys, 1988). When managers read the environment, they identify emerging national, state, and local trends and anticipate their impact on the agency. Strategic planning is the work managers do to create a vision and purpose for the agency and to make the vision actionable through the efforts of others. Managers are innovative when they introduce or encourage others to introduce innovation and change within the agency.

Manager as Organizer

Turbulent environments require organizations to change their internal structures, processes, and/or conditions in order to adapt. This is referred to as aligning (Menefee & Thompson, 1994). Aligning includes organizing, delegating, and staffing. Organizing is the work managers do to arrange and structure the work of the agency so as to optimize the use of its human and material resources. Organizing involves a full range of skills including establishing an organizational structure, developing formal work relationships among positions, determining workflow, and redesigning jobs for individuals and groups (Bennett, Evans, Tattersall, 1993; Hartman & Feinauer, 1994; Schmid, 1992). In delegating work, managers assign formal responsibility and authority to those whose role it is to perform the work. Managers help to clarify the role of the job incumbent and review their performance expectations, holding employees accountable for predetermined outcomes. The ability to recruit, hire, orient and train, reward, and discipline people effectively is called staffing or human resource management. Staffing is a critical skill for social work managers (Levine, 1995; Musser-Granski & Carrillo, 1997; Perlman, 1994). It involves successful creation of a high-performing human resource team that comes to the agency not by accident, but by careful and purposeful matching of the right skills with the job requirements. Good staffing maximizes the contributions of the worker to the team and to the organization (Berry, 1989; Kraus & Pillsbury, 1994; McNeely, 1988).

Manager as Resource Administrator

Managers must also acquire and manage the resources necessary to operate the agency and serve the client. Leveraging resources (Menefee & Thompson, 1994) involves securing appropriate inputs including human, financial, information, physical, and the like. Once secured, these resources must be managed efficiently and effectively. We saw earlier how staffing and human resource management are critical functions of social work managers. Managers must also secure and manage revenue (governmental and philanthropic) such that agency funding streams are diversified, thus reducing dependency on any single source (Andron, 1987; Jaffe & Jaffe, 1990; Perlmutter, 1988). Cultivating funding sources often involves developing relationships, networking, and influencing potential contributors over extended periods of time, not just during financial crises. Moreover, managers must be able to track and respond to funding opportunities when they present themselves. This demands a host of skills including research and grant-writing, fund-raising (Kahn, 1978; Sundel, Zelman, Weaver, & Pasternak, 1978), and successful marketing (Kaye, 1994; Segal, 1991; Yankey, Lutz, & Koury, 1986). It also requires that managers represent their agency to the community (Miller, 1981) and the broader environment through effective marketing (Bilbrey, 1991; Segal, 1991), public rela-

tions (Loring & Wimberley, 1993; Schneider & Sharon, 1982), and mass media (Brawley, 1985-1986) campaigns. Maintaining a good image is critical to continued funding (Holmes & Riecken, 1980; Lauffer, 1986). More and more, revenue sources are requiring managers to show evidence of results achieved with donor monies as a condition of continued funding (Courtney & Collins, 1994). Valid and reliable performance data is, therefore, a vital resource for fund development (Crimando & Sawyer, 1983) and other management functions (Caputo, 1986; Mutschler & Hasenfeld, 1986; Poertner & Rapp, 1980). Sophisticated management information systems that inform the agency of internal and external conditions have to be developed and maintained if social work managers are to comply with these requests and take advantage of opportunities in the environment (Berman, 1989; Hanbery, Sorensen, & Kucic, 1981).

Physical resources have to be secured and managed to provide the materials necessary for accomplishing work. Securing and managing these resources requires an understanding of procurement and purchasing, accounting and bookkeeping, and financial planning, budgeting, and reporting (Rosenberg, 1980). Even if managers are not directly involved in these activities, it is necessary that they understand such concepts as break-even analysis, cost accounting, alternative choice decisions, pricing, operations budgeting, and interpretation of financial reports (Anthony & Young, 1994; Hadley, 1996). In fact, in today's complex accountability environment, social work managers who are accountable for the performance of a formal responsibility center (cost, revenue, profit, or investment) must know and apply these technologies well beyond the basic level.

Manager as Evaluator

Evaluating is the work a manager performs to ascertain service needs and determine the agency's effectiveness in providing services (Menefee & Thompson, 1994). Needs assessment is used extensively in human service organizations to design community drug prevention programs (Colby, 1997), identify family service needs (Sung, 1989), plan staff training (Pecora, 1989), improve service-delivery systems (Cheung, 1993), develop cultural sensitivity training (Chau, 1993), assess maternal and child health (Julia, 1992), and so on (Curtner-Smith, 1995; Gerdes & Benson, 1995; Shields & Adams, 1995). Program evaluation is a management tool used to determine the effectiveness and efficiency of individual program components or entire service systems (Grasso & Epstein, 1992; Patti et al., 1987). Although still not a common management practice (McNeece, DiNitto, & Johnson, 1983), this technology is used to investigate program cost-effectiveness (McKay & Baxter, 1980), program stabilization (Bielawski & Epstein, 1984), and a variety of other outcomes (Martin & Kettner, 1996). The research skills for planning and conducting good needs assessments and program evaluations are sophisticated and complex. They include quantitative and qualitative methods such as survey research, experimental and quasi-experimental designs, single-system designs, time-series designs, and field studies (Rossi & Freeman, 1993). Accomplishing these tasks may require managers to develop surveys, perform various statistical operations, interpret statistical tests,

or write research reports for consumers. At the very least, managers should know how to screen, hire, and participate with others in the design, implementation, and interpretation of needs assessments and program evaluations. For the future, however, the basics will not be enough. Recently, management and information systems technologies have converged to shift the evaluation paradigm (Caputo, 1986) from the now-typical annual study to the continuous evaluation of cost and quality at any and all levels of operation (Hicks, 1996; Kinlaw, 1992). Annual assessments are likely to be replaced by monthly performance reviews and ad hoc evaluations, and these will be intimately tied to decisions related to agency legitimization and funding that comes from external sources.

Manager as Policy Practitioner

Policy practice is the work a manager does to develop, interpret, comply with, and influence local, state, and federal policy (Menefee & Thompson, 1994). Managers who engage in policy practice are involved in reading and interpreting federal, state, and local policies and translating these policies into agency structures, conditions, or processes that ensure compliance with federal and state laws (Gryski & Usher, 1980). It is often the case that managers must design and implement new programs and services that either blend with current organizational arrangements or that necessitate their change (Mayntz, 1983). Managers must also act as the policy interpreter for agency employees, helping them understand the implications of new and modified policy for organizational arrangements and for service delivery (Helms,

Henkin, & Singleton, 1989). There is also a need for social work managers to actively participate in the formulation and administration of policy (Wyers, 1991) at both the state and federal level. Because agencies, their managers, staff, and clients are the recipients of social policy legislation, they need to have a hand in crafting policy by influencing policy-making groups with their knowledge and experience in social problems (Wyers, 1991). In addition, social work managers need to be savvy in organizing community and advocacy groups for the purposes of influencing federal and state policy. Finally, the role of social work managers in policy implementation analysis overlaps their role as evaluators (Copeland & Wexler, 1995).

Manager as Advocator

Advocating is an essential activity of social work managers (Menefee & Thompson, 1994). Managers must perform such activities to ensure that individuals and groups are properly and accurately represented in an economic and political system that affords differing opportunities to different people and different classes of people. Advocating is the work managers perform to further the cause of individuals or groups before major stakeholders. Managers may advocate inside the organization or in the environment; and they may do so at the case or class level (Ezell, 1991). Case advocacy pertains to representing or lobbying for individual rights, whereas class advocacy is concerned with representing or lobbying for the rights of groups. Skills include representing significant others; representing the agency; expressing management's viewpoint to staff and vice versa; lobbying at local, state, and national levels; tes-

tifying; and establishing contact with legislators and government administrators (Ezell, 1991). Using these skills, managers may advocate for community services (Mancoske & Hunzeker, 1994), high-risk clients (Klein & Cnaan, 1995), Medicaid-managed care recipients (Perloff, 1996), environmental health (Landrigan & Carlson, 1995), and other important arenas where the disenfranchised may not have the capacity to speak for their own rights. In the future, social work managers as a group must take a more organized and proactive approach to influencing the premises on which social policy is founded as well as the substance, implementation, and evaluation of that policy.

Manager as Supervisor

Supervision is regarded as the cornerstone of clinical practice (Pepper, 1996). The overall objective of supervision is to maximize service effectiveness and efficiency through the day-to-day operations of the unit. Supervising is the work managers do to direct and guide the delivery of services while simultaneously attending to the socioemotional needs of the workers. Kadushin (1992) presents a model of social work supervision that includes three functions, administrative, educational, and supportive. Menefee and Thompson (1994) support this observation with empirical evidence that supervision is composed of coordinating, supporting, and consulting/advising activities. Much of the literature on supervision can be organized using this framework. Effective supervision demands skills in motivating employees (Walsh, 1990), coordinating work and workload (Rauktis & Koeske, 1994), setting goals and limits (Kurland & Salmon, 1992), giving corrective feedback (Latting & Blanchare, 1997), monitoring and improving work processes, educating and consulting with employees (Greene, 1991), controlling outcomes (Austin, 1981), and supporting the socioemotional needs of staff. Today's traditional form of supervision will gradually give way to a supervisory partnership between workers who perform tasks and a person who coordinates, supports, and advises workers. Some authors have even suggested that, in the near future, the supervisory function will be in jeopardy, with the advent of self-directed work teams (Orsburn, Moran, Musselwhite, & Zenger, 1990).

Manager as Facilitator

Facilitation includes all of the strategies managers use to enlist the efforts of workers in accomplishing the vision, mission, and goals of the agency. Facilitating is the work managers perform to orient and enable others to carry out the work required (Menefee & Thompson, 1994) to achieve agency goals. Although this definition sounds much like leadership, we have divorced it from the concept as a precaution to avoid confusion with other multiple and vague definitions of that term (Bass, 1990). Activities associated with facilitating are empowering, developing, and modeling. Social work managers empower their employees by helping them influence agency operations, programs, and services (Staples, 1990). When staff are empowered, they perform better and are more innovative (Guterman & Bargal, 1996; Shera & Page, 1995). Collaborative practice, staff development, and supervisory leadership are all-important elements in building and maintaining an agency that is empowered (Gutiérrez,

GlenMaye, & DeLois, 1995). Furthermore, an agency that is empowered will promote greater job satisfaction and service effectiveness (Shera & Page, 1995). Managers also develop their employees by providing training and education opportunities that improve their expertise (Berman, 1994; Doueck & Austin, 1986; Wright & Fraser, 1987). Lee (1984) offers managers a process for implementing staff development programs. Using staff participation, training needs are assessed (Doelker & Lynett, 1983), developmental priorities are identified, training programs are designed, resources are acquired, training efforts are initiated, and outcomes are subsequently evaluated (Rooney, 1985). Staff training is also used as a strategy for developing the organization (Doueck & Austin, 1986; Gibelman & Pettiford, 1985) as well as its management practices (Baron, Leavitt, & Watson, 1984). Finally, social work managers model the practices, beliefs, values, and ethics to which all other employees aspire. Modeling is one of the most important roles of social work managers because through modeling, workers learn and internalize appropriate behaviors, values, and ethics in the workplace. Collectively, these behaviors, values, and ethics compose what is known as the organizational culture (Deal & Kennedy, 1982). Active and conscious management of the organizational culture will become increasingly important as the American nonprofit workforce continues to diversify.

Manager as Team Builder-Leader

Social work managers make extensive use of administrative and clinical groups in agencies and in communities (Gummer, 1995; Toseland

& Ephross, 1987) to accomplish the work of their agency. Coalition and team building is what a manager does to organize and enlist the work of groups to ensure that agency operations are effective and services are available (Menefee & Thompson, 1994). Teams take many forms. They may be interagency (Iles & Auluck, 1990), multidisciplinary (LeBlang, 1979; Whiting, 1977), interdisciplinary (Gibelman, 1993), or intradisciplinary (Weganast, 1983). Managers use teams for a variety of reasons: to identify, analyze, and solve problems related to agency performance (Hodge-Williams, Doub, & Busky, 1995); to promote creativity and innovation (Pavilon, 1993); to orient and train interdisciplinary service delivery teams (Czirr & Rappaport, 1984); and to accomplish many other goals. Building high-performing teams is no easy task. Managers must be well versed in group processes and able to help groups master the tasks inherent in every stage of development (Ephross & Vassil, 1988). This requires skills in managing the socioemotional as well as the task dimensions of group behavior. In addition, managers need to plan and manage meetings of administrative and clinical groups (Tropman, 1987). They must prepare and disseminate agendas, arrange meeting facilities, notify participants, set meeting objectives, ensure full and balanced participation, focus the group on task, accomplish the intended outcomes, and follow up on meeting decisions. These steps are critical if group members are to have confidence in the value of teamwork. Managers use these same skills to organize coalitions. Coalitions are a major vehicle for organizing and accomplishing social change (Roberts, 1987). Coalitions are used to spearhead citizen rights to housing (Ferlauto, 1991), to improve delivery of services to rural areas (Miner & Jacobsen, 1990),

to expand social work's role in genetic services (Black & Weiss, 1990), to influence urban policy agendas (Sink & Stowers, 1989), and for many other purposes (Gentry, 1987; Roberts-DeGennaro, 1986; Weisner, 1983). Building coalitions and teams is expected to persist as a major social work vehicle for accomplishing change in organizations and communities well into the 21st century.

SOURCES OF VARIATION: WHAT DO WE KNOW?

We have presented a general model of what social work managers do and why they do it. We have not elucidated practice differences or similarities based on such important variables as gender, experience, ethnicity, management level, auspices, and the like. There is an obvious but unfortunate explanation; available research in this area is limited; and, with few exceptions, what is available comes from publications examining these questions not as a primary objective but as secondary analysis. Given this, we present what is known about sources of variation stemming from individual characteristics, organizational arrangements, and environmental conditions.

Individual Characteristics

In the management literature dating back to the early 1950s, it was thought that gender was a determining factor in what managers do and why they do it. More recently, this myth has been dispelled by a number of authors (Ezell, 1993; Maher, 1997; York, 1988) who have shown that males and females do not differ significantly in how often they perform or how important they regard certain management practices. This is not to say that differences based on gender do not exist; they may, but they do not cause significant differences in management behaviors (Ezell, 1993; Zunz, 1995). Still, further research needs to be done in this area because, in the few studies that do exist, little attention is given to controlling for extraneous factors or examining interaction effects. To conclude that gender does not predict differences in management behavior is therefore premature.

Arguello (1984) challenged social work management scholars to investigate ethnicity as an important variable in management. He referred to this area of research as an "obvious void" in our administrative knowledge base. Since then, we have witnessed an increase in the diversity of our workforce like none we have seen before. Furthermore, predictions that this diversity will continue abound. Yet, in the 15 years that followed Arguello's challenge, there has been no research published relating ethnicity to what managers do and why they do it. Thus, by way of explaining how ethnicity influences management practice, the social work management literature is silent.

Education has been heralded by the world of academia as an important influence over what managers do and how they do it, but again, there has been little empirical research to substantiate these claims (Hoefer, 1993). One facet of this research concerns itself with the type of degree best suited for managing social service agencies, the MBA, MPA, or MSW. Arguments have favored and fouled all three degrees depending on whose perspective they entertain, but there is little empirical support for any single viewpoint. Business schools have not been able to demonstrate that managers with MBAs perform significantly different than those with MPAs or MSWs in social service agencies. The same holds true for schools of public administration and schools of social service administration. It is interesting to question popular opinion regarding the superiority of the business school graduate when we see these same schools spawning new concentrations in nonprofit management today (Gummer, 1997). These concentrations are becoming popular because they fill the void created by the lack of commitment to management education and research in the field of social work and in schools of social work across the country. Or, perhaps, it is because, notwithstanding who has managed these organizations, they continue to lack management credibility that business schools look to supply.

Does field of practice predict differences in what managers do? This is the central question posed by Raymond, Teare, and Atherton (1996) in their comparison of management behaviors by field of practice. The results of their study indicate that managers and supervisors essentially engage in the same activities regardless of their specialization or field of practice. A recent study by Thompson, Menefee, and Marley (1999) indicates no significant difference between clinically trained and management-trained social workers in social service organizations with respect to how often they engage in activities related to 12 management practices. Their conclusions support an advanced generalist model of social work education. The research is, however, still in its infancy, and no firm conclusions about field of practice or practice concentration can be drawn from just one or two studies.

Does experience differentiate what managers do? A commonsense response to this question is, "Of course it does!" The more experienced a manager, the better he or she should be at deciding what to do in any given situation. However, a search for empirical studies informing this question reveals a complete void. Research needs to be initiated in this area of inquiry.

Organizational Arrangements

Is management level an important determinant of differences in management behavior? Patti (1977) and Files (1981) tell us that, in general, as we move up the management hierarchy from first-line supervisor to agency director, the amount of involvement in planning, budgeting, negotiating, and representing increases, whereas the activity of supervising declines. Almost two decades later, Zunz (1995) confirms these findings, showing that middle and upper managers spend significantly more time in the coordinator, facilitator, and broker roles than do first-line supervisors and significantly less time in the monitoring role than do first-line supervisors. Together, these studies are informative, but a rather disappointing observation is that only four studies investigating variation in practice by management level were conducted over a 20-year period, hardly adequate for a definitive conclusion regarding this important issue.

Agency auspices may also be a factor explaining variation in what managers do and why they do it. Zunz (1995) found that public and private sector directors differed significantly in the frequency with which they engaged in three out of eight management practices. Private sector managers devoted significantly more time to the roles of broker, innovator, and coordinator than did their public sector counterparts. Twenty years earlier, Patti (1977) found that public managers spent substantially more time in information processing and coordinating than their private sector counterparts. On the other hand, private sector managers spent more time in representation and direct practice activities than did their public sector counterparts. These conflicting findings provide more grist for the research mill, but again, surprisingly little has been done since Patti's initial study.

WHAT MANAGERS DO AND AGENCY OUTCOMES: IS THERE A RELATIONSHIP?

In 1987, *Administration in Social Work* published a special double issue entitled "Managing for Service Effectiveness in Social Welfare Organizations." This issue represented a turning point for social services administration. First, it brought closure to the question of what is the purpose of social welfare administration. Because the raison d'être for a social service agency is to restore, maintain, or enhance the welfare of its clients through its services, service effectiveness is the central concern of social administration (Patti, 1988). This conclusion begs the questions of how well administrative practice performs its role of promoting effective services and how does an agency define effectiveness. Second, the issue emphasizes the need for further research into the relationship between what managers do and the outcomes they accomplish. From a research perspective, we are on the right track, but as we shall see, our progress has been snail-like.

It is a critical and formidable task that we learn more about the specific effects, if any, of manager behavior on agency outcomes. This knowledge provides managers with the capacity to vary what they do to improve productivity, service quality, service effectiveness, and client satisfaction. Ezell, Menefee, and Patti (1989) conducted one of the only deliberate studies investigating the relationship between what managers do and what effects their practice has on agency outcomes. They explored the direct and indirect effects of 13 management activities on the scope and sufficiency of services provided by hospital social work units. With the exception of "interacting with hospital officials," they found that management activities affect scope and sufficiency indirectly through their effects on unit structure and status. More specifically, unit structure and status are enhanced by management decision making and problem solving but diminished by planning, coordinating, and managing conflict. Structure alone is negatively affected by disciplining and correcting. Status alone is positively affected by socializing. In turn, both structure and status positively affect scope and sufficiency.

Subsequent literature contains studies explicating relationships between specific aspects of managerial behavior and correlates of agency effectiveness. For example, Shin and McClomb (1998) investigated the relationship between leadership behaviors and organizational innovation. They found that leadership style was a stronger factor than agency, environmental, or leader characteristics in determining the frequency of innovation. Similarly, Boettcher (1998) reports those agencies using TQM as a

management approach improved performance in seven out of eight major agency outcomes. The TQM method of management improved client satisfaction, reduced the frequency of complaints, enhanced relationships between the agency and its funders and special interest groups, improved employee morale, reduced employee complaints, and increased employee acceptance of change. Poulin (1994) implies that a manager's capacity to design jobs effectively relates directly to the level of satisfaction experienced by employees. Glisson (1989) hypothesizes that three components of leadership (maturity, power, and intelligence) influence the degree of commitment and satisfaction employees experience on their jobs. He found that maturity was significantly related to employee job satisfaction and commitment, whereas power and intelligence of the leader were highly correlated only with organizational commitment. The more mature the leader, the more satisfied and committed the workers; and the greater the leader's power and intelligence, the more likely the worker would commit to the organization. These studies represent an important but limited body of knowledge relating management practice to agency outcomes.

THE STATUS AND FUTURE OF SOCIAL SERVICE MANAGEMENT RESEARCH

Fifteen years ago, Rapp, Hardcastle, Rosenzweig, and Poertner (1983) published an article in *Administration in Social Work* entitled "The Status of Research in Social Service Management." The article cites three major deficits in our research: (a) the volume of empirical studies is minimal, (b) the main focus of these studies is on other issues rather than on management practice, and (c) the research is summarily weak. They suggest that scholars focus future research efforts on defining what managers do, why they do it, and what effects they have on agency outcomes.

Today, we know little more about effective social service management practices and outcomes than we did in 1983. Why? First, the profession has insufficient "intellectual resources" (Patti, 1998) to do the job; there simply are not enough scholars available to expand the scope and depth of practice research. Second, the existing cadre of scholars has not agreed on a research agenda that informs the relationship between management practices and agency outcomes. Third, the research is scattered over too wide a subject area such that no recognizable body of practice knowledge emerges from a thorough review of the literature (Au, 1994). Fourth, we have been producing research that is primarily exploratory or descriptive in nature rather than explanatory. Fifth, there are very few replication studies that either refute or support previous findings. Sixth, the empirical strength of most of the research to rule out alternative explanations for major findings is questionable. Finally, the social work profession and its educational institutions have still not recognized and invested in social work administration as a vehicle for preserving control over their own professional domain.

If social work management is to survive and thrive, it must be able to compete effectively with other professions (business administration, public administration, health care administration, etc.) in preparing people for the practice of management. The competition will demand that social work managers have a firm grip on effective management practices in both the technical and social arena. This will happen only if students of social work management receive a complete and thorough education in the theory and practice of social work administration. Such an education will be based on sound empirical research that informs what managers do, why they do it, and with what effects (Au, 1994). A strong research agenda aimed at informing these questions will emerge only when the social work profession formally recognizes that it has a strategic role in and responsibility for managing social services. Alternatively, imagine building the Great Society, launching the Civil Rights Movement, or implementing welfare reform without the leadership of *business administrators*. Huh? "Impossible!" you say?

REFERENCES

Andron, S. (1987). Setting funding priorities in the voluntary sector: A case study from the Jewish Federation Council of Greater Los Angeles. *Journal of Sociology and Social Welfare, 14*(1), 55-72.

Anthony, R. N., & Young, D. W. (1994). *Management control in nonprofit organizations* (5th ed.). Burr Ridge, IL: Irwin.

Arguello, D. F. (1984). Minorities in administration: A review of ethnicity's influence in management. *Administration in Social Work, 8*(3), 17-27.

Arndt, E. M. (1996). Creating organizational vision in a hospital social work department: The Leitmotif for continuous change management. *Administration in Social Work, 20*(4), 79-87.

Au, C. (1994). The status of theory and knowledge development in social welfare administration. *Administration in Social Work, 18*(3), 27-57.

Austin, M. J. (1981). *Supervisory management for the human services.* Englewood Cliffs, NJ: Prentice Hall.

Baron, R. L., Leavitt, S. E., & Watson, D. M. (1984). Skill-based management training for child care program administrators: The teaching-family model revisited. *Child Care Quarterly, 13*(4), 262-277.

Bass, B. M. (1990). *Bass & Stogdill's handbook of leadership: Theory, research, and managerial applications* (3rd ed.). New York: Macmillan.

Bennett, P., Evans, R., & Tattersall, A. (1993). Stress and coping in social workers: A preliminary investigation. *British Journal of Social Work, 23*(1), 31-44.

Berman, R. I. (1994). Staff development in mental health organizations. *Administration and Policy in Mental Health, 22*(1), 49-55.

Berman, Y. (1989). The structure of information in organizational frameworks—the social service department. *British Journal of Social Work, 19*(6), 479-489.

Berry, P. A. (1989). Application of social work skills to human resource management. *Employee Assistance Quarterly, 5*(1), 67-76.

Bielawski, B., & Epstein, I. (1984). Assessing program stabilization: An extension of the "differential evaluation" model. *Administration in Social Work, 8*(4), 13-23.

Bilbrey, P. (1991). Marketing in mental health services [Special issue]. *Administration and Policy in Mental Health, 19*(2).

Bixby, N. B. (1995). Crisis or opportunity: A healthcare social work director's response to change. *Social Work in Health Care, 20*(4), 1-20.

Black, R. B., & Weiss, J. O. (1990). Genetic support groups and social workers as partners. *Health and Social Work, 15*(2), 91-99.

Boettcher, R. E. (1998). A study of quality managed human service organizations. *Administration in Social Work, 22*(2), 41-56.

Brawley, E. A. (1985-1986). The mass media: A vital adjunct to the new community and administrative practice. *Administration in Social Work, 9*(4), 63-73.

Bryson, J. M. (1988). *Strategic planning for public and nonprofit organizations: A guide to strengthening and sustaining organizational achievement.* San Francisco: Jossey-Bass.

Caputo, R. K. (1986). The role of information systems in evaluation research. *Administration in Social Work, 10*(1), 67-77.

Cashman, J. F. (1978). Training social welfare administrators: The activity dilemma. *Administration in Social Work, 2*(3), 347-358.

Chau, K. L. (1993). Needs assessment for group work with people of color: A conceptual formulation. *Social Work With Groups, 15*(2/3), 53-66.

Cheung, K. F. M. (1993). Needs assessment experience among area agencies on aging. *Journal of Gerontological Social Work, 19*(3/4), 77-93.

Christian, W. P., & Hannah, G. T. (1983). *Effective management in human services.* Englewood Cliffs, NJ: Prentice Hall.

Colby, I. C. (1997). Transforming human services organizations through empowerment of neighbors. *Journal of Community Practice, 4*(2), 1-12.

Copeland, V. C., & Wexler, S. (1995). Policy implementation in social welfare: A framework for analysis. *Journal of Sociology and Social Welfare, 22*(3), 51-68.

Courtney, M. E., & Collins, R. C. (1994). New challenges and opportunities in child welfare outcomes and informal technologies. *Child Welfare, 73*(5), 359-378.

Crimando, W., & Sawyer, H. W. (1983). Microcomputers in private sector rehabilitation. *Rehabilitation Counseling Bulletin, 27*(1) 26-31.

Curtner-Smith, M. E. (1995). Assessing children's visitation needs with divorced non-custodial fathers. *Families in Society, 76*(6), 341-348.

Czirr, R., & Rappaport, M. (1984). Toolkit for teams: Annotated bibliography on interdisciplinary health teams. *Clinical Gerontologist, 2*(3), 47-54.

Damanpour, F., & Evan, W. M. (1984). Organizational innovation and performance: The problem of "organizational lag." *Administrative Science Quarterly, 29*(3), 392-409.

Deal, T. E., & Kennedy, A. A. (1982). *Corporate cultures: The rites and rituals of corporate life.* Reading, MA: Addison Wesley.

Doelker, R. E., & Lynett, P. A. (1983). Strategies in staff development: An ecological approach. *Social Work, 28*(5), 380-384.

Doueck, H. J., & Austin, M. J. (1986). Improving agency functioning through staff development. *Administration in Social Work, 10*(2), 27-37.

Drucker, P. F. (1990). *Managing the nonprofit organization: Principles and practices.* New York: HarperCollins.

Ephross, P. H., & Vassil, T. V. (1988). *Groups that work: Structure and process.* New York: Columbia University Press.

Ezell, M. (1991). Administrators as advocates. *Administration in Social Work, 15*(4), 1-18.

Ezell, M. (1993). Gender similarities in of social work managers. *Administration in Social Work, 17*(3), 39-57.

Ezell, M., Menefee, D., & Patti, R. J. (1989). Managerial leadership and service quality: Toward a model of social work administration. *Administration in Social Work, 13*(3/4), 73-98.

Ferlauto, R. C. (1991). A new approach to low-income housing. *Public Welfare, 49*(3), 30-35.

Files, L. A. (1981). The human services management task: A time allocation study. *Public Administration Review, 41*(6), 686-692.

Gentry, M. E. (1987). Coalition formation and processes. *Social Work With Groups, 10*(3), 39-54.

Gerdes, K. E., & Benson, R. A. (1995). Problems of inner-city school children: Needs assessment by nominal group process. *Social Work in Education, 17*(3), 139-147.

Gibelman, M. (1993). School social workers, counselors, and psychologists in collaboration: A shared agenda. *Social Work in Education, 15*(1), 45-51.

Gibelman, M., & Pettiford, E. K. (1985). An organizational development approach to improving staff development and training. *Journal of Continuing Social Work Education, 3*(2), 15-21.

Ginsberg, L., & Keys, P. R. (1995). *New management in human services* (2nd ed.). Washington, DC: NASW Press.

Glisson, C. (1989). The effect of leadership on workers in human service organizations. *Administration in Social Work, 13*(3/4), 99-116.

Grasso, A. J., & Epstein, I. (1992). Toward a developmental approach to program evaluation. *Administration in Social Work, 16*(3/4), 187-203.

Greene, R. R. (1991). Supervision in social work with the aged and their families. *Journal of Gerontological Social Work, 17*(1/2), 139-144.

Gryski, G. S., & Usher, C. L. (1980). The influence of bureaucratic factors on welfare policy implementation. *Journal of Sociology and Social Welfare, 7*(6), 817-830.

Gummer, B. (1995). Go team go! The growing importance of teamwork in organizational life. *Administration in Social Work, 19*(4), 85-100.

Gummer, B. (1997). Public versus business administration: Are they still alike in unimportant ways? *Administration in Social Work, 21*(2), 81-98.

Guterman, N. B., & Bargal, D. (1996). Social workers' perceptions of their power and service outcomes. *Administration in Social Work, 20*(3), 1-20.

Gutiérrez, L., GlenMaye, L., & DeLois, K. (1995). The organizational context of empowerment practice: Implications for social work administration. *Social Work, 40*(2), 49-58.

Hadley, T. R. (1996). Financing changes and their impact on the organization of the public mental health system. *Administration and Policy in Mental Health, 23*(5), 393-405.

Hall, P. D. (1994). Historical perspectives on nonprofit organizations. In R. D. Herman & Associates (Eds.), *The Jossey-Bass handbook of nonprofit leadership and management* (pp. 3-43). San Francisco: Jossey-Bass.

Hanbery, G. W., Sorensen, J. E., & Kucic, A. R. (1981). Management information systems and human service resource management. *Administration in Social Work, 5*(3-4), 27-41.

Harris, R. G., & Salazar, C. S. (1989). Adopt a house: Building partnerships to save homes. *Public Welfare, 47*(4), 30-35.

Hartman, E. A., & Feinauer, D. (1994). Human resources for the next decade. *Administration and Policy in Mental Health, 22*(1), 27-37.

Hasenfeld, Y. (Ed.). (1992). *Human services as complex organizations.* Newbury Park, CA: Sage.

Healy, J. (1991). Linking local services: Coordination in community centres. *Australian Social Work, 44*(4), 5-13.

Helms, L. B., Henkin, A. B., & Singleton, C. A. (1989). The legal structure of policy implementation: Responsibilities of agencies and practitioners. *Social Service Review, 63*(2), 180-198.

Hicks, D. T. (1996). *Activity-based costing for small and mid-sized businesses: An implementation guide.* New York: John Wiley.

Hodge-Williams, J., Doub, N. H., & Busky, R. (1995). Total quality management (TQM) in the nonprofit setting: The Woodbourne experience. *Residential Treatment for Children and Youth, 12*(3), 19-30.

Hoefer, R. (1993). A matter of degree: Job skills for human service administrators. *Administration in Social Work, 17*(3), 1-20.

Holmes, J., & Riecken, G. (1980). Using business marketing concepts to view the private, nonprofit, social service agency. *Administration in Social Work, 4*(3), 43-52.

Iles, P., & Auluck, R. (1990). Team building, interagency team development, and social work practice. *The British Journal of Social Work, 20*(2), 151-164.

Itzhaky, H. (1987). Social work supervision as a basis for communication and innovation. *Journal of Social Work and Policy in Israel, 1,* 65-77.

Jaffe, E. D., & Jaffe, R. (1990). Resource development and social work: Funding early intervention through homemaker services for brain-damaged children in Jerusalem. *International Social Work, 33*(2), 145-156.

Julia, M. (1992). Understanding how to assess maternal and child health needs in a developing country. *Social Development Issues, 14*(2/3), 28-40.

Kadushin, A. (1992). *Supervision in social work* (3rd ed.). New York: Columbia University Press.

Kahn, E. M. (1978). Strengthening the fund-raising component in social work education. *Journal of Education for Social Work, 14*(2), 53-59.

Kaye, L. W. (1994). The effectiveness of services marketing: Perceptions of executive directors of gerontological programs. *Administration in Social Work, 18*(2), 69-85.

Kenney, J. J. (1990). Social work management in emerging health care systems. *Health and Social Work, 15*(1), 22-31.

Keys, P. R. (1988). Administrative entrepreneurship in the public sector. *Administration in Social Work, 12*(2), 59-68.

Kinlaw, D. C. (1992). *Continuous improvement and measurement for total quality: A team-based approach.* Homewood, IL: Irwin.

Klein, A. R., & Cnaan, R. A. (1995). Practice with high risk clients. *Families in Society, 76*(4), 203-212.

Kraus, A., & Pillsbury, J. B. (1994). Streamlining intake and eligibility system. *Public Welfare, 52*(3), 21-29.

Kurland, R., & Salmon, R. (1992). When problems seem overwhelming: Emphases in teaching, supervision, and consultation. *Social Work, 37*(3), 240-244.

Landrigan, P. J., & Carlson, J. E. (1995). Environmental policy and children's health. *The Future of Children, 5*(2), 34-52.

Latting, J. K., & Blanchare, A. (1997). Empowering staff in a poverty agency: An organization development intervention. *Journal of Community Practice, 4*(3), 59-75.

Lauffer, A. (1986). To market, to market: A nuts and bolts approach to strategic planning in human service organizations. *Administration in Social Work, 10*(4), 31-39.

LeBlang, T. R. (1979). The family stress consultation team: An Illinois approach to protective services. *Child Welfare, 58*(9), 597-604.

Lee, L. J. (1984). Self-study: Organization resource in staff development preparation. *Social Casework, 65*(2), 67-73.

Levine, C. H. (1995). Managing human resources: A challenge to urban governments. *Urban Affairs Annual Reviews, 13,* 1995.

Lewis, J. A., Lewis, M. D., & Souflee, F. (1991). *Management of human service programs.* Pacific Grove, CA: Brooks/Cole.

Loring, M. T., & Wimberley, E. T. (1993). The time-limited hot line. *Social Work, 38*(3), 344-346.

Maher, K. J. (1997). Gender-related stereotypes of tranformational and transactional leadership. *Sex Roles, 37*(3/4), 209-225.

Mancoske, R. J., & Hunzeker, J. M. (1994). Advocating for community services coordination: An empowerment perspective for planning AIDS services. *Journal of Community Practice, 1*(3), 49-58.

Martin, L., & Kettner, P. (1996). *Measuring the performance of human service programs.* Thousand Oaks, CA: Sage.

McKay, A., & Baxter, E. H. (1980). Title XIX, Title XX, and Catch XXII: Cost analysis in social program evaluation. *Administration in Social Work, 4*(3), 23-30.

McNeece, C. A., DiNitto, D. M., & Johnson, P. J. (1983). The utility of evaluation research for administrative decision-making. *Administration in Social Work, 7*(3/4), 77-87.

McNeely, R. L. (1988). Recisions, organizational conditions, and job satisfaction among black and white human service workers: A research note. *Journal of Sociology and Social Welfare, 15*(3), 125-134.

Menefee, D. (1997). Strategic administration of nonprofit human service organizations: A model for executive success in turbulent times. *Administration in Social Work, 21*(2), 1-19.

Menefee, D. T., & Thompson, J. J. (1994). Identifying and comparing competencies for social work management: A practice driven approach. *Administration in Social Work, 18*(3), 1-25.

Miller, D. B. (1981). Community relations in long-term care. *Journal of Long Term Care Administration, 9*(1), 43-52.

Miner, E. J., & Jacobsen, M. (1990). Coalition building in human services: Enhancing rural identity in the shadow of the Big Apple. *Human Services in the Rural Environment, 14*(1), 5-9.

Moore, S. (1992). Case management and the integration of services: How service delivery systems shape case management. *Social Work, 37*(5), 418-423.

Morgan, G. (1988). *Riding the waves of change: Developing managerial competencies for a turbulent world.* San Francisco: Jossey-Bass.

Musser-Granski, J., & Carrillo, D. F. (1997). The use of bilingual, bicultural paraprofessionals in mental health services: Issues for hiring, training, and supervision. *Community Mental Health Journal, 33*(1), 51-60.

Mutschler, E., & Hasenfeld, Y. (1986). Integrated information systems for social work practice. *Social Work, 31*(5), 345-349.

Netting, F. E., & Williams, F. G. (1989). Establishing interfaces between community- and hospital-based service systems for the elderly. *Health and Social Work, 14*(2), 134-139.

O'Looney, J. (1994). Modeling collaboration and social services integration: A single state's experience with developmental and non-developmental models. *Administration in Social Work, 18*(1), 61-86.

Orsburn, J. D., Moran, L., Musselwhite, E., & Zenger, J. H. (1990). *Self-directed work teams: The new American challenge.* Burr Ridge, IL: Irwin.

Patti, R. J. (1977). Patterns of management activity in social welfare agencies. *Administration in Social Work, 1*(1), 5-18.

Patti, R. J. (1983). *Social welfare administration: Managing social programs in a developmental context.* Englewood Cliffs, NJ: Prentice Hall.

Patti, R. J. (1985). In search of purpose for social welfare administration. *Administration in Social Work, 9*(3), 1-14.

Patti, R. J. (1988). Managing for service effectiveness in social welfare: Toward a performance model. *Administration in Social Work, 11*(3/4), 7-21.

Patti, R. J. (1998, October). A conversation with Rino Patti during the Doctoral Chairs meeting at Columbia University School of Social Work.

Patti, R. J., Poertner, J., & Rapp, C. A. (1987). Managing for service effectiveness in social welfare organizations.

Section Three: Social program design. *Administration in Social Work, 11*(3/4), 101-144.

Pavilon, M. D. (1993). Cultural and organizational considerations of TQM: Notes on American and Japanese companies. *Employee Assistance Quarterly, 8*(4), 151-156.

Pecora, P. J. (1989). Improving the quality of child welfare services: Needs assessment for staff training. *Child Welfare, 68*(4), 403-419.

Pepper, N. G. (1996). Supervision: A positive learning experience or an anxiety provoking exercise? *Australian Social Work, 49*(3), 55-64.

Perlman, B. (1994). Personnel management in mental health services. *Administration and Policy in Mental Health, 22*(1), 3-5.

Perlmutter, F. D. (1988). Alternative federated funds: Resourcing for change. *Administration in Social Work, 12*(2), 95-108.

Perloff, J. D. (1996). Medicaid managed care and urban poor people: Implications for social work. *Health and Social Work, 21,* 189-195.

Poertner, J., & Rapp, C. A. (1980). Information system design in foster care. *Social Work, 25*(2), 114-119.

Poulin, J. E. (1994). Job task and organizational predictors of social worker job satisfaction and change: A panel study. *Administration in Social Work, 18*(1), 21-38.

Rapp, C. A., Hardcastle, D. A., Rosenzweig, J., & Poertner, J. (1983). The status of research in social service management. *Administration in Social Work, 7*(3/4), 89-100.

Rauktis, M. E., & Koeske, G. F. (1994). Maintaining social work morale: When supportive supervision is not enough. *Administration in Social Work, 18*(1), 39-60.

Raymond, G. T., Teare, R. J., & Atherton, C. R. (1996). Do management tasks differ by field of practice? *Administration in Social Work, 20*(1), 17-30.

Roberts, D. M. (1987). Patterns of exchange relationships in building a coalition. *Administration in Social Work, 11*(1), 59-67.

Roberts-DeGennaro, M. (1986). Building coalitions for political advocacy. *Social Work, 31*(4), 308-311.

Rooney, R. H. (1985). Does in-service training make a difference? Results of a pilot study of task-centered dissemination in a public social service setting. *Journal of Social Service Research, 8*(3), 33-50.

Rosenberg, G. (1980). Concepts in the financial management of hospital social work departments. *Social Work in Health Care, 5*(3), 287-297.

Rossi, P. H., & Freeman, H. E. (1993). *Evaluation: A systematic approach* (5th ed.). Newbury Park, CA: Sage.

Salamon, L. M. (1997). *Holding the center: America's nonprofit sector at a crossroads.* New York: Herlin.

Schmid, H. (1992). Relationships between decentralized authority and other structural properties in human service organizations: Implications for service effectiveness. *Administration in Social Work, 16*(1), 25-39.

Schneider, R. L., & Sharon, N. (1982). Representation of social work agencies: New definition, special issues, and practice model. *Administration in Social Work, 6*(1), 59-68.

Schwartz, A. Y., Gottesman, E. W., & Perlmutter, F. D. (1988). Blackwell: A case study in feminist administration. *Administration in Social Work, 12*(2), 5-15.

Segal, U. A. (1991). Marketing and social welfare: Matched goals and dual constituencies. *Administration in Social Work, 15*(4), 19-34.

Shera, W., & Page, J. (1995). Creating more effective human service organizations through strategies of empowerment. *Administration in Social Work, 19*(4), 1-15.

Shields, G., & Adams, J. (1995). HIV/AIDS among youth: A community needs assessment study. *Child and Adolescent Social Work Journal, 12*(5), 361-380.

Shin, J., & McClomb, G. E. (1998). Top executive leadership and organizational innovation: An empirical investigation of nonprofit human service organizations. *Administration in Social Work, 22*(3), 1-21.

Sink, D. W., & Stowers, G. (1989). Coalitions and their effect on the urban policy agenda. *Administration in Social Work, 13*(2), 83-98.

Skidmore, R. A. (1983). *Social work administration: Dynamic management and human relationships.* Englewood Cliffs, NJ: Prentice Hall.

Slavin, S. (1978). *Social administration: The management of social services.* New York: Haworth.

Staples, L. H. (1990). Powerful ideas about empowerment. *Administration in Social Work, 14*(2), 29-42.

Steiner, J. R., Gross, G. M., Ruffolo, M. C., & Murray, J. J. (1994). Strategic planning in non-profits: Profit from it. *Administration in Social Work, 18*(2), 87-106.

Sundel, H. H., Zelman, W. N., Weaver, C. N., & Pasternak, R. E. (1978). Fund-raising: Understanding donor motivation. *Social Work, 23*(3), 233-236.

Sung, K. T. (1989). Converging perspectives of consumers and providers in assessing needs of families. *Journal of Social Service Research, 12*(3/4), 1-29.

Thompson, J. J., & Kim, Y. W. (1992). Forecasting AFDC caseloads and expenditures. *Social Work Research and Abstracts, 28*(4), 27-31.

Thompson, J. J., Menefee, D., & Marley, M. (1999). A comparative analysis of social workers' macro practice activities: Identifying functions common to direct practice and administration. *Journal of Social Work Education, 32*(1), 1-10.

Toseland, R. W., & Ephross, P. H. (Eds.). (1987). *Working effectively with administrative groups.* New York: Haworth.

Tropman, J. E. (1987). Effective meetings: Some provisional rules and need research. In R. W. Tosland & P. H. Ephross (Eds.), *Working effectively with administrative groups* (pp. 41-55). New York: Haworth.

Tucker, D. J., Baum, J. A. C., & Singh, J. V. (1992). The institutional ecology of human service organizations. In Y. Hasenfeld (Ed.), *Human services as complex organizations* (pp. 47-72). Newbury Park, CA: Sage.

Vogel, L. H., & Patterson, I. (1986). Strategy and structure: A case study of the implications of strategic planning for organizational structure and management practice. *Administration in Social Work, 10*(2), 53-66.

Walsh, J. A. (1990). From clinician to supervisor: Essential ingredients for training. *Families in Society: The Journal of Contemporary Human Services, 71*(2), 82-87.

Webster, S. A., & Wylie, M. (1988). Strategic planning in human service agencies. *Journal of Sociology and Social Welfare, 15*(3), 47-53.

Weganast, D. (1983). *Team building: An application of group leadership skills to case management in child protective services.* Unpublished doctoral dissertation, City University of New York.

Weiner, M. E. (1982). *Human services management: Analysis and applications.* Homewood, IL: Dorsey.

Weisner, S. (1983). Fighting back: A critical analysis of coalition building in the human services. *Social Service Review, 57*(2), 291-306.

Whiting, L. A. (1977). A community multidisciplinary child protection team. *Children Today, 6*(1), 10-12.

Wodarski, J. S., & Palmer, A. (1985). Management applications of behavioral science knowledge. *Social Casework: The Journal of Contemporary Social Work, 66*(5), 293-303.

Wolk, J. L., Way, I. F., & Bleeke, M. A. (1982). Human service management: The art of interpersonal relationships. *Administration in Social Work, 6*(1), 1-10.

Wright, W. S., & Fraser, M. (1987). Staff development: A challenge of privatization. *Journal of Sociology and Social Welfare, 14*(4), 137-160.

Wyers, N. L. (1991). Policy-practice in social work: Models and issues. *Journal of Social Work Education, 27*(3), 241-250.

Yankey, J. A., Lutz, C., & Koury, N. (1986). Marketing welfare services. *Public Welfare, 44*(1), 40-46.

York, R. O. (1988). Sex role stereotypes and the socialization of managers. *Administration in Social Work, 12*(1), 25-40.

Zunz, S. J. (1995). The view from behind the desk: Child welfare managers and their roles. *Administration in Social Work, 19*(2), 63-80.

CHAPTER THIRTEEN

Managing for Service Outcomes: The Critical Role of Information

JOHN POERTNER

This chapter reviews the literature on the role of information in management. It includes consideration of the categories of performance information that managers need and a brief review of measurement in each of these performance areas. Finally, the literature on feedback in organizations is used to suggest ways that managers can use information to empower staff and improve program performance. The emphasis here is on the practical dimensions of the "right" information for these tasks and the specifics of using performance information to enhance organizational performance.

Management scholars are increasingly recognizing the importance of information to the design and management of organizations. For example, Peter Drucker (1995) has devoted nearly one quarter of *Managing in a Time of*

Great Change to the information-based organization. In *Competing by Design: The Power of Organizational Architecture,* Nadler, Tushman, and Nadler (1997) conclude that a fundamental concept that applies to organizational design at every level "is the notion that the primary work of modern organizations is the gathering, channeling, and processing of appropriate information" (p. 228). Edward Lawler III (1996) suggests that measurement and communication are critical to creating a high-performance organization because lateral processes are key to organizational effectiveness, and involvement is the most effective source of control.

This literature is not specific to social work agencies. Yet, what is more information-intense than social work? It is the knowledge and skills of a worker engaging with clients that produce mutually agreed-on benefits to clients. Social administrators have the responsibility for assuring the success of this transaction, even though the client and worker engage in a private place, rarely observed by others.

At the same time that social administrators need to focus on the client-worker transaction, they are encountering environmental changes that are critical to organizational survival and effectiveness. Changes in social policies such as Temporary Assistance to Needy Families (TANF) and the Adoption and Safe Families Act now set time limits for clients. New funding mechanisms such as managed care and performance-based contracting attempt to link reimbursement, social work effort, and client outcomes.

MANAGEMENT, INFORMATION, AND PERFORMANCE

Managers seeking ways to enhance organizational effectiveness are bombarded with material on such topics as Total Quality Management (TQM) and re-engineering. Recently, the U.S. Army Research Institute asked the National Research Council to form a committee to examine what is known related to improvement of individual and group performance in organizations (Druckman, Singer, & Van Cott, 1997). They examined the literature on TQM, downsizing, and re-engineering, finding that none of these approaches appears to have a consistently positive relationship with organizational effectiveness. Some efforts are successful, and some are not. These scholars suggest that what may be more important to organizational effectiveness is the manager's ability to provide leadership, shape organizational culture, and attend to interorganizational relationships. Information is essential to these management tasks.

Much has been written on leadership and the knowledge, skills, and abilities needed by leaders. This literature consistently emphasizes that managing information is an essential component of leadership (e.g., Kim & Yukl, 1995; Locke et al., 1991; Peters & Austin, 1985). In the model put forth by Locke et al. (1991), leaders' motives, traits, knowledge, skills, and abilities are the necessary background for formulating a vision and implementing the vision. Managing information is essential to creating and implementing the vision. (See Chapter 16 for further discussion of leadership.)

Managing information begins with collecting data on performance and turning this into information that influences behavior in the direction of improving program performance. Data on organizational performance comes from formal and informal sources both within and outside the organization. It is the manager's responsibility to select the most important data from these sources and disseminate information to everyone who plays a role in program performance. This includes key individuals external to the organization as well as those within.

In the context of a social program, the vision specifies the client outcome that is a key performance category. The range of people who are needed to achieve the outcome make up the web of communications channels that the leader uses to collect and disseminate information. Clients are heard, and the desired outcomes are measured on a regular basis. Leadership includes collecting and giving information to those individuals who directly influence the client outcome. This may be a landlord, a judge, a school teacher, or a social worker in another agency. Leaders also collect information from and disseminate it to all of the other people who contribute indirectly to results for clients. These include the United Way, the state or county agency contracting for services, and the citizens of the community.

Information is also an essential element of organizational culture. The culture of an organization, like other cultures, consists of the values and norms that shape people's behavior. These values and norms affect the behaviors of members of the organization who produce performance. As in other cultures, the stories, symbols, rites, and rituals of the group transmit the values and norms that affect behavior.

The management literature includes many debates about organizational culture, including what it is and how it is influenced or changed. As Druckman et al. (1997) comment,

> Most organizational researchers agree on six aspects of organizational culture:
> 1. Cultures are a property of groups of people and not individuals.
> 2. Cultures engage the emotions as well as the intellect.
> 3. Cultures are based on shared experiences and thus on the histories of groups of people; to develop a culture takes time.
> 4. Cultures are infused with symbols and symbolism.
> 5. Cultures continually change because circumstances force people to change.
> 6. Cultures are inherently fuzzy in that they incorporate contradictions, paradoxes, ambiguities, and confusion. (p. 69)

As people in organizations share experiences, react to symbols, and engage their emo-

tions and intellect, their behavior either enhances or hinders organizational effectiveness. Organizational culture is a powerful management tool. It is a management task to shape the culture so that members' behavior enhances organizational performance.

Information is a key element in shaping organizational culture. A poster that records the number of clients who achieved an important outcome last month is a powerful symbol that communicates an essential element of organizational effectiveness. A discussion in a monthly report that includes the amount of time staff spent directly with clients communicates an important organizational value that is likely to contribute to a focus on staff working with clients. Working together to problem-solve about how to obtain the cooperation of another community institution to enhance performance is an important shared experience that influences future behavior. As Druckman et al. (1997) observe, "Cultures are clearly repositories of information and knowledge and, as such, can help or hinder work performance" (p. 76).

FOCUSING ON THE "RIGHT" INFORMATION

Although it is clear that managers need information of a variety of types, it is far less clear what is the right information. The literature (Drucker, 1973, 1995; Lawler, 1996) has consistently emphasized that determining what information is needed to manage for performance is a continuous process of responding to changes within the organization, as well as in the environment. Organizations and environments change in unpredictable ways that require continual modification of information requirements. For example, information needs under the Adoption Assistance Act of 1980, which emphasized knowing where the children are placed, making reasonable efforts to maintain children at home, and returning children to their home, are clearly different than those required under the Adoption and Safe Families Act of 1997, which places an emphasis on children exiting the child welfare system through return home or adoption within certain time frames.

In addition to a dynamic environment, social services, like other public programs, have multiple constituents whose interests must be considered (Martin, 1988). Anspach (1991) demonstrated that these constituents may have very different definitions of organizational effectiveness. This requires management to tailor the information provided to constituents and to their particular interests and definitions.

Managed care and performance contracting are placing different information demands on managers. With fee-for-service contracts, information needs are related to counting service units and using this count to acquire funds. With performance-based contracting, information needs depend on the contract's definition of performance. With a capitated funding mechanism, managers share the financial risk of overspending on services so that the right information is different.

Although categories of information in social services will change in response to evolving policies, funding mechanisms, and constituents, Martin and Kettner (1996) and Rapp and Poertner (1992) propose somewhat different but overlapping program performance categories that are useful for identifying the social ad-

ministrator's need for information. The performance areas proposed by Rapp and Poertner (1992) will be used here.

Client outcome. If the key transaction in the social work agency is the worker and client engaging in a process to achieve a mutually agreed-on goal, then the result of this transaction is the bottom line for the social administrator. This is the distinguishing feature of social administration. Information on client outcomes is important to managers to judge program performance, motivate and direct staff, and acquire resources from the environment.

The bottom line for modern business organizations is different. The popular business techniques of downsizing, re-engineering, and TQM have renewed the focus of the business organization on the customer who purchases a product or service and generates the income that is key to organizational survival. As Peter Drucker (1995) says, "The only profit center is a customer whose check has not bounced" (p. 137). These management techniques generate companion concepts such as customer satisfaction, continuous quality improvement, and cost reduction. All of this is intended to result in someone buying the product or service at the best possible price, generating income and resulting in profit.

The connection between the service transaction and income may become more direct in the social services as social policy specifies a client outcome that has broad public agreement and funding mechanisms are directed at these outcomes. However, this is still not the norm. At the current stage of development, the social administrator's job is more complex than that of the business administrator because the client-worker transaction does not always generate revenue directly. Social administrators are in business to make a difference in people's lives, satisfy a complex group of constituents, and acquire resources of many types from multiple sources.

Service events. Positive results for clients occur primarily through the client and worker transaction. This is the service event. Martin and Kettner (1996) also refer to this as outputs. The service event is to the social administrator as the sales call is to the manufacturer. Without the sales call, the sale is unlikely, and revenue and profit drop. Without clients and workers engaged in mutually beneficial activities, the program will not achieve its bottom line. Information on these events assures the manager that the social program is operating as intended.

When a worker visits a parent and jointly develops a plan that allows the parent to safely care for a child, child safety is enhanced. When a case manager visits a person with severe mental illness at a fast-food restaurant and works jointly to identify the next steps in getting or keeping a part-time job, the consumer's quality of life is enhanced. Although the connection between the service event and the outcome in these two examples is arguable, it is our empirical knowledge of this connection that is debatable, not the idea that the client benefit occurs through contact and joint efforts.

The importance of the service event suggests several roles for managers. Social administrators need to continue to find information on the most effective interventions and encourage staff to incorporate these techniques to improve their practice and results for clients. In addition to skills and knowledge, social administrators need to remove organizational or environmental barriers to workers engaging effectively with clients.

As social administrators attend to results for clients, they also need to focus attention on the timing, duration, and number of service transactions within a program so that clients get the full benefit of workers' knowledge and skills. Clearly, none of this can be done without information of a variety of types.

Resources. The service transaction and accompanying benefits to clients cannot occur without a variety of resources. The acquisition and efficient use of resources is a widely recognized responsibility of social administrators. Information about resources is critical not only to maintaining the program but also to assessing other results. For example, a manager cannot help a program become more efficient without linking costs to outputs or client outcomes.

The range of resources required to support the client and worker transaction is very large. Managers need not only information on funds and personnel but also the latest knowledge of the most effective interventions. Child welfare workers, for example, need to know what treatments are most effective for helping mothers addicted to cocaine. Managers need knowledge of the network of resources and relationships required to obtain positive results for clients. For example, community tenure for individuals with severe and persistent mental illness is linked to certain actions by employers and landlords. An agency that relies on community support for money or clients also needs information on the community's perception of the agency. This is not an exhaustive list but illustrates the range of information required by social administrators.

Staff morale. Although staff morale receives considerable attention in management research and literature (Spector, 1997), and it has been linked to concepts such as burnout (Jayaratne & Chess, 1984), there is a noticeable lack of findings linking staff morale and client outcomes. Only recently, Glisson and Hemmelgarn (1998) conducted groundbreaking research that linked organizational climate to positive outcomes for children. Their definition of organizational climate included several elements related to job satisfaction as well as a direct measure of job satisfaction.

The results of one study do not warrant strong claims of a positive connection between staff morale and client outcomes. However, even if the connection between staff morale and client outcomes is not well established, social administrators seek high staff morale because direct service workers are among the most important resources in the social agency. Direct service workers interact directly with clients. Monitoring this important resource is as important as monitoring other resources essential to the effectiveness of the organization.

Efficiency or productivity. The fifth performance category is efficiency (see the 1991 special issue of *Administration in Social Work,* Volume 15, Nos. 1/2, entitled "Efficiency in the Social Services"). With limited resources and large social problems, social agencies that become more efficient in their operations can expand their services and results. Social administrators who can maintain or increase client outcomes through improved service events using fewer resources can redirect needed resources to serving additional clients (Pruger & Miller, 1991).

Social services operate differently in this regard than businesses that sell products or services. An emphasis in businesses is the need to get the best product or service to the consumer at the lowest price. Consequently, efficiency is directed at cutting costs while maintaining quality. The customer buys the product, and the revenue stream is maintained.

The relationship between quality and resources in social services is much more complex. Martin and Kettner (1996) have an entire chapter devoted to considerations of quality in social services. They discuss the difficulties of identifying quality social services and identify 15 potential dimensions of quality. At the same time, some managed care systems are attempting to link quality outcomes and resources. If the nature of quality outcomes can be agreed on, this aspect of managed care has considerable potential to increase the efficiency of social services. The debate and much of the displeasure about managed care are primarily about the connections among resources, services, and outcomes. When the managed care system pays more attention to the cost of service events than to results for clients, these systems are problematic. It is not the desire to produce better client outcomes with fewer resources that creates difficulties.

Regardless of the funding system that a social administrator is operating within, information is the key to concerns about program efficiency. This includes a need for the best available information on client outcomes, information on frequency and quality of service events, and data on all of the resources needed to maintain the program. This provides the social administrator with the tools necessary to have a client-centered focus on efficiency.

MEASURING RESULTS

Identification of the right information is the beginning of using information to manage for results. Several factors make this task challenging. First, measuring results takes considerable time and other resources (Martin & Kettner, 1996). Second, there is a tendency to try to measure too many elements within each category. This makes the task even larger, and ironically the results may be less effective. A system of many measures produces information overload for the audience, draws attention away from the most important aspects of performance, and allows individuals to choose the data that assure them that their performance is adequate (Rapp, 1984). Third, in most cases, the best possible measure does not exist.

The daunting task of measuring results can be put into perspective by remembering the following.

- The ideal information system includes the fewest pieces of information that accurately depict the performance of the program it is modeling.
- Some of this information already exists within the organization.
- Information system development begins with using existing information and augmenting this through ongoing investment of new resources.
- Information system development is an iterative process requiring continuous modification of measures and indicators.

Measuring results refers to selecting valid and reliable measures in each of the five categories of program performance discussed in the previous section. Selection of measures requires balancing validity and reliability with cost and feasibility. This requires balancing inclusiveness with careful selection of the most important measures. This also requires continual investment in development of measures and data collection strategies. Fortunately, there is an increasing body of useful literature to assist managers in selecting measures (e.g., Martin & Kettner, 1996; Yates, 1996).

Client outcomes. Measuring outcomes for clients is the most important part of managing for results in social service programs. It is also the most difficult. Some of these difficulties include the following:

- Agencies do not typically have existing data on client outcomes.
- For most programs, clients and workers are trying to achieve many different types of outcomes.
- It is not easy to determine how to measure a particular type of client outcome.
- For many types of outcomes, it is a very expensive process to design and collect this information.

Considering the common types of client outcomes can facilitate identifying client outcome measures. Rapp and Poertner (1992) provide a useful typology identifying client outcomes and measures. This typology identifies client outcomes as

- Changes in affect
- Changes in knowledge
- Changes in behavior
- Changes in environment
- Changes in status

A different type of instrument measures each type of outcome. For example, an attitude scale may measure changes in affect (e.g., Child's Attitude Toward Mother; Hudson, 1982). True/false, multiple choice, or short-answer questions may measure changes in knowledge. Behavior change may be assessed through the use of a behavioral checklist (e.g., Preschool Behavior Rating Scale; Barker & Doeff, 1980).

In some cases, existing measures match the desired outcomes of a program. Where this is the case, the next challenge is the collection of these data. In the ideal situation, the measurement is integrated into practice. For example, the clinical scales developed by Walter Hudson (1982) are designed to be an integral part of practice. This permits relatively unintrusive and inexpensive collection of outcome data.

Environmental change measures are less well developed. Given the emphasis in social work on the person in the environment, it is ironic that there are few measures of this type. Licensing standards include consideration of the physical environment for day care centers, foster homes, and institutions. However, less is known in other areas, such as the environmental components that support adults with serious mental illness in the community. There is even less known about nonphysical aspects of the environment. This is clearly an area requiring development.

It may be easiest for managers to begin development of client outcome information by using status change measures. Status refers to a set of mutually exclusive and exhaustive conditions that reflect a condition or conditions of clients (Taber & Poertner, 1981). Many programs are designed either to assist people to move from a less desirable current condition to a more desirable condition or to maintain a current desirable condition. In child welfare, for example, the movement of children to a permanent and safe home is a primary goal. Therefore, movement from living in a substitute care arrangement to return to a safe home is a desirable status change.

Status change measures are appealing for several reasons. First, as in child welfare, public policy in many areas is framed around changes in status. Acquiring employment sufficient to live above the poverty line, living safely and independently in a community, and maintaining "at risk" children in school are additional examples. Second, status change measures already exist within many social service agencies. Child welfare agencies record where children are living so that development of an indicator of children moving from substitute care to adoption is not difficult or expensive. Third, a wide range of constituents easily understands status change indicators.

Some difficulties are associated with status change measures. Some people argue that they are not adequate indicators of the condition of the client. For example, knowing the number of children who returned to a safe home does not indicate anything about the health and well-being of these children. In addition, some status change measures may be subject to administrative manipulation. A child welfare administrator could embark on a program of returning children to their homes of origin with little consideration of child safety or well-being.

Service event. Positive results for clients occur through the efforts of workers and clients engaging in the helping process. Managing by performance requires paying attention to these client and worker encounters or service events. This includes tracking service events in the information system and using this feedback with staff.

Although measurement of client outcomes is problematic, the measurement of service events is much easier. The frequency and duration of the service event are included in the information system. In regard to service events, the challenge for managers is selecting the most important events. For a given program, there is likely to be a variety of different types of client and worker encounters. To achieve an information system that includes the fewest possible indicators, it is necessary to identify the service event or events that are most important in producing the client outcome. For example, if a program is seeking to return children to a safe home, the most important service event is probably the time a worker spends engaged with the parent. In this case, the information system would need to keep track of an indicator such as the number of hours that workers spent with parents.

Resources. Measurement of resource needs is not a difficult task. The resources needed to maintain a program and produce positive results for clients include personnel, clients, funds, public support, and knowledge. The difficulty in this area is identifying a few indicators from within the large number of possible resources that are needed to maintain a program. For a particular program, each of the major types of resources can include a vast array of subcategories. If managers were to systematically list all of the resources that are needed to maintain a program, the list would likely include 20 or more resources.

The manager's challenge is selecting from the universe of possible resources those that need to be monitored. Inattention to some resources will lead to shortages and declining program performance. Inattention to others has little impact on the program. For any program, the list of needed resources can be broken down into those that need less attention and those that need continual monitoring. It is this later group that is measured in this category.

For example, a manager would achieve little benefit from monthly monitoring of income for a program funded by an annual appropriation or contract. However, monthly monitoring of income for a program that relies on periodic donations is critical to assure that the program has sufficient funds to operate. A similar examination of each resource needed to maintain a program can identify those resources and measures that fit the program structure and need to become part of managing for results.

Staff morale. It is very unusual for managers to measure staff morale in a periodic and systematic manner. Most managers rely on secondary indicators such as staff turnover or their own informal interactions to gauge staff morale. However, so many variables can explain staff turnover that this is not likely to be a good indicator of staff morale (Spector, 1997).

If the most important transaction for producing positive results for clients is the interaction between workers and clients, one could argue for a more systematic method of assessing staff morale. For purposes of measurement, staff morale is defined as the degree to which staff experience having their job values satisfied. Job values are those elements of the job that are important to maintaining interest and enthusiasm in the work. Although each person has a unique set of job values, others share many of these in the workplace. The fit between staff expectations and common job values can be periodically and systematically measured.

For a small work unit, one simple way to assess staff morale is to periodically ask staff to identify what is going well for them on the job and what they would like to see changed. This can be done by giving each staff member three note cards of one color and three of a different color. Staff are asked to list the three most important things that are going well on cards of one color and three things they would like to see changed on the other color cards. A clerical person then types up the lists. Although technically, this is not a measure unless the items on each list are counted, it may be an effective way to take a reading on what job values staff feel are being satisfied and what values need attention. Management response to these items in terms of recognition and action is probably more important than producing a score.

The open-ended nature of the note cards makes compiling responses less feasible for units with large numbers of staff. In these cases, the use of a standard job satisfaction instrument is indicated. A large number of job satisfaction measures can be found in the literature. Spector (1997) developed the Job Satisfaction Survey (JSS), which includes 36 items covering nine dimensions of job satisfaction. Spector has demonstrated good reliability and validity for this measure. An older measure that is easy to score and includes most of the common job values is the Job Description Index (Smith, Kendall, & Hulin, 1969).

Efficiency. Efficiency measures are quotients of inputs and outputs. All of the resources required to maintain a program are the inputs. Client outcomes, service events, and staff morale are the outputs. Dividing any of these inputs by any of the outputs identifies possible efficiency measures. However, this produces an immense array of efficiency measures. Most of these measures are not useful or important to monitor. The management challenge is to select the most important indicators (McCready, Pierce, Rahn, & Were, 1996; Pruger & Miller, 1991). It is likely that only a few of these indicators are important to the performance of a program. For example, because the time workers spend with clients produces the client outcome, the percentage of worker time spent with clients is likely to be an important efficiency indicator. Similarly, for agencies with limited resources, the cost of a client outcome is likely to be an important indicator.

Management judgement is required to select the most important efficiency indicators. At the same time indicators are selected and used, they need to be continuously examined to assure that they are helping the program improve results. Similarly, as program performance results identify problems, it is likely that new or revised efficiency indicators will be identified.

USING RESULTS TO EMPOWER STAFF

As staff work together to assist clients to achieve mutually agreed-on goals, the energy and enthusiasm that are needed to continue this difficult work comes from many places. One of the most important sources of motivation is the information or feedback people receive about their work. Taylor (1987) reviewed the organizational feedback literature and commented, "Feedback or information about the effectiveness of one's work behavior is a necessary component of the individual learning process in organizations" (p. 191).

Using information to empower staff requires an understanding of the effects of feedback in organizations. The analogy of the operation of a thermostat is often used to convey the essential elements of a feedback system. The thermostat receives information about the temperature of the room (feedback) and compares it to the current setting (the standard). If the thermostat senses a discrepancy, it sends a signal to the furnace or air conditioner to take action. When the temperature returns to acceptable boundaries, the thermostat signals the process to stop.

The simplicity of this analogy belies the complexity of such systems in organizations. Whereas the thermostat operates effectively with a single standard, people operate with multiple hierarchical standards, which are individual as well as organizational and sometimes based on contingencies (Taylor, 1987). It is as if the thermostat were intelligent and could sense temperature and humidity and make different decisions based on the combination of the two. The system is more likely to perform well when individual standards, organizational standards, and contingencies are consistent.

A second complexity is the data-rich environment of organizations. The thermostat attends to a single data source. People in organizations can choose to attend to a few, if any, of the many possible data sources. These data sources contain information of varying degrees of accuracy and carry different levels of importance for workers. Some individuals place more value on the feedback from a co-worker than a supervisor or an information system.

Third, thermostats are nonfeeling mechanical systems that are designed to react to discrepancies between standards and current readings (feedback) in the same way every time. People have a range of affective responses (Taylor, 1987). Many people avoid negative feedback and perceive it as a threat to self-esteem. Another response to feedback that is not consistent with standards or expectations is to judge the data as inaccurate and lower the credibility of the feedback source. People also react to feedback differently depending on whether it is attributed to external or internal causes. Negative feedback attributed to external causes such as lack of community resources or an incompetent worker in another agency is more easily dismissed. Feedback, either positive or negative, that is attributed to personal causes receives a more intense emotional reaction.

The differences between people and thermostats suggest several implications for managers. First, managers can use mechanisms such as organizational culture as well as information systems to clearly communicate organizational standards and contingencies. This includes clearly communicating the specific client outcomes that the program seeks to achieve, the levels of performance that are expected, and the rewards available for individuals and units who achieve or exceed standards for performance.

Second, because people in organizations have a number of sources of feedback to select from, managers can indicate to staff those sources that are most important. The organizational culture can also be used to shape the feedback provided by coworkers and supervisors. Reinforcing a positive client-centered culture that places an emphasis on workers and supervisors rewarding individuals for client achievements is an example. The information system can provide other types of feedback to work units. For the information system to have the desired impact, managers must develop reports that are well focused (few pieces of the most important data) and are designed to draw workers' attention to performance.

Third, managers can avoid attributing performance to external causes. It is frustrating to see less than desired performance that seems to be consistently linked to a public policy or a key actor in the community. However, rather than discounting negative performance by focusing on the link to an external source, it is more useful to address this through brainstorming alternative interventions at other levels. For example, strategies can be developed to intervene at the community level, or professional organizations can be supported to advocate with legislative bodies.

Although these strategies can help influence people to use feedback to change and improve their performance, this is not an automatic reaction. Current research suggests that one of the important considerations in individuals' use of feedback to improve performance is their feedback-seeking behavior (Madzar, 1995). For example, VandeWalle and Cummings (1997) found that goal orientation influenced feedback-seeking. That is, individuals with an orientation toward learning and improvement tend to seek feedback and are more likely to use it for performance enhancement.

Building an environment of learning and growth can reinforce this orientation in staff. The organizational culture can be useful in this regard. All areas of social work are confronted with difficult client situations for which there is no obvious correct response. Recognizing these difficult situations through client stories and rewarding staff for creativity can reinforce a learning environment.

Northcraft and Ashford (1990) also found that individuals with low performance expectations sought less feedback than those with high expectations. A finding that may be useful for this situation is that feedback-seeking occurs through both direct inquiry and monitoring (Ashford & Cummings, 1983). Inquiry is the process of directly asking for feedback on performance, whereas monitoring is observing the environment to identify cues about performance. Managers who make performance expectations clear and communicate them using a variety of strategies may positively influence staff with low performance expectations. Team and unit goals, posters, and performance reports are all opportunities to cue workers about performance expectations.

A factor that may be related to seeking feedback directly or by monitoring is the cost of the decision. Several studies (Ashford & Cummings, 1983; Ashford & Northcraft, 1992; Fedor, Rensvold, & Adams, 1992) suggest that perceived cost is a primary determinant of a person's decision to seek feedback. These perceived costs include self-esteem, self-definition, and the need to stop doing something that is routine and learn some new process or procedure.

This has important implications for the changing world of social services. For example, workers used to having what seemed to be unrestricted time to help people find jobs or return children to their parents are now confronted with time limits. Some staff will find this an opportunity to learn and grow. Other staff will find the personal costs of change too high to use feedback to improve performance, even when performance expectations are clearly communicated.

This suggests that managers need to find ways to tailor feedback to the individual reactions of staff. Workers who actively seek feedback and are oriented to learning need little attention other than the usual rewards. However, managers need to react differently to workers who perceive a significant cost to using feedback. In these cases, managers need to identify the perceived costs and assist workers to reduce these costs. This may include assurance that although the world is changing, the worker is still a valued member of the team. Some workers will need assistance giving up processes or procedures that are not producing results and then learning new methods.

Ashford and Northcraft (1992) found that people sought less feedback in public than in private conditions. Because much of the work of the manager is done in public, the recognition that feedback-seeking occurs more often in private has obvious implications. Carefully listening for workers seeking feedback in private meetings will help identify those who are more likely to use feedback to enhance performance. Once they are identified, it is easier to tailor performance feedback to these individuals. In addition, when managers use feedback in public settings, a focus on positive feedback is likely to be well received.

The literature also recognizes the differential use of feedback in situations with complex tasks. Two findings of Korsgaard and Diddams (1996) are particularly relevant. First, performance improvement for complex tasks occurred only when process feedback was available. Second, individuals performed better on complex tasks to the extent that they developed multiple distinct goals. Individual propensity to set multiple goals depended on the availability of process feedback.

Managers can use the collaboratively developed individual staff development plan as an opportunity to address this complexity. Beginning with performance feedback, managers can identify workers requiring learning goals related to key processes as well as those linked to client outcomes. This plan would also include mechanisms to assure that workers receive the necessary feedback and rewards for both the processes and the outcomes. For example, the child welfare worker who has difficulty achieving family reunification results may also have difficulty developing case plans with clients. This worker's staff development plan could include methods for improving case-planning techniques as well as making reunification decisions. This development plan also needs to include mechanisms for the worker to receive ongoing feedback on his or her case-planning skills.

SUMMARY

Information is an important element in managing for performance. It is an essential consideration in organizational design. Information is a central ingredient for leadership. Information is critical to shaping and maintaining a client-centered and performance-driven organizational culture.

At the same time, effective management use of information involves a complex set of considerations. It is essential to focus on the right information. From a performance perspective, it is suggested that the areas of client outcome, service events, resources, staff morale, and efficiency guide identification of information needs. Within each of these categories, managers need to carefully select the fewest possible and best indicators of performance.

Finally, the use of information to enhance performance is a complex task. The literature on feedback-seeking behavior and individual responses to information suggests that managers need to use a variety of strategies to produce desired results. Along with the information system, conscious use of elements of organizational culture can be effective in helping staff to use performance feedback. In addition to strategies focused on the program or unit, managers also need to identify individual reactions to feedback and use staff-development strategies to assist individual workers to respond positively to performance feedback.

REFERENCES

Anspach, R. R. (1991). Everyday methods for assessing organizational effectiveness. *Social Problems, 38*(1), 1-19.

Ashford, S. J., & Cummings, L. L. (1983). Feedback as an individual resource: Personal strategies of creating information. *Organizational Behavior and Human Performance, 32,* 370-398.

Ashford, S. J., & Northcraft, G. B. (1992). Conveying more (or less) than we realize: The role of impression management in feedback seeking. *Organizational Behavior and Human Decision Process, 53,* 310-334.

Barker, W. F., & Doeff, A. M. (1980). *Preschool behavior rating scale: Administration and scoring manual.* New York: Child Welfare League of America.

Drucker, P. (1973). Managing the public service institution. *The Public Interest, 33,* 43-60.

Drucker, P. (1995). *Managing in a time of great change.* New York: Truman Talley.

Druckman, D., Singer, J. E., & Van Cott, H. (1997). *Enhancing organizational performance.* Washington, DC: National Academy Press.

Fedor, D. B., Rensvold, R. B., & Adams, S. M. (1992). An investigation of factors expected to affect feedback seeking: A longitudinal field study. *Personnel Psychology, 45,* 779-805.

Glisson, C., & Hemmelgarn, A. (1998). The effects of organizational climate and interorganizational coordination on the quality and outcomes of children's service systems. *Child Abuse and Neglect, 22*(5), 401-421.

Hudson, W. W. (1982). *The clinical measurement package: A field manual.* Chicago: Dorsey.

Jayaratne, S., & Chess, W. (1984). Job satisfaction, burnout, and turnover: A national study. *Social Work, 46,* 448-453.

Kim, H., & Yukl, G. (1995). Relationship of self-reported and subordinate-reported leadership behaviors to managerial effectiveness and advancement. *Leadership Quarterly, 6,* 361-377.

Korsgaard, M. A., & Diddams, M. (1996). The effect of process feedback and tasks complexity on personal goals, information searching, and performance improvement. *Journal of Applied Social Psychology, 26,* 1889-1911.

Lawler, E. E. (1996). *From the ground up: Six principles for building the new logic corporation.* San Francisco: Jossey-Bass.

Locke, E. A., Kirkpatrick, S., Wheeler, J. K., Schneider, J., Niles, K., Goldstein, H., Welsh, K., & Chan, D. (1991). *The essence of leadership: The four keys to leading successfully.* New York: Lexington Books.

Madzar, S. (1995). Feedback-seeking behavior: A review of the literature and implications for HRD practitioners. *Human Resource Development Quarterly, 6*(4), 337-349.

Martin, L. L., & Kettner, P. M. (1996). *Measuring the performance of human service programs.* Thousand Oaks, CA: Sage.

Martin, P. Y. (1988). Multiple constituents and performance in social welfare organizations: Action strategies for directors. In R. Patti, J. Poertner, & C. A. Rapp (Eds.), *Managing for service effectiveness in social welfare organizations.* New York: Haworth.

McCready, D. J., Pierce, S., Rahn, S. L., & Were, K. (1996). Third-generation information systems: Integrating costs and outcomes. Tools for professional development and program evaluation. *Administration in Social Work, 20*(1), 1-15.

Nadler, D. A., Tushman, M. L., & Nadler, M. B. (1997). *Competing by design: The power of organizational architecture.* New York: Oxford University Press.

Northcraft, G. B., & Ashford, S. J. (1990). The preservation of self in everyday life: The effects of performance expectations and feedback context on feedback inquiry. *Organizational Behavior and Human Decision Processes, 47,* 42-64.

Peters, T. J., & Austin, N. (1985). *A passion for excellence: The leadership difference.* New York: Random House.

Pruger, R., & Miller, L. (1991). Efficiency and social services: Parts A and B. *Administration in Social Work, 15*(1/2), 5-23, 25-44.

Rapp, C. A. (1984, Summer). Information, performance, and the human service manager of the 1980s: Beyond housekeeping. *Administration in Social Work, 8*(2), 69-80.

Rapp, C. A., & Poertner, J. (1992). *Social administration: A client-centered approach.* White Plains, NY: Longman.

Smith, P. C., Kendall, L. M., & Hulin, C. L. (1969). *The measurement of satisfaction in work and retirement: A strategy for the study of attitudes.* Chicago: Rand McNally.

Spector, P. E. (1997). *Job satisfaction: Application, assessment, causes, and consequences.* Thousand Oaks, CA: Sage.

Taber, M., & Poertner, J. (1981). Modeling service delivery as a system of transitions. *Evaluation Review, 5*(4), 546-566.

Taylor, M. S. (1987). The effects of feedback on the behavior of organizational personnel. In R. Patti, J. Poertner, & C. A. Rapp (Eds.), *Managing for service effectiveness in social welfare organizations.* New York: Haworth.

VandeWalle, D., & Cummings, L. L. (1997). A test of the influence of goal orientation on the feedback-seeking process. *Journal of Applied Psychology, 82*(3), 390-400.

Yates, B. T. (1996). *Analyzing costs, procedures, processes, and outcomes in human services.* Thousand Oaks, CA: Sage.

CHAPTER FOURTEEN

Interorganizational Collaboration in the Task Environment

CATHERINE FOSTER ALTER

No organization or agency can survive today completely on its own. Regardless of their organization's size, public or private affiliation, or range of services provided, successful managers know that partnerships and collaborations are important for the success of their organization. They are one means for managing the task environment and adapting to fast-changing conditions. More than ever, the resources essential for the survival of a human service organization lie outside its boundaries and beyond a manager's control. Thus, today, most successful organizations are part of a web of lateral and/or horizontal connections such as partnerships, consortia, networks, and service-delivery systems (Alter & Hage, 1993; Considine, 1988). Likewise, successful managers spend a significant part of their time developing and maintain-ing interorganizational alliances between their organizations and others. In today's world, these forms of collectivity are not an option; they are a necessity. If the capacity to network and collaborate is not among an organization's competencies, management needs to get busy.

Before reading the rest of this chapter, a few caveats. First, partnerships and networks are not a panacea for every ill that organizations experience; they cannot overcome managerial stagnation nor organizational error (Argyris, 1982). What they can do, under the right circumstances, is extend the existing competence of organizations so they can accomplish objectives beyond their current reach. Furthermore, more than a superficial understanding of strategic thinking and innovative organizational structures is needed to make them work to advantage. Wise managers do not enter into strategic networks without the capability and resources to take a longitudinal approach to goals because collaborations are not a quick fix. The long-term advantages of collaboration require time and patience, as the solutions and added value unfold over time.

Partnerships and networks also require a considerable financial investment. Funders, however, are seldom willing to include the actual costs of collaboration in contracts and grants. For example, community organizations are told to cooperate in the delivery of categorically funded programs to reduce duplication, plug gaps, and create "seamless" systems, as if local collaboration could undo federal and state fragmentation. Local providers must demonstrate a capacity to coordinate their delivery of services before being let into the new privatized "managed networks" of state-funded service-delivery systems. In these top-down managed forms of collaboration, the additional costs of interagency communication are seldom included in the unit costs or capitation rate.

Despite the difficulties associated with building partnerships, ample anecdotal and empirical evidence exists to indicate that managers spend as much time "facing outward" as they do handling internal management tasks. For example, Menefee and Thompson (1994) concluded that "the role of the social work manager has undergone a major transformation in the last 10 years" (p. 19), now including an equal emphasis on managing the task environment and managing intraorganizational processes. No longer do administrators face only inward; rather, as parts of subsystems of service systems, they are affected by complex sets of stakeholders and multiple funding streams (Menefee & Thompson,

1994). To survive in this increasingly complex environment, managers must understand that these forces are best thought of as reciprocal. Organizational survival today requires that managers influence and shape their organizations' environments as much as they are influenced and shaped by them.

A word about terms. This chapter describes a set of general principles and practices that apply to all situations where one organization is associated with one or more other autonomous organizations to achieve a goal none could achieve on its own. Undoubtedly, collaborative and integrative efforts can take place within a single complex organization, but the focus of this chapter is collaboration across the boundaries of organizations (Hassett & Austin, 1997; Mathiesen, 1971). Many nouns are commonly used to describe these inter- and intraorganizational structures—*partnerships, teams, strategic alliances or relationships, consortia, collectives, networks,* and so on—depending on the number of participants, the purpose, and the structure of the association. Similarly, numerous verbs are employed to describe the act of creating and maintaining interorganizational relationships. Terms such as *collaborating, boundary spanning, cooperating, coordinating,* and *networking* are often used interchangeably. No agreement exists in the literature about standard definitions of these terms, although a number of taxonomies have been designed with this goal in mind (Alter & Hage, 1993; Astley & Fombrun, 1983). For the purposes of this chapter, *partnerships* is used to refer to joint ventures with limited numbers of members whereas *networks* refers to those associations with larger numbers. The primary strategy for building these interorganizational arrangements is termed *collaborating* (Henneman, 1995; Henneman, Lee, & Cohen, 1995; O'Looney, 1994).

Little has been written about the process of building partnerships and networks (for exceptions, see Bergquist, Betwee, & Meuel, 1995; Doz & Hamel, 1998; Gray, 1985; Hahn & Alter, 1985; O'Connor & McCord, 1990/1991). We need a better understanding of how managers successfully pull organizations together, achieve agreement about purpose and methods of collaboration, and then channel the available resources toward a common goal.

We also need a better understanding of how managers successfully maintain their partnerships, once they are operational. What needs to happen for partnerships to survive and adapt to changing conditions? What challenges do they typically face? How do they meet these challenges? These processes are described in the latter half of this chapter. First, we consider why partnerships and networks are increasingly important to organizational survival, and we discuss their advantages and risks.

THEORETICAL CONTEXT

Nothing about interorganizational partnerships is new; they have been in use since formal organizations were invented during the Greek and Egyptian civilizations. What is new is their scope and number. The use of partnerships and networks in commerce and human-service delivery increased dramatically during the last two decades (Alter & Hage, 1993). We do not have good documentation of this increase, but all around us are examples. The U.S. government joins the big three automakers in a $1 billion research and development effort to design more fuel-efficient cars. The Colorado Symphony, more than $5 million in debt in 1989, transforms itself into a cooperative with linkages to the community and private industry and becomes remarkably successful in building support, increasing ticket sales, and becoming a vital member of the City of Denver. And, in child welfare systems, public and private agencies jointly establish common referral networks and case management projects to improve the quality of their services. Across government, commerce and industry, and human services, autonomous organizations increasingly form partnerships and networks to accomplish supraordinate goals.

The Changing Environment

The force driving partnership and network formation is multifaceted change, which increases in speed and intensity by the year (Morrison, 1996). Like the Santa Ana winds, this change is constant, intense, and unpredictable, and it affects every aspect of organizations and their environments. Today, managers can be heard to say, "In the old days . . . last year that is . . ."

The rapid pace of change, in turn, is fueled by the continuous growth in knowledge. One of the most important factors shaping the structure and process of service delivery is the growth of knowledge and the resulting new technologies (Alexander & Randolph, 1985). These factors are important determinants of the ways in which professionals and organizations work together. As our knowledge base grows, society's perceptions of human and organizational behavior become increasingly more complex (Hage & Powers, 1992), and this has two impacts on human service professions and their organizations. The first is society's increasing willingness and capacity to identify and respond to new social problems; the second is society's unwillingness to adequately fund solutions for these problems.

As understanding of human problems improves, society views them more complexly and holistically (Lefton & Rosengren, 1966). We identify many more human conditions as constituting a community problem than in the past. An empirical study of eight interorganizational service-delivery systems in 1984 found that six of the services had been developed only in the previous 15 years (hospice care, special needs adoption services, child protection services, rape/domestic violence intervention, community support/care for chronically mentally ill adults, and prevention of institutionalization for frail elderly; Alter & Hage, 1993). The two services that had existed in these communities prior to 1970 were prenatal care for at-risk pregnant teens and juvenile correctional programs. The increase in identification of and response to new societal problems is the dynamic force that causes an increase in the number of human service organizations in American communities.

Society is also more sophisticated about intervention and treatment. We more readily accept that most human problems are multidimensional (Perlman, 1975) and that categorical programs focusing on only one behavior are, in most cases, less effective than those that take a comprehensive approach to individuals and families (Dryfoos, 1991). Thus, federal, state, and local communities strive to develop multidisciplinary approaches to a wide range of human problems. Not surprisingly, professions, disciplines, and organizations are exhorted to

engage in interdisciplinary research and practice, and organizations are mandated to form interorganizational alliances to provide more comprehensive and "seamless" service. As the knowledge base of the helping professions has broadened, policy makers and program planners see more clearly the connections between problems and solutions.

The explosion of knowledge also causes major changes in the technologies of intervening—the methods used to accomplish service goals (Provan, 1984). We need only pick up a newspaper or academic journal to learn about new behavioral, cognitive, social, and medical approaches to almost every problem, as well as how each approach embraces several theoretical perspectives, each with a range of models. The result of this growth in specialization at the community level is fragmentation (Kamerman & Kahn, 1990).

As new knowledge of human behavior increases and the pace of social and technological change quickens, the proliferation of human services, human service organizations, and professions results in further fragmentation of the human services. Postindustrial society is characterized by an exponential growth in knowledge and technology (Hage & Powers, 1992), made possible by our increasing capability to think in more complex ways—that is, multivariate cognitive processes, dialectical thinking, cause/effect analysis. Multisystemic thinking is another by-product of the knowledge explosion and an important prerequisite to building successful partnerships and networks. Even when organizations are driven toward collaboration by the needs discussed below, managers will probably be resistant and/or unsuccessful if they lack an appreciation of environmental complexity and/or lack the ability to think in multisystem ways.

Partnerships and Networks: One Response to Change

If an organization has all the resources it needs to fulfill its mission—that is, human assets such as knowledge and skills, state-of-the-art technologies, positive community image and sanction, a supportive policy environment—then administrators need not consider networking a necessity. If, however, resources are inadequate for strengthening a service, breaking into a new service market, or accomplishing a policy objective in the wider environment, then collaboration can play a key role (Bell & Dennis, 1991). Managers most often form partnerships and networks for the purpose of obtaining needed resources, sharing risk, co-opting or competing with competitors, improving adaptability, and achieving economies of scale.

The need for resources. The most frequently cited reason for interorganizational collaboration is the need for resources to enable the accomplishment of organizational objectives. In many instances, collaboratives are an efficient way of gaining resources, especially those that are highly specialized, tacit, or dependent on political and policy experience. Once embedded within an organization, these competencies can be leveraged into expanded activities of the alliance (Benson, 1975). For example, a community-based economic development organization in a Midwestern state needed to start a self-employment program for women receiving Aid to Families With Dependent Children (AFDC). It learned, however, that the state welfare rules on asset accumulation made success almost impossible. The organization allied itself with the trade association of the banking industry and, through education and the influence of several of its board members, enticed the association into working for legislative reform. An AFDC waiver was adopted by the legislature, and the program was launched. Now, after almost 10 years, the state has over 800 small businesses owned by formerly low income women, and the state has a high level of commercial lending to start-up micro enterprises (Institute for Social and Economic Development, 1998).

The need to expand. In the business sector today, companies are being compelled by market forces to downsize and focus on a narrow range of activities, but simultaneously, they must enter new markets (Bergquist et al., 1995). This presumes that a single company will have "in shop" all of the resources it needs and makes it less likely that it can risk what it does have to exploit new opportunities. A solution is found by combining separate resources to produce new activities that are better than the sum of the previous parts (Yuen & Owens, 1996). Although research is scanty in the nonprofit sector, anecdotal data suggest that the same circumstances are currently present in many health and welfare organizations. For example, a hospice organization on the East Coast decided to establish a specialized program for terminally ill AIDS patients, but it was reluctant, because the needed specialized knowledge and skill were lacking. Members of the hospice board located a university teaching hospital that had a specialization in immune deficiency disease and was willing to provide technical consultation and supervision in return for an opportunity to develop medical internships. Some time after the AIDS hospice began, the organization leveraged its newly gained knowledge by initiating an extensive 10-state training program for AIDS caregivers.

The need to compete. Of course, it is not always necessary to turn a potential competitor into an ally via collaborative activities. Circumstances occur where Organization A needs to neutralize or block Organization B before it can successfully achieve an objective. In this circumstance, Organization A's least costly means of overcoming Organization B may be co-option—making Organization B an ally. Then again, competing with Organization B by forming an alliance with Organization C may be more advantageous (Gargiulo, 1993). In an age of managed care, competing successfully may be the difference between an organization that closes its doors and one that creates new stability and growth. For example, a community-based mental health organization decided to compete for a large statewide behavioral managed care contract in order to survive, but its chances of winning were slim compared with the other mental health organization in town—a large for-profit hospital owned by a national corporation. After a thorough community-needs assessment, this organization partnered with the local Latino service organization, and they submitted an integrated proposal that won the bid. The components of diversity and community embeddedness offered by the local partnership outweighed the advantages offered by the national corporation.

The need to move quickly. Grant-funding and managed care systems often require organizations to move with speed. Unfortunately, adaptability and speed require excess organizational capacity not available in many health and welfare organizations today. One way to overcome this barrier of speed is to form interorganizational collaboratives with agreed-on divisions of labor. In a partnership among three family service organizations, each hired one specialist—a social welfare planner/policy analyst, a researcher/statistician, and a grant writer/editor. These three, working as a team and in concert with their three managers, developed an annual work plan that benefitted each organization equally. The cost-benefit ratio of this pooling of resources was highly successful from the first year.

The need to achieve economies of scale and contain costs. At this time, we have little conclusive evidence about whether collaboration is an effective strategy for achieving economies of scale and containing costs. The expectation has been that collaboration should result in significant savings (Hassett & Austin, 1997), an expectation that was not realized in the Services Integration Targets of Opportunity (SITO) projects of the 1970s (Agranoff, 1991; Agranoff & Pattakos, 1979) nor documented since then. On the other hand, little or no data exist on small, successful, community-based service integration to determine if economies of scale across participating programs have been achieved. Common sense dictates that case coordination, as an added value, certainly must add cost. But what about real service integration? When several community-based organizations who serve the same client population can eliminate the duplication of program components such as intake, assessment, and case planning, common sense also dictates that overall service costs will be lowered.

Potentially, interorganizational collaboration has a number of important strategic advantages—acquiring scarce or specialized human assets that enable organizations to improve their speed and adaptability and thus compete more successfully over time. Interorganizational

TABLE 14.1 Calculus of Interorganizational Collaboration

Cost	Benefit
Loss of resources: loss of time, money, and information (Benson, 1975; Litwak & Hylton, 1962)	Gain of resources: time, money, and information (Litwak & Hylton, 1962), utilization of unused organizational capacity
Linkage with failure: sharing of the costs of failing such as loss of reputation, status, legitimacy, and financial position	Sharing the risks of program development: split the costs of failure—to move quickly enough, to develop program of sufficient quality or acceptance, to gain sufficient market share (Bergquist, Betwee, & Meuel, 1995)
Loss of technological superiority: loss of human assets with technological edge or with specialized intervention skills (Provan, 1984)	Opportunities to learn and to adopt new technologies, develop competencies, or jointly develop new services
Loss of autonomy (Gouldner, 1960): loss of ability to unilaterally control outcomes (Gray & Hay, 1986), goal displacement (Beder, 1984)	Increased influence over domain: ability to penetrate new markets, competitive positioning with new service in current markets
Loss of stability: increase in feelings of uncertainty and dislocation, loss of known time-tested technology (Beder, 1984)	Ability to manage uncertainty: to solve complex problems (Hage, 1988), to specialize or diversify (Alter, 1988), to fend off competitors (Sosin, 1985)
Conflict over domain, goals, methods (Alter, 1990)	Increased synergy: increase in mutual support and harmonious working relationships (Bergquist, Betwee, & Meuel, 1995)
Delays in solutions due to problems with communication and coordination; frustration over delay in seeing outcomes	Improvement in response rate: rapid response to changing market demands, less delay in use of new technologies

SOURCE: Adapted from Alter and Hage (1993, pp. 36-37).

collaboration also has both costs and benefits that need to be clearly understood.

The Calculus of Interorganizational Collaboration: Balancing Risk and Gain

A summary of the costs and benefits of collaboration are shown in Table 14.1. This is meant to be not an exhaustive list but a brief summary of the many costs and benefits that have been identified in the literature.

Each item in Table 14.1 has a quid pro quo, but this does not mean there is a potentially equal loss or gain in each area. It does suggest that smart managers, either consciously or unconsciously, estimate the overall costs and benefits of collaboration and conclude that the benefits outweigh the costs before they move ahead with collaborative efforts. For example, a perceived loss of autonomy may be offset by a newfound ability to specialize, and with greater specialization, there is less likelihood of direct competition.

A wide range of motivators and risks are associated with collaborative relationships. Depending on the circumstances, different writers have focused on different aspects of this calculus. Benson (1975), for example, placed a much greater emphasis on the potential loss of resources; McCann and Gray (1986) focused on power in collaboration; Litwak and Hylton (1962) saw opportunities in the same situation. Tjosvold (1986) focused on the opportunities to gain information and expertise rapidly, thus creating the capability for program expansion. Others tend to emphasize the economics of services integration (Hassett & Austin, 1997).

Differentiating Collaborative Forms

Managers also need to understand the different types of collaboration, ranging from loosely linked forms that require little investment of time and money to those that are tightly linked and require a huge commitment. At the outset, however, a Cadillac may be unnecessary if a Chevy will do. One way to understand this hierarchy of collaborative forms is to categorize their functions as follows.

Obligational partnerships. Partnerships and networks that come together to exchange resources can be termed *obligational* collaborative forms. They are loosely linked, informal, and often based on personal and friendship relationships. They enable managers to be better boundary spanners. They provide a means of obtaining, via exchange relationships, critical resources such as information and knowledge that are unobtainable through other channels (Bell & Dennis, 1991). Obligational partnerships and networks are built on the principle of reciprocity—you give me something of value, and I will return the favor. They can be ad hoc, formed to meet a time-limited need, or maintained for many years as a useful form of mutual exchange (Mathiesen, 1971). One example is community welfare councils, which survive for decades because they are a good medium of information exchange.

Promotional partnerships. Partnerships and networks that form to accomplish a goal or objective that no single partnership could accomplish on its own, by necessity, must be more tightly linked and formal (if significant investments are required), and they must enable managers to pool their resources through various means (co-location, interagency teams with formal specialization of roles, etc.). Because they function to accomplish an objective, they require a good measure of task coordination as opposed to simple exchange of resources. They can be ad hoc, as when a specific political or legislative objective is tackled and accomplished, or they can survive for long periods of time, but in either case, they represent a meshing of resources and joint action.

Systemic partnerships. Partnerships and networks that form to enable organizations to jointly provide a service or product are a systemic form of collaboration. They are the most tightly linked and formal, and they allow organizations to integrate their resources and human assets. For example, in an integrated service-delivery system, agencies work together via common plans and protocols, and their staffs work together face-to-face from intake through termination. In integrated service systems, clients are not aware of what agency is serving them, nor are they able to differentiate workers in terms of their employers. This form of collaboration is said to be seamless.

Before managers are willing to surrender their autonomy and enter into interdependent relationships with other organizations, they must be convinced that one or more of their organization's needs are paramount. Perceptions about these needs occur singly and in degrees, but when they occur together and are seen as linked together, then their interaction creates greater pressure that forces administrators into collaborative activities (Light, 1997). Which form and function the collaboration takes depends on which of these needs is being sought, and it is an evolutionary process that emerges over time.

The differences among these three forms of collaboration may be difficult to discern because in reality they often overlap. Together, these three basic forms constitute a framework that describes a continuum of collaborative forms, each with different purposes, structures, operations, and outcomes (Alter & Hage, 1993). In simplified form, the theory postulates that interorganizational collaboration requires organizations to communicate and exchange information effectively, and then coordinate resources in joint activities effectively, before they can integrate resources and action effectively. This framework is not intended to be a rigid developmental sequence, however. It is theoretically possible, for example, for a partnership or network to originate as a production system, especially if mandated by law, as in juvenile justice systems. What the theory does assert is that the collective tasks necessary for the first form are also necessary for each succeeding form, for it to be successful.

COLLABORATING AND NETWORKING

New ventures in interorganizational arrangements can produce a broad range of emotions, from great excitement to great anxiety. Managers and staff react in different ways depending on their personalities, worldviews, and experiences with past interorganizational efforts. At the outset, managers as well as staff need to be sanguine about the investment that is necessary to initiate a collaborative effort and realistic about their capacity to take a loss on their investment.

Prerequisites of Collaboration

The strategies of organizational survival discussed above may be obvious to all organizational members, but without certain prerequisites, the chances of success can be limited. The two most important prerequisites are (a) the necessary resources (Litwak & Hylton, 1962) and (b) a willingness to be a risk-taker (Hudson, 1987).

Considerable amounts of time and money are necessary to establish and then maintain interorganizational relationships, and the investment increases from obligational, to promotional, to systemic partnerships. Managers must invest enormous amounts of time in seemingly unproductive social and community activities before ideas and opportunities present themselves. Initial meetings are often unproductive, and numerous starts and stops commonly occur as organizations search for allies who can create truly synergistic and creative relationships. Thus, stakeholders must be realistic about the true costs before initiating collaborative efforts.

Administrators must also have an innate sense of adventure, be horizon scanners, possess a positive attitude toward change, and provide a vision of a different future. They need to view innovation as an evolutionary process that adds value to previous initiatives (Ashkenas, Ulrich, Jick, & Kerr, 1995). To initiate collaboration, managers must not only initiate, motivate, and lead within their own organizations, they must also accomplish the same future-oriented processes with colleagues in other autonomous organizations. Partnerships always require some risk-taking. As in marriage, where each spouse simply trusts the intentions and competencies of the other, so managers must be able to make a similar commitment to an organizational relationship that has no guarantee of success. The capacity to tolerate a degree of uncertainty has always been required to some extent in marriage, as well as in community and policy development arenas. Now, it is also true across the boundaries of organizations.

Initial Phase: Seeking Partners

Developing partnerships and networks is essentially a political process, because power in a partnership or network must be shared. Especially in the initial phases of collaboration, power struggles can erupt between those who are best served by the status quo and those who want to introduce an innovation. Regardless of whether power or persuasion is used, overcoming resistance to change is a political process that requires strategic thinking and skill in negotiation and conflict resolution. This process is also complex because organizations have

mixed motives: that is, organizational members often share some common interests, but also hold some conflicting ones; the resulting relationships are, therefore, simultaneously interdependent and conflicting. Making sense of these cross-cutting motives can be an analytical challenge, but understanding them is essential in building interorganizational partnerships.

Gray (1985) described an approach that is particularly useful in the initial phase of building interorganizational partnerships because it focuses on managers' interpersonal skills. Her approach conceptualizes three basic tasks that must be accomplished if partnerships are to develop successfully: (a) establish communication, (b) develop a shared vision, and (c) establish permanence through trust. As in all political processes, these tasks are not performed in a linear fashion, although that is the way they are described below. In reality, they are integrated parts of a circular process characterized by a considerable amount of reformulation and mutual adjustment. Accomplishment of these tasks is essential for all types of collaboration, whether voluntary or mandated, because all working relationships are hampered without open communication and trust. Although it is true that resistance may be greater when collaboration is mandated, it can certainly occur in any situation. It should be noted that many so-called voluntary associations, when initiated to obtain badly needed resources, may be infused with as much conflict as any mandated relationship. The lesson is that all types of networking require a high level of communication and conflict resolution skills.

Task 1. Establish communication through negotiation and conflict resolution. The first step in seeking new partners is initiation of communication with organizations that may be a "good fit" in terms of unmet goals, history and experience, commonality of vision and values, and complementary resources. To identify likely partners, managers should study the distribution of power and resources horizontally and vertically throughout the community or region. They seek to discover the organizations that have something to gain or lose by the implementation of the collaborative idea, and then they approach those who would profit from it. This identification of potential stakeholders and their enlistment in negotiation is a crucial step, and if important stakeholders are inadvertently left out of the process, sanction for the collaboration may never be obtainable. On the other hand, if organizations are wrongly identified as stakeholders and brought into negotiation, the process can become sidetracked and/or sabotaged. Likewise, if too many organizations are included, the process can be unwieldy. In the initial stage, there is a tendency to include all potential partners for fear of alienating someone; this tendency should be avoided because the process will become so unwieldy it can threaten success.

This sorting out of nonessential actors is vital for successful collaboration and requires skill and patience. Effective sorting is best achieved in an incremental process that occurs in an incredibly large number of interactions both between individuals in informal settings and among groups in semiformal and formal meetings.

Once potential partners are identified and sorted, the objective is to entice stakeholders into a conversational process that centers on the proposal. As discussion proceeds, the task is to analyze potential partners' motives for joining (or not joining) and agreeing to work together toward a common goal. Managers must realize that partner interests may vary along a continuum that ranges from highly objective, such as financial considerations, to very subjective, such as socially constructed values concerning the "right way of doing things." The object of this process is to reconcile potential partners' seemingly divergent motives by identifying where trade-offs can be found. By this process, dissimilar interests may not be so in conflict that they would require partners to compromise on uncompromisable interests. To find this common ground, it is necessary to envision potential partners collectively as a field of mixed motives (Alter, 1990). Managers must place themselves in the middle of these often dissimilar interests. This negotiation process establishes the common ground on which to build the partnership.

Task 2: Develop a common cognitive structure. Once common ground is established, it is essential to develop a "common cognitive structure" (Gray, 1985). Sometimes termed a "shared vision," this is achieved by a process that is often mistakenly overlooked or given short shrift. Careful attention must be given to this process because it ensures that participants have a similar definition of the problem and a common definition of its solution: of what they intend to do and how they intend to do it.

Almost always, people have different cognitive conceptions about the same phenomenon, even though they use similar terms. For successful partnering in the initial stage, all participants must have similar images and definitions of those images. Sometimes, a fully fleshed-out cognitive picture of the goal is all that is needed, but most often a shared and clear understanding of the problem is also necessary. It can also be the case that stakeholders are operating with extremely broad concepts of their goal, such as comprehensive, integrated, and multidisciplinary, and are not aware that going from such an abstraction to an operational model can be difficult and time consuming. Considerable intellectual effort is often needed to translate abstract mental images into concrete plans that are feasible and cost-effective. Managers may be unaware they do not have an implementable model, and thus their expectations of the partnership and the collaborative process may be unrealistic. When operations finally commence, they quickly become frustrated and withdraw prematurely from the partnership. For both of these reasons, time spent on cognitive mapping and logic modeling (Alter & Egan, 1997) is time very well spent.

In communities where partnerships and networks have been tried and failed, the forging of a common cognitive structure can be dominated by retrospective and negative recitals of past failure. Then, the goal becomes avoiding failure—a tautology that is self-defeating. If this is the case, managers should start the planning process by seeking agreement on the goal without specifying the problem. "How can we achieve a place at the table in the managed care environment?" "How can we together provide the best care and support of homeless families in our community?" This is a normative process (Gilbert & Specht, 1977) and is preferable in many situations when it is not necessary to focus on a problem and its causes.

Conflict is often a part of negotiating and a necessary part of achieving common cognitive structures. Managers need to be sensitive to the potential for conflict as well as the potential of using conflict to push the negotiation forward. Differences and incompatible ideas must be resolved, and managers can sometimes use anger to expose contradictions that potential partners would rather hide. Conflict is often necessary to stimulate creative processes whenever change is proposed; it becomes destructive only if it escalates beyond a level at which it can be controlled (Alter, 1990).

Through negotiating communication, then, the potential partners accomplish the process of defining a common cognitive structure. Clearly, and in detail, they must describe the effort they wish to undertake. Considerable time and energy are usually spent in developing a common cognitive structure, because during this phase, the basic ideas about efficacy are thrashed out. Negotiations may at times seem frustrating and futile. These feelings can be tempered if managers remain focused on the goal and keep the development process moving. As the plan is revised through many discussions in which there is a conscious dialectic of conflict and resolution, managers will be able to work potential partners toward a common vision of how a workable collaboration should and could function. Although skeptical in the initial phase of this process, the partners will gradually become more cooperative and enthusiastic.

Achieving a shared cognitive structure also requires that a mutual understanding be reached by all participants regarding their contributions to the joint project and their expectations regarding payoffs for their cooperation. In simple terms, this means that administrators and policymakers, supervised employees, and line staff must be clear about what they are agreeing to do and, in turn, what benefits they expect to receive from their efforts.

Task 3: Achieve trust. There is anecdotal evidence that many partnerships and networks fail or never achieve their potential because the initial phase was never completely addressed or completed. The outcome of successfully reaching consensus on a common cognitive structure is a deeper understanding of each other. This process leads to mutual respect and the concomitant ability to make a substantial commitment to the partnership. This process is called achieving trust.

In a study of collaboration, Bergquist et al. (1995) compiled 55 case studies of partnerships and found they often succeeded or failed, not because of tangible elements such as resources or expertise, but because of the quality of interpersonal relationships. They concluded that successful partners must share something more than the basic bargain they forged.

> Sometimes this is an appreciation for the complementary skills or perspective a partner brings to solving problems . . . or common values or goals . . . or basic human qualities such as integrity, loyalty, kindness, humor, and tolerance . . . or desire to learn from each other. Typically, it is a rich combination of some or all of the above. (Bergquist et al., 1995, p. 65)

One result of fully knowing and understanding a potential partner is that managers begin to identify these desirable resources and qualities and begin to rely on them; to rely on others is to trust them.

Bergquist et al.'s (1995) analysis of trusting relationships is helpful because it is multidimensional; they propose at least three components to a fully trusting relationship. First is trust in intentions. If managers feel that potential partners are interested in every organiza-

tion's welfare, not just their own, then managers will tend to believe that the relationship is based not only on self-interest but also on mutual interest. There is a belief that the partners are committed to an effort in which all will benefit. Second is trust in competency. Managers may believe that a potential partner is very committed to their organization's future, but if they are not convinced the partner has the knowledge and skill to benefit their organization, then they will be reluctant to put their organization's future in the partner's hands. Third is trust in perspective. Managers may have trust in a potential partner's intentions and competence, but if they believe that the partner's worldview is different from theirs and that agreement on a common cognitive structure cannot be embedded within the culture of their organization, then the probability is that in time the partnership will founder on discord and conflict. When managers feel uncertain about a potential partner, it may be because one of these dimensions is missing or perhaps because there is a dissonance between organizations' perspectives. This is a particularly important form of trust when partnerships are composed of individuals from diverse cultures and ethnicity.

In building successful partnerships and networks, the object is to grow trusting relationships into group solidarity and esprit de corps, such that single organizations are willing to surrender autonomy and invest resources. Hechter (1987) believes that group solidarity is a function of two independent elements: (a) the extensiveness of the normative obligations individuals are willing to assume by virtue of their participation in a given group and (b) the extent to which they actually comply with these normative obligations. Hechter's theory holds that the greater the average proportion of each partner's private resources contributed to the collective goal, the greater the solidarity of the group. In other words, partners will give up resources to gain access to collective ones, and they will act in ways consistent with collective standards of conduct out of fear of losing their investment. Thus, when the extensiveness of the obligation is high, solidarity will be high, and vice versa. The emphasis of this model is on the costs and benefits of joining partnerships and networks; the potential loss of autonomy is one of the costs that partners must bear to achieve the group goal.

Of course, interorganizational partnerships and networks are not groups of individuals but task institutions developed to achieve supra-organizational goals. However, the idea that there is a built-in incentive to trust and to be solidly committed to a partnership makes intuitive sense. Managers all have felt at times that they have so much invested in a project that they cannot afford to abandon it. Once time (and time *is* money) is spent on developing a collaboration, there is a correlation between the partners' willingness to trust and stick with the process and the amount of the investment (Hechter, 1987). Although it is not a perfect correlation, leadership can use this inevitable dynamic in subtle ways to keep things together when the going gets tough.

Although the foregoing generalizations regarding trust and commitment seem to apply more to small partnerships, researchers have found that they apply equally to large, interorganizational networks (Bergquist et al., 1995; Tjosvold, 1986). Like individuals, organizations have personalities, values, specific ways of looking at opportunities, and other attributes that make up what is known as organizational culture. Similarly, then, they can clash just as fiercely as two people involved together in a small business. Therefore, establishing open communication systems that can manage conflict is essential for successful partnering between organizations. Likewise, achieving consensus on a shared vision and building trust are also basic ingredients of successful partnerships. Partnerships often fail in part because insufficient time is devoted to these basic tasks, which, if accomplished, lay the foundation for effective and rewarding relationships.

Implementation Phase: Establishing Operational Plans

"Turning vision into value" is the effective management of the relationships that are central to any organization. To be successful, managers need to consider carefully their reasons for forming the partnership and then design structures and processes appropriate and effective for achieving their mission. Of course, governance structures are necessary, but control and coordination of horizontally linked autonomous organizations is distinctly different than the same functions within a single organization. In addition, given different degrees of task integration, decisions about integrative processes should be based on the nature of the work and not on abstract notions about the desirability of integration for its own sake.

Task 1: Establish stable yet flexible governance structures. To maintain a partnership and its shared vision of the future, clear and permanent governance structures and operational processes are necessary. Maintenance of any program requires a governance structure that controls the ongoing operation so that the shared vision will be developed and maintained (Considine, 1988). To minimize program slippage, implementation needs to include decisions about who controls what, when, and how.

The management and leadership role in traditional, hierarchical organizations is one of monitoring and controlling the ongoing operations of the organization (Considine, 1988). By contrast, management of interorganizational arrangements is a matter of achieving control through various methods of collaboration: that is, linking, coordinating, and integrating. Kanter (1994) describes leadership across the boundaries of organizations as essentially one of integration, the most intense form of collaboration. She describes five discrete types of integration: strategic, tactical, operational, interpersonal, and cultural. Achieving strategic integration requires leaders to keep stakeholders informed so that all are fully aware of all aspects of the operation and can, therefore, help one another make decisions and solve problems. Mid-level managers and supervisors accomplish tactical integration by working with their counterparts in developing and implementing the plans and protocols that enable staff to work together effectively and efficiently across the boundaries of their organizations. The third type, operational integration, occurs when adequate resources are provided for day-to-day operations and when the activities of staff are facilitated in a manner that allows them to achieve maximum performance. Interpersonal integration is the development of friendship and trusting relationships among all staff across all levels, which ultimately produces a shared interorganizational culture across the boundaries of all the organizations.

Finally, Kanter (1994) and Bergquist et al. (1995) assert that the most important function of managers' leadership is to empower their employees to use changing environmental conditions in positive ways and to endure the risks of change. As Bergquist et al. note,

> We have consulted to many organizations . . . that were poised on the brink of change, in response to shifting conditions within and surrounding the organization. Yet this change never occurred, in large part because there was neither the courage nor the commitment of leaders in the organization (at all levels) to the necessity of change or to the learning that inevitably accompanies any change process. (p. 45)

When managers join with others to achieve a common goal, they are inevitably forced into change. Exposed to different perspectives and methods, while challenged to find compatible ways of working with new partners, managers must adapt and adjust their methods to be complementary and compatible. Managers should not enter into working agreements with others unless they are willing to integrate their efforts; avoidance of change will almost certainly doom the most altruistic or pragmatic of joint efforts.

Thus, partnerships must have flexible rather than rigid governance structures. Partnerships have a distinct advantage over intraorganizational forms precisely because they can be shaped and reshaped by the partners in response to their changing environments. This emphasis on the necessity to build adaptive interorganizational governance structures seems to contradict the stated need to design clear, permanent mechanisms of control, and to some degree, it does. In fact, partnership structures need to simultaneously control and be flexible. Gray (1985) suggests that as a sense of interdependence among partners increases (Wageman & Baker, 1997), the will to remain steadfast in pursuit of the shared vision while si-multaneously changing and adapting to new contingencies also increases. Creating governance structures that will achieve this dual goal is the major aim of the implementation phase.

Task 2: Establish effective work processes. Above, we asserted that postindustrial society has seen a steady movement toward more complex institutional arrangements and complex collaborative mechanisms. The growth of knowledge in social and biological sciences has meant the recognition of more complex medical and social problems, producing a proliferation of new interventions, agencies, and interorganizational arrangements. Over 30 years ago, Lawrence and Lorsch (1967) hypothesized that as the environment changes rapidly, new and different demands are made of organizations—demands for higher quality and broader ranges of services at lower costs. To meet these demands and compete successfully in the changing environment, organizations must become more complex and differentiated while the tasks that staff perform will become increasingly specialized. Various units and departments take on roles, responsibilities, and styles of operation that differentiate them from other units and departments to which they were previously similar. Many writers point out that this trend is not only inevitable but can be a healthy development for organizations (Alexander & Randolph, 1985). Increasing specialization and task complexity (Brown & Konrad, 1996) leads to interdependencies because workers can no longer perform all of the necessary tasks and must rely on others to accomplish the work of the organization. Thus, the greater the specialization and division of labor of the whole, the greater the need for interdependent parts. Put simply, in complex organizational structures, we need and have to depend on each other.

This trend toward increasing differentiation and specialization applies especially to partnerships and interorganizational networks. The central idea—that structural differentiation demands increasing levels of collaboration and that differentiation and collaboration must increase in tandem for organizations to avoid poor performance—is probably more true of interorganizational collaborations than it is of single organizations (Alter & Hage, 1993). Given this thesis, processes and methods that achieve increasing levels of coordination across the boundaries of organizations must be identified. Put more simply, the more complex the efforts of partnerships and networks, the greater the level of collaboration that must be accomplished.

Above we identified three types of partnerships or networks—obligational, promotional, and systemic—each requiring progressively more complex forms of interorganizational structures and processes. Furthermore, we asserted that partnerships will not be successful until all levels of the participant organizations are working together in a complementary manner. Putting these two ideas together produces Table 14.2, which lists methods for achieving increasing levels of collaboration in service delivery horizontally across the administration/policy-making, program management/supervision, and direct practice levels of autonomous organizations. It should be noted that as the intensity of collaboration increases, the costs of collaboration also increase.

As an example of how the intensity of collaboration can increase, Table 14.2 contrasts refer-

TABLE 14.2 Methods for Increasing Levels of Collaboration in Interorganizational Service-Delivery Systems

Obligational Partnerships/Networks: *Methods of Exchanging and Linking*	*Promotional Partnerships/Networks:* *Methods of Pooling and Meshing*	*Systemic Partnerships/Networks:* *Methods of Integrating*
Policy making/administration		
Referral agreements concerning which agencies (units) will accept what clients under what conditions	Coalitions that make and clarify policies, do collaborative needs assessment and planning, and solve systemic policy problems when they arise	Interagency executive committees that develop seamless services through the pooling of resources and co-location of staff
Resource, acquisition that provides resources needed for interagency referral systems, i.e., MIS systems, computer networks, sufficient staff	Resource acquisition that provides resources necessary for filling service gaps and implementing policies and plans	Joint resource acquisition that provides new resources that benefit the whole system and that support integrated services
Program management/supervision		
Protocols that operationalize the mechanics of a referral system such as information required by all participating agencies, forms to use, procedures to follow, timing, and so on	Program plans that implement coordinated service delivery; define the roles of participating agencies in terms of intake, assessment, and treatment services; and ensure that all program components of the system operate smoothly	Management tools that support the collaborative operation of services: procedures for integrating the hiring, supervising, and evaluating of pooled staff; integrated budgets and operating plans, methods for integrated program evaluation
Direct practice		
In-service training for staff of all participating agencies (units) that provides comprehensive information about services available to clients of the system	Case conferences/interagency staffings that share information about client assessment, planning, and intervention and offer mutual case adjustment/planning opportunities	Interagency teams that jointly do client assessment and develop and implement an integrated case plan
Social and professional functions that promote mutual awareness and understanding between staff who make and receive referrals in participating agencies (units)	Case coordinators who ensure that all necessary client information is shared, detect intervention problems, and negotiate adjustments in participating agencies' case plans if necessary	Case integrators who ensure that all necessary information is shared among participating team members, monitor team members' compliance with the case plan, and mediate changes in the case plan if necessary

ral agreements, coalitions, and interagency executive committees as methods of bringing increasing collaboration to the policy-making and administrative functions of partnerships and networks. Likewise, Table 14.2 contrasts in-service training of participants' staff, interagency case conferences, and permanent interagency teams as means of achieving increasing collaborative intensity among the direct practice staffs of member organizations.

This illustration is cast in the language of service systems—those that collaborate via referral agreements, coordinated service delivery, and truly integrated seamless systems. Nevertheless, it lays out a framework of collaborative methods that can be applied to many other types of interorganizational collaboration.

When partnerships and networks are being implemented, the primary task is to create stable yet flexible governance structures that will support frequent and open communication among partners and preserve the shared vision that brought them together in the first place. The other major task is to create work processes that fit the necessary degree of specialization and produce the required level of collaboration. It is certainly possible to install overly integrative methods that are a waste of resources and everyone's time and energy; it is more likely that insufficient levels of collaboration are used during start-up and implementation. These principles are similar to management practices within all types of complex organizations. The major difference is the absence of traditional management control in networks, which must be replaced by various methods of collaboration, of which there is a vast range.

LESSONS LEARNED

Societies are weak in their interorganizational capability, as compared with their capability at the level of the single organization, though here also, the higher level of interdependence present in the contemporary environment is rendering traditional bureaucratic models dysfunctional. Debureaucratization of single organizations is necessary but not sufficient. Needed also are ad-
vances in institution-building at the level of interorganizational domains.

Eric Trist, 1983

The art of interorganizational practice has not progressed significantly since Eric Trist (1983) wrote 17 years ago that "societies are weak in their interorganizational capability" (p. 283). The problem is that little empirical evidence exists regarding the efficacy of interorganizational partnerships and networks.

The SITO evaluation is one of a limited number of formal interorganizational projects that we have (Agranoff, 1991; Agranoff & Pattakos, 1979). The major findings from these projects were that (a) few projects were implemented quickly enough to satisfy all stakeholders, (b) expectations that service integration would result in cost savings were dashed, and (c) resistance from staff contributed to significant program slippage (Hassett & Austin, 1997).

Based on these findings, the following advice is certainly intuitive if not validated by multiple scientific studies. First, managers and program planners need to have a long-term vision of the possibilities and probabilities of their interorganizational efforts. It can take several years of cultivation and relationship building for a common cognitive structure and trust to develop. This is an incremental process. Small successful efforts that build sequentially toward the goal are absolutely necessary to keep the potential partners engaged and willing to continue their investment. Second, all partners need to have realistic expectations about the short- and long-term outcomes. We would never expect to create a complex social service organization and have it up and running with favorable benchmarks in place within a year. Why, then, would we expect the same or more of partnerships and networks, which must be created without the advantage of intraorganizational control? It depends, of course, on the depth and scope of the collaboration, but effective operational systems take more time and a greater investment across organizational boundaries than within them. Third, if it is important to have clearly defined and behaviorally specific objectives for human service organizations today, then this is especially true of collaborative partnerships. Logic models, if carefully constructed during the planning process by all who will have responsibility for delivering the product, put all stakeholders on the same page and may avoid serious misunderstandings and program slippage as the partnership develops. Fourth, potential partners should prepare at the outset for exit. They should construct ways and means of dissolving the partnership if it does not work. In much the way that a prenuptial agreement can save unnecessary arguments at the time of marital separation or divorce, so preconstructed methods of exit can eliminate misunderstandings and hard feelings when an organizational partnership is forced to dissolve.

The knowledge and documented experience of interorganizational collaboration is limited, partly because federal agencies have only been interested in funding evaluations of large-scale, top-down, integrated service-delivery systems. The fact is that these projects are only the visible tip of the iceberg. In every community and in every service sector, multiple networks of informal, reciprocal, friendship relationships exist among line workers and staff; without them, client services would be far less effective and efficient than they actually are. In building formal interorganizational systems, managers would do well to identify, learn from, and build on the relationships that already exist.

REFERENCES

Agranoff, R. (1991, November/December). Human services integration: Past and present challenges in public administration. *Public Administration Review* (No. 6).

Agranoff, R., & Pattakos, A. N. (1979). Human services integration: Past and present challenges in public administration. *Public Administration Review, 51*(6), 533-542.

Alexander, J., & Randolph, W. A. (1985). The fit between technology and structure as a predictor of performance in nursing subunits. *Academy of Management Journal, 28*(4), 844-859.

Alter, C. (1988). Function, form and change of juvenile justice systems. *Children and Youth Services Review, 10*(2), 71-99.

Alter, C. (1990). Conflict and cooperation in interorganizational service delivery systems. *Academy of Management Journal, 33*(3), 478-502.

Alter, C., & Egan, M. (1997). Logic modeling: A tool for teaching critical thinking in social work practice. *Journal of Social Work Education, 33*(1), 85-102.

Alter, C., & Hage, J. (1993). *Organizations working together.* Newbury Park, CA: Sage.

Argyris, C. (1982). *Reasoning, learning, and action: Individual and organizational.* San Francisco: Jossey-Bass.

Ashkenas, R., Ulrich, D., Jick, T., & Kerr, S. (1995). *The boundaryless organization: Breaking the chains of organizational structure.* San Francisco: Jossey-Bass.

Astley, W. G., & Fombrun, C. J. (1983). Collective strategy: Social ecology of organizational environments. *Academy of Management Review, 8,* 576-587.

Beder, H. (1984). *Realizing the potential of interorgaizational cooperation.* San Francisco: Jossey-Bass.

Bell, G. H., & Dennis, S. (1991). Special needs development, networking, and managing for change. *European Journal of Special Needs Education, 6*(2), 133-146.

Benson, J. (1975). The interorganizational network as a political economy. *Administrative Science Quarterly, 20*(2), 229-249.

Bergquist, W., Betwee, J., & Meuel, D. (1995). *Building strategic relationships: How to extend your organization's reach through partnerships, alliances, and joint ventures.* San Francisco: Jossey-Bass.

Brown, D. W., & Konrad, A. M. (1996). Task complexity and information exchange: The impact of nurses' networking activities on organizational influence. *Sociological Focus, 29*(2), 107-124.

Considine, M. (1988). Bureaucracy and the structure of collaboration. *Australian Journal of Public Administration, 47*(3), 277-280.

Doz, Y. L., & Hamel, G. (1998). *Alliance advantage: The art of creating value through partnering.* Boston: Harvard Business School Press.

Dryfoos, J. D. (1991). *Adolescents at risk: Prevalence and prevention.* New York: Oxford University Press.

Gargiulo, M. (1993). Two-step leverage: Managing constraint in organizational politics. *Administrative Science Quarterly, 38,* 1-19.

Gilbert, N., & Specht, H. (1977). *Planning for social welfare.* Englewood Cliffs, NJ: Presentice-Hall.

Gouldner, A. (1960). The norm of reciprocity. *American Sociological Review, 25*(2), 161-178.

Gray, B. (1985). Conditions facilitating interorganizational collaboration. *Human Relations, 39*(10), 911-936.

Gray, B., & Hay, T. (1986). Political limits to interorganizational consensus and change. *The Journal of Applied Behavioral Science, 22*(2), 95-112.

Hage, J. (Ed.). (1988). *Futures of organizations: Innovating to adapt strategy and human resources to rapid technological change.* Lexington, MA: Lexington Books.

Hage, J., & Powers, C. (1992). *Post-industrial lives.* Newbury Park, CA: Sage.

Hahn, A. P., & Alter, C. (1985). *Clinicians as program planners: Development of a comprehensive multiple sclerosis clinic as a political process.* Unpublished manuscript.

Hassett, S., & Austin, M. J. (1997). Service integration: Something old and something new. *Administration in Social Work, 21*(3/4), 9-29.

Hechter, M. (1987). *Principles of group solidarity.* Berkeley: University of California Press.

Henneman, E. (1995). Nurse-physician collaboration: A poststructuralist view. *Journal of Advanced Nursing, 22,* 359-363.

Henneman, E., Lee, J. L., & Cohen, J. (1995). Collaboration: A concept analysis. *Journal of Advanced Nursing, 21,* 103-109.

Hudson, B. (1987). Collaboration in social welfare: A framework for analysis. *Policy and Politics, 15*(3), 175-182.

Institute for Social and Economic Development. (1998). *Annual report.* Iowa City, IA: Author.

Kamerman, S. B., & Kahn, A. J. (1990). Social services for children, youth, and families in the United States. *Children and Youth Services Review, 12*(1/2), 1-179.

Kanter, R. (1994, July/August). Collaborative advantage. *Harvard Business Review,* 96-108.

Lawrence, P. F., & Lorsch, J. W. (1967). Differentiation and integration in complex organizations. *Administrative Science Quarterly, 12,* 1-47.

Lefton, M., & Rosengren, W. (1966). Organizations and clients: Lateral and longitudinal dimensions. *American Sociological Review, 31*(6), 802-810.

Light, D. W. (1997). From managed competition to managed cooperation: Theory and lessons from the British experience. *The Milbank Quarterly, 75*(3), 297-341.

Litwak, E., & Hylton, L. F. (1962). Towards the theory and practice of coordination between formal organizations. In W. Rosengren & M. Lefton (Eds.), *Organizations and clients* (pp. 137-186). Columbus, OH: Charles E. Merrill.

Mathiesen, T. (1971). *Across the boundaries of organizations.* Berkeley, CA: Flendessary Press.

McCann, J. E., & Gray, B. (1986). Power and collaboration in human service domains. *The International Journal of Sociology and Social Policy, 6*(3), 58-67.

Menefee, D. T., & Thompson, J. J. (1994). Identifying and comparing competence for social work management: A practice driven approach. *Administration in Social Work, 18*(3), 1-25.

Morrison, T. (1996). Partnership and collaboration: Rhetoric and reality. *Child Abuse & Neglect, 20*(2), 127-140.

O'Connor, G. G., & McCord, L. (1990/1991). Networking among social service providers: An expanded and transformed practice. *The Journal of Applied Social Sciences, 15*(1), 7-29.

O'Looney, J. (1993). Beyond privatization and service integration: Organizational models for service delivery. *Social Service Review, 4,* 502-534.

O'Looney, J. (1994). Modeling collaboration and social services integration: A single state's experience with developmental and nondevelopmental models. *Administration in Social Work, 18*(1), 61-86.

Perlman, R. (1975). *Consumers and social services.* New York: John Wiley.

Provan, K. G. (1984). Technological and interorganizational activity as predictors of client referrals. *Academy of Management Journal, 27*(4), 811-829.

Sosin, M. (1985). Social problems covered by private agencies: An application of niche theory. *Social Service Review, 59,* 75-93.

Tjosvold, D. (1986). The dynamics of interdependence in organizations. *Human Relations, 39*(4), 517-540.

Trist, E. (1983). Referent organizations and the development of interorganizational domains. *Human Relations, 36*(1), 269-284.

Wageman, R., & Baker, G. (1997). Incentives and cooperation: The joint effects of task and reward interdependence on group performance. *Journal of Organizational Behavior, 18,* 139-158.

Yuen, F., & Owens, J. (1996). Power in partnership. *International Journal of Nursing Practice, 2,* 138-141.

CHAPTER FIFTEEN

The Manager as Leader

DAVID BARGAL

Managerial leadership plays a central role in the administration of organizations in general, and social service organizations in particular. It assumes the main responsibility for their establishment and maintenance, as well as for their adaptation to changing conditions. The indispensable role of managerial leadership is also highlighted by the changing internal and external conditions of the organization's environment. Human service organizations, which aim at changing people and/or the social conditions in which they live, operate within very uncertain circumstances and use indefinite technologies. Thus, the role of human service managerial leadership has become even more pivotal, as will be pointed out in this chapter.

The first section will present definitions of leadership and managerial leadership, as developed in the context of business organization theory and social psychology, with emphasis on differences between leadership and management. The issue of effectiveness in the managerial role will be discussed with respect to organizations in general and human service organizations in particular. Four major leadership approaches formulated during the 20th century will be discussed: the trait approach, the leadership-style approach, the contingency approach, and the new leadership approach. In the context of the new leadership approach, emphasis is placed on the distinction between the transactional and transformational types. In addition, feminine leadership theory will be described briefly. The main part of the chapter will deal with components of leadership effectiveness in human service organizations. The chapter will conclude with the implications of leadership theories for selecting, developing, and fostering managers in human services and suggestions for further needed research.

DEFINITIONS OF LEADERSHIP

The theoretical and empirical literature dealing with the manager's role in organizations draws largely on knowledge developed under the rubric of leadership (Yukl, 1994). Theoreticians define leadership according to their individual orientation and the aspect of the construct on which it focuses. In this connection, Stogdill (1974) concluded that "there are almost as many definitions of leadership as there are persons who attempted to define the concept" (p. 259). A recent review lists over 7,000 books, articles, and presentations dealing with the subject (Bass, 1990).

Nonetheless, numerous definitions emphasize influence processes as the core behavior of leaders. For example, Hogan, Curphy, and Hogan (1994) maintain that

> Leadership involves persuading other people to set aside for a period of time their individual concerns and to pursue a common goal that is important for the responsibilities and welfare of a group. . . . Thus, leadership concerns building cohesive and goal-oriented teams; there is a causal and definitional link between leadership and team performance. (p. 493)

This definition represents the traditional social psychological research perspective of leadership and leadership processes.

Burns (1978) offered a different definition of leadership, which represents the new leadership paradigm to be elaborated on below:

> Leaders induce followers to act for certain goals that represent the values and motivations—the

wants and needs, the aspirations and expectations—*of both leaders and followers* [emphasized in the original], and the genius of leadership lies in the manner in which leaders see and act on their own and their followers' values and motivations. (p. 19)

Burns's definition represents a different school of thought and reflects an approach based on holistic, humanistic, and transactional perspectives. Followers and leaders are perceived as possessing values, needs, and aspirations. Those exhibiting leadership aim toward mutual fulfillment of both parties' needs. However, as emphasized in the definition, there are also qualities of behavior that reflect the so-called "genius of leadership" and distinguish between those who actually achieve leadership and those who fall short of it.

These definitions represent two poles on a continuum of leadership types. At one end, leadership is portrayed in terms of influence processes, group cohesiveness, and goal attainment; this is one of the dominant research paradigms in much of the leadership literature. At the opposite end, represented by Burns's definition and its derivatives, are transactional and transformational leadership types in the new leadership paradigm. These two leadership paradigms represent, in large measure, the history of research and theory on leadership to be discussed briefly in the section on "Leading Schools of Research on Leadership."

LEADERSHIP AND MANAGEMENT

One of the ongoing controversies in the leadership literature focuses on the distinction between leadership and management. Yukl (1989), for example, maintains that a person can be a leader without being a manager and that a person can be a manager without leading. In line with this notion, Bennis and Nanus (1985) suggest that "managers are people who do things right, and leaders are people who do the right things" (p. 21). The first sharp distinction between leaders and managers was made by Zaleznik (1989), who claimed,

> The crucial difference between managers and leaders is in their respective commitments. A manager is concerned with how decisions get made and how communication flows; a leader is concerned with what decision gets made and what he or she communicates. (pp. 19-20)

In contrast, Yukl (1989, 1994) maintains that there is a considerable overlap between leadership and management. According to this view, it is impossible to resolve the controversy about the distinction between leadership and management at this stage of the development of the discipline. He therefore proposes that the terms *manager* and *leader* be used interchangeably, as in the following list of manager/leader activities:

> Influence processes affecting the interpretation of events for followers, the choice of objectives for the group or organization, the organization of work activities to accomplish the objectives, the motivation of followers to achieve the objectives, the maintenance of cooperative relationships and teamwork, and the enlistment of support and cooperation from people outside the group or organization. (1994, p. 5)

This definition encapsulates many components introduced by the leading schools of research on leadership, as described in the following section.

LEADING SCHOOLS OF RESEARCH ON LEADERSHIP

Four major approaches formulated during the 20th century focus on the explanation of the leadership phenomenon: trait, style, contingency, and the new leadership paradigm. The first three approaches represent the components of the earlier, dominant definition of leadership in the professional literature: influence processes, group cohesiveness, and goal accomplishment. To the other extreme, the new leadership paradigm is characterized in reciprocal terms, that is, the needs and values of leaders and followers, as well as in terms of the rich and complex interrelationships that take into account symbolic communication as well as contextual factors such as the economic, historical, and political conditions in which the organization operates (Bargal & Schmid, 1989). The following analysis will begin with the trait approach, the earliest approach, which has recently gained renewed interest.

The Trait Approach

The trait approach, which prevailed from 1930 to 1950, emphasizes the personal attributes of leaders on the assumption that "leaders are born rather than made." Research based on this approach has focused on personal characteristics of leaders such as physical appearance, intelligence, need for power, achievement, and dominance.

At the end of the 1950s, the trait approach was abandoned owing to lack of valid research results revealing a pattern of traits that could predict effective leadership and management behavior. With the advancement of personality research and theory in the mid-1970s, the contribution of traits to understanding leadership and management behavior has been reconsidered. In a review of findings from studies based on the trait approach, House and Aditya (1997) emphasize the following three points. First, a number of traits appear to consistently differentiate leaders from others: physical energy, a higher level of intelligence than followers, and prosocial influence motivation (House & Baetz, 1979), as well as adaptability, flexibility, self-confidence, and achievement motivation. Second, the impact of traits on the effectiveness of leaders depends on the extent to which the traits are relevant to the situation at hand. For example, achievement motivation may predict effectiveness and success when the tasks are challenging and require a high degree of initiative and personal responsibility. Third, traits have a stronger impact on the behavior of leaders when the situational characteristics allow for expression of the individual dispositions. In sum, these findings suggest that personality is an important predictor of performance effectiveness and should therefore be carefully considered in the process of selection and promotion of organizational managers.

The Style Approach

During the late 1940s and early 1950s, the focus of research shifted from leadership traits to patterns of behavior, or leadership styles. The style approach, formulated by Bales (1954), Stogdill and Coons (1957), and Likert (1961), still influences contemporary leadership theory, training, and development. Bowers and Seashore (1966) examined subordinates of leaders in various organizations. Subjects completed a questionnaire consisting of a list of general statements about leadership behavior and were asked to indicate the extent to which each statement reflected the behavior of their own leader. Analysis of the responses revealed two main patterns of leadership behavior: One pattern, *consideration,* characterizes a style in which leaders are concerned about their subordinates as individuals. These leaders are trusted by their subordinates and promote good interpersonal relationships within the organization. The other pattern, *initiating structure,* refers to a leadership style that defines the subordinates' tasks and actively monitors their performance. Scores for leaders were calculated along these two dimensions. The main criticism of the style approach is that "little thought was given to the specific role demands of leaders, the context in which they functioned, or differences in dispositions of leaders and followers" (House & Aditya, 1997, p. 421).

The Contingency Approach

The contingency approach, developed during the 1960s, views situational variables as the most important for understanding leadership behavior. The following are the main theories representing this approach: the contingency theory of leadership (Fiedler, 1967, 1971), path-goal theory of leadership effectiveness (House, 1971; House & Mitchell, 1974), life-cycle theory (Hersey & Blanchard, 1982), cognitive theory (Fiedler & Garcia, 1987), and decision process theory (Vroom & Yetton, 1973).

In a later evaluation of these leadership theories, Yukl (1989) points out some of their limitations. Specifically, it was found that the key variables are usually defined in general terms and are difficult to measure. Moreover, all the contingency theories address situational variables but are often ambiguous (e.g., task complexity). Moreover, according to Yukl (1989), managers may find these variables difficult to translate into specific guidelines—although the main contribution of this approach is its recognition of the leader's need to take contextual factors into account.

The New Leadership Approach

In contrast to the three schools of leadership described above, which were derived from the social psychological tradition, the new leadership approach is anchored in Burns's (1978) concept of leadership. According to Burns, leaders "see and act on their own and their followers' motivations" (p. 19). The term *new leadership* encompasses several approaches toward leadership that originated in the mid-1980s and focus on common themes (Bryman, 1992). Specifically, Bargal and Schmid (1989) refer to the following categories of leadership: the leader as a creator of vision and strategic architect (Bennis & Nanus, 1985; Mintzberg & Waters, 1983; Sashkin, 1988; Westley & Mintzberg, 1989), the leader as creator and changer of organizational culture (Schein, 1985, 1992), and transactional and transformational leadership (Bass, 1985; Bass, 1997; Tichy & Devana, 1986).

The leader as creator of vision, culture, and strategic architect. The leader has been perceived and described as the creator of vision for the organization. According to Bennis (1983) and Bennis and Nanus (1985), vision is the capacity to create and communicate a compelling picture of a desired state of affairs, to impart clarity to this vision (paradigm, context, frame),

and to induce commitment to it. Bennis and Nanus (1985) based their findings on unstructured interviews with 90 executive directors whose records revealed extraordinary organizational achievements. About 30 of the directors were drawn from public organizations, including cultural and artistic foundations.

Mintzberg and Waters (1983) used the term *strategy building* to describe a process similar to that of creating vision. Future plans, or strategies, are developed as a consequence of interacting processes originating in the environment, the organization, and its leaders. Leaders who engage in conceiving strategies are described by Mintzberg and Waters (1983) as concept attainers.

According to this approach, the leaders create and change their group's culture (Schein, 1985, 1992). Schein maintains that leaders play a central role in creating and instilling organizational values, ideology, and norms in the organizational setting. Particularly at the founding stage, the leader's guidance regarding preferred ways to cope with problems also reduces anxiety among group members and helps them deal with the new reality. This contributes both directly and indirectly toward better accomplishment of goals.

In the same vein, Pondy (1978) proposed that leadership should be perceived as the shaping of meanings and the creation of language. According to this view, leadership effectiveness is based on the leader's "ability to make activity meaningful for those in his role set—not to change behavior but to give others a sense of understanding of what they are doing, and especially to articulate it, so they can communicate about the meaning of their behavior" (p. 94).

Transformational and transactional leadership. Bass (1985) formulated a typology of transformational and transactional leadership. Although the typology derives from Burns's (1978) conceptualization, it is anchored in empirical research. In these studies, business executives, agency administrators, and U.S. army colonels responded to a list of statements regarding leadership behavior (Bass, 1985, 1997; Bass & Avolio, 1993).

These studies revealed four interrelated components of transformational leadership behavior: idealized influence, inspirational motivation, intellectual stimulation, and individualized consideration (Bass, 1997). *Idealized influence* refers to the ability of leaders to display conviction, emphasize trust, take stands on controversial issues, present their most important values, and emphasize the importance of purpose, commitment, and ethical consequences of decisions. From this point of view, leaders are admired as role models; generate pride, loyalty, and confidence; and mobilize support in pursuit of a common cause. *Inspirational motivation* refers to the ability of leaders to articulate an appealing vision of the future, to challenge followers with high standards, to express enthusiasm, and to provide encouragement. *Intellectual stimulation* refers to the ability of leaders to question old assumptions, traditions, and beliefs; to stimulate new perspectives and ways of doing things in others; and to encourage expression of new ideas and reasoning. *Individualized consideration* refers to the ability of leaders to deal with others as individuals; to consider individual needs, abilities, and aspirations; to listen attentively; and to further the development of individuals, as well as to advise, teach, and coach (Bass, 1997).

Similarly, four components of transactional leadership were defined, as follows: *Contingent reward:* Leaders engage in exchange of rewards for performance, clarify expectations, and negotiate for resources. *Active management by exception:* Leaders monitor followers' performance and take corrective action if deviations from standard occur. *Passive management by exception:* Leaders fail to intervene until problems become serious. Action is not taken until mistakes are brought to their attention. *Laissez-faire leadership:* A non-leadership behavior, in which leaders avoid accepting their responsibilities, are absent when needed, fail to follow up requests for assistance, and resist expressing their views on important issues.

Regarding the various components of the two types of leadership, the researchers have concluded that "transformational leadership tends to be most effective, followed in order of effectiveness by contingent reward, active management by exception, passive management by exception, and laissez-faire leadership" (Bass, 1997, p. 134). In the existing research literature, little attention has been paid to contextual influences on transformational leadership. In this connection, a recent study by Pawar and Eastman (1997) presents four contextual factors that may affect organizational receptivity to transformational leadership:

1. The organization performs during a period of change and development.
2. The organization engages in environmental exchanges (boundary-spanning).
3. The organizational structure is simple rather than bureaucratic.
4. The mode of governance is clan-type (Wilkins & Ouchi, 1983), where members of the orga-

nization emphasize strong identification with collective values.

FEMININE LEADERSHIP THEORIES

The title of this section is an umbrella term encompassing different perspectives for analysis of women's leadership roles in organizations. Calas and Smircich (1996) take this concept to an extreme in their assertion that there are different theories (liberal, radical, psychoanalytic, Marxist, socialist, post-structuralist, and third-world approaches) that deal not only with leadership issues of women but with "feminist approaches to organization studies." The authors further contend that "despite their diversity, most feminist theories share some assumptions, notably the recognition of male dominance in social arrangements and a desire for changes from this form of domination" (p. 219). Owing to the wealth of literature dealing with feminine theories of leadership and organizations, the current chapter will limit itself to the above general description and later mention some implications of this approach for executive behavior in human service organizations (for a detailed, comprehensive discussion of women's leadership issues, see Calas & Smircich, 1996).

LEADERSHIP THEORIES AND EFFECTIVE PERFORMANCE IN HUMAN SERVICE ORGANIZATIONS

There is a dearth of literature on leadership and management effectiveness, despite the central importance of this issue to organizations (Yukl, 1994). The complexity of the issue is highlighted by the unique structural features of human service organizations. The following discussion will begin by examining leadership effectiveness and its evaluation in the general organizational literature. Afterward, the specific context of human services will be explored.

Yukl (1994) refers to leadership effectiveness "in terms of the consequences of the leaders' actions for followers and other organizations' stakeholders" (p. 5). According to this view, research on leadership should include "a variety of different criteria . . . and examine the separate impact of the leader on each criterion over an extended period of time" (p. 7). Campbell, Dunnette, Lawler, and Weick (1970) proposed a person-process-product model of managerial effectiveness. In this model, *person* refers to managers' competencies, such as motivation, communication, and problem solving; *product* refers to an organizational outcome, such as productivity or volume of sales; and *process* refers to the manager's influences on job activities.

Several research findings have revealed contributing factors to leadership effectiveness. Allen (1981) found that successful outcomes of a school principal's performance depend on his or her selection of appropriate roles to enact for a given situation. Similarly, a study of 24 managers in a medical insurance company (Komaki, Zlotnik, & Jensen, 1986) revealed that effective leaders are more active than ineffective leaders. In addition, it was found that these managers were closer to their employees and provided contingent reinforcement. In a study of 109 chief executive officers (CEOs), Stagner (1969) found that time spent in organizational planning was related to firm profitability. In a comparison of 30 effective and 30 ineffective executives, Williams (1968) found that planning activity contributes toward organizational effectiveness. Bray, Campbell, and Grant (1974) found that planning skills measured in AT&T assessment centers was one of the best predictors of subsequent managerial success. In a similar vein, Lake and Martinko (1982) found that highly effective principals spent more time with people outside of the school and were more active in initiating those contacts than moderately effective principals. Numerous additional studies cite evidence of different positive correlations between some of the independent variables and criteria for effectiveness.

Human service organizations are characterized by some unique features that differentiate them from business organizations. Their main objective is to "change people and/or the social conditions in which they live" (Patti, 1987, p. 7); their raw material is personality, attitudes, perceptions, and emotions. Technologies employed to change people and their social conditions are uncertain and often ambiguous. The main vehicle for effecting change is professionals and their repertoire of interventions. Given the human raw material and the uncertain intervention technologies, it is even more difficult to measure effectiveness (D'Aunno, 1992; Hasenfeld, 1983, 1992).

According to Poertner and Rapp (1983), the impact of directors on effectiveness of social service agencies is reflected in three kinds of outcomes: success in effecting changes in the clients served and in their environmental conditions; "service quality, or the extent to which the organization is competently implementing methods and techniques that are thought necessary to achieve service objectives" (p. 8); and client satisfaction with the services rendered to them. This list also includes measures of work-

ers' satisfaction, professional competencies, and a relatively lower rate of burnout and turnover (Glisson, 1989; Guterman & Bargal, 1996; Malka, 1989).

Campbell et al.'s (1970) person-process-product model of managerial effectiveness was applied as follows to the arena of human service organizations. The components of the model derive from leadership and management theory, as well as from theory and research presented in previous sections of this chapter. In addition, the model applies literature on social work practice and research in an attempt to understand how to promote effective performance in social service agencies. It should be noted that there is no linear correspondence between the columns in Figure 15.1.

Figure 15.1 presents a model of leadership effectiveness in human service organizations, which focuses on three main categories of components: person, process, and products. The model assumes that personality traits, knowledge, and skills combine with performance of appropriate managerial activities to yield organizational products that are considered effective outcomes according to the organizations' mission and goals (Patti, 1987).

The following description elaborates on the three categories of components listed in Figure 15.1, beginning with column A.

Motives and traits. As mentioned, trait theory assumes that the motives and traits of managers and leaders play an important role in predicting their effectiveness. A motive, according to Locke et al. (1991), is a wish that moves a person to action. Locke et al. (1991) use the term *drive* in reference to several motives. The literature documents findings indicating rela-

Person (A)	Process (B)	Products (C)
1. Motives and traits: • Drive (achievement, ambition, initiative) • Self-confidence • Flexibility • Charisma • Professional worldview 2. Knowledge • Formal education in social welfare and social work • Knowledge of the particular human service organization and its intervention 3. Skills • Management skills: goal setting, planning, problem solving, managing resources, managing organization-environment relations • Interpersonal skills: listening, communicating, networking	1. Task-oriented activities • Creating a vision • Creating a professional culture • Intellectual stimulation • Delegating authority • Empowering • Involving subordinates in decision making • Inspiring 2. Relations-oriented activities • Individualized consideration, mentoring • Conflict management • Support • Rewards	1. Changes in clients served and their environmental conditions 2. Service quality 3. Client satisfaction 4. Highly satisfied and committed professional staff who reveal low rates of burnout and turnover

Figure 15.1. Components of Leadership Effectiveness in Human Service Organizations

tively high achievement motivation among leaders (Bass, 1990), in addition to high ambition, energy, and initiative. Leaders or managers in human service organizations are called on to carry out their mission in the face of many obstacles. Meinert, Ginsberg, and Keys (1993) present data from 92 CEOs at state social, mental health, and corrective service departments. When asked about the serious problems they face in their organizations, over 50% of the respondents cited inadequate resources, insufficient staff, poor public reputation, and federal policy restrictions and regulations. In a narrative account called "Reflection on Effective Leadership," Susan Blumenfield (1995), director of the Department of Social Work Services

at Mount Sinai Hospital in New York City, wrote the following:

> Leadership in today's health care social work may require the energy and strategic skills of an Attila (the king of the Hun), but it must be tempered with the vision of Jane Addams, the intellect of Gordon Hamilton, and the know-how of a Harvard MBA. (p. 21)

Self-confidence is another important trait characterizing successful leaders. This trait, which is defined as having assurance in one's own ideas and skills (Bennis & Nanus, 1985; Burns, 1978), plays a central role in making decisions, persuading subordinates, and empowering others. Reflecting on his effective leadership as a social work director in health care, Spitzer (1995) writes, "It is up to the director to have a sense of self-confidence as well as communicate a sense of belief in other's capacities" (p. 106).

Flexibility is a trait needed by human service leaders to deal with rapid changes in their organizational environments (Bass, 1990). If human service leaders are too set in their ideas, the organization may not adapt to changes in its environment and may end up with fewer resources to cope with their clients' needs.

Charisma, which was first introduced into the organizational literature by Weber (1947), has recently become a widely studied trait of leadership (Bass, 1985; Conger & Kanungo, 1987, 1988). Charisma can be defined as the power to arouse emotions in others, and it is an inherent aspect of relations between leaders and followers. The greatest merit of charisma is its role in reducing "resistance to attitude change in followers . . . arousing emotional responses toward the leader and a sense of excitement and adventure" (Bass, 1985, p. 56). Professional worldview is a characteristic shared by all human service professionals, providing them with a rationale for intervention in human misery (Meinert et al., 1993). According to Bargal (1982),

> It means that its protagonist applies a system of value judgment to a whole range of subjects which encompass four main elements (Levy, 1973): Preferred images of people; goals to be striven for with respect to those who are the objects of his or her concern; the means to be used to achieve the professional goals and a social vision, that is a future plan concerning human beings in their environments. (p. 11)

In human service organizations characterized by goal ambiguity and uncertain intervention

technologies, it is particularly important to have a leader with an innovative and inspiring worldview.

Knowledge. Component 2 in column A, *person,* refers to knowledge. As can be seen, knowledge is an important part of leadership success. Two types of knowledge are presented here: formal education in social welfare and related fields, including policies, financing, and institutional arrangements in particular fields of service that constitute important elements of the task environment; and knowledge of the particular human service organization one heads.

Meinert et al. (1993), who focus on performance characteristics of CEOs in social services, found that they have formal education and training in social work and related areas. However, in reference to directors of business organizations, Bennis and Nanus (1985) report that only 40% of the effective leaders participating in their study had received degrees. Kotter (1982) and Garbarro (1987) found that successful managers had in-depth knowledge about the organization they headed. With regard to human service managers, these findings emphasize the importance of understanding the intricacies of their organization's administrative structure and the clinical services provided by the organization. These conclusions are also in line with Gowdy, Rapp, and Poertner's (1993) approach toward organizational performance, which focuses on client-centered practice.

Skills. The third component in column A, skills refers to training and competence in two realms: managerial and interpersonal. Managerial skills are crucial for carrying out the daily activities of the human service agency or organization (Ezell, Menefee, & Patti, 1989;

Glisson, 1989; Kotter, 1982; Menefee & Thompson, 1994; Patti, 1977; Patti & Rauch, 1978). Whereas Ezell et al. (1989) and Glisson (1989) emphasize more traditional management skills of managers in social service organizations, Menefee and Thompson (1994) reveal a major shift in prioritizing of managerial functions by social service managers. To quote the authors,

> The study suggests a transformation in the role of the social work manager that is evidenced by substantive changes in the scope, complexity, and priority of the competencies and skills required. . . . The role has shifted from one focused on internal operations to one that is strategically oriented. . . . They now give equal if not more attention to the entire context of service delivery by actively monitoring and managing the boundary between the external environment and internal organizational arrangements. (pp. 13-14)

Interpersonal skills are important for leadership behavior, which focuses continuously on interaction between the leader and followers. Research has shown that successful leaders generally have highly developed interpersonal skills, are sensitive to others, and can communicate emphatically with colleagues and subordinates (Bennis & Nanus, 1985; Menefee & Thompson, 1994; Yukl, 1994).

Column B of Figure 15.1 represents the main activities that leader-managers of human service organizations are expected to perform. Most of the components in this column are based on the new leadership approach, although the categories *task-oriented activities* and *relations-oriented activities* derive from the leadership-style approach (see description above). The leadership-style components *initiation of structure* and *consideration* appear in the same column, to emphasize their combined impact on the activities of the human service

manager. Each of these components is elaborated on in column B.

Task-Oriented Activities

Creating a vision: Leaders of the human service organizations are expected to formulate their vision (Bennis & Nanus, 1985). For this purpose, they need to accomplish the following (Locke et al., 1991): gathering information, processing information, conceptualizing the vision, and evaluating the vision. Information is gathered both inside and outside the organization. Afterward, the leader analyzes and synthesizes the information and formulates a proposed plan, or defines "a clearly articulated vision of the purpose that is at once simple, easily understood, clearly desirable and energizing" (Bennis & Nanus, 1985, p. 103). The vision statement should be brief, clear, abstract, and future-oriented. It is subject to continuous evaluation and modification as it is implemented and as internal and external conditions of the organization change (Locke et al., 1991). In a study of 168 top executive directors of nonprofit human services, Shin and McClomb (1998) defined four different leadership styles that affect the leader's tendency to innovate: motivator, analyzer, vision setter, and task master. Of the four styles, the vision setter was found to be strongly related to frequency of innovation. Based on these findings, the authors concluded "that leadership style is a dominant factor in organization innovation when compared to other possible influences such as organizational characteristics and environmental pressure" (p. 16). In line with these results, Steiner, Gross, Ruffolo, and Murray (1994) refer to the vision-building phase as part of the strategic planning process in human services.

Creating a professional culture within human service organizations plays an important role in achieving effectiveness. Professional culture can promote client-centered practice (Gowdy et al., 1993) as well as continuous development, training, and supervisory support for staff. When the professional culture is congruent with organizational goals and needs of personnel, turnover rates will be substantially reduced (Sheridan, 1992). In this organizational culture, the manager also plays a key role in lending significance and logic to the often frustrating task of human service providers, not to mention the manager's central contribution toward introducing new ideas and knowledge. Grasso (1994) studied the relationship between treatment-team supervisory management style, service effectiveness, and job satisfaction in a family treatment and child care agency. Whereas the supervisory management style correlated positively with workers' satisfaction, it did not correlate positively with service effectiveness.

Regarding the component of *intellectual stimulation* (Bass, 1997), managers play a key role in providing social workers with new knowledge to be applied for the benefit of clients. In the same vein, Shera and Page (1995) maintain that by empowering followers (i.e., human service staff), managers can enable them to improve their performance with clients. The authors suggest "detailed structural relational and technological strategies that can be used to empower workers in human service organizations" (p. 2). These strategies highlight the importance of involving human service professionals in the agency's decision-making processes. However, the few systematic studies on this topic (Packard, 1993; Ramsdell, 1994) reveal a low rate of staff participation in decision making at social service agencies. Schmid

(1992) found a relationship between decentralized authority and organizational effectiveness, which also speaks for delegation of managerial power and involvement of staff in administrative processes.

Relations-Oriented Activities

The second section of column B in Figure 15.1 deals with relations-oriented activities of leaders in human service organizations. *Individualized consideration* is described above as part of the repertoire of transformational leaders (Bass, 1997), and *mentoring* is defined by Yukl (1994) as providing coaching, career advice, and facilitation of skills acquisition and professional development of staff members. In the field of social work, professional development takes place continuously on the job, owing to uncertain intervention technologies and the changing client population. Schon (1984) referred to this type of professional development as "reflection in action," which may be promoted by systematic professional mentoring. Several studies have shown that support from supervisors and managers contributes toward preventing burnout, increasing job satisfaction, and reducing tendency to leave jobs among social service workers (Bargal & Guterman, 1996; Himle, Jayaratne, & Thyness, 1989; Jayaratne, Tripodi, & Chess, 1983). The final component of managerial activity in this category focuses on conflict management. Two main types of conflicts arise in organizations: personal and ideological. Personal conflicts may ensue as a result of interpersonal differences between employees and team leaders. The second may reflect differences in prioritizing objectives, choosing intervention strategies, and formulating policy principles. Social service managers are called on to facilitate constructive resolution of these conflicts and encourage cooperation and identification with the goals of the service as a whole (Yukl, 1994).

The four categories of components in column C of Figure 15.1 (Products), which represent effective performance in human services, focus mainly on fulfillment of the organization's goals, that is, changing clients and environmental conditions through high-quality service that satisfies consumers. The literature regarding changes in clients' attitudes and behavior is controversial. Because clients of human service organizations are rarely asked to provide feedback about the treatment they receive, very little is known about the extent of their satisfaction with the services rendered or about their evaluations of service quality. Most of the research on relationships between leadership inputs and organizational performance relates to employee satisfaction, support, and prevention of burnout and turnover (Bargal & Guterman, 1996; Glisson, 1989; Grasso, 1994; Guterman & Bargal, 1996; Malka, 1989).

SUMMARY AND DISCUSSION

The review of research on leadership theories during the 20th century provides human service managers with a wealth of information that may improve their performance and contribute to better service effectiveness. House and Aditya's (1997) conclusions about the contribution of certain traits to successful performance of leaders reflect selection criteria that may be applied toward recruitment and selection of human service managers. The leadership-style model highlighted the importance of combining task-oriented and relationship-oriented activities in management of social service agencies. The new leadership paradigm and its main representatives (Bass, 1985, 1997; Bennis & Nanus, 1985; Schein, 1992) have proposed a set of activities (e.g., individualized consideration and inspiration) that may change the quality of leadership in human services but are not easily found in ordinary managers. Pawar and Eastman's (1997) theoretical propositions reveal the contextual conditions for optimal application of the paradigm.

On the whole, Figure 15.1 reflects the difficulty of designing research that can evaluate the multifactorial relationships between person-process and products as measures of leadership effectiveness in human services. In the same vein, Grasso (1994) arrived at the same conclusions regarding future research designs for measurement of leadership effectiveness in the human services. An alternative research strategy that has yet to be applied in human service organizations may be modeled after Peters and Waterman's (1982) study of 10 successful business organizations. In the same vein, recent research conducted by Porras and Collins (1994) was based on a holistic case study approach to study entire systems of successful business organizations and formulate a set of generalizations that may be applied by theorists and organizational leaders in different settings. A comprehensive longitudinal study might examine different types of social welfare organizations according to the categories proposed by Patti (1987): social control, social care and maintenance, socialization and prevention, restoration and rehabilitation, and advocacy and social change. The model proposed in Figure 15.1 could then be analyzed in an attempt to ascertain the relationships between its components, particularly those deriving from the new leadership approach (Bass, 1997; Bass & Avolio, 1993).

Additional issues relate to social service managers as leaders, women and leadership in the social services, and training for leadership in social service organizations.

Regarding women and leadership in social services, research findings reveal that the percentage of women in managerial positions in U.S. industries has risen from 18% in 1970 (Johnston & Packer, 1987) to about 40% in 1989 (Jacobs, 1992). At the same time, however, the proportion of women in administrative social work positions is on the decline (Chess, Norlin, & Jayaratne, 1987; Haynes, 1989). Although the reason for this decline is unknown, it may be attributed to budgetary cutbacks and layoffs in the social services. It may also reflect a biased approach toward women in management, rooted either in political-economic conditions (Martin & Chernesky, 1989) or in social-psychological stereotypes (Ezell, 1993). Recent literature on women and managerial effectiveness rules out gender-based inferiority (Eagly, Karau, & Makhijani, 1995) and suggests that the biased approach should be changed in light of women's massive presence in the helping professions.

Finally, regarding the likelihood of training and developing managers into leaders in human service organizations, it should be noted that because social work is based on belief in the ability of individuals to change (e.g., clients, family members, community leaders), the same principle may be applied to social service managers. The literature regarding business organizations reports tremendous investment in leadership training. Bass and Avolio (1993) express considerable optimism about the prospects of turning nonprofit managers into effec-

tive transformational leaders. In line with these findings, Conger (1992) also suggests four main approaches to leadership training: personal growth approaches, conceptual approaches, feedback approaches, and skill-building approaches.

In sum, the evidence indicates that leadership can be learned, or at least the functioning of leaders can be considerably improved through careful training and coaching. This is encouraging for clients and employees of human service organizations. If transformational and effective leaders can be developed in those organizational settings, the result will be, as Burns (1978) described it, "a relationship of mutual stimulation and elevation that converts followers into leaders and may convert leaders into moral agents" (p. 4). Indeed, this is the leadership style so badly needed by human services at this time.

REFERENCES

Allen, P. (1981). Managers at work: A large-scale study of the managerial job in New York City government. *Academy of Management Journal, 24,* 613-619.

Bales, F. (1954). In conference. *Harvard Business Review, 32*(2), 44-50.

Bargal, D. (1982). *Social work as a professional career: Renewal vs. erosion* (Arnulf M. Pins Memorial Lecture). Jerusalem: Hebrew University of Jerusalem, The Paul Baerwald School of Social Work.

Bargal, D., & Guterman, N. (1996). Perception of job satisfaction, service effectiveness, and burnout among Israeli social workers involved in direct practice [in Hebrew]. *Society and Welfare, 16*(4), 541-566.

Bargal, D., & Schmid, H. (1989). Recent themes in theory and research on leadership and their implications for management of the human services. *Administration in Social Work, 13*(3/4), 37-54.

Bass, B. (1985). *Leadership and performance beyond expectations.* New York: Free Press.

Bass, B. (1990). *Bass and Stogdill's handbook of leadership: Theory, research, and managerial applications* (3rd ed.). New York: Free Press.

Bass, B. (1997). Does the transactional-transformational leadership paradigm transcend organizational and national boundaries? *American Psychologist, 52*(3), 130-139.

Bass, B., & Avolio, B. (1993). Transformational leadership: A response to critiques. In M. Chemers & R. Ayman (Eds.), *Leadership theory and research: Perspectives and directions* (pp. 49-88). San Diego, CA: Academic Press.

Bennis, W. (1983). The art form of leadership. In S. Srivasta (Ed.), *The executive mind: New insights on managerial thought and action* (pp. 15-24). San Francisco: Jossey-Bass.

Bennis, W., & Nanus, B. (1985). *Leaders: The strategies for taking charge*. New York: Harper & Row.

Blumenfield, S. (1995). Reflections on effective leadership: Strains and successes, strategies and styles. *Social Work in Health Care, 20*(4), 21-37.

Bowers, D., & Seashore, S. (1966). Predicting organizational effectiveness with a four-factor theory of leadership. *Administrative Science Quarterly, 11*, 238-263.

Bray, D., Campbell, P., & Grant, D. (1974). *Formative years in business: A long-term AT&T study of managerial lives*. New York: Wiley-Interscience.

Bryman, A. (1992). *Charisma and leadership in organizations*. London: Sage.

Burns, J. (1978). *Leadership*. New York: Harper & Row.

Calas, M., & Smircich, L. (1996). From the woman's point of view: Feminist approaches to organization studies. In S. Clegg, C. Hardy, & W. Nord (Eds.), *Handbook of organization studies* (pp. 218-258). London: Sage.

Campbell, M., Dunnette, M., Lawler, E., & Weick, K. (1970). *Managerial behavior, performance, and effectiveness*. New York: McGraw-Hill.

Chess, W., Norlin, J., & Jayaratne, S. (1987). Social work administration 1981-1985: Alive, happy, and prospering. *Administration in Social Work, 11*(2), 67-78.

Conger, J. (1992). *Learning to lead: The art of transforming managers into leaders*. San Francisco: Jossey-Bass.

Conger, J., & Kanungo, R. (1987). Toward a behavioral theory of charismatic leadership in organizational settings. *Academy of Management Review, 12*, 637-647.

Conger, J., & Kanungo, R. (1988). *Charismatic leadership: The elusive factor in organizational effectiveness*. San Francisco: Jossey-Bass.

D'Aunno, T. (1992). The effectiveness of human service organizations: A comparison of models. In Y. Hasenfeld (Ed.), *Human services as complex organizations* (pp. 341-361). Newbury Park, CA: Sage.

Eagly, A., Karau, S., & Makhijani, M. (1995). Gender and the effectiveness of leaders: A meta analysis. *Psychological Bulletin, 117*(1), 125-145.

Ezell, M. (1993). Gender similarities of social work managers. *Administration in Social Work, 17*(3), 39-57.

Ezell, M., Menefee, D., & Patti, R. (1989). Managerial leadership and service quality: Toward a model of social work administration. *Administration in Social Work, 13*(3/4), 73-98.

Fiedler, F. (1967). *A theory of leadership effectiveness*. New York: McGraw-Hill.

Fiedler, F. (1971). Validation and extension of the contingency model of leadership effectiveness: A review of empirical findings. *Psychological Bulletin, 76*, 128-148.

Fiedler, F., & Garcia, J. (1987). *New approaches to leadership: Cognitive resources and organizational performance*. New York: John Wiley.

Garbarro, J. (1987). *The dynamics of taking charge*. Cambridge, MA: Harvard School of Business.

Glisson, C. (1989). The effect of leadership on workers in human service organizations. *Administration in Social Work, 13*(3/4), 99-116.

Gowdy, E., Rapp, C., & Poertner, J. (1993). Management is performance: Strategies for client-centered practice in social service organizations. *Administration in Social Work, 17*(1), 3-22.

Grasso, J. (1994). Management style, job satisfaction, and service effectiveness. *Administration in Social Work, 18*(4), 89-105.

Guterman, N., & Bargal, D. (1996). Social workers' reports of their power and service delivery outcomes. *Administration in Social Work, 20*(3), 1-20.

Hasenfeld, Y. (1983). *Human service organizations*. Englewood Cliffs, NJ: Prentice Hall.

Hasenfeld, Y. (1992). *Human services as complex organizations*. Newbury Park, CA: Sage.

Haynes, K. (1989). *Women managers in human services*. New York: Springer.

Hersey, P., & Blanchard, K. (1982). *Management of organizational behavior: Utilizing human services*. Englewood Cliffs, NJ: Prentice Hall.

Himle, D., Jayaratne, S., & Thyness, P. (1989). The effects of emotional support on burnout, work stress, and mental health among Norwegian and American social workers. *Journal of Social Service Research, 10*(1), 41-56.

Hogan, R., Curphy, G., & Hogan, J. (1994). What we know about leadership: Effectiveness and personality. *American Psychologist, 49*(6), 493-504.

House, R. (1971). A path goal theory of leader effectiveness. *Administrative Science Quarterly, 16*, 321-338.

House, R., & Aditya, R. (1997). The social scientific study of leadership: Quo vadis? *Journal of Management, 23*(3), 409-473.

House, R., & Baetz, M. (1979). Leadership: Some empirical generalizations and new research directions. In B. Staw (Ed.), *Research in organizational behavior* (Vol. 1, pp. 341-423). Greenwich, CT: JAI Press.

House, R., & Mitchell, T. (1974). Path goal theory of leadership. *Journal of Contemporary Business, 3,* 81-97.

Jacobs, J. (1992). Women's entry into management: Trends in earnings, authority, and values among salaried managers. *Administrative Science Quarterly, 37,* 282-301.

Jayaratne, S., Tripodi, T., & Chess, W. (1983). Perceptions of emotional support, stress, and strain by male and female social workers. *Social Work Research and Abstracts, 19,* 19-29.

Johnston, W., & Packer, A. (1987). *Workforce 2000: Work and workers for the twenty-first century.* Indianapolis: Hudson Institute.

Komaki, J., Zlotnik, S., & Jensen, M. (1986). Development of an operant-based taxonomy and observational index of supervisory behavior. *Journal of Applied Psychology, 71,* 260-269.

Kotter, J. (1982). *The general managers.* New York: Free Press.

Lake, D., & Martinko, M. (1982). *The identification of high performing principals* (Working paper). Tallahassee: Florida State University.

Levy, C. (1973). The value base of social work. *Journal of Education for Social Work, 9*(1), 34-42.

Likert, R. (1961). *New patterns of management.* New York: McGraw-Hill.

Locke, E. A., Kirkpatrick, S., Wheeler, J. K., Schneider, J., Niles, K., Goldstein, H., Welsh, K., & Chan, D. (1991). *The essence of leadership: The four keys to leading successfully.* New York: Lexington Books.

Malka, S. (1989). Managerial behavior, participation, and effectiveness in social welfare organizations. *Administration in Social Work, 13*(2), 47-65.

Martin, P., & Chernesky, R. (1989). Women's prospects for leadership in social welfare: A political-economy perspective. *Administration in Social Work, 13*(3/4), 117-143.

Meinert, R., Ginsberg, L., & Keys, P. (1993). Performance characteristics of CEOs in state departments of social service, mental health, and correction. *Administration in Social Work, 17*(1), 103-114.

Menefee, D., & Thompson, J. (1994). Identifying and comparing competencies for social work management: A practice driven approach. *Administration in Social Work, 18*(3), 1-25.

Mintzberg, H., & Waters, J. (1983). The mind of a strategist. In S. Srivasta (Ed.), *The executive mind: New insights on managerial thought and action.* San Francisco: Jossey-Bass.

Packard, T. (1993). Managers' and workers' views of the dimensions of participation in decision-making. *Administration in Social Work, 17*(2), 53-66.

Patti, R. (1977). Patterns of management activity in social welfare agencies. *Administration in Social Work, 1*(1), 5-18.

Patti, R. (1987). Managing for service effectiveness in social welfare agencies: Toward a performance model. *Administration in Social Work, 11*(3/4), 7-21.

Patti, R., & Rauch, R. (1978). Social work administration graduates in the job market: An analysis of managers' hiring preferences. *Social Service Review, 52*(4), 567-583.

Pawar, S., & Eastman, K. (1997). The nature and implications of contextual influences on transformational leadership: A conceptual examination. *Academy of Management Review, 22*(1), 80-109.

Peters, T., & Waterman, R. (1982). *In search of excellence: The leadership difference.* New York: Random House.

Poertner, J., & Rapp, C. (1983). Organization learning and problem finding. In M. Dinerman (Ed.), *Social work in a turbulent world.* Silver Spring, MD: NASW Press.

Pondy, L. (1978). Leadership is a language game. In M. McCall & M. Lombardo (Eds.), *Leadership: Where else can we go?* Durham, NC: Duke University Press.

Porras, J., & Collins, J. (1994). *Built to last: Successful habits of visionary companies.* New York: Harper Business.

Ramsdell, P. (1994). Staff participation in organizational decision-making: An empirical study. *Administration in Social Work, 18*(4), 51-72.

Sashkin, M. (1988). The visionary leader. In J. Conger & R. Kanungo (Eds.), *Charismatic leadership: The elusive factor in organizational effectiveness* (pp. 122-160). San Francisco: Jossey-Bass.

Schein, E. (1985). *Organizational culture and leadership: A dynamic view.* San Francisco: Jossey Bass.

Schein, E. (1992). *Organizational culture and leadership: A dynamic view* (2nd ed.). San Francisco: Jossey-Bass.

Schmid, H. (1992). Relationship between decentralized authority and other structural properties in human service organizations: Implications for service effectiveness. *Administration in Social Work, 16*(1), 25-40.

Schon, D. (1984). *The reflective practitioner: How professionals think in action.* New York: Basic Books.

Shera, W., & Page, J. (1995). Creating more effective human service organizations through strategies of empowerment. *Administration in Social Work, 19*(4), 1-15.

Sheridan, J. (1992). Organizational culture and employee retention. *The Academy of Management Journal, 35*(5), 1036-1056.

Shin, J., & McClomb, G. (1998). Top executive leadership and organizational innovation: An empirical investigation of nonprofit human service organizations (HSOs). *Administration in Social Work, 22*(3), 1-21.

Spitzer, W. (1995). Effective leadership: The health care social work director. *Social Work in Health Care, 20*(4), 89-109.

Stagner, R. (1969). Corporate decision-making: An empirical study. *Journal of Applied Psychology, 46,* 350-357.

Steiner, J., Gross, G., Ruffolo, M., & Murray, J. (1994). Strategic planning in nonprofits: Profit from it. *Administration in Social Work, 18*(2), 87-106.

Stogdill, R. (1974). *Handbook of leadership: A survey of literature.* New York: Free Press.

Stogdill, R., & Coons, A. (1957). *Leader behavior: Its description and measurement.* Columbus: Ohio State University Bureau of Business Research.

Tichy, N., & Devana, M. (1986). *The transformational leader.* New York: John Wiley.

Vroom, V., & Yetton, P. (1973). *Leadership and decision making.* Pittsburgh, PA: University of Pittsburgh Press.

Weber, M. (1947). *The theory of social and economic organizations.* New York: Oxford University Press.

Westley, S., & Mintzberg, H. (1989). Visionary leadership and strategic management. *Strategic Management Journal, 10,* 17-32.

Wilkins, A., & Ouchi, W. (1983). Efficient cultures: Exploring the relationships between culture and organizational performance. *Administrative Science Quarterly, 28,* 468-481.

Williams, E. (1968). *An analysis of selected work duties and performances of the more effective versus the less effective manager.* Doctoral dissertation, Ohio State University, Columbus.

Yukl, G. (1989). Managerial leadership: A review of theory and research. *Journal of Management, 15*(2), 251-289.

Yukl, G. (1994). *Leadership in organizations* (3rd ed.). Englewood Cliffs, NJ: Prentice Hall.

Zaleznik. A. (1989). *The managerial mystique: Restoring leadership in business.* New York: Harper & Row.

CHAPTER SIXTEEN

Managing Information for Decision Making

DICK SCHOECH

Until recently, social welfare management involved managing primarily human, physical, and financial resources. However, modern management places a heavy emphasis on managing with information and, consequently, managing the information resources of an agency. The primary reason for this new emphasis is that powerful information technologies have been transforming the workplace. Computers and telecommunications have had substantial impact on management in the corporate sectors. The same is happening in the nonprofit and social welfare sectors. However, because of the complexity of social welfare agencies and their environment, the task of managing their information resources is more difficult than the same task in business.

Other pressures exist for using technology. One is the Government Performance and Results Act (GPRA). GPRA is a federal law that requires (a) strategic plans, (b) annual performance plans that establish accountability for results (i.e., targeted performance levels, indicators), and (c) measurement systems to collect data on performance (http://www.erols.com/jjjams/00000006.htm). Another pressure stems from the privatization and contracting of services associated with managed care. The man-

AUTHOR'S NOTE: This chapter contains information from Dr. Schoech's book, titled *Human Services Technology: Understanding, Designing, and Implementing Computer and Internet Applications in the Social Services* (2nd ed. of *Human Services Computing: Concepts and Applications*), which is available from Haworth Press, 1999.

aged care model requires providers to have information about services and clients to determine capitation rates. Managed care companies also like to contract with providers for a large number of clients. This encourages small independent providers to form coalitions and develop sophisticated information systems so they can gain large service contracts. In addition to managed care, almost all new management initiatives are based on the availability of good information about clients and services.

This chapter presents the basics of information management. The intent is to have managers see information as a core agency resource and information management as a core function similar to managing the other basic agency resources of money, people, and facilities.

BASIC CONCEPTS

Terminology. Before beginning the discussion of information technology (IT), some basic definitions are useful to aid understanding. It would be useful to review the definitions in Appendix A before continuing.

Information technology as change. IT applications involve changes in processes and people. The extent of change depends on factors such as the number of processes affected by the application, the extent of change from the old to new system, and the number of people affected.

According to the National Science Foundation, hardware typically absorbs 10% of the overall IT application costs, software and software development absorb 40%, and implementation and training absorb 50% (Neilson,

1985). As technology has become more pervasive, many would change these percentages to 10/30/60. This rule of thumb suggests that getting people to use processed information in their work is more difficult than designing the IT application. However, when developing IT applications, agencies often expect to spend resources in the reverse proportion. That is, they budget 50% for hardware, 40% for software and software development, and 10% for implementation and training. Consequently, much of the training and implementation is added on to existing workloads, thus causing frustration and resentment regarding the IT application.

Much of the information on change and change management is familiar to human service professionals. We are experts in changing clients and their environments. However, human service professionals tend to become fascinated with technology and neglect people change. The situation is similar to the adage about the cobbler's son not having shoes. This neglect of people change coupled with the management focus of many initial IT applications has also resulted in a negative attitude and resistance by social welfare agency staff.

The impact of change can be minimized if users are well informed and involved in the process and if the change is gradual and aligned with user values. Being able to visualize the completed application also helps reduce resistance. The guidelines for IT success will be addressed later in a more substantive manner.

Information management as a basic organizational function. Information is the primary resource used in delivering human services. Essential to managing agency IT is viewing information as a resource capable of being managed. Managing information is an organizational process as important to agency success as managing money, personnel, and property. Failure to manage information is wasteful. It causes poor decision making and results in poor goal achievement. The management of information implies that someone is responsible and that the appropriate technology is used to collect, store, manipulate, and distribute information.

Another aspect of IT management is that agency systems rarely operate in isolation. Even a small application, such as a computerized mailing list, will influence other agency processes. Because IT rarely exists in isolation, a conceptual understanding of overall agency IT is desirable before any application is developed. Detailed plans for specific applications need to be developed within the framework of an overall IT strategic plan. IT that follows a planned change process has a better chance of success.

The change process and change management. IT development follows a process similar to other agency changes. The process of planned change is well researched. At its simplest, the stages of any planned change effort involve feasibility, assessment, implementation, and evaluation. The following quotation compares the changes associated with developing IT to those associated with psychotherapy.

> Just as psychotherapy begins with an analysis and assessment of the client's psychological needs, the system development process begins with an analysis of information needs. The psychotherapy process proceeds to helping the client discover and design new ways to meet his or her psychological needs; the information system development process proceeds to the design of a system of gather-

ing, processing, and producing information. Psychotherapy concludes with the successful integration of new attitudes and patterns of behavior; information system development concludes with the installation of a new, successful information system. (Zefran, 1984, p. 21)

Although the change process can be stated simply and logically, implementing change often becomes a process of "muddling through." In muddling through, the overall plan is kept in mind as one struggles to find the most appropriate solutions to day-to-day problems.

DESIGNING AND DEVELOPING INFORMATION TECHNOLOGY APPLICATIONS

Agencies progress through major stages, activities, and decisions when developing IT applications. Figure 16.1 summarizes the activities involved at each stage of the application development process. The process is both sequential and repetitive. As decisions are made throughout the process, some stages are repeated as other new stages are entered. Each stage builds on and amplifies the activities of the previous stage and addresses some of the tasks in future stages. For example, the first stage, preparedness and feasibility, must be given repeated consideration throughout the process. In addition, success criteria developed in the feasibility stage are used during the evaluation stage.

Each stage in Figure 16.1 begins with the setting of goals, objectives, tasks, schedules, checkpoints, responsibilities, and completion criteria for that stage. Each stage ends with the documentation of all activities in a report. This re-

Stage 1: Exploration of Feasibility and Preparedness

Communicate about the IT effort to all staff

Establish an agency steering committee and application-specific subcommittees

Define the application's purpose, development timetables, and responsibilities

Estimate resources for change, that is, money, time, expertise, and commitment of key individuals

Estimate improved application impacts (positive and negative)

Assess the expectations and reactions of those who will be affected by the application

Draft continuous improvement mechanisms and success measures

Prepare and circulate preparedness and feasibility report

Decide to proceed or terminate effort

Stage 2: Assessment (Systems Analysis)

Identify the major needs and decisions the application will address

Define the characteristics of the information needed, its source, and collection methods

Analyze current and future data input, processing, and output operations and requirements, for example, forms, data manipulations, files, reports, and flow of information from collection to dissemination

Evaluate problems with how things are currently done

Identify resources on which to build the new application

Collect baseline data on success measures

Review similar efforts in other agencies and request help from national or state associations

Prepare and circulate assessment

Decide to proceed or terminate effort

Stage 3: Conceptual Design

Finalize application scope, goals, objectives, continuous improvement measures, and success measures

Develop alternative conceptual designs, that is, fields, records, files, data manipulation, forms, reports, and graphics

Apply design specifications such as flexibility, reliability, processing and statistical requirements, growth potential, life expectancy, and tie-in with other applications

Apply restrictions to designs, that is, required and desired data frequency, volume, security, confidentiality, turn-around time, money, time, and expertise

Design mechanisms to collect and report continuous improvement information

Translate designs into software, hardware, and networking configurations

Detail the advantages, disadvantages, and assumptions of alternate designs

Prepare and circulate conceptual design and decide to proceed or terminate effort

Stage 4: Detailed Design and Development

Set up controls and technical performance standards for chosen design

Select the software for the chosen design

Select the hardware to match the software

Select the necessary networking and communications

Design and develop data collection forms, data manipulation, operations, file specifications, database structures, error checks, storage mechanisms, backup procedures, and output reports

Prepare documentation and instruction manuals

Figure 16.1. Stages in the Process of Developing an Information Technology (IT) Application

SOURCE: From "Strategies for Information System Development," by D. Schoech, L. L. Schkade, & R. S. Mayers, (1982), in *Administration in Social Work, 5*(3/4), 25-26. Copyright 1981 by Haworth Press. Adapted by permission.

port then becomes the basis for deciding whether to proceed to the next stage. Completing all stages for a relatively small application may take several months. For large applications, such as the development of a comprehensive information system, the process

Stage 5: Testing and Preparation
   Prepare system operators, users, and others to
      receive the application
   Develop agency policy and procedural changes
      necessary for the new application
   Develop performance specifications and testing plan
   Test programming, forms, operational procedures,
      instructions, reports, and the use of outputs
   Educate and train system operators, data users, and
      others affected

Stage 6: Implementation
   Develop and approve conversion plan, for example,
      stop old system when new system starts or run
      old and new systems simultaneously for
      comparison
   Incorporate application into standard operating
      procedures, for example, performance appraisals,
      new employee orientation, and training
   Reorganize staff and space if necessary
   Convert from old to new equipment, new processing
      methods, and new procedures
   Ensure all systems and controls are working

Stage 7: Monitoring and Evaluation
   Compare application performance with initial
      application objectives, for example, outputs used
      in decision making, users satisfied, client services
      improved
   Relate benefits and costs to initial estimates
   Ensure continuous improvement mechanisms are
      working and remedial action is taken

Stage 8: Operation, Maintenance, and Modification
   Prepare backup and emergency plans and procedures
   Complete documentation, for example, instructions
      for adding to, deleting from, or modifying
      application
   Assign people responsible for data integrity, system
      maintenance, backup, new software
      appropriateness, virus protection, and so on
   Provide continuous training of users
   Continue to add desired enhancements and to
      maintain and debug the application
   Begin Stage 1 if additional subsystems are to be
      developed

Figure 16.1. *Continued*

may take several years. In some cases, the time required to develop a complex application is so long that the application is never completed before a redesign is considered.

The time devoted to each stage can vary substantially depending on the size and complexity of the application. The 80/20 rule suggests that 80% of an application can be completed using only 20% of total resources. However, to complete the remaining 20% of the application requires 80% of total resources. This final 20% can cause frustration, especially among users who see little progress as they eagerly wait for the completed application. The 80/20 rule applies to IT primarily because the user interface

for system features is much easier to design than the detailed programming required to make the features work bug-free.

Going through the stages in the development process may appear scientific and precise, but doing so is more of an art than a science. The time and effort devoted to each activity varies for different applications. For example, if an agency purchases an information system from a vendor, it may skip some design phase activities because the vendor completed them. However, the agency should compile documentation on all stages no matter when, where, or who completed them (see document preparation under each stage of Figure 16.1).

INFORMATION
MANAGEMENT CONSIDERATIONS

There are different ways for agencies to approach the development process.

Structuring IT in the agency. To develop and
manage information, an agency must create the
appropriate organizational structure and assign
the necessary responsibilities and tasks to key
people. The seven groups involved in information management are:

1. Agency management
2. The agency-wide IT committee
3. The application task force
4. The IT manager
5. Users
6. Those affected by the application
7. Technicians and specialists

If one of these participants is not involved,
the potential for successful information management decreases. In nonprofit agencies, an IT advisory committee of the board may involve other
important stakeholders such as members of the
parent organization, funding sources, and client
advocate groups. The responsibilities and tasks
of each group will be discussed further.

Top management appoints the steering committee, approves contracts with vendors and
consultants, adjusts workloads, establishes and
maintains open lines of communication, and
balances the conflicting needs of all agency
components requiring IT resources. Top management should communicate its expectations
and involvement to all in the agency.

The IT committee includes representatives
of all parts of the agency and performs an advisory role to top management. This ensures that

the overall IT effort is consistent with agency
plans and coordinated across departments. The
major task of the committee is to develop an information management plan that contains (a)
IT goals and priorities; (b) IT policies, procedures, and integration standards; (c) challenges,
issues, and risks; and (d) hardware, software,
networking, and training implications. Committee members should communicate information and concerns about IT to and from the staff
they represent. The IT committee may appoint
task forces to work on special projects or issues,
such as confidentiality.

When the agency develops a new application, the IT committee should appoint an application task force that represents all affected parties in the development process, sets overall
policy, and monitors development. The application task force fosters communication, reduces resistance, and improves the chances that
the application will meet the needs of all involved. The task force must ensure that communication channels are established and open
and that feedback is obtained from all levels of
the organization. If conflicts arise, the task
force should help resolve them or refer difficult
matters to the IT committee or top management for resolution. For agencies with a few applications, the IT committee may function as
the application task force.

The IT manager is sometimes called a data
administrator, information manager, management information system (MIS) director, or
chief information officer (CIO). This person is
responsible for developing and documenting
the application, managing and coordinating information on a day-to-day basis, and providing
user training and support. The IT manager
should understand all departments of the
agency as well as technology and application

development. The role is primarily that of development, maintenance, coordination, control, and liaison. Therefore, the IT manager needs managerial, technical, and communication skills. For communication and coordination purposes, the IT manager should be a member of the IT committee and the application task force but probably not the chair of these committees.

Users are the most important group to be involved in IT development. Many techniques to involve users exist, for example, involving users on the IT committee and application task force, teaming users with consultants, and prototyping. Those affected by an application can vary substantially. An information system may affect almost every group and department in an agency. However, a performance support system that focuses on one process or body of knowledge can be designed and implemented without substantially affecting other parts of the agency.

Although involving users is essential, others affected by the application can provide valuable input. If possible, clients or client representatives should be members of the IT committee or application task force. They provide a perspective that cannot be obtained inside the agency. Due to accountability, boards and funding sources may play a role in agency information management. For example, an agency board member may have computer, networking, or information management expertise. Or, a funding source may require an agency to use its service definitions or software to collect and process its information. Funder requirements should not drive information systems design, because they are based on funder needs rather than agency needs. Although external needs may influence application design, an applica-

tion should rarely be designed based on outside information needs. An application should primarily contain information and processes that model what occurs in the agency. This information should then be translated into reports for those outside the agency. Computerizing basic agency information offers flexibility because it can always be combined into categories. For example, a funding source may ask for the number of clients served by age categories. The agency should collect date of birth and then have the computer process date of birth into age categories.

Technical specialists supply the hardware and software expertise needed to develop and manage computer applications. The technical specialists may be in-house personnel, outside consultants, or a combination. At present, IT personnel have many employment opportunities and often experience rapid job changes. Agencies can rarely compete with the private sector for permanent IT expertise. Because human service specialists can usually understand IT more easily than IT specialists can understand human services, it is often feasible to develop IT generalists and managers from existing staff and then hire or contract for the specialized expertise that varies with each application. Another strategy is for a coalition of agencies to share technical expertise.

Tools. Many tools are available to aid system development. The request for proposal (RFP) provides a format for communicating application requirements and ensuring comparable proposals. At least three vendor responses are recommended. The response to the RFP should become part of the contract with the chosen vendor. A formal signed vendor contract helps remove optimistic promises and "sales talk" from the proposal. The vendor contract reduces misunderstanding and becomes the agency's only assurance that it will receive the specified application. It specifies responsibilities, jobs, prices, and recourses, should things not go as planned. The contract can also address the issue of securing expertise and controlling the scope of the application (see subsequent discussion). A vendor contract ensures that both parties understand the nature of the arrangement and eliminates the reliance on general purpose contracts. General purpose contracts can be confusing to the agency and may not contain details pertinent to the application. If the application is large and complex, a bidders' conference allows vendors to tour current operations and ask questions about the potential application. Buying an application can be compared to marriage, because the agency and vendor are entering a long-term arrangement. This is especially true if the application solves a large agency problem.

Techniques. Large system development efforts, such as automating a state child protective services or mental health department, can use analysis and design techniques that have been developed in business over many years. These techniques, called structured methodology, organize the systems analysis and conceptual design stages by using a series of increasingly detailed refinements (Perrone, 1997; Schoech, 1999; Yourdon, 1991). These techniques are important, but beyond the scope of this chapter.

Skills. Developing applications requires a unique blend of technical and people skills. Also essential are good fact-finding techniques, such as listening, observing, interviewing, analyzing documents, constructing questionnaires, and using sampling methodologies. Good communication and training skills ensure that all affected staff have a chance to learn what is happening. Miscommunication or lack of information can lead to rumors, fear, and resistance. Computer technicians, systems designers, managers, and direct service providers often use jargon that is peculiar to their jobs. The jargon of both groups should be defined in writing and circulated to improve communications between agency staff and system developers. A cardinal rule in organizational change is "no surprises." This means that people should have easy access to information as it becomes available, unless a very good reason for withholding information exists. A web site is an excellent way to make this information readily available. Communication is often more difficult than anticipated. For example, in one agency, the developers bragged about their representative application advisory committee. In interviews, workers on the advisory committee said that the meetings were interesting but took time away from their work. These workers rarely discussed committee deliberations with colleagues. They did not understand that their role was to foster two-way communication between the developers and their peers. They did not see the importance of this role nor were they, or their supervisors, aware of the extra time it should take. Consequently, the developers had an overly positive view of how agency workers viewed the system and its usefulness.

POSITIONING INFORMATION TECHNOLOGY IN THE AGENCY

Some key issues in developing an application include how the agency is going to approach the development process, secure the needed expertise, and structure the expertise within the agency.

Development approaches. Three common development approaches are top-down, bottom-up, and prototyping. Rarely do agencies use these three approaches in their pure form. Agencies often use a continuous mix of the three approaches.

In a top-down approach, an agency first designs a model of the total system and then develops subsystems as integral parts of the total application. This traditional, logical approach typically occurs in large government agencies. In this approach, the person in charge of the development effort proceeds through a structured process of identifying needs and application specifications before soliciting vendors with an RFP.

In a bottom-up approach, an agency develops small, well-focused applications based on immediate needs. Agencies combine applications into a total system only when the need arises. Typically, in this approach, a worker or middle-level manager/department finds available hardware, software, and networking capabilities and starts to develop and implement an application that addresses an immediate problem. Although all the stages in Figure 16.1 may be completed, other systems and overall agency needs may be ignored. Activities may not be as formally developed, and top-level sanction and support may not exist. After several bottom-up approaches are taken, coordination and compatibility problems may force the agency to take a more top-down approach. Social work departments in hospitals typically use this approach when they develop a hospital social work system, which is eventually integrated into the hospital information system.

In a prototyping approach, an initial "quick and dirty" application is developed and given to key personnel for testing and evaluation. The application specifications and design features are developed not through a formal assessment and consideration of the options (Stages 2 and 3 of Figure 16.1) but through repeated cycles of quick analysis, development, trial use, evaluation, and refinement. The emphasis during prototyping is on quickly programming a trial solution. Conventional wisdom and standard practices are ignored for "what works." Prototyping allows users to agree on the look and feel of the application before developers fully define the specifications. The final application may not resemble the original information needs or the initial design. Prototyping allows users and system development specialists to educate each other about their respective needs and capabilities. Prototyping often occurs when no similar application exists, such as in an application that supports direct intervention with clients, for example, delivering human services in clients' homes via Internet-based two-way video.

Each approach has its advantages and disadvantages. In the human services, traditional top-down development is more appropriate for applications that address the routine and well-structured problems of middle management. In top-down development, the tendency exists to address only well-defined information needs. An organization may advocate a bottom-up approach when it has the opportunity to implement several needed applications but does not have the time or expertise to develop an overall IT strategy. Prototyping may be combined with top-down development to overcome this tendency. Prototyping is especially useful when a top-down approach is taken with applications that support the non-routine and ill-structured problems at the top management, policy, and direct service levels. For complex applications, it may be desirable to combine all three approaches. For example, a drug treatment agency may use a top-down approach to develop a strategic plan for agency-wide technology. A new halfway house program may provide the funds and opportunity to develop an information system that tracks the progress of clients in the halfway house. This system could be developed from the bottom up, that is, the information requirements of other programs of the agency may not be considered. The agency may realize that the halfway house information system will need to be changed when an overall agency information system is developed. The halfway house program evaluator might use prototyping to design an application system that advises staff on the potential problems of new clients based on an analysis of similar past cases. Variables found important in this prediction system, such as a client having a concerned relative living within 5 miles of the halfway house, might become part of an overall agency information system that is later developed using a top-down approach. This overall system could integrate the halfway house information system and other applications.

Securing and structuring expertise. Agencies can obtain expertise from within the agency, from outside consultants, or from a combination of both. Use of internal expertise alone may produce an application that is useful but technically limited and difficult to support. Use of only outside consultants may produce an application that is technically appropriate but of limited usefulness. Moyer (1997) advocates relying on internal expertise and handling the

technical proficiency versus usefulness issue by placing outside consultants under the control of internal staff. This combination is especially good at controlling the scope of an IT application, which often tends to expand uncontrollably. Although users can best define the scope, outside contractors are good at curbing users' and managers' appetite for expanding the application scope.

Once expertise is secured, it must be organized within the agency. Possible relationships of top management and the IT manager to the IT committee and the application task force are presented in Figure 16.2.

Balancing centralized management with end-user planning and control. One of the most significant management challenges is to foster end-user involvement and creativity while controlling the tendency of end users to develop and operate applications independently. The term often used to describe end user development is *distributed IT* because IT is distributed out to individual end users. It may seem paradoxical at first, but the best route to a properly functioning distributed IT environment is centralized planning, control, standardization, and training. To avoid the protectionist attitude and independent development of many distributed IT groups, top management, via the IT committee, must decide the desirable balance of distribution and central control. Then, it must provide central staff with the authority necessary to implement this balance. The intent is not to create an adversarial relationship between distributed IT units and the central unit. Rather, the intent is to administer the entire distributed network as one integrated system that takes into account the needs of users and other stakeholders. Although centralized control removes

Structure 1

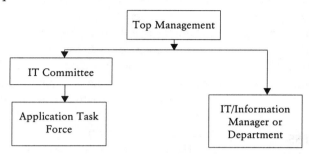

In Structure 1, a balance of power exists between the IT committee and the IT/information manager. Top management settles disagreements.

Structure 2

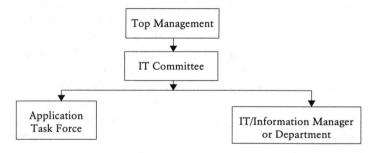

In Structure 2, the application task force and IT/information manager report directly to the IT committee. This structure is recommended.

Structure 3

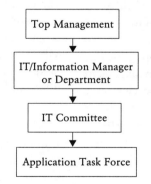

In Structure 3, all IT committees are under the IT or information management department. This structure is not usually recommended because it gives too much control to the IT/information manager and makes access to top management by user representatives more difficult.

Figure 16.2. Ways to Structure the Information Technology (IT) Application in an Agency

some of the advantages of distribution, for example, complete independence of end users, the gains far outweigh the losses. Without central control, many systems may compete for scarce IT resources, avoid common taxonomies, and resist information sharing.

GUIDELINES FOR SUCCESS

This section summarizes conventional wisdom and guidelines for IT success. If followed, these guidelines should help an agency to avoid disruption and anticipate problems before they occur.

Begin by planning. Planning is consistently mentioned as a key factor in successful IT implementation. A 3- to 5-year plan should address how applications will be tied together to form an overall system that achieves agency-wide goals. Planning allows modular implementation, which lessens risks, increases flexibility, spreads out costs, and provides time to react and adjust. Agencies that are highly influenced by their environment should view applications as part of a larger community IT system. The IT plan should address how an agency will integrate its applications into this larger system. For example, case management applications that match clients to services may require continuous updating of the community services available. Agencies could cooperatively update a community services information system using the Internet.

Place IT in a separate, top-level department and base the design on client services. Because information cuts across departmental and orga-

nizational boundaries, the IT department should be a separate, high-level department. This advice is not often followed, because the tendency exists to place the information management function in the department that first computerizes. Creating a separate high-level unit is considered only after an agency develops several applications. For example, because an accounting application is typically installed first, the budget officer is often responsible for information management. This problem is especially serious in the human services, where contracts and grants provide funds that are not tied to customer outcomes and satisfaction. Many funding sources will provide agencies with information systems designed around their programs. Thus, an agency can quickly develop an information system designed around accounting, funding, or one program rather than client services. Because IT applications become information models of organizations, they should reflect the agency's mission or client services. An overall design that is based on an agency's natural way of providing services will serve the agency better than a system constructed of many separate applications that were designed to meet outside needs. An overall design that is determined through a formal analysis of the total agency (Figure 16.1, Stages 1 and 2) can also be much simpler to develop, understand, and maintain.

Involve and prepare stakeholders. An agency should be prepared psychologically and financially for designing and implementing an IT application. The agency that is most successful in designing and implementing an IT application will already be functioning well, so it can take the time and risks associated with the changes required. An organization in crisis or one barely surviving may not have the necessary time, energy, or morale, although it may be highly motivated to change. An agency should have formalized and stable goals, procedures, and operations, because IT applications become information models of the operations they automate. An agency with frequently changing goals, structures, and procedures will find its IT application quickly outdated and expensive to maintain.

Application success increases when the entire range of people affected by the application are involved in its design and implementation. This is difficult advice to follow because involvement is time-consuming and "messy," and the payoffs are long-term and hard to measure. Involvement is particularly important where agencies quickly purchase and implement prepackaged applications. Purchasing IT bypasses much of the learning that occurs when an agency develops its own application. If the agency purchases sophisticated applications, it must substitute other learning experiences for those that occur with custom applications development, for example, staff could visit similar applications in other agencies.

Demonstrate top-level involvement and commitment. The success or failure of most IT applications can be traced back to the clear, consistent, and visible involvement of a key leader. Top-level decision makers can demonstrate leadership by doing the following:

- Educate themselves so as not to be dazzled by technology and vendor promises
- Make certain the organization is reasonably stable

- Maintain control over the development effort
- Ensure that accountability for results is clearly assigned and openly understood and that those accountable have the necessary authority to take initiatives and make decisions that affect results
- Expend the extra time and energy required throughout the application development and implementation process
- Ensure that those developing an application receive the necessary release time from normal duties
- Guarantee that all users are provided education and training
- Demonstrate that the information, data, and power inherent in any application will not be used for personal gain or punishment of employees
- Separate IT changes from other changes; that is, do not blame IT for organizational changes that management has been reluctant to make
- Assume responsibility for resolving conflicts that arise during implementation
- Openly demonstrate commitment and involvement by attending important meetings, assigning quality personnel to the development effort, and making timely and firm decisions

Employees will not support an application if the organization's leaders do not take it seriously.

An example will illustrate the importance of top management to the IT development process. The clinical training committee of a mental health provider sought the assistance of a consultant to help integrate clinical IT applications into the organization. Staff members brought in the consultant because they feared the accounting department was controlling and restricting the scope of clinical IT. The executive director took a hands-off approach because he did not understand the subtleties of technology and the control issues IT raises. However, major IT change could not move forward without this dispute being resolved.

Consider agency sophistication. Because an IT application is typically more complex than its manual counterpart, it requires a higher level of sophistication on the part of agency operations and the user. One example of this sophistication is the standardization that accompanies any application. Standardization takes many forms, such as the definition of terms, common operational procedures regarding information, and centralized control and access to information. An agency must generally impose far more discipline throughout the organization when IT applications are used.

Most human service organizations should avoid implementing the latest IT developments. The history of technology is littered with pioneering IT applications that were rarely used. Success is most often reaped by settlers who follow closely behind the pioneers and make substantial improvements while avoiding the mistakes. Although being in the forefront of IT can be exciting, it is usually frustrating and costly in terms of agency time, effort, and morale. In addition, problems often plague newly developed applications. Cautiously implementing proven applications is safer for agencies not capable of withstanding the bleeding that occurs on the cutting edge. Agencies best able to withstanding the stress of pioneering are those that are either successful or failing. Successful agencies can more easily withstand the accompanying changes; failing organizations are often more open to large change. Pioneering in IT is best left to those who can take risks, for example, university researchers and vendors.

Avoid overreliance on a few isolated technical specialists. Reliance on one or several people for IT development and implementation presents serious risks for an agency. A consultant may change firms and leave an agency stranded. An in-house designer may quit and set back the IT effort. Agencies must assure continuity for the 2 or 3 years a major application requires, regardless of the personnel changes that occur. Building a strong application task force and teaming consultants with in-house staff ensure that consultants do not foster agency dependency. In choosing the staff to team with outside specialists, select employees who will be with the agency for a long time. Training the brightest, most interested, and younger members of the staff may seem logical. However, these are more likely to leave the agency with their newly developed expertise.

Another way to lessen dependence is to have good documentation, for example, on-line help, user manuals, and design specifications. Managers neglect documentation because its value is not immediately recognizable. Application designers neglect it because documentation is a boring and time-consuming task. However, documentation is the basis for evaluating and controlling the IT effort as well as for building additional applications. Documentation is also the key to continuity, especially when technology is changing rapidly and knowledgeable IT personnel change jobs frequently. Agencies with good documentation are better able to handle problems such as ensuring that all systems can share common data such as a client's name.

Select software before hardware. In developing an application, hardware is a less crucial factor than software. If hardware and software are purchased separately, choose software before purchasing hardware and base software selection on a needs analysis. For example, whether an agency selects to implement a local area network or use an intranet should be based on a well-defined needs analysis developed by key staff throughout the organization.

One way to seek software is to obtain the names of comparable agencies that have similar applications. A telephone call to state and national associations or a site visit to a similar application can provide valuable information. The Internet contains numerous links to software, and Internet discussion lists allow communication with many experts who use software packages.

The tendency often exists to custom-design a solution when a packaged solution could be purchased. Even if internal developments seem less costly, an outside package should be considered because the purchase/build decision can affect agency IT for many years. Once made, this decision and its consequences are difficult and expensive to reverse. This decision is similar to the automobile purchase decision. A customized one-of-a-kind car may fit the driver's needs best. However, a common car will be easier and less expensive to repair and maintain. Even with custom-programmed software, the agency should encourage the use of generic tools such as those associated with database management systems and intranets. The money invested in these tools often results in less overall programming time and less dependence. Application developers have incentives to custom-develop every part of the application, because custom-developed applications ensure job security.

Working with vendors is not always easy. Vendors often use terms loosely and often advertise products that are not currently available to attract buyers away from competing products. It is common to wait for an essential piece of software that was promised months earlier. Vendors can change products and marketing strategies and leave those waiting stranded. A rule of thumb is that software does not exist until it is running on your computers. When considering software from vendors, ask for a list of organizations presently using the software and randomly contact several. Be sure that the vendor does not limit the potential list by recommending only a few well-screened possibilities. Also, ensure that the agency will have access to the application source code if the vendor goes out of business or is unable to support the product. The above comments are not intended to reflect negatively on vendors. However, human service professionals should not confuse the helping relationship between practitioners and their clients with the business relationship between vendors and their clients.

Safeguard security and confidentiality from the beginning. IT applications can be secure and protect the confidentiality associated with client information as well as any paper and pencil system. However, this is true only if security and confidentiality are part of the initial design and if the agency establishes and follows appropriate policies and procedures. Often, security is lax until after a violation has occurred. Establishing security and privacy safeguards after an application is developed can be expensive and time-consuming.

IT applications have a tendency to make private information public, and mistakes tend to be big. For example, a private e-mail may be accidentally distributed to the whole agency, or staff may obtain gossip by snooping into computer files. The training of users on protecting security and privacy is equally as important as passwords, encryption, audit trails, and requests that users verify the last recorded use under their names. Training can address problems such as passwords taped on the display and spouses' names as passwords.

Build in continuous improvement mechanisms. Continuously monitoring and openly sharing feedback about key activities and results with stakeholders are beneficial, especially with complex applications (Hile, 1998). Many feedback measures can be derived from the application's goals and objectives. Other measures that should be tracked concern efficiency, effectiveness, satisfaction, and application success. These measures and feedback mechanisms must be built into the application-development process from the very beginning. Measures are more powerful if they are positive rather than negative and address application output rather than input.

Expect the development effort to be frustrating and time-consuming. Designing and implementing IT applications is not an easy process. Problems multiply as the size of the application and the complexity of the tasks supported increases. Developing a routine application can be difficult, and developing a complex application, such as an agency information system or web site, can be a long-term process requiring many revisions. Estimates of the time and work involved are often inaccurate. For example, when building a web site, the number of tasks to be completed seems to grow exponentially as the number of pages in the site increases, rather than growing geometrically.

CONCLUSION

The preceding discussion is rooted in computer technology. However, the era of computers driving IT change is giving way to communications between computers driving IT change (Kelly, 1997). In the 1967 movie *The Graduate,* the one word of advice given to the graduating senior was "plastics." Today that word of advice would be "connectivity."

For social welfare agencies, which typically have decentralized and collaborative structures, IT connectivity will have significant impacts. The Internet allows coalitions of agencies, such as homeless shelters, to be connected to share client information. These new arrangements require a rethinking of the meaning of case management, privacy, confidentiality, informed consent, and client involvement. Extranets will allow agencies to connect with constituents and stakeholders. For example, a Texas Department of Protective and Regulatory Services extranet allows local judges to tap into the agency database and view the files of children under their conserveratorship. This immediate access to agency records by those outside the agency will have significant implications for decision making and agency performance. Telehealth applications, which use low-cost, Internet-based, interactive video, have proven effective for connecting service-delivery professionals with clients in rural areas and those with disabilities (http://catelehealth.org/sect1.html). Removing the geographic limitations on service provision will have substantial impact on the ability to interact quickly with clients globally and on client choice of service provider. Virtual therapy over the Internet has successfully connected many clients to treatment and will grow as an adjunct to traditional counseling and as a new counseling form. Internet-delivered instruction is proving to be an effective and flexible way to connect students to universities in ways that rival the traditional classroom for many human service topics (http://www.csun.edu/sociology/virexp.htm). Finally, clients are able to connect to Internet resources to quickly obtain more up-to-date expertise on their problem than that possessed by their practitioner. Most social welfare professionals are not prepared for information-empowered clients who demand to take a more active role in their treatment based on a narrow but up-to-date understanding of their problem.

The implications of these coming changes for managers and practitioners have yet to be researched. The pressures on IT developers to produce well-functioning applications are so great that they rarely research their applications. One traditional source of research is graduate students. However, the specialized expertise needed to guide student IT research is not available in many graduate schools. Virtual dissertation committees could be a solution, but issues of compensation and accreditation have yet to be worked out.

We enter the 21st century trying to adapt to a technology-driven world. The unconnected social welfare agency is disappearing like the "mom and pop" restaurant. Most practitioners and agencies are not ready to enter the brave new world of IT, even though the pace of technology shows no sign of slowing. Our task, then, is to make wise choices regarding current IT as we struggle to understand and assimilate future technological developments.

APPENDIX

Basic Information Technology Terms

Term	Definition
Application	Systems composed of people and procedures that solve a problem. Cars and trucks are transportation applications just as word processors and treatment planners are information technology (IT) applications.
Computer	An electromechanical device that accepts data and instructions, manipulates the data according to the instructions, and outputs the results.
Computer network	Linked software and hardware systems that share resources. Computers on a network are called nodes. Local area networks (LANS) link many computers in the same geographic area. Wide area networks (WANS) link nodes separated geographically.
Computing	The total process of collecting, storing, manipulating, communicating, and disseminating information in electronic form.
Confidentiality	The level of secrecy assumed or formally agreed on by two or more parties with the expectation that shared information will be used consistent with this agreement. Confidentiality is a matter of proper levels of authorization, access codes, encryption, and other measures.
Connectivity	The extent of the linkages and the sharing of IT resources between two or more systems.
Data	Numbers that have no inherent meaning. For example, the numbers 76019 are data, for they have no meaning other than their arithmetic value.
Data processing	The capturing, storing, manipulating, and communication of data.
Decision support system	An interactive IT application designed to assist users in making complex decisions. A decision support system usually answers "what if" type of questions.
Documentation	Descriptive information, in written or electronic form, that explains the development, use, operation, and maintenance of a computer or application.
Extranets	Interagency networks that use Internet tools.
Hardware	The physical, tangible components of a computer, for example, a monitor. One can touch and see hardware.
Information	Data organized to communicate a meaning. If 76019 is a zip code, then one could discover that this arrangement of numbers denotes the University of Texas at Arlington.

Term	Definition
Information system	A system of people, procedures, and equipment for collecting, manipulating, retrieving, and reporting information.
Information technology	Technologies that collect, process, manipulate, and disseminate information. For example, a book is a paper-based information technology whereas a computer is an electronics-based information technology.
Internet	A network of networks that is independent of any application or organization.
Intranets	Intra-agency networks that use Internet tools.
Knowledge	Information in the form of descriptions and relationships. For example, the fact that the University of Texas at Arlington is part of the state university system is a piece of knowledge.
Performance support system	An IT application designed to improve staff performance by providing content-specific advice when it is needed and in the format in which it is needed.
Security	The protection of hardware, software, and data by passwords, backup procedures, restricted physical admittance, firewalls, duplicate storage, and protection from fire and electrical interruption.
Privacy	The rights of individuals to keep their possessions, including information about themselves, away from others.
Software	Instructions that guide the computer's operations and their accompanying documentation.
Technology	The combination of tools and actions that are grounded in scientific knowledge, practice, or ideology and that direct or supports one's activities and decisions, for example, interviewing protocols or computer systems.
Wide Area Network (WAN)	A network that connects computers to share IT resources in many agencies.

REFERENCES

Hile, M. (Ed.). (1998). The history and function of the target cities management information systems [Special issue]. *Computers in Human Services, 14*(3/4).

Kelly, K. (1997). New rules for the new economy: Twelve dependable principles for thriving in a turbulent world. *Wired, 5*(9), 140-197.

Moyer, D. (1997). Journey to the brave new world of data automation technology—are we ready. *Computers in Human Services, 14*(2), 17-34.

Neilson, R. (1985). The role of the federal government in social service systems development. *Computers in Human Services, 1*(2), 53-63.

Perrone, G. (1997). *Structured analysis with case tools.* Englewood Cliffs, NJ: Prentice Hall.

Schoech, D. (1999). *Human services technology: Understanding, designing, and implementing computer and Internet applications.* New York: Haworth.

Yourdon, E. (1991). *Modern structured analysis.* Englewood Cliffs, NJ: Prentice Hall

Zefran, J. (1984). Analysis of the information needs of a private practice. In M. Schwartz (Ed.), *Using computers in clinical practice* (pp. 19-39). New York: Haworth.

CHAPTER SEVENTEEN

Managing the Planning Process

MICHAEL J. AUSTIN

JEFFREY R. SOLOMON

For most human service agencies, planning is viewed as a luxury, especially when the demand for services exceeds the supply. In our recent history (1945-1980), the limited amount of planning was usually long-range planning that paralleled the growth of the economy and social programs. However, with government cutbacks in social programs, the expansion of military expenditures, and the global competitiveness that fostered the trend of downsizing and mergers in the 1980s, long-range planning was replaced by strategic planning in both the for-profit and non-profit sectors. Long-range planning was characterized as *extrapolational,* in essence extrapolating from current realities and trends 10 to 15 years into the future, assuming continued growth. This was logical in the post-World War II environment of steady economic growth and the steady expansion of government-supported social programs.

With the oil crisis of the 1970s and the military build-up of the 1980s, economic growth was linked to the global economy, and the growth of social programs was curtailed throughout the Reagan Era of 1980 to 1992. These changes fostered a new era of strategic planning, which was characterized as *transformational,* in essence a planning process designed to transform organizations in the short term (3 to 5 years), not long range. Such transformational planning is far more strategic with respect to external competition, environmental forces (threats and opportunities), and internal forces (strengths and weaknesses).

In the post-World War II period, planning has shifted dramatically from being a luxury in an era of long-range planning to being a necessity in an era of strategic planning. Some of the profound changes in the economy of social welfare need to be noted here, even though they are beyond the scope of this chapter. The arrival of managed care in the health care sector has led to significant changes in the financing, organization, patient care, and management of health and mental health services. Strategic planning has become essential as health care institutions are restructured, merged, closed, centralized, decentralized, and capitated. Similarly, the arrival of welfare reform has led to the restructuring of state and local social service agencies as well as community-based nonprofit contract provider agencies. The shift from benefit eligibility to job-ready employability has had a profound impact on redefining clients as future employees and social service personnel as employment and workplace-support specialists.

With this brief historical overview, it is possible to see how strategic planning provides an important tool for understanding how public and nonprofit social and human service agencies can address their respective futures. Planning has changed fundamentally to meet the demands of the modern era. The following characteristics of planning suggest the critical role that planning plays in enabling organizations to deal with an uncertain and changing environment:

- Planning involves adjusting the internal structures and processes to account for changes in the external environment, especially acquiring the tools and capabilities to assess the external environment in terms of legislation, economic forecasts, changes in housing and transportation, the changing demand for support services such as child care and health care, and the emerging role of faith-based organizations in the delivery of human services.

- Planning involves increased interest in organizational learning and strategic management, which are necessary to position agencies to be relevant and responsive to the changing needs of client populations.

- Planning involves a profound shift in management philosophy from reactive crisis management to proactive strategic management, in which middle and senior managers create more balance between their concerns for efficient internal operations and effective external community relations.

- Planning involves renewed interest in understanding and assessing the community context of human service organizations; directors of public social service agencies spend far more time educating elected officials and opinion leaders, and nonprofit agency directors devote more time to educating and shaping a more externally oriented board of directors (networking, fund-raising, lobbying, marketing, and so on).

- Planning involves shifting from plans being an end goal/document to plans becoming the first step in a larger process of change: Strategic issues/directions/initiatives are translated into specific action plans, which rely on strategic management and ultimately lead to the measurement of outcomes in terms of both quality and quantity.

- Planning involves new roles for program managers and agency directors; they need to be more significantly involved than ever before in at least four areas of agency planning: (a) strategic planning, (b) strategic management related to implementing the plan, (c) operations and program planning related to restructuring current programs/systems and developing new service programs and systems, and (d) evaluation planning, which involves the design and implementation of new information systems and policy analysis capabilities.

With these significant changes in mind, this chapter focuses on strategic planning, implementation of the plan in the midst of ongoing operations/program planning, and the relationship between planning and implementation. Case examples will be used to illustrate key planning activities, and the chapter will conclude with a discussion of the challenges facing agency-based planning. Strategic planning is only as good as the process used to implement the plan and monitor the change process. Therefore, the dual perspective of planning and implementation is a central theme throughout this chapter. Each perspective will be defined, along with the nature of the relationship between planning and operations.

DEFINING STRATEGIC PLANNING

As Berman (1998) has noted, strategic planning is a set of procedures that help organizations and communities to align their priorities with changing conditions and new opportunities. He approaches strategic planning from both a community and organizational perspective and notes that it is used

- to design a future that better meets their needs and to develop paths and guideposts
- to build consensus among often disparate individuals and organizations and to shape different points of view (board, staff, clients, community, etc.)
- to motivate organizations to respond to a changing environment
- to address the need for consolidation, reorganization, or restoration of balance among different organizational services

From a slightly different perspective, Bryson (1995) views strategic planning as a disciplined effort to produce fundamental decisions shaping the nature and direction of organizational activities. He notes that strategic planning

- can help revitalize, redirect, and improve organizational performance
- can provide an opportunity to make connections and changes across programs, as well as integrate policies and programs
- can build bridges with individuals and groups who are affected by or can affect the future of the organization
- can help make important decisions related to four fundamental questions: (a) Where are we going (mission)? (b) How do we get there (strategic programs)? (c) What is our blueprint for action (budgets)? and (d) How do we know if we are on track (monitoring and assessment)?
- can be effectively used in highly politicized environments, provided extra attention is give to both client/member and stakeholder analysis

Bryson notes that the most important feature of strategic planning is promoting the development of strategic thinking. This characteristic is what clearly distinguishes the old approaches of long-range planning from the new methods of strategic planning. Thinking strategically is somewhat like thinking critically. Individuals and groups acquire three important capacities: (a) developing a keen awareness of organizational cultures, histories, and external environments; (b) pursuing an intense examination of assumptions underlying different aspects of organizational life; and (c) engaging in imaginative speculation in which alternatives and viable options are generated. Strategic thinking also involves assessing how others view strategic planning, the topic of the next section.

THE KEY ELEMENTS OF STRATEGIC PLANNING

Based on a review of the limited literature on strategic planning and management in the human services, it is possible to identify three general themes. One segment of the literature focuses on the definition of strategic planning, the specific planning steps, and the benefits of strategic planning (Eadie, 1983; Julian & Lyons, 1992; Kaufman & Jacobs, 1987; Koontz, 1981; Sorkin, Ferris, & Hudak, 1984; Steiner, Gross, Ruffolo, & Murray, 1994; Ziegenfuss, 1989). Another segment includes discussions of the relationship among organizational characteristics, strategic planning, and performance (Siciliano, 1997; Vogel & Patterson, 1986; Webster & Wylie, 1988a, 1988b). A third segment focuses on some of the administrative and supervisory issues that need to be taken into account when implementing a strategic plan (Eldridge, 1983; Gowdy & Freeman, 1993).

With regard to the definition and relevance of strategic planning, Steiner et al. (1994) have identified certain internal and external factors. Among the most important external factors are (a) decreased funding; (b) changing social political and economic priorities in the external environment; (c) increased competition; (d) societal demographic, social, political, and economic changes; and (e) changing regulatory requirements. The most important internal conditions include (a) change in leadership or high turnover; (b) conditions of stagnancy, crisis, or loss of focus, and (c) rapid increases or decreases in demand for services. All of these factors also contribute to legislative pressures on public and nonprofit social services agencies to become more accountable (Siciliano, 1997; Steiner et al., 1994; Webster & Wylie, 1988b). Consequently, social services agencies have been placing greater emphasis on strategic planning over the past two decades (e.g., by 1984, 62% of the 800 member organizations affiliated with the United Way had initiated a strategic planning process).

With respect to linking strategic planning to organizational characteristics, Webster and Wylie (1988a) found that agencies receiving funds from the United Way were more likely to engage in strategic planning if (a) their client population was changing rapidly, (b) they experienced pressures from regulatory agencies to plan, and (c) they had attended a workshop on strategic planning. Almost 90% of the agencies felt that they had benefitted from the strategic planning process by changing their mission, adding/eliminating services, and/or restructuring the organization, with almost 50% of the agencies characterizing the benefits as major. Webster and Wylie also found that large agencies using outside consultants to develop a comprehensive strategic planning process reported major changes as a result of the process. In addition, it was found that, in some cases, eliciting widespread stakeholder participation detracted from securing major changes and was associated with lower agency satisfaction with the process.

Similarly, in a survey of 240 YMCAs, Siciliano (1997) found that (a) the active involvement of board members can enhance the effectiveness of the strategic planning process, especially through their involvement on strategic planning committees; (b) financially secure organizations were more likely to engage in effective strategic planning; and (c) effective strategic planning leads to better financial and operational performance.

With respect to implementing strategic plans, Eldridge (1983) identifies the following factors that can keep the agency from fully benefitting from the plan: (a) inadequate staff involvement, (b) inability to anticipate and manage conflicts, (c) insufficient teamwork and coordination, (d) lack of staff empowerment, and (e) poor use of procedures to implement a plan (timelines, delegated responsibilities, and decision-making authority). As Gowdy and Freeman (1993) note with respect to program supervision, it is one thing to create a new program (or strategic plan) and quite another thing to change or reshape a program (or agency) to be responsive to changing conditions.

STEPS IN STRATEGIC PLANNING

The specific activities involved in developing an effective strategic plan vary considerably depending on the focus, size, location, and external and internal environment of an agency. However, certain broadly defined activities, usually carried out simultaneously, are common to the development of an agency's strategic plan; namely, (a) reassessing the agency's mission and developing a future vision of the agency, (b) assessing the external environment and competition, (c) assessing the internal operations and client services, and (d) developing a plan that includes strategies, tasks, outcomes, timelines, and implementation steps (Allison & Kaye, 1997; Bryson, 1995; Eadie, 1983; Julian & Lyons, 1992; Steiner et al., 1994). These broadly defined activities can be itemized in terms of key questions to be addressed, as noted in Figure 17.1.

Clarifying mission, goals, and objectives. One of the initial steps in the strategic planning process is to reassess the organization's mission statement. If this process has not been done since the agency was established, it means a return to its charter or articles of incorporation to find the stated purpose of the organization. The mission statement often includes the agency's major goals. However, in periods of rapid external and internal change, some goals may have become obsolete or require clarification in relationship to changing client needs, new regulatory requirements, funding priorities, and/or societal values. To be effective, agency goals need to be achievable, manageable, operational, and small in number. The process of clarifying goals should involve all relevant stakeholders (staff, clients, advocacy groups, funding organizations, and regulatory agencies) to develop a sense of ownership. A clearly articulated, generally accepted, and comprehensive set of goals in a mission statement is important for generating energy, cohesion, and motivation to deal with internal and external challenges.

As noted in Figure 17.2, the mission statement for a large Jewish fund-raising organization in New York City includes four components: (a) a brief history of the organization, reflecting its roots and traditions; (b) a listing of its core values, which are used to guide daily operations; (c) a listing of the primary goals that structure the current operations; and (d) a listing of the methods used to achieve those goals. Not all mission statements are this elaborate, and some agencies pride themselves on the use of very brief mission statements. For example, a brief mission statement drawn from Figure 17.2 might be: To ensure the continuity of the Jewish people, to enhance the quality of Jewish life, and to build a strong and unified Jewish community—in New York, Israel, and throughout

Strategic Planning Guide

I. Mission Statement Development/Review

1. Does it reflect the organization's strengths and areas for continuous improvement?
2. Does it adequately describe the clients, major programs/services, staff, and board?
3. Does it reflect the unique assets of the organization?
4. Does it reflect the organization's history and philosophy in terms of core values?

II. Assessing the External Environment

1. What are some of the local and national factors affecting the organization: (a) social and political factors (shifting values, rising expectations, emerging groups, changing demographics, etc.), (b) economic factors (financial markets, local economy, tax policies, housing market, etc.), and (c) technological factors (information systems, Internet, cellular communications, etc.)?
2. Given these external factors, what are the organization's major opportunities and threats?

III. Identifying Best Practices and the Nature of Our Competition

1. What are some of the best practices (programs, processes, procedures) being carried out in similar organizations locally, regionally, nationally, and internationally?
2. How do we compare with the competition in terms of (a) client services/fees, (b) staff salaries, (c) facilities, (d) reputation, and (e) administrative capacities (program development, marketing, and service effectiveness/efficiency)?

IV. Client /Stakeholder Analysis

1. Who are the clients/stakeholders, and how have they changed over the past 5 years (age, ethnicity, gender, urban/suburban, occupations, incomes)?
2. Why do they seek/use the organization's services (satisfaction/expectations)?
3. What do staff/board want to change (programs, service mix, staff/volunteer roles, etc.)?
4. What are our efforts to reach prospective clients/stakeholders?

V. Assessing Internal Operations

1. How well do we manage our operations: (a) finances (budgetary trends over past 5 years), (b) facilities (space utilization and building maintenance), (c) staff (personnel systems and professional development), (d) volunteers (recruitment, training, deployment, evaluation, recognition), (e) service programs (design, update, market, implement, evaluate), (f) communications (printed, information, and referral coordination), and (g) board leadership (board development and leadership succession) and client relations (including outreach)?
2. How well do we plan and evaluate service programs?
3. What are the major strengths and limitations of our organization's internal operations?

VI. Developing the components of the plan

1. What are the cross-cutting themes that emerge as new directions/initiatives from items I to V?
2. What strategies, tasks, and outcomes can be identified to address each initiative?

Figure 17.1. A Strategic Planning Guide

Mission Statement of the United Jewish Appeal

Our History

UJA-Federation, the primary philanthropic arm of the Greater New York Jewish community, continues long and distinguished traditions of serving the Jewish community in New York, Israel, and throughout the world.

Since its founding in 1917, the Federation of Jewish Philanthropies of New York helped—through united fund-raising and other means—a diverse and growing network of agencies to minister the human service needs of the Jewish community and to advance and improve Jewish education.

In 1938, as a direct reaction to Kristallnacht and the Nazi threat to Jewish survival, the United Jewish Appeal was founded to finance the rescue, relief, and rehabilitation of Jews in Nazi Germany and throughout the world. In 1948, with the establishment of the State of Israel, UJA became the principal means for American Jews to assist in the absorption of Jewish immigrants and the building of the Jewish State.

In 1973, as the Yom Kippur War threatened the existence of the State of Israel, UJA and Federation united their fund-raising efforts but retained their separate administrative and other operations. In 1986, to further the interests of the Jewish community, the merger of the two organizations was completed.

Our Values and Commitments

UJA-Federation exists in the largest and most diverse Jewish community in the world. We strive to advance the shared values and commitments of the overwhelming majority of that community:

- Philanthropy as an act of righteousness (tzedakah); the historic Jewish ideal of social justice for all; and the responsibility of Jews everywhere, each for the other
- The profound importance and vital role of Israel in Jewish history and Jewish life today
- The responsibility to help, rescue, and liberate Jews everywhere they may be in danger
- The unity of the Jewish people, while maintaining respect for the diversity of Jewish experience and ideas
- The importance of Jewish education and the synagogue to convey Jewish identity and values

Our Mission

It is the Mission of UJA-Federation:

- To ensure the continuity of the Jewish people, to enhance the quality of Jewish life, and to build a strong and unified Jewish community—in New York, Israel, and throughout the world
- To help, through a network of affiliated agencies, individuals and families in need—the old and young, the unemployed, the homeless, the sick and poor—and to resettle those who are persecuted or oppressed
- To help meet human needs in the State of Israel and to strengthen the relationship between the people of Israel and the Diaspora

In order to fulfill our Mission, we must:

- Strengthen the UJA-Federation role as the primary arm of the Jewish community of Greater New York for fund-raising, communal planning, and allocation of resources
- Strengthen our partnership with the network of human and community service agencies, synagogues, Jewish education, and rescue agencies serving New York, Israel, and other countries; seek the active participation of all sectors of the Jewish community and bring all Jews more closely together
- Work in concert with government, other voluntary agencies, and other ethnic and religious communities in New York
- Educate the members of the Jewish community about the importance of supporting—with their talent, energy, and material resources—the UJA-Federation Mission

Figure 17.2. Mission Statement of the United Jewish Appeal—Federation of Jewish Philanthropies of New York, Inc. Approved November 30, 1989

the world. However, such brief statements do not always help others understand the full dimensions of an organization's mission.

Whereas a mission statement focuses primarily on the present and immediate future of the agency, a vision statement is designed to help the organization envision a time in the distant future (e.g., 15 years out) by encouraging all parties in the planning process to dream. The primary assumptions underlying the development of a vision statement are that the agency will have all the resources it needs (money, staff, facilities, etc.) to create and operate an ideal set of services for a target audience with a particular reputation and core set of values readily apparent to the community. For many, vision statement development is extremely challenging and time-consuming, given the extensive preoccupation with the opportunities and threats of the present. However, the exercise can be very informative as it stretches the best minds in the organization to envision a future condition that could provide a roadmap into the future.

Scanning the environment. One of the factors that distinguishes strategic planning from long-range planning is the active scanning of the external environment. Identifying threats and opportunities due to social, political, and economic changes provides important information for continuously testing the relevance and feasibility of the agency's goals. Scanning can also identify problems and prospects that an agency may face in the future. These issues include the general condition of the economy, immigration trends, corporate policies, technological changes, and changes in societal values. These issues could affect the size of caseloads,

contribute to changing client needs, and/or influence the flow of future funding. Consequently, agencies need to develop the capacity to foresee the impact of a broad range of factors on their agencies and client populations.

Environmental scanning is most effective when it is carried out on a continuous basis, especially during periods of rapid change. It requires access to sources of information to track relevant social, economic, and political changes at the local, state, and federal levels. Although newspapers and magazines can be important sources of information, other sources include informal channels of information used by the agency's board of directors, local leaders, advocates, and public officials. For example, community leaders may provide useful insights about the changing nature of client problems, whereas legislators may provide useful information about impending changes that may affect the revenue base of an agency. Assessments of the complex external environment are usually difficult and expensive for social services agencies to purchase, and therefore, senior agency staff need to acquire the expertise to engage in effective environmental scanning. Scanning the environment could be one of the most important components of the strategic planning process.

In addition to the ongoing comparative assessments, which agencies conduct informally with similar agencies in their fields of service, another aspect of scanning the environment includes assessing competition and best practices. Although most human service agencies do not conceive of themselves as operating in a competitive environment, it is clear that such environments exist and may be increasing with the arrival of managed care and welfare reform.

Most public agencies are instrumental in creating boundaries around competition through the use of contracting with providers who can deliver services most efficiently, effectively, and cheaply. In contrast, nonprofit agencies are experiencing considerable competition as they seek multiple sources of funding, including funds from foundations, and find themselves under increased pressure to collaborate with other agencies, co-locate service, merge with or acquire other agencies, or go out of business.

One of the most productive approaches to assessing the competition in these times is to view the process as identifying best practices. This approach assumes a more open exploration of the environment by learning about the effective practices, policies, and/or procedures used by other agencies locally, regionally, nationally, and internationally. By comparison, agencies are then able to modify their own services to adapt and/or include some of the best practices learned through scanning the environment.

Assessing operations. To achieve its mission and goals within the context of the external threats and opportunities, an agency must develop a comprehensive understanding of its own strengths and the limitations of its operations in relationship to its resources (services, finance, personnel, facilities, communications, policies/procedures, and governance).

It is important to fully involve all levels of agency staff and board members to benefit from their observations about the agency's strengths and limitations. Top management needs to provide staff with the opportunity to assess organizational strengths and limitations to foster open dialogue, criticism, self-reflection, and an assessment of staff roles in relationship with the rest of the organization. Participation in program and strategic planning helps staff members transcend the narrow perspectives of their own jobs and become less defensive about evaluation activities as they comprehend the larger systemic issues that influence their individual practice (Gowdy & Freeman, 1993). Similarly, dialogue and feedback from clients, advocacy groups, and the general community are necessary to acquire other points of view. Frequently, a facilitator or organizational development consultant can be useful in developing a comprehensive balance of organizational strengths and limitations, as well as assisting with the environmental assessment and the construction of the strategic plan.

Most strategic plans include a set of strategies or directions that the organization has chosen to pursue. An example of one of these strategies is noted in Figure 17.3 related to a national Jewish women's organization (Hadassah), namely strengthening organizational structures and processes, which is one of five strategies. The others are related to expanding membership and fund-raising, increasing targeting of programs at the local level, improving governance, and strengthening the volunteer-staff relationship.

Central to assessing internal operations is the process of analyzing the client or stakeholder population. As noted in Figure 17.1, many questions can be addressed in constructing a picture of the population currently being served as well as previous populations. It is important to know how the client or stakeholder population has changed over time. When looking back over the past 5 years, has the population become older or younger, have the needs/interests

Strategy 3—Organizational Structure and Processes

Throughout the strategic planning committee reports, there was a consistent theme that the current organizational structure did not facilitate effective communication, flexibility in programming, quick response to changing environments and issues, and a personal sense of job enrichment. The following action plans need to be designed and implemented to address Strategy 3:

- Developing an interdepartmental structure for conducting annual or every-other-year evaluations of Hadassah programs, including all Israel and American projects, to assess levels of success and the potential for new ventures. Included in the structure needs to be a mechanism for evaluating new pilot proposals and the review of existing pilot projects.

- Conducting an in-depth assessment of Hadassah's current organizational structure in New York (the need for specific departments under a particular division, the need for eight divisions, role of the division coordinator, etc.) linked to an assessment of the structure of regions, the potential for satellite offices, and the role of regional consultants.

- Developing specific processes to foster greater interdepartmental communication to share annual work plans reflecting goals and measurable objectives as well as share departmental assessment of needs in the regions. In addition, it is important to address the multiple issues of improving meeting management within and between departments (e.g., use of agendas, coordinated meeting schedules, clarity about volunteer and/or staff participation, use of visuals, etc.).

- Conducting a communications audit to assess Hadassah's public relations capacity to share successes and important human interest stories, assess the merits of a Hadassah House newsletter, and investigate the capacity to test-market issues and program ideas on a national bias. Special attention should be given to how Hadassah House communicates with chapters and regions.

- Conducting an office management audit to assess the adequacy of office equipment (desk-top publishing, teleconferencing, word processing, electronic mail, etc.) and the efficiency of current methods of managing the mail, distributing materials, and recycling.

Many of these issues should be handled by a senior management group responsible for the overall management of Hadassah House operations.

Figure 17.3. Hadassah Strategic Plan (1993)

NOTE: Hadassah is an American Jewish women's organization with 300,000 members, which provides educational programs and generates financial support for health, education, and community services in Israel.

of clients or members changed, and is the organization responsive to any of these changes? This form of client/stakeholder analysis relies heavily on satisfaction surveys, recent focus-group meetings, interviews, and/or a review of client/member records. Although most human service organizations possess an immense amount of client data, it is rarely reviewed from the perspective of contributing to a strategic plan. As a result, client analysis is an essential component of assessing internal operations.

Constructing the strategic plan. The previous steps on assessing the environment and internal operations involve collecting relevant information for use in developing the written plan. The final step in the strategic planning process includes the design of specific strategies to achieve the agency goals. It is based on an analysis of the internal strengths and weaknesses and external threats and opportunities. For example, the three major themes and the nine directions in the strategic plan of a public social service agency are noted in Figure 17.4. Each one of the nine directions would require considerable staff energy and a timeline of several years to implement. Simply communicating the considerable ramifications of the plan with all levels of staff, let alone the community, can be a significant challenge for senior management.

The formulation of strategies involves specifying what will be done, how it will be done, by whom, and when. Strategies involve concrete programs, policies, procedures, and action plans. These all flow from the agency's updated mission statement and reflect detailed and specific guidelines for future action. Once the overall strategic plan is ready, the next step is to design an implementation plan that links the strategic plan to the regular operations of the agency (Ziegenfuss, 1989). This includes the process of developing specific and measurable objectives, outcomes, and performance indicators for each program. These indices should serve as useful benchmarks for annually evaluating the implementation of the strategic plan. A key element of the implementation plan is the identification of the specific human and physical resource requirements for each objective. This element provides the basis for developing the budget needed to implement the strategic plan.

The budget and its justification must specify the proposed expenditures for each program, department, and activity based on the resource requirements and assigned responsibilities. The next component is allocating the responsibility for implementation and monitoring. Despite the growing popularity of strategic planning for social service organizations, the following factors continue to restrict the ability of the agencies to fully benefit from such planning (Eldridge, 1983):

- Inadequate staff involvement, including insufficient authority to make decisions, lack of access to analytical tools, lack of available information, and insufficient attention by top management to involve staff who have the relevant information

- Inability to anticipate and manage conflicts, especially within the strategic planning teams, where members may have different disciplines/backgrounds and senior administrators are unable to manage these conflicts

- Insufficient teamwork and coordination, especially when the planning teams are too large and unwieldy to function effectively (small teams of staff with different responsibilities can ensure more productive participation)

- Lack of empowerment, especially when the planning team is overwhelmed by the external demands on the agency and perceives little room for devising creative solutions

- Poor use of the planning procedures, especially when the deadlines for different tasks, responsibilities, and decisions are not clearly defined, resulting in haphazard, random, and biased decision making

In a case study of a youth agency, Vogel and Patterson (1986) found that a team-based organizational structure can contribute to more effective strategic planning where work tasks and worker skills are combined to achieve goals. In contrast to the top-down bureaucratic approach, the team-based approach can greatly

Theme I: Implement a Proactive, Outcomes-Oriented, High-Impact Philosophy of Service

Strategic direction 1: We will promote a proactive, outcome-oriented approach to meeting consumer needs through continuous training and support for Human Services Agency (HSA) and other service provider staff to provide assistance to consumers in advocating for their own needs.

Strategic direction 2: Policymakers, program managers, and individual service providers at all levels (private, public, volunteer) will make decisions on the most effective utilization of resources by considering a common set of values:

   a. We will achieve the most long-term, widespread impact at the lowest cost, as determined by the best available consumer-defined outcome measures.
   b. We will focus on prevention and the earliest possible intervention, promote self-sufficiency, and strengthen families and individuals within their familial and support environments.
   c. We will treat all consumers with respect.
   d. We will assure, at a minimum, that all consumers receive assistance in identifying their needs and information and referral on available options for food, clothing, shelter, and health care.

Theme II: Extend the Boundaries of the Human Services System

Strategic direction 3: We will create a seamless system of public/private service by fostering cooperation and partnerships among government, nonprofit, and private sector organizations and individuals through the development of shared vision and values, common interests and objectives, and coordinated implementation strategies.

Strategic direction 4: We will build support for addressing human service needs through separate and joint public education efforts.

Strategic direction 5: We will promote waivers and legislation that remove disincentives to prevention and early intervention services, attainment of consumer self-sufficiency, and provision of assistance that strengthens consumers' family and support environments.

Theme III: Deliver Services That Respond to the Self-Identified Needs of Consumers

Strategic direction 6: We will develop an integrated single intake system, with multiple physical entry points, that provides consumer access to all available resources, both public and private, as well as a system of needs assessment, information, and referral that supports a coordinated delivery of services and offers consumers choices in both definition of needs and selection and design of solutions.

Strategic direction 7: We will create accessibility to services for all consumers.

Strategic direction 8: We will use data collected while serving consumers to plan, operate, and evaluate human services programs and activity.

Strategic direction 9: We will make changes needed to expand service delivery of child care, affordable housing, and job training to consumers identified as the "working poor."

Figure 17.4. Strategic Planning Directions—San Mateo County (California) Human Services Agency (1993)

facilitate the development of strategic plans that call for changing the internal environment of the agency in response to external demands.

As noted earlier in the chapter, developing a strategic plan is one thing, but implementing it can be quite challenging. The implementation process usually occurs while staff are carrying out ongoing agency activities and programs. Implementing the plan can be seen as an added burden (sometimes likened to changing a tire on your car while proceeding down the road at 60 mph). In the next section, we explore the issues of strategic management associated with planning and implementing ongoing operations and programs.

KEY ELEMENTS OF OPERATIONS/ PROGRAM PLANNING

While strategic planning provides a framework for setting agency directions with a focused mission statement, program and operations planning are the key components of day-to-day agency life. They tend to be tactical and emerge from four compelling sources: (a) the strategic plan itself, (b) ongoing program evaluation, (c) contingency planning, and (d) annual budget planning.

STRATEGIC PLAN IMPLEMENTATION

Operational planning involves the transformation of the major initiatives in a strategic plan into specific goals and objectives that include action steps for staff and others to carry out. It is generally assumed that the implementation teams include many more people than the number who developed the strategic plan. Similarly,

it is necessary to identify a range of resources needed to implement the initiatives in the strategic plan. In many settings, strategic plan implementation is driven by a conscious effort to involve busy staff and others in either changing the way they do business or to add new expectations to existing workloads. As Stacey (1992) notes, the controlled behavior (of staff and others) needs to have some overall coherence or pattern; that is, it is internally connected and constrained—it is the opposite of haphazard, unconnected thinking and acting without any pattern, or unconstrained explosively unstable behavior. Consequently, strategic plan implementation is built on the assumption that organizations need to change. Therefore, the operational plans for each initiative in the strategic plan need to be spelled out. Many agencies, especially public agencies, link the implementation of a strategic plan to its ongoing annual operations plan, which generally includes the following components (Allison & Kaye, 1997):

- Specified process and outcome objectives
- Identified staff responsible for implementing the plan
- A user-friendly monitoring template to note progress made
- Continuous reference to operationalizing the strategic plan
- Continuous assessment to make sure that the operational plan is realistic
- Continuous opportunities to provide suggestions for future annual plans

The most common error in strategic planning is to believe that the task is completed when the plan is approved. Agency staff members can use a variety of techniques to assure that the plan is continuously cited throughout

Recommendation 1 1.1 1.2	Action Steps 1. 2. 3.	Outcomes 1. 2. 3.	Due Dates 1. 2. 3.	People Responsible 1. 2. 3.
Recommendation 2 2.1 2.2				
Recommendation 3 3.1 3.2				

Figure 17.5. The Operational Steps Needed to Implement the Strategic Plan

the implementation process. For example, a simple, self-monitoring approach can be used when the key elements of the strategic plan are "boiled down" into specific action steps with projected outcomes, due dates, and people responsible for completing the work, as noted in Figure 17.5. This chart could be updated monthly and shared with the agency board of directors on a quarterly basis, with a discussion focused on the status of each recommendation and the barriers preventing full implementation. The combination of board oversight with staff accountability helps to maintain the focus and momentum needed to implement the strategic plan.

PROGRAM PLANNING AND EVALUATION

Well-administered, disciplined agencies engage in serious program planning and evaluation as part of their ongoing functioning. It is critical to formally create a feedback loop from evaluation to program planning to assure that the lessons learned in these evaluative activities are translated to program and agency policies and procedures. For example, in the geriatric mental health program of a South Florida agency, accessibility was an important part of assessing client services. In looking at the populations served by the agency as compared to the target population in the catchment area, it was discovered that both men and Hispanics were significantly underrepresented in the client population. Through formal program planning sessions involving senior management, program evaluators, and clinical and supervisory staff to identify potential reasons for an underrepresentation of men, it was concluded that the center's hours of operation (8:30 a.m. to 5:30 p.m. Monday through Friday) might be a barrier to the employed older, disproportionately male population. Data from a review of intake inquiries suggested that, indeed, this might be a factor, and the hours of operations were changed to include evening hours, which helped to increase male service utilization (Austin, 1983; Kettner & Daley, 1988).

Even though the program was multilingual (including Spanish), a focused outreach effort was developed based on concepts of *personalismo,* a concept that suggested the personal relationship between referral sources and Spanish-speaking clinical staff was more important than traditional institutional liaison arrangements. Again, the operational changes, which included the outreach of Spanish-speaking clinical staff to traditional referral sources, resulted in significantly greater service accessibility for the Latino population. The measurement of service outcomes, program accountability, and information management are addressed elsewhere in this volume. They are critical elements for effective operations planning (Szapocnik, Solomon, Faletti, & Perry, 1979).

CONTINGENCY PLANNING

Day-to-day agency life is filled with the drama of unexpected events. Despite the finest strategic and operational plans, effective organizations are not always able to respond quickly and opportunistically to sudden environmental shifts. A mid-year reduction in public support, a fire in an agency facility, a serious untoward incident involving an agency client, an agency labor dispute, an inability to find qualified credentialed staff to fill vacant positions—these are among the myriad reasons that contingency planning often becomes a critical component of potential agency success. As a form of opera-

tions planning, contingency planning involves the converting of crises into organizational opportunities. This requires special attention to using a disciplined approach to systematically (a) refer to the agency mission on a regular basis, (b) seek out available information, (c) promote the active participation of appropriate staff and lay leaders, and (d) engage in extensive monitoring and follow-up. Contingency plans are much easier to implement if a strategic plan provides overall guidance for the future allocation of scarce agency resources.

Perhaps the most common contingency is a change in the flow of agency revenues that threatens the survival of the agency and its programs. In the case of a large city fund-raising agency that allocates funds annually to a group of beneficiary agencies, experience with agency financial failures led to the development of a management tool that eliminated the need for crisis management and focused the agency's board of directors and senior management on rational contingency planning tied to agency mission and plan. The tool was an early warning system that uses a combination of financial analyses (balance sheet ratios), agency-by-agency trend data, assessment analyses, and comparisons to identify those agencies that were within 1 to 2 years of crisis. In many cases, this led to contingency financial planning that altered the direction of the agency. In some cases, the agency mission could best be served by beginning discussions on the value of a merger with another agency.

Most human service managers believe strongly in their agency mission and the value of its services, and they tend to view budgetary threats with unfettered optimism. However, budgets are projections that cannot always take into account changes in the external funding environment. As a result, managers tend to delay serious cuts as long as possible and to limit those cuts to overhead expenses rather than direct service delivery or across-the-board cuts in service expenditures, waiting for each contingency to become a crisis before acting. Ironically, fiscal crisis is often an unusual opportunity to reshape the agency in line with strategic planning recommendations. Fiscal crisis provides management with the ability to move far more decisively and quickly than in times of stability. The availability of time is a critical factor in contingency planning. If there is not enough time to meet the monthly payroll due to the financial crisis, it may be too late for continency planning and drastic measures may be needed.

BUDGETARY PLANNING

Annual budgets represent the major link between implementing a strategic plan and the ongoing priorities reflected in the annual operations plans that accompany most budgets. Many organizations do program and operations planning on the basis of the agency's fiscal year. The budgetary allocation of funds often requires clear and measurable objectives and the resources needed to achieve the goals and objectives, which need to be financially quantified in terms of revenues and expenses. This form of budgeting helps to assure that the budget preparation process is driven more by agency program and mission considerations than simply by the availability of financial resources (program driven rather than finance driven). Effective managers use budget planning as a valuable adjunct to implementing a strategic plan.

For example, a national planning and service agency recently conducted a strategic plan that built the budgetary process into the planning process. The technique involved the use of a parallel budgetary planning process conducted at the same time as the strategic plan was being developed. The strategic planning included six major task forces. As each task force developed its recommendations, management was asked to prepare budget projections related to each of the recommendations, and agency department heads were asked to identify the implications of each recommendation for staff implementation. By linking the planning and budgeting processes together, this agency improved its capacity to understand the implementation implications of the proposed components of the plan. At the same time, it involved the financial staff in thinking carefully about the financial and human resource implications of each recommendation in the strategic plan. In gaining board approval of the plan, a budget template was used to demonstrate the budgetary changes needed to implement each recommendation; this technique helped to raise the level of confidence among all involved with respect to the realistic possibilities of implementing the strategic plan.

REVISITING THE RELATIONSHIP BETWEEN STRATEGIC PLANNING AND OPERATIONAL PLANNING

The culture of strategic and operational planning requires agency leadership that is prepared to openly and objectively look at its current practices with the expectation and belief that things can be better. Quality strategic planning is an interactive process that invites all stakeholders to participate actively in constructive criticism. The best planning processes have as many stakeholders as possible feeling that they are contributing to the activities. Whether it is in the process of holding formal hearings or engaging in focus groups, town meetings, and other methods of reaching all stakeholders, communication is a key element to planning.

An effective planning process is not simply an analytic exercise. It is one that blends art with science: the science of an analytic mind-set to complete a comprehensive organizational assessment with the artistry to foster the broadest level of participation, touching the hearts and minds of all stakeholders with core organizational values and hopes for the future. Strategic planning involves change and managerial leadership. To paraphrase an observation by Lao Tse centuries ago, "leaders are individuals whom the people hardly know exist; but good leaders, when their work is done, their aims fulfilled, become truly invisible when the people say 'We did this ourselves.'" The quest for continuous improvement can motivate staff and board members alike, especially when they build together an environment where creativity leads to shared satisfaction and the status quo is not an acceptable condition.

CONCLUSION

In this chapter, we have explored the dynamics of strategic planning and operations planning and implementation. We have emphasized the linkage between planning and implementation and the importance of involving staff and board members throughout the process. Strategic planning is characterized as proactive and linear in that it seeks to analyze data from a variety of sources to develop a course of action. Not everyone identifies with the importance of planning. In the for-profit arena, an increasing number of entrepreneurs tend to minimize planning in order to be able to respond to opportunities that could not have been foreseen (Mintzberg, 1994). Some human service administrators identify with this entrepreneurial model, either because of the presumed flexibility involved or because the planning process is seen as too labor-intensive and costly when involving staff, board members, and/or a consultant/facilitator. These reactions to planning call for more research on the process and outcomes of strategic planning. Although there is research on the benefits of strategic planning, there is little research to document the consequences of not planning, except maybe for case studies of failed businesses or agencies. We need more information about when and why strategic planning works in human service organizations.

The operational and program planning required to implement a strategic plan clearly requires staff to understand the full context and details of the strategic plan to develop a sense of ownership. This ownership is critical if the unanticipated changes and crises that emerge daily in human service agencies are not to be allowed to derail the implementation process. This is easily said but not easily done. Both planning and implementation are creative processes. The analytic aspects of a strategic plan need to be matched by the interactional skills of managers and staff, if the future vision of the agency is to have any meaning within the daily realities of organizational life. There is an artistry to both planning and implementation. This observation has become even more relevant as agencies seek to implement strategic plans by paying attention to the processes of change management.

Change management is an organizational process that recognizes the importance of involving staff at all levels in "modifying the way we do business" (sometimes likened to the process of moving a graveyard). The forces for change and the forces of resistance need to be managed. Although change management is a topic for another chapter (McLennan, 1989; O'toole, 1995; Senge, 1990), it is important to note that some human service organizations are recognizing the need for internal organization development specialists to assist with the team-building, communications enhancement, and intra-organizational restructuring that are often called for in the implementation and monitoring of strategic plans.

The value of strategic planning as a managerial tool has increased dramatically in the context of reinventing government and redefining the role of human services. As we move from an industrial society to a service and information society, the informational tools that allow us to look at our practices more systematically have become both widespread and inexpensive. These tools can be used quite successfully to inform the strategic planning process. Finally, with the end of the Cold War, the globalization of the economy, and a long period of sustained economic growth, service consumers have increased their expectations for high-quality services. The human service administrator has a responsibility to anticipate and respond to this expectation through the use of strategic and operational planning as an essential component of human services management.

REFERENCES

Allison, M., & Kaye, J. (1997). *Strategic planning for nonprofit organizations.* New York: John Wiley.

Austin, D. (1983). Program design issues in the improved administration of human services programs. *Administration in Social Work, 7*(1), 1-11.

Berman, E. M. (1998). *Productivity in public and nonprofit organizations.* Thousand Oaks, CA: Sage.

Bryson, J. M. (1995). *Strategic planning for public and nonprofit organizations.* San Francisco: Jossey-Bass.

Eadie, D. (1983, September/October). Putting a powerful tool to practical use: The application of strategic planning in the public sector. *Public Administration Review,* pp. 447-452.

Eldridge, W. (1983, March). Aids to administrative planning in social agencies. *Child Welfare,* pp. 119-127.

Gowdy, E., & Freeman, E. (1993). Program supervision: Facilitating staff participation in program analysis, planning, and change. *Administration in Social Work, 17*(3), 59-79.

Julian, D., & Lyons, T., (1992). A strategic planning model for human services: Problem solving at the local level. *Evaluation and Program Planning, 15,* 247-254.

Kaufman, J., & Jacobs, H. (1987, Winter). A public planning perspective on strategic planning. *Journal of American Planning Association,* pp. 23-33.

Kettner, P., & Daley, J. (1988, March). Designing effective programs. *Child Welfare,* pp. 99-111.

Koontz, H. (1981). Making strategic planning work. In L. Reinharth, H. Shapiro, & E. Kellman (Eds.), *The practice of planning: Strategic, administrative, and operational.* New York: Van Nostrand Reinhold.

McLennan, R. (1989). *Managing organizational change.* Englewood Cliffs, NJ: Prentice Hall.

Mintzberg, H. (1994). *The rise and fall of strategic planning: Reconceiving roles for planning, plans, planners.* New York: Free Press.

O'toole, J. (1995). *Leading change: Overcoming the ideology of comfort and the tyranny of custom.* San Francisco: Jossey-Bass.

Senge, P. (1990). *The fifth discipline: The art and practice of the learning organization.* New York: Doubleday.

Siciliano, J. (1997). The relationship between formal planning and performance in nonprofit organizations. *Nonprofit Management and Leadership, 7*(4), 387-403.

Sorkin, D., Ferris, N., & Hudak, J. (1984). *Strategies for cities and counties: A strategic planning guide.* Washington, DC: Public Technology.

Stacey, R. D. (1992). *Managing the unknowable: Strategic boundaries between order and chaos in organizations.* San Francisco: Jossey-Bass.

Steiner, J., Gross, G., Ruffolo, M., & Murray, J. (1994). Strategic planning in nonprofits: Profit from it. *Administration in Social Work, 18*(2), 87-106.

Szapocnik, J., Solomon, J., Faletti, M., & Perry, P. (1979, March). Reaching out to Hispanic elders in need of mental health services. *Journal of Hispanic Behavioral Services, 3*(1).

Vogel, L., & Patterson, I. (1986). Strategy and structure: A case study of the implications of strategic planning for organizational structure and management practice. *Administration in Social Work, 10*(2), 53-66.

Webster, S., & Wylie, M. (1988a). Strategic planning in competitive environments. *Administration in Social Work, 12*(3), 25-43.

Webster, S., & Wylie, M. (1988b). Strategic planning in human service agencies. *Journal of Sociology and Social Welfare, 15*(3), 47-64.

Ziegenfuss, J. (1989). *Designing organizational futures.* Springfield, IL: Charles C Thomas.

CHAPTER EIGHTEEN

Manager as Resource Developer

PHILIP McCALLION

For many agencies, fund-raising and grant writing are reactive processes. Proposals are developed to rescue programs that lose their traditional funding, to replace physical plant or equipment that has outlived its usefulness, and to address new priorities identified by funders through request for proposal (RFP) processes. Agencies often find themselves disadvantaged because their efforts are not timely, pressing needs can rarely be matched with available opportunities, and allocated resources are not sufficient for the task. Responding to the challenge for change in an RFP represents an opportunity for renewal for some agencies, causing them to re-examine their mission and the relevance of their programs. However, there is a long-standing concern that agencies that are successful in

obtaining new and more resources often encounter problems over time, as pursued funders' priorities reshape the agency's own mission and goals, leading to goal displacement and conflict with other agency constituencies (Kettner & Martin, 1996). This chapter will challenge social work managers to consider the changing resource picture and the resource dilemmas they must proactively resolve to maintain their agency missions and to provide needed and valued services to consumers. Matching management skills with resource development requirements will also be discussed. Key points will be illustrated using a case study. The primary audience for this chapter will be managers of private not-for-profit agencies (NPOs). However, many of the issues raised also apply to managers of for-profit and public human service programs. The chapter will assume that the majority of resources used by managers of private agencies will be from public sources.

For the purposes of this chapter, the following definitions of agency mission, contracts, and grants will be assumed. Agency mission refers to the general statement of the purposes of an NPO. Often, this was established by the board of directors or by a manager previous to the current office holder. The mission statement legitimizes the activities undertaken by an agency, and all programming should be consistent with that mission (Weinbach, 1998). The missions of many NPOs were written to further important social goods for the most needy and vulnerable in society, reflecting the intentions of an initial donor or the desires of the individuals who came together to form the agency (Gronbjerg, 1993; Weinbach, 1998). Contracts are formal arrangements between public agencies and private providers to provide specified services, sometimes with predetermined expected outcomes, to a fixed number of consumers for an agreed cost. Such arrangements are at the convenience of public funders, are subject to their oversight, and are renewable, usually on an annual basis. Continuity of services for consumers usually encourages the renewal of contracts and the ongoing provision of the same menu of services, but requirements for innovation and a willingness not to renew contracts by some public agencies make some contracts look more like grants. Grants are time-limited opportunities to demonstrate new approaches, to assist new providers to demonstrate competence, or to supplement existing contracted programs. Grants may be for more than 1 year but are generally

not renewable. However, there may be opportunities to later convert grants to contracts.

THE CHANGING RESOURCE ENVIRONMENT

Social service agencies today are faced with changing environments that have a direct impact on resources. Among the changes are (a) changing demographics and social structures; (b) changing role of government, increased accountability, and increased competition; (c) real-dollar reductions in private resources; (d) ramifications of previous deinstitutionalization; (e) consumer choice initiatives; (f) restructuring of health care delivery, oversight, and payments; and (g) competition from for-profit entities.

Changing demographics and social structures. A variety of forces are reshaping society to present more challenges to human service organizations, including more and more pressing social problems and reductions in resources, particularly volunteers and donations. Rising numbers of homeless people, the epidemic of drugs, greater awareness of the impact of alcohol, and the attention being focused on AIDS/HIV all represent human service areas that have grown in significance in recent decades, increasing the impact of other social problems and consuming resources (Menefee, 1997; Stern & Gibelman, 1990). Newly recognized populations contribute to an environment of more pressing social problems and increase competition for resources.

Other demographic trends demand reallocations of resources. For example, the number of elderly people in the United States has almost doubled from nearly 17 million in 1960. The most rapid growth will occur among those 85 and above (Biegel & Blum, 1990). The number of people age 65 and older who are experiencing difficulty with activities of daily living and therefore may need services is expected to increase from 8.7 million in 1990 to 11.5 million by 2010 (Jette, 1996). At the same time, the relative number of younger people is declining, raising concerns about the future ability of U.S. society to support this burgeoning elderly population. There are already conflicts between the generations for resources (Winbush, 1993). The population of people of color is also projected to increase in the coming decades, becoming the majority of the population. This reflects improving mortality pictures, higher comparative birth rates, and the impact of continued immigration trends. Services and service providers are not currently organized to recognize this reality. A greater range of services is being demanded (Aponte & Crouch, 1995; McCallion & Grant-Griffin, in press).

There are growing numbers of two-earner families and single-parent households, reductions in family size and extended family interactions, and increasing disparities between rich and poor (Barnet & Cavanaugh, 1994). The result is an increasing number of American families at risk (Children's Defense Fund, 1996). Also, among American families who see themselves as middle class, there are increased feelings of financial strain that encourage/require more employment, particularly for women, and reduce traditional levels of volunteer activities by both men and women (Fost, 1996). Donations are also remaining at current or reduced levels when adjusted for inflation (Gronbjerg, 1993). Agencies must, therefore, face greater

challenges with fewer of the private resources on which they have relied.

Changing role of government, increased accountability and competition. There has been a steady reduction in the role of federal, state, and local agencies in the provision of services. More recently, in the pursuit of balanced federal and state public funding, support for private agency programs has also declined, and expectations of the services that agencies must provide to continue receiving funds have increased (Kettner & Martin, 1996). Some areas have fared better than others. For example, there have been increases in funding for AIDS-related programs, whereas support for welfare, children, mental health, and employment programs has declined. Gummer (1990) argued that the 1980s saw a major cultural shift in the public funding and administration of human service programs. Previously, historical ambivalence about helping the needy was balanced by a belief in the value of addressing the needs of the less well-off. The 1980s, he argued, saw the rise to prominence of a business culture that emphasizes productivity and efficiency, cost containment, reduction of government roles, and movement of dependent people into work roles. This trend has limited resources and how they are expended, increased uncertainty about future resources, and changed accountability expectations (Gummer, 1990; Menefee, 1997).

Historically, accountability procedures associated with contracts between public funders and private providers of services focused on process issues such as numbers served, verification of delivery of contracted services using prescribed modalities, and completion of required paperwork. Increasingly, however, there are also performance expectations regarding volume and unit cost of services, completion rates for consumers, and the attainment and sustaining of expected outcomes for consumers at the end of programs (Kettner & Martin, 1993). External reviews of the attainment of performance indicators are influencing the renewal of contracts and restricting providers' abilities to establish their own goals and success criteria.

Another important change has been growth in the number of private agencies seeking public funding. This growth has been directly encouraged by public funders, for example, in establishing across the United States community mental health centers, group homes, and other community service providers for people with mental illness or developmental disabilities. However, even as resources have declined, there has been continued growth in the number of agencies seeking that funding. For example, between 1987 and 1995, the number of agencies recognized as nonprofits (i.e., 501[c][3]) by the Internal Revenue Service has grown from 389,415 to 576,133 (Standley, 1998). The combination of shrinking resources and increasing numbers of providers means increased competition for resources.

One competitive outcome is that agencies are increasingly focused on recruiting and serving high- and full-pay consumers in their service sector and are less focused on the growing service needs and demands of lower-pay and no-pay consumers. This leads to further competition between agencies. Positioning for competitive advantage with high-pay consumers also encourages goal displacement among agencies whose missions originally responded to the needs of consumers now seen as low- or no-pay (Netting, McMurtry, Kettner,

& Jones-McClintic, 1990; Stern & Gibelman, 1990).

Real-dollar reductions in private resources. For many agencies, reliance on public dollars from the beginning means they have paid little attention to developing alternative resources. Existing private dollars have also shrunk as a percentage of many agencies' budgets (Netting et al., 1990), and the value of those resources has been reduced in inflation-related terms.

Ramifications of previous deinstitutionalization. The 1960s, '70s, and '80s were marked by the deinstitutionalization of people with mental retardation and other developmental disabilities and people with mental illnesses. Many of the institutions closed (Hadley, 1996). This means community settings are serving both the previously institutionalized and people who in the past would have entered institutions. In addition, improvements in health care and other service provisions are increasing the life spans of people with disabilities and mental illnesses (McCallion & Tobin, 1995). These trends place increasing demands on community-based service agencies to provide more services to a greater number of consumers.

Consumer choice initiatives. On a limited scale, increasingly empowered consumers and communities are asserting that they are better able to determine what their needs are and can deliver better services than established agencies (McCallion, Janicki, & Grant-Griffin, 1997). For example, families of people with disabilities have demonstrated in a number of states that cash subsidies are a more cost-effective way of delivering respite services than agency-based programs (Agosta & Melda, 1996). Newly formed grassroots agencies and consumer groups participating in these initiatives do not have the expense of infrastructure and staff investments faced by established agencies. In cost-conscious environments, their low-cost offerings may threaten the services provided by those agencies.

Restructuring of health care delivery oversight and payments. Managed care has grown significantly in recent decades (McLeod, 1993). It represents an effort to control costs that began in health care and has spread to other human service areas. This goal is achieved by controlling use and payments for care and by shifting some of the economic risks from payers to patients and providers (Cornelius, 1994). For human service NPO providers, these forces are shaping the auspices under which services may be delivered; limiting payments indepen dent of level of services actually delivered; and determining who may deliver and who may receive services, what services and what levels of services will be reimbursed, and what outcomes are expected in what time frames (Strom & Gingerich, 1993).

Competition from for-profit entities. The trend to greater privatization in the delivery of human services has made providing services attractive to for-profit agencies. They, in turn, have become a preferred option for some public funders, because their for-profit orientation seems more consistent with accountability and cost-containment concerns than the consumer orientation of NPOs (Netting et al., 1990). Furthermore, the growth of managed care has encouraged both the development of for-profit

providers and the expansion of their service systems into traditional NPO arenas to achieve economies of scale and other cost-containment goals (Cornelius, 1994). An additional consequence is that for-profit providers are particularly targeting full-pay and low-demand consumers, leaving the more difficult consumers and those for whom there is low reimbursement to NPOs and public providers (Burke & Rafferty, 1994; Netting et al., 1990). This increases the financial risks for NPOs.

The trends are exemplified in the following case example.

Case Example, Part I

In the early 1960s, the executive director of a nationally known residential facility for people with developmental disabilities persuaded his board that the agency should exclusively serve private-pay consumers. Up to that point, about 40% of consumers served were funded by public dollars, with the remainder supported by trust funds or direct contributions from families. The executive director was becoming increasingly concerned that growing public regulation and oversight was requiring the agency to move programming in directions that were not consistent with the history of the agency. The agency's reputation was that of an idyllic "safe haven" for people with disabilities, protecting them from the traumas of mainstream life. State agencies were requiring planned movement of consumers into the community and, although only some of the consumers served were publicly funded, the state was applying these requirements in its licensing review of care for all consumers at the agency. The board agreed with the executive director that removal of the publicly funded consumers would diminish much of this oversight and return the agency to its mission. Public agencies were given 3 months to remove the consumers they were funding.

Within 3 years of the discharge of publicly funded consumers, the agency found itself in serious financial difficulties and began to draw heavily on its endowments. Within another 2 years, the decision was made to again accept publicly funded consumers. Public agencies needed the slots available at the private agency and responded positively to the reopening of acceptances. However, key staff at the public agencies remained angry about what had happened previously and proved to be tough negotiators on the application of regulations and determination of appropriate payment rates for placements.

The board and executive director reaccepted public consumers reluctantly and continued to struggle with state regulators to preserve their vision of the agency. This caused them to commit endowment and other raised funds to support activities not covered by public funding and to provide assistance to private-pay families experiencing financial difficulties.

Over the next 5 years, the proportion of publicly supported consumers at the agency rose to 60%. This resulted from increased public referrals to this private agency because its rates were lower than those at comparable public agencies. Slots for an increased number of publicly funded consumers became available because of the aging and death of some private-pay consumers; the growing inability of private-pay families to meet the increased costs associated with newly required programming, resulting in disenrollments; movement of some existing consumers into the community; and a cost-driven dramatic reduction in new private-pay applications. These trends continued and were compounded by the flight of many experienced and talented staff, who saw decisions at the agency increasingly influenced by financial considerations. Within 15 years of the original decision to disenroll all publicly funded consumers, this nationally known agency found itself on the verge of bankruptcy, its endowments spent and its properties mortgaged. The public and private rates it received did not cover the costs of the services it was required to deliver, and it was not judged to be adequately delivering those services. The agency was about to close. . .

With hindsight, it was relatively easy to reconstruct the decline of this agency. However, the decline occurred over 15 years, and there were times when the problems were not so pressing, and improvement could be surmised. Also, changes over time in executives and in board composition, and recognition of acrimonious relationships with public regulators and funders, left room for attribution of blame to the role of previously involved individuals and the hope that personnel changes would lead to improvement. What is clear, however, is that over those 15 years, the agency continued to focus on what it perceived to be its core mission, assumed that its ability to attract and use resources would remain the same, and sought to maintain or return to the state of affairs and goals that engendered its mission. Meanwhile, funding mechanisms, regulatory expectations, the service environment, and political realities changed around it. Also, as a well-endowed agency, this facility thought it could ignore, then tried to thwart changes being imposed by funding and regulatory sources. It ended up expending resources and failed to find ways to replenish what was being expended.

The experience of this agency raises important questions about the relationship between public and private agencies and about the ability and responsibility of private agencies, particularly NPOs, to pursue privately versus publicly defined missions and approaches to service. It also challenges us to think about whether or not agency constituencies are served when the definition and implementation of an agency's mission remain static. In addition, for the purposes of this chapter, it points out the imperative of developing resources and the consequences of receiving resources from others, particularly from the public arena.

RESPONDING TO RESOURCE ENVIRONMENT CHANGES

Resource environment changes have created five dilemmas that human service managers must resolve to successfully manage their agencies: (a) meeting funder and agency goals, (b) balancing resource development with resource allocation, (c) balancing long- and short-term resource needs, (d) diversifying resources, and (e) competing with uneven rivals.

Meeting funder goals and agency goals. An emerging profile of NPOs—particularly in the areas of children's services, mental health, developmental disabilities, drug and alcohol treatment, and health—shows them competitively receiving 80% to 100% of their funding from public agencies or managed care providers (Netting et al., 1990). Also, those funders have increased expectations about how recipient agencies should deliver services, with specified outcomes. Financial expansion of agencies, in particular, and financial viability in general may be predicated on the openness of providers to pursue goals established by funders and regulators. In a political environment, funders' goals may themselves be contradictory, and they often change over time. Outright inconsistency with an agency's own goals will be obvious and is more likely to be addressed by managers and boards of directors. More subtle will be gradual changes driven by reconciling the desires of a number of funders and accepting changes over

time in particular funders' goals. Yet, each NPO was founded for a particular purpose and with a specified mission, often dedicated to the most vulnerable in society (Weinbach, 1998). Sometimes, the change pressures and process are helpful. An agency may recognize that its original mission is no longer viable or meeting as critical a social need. It is more likely, however, that managers and board members must weigh pursuing funding that, although offering financial viability, also encourages pursuit of new or increasingly selected populations or service modalities. In particular, consideration must be given to the consequences of such choices for needy, oppressed, and vulnerable populations, which are less likely to be priorities under these funding mechanisms. Similarly, the appropriateness of specified treatment modalities, their purposes—for example, to change individuals as opposed to changing environmental constraints on individuals—and the adequacy of levels of service funded must also be weighed against the hopes and goals for consumers outlined in an agency's mission statement.

Allocating resources to support resource development while maintaining allocations of service-delivery resources. Traditionally, agencies have prided themselves on allocating the highest possible percentage of resources to direct services to consumers. Indeed, there have been concerns raised about not-for-profits that dedicate particularly high proportions of their resources to administrative and other resource development costs (Milofsky & Blades, 1991). The emergence, however, of a "contract culture" (Kramer, 1994), the competitive pursuit by private agencies of public dollars available through time-limited contracts, requires the allocation of at least some resources to contract development, management, and renewal. For example, the process of grant writing, of responding to requests for proposals, requires staff time and other resources to develop and express goals, strategies, expected outcomes, and other required components of proposals. The amount of work is increased by short time frames for responses as well as different due dates, length of contracts, contract expectations, and other contract components for different funders (Gronbjerg, 1991). Also, not every proposal is successful. Resources are often needed to support the submission of multiple proposals. The pursuit of nonpublic resources often requires similar resource investments to facilitate the development of income-generating events, planned giving, foundation grants, and individual gifts.

Balancing long- and short-term resource needs. Grant writing and contract negotiation often occur in a context of imminent loss of funds for the agency and services for the consumer. Therefore, managers' attention is rightly focused on these short-term goals. However, a continued focus on short-term survival often creates an environment that leads to gradual goal displacement over the long term through pursuit, receipt, and implementation of successive and different contracts and grants. Equally, short time frames for responses, up-front resource requirements, and the need to demonstrate an ability to carry out a proposed contract's requirements often restrict agencies from participating in the competition for more or new sources of funds (Gronbjerg, 1993; Schlesinger, Dorwart, & Pulice, 1986). Effectively positioning an agency in new or expanded funding requires planning, recruitment

of needed staff, and the development of indicators that suggest an agency will be successful in meeting the requirements of contracts. This is likely to be a long-term development effort, sometimes taking resources from other activities that may produce more immediate returns.

Diversifying funding resources while acknowledging growing dependence on single-source funding. Most not-for-profit agencies receive the majority of their funding from one source (Gronbjerg, 1993). There are costs to the provider's independence that diversification of funding may remediate. However, public agencies have carved out unique services areas, for example, mental health or drug and alcohol services, and usually target funds toward agencies that share their service perspective and consumer focus. Service perspectives, regulations, and funding practices frequently differ by public agency, making it difficult for one provider to maintain substantial contracts from different funders. Indeed, successful aggressive pursuit of other public funds may cause a private provider to offer an inconsistent profile to all its funders. For example, an AIDS/HIV housing provider recently expanded into housing options for people with mental health issues and people with developmental disabilities. Dealing with three sources of funding and three sets of regulations has proved more time-consuming than managers expected, largely because of increased scrutiny resulting from the suspicions of each funder that other funders' perspectives are paramount at the agency.

Dependence on one funding source can be attractive because it provides more certainty about how an agency will be paid, by whom, for what services, and with which expected outcomes. However, it also increases an agency's financial vulnerability, for example, when contracts are not renewed or expected increases are not received. The difficulties associated with nurturing alternative funding sources notwithstanding, their development reduces financial vulnerability (see Chapter 7, this volume). Over time, with single-source funding, there is also a likelihood that the private agency will become an extension of the primary funder, fulfilling the funder's mission in the selection and provision of services, types of consumers served, and outcomes sought. Rejection of the funder's mission and "guidance" will clearly jeopardize continued critical funding. However, the presence of other funding increases an agency's ability to support missions not valued by the primary funding source. Managers and boards of directors have an opportunity to actively consider how their agency is being reshaped by their primary funder, allowing them to make choices rather than succumb to mission drift. The process of recognizing mission drift and displacement helps to identify where additional resource development efforts should be directed.

Competing with unequal rivals in an increasingly competitive resource arena. Public agencies have turned to the private sector for the provision of social services because of beliefs that such agencies are most cost-effective, have alternative strategies to offer, and can respond to changing needs (Burke & Rafferty, 1994). There is also a belief that competition among private agencies will produce more innovation and attention to cost issues. However, from the beginning of the present thrust toward privatization and a market approach to service provision, there have been concerns that true competition does not and perhaps cannot exist. There

are a number of reasons. Larger agencies are more likely to have the experience and resources to submit proposals within short time frames. Accountability concerns encourage staying with providers and treatment approaches that have been used in the past. Payments in arrears and 1-year renewable contracts represent a greater financial risk for new as opposed to established providers. These are important challenges for NPO managers seeking to maintain or expand funding.

The advent of for-profit providers, on the one hand, has increased the number of providers able to compete. On the other hand, it has placed smaller and newer NPOs at a greater disadvantage in the competition for funds. Also, for-profit providers, lacking mission statements committing them to serve the most vulnerable consumers, are accused of targeting high-pay and low-need consumers, leaving NPO providers to serve those with highest needs for the lowest revenue returns (Burke & Rafferty, 1994; Netting et al., 1990). The extension of managed care into behavioral health and other human service arenas has also increased the profile of hospital systems as providers. Whether under for-profit or NPO auspices, they contribute to the competition, as they are a resource-laden competitor for both public and private funds, attract high-pay consumers, and function themselves as funders of services or gatekeepers of consumers for agencies with which they are competing for other resources.

Returning to the case example, how one agency reconciled these forces is illustrated.

Case Example, Part II

Faced with imminent bankruptcy and closure, the board of directors turned to a larger and more successful NPO with a similar mission. The basis of the appeal was immediate concern for the welfare of the 300 consumers receiving residential services and the negative impact on the service network and the range of services offered consumers through the loss of this agency. The larger agency entered into a management contract and committed private resources to sustain the agency for an interim period.

The conflict between funders of services and the agency was immediately targeted. A meeting was convened of past and present board members, national leaders in the services field, funder representatives, staff, families, and advocates to consider the funders' priorities, the agency's existing mission statement, and developments in the services field. A strategic plan for the agency emerged that established core agency mission values. Some changes to the mission statement were agreed to that responded to funder priorities and reflected advances in services nationally. For example, the mission statement was changed to encourage pursuit of community-based rather than institutional living and service options. However, the mission statement's emphasis on offering lifelong access to the agency for consumers and their families was maintained, although funders preferred and would fund time-limited programming. It was recognized that this part of the mission could only be sustained through soliciting new resources from nonpublic sources.

The discussion then turned to the resources the agency currently received. For the first time, it was recognized that reliance on public agency funding for people with developmental disabilities offered overall budget stability. Other funding sources were examined and continued on the basis of the extent to which their requirements were consistent with the primary funding source, they protected the agency from the financial vulnerability of overreliance on one funder, or they offered resources to support mission-related activities not supported by the primary funder. Consistent with this model, plans were made to pursue expanded access to resources from the primary funding agency and to expand efforts to acquire other funding.

The precarious state of some of the agency's programs seemed to call for all resources being dedicated to their restoration. However, the decision was made to divert some resources to establish a development office to pursue private and public funds and plan for the next level of programs at the agency. Given recent history, it was recognized that the agency was disadvantaged compared to other private agencies in competing for general service contracts. Indeed, the agency's difficulties had encouraged other providers to compete for contracts it had previously held. Also, the agency was having difficulties matching the cost efficiencies of its rivals. Attention was focused on addressing these competitive disadvantages. Also, it was decided to target several specialized populations of people with developmental disabilities. Serving these subpopulations was determined to be consistent with the agency's mission and met an important need for the funder. It was decided to make investments in specialized staff that would position the agency to compete effectively for new and expanded contracts to serve these consumers. Finally, plans were laid for periodic reports by the new executive director to the board of directors on progress with the strategic plan and on implications of its implementation for continued adherence to the newly stated agency mission.

MANAGEMENT SKILLS FOR RESOURCE DEVELOPMENT AND MAINTENANCE

Successfully resolving resource dilemmas calls for the application of a number of management skills:

Finding the fit between resource development opportunities and the agency's mission. Decisions about the intent, structure, and priorities for funding streams are often made through political processes that pay little regard to the consumers who will be affected or the provider agencies who will be given the opportunity, through competitive grants and contracts, to meet consumer needs (Jansson, 1998). Faced with funders' parameters, before responding to the request for proposals, managers must consider which funding priorities are consistent with their mission, which can incorporate their mission, and which present problems for their mission.

Board and constituency involvement and development. Board members are charged with the definition and maintenance of the agency's mission. They have responsibilities to be active in reviewing compliance with the mission, assisting the manager in securing resources to carry out the mission, and promoting goodwill in the community in support of the agency (see Chapter 6). Managers and board leaders must consider these issues in the formation of the board, provide opportunities for the discussion of these issues, and accept the board's oversight.

The newly appointed director of an agency came up with a creative but legal way to make his consumers eligible for a source of funds with which he had considerable experience at a previous agency. Board members expressed concerns that this was moving the agency in a new and different direction. Discussion was tabled until the next meeting. However, the application deadline was at hand, and the executive director went ahead and applied. The grant was successfully awarded the day before the next board meeting. At the board meeting, board members voted not to accept the funds and, within a short time, the executive director was asked to leave.

This is a good example of a manager who neither recognized the role of the board, nor worked with the board to consider how new re-

sources may or may not fit with the agency's mission.

Staffing for resource development. Successful resource development is critical to an agency's survival and growth. Time and expertise must be allocated to identifying funding trends, including opportunities for funding expansion, and threats to existing funding. Writing grants, scanning the environment for opportunities, organizing special events, building partnerships and coalitions, and managing boards are all skills. Professional development staff bring the writing skills and orientation to achieve this.

Grant proposals are most effective when they are responsive to the funder's request for proposal, comply with the proposal requirements, and demonstrate the agency's capability to deliver what it is promising. A particular challenge for managers faced with the imminent loss of funds for a program is to respond to requests for innovation and change when their primary desire is to preserve what they have already established. The development staff people must be able to separate from day-to-day concerns and focus on what is required, yet, they must also be connected to the agency to reflect its values and its desires. The ability to view programs objectively is also important if development staff are to develop the evaluation components called for in grants. However, managers should not simply relinquish design of evaluations to such staff. Evaluation should be designed to assess how well the agency is fulfilling its mission and meeting consumer goals, not just to reply to funder mandates. Finally, no matter how well intentioned, programs that lose money jeopardize the entire agency. Development staff must work closely with financial management and program staff to ensure the relevance and financial viability of what is being proposed. For example, all costs must be covered not only for personnel and program but also for the administrative and support needs of the new program. Also, the implications of payment schedules that hold monies until after the delivery of services, requirements for cost sharing and in-kind contributions for borrowing, and other financial needs of the agency must be considered.

Development is not necessarily a role that can be filled by a "good" employee from within or that can be successfully shared with other job responsibilities. To an equal degree, spending large amounts of money on development staff or outside consultants does not guarantee resource development success. Managers and boards must establish their resource development needs and goals, recruit the skills needed, and dedicate sufficient time and other resources to support the development person's activities.

Shaping and influencing funders' priorities. It is true that much of the resource picture is determined by political processes over which providers have little control, but that is not to say providers are without influence. Prohibitions against use of public funds for political purposes and conflict of interest policies notwithstanding, managers do have opportunities to share success stories, demonstrate cost-effective yet consumer-sensitive approaches, and suggest add-ons and modifications to existing programs. Failure to do so leaves the door open to those opposed to the funding of human services to make their case unopposed (Kettner & Martin, 1996). Education and influence efforts by managers should be directed toward the public at large, public agency staff, and legislative decision makers. This is often an area

where board members and consumers can play important roles as spokespeople and advocates. It requires managers to use such people effectively, to provide them with the needed information, and to coordinate efforts within the agency and with other private agencies.

Planning for when the grant (or contract) ends. One attractive feature of grants for public funders is that they are time-limited (Gronbjerg, 1993). Changing budget priorities and desires to balance budgets and cut taxation also increase the likelihood that contracts may not be renewed or may not include sufficient resources to continue programs at the same level of service. On receipt of notification of an award, a manager must begin to plan for when the grant or contract ends. There are three options: (a) convince the funder to provide continued and sufficient funding, (b) end the program's activities and lay off or reassign the staff when the grant ends, or (c) identify a new grant or source of funding that the agency will be positioned to apply for before the grant or contract ends. The first option is unlikely to occur for grants but may for contracts, and the second will affect consumers and staff negatively. The third option requires planning, scanning of the environment for new opportunities, and developing new proposals when such opportunities are identified.

Identification and cultivation of long-range alternate funding resources. Alternate funding sources include foundation grants, private donations, corporate support, special event fundraising, community solicitation, participation in federated campaigns, bequests, consumer fees, and generation of income from for-profit activities. Such resources can support mission-related activities that public funding will not support or does not support adequately, protect agencies from the financial vulnerability of relying on one source of income, provide seed funding for new and innovative programs that may eventually attract public funds, serve as a bridge when one source of funds is lost so that a new source can be located and applied to, and provide capital funds for buildings and equipment essential to programs but beyond the financing means of the agency. However, these sources often have guiding philosophies, find some populations more attractive than others, and rarely represent ongoing funding. Charging consumer fees, in particular, directs agencies toward a select group of consumers, those who are able to pay (Hardina, 1990). Managers must determine which alternate sources are consistent with the agency's mission. For example, regardless of the funding offered, some agencies may not be willing to accept funds from certain corporate sponsors.

As in grant writing for public contracts, managers must then develop proposals to meet sponsor guidelines and to present a fundable picture. More than that, managers must invest through staff, board members, and other volunteers in connecting with donors on a personal level to cultivate recognition and support of agency activities. Investing in a long-term effort is more likely to produce results than launching a crisis-driven appeal. Special events such as gala dances, raffles, bingo, bake sales, and annual fund drives pose their own issues for managers. These are often labor-intensive events with a small return compared to a successful grant or contract proposal. However, for many agencies, the small return may be more predictable than success in writing a grant. Also, the funds accrued may be critical to supporting pro-

grams for which there are no other available external funds. Nor should managers fail to recognize the community relations value of these activities, often raising the agency's and consumers' profile in ways that are helpful for securing other funds.

Developing financing alternatives and for-profit opportunities. Much of NPO resource development is focused on procuring external rather than internal resources. Yet, internal economies can be realized through contract-chargeable leasing of furniture, buildings, vehicles, and equipment and through access to bond issues and other low interest loans (Stowers, 1990). Income can also be generated by selling services such as payroll or computer support to other agencies and renting out or selling off underused capital assets. Costs can be reduced by sharing services and staff. There are also profit-making opportunities that may subsidize not-for-profit activities. For example, a not-for-profit hospital was able to support services for those unable to pay through profits generated by services targeted to higher income consumers (Perlmutter & Adams, 1990). Other agencies have developed businesses that offer employment opportunities for consumers and generate income to support program activities. All of these require attention from managers to develop such options and to ensure they produce ends that are consistent with the agency's purposes and position the agency favorably for the future, rather than develop potential liabilities and conflicts.

Stewardship of existing resources. Many agencies benefit from bequests, other gifts, and trust funds. These funds often have the advantage of being unrestricted in purpose, that is, the agency can choose how best to expend them. They may also be set up to be available over a number of years. The receipt of gifts is an opportunity and a responsibility. Gifts can be used to address short-term problems and to secure the immediate financial position of the agency. Or, they can be held for critical periods to help the agency fund expansions, to support mission-related activities that are unfunded, or to support other financial transactions. Holding such funds for a long period challenges managers and board members to consider how best those monies should be invested. Generally accepted accounting principles recommend a conservative approach to investing (Blazek, 1996). Reliance on insured deposits and government-backed instruments is recommended. However, over recent years, this has meant low returns. Others suggest managers invest such funds more aggressively to generate income to support agency activities, while preserving the principal for future needs. In Orange County, California, funds were invested in high-risk derivatives for spectacular gains initially, followed by bankruptcy-inducing losses. Managers miss an opportunity to generate resources when they do not pay attention to investment policies (Heimerdinger & Davidowitz, 1992). However, the Orange County experience points out the importance of responsible practices, consistent with the agency's mission and supported by board oversight (Kearns, 1995).

CONCLUSION

In recent years, public agencies have divested themselves of their service-provision responsibilities, seeking to introduce greater elements of competition among private agencies who are now increasingly those providers and to reduce the presence of public funds in the support of consumers not able to support themselves. Meanwhile, needs and demands for services have increased, as have the number of agencies who wish to be providers. Maintaining and enhancing the resources a private agency requires to meet the needs of the consumer groups its mission targets have become critical roles for agency managers. To be successful, managers must be effective competitors in the contract culture—this requires the allocation of resources and the presence of grant- and contract-procurement skills. To be true to their agency's mission, however, managers must also be effective in locating and procuring complementary resources, making maximum use of the resources they have, and shaping the agendas of those on whom they rely for funds.

REFERENCES

Agosta, J., & Melda, K. (1996). Supporting families who provide care at home for children with disabilities. *Exceptional Children, 62*(3), 271-282.

Aponte, J., & Crouch, R. (1995). The changing ethnic profile of the United States. In J. F. Aponte, R. W. Rivers, & J. Wohl (Eds.), *Psychological interventions and cultural diversity* (pp. 1-18). Boston: Allyn & Bacon.

Barnet, R., & Cavanaugh, J. (1994). *Global dreams: Imperial corporations and the new world.* New York: Simon & Schuster.

Biegel, D., & Blum, A. (Eds.). (1990). *Aging and caregiving: Theory, research, and policy.* Newbury Park, CA: Sage.

Blazek, J. (1996). *Financial planning for nonprofit organizations.* New York: John Wiley.

Burke, A. C., & Rafferty, J. A. (1994). Ownership differences in the provision of outpatient substance abuse services. *Administration in Social Work, 18*(3), 59-81.

Children's Defense Fund. (1996). *The state of America's children yearbook.* Washington, DC: Author.

Cornelius, D. S. (1994). Managed care and social work: Constructing a context and a response. *Social Work in Health Care, 20*(1), 47-63.

Fost, D. (1996). Farewell to the lodge. *American Demographics, 18*(1), 40-45.

Gronbjerg, K. A. (1991). Managing grants and contracts. *Nonprofit and Voluntary Sector Quarterly, 20*(1), 5-24.

Gronbjerg, K. A. (1993). *Understanding nonprofit funding: Managing revenues in social services and community development organizations.* San Francisco: Jossey-Bass.

Gummer, B. (1990). *The politics of social administration.* Englewood Cliffs, NJ: Prentice Hall.

Hadley, T. R. (1996). Financing changes and their impact on the organization of the public mental health system. *Administration and Policy in Mental Health, 23*(5), 393-405.

Hardina, D. (1990). The effect of funding sources on client access to services. *Administration in Social Work, 14*(3), 33-46.

Heimerdinger, J. F., & Davidowitz, R. G. (1992). Trusts and estates: A management stepchild. *Administration in Social Work, 16*(1), 81-87.

Jansson, B. S. (1998). *Reluctant welfare state.* Pacific Grove, CA: Brooks/Cole.

Jette, A. (1996). Disability trends and transitions. In R. H. Binstock & L. K. George (Eds.), *Handbook of aging and social sciences* (4th ed., pp. 94-116). New York: Academic Press.

Kearns, K. (1995). Accountability and entrepreneurial public management: The case of the Orange County Investment Fund. *Public Budgeting and Finance, 15,* 3-21.

Kettner, P. M., & Martin, L. L. (1993). Performance, accountability, and purchase of service contracting. *Administration in Social Work, 17*(1), 61-79.

Kettner, P. M., & Martin, L. L. (1996). The impact of declining resources and purchase of service contracting on private, nonprofit agencies. *Administration in Social Work, 20*(3), 21-38.

Kramer, R. M. (1994). Voluntary agencies and the contract culture: Dream or reality. *Social Service Review, 68*(1), 33-60.

McCallion, P., & Grant-Griffin, L. (in press). Redesigning services to meet the needs of multicultural families. In M. P. Janicki & E. Ansello (Eds.), *Aging and developmental disabilities.* Baltimore, MD: Paul Brookes.

McCallion, P., Janicki, M., & Grant-Griffin, L. (1997). Exploring the impact of culture and acculturation on older families caregiving for persons with developmental disabilities. *Family Relations, 46*(4), 347-358.

McCallion, P., & Tobin, S. S. (1995). Social worker orientations to permanency planning by older parents caring at home for sons and daughters with developmental disabilities. *Mental Retardation, 33*(3), 153-162.

McLeod, G. K. (1993). An overview of managed health care. In P. R. Kongstvedt (Ed.), *The managed health care handbook* (pp. 3-11). Gaithersburg, MD: Aspen.

Menefee, D. (1997). Strategic administration on nonprofit human service organizations: A model for executive success in turbulent times. *Administration in Social Work, 21*(2), 1-19.

Milofsky, C., & Blades, S. D. (1991). Issues of accountability in health charities: A case study of accountability problems among nonprofit organizations. *Nonprofit and Voluntary Sector Quarterly, 20*(4), 371-393.

Netting, F. E., McMurtry, S. L., Kettner, P. M., & Jones-McClintic, S. (1990). Privatization and its impact on nonprofit service providers. *Nonprofit and Voluntary Sector Quarterly, 19*(1), 33-47.

Perlmutter, F. D., & Adams, C. T. (1990). The voluntary sector and for-profit ventures: The transformation of American social welfare. *Administration in Social Work, 14*(1), 1-13.

Schlesinger, M., Dorwart, R., & Pulice, R. (1986). Competitive bidding and states' purchase of services: The case of mental health care in Massachusetts. *Journal of Policy Analysis and Management, 5*(2), 245-263.

Standley, A. P. (1998). *Voluntary health associations' strategies for succeeding in an increasingly competitive environment.* Chicago: Alzheimer's Association.

Stern, L. W., & Gibelman, M. (1990). Voluntary social welfare agencies: Trends, issues, and prospects. *Families in Society: The Journal of Contemporary Human Services, 71*(1), 13-23.

Stowers, G. N. (1990). Innovations in human services financing. *Public Budgeting & Finance, 10,* 26-35.

Strom, K., & Gingerich, W. J. (1993). Educating students for the new market realities. *Journal of Social Work Education, 29*(1), 78-87.

Weinbach, R. W. (1998). *The social worker as manager.* Boston: Allyn & Bacon.

Winbush, G. (1993). Family caregiving programs: A look at the premises on which they are based. In L. Burton (Ed.), *Families and aging* (pp. 129-133). Amityville, NY: Baywood.

CHAPTER NINETEEN

Financial Management

MARK EZELL

There is little debate about the importance of financial management among the numerous responsibilities of social work administrators. Every agency constituent group has a sizable stake in the effective management of fiscal resources during all stages of the budget cycle. Clients are concerned—probably in a somewhat indirect manner—about financial management, because quality services and intended outcomes cannot be achieved without good budget planning, implementation, control, and assessment. Agency staff have a personal and professional stake, in that their salaries and work conditions depend on the prudent use of dollars, as does their ability to serve those in need. It goes without saying that funders are interested in the effective use of funds for such reasons as the accomplishment of client service objectives and community support.

Notwithstanding the importance of financial management, social work students contemplate their budgeting class(es) with great trepidation. Social work managers, often promoted from the ranks of direct service workers, share these feelings. Whether the trepidation stems from math phobia or the sometimes technical nature of this work remains to be seen, but as Lohmann (1980) rightly points out, managers "must eventually come to terms with these topics. For the truth is that management knowledge cannot be considered complete without some knowledge of the working of financial resources in organizations and of the decisions which regulate their movement" (pp. 123-124). Twenty years after Lohmann's statement, it seems clear that it should be changed from *some* knowledge to *extensive* knowledge.

Even though budgeting duties are important and frequently time-consuming, one of the major challenges facing social work managers is to avoid "budget obsession" and simultaneously to consider several other important factors with financial concerns when making decisions. All too often, expenditure budgets are treated as immutable law and become of singular importance in agencies. Budgets and budget compliance should be seen as means to facilitate all aspects of service effectiveness (Patti, 1985) and employee satisfaction. The relevance and value of budgeting and other financial management functions should be evaluated in terms of how well they contribute to positive client outcomes, service quality and program integrity, client satisfaction, and positive staff morale. "The more the organization knows about where and how it uses resources, the better service job it can do" (Vinter & Kish, 1984, p. 2).

This chapter begins with a discussion of the fiscal and regulatory context within which social welfare agencies operate. Contextual factors such as managed care and purchase of service contracting are reviewed, as are federal laws and regulations and unrelated business income. The next section explains numerous fiscally related administrative tasks organized around the major stages of the budgeting cycle. The final section includes an in-depth discussion of two common financial management issues faced by social work organizations, projecting revenues and monitoring expenditures and revenue. Several exemplary approaches to deal with these issues are suggested.

CONTEXT

Social agencies are primarily accountable to external constituencies for how they use and record their financial resources. The most prominent external constituencies are the various funders, whether funding comes from public or private sources. To a large degree, the funders dictate budget formats, report types and frequencies, and accounting and auditing procedures. Nonprofit social welfare organizations also need to comply with the policies and procedures of their boards of directors and the Internal Revenue Service (IRS). Even without all these specific dictates, social agencies must have well-developed financial management systems to compete in the current fiscal and policy environment.

Besides facing the requirements of specific funders, social welfare agencies and their managers operate in an environment strongly shaped by contemporary funding mechanisms such as managed care and different contracting approaches (e.g., fee-for-service, case rate, etc.). It is becoming very rare for social welfare nonprofits to have single sources of funding, such as United Way. It is very common for both large and small nonprofits to rely on multiple funding streams, including government and foundation grants, government contracts, managed care agreements, individual donations, and proceeds from endowments.

Bidding for private insurance and public contracts is increasingly competitive, and when reimbursement rates are part of the bid, social welfare administrators need to know how much it costs to deliver services to particular types of clients and how many clients are needed for a specific program to break even (Meyer & Sherraden, 1985). Agencies that bid successfully will need to develop and operate financial and client information systems that can invoice the payer(s) for the specific set of services provided to each client at the agreed-upon rates. The author is aware of state contracts with private providers (both for-profit and nonprofit) that reimburse on an hourly basis depending on the nature of the service delivered (e.g., transportation, therapy, etc.) and on the type of staff delivering the services (e.g., professional, paraprofessional, etc.). This requires detailed record keeping, billing, and monitoring systems.

Public and private agencies receiving federal funding must comply with Circular A-133, "Audits of States, Local Governments, and Non-Profit Organizations" (Office of Management and Budget, 1997). Circular A-133 is intended to unify auditing standards used by the federal government when auditing nonfederal organizations that expend federal funds. In most cases, nonfederal agencies do not have to conduct audits as specified in the Circular if they receive less than $300,000 of federal awards per year. If agencies are subject to the provisions of Circular A-133, they must prepare certain financial statements. The audits seek to determine the following: (a) are the financial statements prepared in accordance with generally accepted accounting practices? (b) do internal controls ensure compliance with relevant laws and regulations? (c) has the agency complied with laws, regulations, and the provisions of contracts or grant agreements? and (d) has the agency corrected problems identified in prior audits (Kalin, Hardiman, Corfman, & Hunter, 1990). Because audits may be conducted on the entire operation of the agency and not just the organizational units that expend federal funds, agencies are strongly encouraged to design fiscal systems that are consistent with expectations outlined in Circular A-133.

Another context affecting financial management in social work organizations is the growing and maturing movement toward performance measurement. Joyce (1997) discusses whether and how performance measures can be used in the budgeting process. He reminds us that zero-based budgeting as well as program budgeting, both of which have been around for quite a while, require a great deal of work. Performance budgeting, discussed in more detail below, attempts to use program results for budgeting purposes, but this approach to date has received mixed reviews. At the federal level, agencies are required to report on performance measures as part of their annual budget requests. This requirement was included in the Government Performance and Results Act of 1993 (P.L. 103-62; Martin & Kettner, 1996). Similar requirements will affect states and are included in Performance Partnership Grants (PPG). "Under a negotiated PPG agreement, as currently proposed, DHHS [Department of Health and Human Services] and each state would agree on a set of objectives and performance measures for individual federal-state grants" (Perrin & Koshel, 1997, p. 5). It remains to be seen how much these requirements will change agency budgeting practices. At this point, it only appears that performance measures are to be included as part of annual budget requests but not integrated into budgets.

Just like individuals, nonprofits have to file income tax returns with the IRS. Specifically, they must file Form 990. As a result of the policy and fiscal environment of the last two decades, many nonprofits engage in revenue-generating activities that are unrelated to their exempt purposes (Ezell & Wiggs, 1989). Administrators should seek expert advice on the definition of "unrelated business income" and whether it applies in their specific situation because the regulations are complex. Business activities that are not directly related to the exempt purposes of the organization and are regularly carried on may generate a profit on which the nonprofit must pay unrelated business income tax. Even if the profits from the unrelated activities are used to subsidize underfunded, exempt activities, income tax will still be due.

Instead of operating unrelated businesses within nonprofit corporations, many organizations have opted to create for-profit subsidiaries to generate revenues for the nonprofit (Goldstein, 1998). The advantage of this arrangement is that the nonprofit receives tax-free income from the for-profit subsidiary, and the subsidiary writes off its charitable donation. Tax laws and accounting practices are different for these types of corporations. Obviously, unrelated business activities—whether housed in the nonprofit or a subsidiary—can consume a great deal of administrators' attention, as well as other resources, and might draw attention and focus away from the central social welfare mission of the organization. In either case, administrators should proceed with great caution and should seek advice from tax attorneys and certified public accountants.

Inherent in the discussion to this point is that agency auspice is a significant contextual factor. The financial management differences between public and private agencies are profound, as are those between the private for-profits and private nonprofits. Also, although not all private agencies are small, almost all public social welfare agencies are large. Auspice in combination with agency size creates one of the major differences in managing public versus private agencies. Public social work managers generally have less input into the design of the financial management systems. Those responsible for recording, reporting, and monitoring financial transactions are likely to be in a separate organizational unit than those delivering services, giving the social welfare manager less influence over the form and frequency of financial reports. The author's experience is that monthly financial statements in public agencies, for example, are less user-friendly than similar reports in nonprofits, largely because the reports are prepared by and primarily for the use of budget specialists.

Internally, nonprofit social agencies are accountable to boards of directors where ultimate legal fiduciary responsibility rests. Many boards create finance committees to work closely with agency staff and to save the remainder of the board from having to review numerous detailed financial reports. The division of labor between the board and the staff is a delicate, evolutionary dynamic. As a staff person, the author has felt that board members tried to micro-manage; as a board member, he has felt that staff were too involved in policy making. Nevertheless, the organization as a whole benefits, and the manager is best protected, when board members are actively involved in all stages of the budget cycle. One issue that especially needs board involvement is the challenge of what to do with cash reserves and endowments. Wolf

(1990) advises that when reserve funds grow large, "the board [should] designate a portion of the reserves as 'funds functioning as endowment'" (p. 149). Endowments, whether created from reserves or specific contributions, involve investing the principal and only spending the earnings for specified purposes. Clearly, managers need to work with and depend on their boards to establish investment policies regarding whether to invest endowment funds and cash reserves in savings accounts, mutual funds, or other investment vehicles.

FISCAL RESPONSIBILITIES OF THE SOCIAL WORK ADMINISTRATOR

Being accountable to internal and external constituents is only one aspect of financial management. Managers' time will also be devoted to planning, monitoring, and evaluating the use of financial resources in such a way as to achieve the goals and service objectives of the agency. This section will explain the three major stages of the budget cycle and the associated managerial tasks of each. Because another chapter is devoted to fund-raising, (see Chapter 18), this chapter will treat that task as a *fait accompli* (and wouldn't it be nice if that was always the case?).

The stages of the budget process are not as linear as this chapter and many books seem to depict. At any given time, administrators are simultaneously concerned with at least three different fiscal years—prior, current, and next. The exception to this, of course, is when an agency or program is brand new, for example, when a grant proposal is being written for a new service. Next year's budget, the continuation budget, must be developed long before the current fiscal year is complete. A fiscal year has to be completed and all expenses and revenues recorded before an audit or a cost analysis can be done. This doesn't happen until a new budget year is well under way.

Figure 19.1 illustrates this scenario, but because of the limits of two-dimensional illustrations, the stages appear to be sequential when they often are not. The scenario is frequently even more complicated because many agencies and programs have multiple funding sources that are operating on different fiscal years. Standard fiscal years are October 1 to the end of the following September (e.g., federal government), July 1 to June 30 (state governments), and January 1 to December 31 (many United Ways). The timetables for the stages and tasks, therefore, are dictated by the funding sources. One highly recommended technique to cope with the mélange of due dates is to develop a budget calendar that includes the elements presented in Figure 19.2. This is easily done with planning software.

Before discussing each budget stage and its associated managerial tasks specifically, two important notes are warranted. First, the following discussion focuses on *what* has to be done, not *how* to do it. It is neutral as to management style. A specific manager's style might be unilateral and top-down, or it might be a participative style. The choice of management style, or combinations of styles, is constrained by time, energy, staff and their skill level, and other programmatic obligations. Second, although administrators do not necessarily do all budgeting tasks personally (e.g., bookkeeping), they must, at least, oversee the following: hire and supervise appropriate personnel, be able to talk the language of and communicate with fiscal staff,

FY–1 (prior)			FY 0 (current)			FY +1 (next)		
Assess FY –2	*Implement* FY –1	*Plan* FY 0	*Assess* FY –1	*Implement* FY 0	*Plan* FY +1	*Assess* FY–0	*Implement* FY+1	*Plan* FY+2
			Audit	Allocate funds	Project revenues			
			Analyze costs	Manage	Plan program and budget			
			Report	Control	Estimate costs			
				Adjust	Negotiate			
				Report				

Figure 19.1. Three Fiscal Years (FY) of Concern and Budget Stages

associate fiscal issues with program matters and client concerns, translate fiscal reports to appropriate audiences, and ensure quality control of the financial systems.

Planning and development stage. The first stage of the budget cycle is planning and development. The specific managerial tasks in this stage will differ depending on whether a budget is being prepared for a new or continuing program, as well as on the specific budgeting process used. The most common and simplest budget process is incremental—or, unfortunately, decremental—where an agreed-on percentage, frequently an inflationary factor or change in the cost of living, is added to or subtracted from the prior year's budget. Two other well-known budget processes, zero-based budgeting (ZBB) and planning programming budgeting system (PPBS), are too complex to explain fully here and are rarely used in their entirety. Both are de-

rived from a rational planning model and are time-consuming. ZBB, unlike incremental budgeting, does not take the prior year's budget as its starting point but rebuilds budgets and programs from the ground up. Mayers (1989) discusses the strengths and weakness of each of these budgeting processes and makes an important distinction between budget processes (i.e., how the budget is planned) and budget documents or formats (i.e., the layout of the budget on paper). Frequently, programs combine the best and most convenient features of different budget processes and use different budget formats for various audiences and purposes.

The most common budget format is a line-item budget, also known as an object classification budget (Granof, 1998). This form of budget includes a vertical listing of the sources of revenue (e.g., grants, donations, fees, etc.) and the input items to be purchased to run the program (e.g., salaries, benefits, travel, rent, etc.).

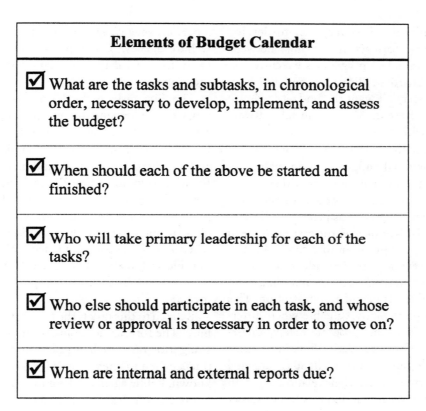

Elements of Budget Calendar

☑ What are the tasks and subtasks, in chronological order, necessary to develop, implement, and assess the budget?

☑ When should each of the above be started and finished?

☑ Who will take primary leadership for each of the tasks?

☑ Who else should participate in each task, and whose review or approval is necessary in order to move on?

☑ When are internal and external reports due?

Figure 19.2. Elements of a Budget Calendar

The horizontal axis frequently includes columns that represent the prior year and the current year's budget for each of the revenue and expense items. This allows a year-by-year comparison of changes. In the case of an agency with multiple programs or services, a line-item budget makes it impossible to determine which services are being increased or decreased. A line-item budget directs one's attention toward agency inputs and reveals little about programs, policies, or priorities.

A common alternative to this format shows the same line items listed down the first column, but the horizontal axis shows either programs or organizational units. For example, a children's agency might have programs such as recreation, tutoring, and counseling; each of these would have a column. A public child welfare agency would have organizational units such as child protective services, foster care, adoption, and family preservation. One of the great contributions computers have made to financial management is that it is very easy to develop these different formats and change between them. For example, an agency's executive director, the board of directors, and the local United Way may all want the budget layout to be slightly different. Most financial software can do this with ease.

Vinter and Kish (1984) are strong proponents of functional budgeting as a way to allocate, control, and analyze costs within a program but across functions or sets of activities. Wolf (1990) refers to this as project budgeting. Vinter and Kish's book uses the case example of a youth diversion program that can be broken down into several interdependent functions: screening and intake, referral, counseling, consultation and referral, and administration. This approach is particularly valuable when different clients of the same program receive different packages of services. As in Vinter and Kish's case example, above, every client is screened and, for a certain subset, their relationship with the program ends at that point. Another subset of clients receives screening and intake and then is referred for services to another agency. Still another receives screening and intake and then counseling. As is probably obvious, functional budgeting coupled with an understanding of different client case flows allows managers to conduct cost analysis (to be discussed below).

The final form of budgeting to be discussed here is performance budgeting, which has recently regained some of its lost popularity. This is a budget that focuses on an organization's or program's outputs (such as workloads), efforts, or outcomes, emphasizing units of work produced and their cost per unit. Figure 19.3 shows a performance budget for a hypothetical child welfare agency. This type of budget is most likely to be used in combination with one of those above.

The first task in the budget development stage is to understand the agency's or program's revenue sources, amounts, and related policies. Questions such as the following should be asked and answered: How much funding is approved for what amount of time? How is the revenue received (e.g., reimbursed on a per client basis, periodic lump sums, etc.)? In what instances does the manager have budget discretion, and when is prior approval needed? What are allowable and unallowable costs? And, what are the fiscal and programmatic reporting requirements?

Related to this task is the forecasting of revenues. The forecast for some revenue sources is straightforward, such as grants and some contracts, when the next year's level of funding is known. Public agencies depend on a somewhat unpredictable legislative process to establish their revenue levels. In other instances, however, when revenue is based on factors such as the volume of services delivered, fund-raising efforts, the number of clients, client fees, and reimbursement rates, the trends need to be studied and projection techniques used. Three pieces of advice are offered here. First, estimate revenues conservatively and expenses liberally so that the agency will be protected if you are wrong in both cases. Second, forecast revenues before estimating expenses. When expenses are estimated first, there is a strong tendency to project revenues at a level to match or exceed expenditures as opposed to a more realistic and safer level. Finally, Wolf (1990) suggests

Program Activity	**Budget**
➢ Investigate 30,000 reports of child abuse and neglect.	$30,000,000
➢ Provide 2,007,500 days of foster care.	$180,675,000
➢ Recruit 500 new foster homes.	$500,000
➢ Train 750 foster parents.	$250,000
➢ Prevent foster care placement of 500 children.	$1,750,000
➢ Place 300 children for adoption.	$4,200,000

Figure 19.3. Performance Budget of a Hypothetical Child Welfare Agency

that managers include a contingency/reserve line item in their budgets that should be as high as 5%, especially if revenue sources are unpredictable. Using a line item such as this is another instance in which board policy is needed to guide decisions on when reserve funds can be spent.

Program planning is another task during this stage. The program plan must include an estimate of the number of clients to be served and must be specific enough to allow an estimation of how much of different types of resources is needed. In social work programs, the major resource is almost always staff, so that is a good place to start. What types of staff (e.g., BSW, MSW, etc.) are needed to deliver the intended

service? How many of each is needed, and what will be their level of compensation? After those determinations, it is fairly straightforward to estimate the costs of fringe benefits and payroll taxes. To estimate the next set of costs, ask what types of facilities, space, and materials are necessary to deliver the intended services and how much of each will be needed to serve the estimated number of clients. For example, if a counseling program will use treatment groups, they will need offices that are conducive to this type of intervention. This, of course, will only provide managers with estimates of the basics. A strong reminder for this task is that the cost estimates cannot be made without adequate program plans. Program staff and financial staff should not work in isolation from one another but should sit down together and circulate drafts of the budget and program plan. Here is where the important link between programming and budgeting is often lost.

The final managerial task in this stage of the budget cycle is negotiation. Whether the budget is being submitted to external funders, legislative bodies, or a board of directors, these bodies are frequently looking to cut costs and increase efficiencies and productivity. Managers must defend their budget requests and their programs, advocating for their clients and staff (Ezell, 1991). Although there are many different ways to be persuasive in these situations, social work managers will be well-served if they have program evaluation results that demonstrate service effectiveness, cost-analysis findings to substantiate budget requests, and needs-assessment statistics to show the necessity of their program.

Implementation. The next stage of the budget cycle begins once the budget and program have been approved by the appropriate powers-that-be and the program start date occurs. An early task in this stage is the allocation of funds to specific program activities (i.e., functions) and cost centers. "Cost centers represent clusters of distinguishable activities that accrue costs, to which expenditures can be assigned" (Vinter & Kish, 1984, p. 114). Allocating resources in this manner firmly establishes which and how much of the different resources (e.g., staff time, space, client financial assistance, etc.) will be devoted to various program activities. A functional budget facilitates this task, just as this task supports the control function.

Exercising programmatic and fiscal control requires managerial vigilance. It is easy to understand the importance of fiscal control by remembering that revenues were projected, programs planned, and costs estimated far in advance—sometimes more than a year—of the actual delivery of services. Much can change between the planning and the implementation stage. Also, largely unique to the social work enterprise is the fact that all clients are different, and each brings a different set of strengths and challenges that will consume more and different resources than anticipated. Control consists of three activities: (a) monitoring revenues and expenditures, (b) comparing the data collected from monitoring to standards or benchmarks, and (c) taking corrective action if necessary. The budget, broken down into monthly or quarterly increments, provides the benchmarks. Managers need to develop the procedures, oversee the necessary recording of revenue and expenses, and install a system that will produce timely financial statements that include variances from budget and year-end estimates. The reports need to be detailed so that warning flags pop up easily and early; once a warning flag comes up, the manager needs to start asking questions. A warning flag does not mean that something untoward is happening but may only reveal that the original budget needs adjusting due to unforeseen rate hikes (e.g., postage, insurance). It may indicate that services are being implemented differently than planned or that fund-raising activities are being less productive than hoped. Warning flags might also announce that the client population is harder to reach and serve than anticipated. Flags should pop up when revenue collections are falling short and when expenditures are both over and under budget.

This stage includes financial reporting to both internal and external constituents. Nonprofits provide financial reports to the IRS (Form 990), funders, boards of directors, and members. Public agencies report to their respective legislative bodies and to other governmental agencies, such as the federal government, when a state has a federal grant. This stage of the budget cycle, like the previous one, can involve more negotiations. Funders' permission to amend the expenditure budget may be sought when major changes are necessary. Most funders allow managers a certain amount of budget discretion without review, but commonly, if any line item needs to be reduced or increased by more than 10%, prior approval is required. If revenue collections are falling below budget, expenses will need to be cut unless reserve funds can be tapped. Undoubtedly, this will require internal negotiations among staff and various programs as well as legislative bodies and boards of directors.

Assessment. The third stage of the budget cycle begins once the fiscal year has been completed, and all income and expenditures have been recorded. Managers need to file end-of-year program and financial reports with the appropriate authorities and demonstrate that objectives were met and funds used appropriately. It is at this point that managers either choose to conduct an audit or are informed that their agency/program will be audited. There are many different definitions of auditing (McKinney, 1995), many types of audits, and numerous agencies that can serve as auditors, ranging from accounting firms to legislative and governmental auditing offices.

> *Financial and compliance audits* or *fiscal audits* [emphasis in original] assess whether financial operations are properly conducted. They evaluate whether an entity's financial statements are presented fairly and in compliance with applicable laws, policies, procedures, and regulations. (McKinney, 1995, p. 407)

It should go without saying that social welfare administrators are expected to give their full cooperation to auditors. The author's experience is that auditors hired by the agency can be extremely helpful, especially when they review and make suggestions regarding the adequacy of internal fiscal controls. Nonprofit managers and boards are frequently hesitant to pay for audits every year, but such practices represent false economies. It is far better to get critical feedback from accountants who are working for you rather than unexpectedly to be handed a list of audit exceptions by auditors for the IRS, the General Accounting Office, or other governmental bodies whose loyalties are elsewhere.

The final managerial task to be discussed here is cost analysis. Far too few social work agencies conduct appropriate analysis of their costs and, therefore, lack the ability to state what it costs to serve different kinds of clients. In our current world of managed care, privatization, and fee-for-service contracts, this puts social work agencies at a huge disadvantage. Cost analysis is a technique that calculates the use of resources by different types of clients, outputs, or outcomes. This process links expenditures with program operations and outcomes.

For a single program in which all clients receive the same package of services, the *per-client program cost* is easily calculated by dividing the number of clients served into the total program cost (Mayers, 1989, p. 142). When different clients receive different combinations of services or when service units are defined as something other than clients served (e.g., counseling session, meals delivered, etc.), cost analysis is more challenging. Flowcharts tracing client careers (Vinter & Kish, 1984, p. 258) and functional budgets are necessary to disaggregate program components and determine the cumulative costs for different client careers. A word of caution is warranted here about using the results of a cost analysis to negotiate contracts. As previously mentioned, social welfare administrators are disadvantaged without this information, but they may also be in a situation where a little information is a dangerous thing. Do not lose sight of the fact that an analysis of this type calculates the average cost per client or service unit, and *average* is a mathematical concept and does not represent a "real" client or service unit. This means that administrators must not only conduct cost analyses but also be familiar with the characteristics of and challenges involved in serving the intended client population. Again, knowing just the dollars is not enough.

The example above describes how to calculate the cost per unit of output as opposed to outcome. The number of youth who complete a delinquency rehabilitative program is the amount of output, but the number of these youth who remain crime-free for a year, for example, is the amount of positive outcomes. More and more funders are insisting that outcomes be specifically defined and reported. Equally concerned about outcomes are those agencies that have signed performance contracts, who may be required to return funds if they fail to reach agreed-on levels of success (Else, Groze, Hornby, Mirr, & Wheelock, 1992). Analyzing costs per positive outcome parallels the example above, and it will require agencies to collect one or more outcome measures for clients served. (For a useful example of a technique to associate costs with outcomes, see McCready, Pierce, Rahn, & Were, 1996.)

COMMON FINANCIAL MANAGEMENT ISSUES

Social service agencies tend to have several financial management challenges in common. For over 10 years, the author has worked with numerous public and private agencies as they wrestled with financial management challenges in a changing policy and fiscal context. Based on that experience, it is possible to identify frequent challenges and exemplary financial practices designed to solve them. Although cautions and small tidbits of advice were offered above, this section discusses two challenges in more detail.

The first issue involves revenue forecasting. As discussed earlier, if grants have been awarded, the amount of revenue is known. However, other funding mechanisms reimburse based on the volume of services delivered within the agreed-on ceilings defined in the contracts. The challenge becomes predicting volume, and in most cases, this means the number of clients served. Many managers develop their estimates

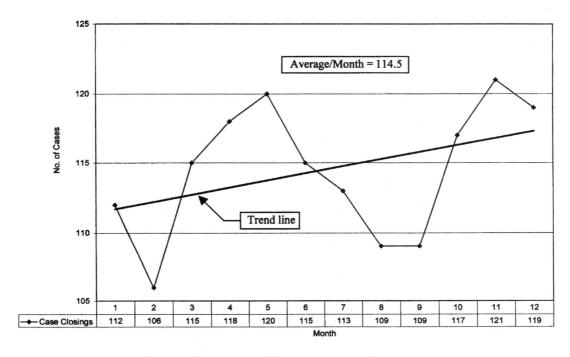

Figure 19.4. Fiscal Year 98: Case Closings Per Month (Hypothetical Data)

rather unsystematically with "guesstimates" based on unknown factors. Sometimes, they project the number of cases that just happens to balance their budget.

Many social work administrators have begun using simple mathematical projections and have found them useful. They absolutely do not depend on these as their sole source of estimates but weigh them along with their practice wisdom; knowledge of the field, clients, and the near future; and conversations they have with the funding and referral sources. Figure 19.4 includes 12 months of hypothetical data on case closings and graphs them over time. This hypothetical example is relevant in situations when funders reimburse providers and/or collect client fees. The specific question confronting the manager is how many cases will we close next fiscal year and, therefore, how much revenue will that generate.

Fiscal Year 98 case closings averaged 114.5 per month. The manager could use that average to project next year's number. This is often done, eyeballed, and then increased by some factor—often 5% or 10%. This ignores the overall trend of increased closings as the year progressed and the real possibility that they will continue to increase next year. This trend can be easily identified with spreadsheet software, as was done in Figure 19.4. It is easy to graph the FY98 data and use the software to add a trend line to it. (Microsoft Excel was used here.) In high school math, we learned that this line has an equation that describes it (in this case, $y = .5105x + 111.18$, where x is the month number and y the number of case closings). This equation can be used to estimate how many cases will be closed in months 13 through 24. Totaling these for the next fiscal year provides an estimate that a total of 1,448 cases will be closed, an annual increase of 5.3%, and an average of 120.6 closings per month. The software does almost all the work.

The second issue of concern is the preparation and formatting of periodic reports used to monitor revenues and expenses. A number of common practices make these reports less useful than they could be and cause them to fail to provide early warnings of financial problems. First, it seems obvious that if monitoring reports are prepared monthly, for example, then the original revenue and expense budgets should be broken down into monthly increments so that useful benchmarks are established. All too often, these are developed as if one-twelfth of the revenues will come in every month and one-twelfth of the expenses will occur. This may be a reasonable assumption on some line items, such as salaries and benefits, but travel, insurance and tax payments, and a number of other items are expended on different and variable schedules. Much depends on the type of program and when certain activities occur. Also, if the organization holds one major

fund-raising event per year, both the costs of putting it on and the revenue generated will occur irregularly. Because of this, managers frequently review and act on monthly statements based on faulty benchmarks.

A similar problem occurs when managers use monitoring information to project their end-of-year financial position. This is an ongoing managerial concern as they ask, Will I be over or under budget at the end of the year? Monitoring reports frequently include a column that shows—item by item, program by program, or both—how much has been spent (or received) year-to-date. Another column indicates the remainder left to be spent or amounts to be collected based on the approved budget. There is nothing to help managers project their year-end balances.

Many administrators have learned that adding a column that represents their best projection of how much will be spent or received in the remaining months makes the year-end projections much more accurate. This column is not created mathematically but is derived by asking several questions. For example, if managers review the midyear monitoring report, they will ask these questions to create this *accrual column*: (a) will the last 6 months' spending pattern on this item continue? (b) do program plans anticipate more or less spending on this item in the next 6 months? and (c) are any rate changes expected in the next 6 months? The figure derived from this thought process, added to the amount already spent, shows an estimate of how much will be spent by the end of the year. This is the figure that should be compared to the original budget to estimate over- or underspending.

A challenge associated with monitoring revenues and expenditures is managing cash flow. Unfortunately, even though social welfare administrators may have successfully negotiated a contract and a fair reimbursement rate, it can take 1 to 3 months after invoicing to receive payment. For the specifics of how to conduct cash flow projections, see Wolf (1990), but a small addition to the monthly monitoring reports can be immediately useful. Show the cash balance at the beginning of the month, the monthly net of revenue and expenses, the cash balance at the end of the month, and finally, the projected net of revenue versus expenses for the next month. Comparing the end-of-month cash balance with next month's projection will reveal whether there will be cash on hand at the end of the month or if funds need to be moved from the reserve account. Besides projecting and monitoring cash flow, lengthy delays in payments require that agencies have sizable cash reserves or lines of credit.

Finally, the formatting of these types of reports makes them difficult to use (Oster, 1995). Frequently, a lot of numbers are jammed onto a page that is poorly labeled. Consider different formats for different audiences. The administrator with program responsibility can be given detailed reports, whereas the board of directors might receive a report with aggregated numbers. For example, although it is possible to report expenditures line item by line item, they can also be summarized into categories such as personnel (salaries, benefits, and employee taxes) and operating costs (e.g., rent, travel, supplies, equipment, etc.). Graphics such as line charts and bar graphs are also very useful when making comparisons.

CONCLUSION

This chapter serves as an introduction to the financial management responsibilities of social work administrators. Many of the necessary skills, knowledge, and related issues were presented by first discussing the fiscal, regulatory, and policy context that influences this particular aspect of administrative practice. Second, the chapter explained the three major stages of the budget cycle and specific tasks that managers must accomplish during each stage. Finally, two major financial management issues were discussed in greater depth. The chapter would not be complete, however, without comments on ethics and financial management and on the budget requisites needed to build and maintain a culturally diverse staff.

Unlike the previous version of the National Association of Social Workers (1996) Code of Ethics, the new code has several specific standards devoted to administration [3.07(a) through 3.07(d)]. Administrators with budget responsibilities will be challenged to stay in compliance with these and all the other ethical standards. A general reminder provided by the code is the central importance of clients.

Of all the financial tasks implemented by managers, budget cutting may create more ethical dilemmas than any other situation, especially if staff layoffs or service rollbacks are involved. Having strong personnel policies is of utmost importance in these situations. They can guide decision making. There are two potential ramifications of budget cuts that managers should examine before implementing the cuts. First, will the possible cuts affect certain staff more than others, and, second, will particular client groups be disproportionately affected? In both cases, managers must avoid "discrimination on the basis of race, ethnicity, national origin, color, sex, sexual orientation, age, marital status, political belief, religion, or mental or physical disability" (NASW, 1996, pp. 22-23).

Building a diverse agency staff and serving a diverse clientele are related to the ethical management of agency resources in many ways. Recruiting diverse staff and clients and increasing the cultural competence of all organizational members are frequently discussed topics in the profession and in agencies. An agency's efforts and commitments in this area should be reflected in its budget. It is difficult, at best, to recruit and hire a diverse staff if job announcements are only listed in mainstream media; funds must be included in the budget to advertise in alternative, community, and ethnic publications. The cultural competence of staff is difficult to achieve and maintain without funds for training, consultation, and supervision. Certain hard-to-reach clients, such as children with disabilities, will not receive services without funds to reimburse staff for mileage. Facilities must be remodeled to accommodate staff and clients with disabilities. The list can go on and on. The important point is that sincere efforts to increase organizational diversity will require that funds be included in program budgets.

Managing the finances for a social welfare program is a major responsibility that involves many large and small decisions, the use of influence and power, and the need for creative thinking. The effectiveness of financial management should be judged on the basis of how well it contributes to service effectiveness, to staff morale, and to the continuing viability of the agency in the community. Balancing the budget, staying "in the black," cannot be ignored, by any means. The budget, which is merely a plan of how to use resources, should be handled as a powerful tool to help accomplish service objectives and social welfare goals.

REFERENCES

Else, J. F., Groze, V., Hornby, H., Mirr, R. K., & Wheelock, J. (1992). Performance-based contracting: The case of residential foster care. *Child Welfare, 71*(6), 513-526.

Ezell, M. (1991). Administrators as advocates. *Administration in Social Work, 15*(4), 1-18.

Ezell, M., & Wiggs, M. (1989). Surviving the threats from small business advocates. *The Child and Youth Care Administrator, 2*(1), 47-53.

Goldstein, H. (1998, April 9). Making charities' for-profit arms more accountable. *The Chronicle of Philanthropy* [On-line]. Available: http://philanthropy.com/premium/articles/v10/i12/12004501.htm

Granof, M. H. (1998). *Government and not-for-profit accounting: Concepts and practices.* New York: John Wiley.

Joyce, P. G. (1997). Using performance measures for budgeting: A new beat, or is it the same old tune? In K. E. Newcomer (Ed.), *Using performance measurement to improve public and nonprofit programs* (pp. 45-61). San Francisco: Jossey-Bass.

Kalin, D. H., Hardiman, P. F., Corfman, S., & Hunter, C. (1990). Auditing nonprofit entities under Circular A-133. *The CPA Journal, 60*(2), 32-43.

Lohmann, R. (1980). Financial management and social administration. In F. D. Perlmutter & S. Slavin (Eds.), *Leadership in social administration* (pp. 123-141). Philadelphia: Temple University Press.

Martin, L. L., & Kettner, P. M. (1996). *Measuring the performance of human service programs.* Thousand Oaks, CA: Sage.

Mayers, R. S. (1989). *Financial management for nonprofit human service agencies.* Springfield, IL: Charles C Thomas.

McCready, D. J., Pierce, S., Rahn, S. L., & Were, K. (1996). Third-generation information systems: Integrating costs and outcomes. Tools for professional development

and program evaluation. *Administration in Social Work,*
20(1), 1-15.

McKinney, J. B. (1995). *Effective financial management in*
public and nonprofit agencies (2nd ed.). Westport, CT:
Quorum Books.

Meyer, D. R., & Sherraden, M. W. (1985). Toward improved financial planning: Further applications of
break-even analysis in not-for-profit organizations. *Ad-*
ministration in Social Work, 9(3), 57-68.

National Association of Social Workers. (1996). *Code of*
ethics. Washington, DC: Author.

Office of Management and Budget. (1997). *Audits of states,*
local governments, and non-profit organizations (Circular No. A-133). Washington, DC: Author.

Oster, S. M. (1995). *Strategic management for nonprofit or-*
ganizations: Theory and cases. New York: Oxford University Press.

Patti, R. J. (1985). In search of purpose for social welfare administration. *Administration in Social Work, 9*(3), 1-14.

Perrin, E. B., & Koshel, J. J. (Eds.). (1997). *Assessment of*
performance measures for public health, substance
abuse, and mental health. Washington, DC: National
Academy Press.

Vinter, R. D., & Kish, R. K. (1984). *Budgeting for not-for-*
profit organizations. New York: Free Press.

Wolf, T. (1990). *Managing a nonprofit organization.* New
York: Fireside.

CHAPTER TWENTY

Managing Personnel

PETER J. PECORA
MICHAEL WAGNER

In the human services field, line staff and supervisors constitute one of the most important resources for maximizing agency productivity and effectiveness. Personnel management
in social work agencies involves key functions
that must be performed to develop and maintain a group of skilled, productive, and satisfied
employees, namely:

- Recruiting, screening, and selecting social
  work and other personnel
- Specificying and allocating job tasks to design
  position descriptions and staffing patterns and
  requirements

- Designing and conducting performance ap-
  praisals
- Orienting, training, and developing staff
- Supervising and coaching ongoing task perfor-
  mance
- Handling employee performance problems
- Enforcing employee sanctions and, when nec-
  essary, dismissing workers

There are a host of issues and tasks associated with these key personnel management
functions, such as job classification and wage
setting, support of work teams, worker job motivation and productivity, employee health and

AUTHORS' NOTE: This chapter is adapted from Pecora, (in press). Recruiting and selecting effective employees. In R. L.
Edwards & J. A. Yankey (Eds.), *Skills for effective management of non-profit organizations*. Washington, DC: National
Association of Social Workers. The authors thank Stacy Radley and Gloria Rendon at the University of Utah, Michael J. Austin of
the University of California at Berkeley, Nigel Bristow of Targeted Learning Inc., and members of Recruitment and Selection
Competencies Work Group at The Casey Family Program for sharing their innovative personnel management materials.

safety, labor-management relations, personnel administration law, and merit system reform. Personnel management overlaps greatly with supervision of staff in that many supervisory responsibilities include functions such as promoting teamwork, setting unit goals, promoting and supporting ethnic and cultural diversity, negotiating organizational demands, and managing conflict. (See, e.g., Brody, 1993; Patti, 1983; Slavin, 1985; Tambor, 1985; Valdez, 1982; Von der Embse, 1987; Weinbach, 1998; Weiner, 1982.)

Personnel management should be viewed as part of the organization's approach to human resources, which needs to be aligned with the overall organizational mission, vision, and strategy. Bristow (1999b, p. 16) recently conducted a study of 1,030 business organizations to illustrate the value of aligning the following "people systems" with organizational strategy for fiscal success:

- Rewards
- Work design
- Succession/promotion
- Performance management
- Staffing/selection
- Career development
- Training and development

Important efforts are under way in the business and technology fields with respect to competency-based human resource systems that we believe have value for the human services with respect to organizational design and personnel management (see, e.g., Bristow, 1999a, 1999b; Pedigo, 1995a, 1995b). To help obtain a sense of the scope of personnel management, an ex-

ample of the table of contents of a personnel manual is included as Table 20.1. What this high-level table of contents cannot convey is the dynamic and creative work under way in this area—but some of this will be described in this chapter.

A definition of each of the key aspects of personnel management will be presented, along with a brief discussion of their importance for supporting effective social or other services. As part of certain functions, special issues will be briefly addressed, such as affirmative action, equal employment opportunity, protecting Americans with disabilities, and sexual harassment. Because of its importance to the success of the work unit and larger organization, we will focus disproportionately on recruitment, with other sections slightly more narrow in scope. Because affirmative action, equal employment opportunity, and Americans With Disabilities Act guidelines have become so fundamental to management practice, they will be considered first.

AFFIRMATIVE ACTION AND EQUAL EMPLOYMENT OPPORTUNITY

Affirmative Action

Legislation for affirmative action and equal employment opportunity continues to affect the recruitment, screening, and selection of employees in both for-profit and nonprofit organizations. The distinctive components of Equal Employment Opportunity Commission (EEOC) laws are based on Title VII of the 1964 Civil Rights Act and other laws, including the Age Discrimination in Employment Act of 1967;

TABLE 20.1 Typical Table of Contents for a Social Service Agency Personnel Manual

Introduction
    Organization philosophy and mission
    Major organizational goals and objectives
    Organizational programs or types of service
1. Employment
    Hiring authority
    Nondiscrimination and affirmative action policies
       and safeguards (includes safeguards as
       mandated by Equal Employment Opportunity
       Commission, affirmative action, and the
       Americans With Disabilities Act)
    Types of employment (full time, part time,
       temporary, volunteer)
    Probationary period procedures
    Maintenance and access to personnel records
2. Working hours and conditions
    Work schedule and office hours
    Flexible time
    Overtime or compensatory time
    Types of absence and reports
3. Salaries and wages
    Wages and salary structure and rationale
    Paydays
    Deductions
    Raises (merit and cost of living); guidelines and
       rationale
    Compensation for work-related expenses
    Employee access to current salary schedule
4. Employee benefits
    Leaves and absences
    Vacations
    Holidays
    Sick days
    Personal days
    Maternity leave
    Paternity leave
    Leave of absence
    Other excused absences
    Insurance
    Social Security
    Medical insurance
    Life insurance

    Disability insurance
    Unemployment insurance
    Workers' compensation
    Pension or retirement plans
5. Employee rights and responsibilities
    Employee responsibilities
    Employee rights
    Grievance procedures
6. Performance and salary review
    Procedures
    Timing
    Use of probation periods or suspension
    Promotion policies and procedures
7. Staff development
    Orientation of new employees
    Planning process for in-service training and related
       activities
    Educational programs and conferences
8. General policies and procedures
    Outside employment
    Office opening and closing
    Telephone
    Travel
    Personal property
9. General office practices and procedures
    Office coverage
    Smoking
    Use and care of equipment
10. Termination
    Grounds of dismissal
    Resignation
    Retirement
    Release
    Reduction in force
Appendixes
    Organizational chart
    Salary ranges by position
    Equal opportunity guidelines on sexual harassment
    Conflict of interest policies
    Personnel evaluation procedures and forms

SOURCE: Adapted from Cox (1984, p. 275); Wolfe (1984, pp. 63-64); The Casey Family Program (1999).

Sections 503 and 504 of the Rehabilitation Act of 1973, as amended; the Vietnam Era Veterans' Readjustment Assistance Act of 1974; and the Equal Pay Act of 1963.[1] As Klingner and Nalbandian (1985) noted,

> With few exceptions, Title VII (EEO) prohibits employers, labor organizations, and employment agencies from making employee or applicant personnel decisions based on race, color, religion, sex, or national origin. Although it originally applied only to private employers, the concern of EEO was extended to local and state governments by 1972 amendments to the 1964 Civil Rights Act. (p. 64)

Equal opportunity laws reflect a management approach to reducing discrimination against employees by ensuring that equal opportunity is implemented in all employment actions. These laws require nondiscrimination, which involves the elimination of all existing discriminatory conditions, whether purposeful or inadvertent. Nonprofit organizations, because of their tax-exempt status and because they may have government contracts, must carefully and systematically examine all their employment policies to be sure they do not operate to the detriment of any people on the grounds of race, color, religion, national origin, sex, age, or status as a person with a disability, disabled veteran, or veteran of the Vietnam era. Managers must also ensure that practices of those who are responsible for matters of employment, including supervisors, are nondiscriminatory.

In contrast, affirmative action requires that most organizations take steps to ensure proportional recruitment, selection, and promotion of qualified members of groups, such as members of ethnic minority groups and women, who were formerly excluded. Most employers, un-

ions, and employment agencies are required to plan and document, through written affirmative action programs (AAPs), the steps they are taking to reduce the underrepresentation of various groups. Most public and private organizations that provide goods and services to the federal government and their subcontractors must comply with the affirmative action provisions described in Executive Order No. 11246. Guidelines for working with AAPs are found in Title 41, Part 60-2 (known as Revised Order No. 4) of the Office of Federal Contract Compliance (also see Lovell, 1985).

Although both equal employment opportunity and affirmative action seek to eliminate discrimination in employment, the safeguards and improvements mandated by these guidelines in relation to specific practices for recruiting, screening, selecting, and promoting employees vary. For example, a mental health organization may develop a specific campaign to recruit and hire more female supervisors to increase the proportion of female managers in the organization as part of its plan to comply with affirmative action regulations. In contrast, equal employment opportunity organization guidelines cover such areas as the type of questions that can be asked on an employment application or in an interview and emphasize the use of screening or interviewing committees that are composed of a mix of men, women, and people of color.

Knowledge of equal employment opportunity and affirmative action guidelines is essential for designing employment application forms and interviewing protocols that avoid the use of illegal questions. However, court cases and recently passed legislation such as Proposition 209 in California and Proposition 200 in Washington may alter what is permissible under equal employment opportunity and affirmative action guidelines. In fact, some of these state laws have limited the use of affirmative action efforts in college admissions and other areas. Government updates and legal consultations are important resources for assessing the adequacy of procedures.

Equal Employment Opportunity, Affirmative Action, and the Classification of Jobs

In addition to banning certain types of questions on applications or in interviews, equal employment opportunity guidelines forbid any selection process for candidates that has an adverse impact on any social, ethnic, or gender group, unless the procedure is validated through the analysis of jobs or research on the selection of employees. Descriptions and notices of positions that delineate knowledge, skill, ability, education, or other prerequisites require a determination of whether the prerequisites are genuinely appropriate for the job. Some requirements (such as years of experience, certificates, diplomas, and educational degrees) may be considered unlawful on the basis of previous court decisions for a particular position. Proscriptions against discrimination in employment demand that any requirement (education or experience) used as a standard for decisions about employment must have a manifest relationship to the job in question (Meritt-Haston & Weyley, 1983; Pecora & Austin, 1983).

The use of standards that disqualify women, certain racial or ethnic groups, or other groups at a substantially higher rate than white male applicants would be unlawful unless they could be shown to be significantly related to the successful performance of a job and otherwise nec-essary to the safe and efficient operation of the job for which they are used. Educational requirements are defined as a test by the federal government and must be validated in accordance with EEOC's testing guidelines. In addition, if an organization validates its selection criteria, equal employment opportunity guidelines require it to demonstrate that no suitable alternative with a lesser adverse impact is available.

When an adverse impact can be demonstrated with regard to a screening instrument or process (a test or structured interview, for example), employers should use alternative measures that are equally valid but produce a less adverse impact. Unfortunately, little progress has been made in identifying and using screening procedures as alternatives to educational and experience qualifications (Zedeck & Cascio, 1984). Nevertheless, your nonprofit organization should carefully analyze its jobs and clearly define their tasks and requisite knowledge, skills, and abilities. This information is essential for establishing minimum qualifications for various positions so qualified individuals can be recruited and selected. Table 20.2 provides a concise summary, based on equal employment opportunity and affirmative action regulations, of what is acceptable and unacceptable to use in application forms and interview questions. Note that the guidelines for people who have physical disabilities are being revised, and questions must be carefully considered.

AMERICANS WITH DISABILITIES ACT

Overview

The Americans with Disabilities Act (ADA), enacted July 26, 1990, extended broad civil

TABLE 20.2 Guide to Fair Employment Regulations on Pre-employment Inquiries

Acceptable	Subject	Unacceptable
Have you ever used another name? or Is any additional information relative to change of name, use of an assumed name, or nickname necessary to enable a check on your work and education record? If yes, please explain.	Name	What is your maiden name?
What is your place of residence?	Residence	Do you own or rent your home?
Statement that hiring is subject to verification that applicant meets legal age requirements. If hired can you show proof of age? Are you over 18? If under 18, can you, after employment, submit a work permit?	Age	Questions about age, birthdate, dates of attendance or completion of elementary or high school. Questions that tend to identify applicants over 40.
Can you, after employment, submit verification of your legal right to work in the United States? or Statement that such proof may be required after employment.	Birthplace, citizenship	Questions about birthplace of applicant, applicant's parents, spouse, or other relatives. Are you a U.S. citizen? Questions about citizenship of applicant, parents, spouse, or other relatives.
Language applicant speaks, reads, or writes.	National origin	Questions about nationality, lineage, ancestry, national origin, descent, or parentage of applicant, applicant's parents, or spouse. What is your mother tongue? What language do you commonly use? How did you learn to read, write, or speak a foreign language?
Name and address of parent or guardian if applicant is a minor. Statement of company policy regarding work assignment of employees who are related.	Sex, marital status, family	Questions that indicate applicant's sex. Questions that indicate marital status. Number of ages of children or dependents. Provisions for child care. Questions regarding pregnancy, child bearing, or birth control. Name or address of relative, spouse, or children of adult applicant. With whom do you reside? or Do you live with your parents?
	Race, color	Questions as to applicant's race or color. Questions regarding applicant's complexion or color of skin, eyes, hair.
Statement that photograph may be required after employment.	Physical description, photograph	Questions about applicant's height and weight. Requiring applicants to affix a photograph to application. Asking applicants, at their option, to submit to photograph. Requiring a photograph after interview but before employment.

TABLE 20.2 *Continued*

Acceptable	Subject	Unacceptable
Statement by employer that offer may be made contingent on applicant's passing a job-related physical examination. Do you have any physical condition or handicap that may limit your ability to perform the job applied for? If yes, what can be done to accommodate your limitation?	Physical condition, handicap	Questions regarding applicant's general medical condition, state of health, or illnesses. Questions regarding receipt of Workers' Compensation. Do you have any physical disabilities or handicaps?
Statement by employer of regular days, hours, or shifts to be worked.	Religion	Questions regarding applicant's religion or religious days observed. Does your religion prevent you from working weekends or holidays?
Have you ever been convicted of a felony, or arrested? Have you ever been convicted of a misdemeanor that resulted in imprisonment (within specified time period)? (Such a question must be accompanied by a statement that a conviction will not necessarily disqualify the applicant from the job.)	Arrest, criminal record	Have you ever been arrested?
Statement that bonding is a condition of hire.	Bonding	Questions regarding refusal or cancellation of bonding.
Questions regarding relevant skills acquired during applicant's U.S. military service.	Military service	General questions regarding military service such as dates and type of discharge. Questions regarding service in a foreign military.
	Economic status	Questions regarding applicant's current or past assets, liabilities, or credit rating, including bankruptcy or garnishment.
Please list job-related organizations, clubs, professional societies, or other associations to which you belong—you may omit those that indicate your race, religious creed, color, national origin, ancestry, sex, or age.	Organizations, activities	List all organizations, clubs, societies, and lodges to which you belong.
By whom were you referred for a position here? Names of persons willing to provide professional or character references for applicant	References	Questions of applicant's former employers or acquaintances that elicit information specifying the applicant's race, color, religious creed, national origin, ancestry, physical handicap, medical condition, marital status, age, or sex.
Name and address of person to be notified in case of accident or emergency.	Notification in case of emergency	Name and address of relative to be notified in case of accident or emergency.

SOURCE: Based on materials developed by the California Department of Fair Employment and Housing. Adapted from Jensen (1981a, pp. 28-29). Copyright 1981, The Grantsmanship Center. Reprinted with permission.
NOTE: = For a schedule of Grantsmanship Center workshops and for information on how to order their publications, write to The Grantsmanship Center, P.O. Box 17220, Los Angeles, CA 90017 and request a free copy of the Center's Nonprofit Catalog.

rights protection to an estimated 43 million Americans with disabilities. The act contains four major sections: employment (Title I), state and local government services (Title II), public accommodations provided by private entities (Title III), and telecommunications (Title IV). The ADA is neither pre-emptive nor exclusive; stricter requirements of state or federal law will continue to apply. (The following section is adapted from Davis, Wright, & Tremaine Law Firm, 1992. Also see Perry, 1993.)

The purpose of the act is to

- provide a clear and comprehensive national mandate for the elimination of discrimination against individuals with disabilities
- provide clear, strong, consistent, enforceable standards addressing discrimination against individuals with disabilities
- ensure that the federal government plays a central role in enforcing the standards established in this act on behalf of individuals with disabilities
- invoke the sweep of congressional authority, including the power to enforce the 14th Amendment and to regulate commerce, to address the major areas of discrimination faced every day by people with disabilities

The effective date for compliance with specific sections of the ADA varies by topic and by the size of the corporation or entity. The employment provisions became effective July 26, 1992, for employers with 25 or more employees; effective July 26, 1994, for employers with 15 to 24 employees. Under the public accommodations provisions, the compliance dates are January 26, 1992, for large businesses (more than 25 employees and gross receipts of more than $1 million); July 26, 1992, for medium-size businesses (25 or fewer employees and

gross receipts of less than $1 million); January 26, 1993, for small businesses (10 or fewer employees with less than $500,000 in gross receipts).

The ADA is not an affirmative action law. It is an equal employment opportunity law because it addresses discrimination in hiring, accommodation of a disabled person on the job, and access of people with disabilities to public and private facilities. Even if a person has a disability, he or she still must be qualified under the act. A qualified individual with a disability is one who, with or without reasonable accommodation, can perform the essential functions of the job that the person holds or desires. It is a two-step analysis: (a) What are the essential functions of the job? and (b) Can the individual perform the functions with or without a reasonable accommodation?

First and foremost, job requirements should always be expressed in terms of actual job duties and skill requirements and should never be expressed in terms of an applicant's or employee's limitations. The employer should not focus on whether a candidate or employee has a disability or is protected under the act. Rather, an employer should focus on the essential functions of the position and whether a candidate or employee, with reasonable accommodation, will be able to perform the essential functions of the job. Applicants should not be asked about the existence, nature, or severity of a disability but may be asked whether they are able to perform each essential job function.

Employers are still free to hire the most qualified candidate for any particular job. Qualifications of all applicants should be reviewed without regard to the disability of one of the applicants. If the applicant with a disability is the most qualified, then the employer should evaluate whether the disability limits or precludes the performance of an essential function of the job and, if so, whether reasonable accommodation will permit the person to perform the essential functions of the job.

Duty of reasonable accommodation. The concept of reasonable accommodation is the new, unique distinguishing characteristic of employment practices under the ADA. However, the concept is not well defined in the act. In simple terms, a reasonable accommodation is an action taken by the employer that assists a person with a disability to perform the essential job functions. In determining whether a person is qualified for a position, any individual with a disability must be evaluated assuming all reasonable accommodations will be provided. If the individual is then not qualified for the position, he or she may be rejected.

Accommodations provided by private entities. Title III of the ADA prohibits discrimination against individuals with disabilities "in the full and equal enjoyment of goods, services, and facilities of any place of public accommodation by any person who owns, leases (or leases to), or operates a place of public accommodation." A public accommodation is broadly defined and includes places of lodging (excluding facilities with not more than five rooms for rent that is occupied by the proprietor as his or her residence); restaurants and bars; theaters and stadiums; auditoriums, convention centers, or other places of public gathering; sales or retail establishments such as bakeries, grocery stores, clothing stores, and shopping centers; service establishments such as banks, insurance offices, hospitals, and medical offices; public transportation stations; museums, libraries, and galleries; parks, zoos, amusements parks, or other places of recreation; private educational facilities; social services establishments such as day care centers, homeless shelters, food banks, adoption agencies, and senior citizens centers; and places of exercise or recreation such as gymnasiums, spas, and golf courses.

The alterations and new construction provisions of the ADA also apply to commercial facilities intended for nonresidential use whose operations affect commerce. These facilities include office buildings (to the extent they are not covered by the public accommodations provisions of the act), factories, and warehouses.

Discrimination. The ADA requires that services be provided to individuals with disabilities in the most integrated setting appropriate to the needs of the individual. It is discriminatory to deny a person with a disability the opportunity to participate in or benefit from the goods, services, facilities, privileges, advantages, or accommodations offered by an entity or to provide such opportunity in a manner that is not equal to that afforded to other individuals. An entity may provide a service that is different or separate from that provided to other individuals only if such action is necessary to provide a service that is as effective as that provided to others.

RECRUITING AND SELECTING EFFECTIVE EMPLOYEES

Recruitment and screening of staff members are some of the most important components of personnel management. The employee selection process requires both analytical and interpersonal skills, as well as knowledge of affirmative action and EEOC rules. For example, in terms of analytical skills, the position for which the agency is recruiting must be defined in task-specific ways. Task-based job descriptions must be developed, and essential worker competencies (knowledge, skills, abilities, and attitudes) must be identified. Well-developed interpersonal skills are required for interviewing job candidates in a courteous and professional manner.

Recruitment involves generating an applicant pool that provides the employer an opportunity to make a selection that satisfies the needs of the organization. Selection is concerned with reviewing qualifications of job applicants to decide who should be offered the position. Placement involves assigning new employees to positions and orienting them properly so that they can begin working (Shafritz, Hyde, & Rosenbloom, 1986). The major steps involved in recruitment and selection are presented in a checklist form in Table 20.3 and summarized below:

1. Developing a job description that contains information regarding the minimum prerequisite qualifications for the position in terms of personal attributes such as education, experience, and skills

2. Creating position announcements and external advertising

3. Screening job applicants using application forms, resume reviews and checklists, and tests (if appropriate)

4. Conducting both telephone and in-person screening interviews

5. Selecting the successful candidate and notifying other applicants

The interpersonal skills involved include being able to work collaboratively with agency staff to develop common expectations for the position and a common set of interview ques-

tions. Equally important is the ability to reach agreement on what constitutes acceptable responses to various interview questions. Supervisory and other administrative personnel must also be able to interview job applicants in a professional and courteous manner. (For additional information on various aspects of employee selection, see Campion & Arvey, 1989; Mayfield, Brown, & Hamstra, 1980; McCormick, 1979; Mufson, 1986; National Association of Social Workers, 1985; Robertson, 1982; Ross & Hoeltke, 1985; Teare, Higgs, Gauthier, & Feild, 1984; Weinbach, 1998.)

The employment selection process should be considered an important investment of administrative time. If this process is not carried out properly, supervisory staff and managers will spend valuable time and energy unnecessarily—through additional supervisory time overcoming marginal work performance, increased organizational conflict, and the stress involved in transferring or terminating the staff person. Although many local, state, and federal laws affect recruitment, three major sets of law and policy described above help shape what is effective and legal practice in this area: (a) affirmative action, (b) equal employment opportunity, and (c) the ADA. For example, whereas state policies, accreditation standards (Weinbach, 1998), and other factors affect minimum qualifications and other aspects of employee recruitment, these laws remain important guidelines.

POSITION DESCRIPTIONS AND USE OF COMPETENCIES

Specifying Job Tasks and Position Descriptions

Some of the key ingredients of excellence in human service agencies include attention to the

TABLE 20.3 Summary Checklist for Recruiting, Screening, and Selecting Employees

---

Step 1: Developing a Job Description and Minimum Qualifications

    A. Does the job description contain clear and specific task statements that describe the essential duties of this position?

    B. Are the knowledge, skills, abilities, educational degrees (if any), and years of related job experience specified anywhere?

    C. Do the required minimum qualifications for the job match the work to be performed; that is, can you substantiate the connections between the education and experience required and the tasks of the job?

Step 2: Employee Recruitment

    A. Do the job announcements include the necessary details of the position?

    B. Are the announcements clearly worded?

    C. Is the application deadline realistic, given the usual delays in dissemination and publication; that is, does the deadline allow the applicant sufficient time to respond to the announcement?

    D. Have you distributed the announcement to enough community, professional, or other groups? Have you used both formal and informal networks in publicizing the position?

    E. Is a record being kept of how and where the position was advertised or posted, including personal recruitment efforts?

Step 3: Screening Job Applicants Using Application Forms and Tests (If Appropriate)

    A. Does the application form provide information that helps you determine whether the applicant has related education, training, and experience?

    B. Does the application form contain questions that are illegal according to equal employment opportunity laws?

    C. Can you structure the application form and process so applicants are asked to submit a cover letter or other summary statements to highlight how their training and experience qualify them for the position?

Step 4: Conducting the Screening Interview

    A. Have you trained the interviewers in the basic phases and principles of the selection process?

    B. Have you developed a list of standard questions to be asked of each applicant by the same interviewer?

    C. Has a quiet place been set aside for the interview, with phone or other interruptions prevented?

    D. Have you chosen a person to lead the interview through the opening, information gathering, and closing phases?

    E. Have you established a time line for the selection process and informed each applicant of how and when he or she will be notified?

Step 5: Selecting the Person and Notifying the Other Applicants

    A. Have you contacted a sufficient number of applicants' references?

    B. Has the committee weighed carefully all the information gathered to determine the most qualified and committed applicant?

    C. Do you have a firm commitment from the primary candidate before notifying the other applicants?

    D. Is your letter notifying the other applicants worded sensitively to ease their disappointment and thank them for their interest in the position?

SOURCE: Pecora (1998).

details of human service work. For example, the greater the job clarity, the greater the potential for staff members to understand their work and what is expected to be done. As worker understanding is increased, there is greater opportunity to connect observations and feedback about job performance with the job description. As clarity and feedback are increased, it seems reasonable that worker autonomy can also be increased. And as clarity, feedback, and autonomy are increased, there appears to be more opportunity for job enhancement and job enlargement. Job enhancement relates to adding or changing components of the job to further worker growth and development. Job enlargement involves expanding both authority and responsibility to carry out increasingly more complex and/or sophisticated job functions. Both have been linked with employee motivation and productivity (Howell & Dipboye, 1982), along with other job characteristics and factors associated with employee satisfaction and burnout. (See, e.g., Himle, Jaraytne & Thyness, 1989; Vinokur-Kaplan & Bogin, Chapter 9, this volume; Zunz, 1998.) One of the basic tools necessary for increasing job clarity or modifying job responsibilities is an accurate job description.

Over the past 50 years, job descriptions have been viewed by workers and administrators as "necessary evils" in the life of human service organizations. Job descriptions appear to take on importance only when a job vacancy is being advertised and when a new worker appears on the job for the first time. Even at these critical points in the recruitment, selection, and orientation process, most human service practitioners pay very little attention to the job description. There may be several reasons for this

situation. First, job descriptions tend to be written in vague terms because inadequate time is set aside to think through job responsibilities and activities, or the job is defined primarily in terms of the person who fills the position, or the job is based on the assumption that everyone with a BSW or MSW "ought to know" how the job is to be performed. Second, job descriptions are viewed as administrative documents to be filed away and retrieved only when necessary. They are generally not viewed as management tools for helping workers grow on the job or for evaluating job performance.

One approach to assessing task-based job descriptions is to focus on the roles of supervisor and worker (Austin, 1981). This can be a fairly informal process of sitting down with incumbents and identifying their key job responsibilities (what some personnel experts call "key job parts"), or it could involve a more formal job-analysis process that uses a set of steps to analyze the tasks of the job and what it requires to perform them (McCormick, 1979). Experienced supervisors who have learned the job-analysis approach and begun the process of slowly implementing it in their work unit have identified several benefits: (a) it serves as a basis for clarifying job expectations with workers, because the job descriptions are often vague and incomplete; (b) it facilitates worker performance reviews, because there is specific information about job tasks and competencies necessary for assessing outcome; (c) the analysis is job-related and not necessarily worker-specific, so that it provides continuity during staff turnover; (d) it serves as an information base for assessing staffing needs and for requesting additional staff support based on tasks performed in the unit; (e) it serves as a tool for monitoring the relationship between the work performed by staff and the goals and objectives of the agency; (f) the profiles are useful in identifying training needs of workers; (g) it provides consistency of approach across a range of workers in a unit and can serve as a tool for ensuring equitability of work performed and salary levels; and (h) this approach can be implemented in developmental stages (e.g., one worker at a time) and can save time in the long run by reducing the number of supervisor-supervisee meetings needed to clarify the job expectations for new workers.

Not only do the position descriptions provide the foundation for job announcements (see Table 20.4), the task statements also provide a forum for the supervisor to identify performance standards. A major challenge in human service agencies is the development of performance standards that are meaningful to workers. Performance standards linked to a task or cluster of tasks provide a basis for ongoing worker self-assessment and for supervisory troubleshooting when workers do not meet a minimum standard of performance. (See Austin, 1981; McCormick, 1979.)

Use of Competencies in Personnel Management

A competency can be defined as any knowledge, skill, or attribute, observable in the consistent patterns of an individual's behavior, interactions, and work-related activities over time, which contributes to the fulfillment of the mission and accomplishment of the strategic objectives of the organization. Through the understanding and incorporation of both core (organization-wide) and domain (job-related) competencies, staff can develop and apply the means to more effectively

- recruit and select new employees
- assess and enhance their own level of contribution to the organization, as well as assessing and enhancing the level of contribution of those whom they supervise or team with
- focus and manage their own professional development and growth, including setting reasonable goals (Locke & Latham, 1984)

To effectively use a competency platform in your personnel program and practices, every major system needs to have competencies effectively embedded in it. For example, The Casey Family Program has followed the example of a number of major corporations and other types of organizations (Bristow, Dalton, & Thompson, 1996) by adopting nine core competencies for recruiting, supervising, training, and recognizing staff members:

- *Organization and priority setting.* Prioritizes, organizes, and monitors work to ensure that goals, objectives, and commitments are met
- *Flexibility.* Adapts well to changes in direction, priorities, schedule, and responsibilities
- *Two-way communication.* Clearly expresses (verbally and in writing) thoughts, feelings, concepts, and directions; listens effectively to understand communications from others
- *Teamwork.* Works collaboratively and cooperatively in groups for the purpose of achieving shared objectives, consistent with the organization's mission and strategy and individual work goals
- *Relationship building.* Builds and maintains productive associations with others who share a mutual interest in and commitment to achieving Casey's strategic objectives

TABLE 20.4 Sample Position Announcement

POSITION ANNOUNCEMENT
Family Preservation Service Specialist
Children's Services Society
Seattle, Washington

Function and Location. Provides intensive in-home services to families considering out-of-home placement for one or more members. Is on call 24 hours per day to provide crisis intervention and other family services and problem resolution. Will work out of the Wallingford social services office.

Duties and Responsibilities. (Partial List)[a]

1. Provides in-home crisis-oriented treatment and support to families in which one or more family members are at risk of being placed outside the home in foster, group, or institutional care to prevent unnecessary child placement

2. Works a 40-hour nonstructured workweek (including evenings and weekends) to be responsive to the needs of families

3. Provides family education and skills training as part of a goal-oriented treatment plan to prevent the recurrence of or to reduce the harmful effects of the maltreatment of children

4. Advocates for family members with schools, courts, and other social service agencies to help family members obtain financial assistance, housing, medical care, and other services

Qualifications. Master's degree in social work, psychology, educational psychology, or psychosocial nursing is required. Graduate degree in social work preferred. Experience in counseling families and children is required. Knowledge of crisis intervention social casework, communication skills, and family therapy techniques is required. Knowledge of cognitive-behavioral interventions, group work, and functional family therapy is desirable. Must have reliable transportation. Required to live in county served. Salary range: $29,000-35,000

Application Procedures and Deadline. An agency application form, resume, and cover letter describing related education and experience must be submitted. Position closes April 25, 1998. Starting date is tentatively scheduled for May 25, 1998. Please send application materials to

Annette Jandre
Program Supervisor
Children's Services Society
4601 15th Avenue, NW
Seattle, WA 98103
(206) 263-5857

AN EQUAL OPPORTUNITY EMPLOYER—ALL QUALIFIED INDIVIDUALS ARE ENCOURAGED TO APPLY

a. These are key job parts.

- *Valuing diversity.* In the course of accomplishing the job requirements and strategic objectives of Casey, is sensitive to and competent in working with people who are different from one's self

- *Developing self and others.* Recognizes and acts on the need for life-long learning; takes personal responsibility for building professional and organization capability in self and others, consistent with the needs of Casey

- *Critical thinking and judgment.* Gathers, organizes, interprets, and processes information for the purpose of making informed decisions in the course of accomplishing work objectives
- *Technical expertise.* Demonstrates both technical and Casey-specific knowledge required to be proficient in one's profession or job classification (The Casey Family Program, 1998)

A competencies approach can then be linked with a framework for viewing levels of contribution that staff members can make. In fields where employee learning and constant innovation are essential, these are being referred to as *levels of knowledge work:*

Level 1: Acquiring knowledge. The knowledge acquired is in the form of ideas, theories, methods, principles, skills, and information about the organization, the work of the organization, and its customers. The Level 1 contributor seeks and acquires knowledge from two primary sources:

- From supervisors and coworkers (by seeking information, advice, guidance, and feedback)
- From the codified sources of knowledge in the organization (i.e., systems, guidelines, work manuals, operating procedures, policies, etc.)

Level 2: Applying knowledge. Level 2 contributors use acquired knowledge to independently plan and complete value-added work for the organization. They exercise judgment to make their own decisions, rather than deferring those decisions to others. Unless new knowledge is used, it adds little or no value for the organization. By exercising confidence and initiative, Level 2 contributors turn previously acquired knowledge into a value-added resource for the organization. (We tend to think of Level

2 knowledge workers as the "solid performers" in most organizations. Based on our research "star" status is usually only conferred on those knowledge workers who contribute at Levels 3, 4, and 5.)

Level 3: Creating knowledge. The Level 3 contributor creates new knowledge by pushing the boundaries of existing knowledge:

- Asks "what if" questions
- Takes the risk of doing things that have never been done before
- Solves critical problems that have no predetermined solutions
- Invents new products, processes, technologies, or work methods

Level 4: Developing knowledge in others. The Level 4 contributor grows intellectual capital in several different ways:

- Shares knowledge directly with others
- Helps others apply new or existing knowledge to their work
- Provides people with feedback
- Motivates others to create and apply new knowledge
- Communicates a sense of direction and purpose
- Facilitates the face-to-face transfer of knowledge between others

Level 5: Leveraging knowledge. Level 5 contributors help define what the organization does and/or how it does it. They often do this by transforming the knowledge in people's heads into systems that are "owned" by the organization; systems that accelerate the transfer and application of knowledge across the organization. We refer to these systems as structural capital. Although Level 5 contributors may not create this structural capital, they are the ones who get a critical mass of the organization to accept and use the new structural capital. This structural capital could include any of the following:

- New business or technology strategies and directions
- New work methods and expert systems
- New people systems or organization structures
- New training, communication, or information systems (Bristow, 1999a, pp. 5-6)

These kinds of knowledge are what Bristow (1999a, p. 9) and others refer to as "human capital"—part of the assets that an organization can use to generate future returns. In the human services, we might refer to the importance of human capital for providing high-quality services and achieving desired outcomes with our consumers. As part of defining a position and developing the staff that are hired, attention needs to be paid to key competencies that are required and how the employee can grow and contribute to the organization in different ways over time.

As described in Table 20.2, knowledge of EEOC, affirmative action, ADA, job descriptions, and specific key staff competencies are all essential for developing position announcements, screening candidates, and selecting the right candidate. (See American Psychological Association, 1980; Beach, 1975; Campbell, 1983; Eder & Ferris, 1989; Goodale, 1989; Janz, 1989; Latham, 1989; and Lovell, 1985, for more information on these aspects of personnel management.)

ORIENTING AND DEVELOPING STAFF MEMBERS

Orienting, Training, and Developing Staff

The induction process is of critical importance to the new worker and deserves considerable attention by the organization. The impressions generated on entry into the agency are lasting ones, and it is to the agency's advantage that orientation programs be positive experiences. This section will consider the major ingredients that should be included in a sound orientation program from the perspective of the organization and the specific job. Such an orientation would include an introduction to the agency structure and goals, the personnel policies, the director, the job, and the coworkers.

The basic purpose of orientation is to introduce new workers to the organization, its policies and procedures, their colleagues, their role and responsibilities, and the authority structure. The basic components of such an orientation are usually completed in several working days, followed by additional on-the-job orientation that may include reading about policy, agency history, social case-history procedures, and sample case studies.

New workers often enter the agency with only vague notions about its actual programs and procedural operations. Many new workers are not aware of the entry-level skills and knowledge required by human service agencies. Some are hired in public agencies strictly on the basis of good scores on state merit exams. As a result, many human service workers learn about delivering services while on the job. This fact simply underscores the importance of a comprehensive orientation program.

The induction process of new workers should include a complete description of the agency's structure with lines of authority/communication, personnel procedures, and career opportunities. The orientation may be conducted in part by the supervisor and in part by the trainer or staff development specialist. New workers need a full explanation of the purpose, goals, and objectives of the agency. Because most human service agencies are part of a larger network of services, a brief description of the role of the agency in this network is important, including an identification of relevant policies and regulations pertaining to state and federal regulations or agency bylaws. Copies of the organizational chart should be made available to clarify the lines of authority and communication.

Another component of a comprehensive orientation program is the process of familiarizing new workers with the personnel policies of the agency. These policies explain what new workers can expect from the agency and what the agency can expect of new workers. This part of the orientation should be covered by a personnel specialist or another appropriate person who has knowledge of the personnel system. Workers need to be informed of the general rules and regulations concerning annual leave, pay, benefits and services, disciplinary procedures, working hours, grievance procedures, and promotional opportunities. Most agencies provide employees with personnel handbooks containing this information, which should be regularly updated.

Orientation programs should also include an introduction to the agency director. An orientation program also involves supervisors in orienting new workers to the job. Workers who are already oriented to the organization will be better able to grasp their role in carrying out or-

ganizational goals and objectives. Supervisors should be able to relate the goals and objectives of the agency. Information about the unit's role and scope provides workers with a better perspective of the organization's mission and provides the foundation for the supervisor's explanation of how the different positions held by coworkers in the unit help both the unit and the agency to meet goals and objectives. There will probably be few other opportunities for a supervisor to capture workers' openness and receptivity to acquiring a positive attitude toward their job. The orientation process also involves inducting new employees into the culture of the place, norms, folklore, operating assumptions, and other aspects of the organization and work unit. This is done via both informal and formal work systems.

Staff development programs can be viewed from many different vantage points. A program could be a single workshop or a 6-month series of in-service training events. Several programs might be the major components of an agency's annual staff development plan. For workers, a staff development program usually provides opportunities to improve skills and gain new knowledge away from the job. For supervisors, staff development programs may provide an opportunity to improve their own knowledge and skills as well as the capacities of those they supervise. For some administrators, agency staff development programs may be viewed as costly enterprises and only justifiable in terms of disseminating new agency policies and procedures. For other administrators, focused supervision (Weinbach, 1998) and staff training are among the essential strategies for preventing employee obsolescence due to technological, cultural, or social change (see Odiorne, 1984, pp. 218-244) and for helping build critical thinking skills and other key specific competencies (e.g., Nurius, Kemp, & Gibson, 1999). From the perspective of service recipients, staff development programs may be seen as essential if clients are to be served by staff who are up-to-date and knowledgeable about new treatment or service delivery approaches.

The different perspectives suggest the need for a working definition of how to manage the agency staff development process. Staff development program management includes (a) scanning the environment (local, state, and national) for social policies, innovations, and consumer feedback that could influence the service delivery and administrative functions of agency personnel; (b) analyzing the agency as an organization for issues and/or problems that affect either the delivery of services or the administrative supports of such services; (c) assessing the training needs of all staff; and (d) planning, managing, and evaluating programs that are based on the integration of the data gathered from the scanning, analyzing, and assessing activities (Austin, Brannon, & Pecora, 1984).

Although much of the staff training and development literature reflects a heavy emphasis on instructional techniques and participant involvement, very little attention has been given to the principles and practices of managing a staff development program in a human service agency. A systems perspective is useful for understanding the major tasks involved in managing the staff development process: (a) analyzing social policies relevant to the agency's mission, (b) incorporating organizational and worker perspectives, (c) assessing worker learning needs, (d) designing training events, and (e) evaluating training activities.

As noted earlier, the staff development function can be defined as the orienting, updating, and upgrading of agency personnel to provide the highest quality of services to clients. This function can be assumed by many different people in an agency. In some agencies, full-time staff development personnel assume responsibility for managing this function. In other agencies, senior staff members incorporate part-time staff development functions into their overall job requirements. In yet other agencies, staff development responsibilities are delegated to a staff committee for design and implementation. Even when none of these arrangements exist in an agency, supervisory personnel assume some responsibility for the staff development of their subordinates. And finally, in agencies with a flat hierarchical structure and team-delivered services, individual staff members assume considerable responsibility for their own ongoing professional development.

SUPERVISING AND PERFORMANCE APPRAISAL

Supervising Ongoing Task Performance

This function of personnel management encompasses a broad range of tasks that involve helping staff set work priorities, establishing work unit goals, monitoring employee performance, providing supportive and education-oriented supervision (e.g., Austin, 1981; Brody, 1993; Hays & Kearney, 1983; Ivancevich, 1992; Kadushin, 1991; Levy, 1985; Middleman & Rhodes, 1985; Munson, 1993; Weinbach, 1998), supporting self-directed work groups (Dinkmeyer & Eckstein, 1996), and other responsibilities. Here, we focus on performance appraisal because so many personnel management functions affect and are affected by this process.

Designing and Conducting
Performance Appraisals

Overview. Worker performance appraisal is essentially concerned with systematically assessing how well agency staff members are performing their jobs over a specified period of time. Performance evaluations are designed to measure the extent to which workers are achieving the requirements of their position; evaluations should "be based on clearly specified, realistic, and achievable criteria reflecting agency standards" (Kadushin, 1991, p. 329). Superior performance appraisal methods encourage supervisors and workers to set realistic and measurable goals for job performance. Measurable evaluation criteria also help to motivate, direct, and integrate worker learning while providing staff with examples of how they can evaluate their own performance.

The inability of staff members to meet certain performance standards may be due to dysfunctional or unclear agency policies, a shortage of critical resources, inadequate supervisory feedback, or other administrative-related shortcomings. Sound performance evaluations help supervisors and managers to distinguish agency-related problems that should be corrected through some form of organizational change from worker-related performance difficulties that may be corrected by in-service training or formal staff development programs (Mager & Pipe, 1970). Having a systematic approach helps lessen the discomfort of both supervisors and staff (Weinbach, 1998). Evaluating staff on at least an annual basis is important for determining pay raises, suitability for promotion, future assignments, and the need for discipline.

Sound performance-appraisal systems assist agencies in meeting the requirements of equal employment opportunity laws in the areas of promotion or discipline (Brody, 1993; Jensen, 1980; Odiorne, 1984). Finally, given the amount of autonomy and discretion of most social service agency staff, consumers have a right to expect a minimum amount of staff supervision and monitoring as part of agency quality control. As a result of performance evaluations, consumers are more likely to be assured of effective service and protected from continuation of inadequate service (Kadushin, 1991).

Despite the multiple advantages of performance evaluation, human service and other organizations continue to struggle with two primary challenges. First is the challenge of specifying the basis on which a worker's job performance is judged (i.e., the performance standards or criteria to be used). Second, once the criteria have been identified, how and to what extent can they be measured (Howell & Dipboye, 1982)?

A wide variety of process or outcome criteria are being used by human service agencies to evaluate worker performance. Most performance criteria fall into the following general categories: output quality, output quantity, work habits and attitudes, accident rates, learning ability, and judgment or problem-solving ability (Howell & Dipboye, 1982). However, many performance evaluations tend to concentrate too much on subjective personality traits or on the peripheral aspects of the worker's performance (e.g., attitude, punctuality, orientation to managers) and not enough time examining the degree of attainment of specific outcome criteria for the job.

Performance appraisal methods can be categorized into two groups: objective or absolute standards and subjective or comparative standards (Cummings & Schwab, 1973). Objective methods usually focus on some form of economic analysis or examination of concrete outputs (e.g., payment error rates, foster homes recruited, children reunified with parents). Subjective performance evaluation methods use one of the three following approaches to measurement: (a) judging individual performance in comparison to other individuals by using group norms; (b) assessing individual performance based on relatively fixed, independently determined standards; and (c) judging individual performance through careful observation of what people do (Howell & Dipboye, 1982).

Types of approaches. Although there are many appraisal methods, there appear to be 12 major approaches. These approaches can be categorized into five major groups with some overlap between the first two groups:

1. *Personality-based systems:* Lists of personality traits that are assumed to be significant to the job are rated (essay/narrative, graphic rating scales, ranking, forced choice)
2. *Generalized descriptive systems:* Similar to the personality-based systems; terms descriptive of good worker performance are used, such as *organizes, communicates, assesses,* and *motivates,* but often without sufficient definition (essay/narrative, graphic rating, ranking, forced choice)
3. *Results-centered systems:* These systems are especially job-related as supervisors and subordinates mutually define work objectives and measures (management by objectives and results [MBO/MOR] work standards).
4. *Behavioral descriptive systems:* Using detailed job analysis or job descriptions, work behaviors required for success are identified (behaviorally anchored rating scales [BARS], weighted checklist, critical incidents models, assessment centers).

5. *Miscellaneous:* Systems less frequently used that are relatively unique or combine various components of the other methods (forced distribution, field review) (adapted from Odiorne, 1984, pp. 258-259)

The personality-based and generalized description systems, although widely used in human service agencies, have serious limitations. In contrast, research indicates that the results-centered (e.g., MBO) and behavioral description systems (e.g., BARS) provide more job-related and valid measures of performance and withstand litigation well (Cascio & Bernardin, 1981; Holley & Feild, 1982). Each method, however, has various strengths and limitations. For example, the MBO system appears to work best for jobs where workers have a large amount of autonomy and use various technical strategies to achieve performance goals. In contrast, the BARS method appears to be sound for jobs where the work requirements are known, specific, and repetitive (Odiorne, 1984, p. 259).

Choosing a performance appraisal method for your agency. With the exception of certain graphic rating scales, there are no universal appraisal forms in existence today. Most agencies customize a method or form to meet their individual needs. The critical questions we reviewed at the beginning of this chapter should guide managers in choosing the best method for their agency. In choosing a method and in customizing a form, managers should include space on the form to address modifications based on worker or supervisor feedback, as well as to record accomplishments, worker strengths, areas for improvement, and an overall rating of performance. Now that we have reviewed various performance appraisal methods, this last section will discuss some general strategies and principles for conducting performance appraisal interviews.

Planning and conducting performance appraisal conferences. A few general principles for conducting performance appraisals, if followed, result in a much more effective and comfortable process for the worker and supervisor (see Austin, 1981; Jensen, 1980; Kadushin, 1991; Shulman, 1982). For example, staff should be involved in choosing an appraisal system and establishing or modifying evaluation criteria to ensure that more relevant criteria are used; this will increase commitment to the evaluation process and clarify expectations regarding evaluation. The primary, if not the exclusive focus of the evaluation should be on the work performance of the worker rather than any evaluation of the worker as a person. In addition, the appraisal method and criteria should be formulated with some consistency both across workers and supervisors as well as from one evaluation period to the next.

Evaluation should be a continuous process rather than a one-time or occasional event, with time to prepare the assessment prior to the formal evaluation built into the supervision process. As such, evaluation needs to occur within the context of a positive working relationship, and the supervisor should discuss the evaluation procedure in advance with the worker supervised. Evaluations should be conducted with some recognition and consideration of the total range of factors (worker controlled or not) that may be determining the worker's performance. Both worker strengths and areas for improvement should be reviewed in a way that is fair and balanced.

The appraisal conference must be carefully planned, requiring adequate time and a conducive environment free from unnecessary distractions. This implies that the supervisor must move out from behind the desk, postpone visitors and phone calls, and generally show the worker that the appraisal is high priority. The evaluation procedure should be a mutual, shared process with worker participation encouraged, but with both taking some responsibility for reviewing the evaluation form and preparing a preliminary assessment. In preparing draft revisions of the performance appraisal, the supervisor and worker should provide some documentation of their views. To facilitate this process, there should be assurances regarding the confidentiality of what is being said and written.

In conducting performance evaluations, supervisors should not merely list excellent and poor work behaviors but should analyze why certain behaviors are desirable or not desirable as well as set goals for future performance. Evaluations should be viewed as part of a continuous assessment process whereby worker job performance is continuously changing and open to improvement.

Finally, performance evaluation often involves providing both negative and positive feedback as well as negotiating. In providing staff with feedback, it is important to follow some of the principles described by Lehner (as cited in Austin, 1981). Some of these include focusing feedback on behavior rather than on the person, using observational data rather than inferences. It is helpful to focus feedback on description of behavior rather than on judgment, as part of a range of possible behaviors (e.g., more or less) rather than simply making qualitative distinctions (e.g., good or bad). In addition, behavior related to a specific situation should be highlighted (e.g., preferably the "here and now" rather than the "there and then").

Feedback is most effective when it is based on sharing ideas and information rather than on giving advice. Exploring alternatives should be the focus rather than producing answers or solutions. Feedback should be focused on the value it may have to the recipient, not on the value or release that it provides to the person giving the feedback. Concentrate on the amount of information that the person receiving it can use rather than on the amount that the supervisor might like to give. In addition, effective interviewers choose a time and place that is unhurried and comfortable so that personal data can be shared at appropriate times. Finally, during those difficult interviewing moments, they focus feedback on what is said rather than why it is said.

HANDLING EMPLOYEE PERFORMANCE PROBLEMS

Overview

Developing accurate job descriptions, hiring the most qualified personnel, using measurable job-related performance criteria, and conducting effective performance appraisal interviews provide a solid foundation for analyzing and dealing with a variety of employee performance problems. Employee performance problems can be minimized and more easily handled if the personnel functions described in the preceding sections have been adequately addressed. This section will focus on some general principles for handling performance problems, sexual harassment, and employee termination.

Distinguishing Between Worker and Agency Performance Problems

Employee performance problems are often viewed as evidence of a lack of worker knowledge or skill (training need), poor attitudes (a lack of commitment to the job), need for more supervision, or poor use of time. However, employee performance difficulties may be also due to a host of nonworker factors such as unclear agency policies, resource limitations, vague work priorities or performance standards, poor supervision, caseload demands, and assignment of inappropriate cases.

Supervisors and managers need to take a close look at both worker and agency factors before deciding on a course of action. More specifically, in analyzing the performance problem, it is important to determine if the performance difficulty relates to one or more of the following factors:

- Unclear task assignments
- Unclear performance standards
- Lack of worker ability
- Lack of worker knowledge
- Lack of worker skill (or practice)
- Lack of worker motivation (or conversely, lack of agency rewards for performance)
- Mismatch between worker and agency ideology or approach to practice
- Unclear policies
- Lack of resources
- Poor supervision (e.g., little worker feedback, inconsistent monitoring, little technical assistance provided, poor worker-supervisor relationship)
- Unusually large caseloads
- Assignment of inappropriate cases

- Environmental factors such as excessive noise, poor lighting, lack of privacy, depressing decor
- Demeaning or demoralized organizational climate

All of the above factors are common causes of worker performance problems. Once the real causes have been identified, it is much easier to develop a strategy for addressing them.

The Importance of Personnel Policies

Handling worker performance problems requires that certain employee regulations and grievance handling procedures have been specified in the agency's personnel policies. Organizations may use a matrix of discipline procedures for various employee performance problems. Explicit policies provide guidelines for expected employee behavior and consequences for noncompliance. As such, they form a foundation for addressing performance problems within a developmental discipline system. In this system, disciplinary standards and procedures are mutually accepted, designed to shape behavior and not punish, performance focused, and periodically reviewed (see Odiorne, 1984, pp. 205-217).

When workers are clear about their job assignments and performance standards, it is much less likely that such policies will need to be enforced. As the supervisor and worker examine job performance difficulties and possible causes, it is essential as well that the time, place, and nature of the problems have been carefully documented. Effective handling and prevention of performance problems is a characteristic of high-quality supervision. As such, the first line for prevention and remediation is the line supervisor.

Using personnel policies, standard operating procedures, supervision principles, and the job-analysis process described earlier, supervisors can assess the match between worker competencies and the job requisites, seek continuously to clarify performance standards, and remove obstacles to employee success. Supervisors also provide access to training, and monitor and provide feedback and favorable consequences for effective work behaviors (Brody, 1993; Odiorne, 1984). In addition, managers should be sensitive to the possibility that personal factors may be contributing to poor performance. These factors might be a worker's health problems, stress, or other emotional difficulties, non-job related problems (e.g., marital relations, family pressures), and poor work habits (such as unauthorized use of company equipment, carelessness, poor time management).

Human service organizations have a responsibility to assist workers in addressing these problems through referral to medical and mental health programs or, in the case of poor work habits, provision of special on-the-job supervision and coaching. Finally, supervisors should consider whether the employee is "deadwood" (rated as having low performance with no potential for further growth) or just a "problem employee" (performance is at a low level but the potential is considered high; Odiorne, 1984, p. 203). Depending on your management philosophy, you may fire the deadwood employee immediately but institute a variety of measures to assist the problem employee. Thus, in handling performance problems, most agencies rely on progressive discipline consisting of four major phases: (a) counseling and/or training,

(b) written reprimands, (c) final warning and a probationary period, and (d) dismissal.

Employee Termination

The discharging of staff can be one of the most difficult and unpleasant tasks in managing personnel. Supervisors and personnel managers are often given this responsibility with insufficient information and training in planning and carrying out employee terminations. A variety of references provide excellent information and guidelines for handling employee terminations (see, e.g., Coulson, 1981; Jensen, 1981b; Morin & Yorks, 1982; Roseman, 1982; Weinbach, 1998, pp. 171-179). Here are some of the major issues and guidelines for handling the termination process, including the need for explicit policies, common reasons for employee termination, establishment of "just cause," conduct of termination interviews, and the importance of an exit interview.

Clear job specifications and performance standards are essential to evaluating employee performance. Because employee termination can occur for reasons beyond poor performance or misconduct, explicit policies must be developed that describe the conditions under which an employee can be terminated. Written policies provide the operational guidelines for termination, protect staff from arbitrary actions, and help ensure that termination decisions are legal and fair. A host of legal issues surround termination, and nearly all groups of employees have some type of protection under the law that is being enforced by local courts, state human rights agencies, the EEOC, and in the case of unions, the National Labor Relations Board (Ewing, 1983; Lopatka, 1984). For example, the "employment at-will" doctrine allowing termination without notice and cause in nonunion private jobs is increasingly being narrowed by court decisions (Heshizer, 1985). Recent changes in case law provide a powerful incentive for careful development and execution of termination policies in human service organizations.

Termination rationales are typically defined in policy statements as resignation, mutual agreement, reduction in force (job elimination), unsatisfactory performance (including the inability to establish effective working relationships with coworkers), misconduct on the job, and retirement (Jensen, 1981b, p. 38). Supervisors need to be aware of the specific items that should be addressed by the organization's termination policies. For example, policies should contain provisions for severance pay and termination notice and should note whether or not an exit interview is required. In terminating long-time employees, it is appropriate to consider more generous termination pay or notice, "recognizing that older people may have more difficulty in finding other work because many employers still practice de facto age discrimination or because their seniority means that fewer jobs are available at their salary levels" (Jensen, 1981b, p. 38).

Sexual Harassment as Both an Employee Performance Problem and a Grievance

Sexual harassment is discussed here because it has become recognized in recent years as a type of performance problem with significant potential for worker grievance. As in the case of racial harassment, sexual harassment is increasingly recognized as one of the most sensitive employee issues to handle. Agency supervisors and managers, as well as the organization, have been held liable by local and federal courts.

Sexual harassment involves unwelcome sexual advances, request for sexual favors, and other verbal or physical conduct of a sexual nature. Harassment can take many forms including verbal, visual, and physical. For example, visual harassment involves constant leering, suggestive ogling, offensive signs and gestures, or open display of pornographic and other offensive materials. Verbal harassment takes the form of dirty jokes, sexual suggestions, highly personal innuendoes, and explicit propositions. Examples of physical harassment are "accidentally" brushing up against the body, patting, squeezing, pinching, kissing, fondling, forced sexual assault, and/or rape.

The incidence of sexual harassment is much higher than commonly thought. In 1980, the Federal Merit System conducted a survey of 23,000 randomly selected male and female civilian employees with a return rate of 85%. They asked employees whether they had received during the 24-month period of the study (May 1978-May 1980) "any forms of uninvited and unwanted sexual attention" from a person or persons with whom they worked (Merit Systems Protection Board, 1981, pp. 26-37). The forms of behavior identified were:

- Actual or attempted rape or sexual assault
- Pressure for sexual favors
- Deliberate touching, leaning over, cornering, or pinching
- Sexually suggestive looks or gestures
- Letters, phone calls, or materials of a sexual nature
- Pressure for dates
- Sexual teasing, jokes, remarks, or questions

About 42% of the women and 15% of the men reported being sexually harassed during this period. Only 1% reported the severest form (actual or attempted rape or sexual assaults). But that 1% means that almost 12,000 employees of the federal workforce were victimized during that period. Less severe sexual harassment (e.g., letters, phone calls, pressure, touching) was reported by 16% of the respondents, projected to be 300,000 workers. Sexual teasing, jokes, and suggestive gestures were the form of sexual harassment reported by 8% of the respondents, projected to be 150,000 workers. Sexual harassment appears to occur more than once for each victim. These types of findings were also found in studies reported in the popular press and business journals (Collins & Blodgett, 1981; Crull, 1979; Safran, 1976).

The overall finding from these surveys is that sexual harassment is widespread and occurs regardless of a woman's age, marital status, appearance, ethnicity, occupation, or salary level. Based on these studies, it is apparent that many women are treated unequally, are discriminated against, and are abused (Neugarten & Miller-Spellman, 1983).

CURRENT ISSUES

Personnel management functions will need to be refined as part of an approach to practice that emphasizes organizational effectiveness and customer-focused refinement of services (Rapp & Poertner, 1987). Social work administrators must begin addressing key personnel management functions in new ways. For example, performance standards need to be clarified and strengthened from a focus on process to more of a balanced focus on service quality and outcomes. In some cases, practice protocols will need to be used more extensively to help increase consistency in core interventions while allowing maximum worker flexibility in other areas. Recent class-action suits in some areas of social services (e.g., child welfare, mental health) have sometimes resulted in increased paperwork demands with relatively little benefit accrued regarding service quality or outcomes. This has made it difficult for these agencies to implement more streamlined paperwork and other process-monitoring systems while increasing their focus on key results.

How various personnel management practices support or hinder organizational performance is an area that needs more attention. For example, there is growing evidence that supervisors and unit managers are key to policy interpretation and managing change (Resnick & Patti, 1980; Teather, Gerbino, & Pecora, 1996). But more specific knowledge is needed regarding what specific supervisory behaviors most affect worker and program performance, as well as other aspects of continuous quality improvement (Sluyter, 1998).

On a still more micro level, the field needs to be guided by further research on how to minimize biases of various kinds during the employee selection process and how to refine interviewing approaches. Finally, many supervisors and mid-level social work administrators will continue to need skills-based supervisory training to supplement the clinical skills and experience that they bring to these positions.

NOTE

1. See *Civil Rights Act of 1964*, P.L. 88-352, 78 Stat. 241, 28 USC 1147 (1976). A number of laws also support equal opportunity in relation to such factors as age (Age Discrimination Employment Act of 1967, as amended), handicap status (Sections 503 and 504 of the Rehabilitation Act of 1973, as amended), Vietnam service (38 USC 2011-2014, Vietnam Era Veterans' Readjustment Assistance Act of 1974), and equal pay (Equal Pay Act of 1963). See EEOC's (1978) Uniform Guidelines on Employee Selection Procedures (designated as UGESP (1978) Sections 1-18). These guidelines are incorporated into the official regulations of the EEOC, 29 CFR 1607; Office of Federal Contract Compliance Program, 41 CFR 60-3; Department of Justice, 28 CFR 50.14; and the former Civil Service Commission, 5 CFR 300.103(c).

REFERENCES

Age Discrimination in Employment Act of 1967, P.L. 90-202, 81 Stat. 602.

American Psychological Association. (1980). *Principles for the validation and use of personnel selection procedures* (2nd ed.). Washington, DC: Author.

Americans With Disabilities Act of 1990, P.L. 101-336, 104 Stat. 327.

Austin, M. J. (1981). *Supervisory management for the human services*. Englewood Cliffs, NJ: Prentice Hall.

Austin, M. J., Brannon, D., & Pecora, P. J. (1984). *Managing staff development programs in human service agencies*. Chicago: Nelson-Hall.

Beach, D. S. (1975). *Personnel: The management of people at work*. New York: Macmillan.

Bristow, N. (1999a). *The new leadership imperative*. Orem, UT: Targeted Learning. (Available: www.targetedlearning.com)

Bristow, N. (1999b). *Using your HR systems to build organizational success*. Orem, UT: Targeted Learning. (Available: www.targetedlearning.com)

Bristow, N., Dalton, G., & Thompson, P. (1996). *The four stages of contribution* [Mimeo]. Orem, UT: Novations. (Also reprinted in The Casey Family Program, 1996)

Brody, R. (1993). *Effectively managing human service organizations*. Newbury Park, CA: Sage.

Campbell, A. (1983). Hiring for results: Interviews that select winners. *Business Quarterly, 48*(4), 57-61.

Campion, S. E., & Arvey, R. D. (1989). Unfair discrimination in the employment interview. In R. W. Eder & G. R. Ferris (Eds.), *The employment interview—Theory, research, and practice* (pp. 61-74). Newbury Park, CA: Sage.

Cascio, W. F., & Bernardin, H. J. (1981). Implications of performance appraisal litigation for personnel decisions. *Personnel Psychology, 34*(2), 211-226.

The Casey Family Program. (1996). *Competencies at Casey.* Seattle, WA: Author.

The Casey Family Program. (1998, September). *Competencies, recruitment, and selection training manual.* Seattle, WA: Author.

The Casey Family Program. (1999). *Personnel guidelines* (Version 3.0). Seattle, WA: Author.

Civil Rights Act of 1964, P.L. 88-352, 78 Stat. 24.

Collins, E. G., & Blodgett, T. B. (1981). Sexual harassment . . . some see it . . . some won't. *Harvard Business Review, 59,* 76-95.

Coulson, R. (1981). *The termination handbook.* New York: Free Press.

Cox, F. M. (1984). Guidelines for preparing personnel policies. In F. M. Cox et al. (Eds.), *Tactics and techniques of community practice* (2nd ed.). Itasca, IL: F. E. Peacock.

Crull, P. (1979). *The implications of sexual harassment on the job: A profile of the experience of 92 women* (Research Series Report No. 3). New York: Working Women's Institute.

Cummings, L. L., & Schwab, D. P. (1973). *Performance in organizations: Determinants and appraisal.* Glenview, IL: Scott, Foresman.

Davis, Wright, & Tremaine Law Firm. (1992). *Special summary of the Americans With Disabilities Act prepared for The Casey Family Program* [Mimeo]. Seattle, WA: Author.

Dinkmeyer, D., & Eckstein, D. (1996). *Leadership by encouragement.* Delray Beach, FL: St. Lucie Press.

Eder, R. W., & Ferris, G. R. (Eds.). (1989). *The employment interview—Theory, research, and practice.* Newbury Park, CA: Sage.

Equal Employment Opportunity Commission. (1978). Uniform guidelines on employee selection procedures. *Federal Register, 43,* 38920-39315.

Equal Pay Act of 1963, P.L. 88-38, 77 Stat. 56.

Ewing, D. W. (1983). Your right to fire. *Harvard Business Review, 61*(2), 32-34, 38, 40-42.

Goodale, J. G. (1989). Effective employment interviewing. In R. W. Eder & G. R. Ferris (Eds.), *The employment interview: Theory, research, and practice* (pp. 307-324). Newbury Park, CA: Sage.

Hays, S. W., & Kearney, R. C. (1983). *Public personnel administration: Problems and prospects.* Englewood Cliffs, NJ: Prentice Hall.

Heshizer, B. (1985). The new common law of employment: Changes in the concept of employment at will. *Labor Law Journal, 36*(1), 95-107.

Himle, D., Jaraytne, S., & Thyness, P. (1989). The buffering effects of four types of supervisory support on work stress. *Administration in Social Work, 13*(1), 19-34.

Holley, W. H., & Feild, H. J. (1982). Will your performance appraisal system hold up in court? *Personnel, 59*(1), 59-64.

Howell, W. C., & Dipboye, R. L. (1982). *Essentials of industrial and organizational psychology.* Homewood, IL: Dorsey.

Ivancevich, J. M. (1992). *Human resource management* (5th ed.). Homewood, IL: Irwin.

Janz, T. (1989). The patterned behavior description interview: The best prophet of the future is the past. In R. W. Eder & G. R. Ferris (Eds.), *The employment interview—Theory, research, and practice* (pp. 158-168). Newbury Park, CA: Sage.

Jensen, J. (1980). Employee evaluation: It's a dirty job but somebody's got to do it. *Grantsmanship Center News, 8*(4), 36-45.

Jensen, J. (1981a). How to hire the right person for the job. *The Grantsmanship Center News, 9*(3), 21-31.

Jensen, J. (1981b). Letting go: The difficult art of firing. *The Grantsmanship Center News, 9*(5), 37-43.

Kadushin, A. (1977). *Consultation in social work.* New York: Columbia University Press.

Kadushin, A. (1991). *Supervision in social work* (3rd ed.). New York: Columbia University Press.

Klingner, D. E., & Nalbandian, J. (1985). *Public personnel management: Contexts and strategies.* Englewood Cliffs, NJ: Prentice Hall.

Latham, G. P. (1989). The reliability, validity, and practicality of the situational interview. In R. W. Eder & G. R. Ferris (Eds.), *The employment interview—Theory, research, and practice* (pp. 169-182). Newbury Park, CA: Sage.

Levy, C. S. (1985). The ethics of management. In S. Slavin (Ed.), *Managing, finances, personnel, and information in human services.* New York: Haworth.

Locke, E. A., & Latham, G. P. (1984). *Goalsetting: A motivational technique that works.* Englewood Cliffs, NJ: Prentice Hall.

Lopatka, K. T. (1984). The emerging law of wrongful discharge: A quadrennial assessment of the labor law issue of the 80's. *The Business Lawyer, 40*(1), 1-32.

Lovell, E. (1985). Three key issues in affirmative action. In S. Slavin (Ed.), *Managing, finances, personnel, and information in human services.* New York: Haworth.

Mager, R. F., & Pipe, P. (1970). *Analyzing performance problems.* Belmont, CA: Fearson Pitman.

Mayfield, E. C., Brown, S. H., & Hamstra, B. W. (1980). Selection interviewing in the life insurance industry: An update of research and practice. *Personnel Psychology, 33,* 725-739.

McCormick, E. J. (1979). *Job analysis: Methods and applications.* New York: Amacom.

Merit Systems Protection Board. (1981). *Sexual harassment in the federal workplace: Is it a problem?* Washington, DC: Government Printing Office.

Meritt-Haston, R., & Weyley, K. N. (1983). Educational requirements: Legality and validity. *Personnel Psychology, 36,* 743-753.

Middleman, R., & Rhodes, G. (1985). *Competent supervision: Making imaginative judgments.* Englewood Cliffs, NJ: Prentice Hall.

Morin, W. J., & Yorks, L. (1982). *Outplacement techniques: A positive approach to terminating employees.* New York: AMACOM, A Division of the American Management Association.

Mufson, D. W. (1986). Selecting child care workers using the California Psychological Inventory. *Child Welfare, 65,* 83-88.

Munson, C. E. (1993). *Clinical social work supervision* (2nd ed.). New York: Haworth.

National Association of Social Workers. (1985). NASW standards for social work personnel practices. In S. Slavin (Ed.), *Managing, finances, personnel, and information in human services.* New York: Haworth.

Neugarten, D. A., & Miller-Spellman, M. (1983). Sexual harassment in public employment. In S. W. Hays & R. C. Kearney (Eds.), *Public personnel administration: Problems and prospects.* Englewood Cliffs, NJ: Prentice Hall.

Nurius, P. S., Kemp, S. P., & Gibson, J. W. (1999). Practitioner's perspectives on sound reasoning: Adding a worker in-context component. *Administration in Social Work, 23*(1), 1-27.

Odiorne, G. S. (1984). *Strategic management of human resources.* San Francisco: Jossey-Bass.

Patti, R. J. (1983). *Social welfare administration: Managing social programs in a developmental context.* Englewood Cliffs, NJ: Prentice Hall.

Pecora, P. J. (1998). Recruiting and selecting effective employees. In R. L. Edwards & J. A. Yankey (Eds.), *Skills for effective management of nonprofit organizations.* Washington, DC: National Association of Social Workers.

Pecora, P. J., & Austin, M. J. (1983). Declassification of social service jobs: Issues and strategies. *Social Work, 28,* 421-426.

Pedigo, S. L. (1995a). The coming transformation of HR from support to business partner. *Watson Wyatt Communicator, 13*(1), 18-23.

Pedigo, S. L. (1995b). Tying compensation to competencies. *Watson Wyatt Communicator, 13*(1), 34-39.

Perry, P. M. (1993, January/February). Avoiding charges of discrimination against the handicapped. *Law Practice Management,* pp. 34-38.

Rapp, C., & Poertner, J. (1987). Moving clients center stage through the use of client outcomes. *Administration in Social Work, 11*(3/4), 23-40.

Rehabilitation Act of 1973, P.L. 93-112, 87 Stat. 355.

Resnick, H., & Patti, R. J. (1980). *Change from within: Humanizing social welfare organizations.* Philadelphia: Temple University Press.

Robertson, M. A. (1982). *Personnel administration employment interviewing guide for supervisors.* Salt Lake City: University of Utah, Office of Personnel Administration.

Roseman, E. (1982). *Managing the problem employee.* New York: AMACOM.

Ross, A. R., & Hoeltke, G. (1985). A tool for selecting residential child care work initial report. *Child Welfare, 64,* 46-55.

Safran, C. (1976, November). What men do to women on the job: A shocking look at sexual harassment. *Redbook,* pp. 149, 217-224.

Shafritz, J. M., Hyde, A. C., & Rosenbloom, D. H. (1986). *Personnel management in government: Politics and process* (3rd ed.). New York: Marcel Dekker.

Shulman, L. (1982). *Skills of supervision and staff management.* Itasca, IL: F. E. Peacock.

Slavin, S. (Ed.). (1985). *Managing, finances, personnel, and information in human services.* New York: Haworth.

Sluyter, G. (1998). *Improving organizational performance: A practical guidebook for the human services.* Thousand Oaks, CA: Sage.

Tambor, M. (1985). The social worker as worker: A union perspective. In S. Slavin (Ed.), *Managing, finances, personnel, and information in human services.* New York: Haworth.

Teare, R. J., Higgs, C., Gauthier, T. P., & Feild, H. S. (1984). *Classification validation processes for social service positions: Vol. 1. Overview.* Silver Spring, MD: NASW Press.

Teather, E. C., Gerbino, K., & Pecora, P. J. (1996). Making it happen: Strategies for organizational change. In P. J. Pecora, W. Selig, F. Zirps, & S. Davis (Eds.), *Quality im-*

provement and program evaluation in child welfare agencies: Managing into the next century. Washington, DC: Child Welfare League of America.

U.S. Equal Employment Opportunity Commission. (1991). *The Americans With Disabilities Act: Your responsibilities as an employer.* Washington, DC: Author.

Valdez, T. A. (1982). Women in mental health administration. In M. J. Austin & W. E. Hershey (Eds.), *Handbook on mental health administration.* San Francisco: Jossey-Bass.

Vietnam Era Veterans' Readjustment Assistance Act of 1974, P.L. 93-508, 88 Stat. 1578.

Von der Embse, T. J. (1987). *Supervision: Managerial skills for a new era.* New York: Macmillan.

Weinbach, R. (1998). *The social worker as manager* (3rd ed.). Needham Heights, MA: Allyn & Bacon.

Weiner, M. E. (1982). *Human services management: Analysis and applications.* Homewood, IL: Dorsey.

Wolfe, T. (1984). *The nonprofit organization: An operating manual* (pp. 63-64). Englewood Cliffs, NJ: Prentice Hall.

Zedeck, S., & Cascio, W. F. (1984). Psychological issues in personnel decisions. *Annual Review of Psychology, 35,* 461-518.

Zunz, S. J. (1998). Resiliency and burnout: Protective factors for human service managers. *Administration in Social Work, 22*(3), 39-54.

CHAPTER TWENTY-ONE

Managing for Diversity and Empowerment in Social Services

ALFREDA P. IGLEHART

This chapter addresses managing for diversity and empowerment from two perspectives: the internal dynamics of the agency and the agency-community interface. Agency dynamics are crucial for agency functioning and form the foundation from which community practice emanates. Although the agency's structure is the vehicle through which services and programs are formulated and implemented (Rothman & Tropman, 1987), the actual service-delivery process itself is carried out by staff working within those structures. Agency characteristics often determine its capacity to recruit, retain, and manage the staff it needs for organizational maintenance, program imple-

mentation, and goal achievement. To the extent that an agency is involved in service delivery to diverse populations, these characteristics, in turn, determine the agency's capacity to serve these communities effectively.

Effective agency intervention with diverse individuals and communities has been termed multicultural practice, diversity practice, ethnic-sensitive practice, and multicultural competency, among other designations. Garcia (1995) captures the elements of this practice in a definition of multicultural diversity competence that includes the ability to respect, understand, communicate, and collaborate with individuals of diverse cultures. Management for diversity and empowerment at the agency-community interface level suggests that the agency's practice with diverse communities also includes these elements of respect, understanding, communication, and collaboration.

Empowerment practice is viewed as one of the cornerstones of diversity practice competency and holds a great deal of appeal for both administrators and practitioners. Solomon (1976) defines empowerment as a process in which the social worker helps the client to reduce the powerlessness that results from membership in a socially stigmatized group. Hasenfeld (1987, pp. 478-479) expands this definition by adding that empowerment is a process through which clients obtain resources— personal, organizational, and community—that enable them to gain greater control over the environment and to attain their aspirations. Consequently, empowerment practice seems to be a vehicle through which diverse populations that are marginal to and disenfranchised from American society can gain access to goods, services, and rewards to which they feel entitled.

Thus, in the agency, management techniques that minimize marginality, maximize integration, promote an equitable system of rewards, and foster skill development are needed for empowerment practice. In addition, the same or similar techniques are also needed for developing an effective agency-community relationship (Iglehart & Becerra, 1995). The Los Angeles County Department of Children and Family Services, for example, has stimulated the implementation of empowerment practice in its model of family preservation service delivery, which requires collaboration among agencies for the formation of family preservation networks. These networks, composed of a lead agency and several satellite agencies, are re-

quired to provide culturally sensitive services, to use culturally sensitive staff, to create community advisory boards, and to hold regular staff meetings to discuss issues affecting the service-delivery process. Although the participating agencies are committed to serving diverse communities, the lucrative contract with this county agency also serves as an incentive. To a certain extent, agencies have had to alter their management techniques and the manner in which they relate to the communities they serve.

This chapter will cover the following topics: the need to manage for diversity and empowerment, a theoretical foundation for understanding agency-based diversity and empowerment management, those barriers that impede the development of this type of management, and a framework for promoting agency-based diversity and empowerment practice.

WHY MANAGE FOR DIVERSITY AND EMPOWERMENT?

According to Pine, Warsh, and Maluccio (1998, p. 21), demographic shifts in both staff and client pools are amplifying the need to value diversity and to use this diversity as a means of improving service delivery and the workplace climate. Through effective management strategies, administrators can reduce the stress and tension that often accompany the introduction of new, diverse members to the organization. Human resource consultants in the private sector are extolling the benefits of attracting and retaining qualified employees because this human capital represents a significant organizational investment (Gardenswartz & Rowe, 1998; Herman, 1998). With sound management practices, all employees can feel valued and respected, experiencing a promotional system that is fair and open. The organization suffers when workers feel excluded, disregarded, or shut out; time is spent on conflicts and misunderstandings; and communication breakdown occurs because of cultural conflicts (Charlton & Huey, 1992; Gardenswartz & Rowe, 1998). Furthermore, Mor-Barak and Cherin (1998, p. 61) note that a growing body of evidence supports the connection between employees' perception of being accepted by the organization, their job satisfaction, and their organizational commitment. Organizations, therefore, should work to create a civic culture that emphasizes the relational values of equality and respect for differences (Chen & Eastman, 1997). Agency management can facilitate the development of such a culture.

According to Gardenswartz and Rowe (1998), who are diversity trainers/consultants to businesses, diversity is a means of expanding organizational creativity because creativity is often a result of bringing diverse workers together. The authors further maintain that, in an environment marked by continuous change, the organization's resiliency, adaptability, viability, and flexibility are increased through workforce diversity. The organization's overall effectiveness and survivability are expected to increase when management practices support the integration of diverse workers into the organization.

Effective management for diversity and empowerment leads to stronger agency-community interactions and interface. The community experiences the agency through its workers. Social work interventions aimed at developing community partnerships will not work if staff members are not empowered as professionals (Pine et al., 1998, p. 20). Adams and Nelson

(1997, p. 74) also note that partnerships and collaborations mean empowering workers to, in turn, empower families and communities. The same kinds of techniques that support worker empowerment may be used to support community empowerment through the agency's community practice.

THEORETICAL FRAMEWORK

Systems theory is used here to illuminate the agency's internal dynamics and the agency-community interface. Bertalanffy (1974, p. 1100), one of the architects of this framework, asserted that a system is defined as a complex of components in mutual interaction. In an open system, energy is imported from the environment (inputs), transformed to create a technology, and then exported back into the environment (output). Significant features of an open system are interrelatedness of subsystems, boundary maintenance, system equilibrium, system functions (socialization, social control, communication, feedback), system adaptation and maintenance for survival, and the relationship between the system and its environment (Katz & Kahn, 1978).

As an open system, the agency receives inputs from its environment, inputs that are needed for the agency to survive and conduct its daily business. These inputs vary from the tangible (staff, funding) to the intangible (values, beliefs, ideologies). The environment plays a pivotal role in the life of an agency, for it not only provides critical inputs but also confers a legitimacy the agency needs for its existence. The particular manner in which an agency is structured and organized may also be imported from its environment. Consequently, trends in management practices and the identification of "appropriate" management techniques are also imported from and influenced by the environment.

Although an agency is a system unto itself, it is also a system interacting with other systems as well as a subsystem of larger systems. As a bounded, distinct system, the agency interfaces with community systems as it engages in community practice. In addition, the agency and the community are both subsystems of a larger societal system. Many agencies have penetrated a community's boundaries to become part of that community's environment (Ringer & Lawless, 1989, p. 10). Hence, the systems framework permits the examination of agency management practices that address internal agency operations and those that address the agency in relationship to other systems such as communities.

BARRIERS TO DIVERSITY AND EMPOWERMENT MANAGEMENT

Whereas all agencies are confronted with staff diversity issues and the need to respond to diverse communities, responses to these challenges are as varied as the agencies themselves. Some agencies appear to adapt to change with creativity, flexibility, and added growth. Others seem mired in a type of inertia that inhibits change and innovation. Factors that inhibit diversity and management for empowerment are worthy of discussion and seem to grow out of three contexts: societal, professional, and organizational. Understanding these barriers is essential to understanding an empowerment model of administration.

Barriers From Society

Because organizations are subsystems of the larger social system, they import societal values, beliefs, and ideologies that are manifested in the attitudes and behaviors of the staff they recruit and the structures they create. In addition, the dependency of professions on the larger society for legitimacy compels professions and their organizations to accept and mirror problem definitions and problem interventions that may not deviate from prevailing dominant social perspectives.

In the prevailing social context, the ideology of individual merit and the inability to resolve social conflict based on diversity may dictate that organizations can never resolve diversity issues (Donnellon & Kolb, 1994). With an ideology of individual merit that stresses performance as the sole basis for success, administrators may not believe that modifications in management strategies are necessary for a changing and more diverse workforce. Belief in individual merit mutes any consideration of social bias as a contributing factor to the ultimate fate of workers in the agency. In addition, managers may be reluctant to even consider the possibility that any type of social favoritism influenced their own ascendency to power. Furthermore, some managers may believe that conflict is inevitable because issues of race and ethnicity extend far beyond the agency's walls. Social service agencies merely perpetuate many of the tensions and conflicts that plague society in general.

As society generates policy and other legislative responses to the changing social and political climate, these policies find expression in agency procedures and practices. Societal ambiguity surrounding the intent, goals, implementation, and enforcement of these policies often finds expression in social agencies. For example, how agencies interpret policies such as affirmative action and nondiscrimination clauses in contracts is often indicative of societal-level ambivalence about the structural and institutional causes and consequences of discrimination. The variations in agencies' responses to these policies capture much of this ambivalence.

Barriers in the Profession

Many agencies also appear uncertain about methods and approaches for implementing an empowerment perspective whereas others appear to conduct business as usual despite a strong verbal adherence to an empowerment model. Although this ambivalence may have been influenced by a conservative sociopolitical environment, the dominance of casework, direct practice, or micro-social work over indirect practice or macro-social work may have further constrained the evolution of empowerment practice and the evolution of multicultural competency in service delivery.

Part of this confusion about which methods and approaches are most suitable for empowerment management may be attributed to a duality inherent in the empowerment concept and the dimension on which the profession has focused. The mastery, control, and influence supported through empowerment practice may, in fact, be seen as the sense of personal control (Riger, 1993, p. 281). This aspect of the concept addresses psychological (intrapersonal) empowerment rather than concrete empowerment, such as organizational or community empowerment. According to Zimmerman (1995, p. 581), organizational empowerment includes processes and structures that enhance mem-

bers' skills and provide them with the mutual support necessary to effect community level change. Community empowerment entails individuals, organizations, and linkages among organizations working together to improve the community (Zimmerman, 1995). Thus, a primary focus on psychological empowerment appears to minimize the need for empowerment at other system levels.

Psychological empowerment focuses on the beliefs, values, and attitudes of the clients—a familiar domain of the profession. Historically, the profession has stressed the social diagnosis of the individual, and social workers, in general, developed an ideology that supported a psychological orientation to social problems while ignoring institutional solutions. The institutional framework suggests that this conservative ideology was supported by those environmental constituencies controlling resources. This framework proposes that the structure of certain classes of organizations, such as human services, is determined not by technology but by rules emanating from the institutional environment (Hasenfeld, 1992, p. 34). To gain the legitimacy and acceptance that are conferred by the larger society, the profession may have had to endorse a psychological approach to social problem solving (see, e.g., Axinn & Levin, 1982; Gil, 1990; Jansson, 1997; Leiby, 1978; Martin, 1990; Schilling, Schinke, & Weatherly, 1988). This psychological approach may have been endorsed by prevailing public opinion, stakeholders, constituencies, and other groups with the power to shape the development of the profession.

The external or concrete dimension of empowerment—which includes providing tangible knowledge, information, competencies, skills, and especially the resources that enable people to take action (Parsons, 1988, p. 30)—may receive less attention and support in social service agencies. This external dimension captures a more macro approach to practice. This type of empowerment practice seems most consistent with the needs and demands of diverse groups and communities that require information, skills, education, and resources to improve the quality of life. Psychological or personal empowerment alone may be insufficient to bring about the kinds of changes desired by disempowered groups.

Because of the primacy of micro practice, discussions about multicultural competency and empowerment practice often fail to address models of administrative practice that support multicultural competency. Practitioners who seek to develop skills in promoting intrapersonal empowerment among their clients have available to them a range of literature that describes models of empowerment practice and methods of implementing them. On the other hand, those practitioners who seek to facilitate organizational and community empowerment have a more limited array of literature and research to guide them. This imbalance may suggest to some professionals that one type of empowerment has priority over another. Clearly, limitations observed in the field in the implementation of empowerment management techniques may be attributable to the lack of a sound knowledge and research base to guide the development of these managerial practices.

Barriers in the Agency

Agency-related barriers to effective management for diversity and empowerment include agency history, age, mission, degree of bureaucratization, public versus private-nonprofit status, resource level, leadership, the workers themselves, and culture. The grid in Table 21.1 summarizes the manner in which these factors pose a challenge to diversity and empowerment management. This overview of theoretical perspectives and barriers to diversity practice can be used to propose a process for managing and empowering a diverse workforce and for practice with diverse communities.

A FRAMEWORK FOR AGENCY-BASED DIVERSITY AND EMPOWERMENT PRACTICE

Administrative practice that values diversity and embraces empowerment is the underpinning of the agency's management of its staff and of its agency-community relationship. The exploratory framework suggested here is a means of integrating empowerment practice in the agency and with the community. The values inherent in empowerment practice are operationalized through a process that facilitates both worker and community empowerment. With this conceptualization, empowerment practice that fosters appreciation for diversity has unifying elements that link all levels of macro practice. Implicit in this framework is the assumption that empowerment practice in the agency is a necessary precondition for empowerment practice with communities.

This framework uses agency administrators as change agents because they have the power of authority and power over resources. Clearly, agency change does not have to be top-down, and members in lower positions can

TABLE 21.1 Factors in Diversity and Empowerment Management

Factor	Potential Effects
Agency history	Age may reveal a pattern of alienation from particular groups and communities that has perpetuated a negative agency reputation.
Agency's age	Over time, organizations appear likely to experience inertia (Barnett & Carroll, 1995), with routines, structure, and technology so well established that they defy change.
Agency's mission	Mission statements that disregard race, creed, and color as a base for equitable treatment of staff and consumers and statements that espouse "one approach fits all" negate the need to explore alternative management models.
Agency's degree of bureaucratization	Bureaucratic characteristics such as complexity, centralization, formalization, and specialization may block organizational change, depending on the nature of the change under consideration (Barnett & Carroll, 1995; Brager & Holloway, 1978; Hasenfeld, 1983).
Public versus private nonprofit status	Public agencies are generally not lauded for their change ability. Change has long been held as the domain of agencies that could afford to be less responsive to political pressures and more experimental (Brager & Holloway, 1978, p. 43).
Agency resource level	Resource-rich agencies may have the luxury of mounting experimental or pilot efforts to test alternative management styles. With resource-poor agencies, the continuous quest for funds may place the need for more effective empowerment and diversity management low on the priority list.
Agency leadership	Leadership is vital to agency change (Armenakis, Harris, & Mossholder, 1993; Donnellon & Kolb, 1994; Hasenfeld, 1983). Here, the leaders are defined as those individuals who occupy top-level positions in organizations and who will be referred to as administrators. Leaders who do not see value in diversity and empowerment management impede organizational development in this area. The presence of racial/ethnic minority leadership may, for some agencies, pose a unique challenge. For some agencies, the selection of a racial/ethnic minority administrator may be the extent of an agency's empowerment practice. In addition, some racial/ethnic minority administrators may be hesitant to launch dialogue on the subject for fear of being branded as biased in favor of their own group.
Agency staff	Donnellon and Kolb (1994) repeat the often-cited statement that people with power act to retain that power. Change may be perceived as a threat to their power and, hence, workers may resist that change. In addition, Nicolini, Meznar, Stewart, and Manz (1995) note that workers have a general reluctance to move from old learning to new learning. Because of the sensitive nature of discussions of race/ethnicity and cultural diversity, workers may be even more likely to feel threatened and defensive.
Agency culture	Schein (1992, 1996) defines culture as the set of artifacts, values, beliefs, and basic taken-for-granted assumptions that a group shares and that determine its worldview. Agencies with cultures that do not support sensitivity toward and respect for diversity may be the most difficult to change because their members may not recognize their diversity issues or the need to address them.

form change systems and coalitions to engage in collective action (Donnellon & Kolb, 1994; Resnick, 1978). For this discussion, however, the focus is on the strategies and techniques that can be used by administrators.

The elements of the framework presented here will be applied first to the internal agency and then to the agency-community interface. In the discussion of the internal agency, a case example will be presented to illustrate the application of the elements, and the same agency will be used throughout the discussion of the framework.

Leader Orientation

Because administrators are expected to be visionary for the agency and to strive to move the agency closer to that vision, their specific orientation toward diversity is paramount. This orientation is informed by the agency's history and mission so that the vision of the agency's future seems realistic and feasible. If change that alters the fundamental structure, systems, orientation, and strategies of the organization is required, there must be recognition that this type of transformation is slow and tedious. The conceptualization of the change as a series of incremental steps that correct a problem or modify a procedure makes the change more manageable and provides opportunities for monitoring and reassessment (Pearlmutter, 1998).

As was previously indicated, there must be a top-level commitment to diversity practice that propels administrators to take action. Orientation alone, however, is insufficient to begin the change process. Administrators' leadership ability and personal characteristics also shape their power. A change agent's spheres of influence and dominance are enhanced by such attributes of credibility, trustworthiness, sincerity, and expertise (Armenakis et al., 1993). Indeed, Glisson's (1989) research on the effect of leadership on human service workers indicates that a leader's maturity, power, and intelligence can influence workers' level of organizational commitment. Leaders who are change agents should also inspire their workers and demonstrate their own commitment to the vision and values they seek to promote (Posner, 1992).

Because any attempt to change a system can be perceived as a threat to that system's equilibrium, agency resistance should be anticipated. Forces that propel the resistance and forces that counter the resistance should be identified and assessed. Administrators must be aware of the obstacles to be confronted and the strategies that can be effective in overcoming that resistance. The administrator's own risk-taking propensity must also be assessed because resistance can often pose challenges that may test and/or weaken his or her commitment to diversity and empowerment. Administrators' efforts to reduce resistance include using a response style that neutralizes conflict rather than exacerbates it, continuously emphasizing a commitment to worker growth and development, and creating a nonpunitive agency climate that encourages the expression of ideas. These efforts should emanate from the administrator's own values and goals and should, therefore, convey a sincere and honest tone. In some extreme situations, resistance may be strong enough to defeat any change endeavors. For these situations, the change effort may need to focus on creating a climate that at least supports open discussion of change. This may be the first step needed in an incremental process that can conceivably take years to complete.

The agency. Administrators have particular perspectives on the diversity management issues in their agencies. For those with a vision of identifying management techniques that support and encourage diversity, the orientation is to create a stress-free climate in which cultural conflicts are comfortably resolved and workers are at ease with each other. Cultural diversity is perceived as an asset to the agency, enriching the agency for workers and service consumers. Because some type of tension may always exist around cultural diversity issues, administrators who value diversity are concerned with creating a workplace or a system that can effectively address this tension.

A first step in this direction may be the critical review of agency personnel policies and procedures; the employee grievance and appeal process; employee evaluation process; and agency recruiting, hiring, and promotion patterns. In this examination, administrators are seeking to determine whether the agency is doing all it can to attract, retain, and promote workers from diverse groups. Such a task can be undertaken with the assistance of other managers in the agency (see Chapter 20).

In this initial stage, the examination of policies and procedures for the purpose of assessing the agency's hiring and promoting practices may, in itself, increase tension in the agency. Workers may perceive these efforts as an indirect criticism aimed at them. To minimize staff fears and apprehensions, administrators may have to provide some clear explanation to staff of the nature and intent of the review. The extent (detailed or general) and form (verbal or written) of this explanation should be determined by the degree of formality administrators wish to achieve. Clear messages from the administrators are often needed to offset the spec-

ulation, gossip, and innuendo that are likely to arise in the agency.

Case Study

The newly appointed director of a family service agency in a community that was undergoing a demographic shift from primarily African American residents to both Hispanic and African American members was surprised to note that all the staff members were African American, despite increasing requests for services from Hispanic residents. In reviewing agency recruitment and hiring practices, she further observed that policies specifically targeted the hiring of individuals who were knowledgeable about the African American community. The director's orientation supported service delivery to the entire community, and this orientation guided her in the review of agency policy.

The agency-community interface. The administrator's orientation to racial, ethnic, and culturally diverse communities helps determine the agency's relationship with these communities. The agency's history and mission with diverse groups can often be used to explain current relationships. To promote diversity and empowerment in the agency's relationship with communities, administrators see workers as crucial components. Thus, the orientation is to empower workers with the skills, knowledge, and resources necessary for empowerment practice at the community level. Administrators value and respect the diversity of the community and approach this diversity as an asset.

A review of written materials on agency services and programs is undertaken to determine the extent to which they incorporate this value and respect for diversity. Again, other managers can assist in this review. The goal here is to carefully examine program policies and procedures for an articulation of goals and objectives that support diversity. In particular, the review can focus on identifying those goals and objectives that support intrapersonal/psychological, organizational, and community empowerment and diversity practice. Key areas to identify in the review include the improved/enhanced functioning of individual clients, the agency itself, and the community. Although it may seem unusual for services and programs to target agency improvement, numerous programs have the agency as the service beneficiary. Programs and services that involve activities such as staff training, program development, program evaluation, agency-site visits from sponsors, community outreach, community feedback, and community participation provide valuable information about the agency's organizational and community practices.

Information

The policy and program review is preparatory to the gathering of information from primary sources. Although administrators have their opinion of what the agency looks like, how it operates, and what defines its culture, these opinions may be biased and only partially correct. In addition, from the position of administrators, the agency is seen from a top-down vantage point, and others in positions of lesser authority may certainly have a much different set of observations.

The agency. Administrators have to identify those questions and issues that they would like workers to address. These issues and questions should emerge from the policy and program review and from the administrators' vision of the agency's future. These questions may address worker attitudes about the hiring of particular groups of people, service delivery to particular communities, ideologies about diversity, worker issues about diversity, agency directions in this area, and definitions of key elements of the agency's culture.

There are numerous methods for gathering information about the diversity needs of the agency from those within the agency. Surveys, self-administered questionnaires, and focus groups are examples. Administrators should also decide whether this information gathering is to be conducted by individuals within the agency or by outside consultants. Donnellon and Kolb (1994) assert that the organizational diagnosis conducted by insiders is in danger of being too narrow, attempting to avoid conclusions that could possibly stress the system.

This fact-finding mission does not have to be complex, protracted, or expensive. The goal is to obtain candid, open, honest feedback from staff members about the diversity issues administrators have identified, while at the same time allowing workers the opportunity to add, modify, and otherwise comment on diversity in the agency. Each method of information gathering has it own advantages and disadvantages. One-on-one interviews with staff members can provide invaluable information and the safety of confidentiality but may encourage socially desirable, politically correct responses. Even so, this method communicates to the workers the administrator's interest in and commitment to this area. The confidential questionnaire has the advantage of protecting the identity of the respondent and may lead to more candid observations. An outside consultant may be able to stimulate candid discussions from workers that cannot be elicited by those in the agency.

Administrator observations should not be overlooked in this fact-finding phase. By walking around the agency, engaging in casual conversation with staff and clients, and observing what goes on in various parts of the agency, administrators garner additional insights that may serve to further clarify and demystify some of the results obtained through other methods.

Case Study

The director previously mentioned informally surveyed her staff for their opinions about adding Hispanic staff members and serving more Hispanic clients. Although all workers said they were open to such changes, they were also quick to identify the reasons for not undertaking these changes at the present time (i.e., agency had limited resources, other agencies could do a better job of serving Hispanic families, there were so many more pressing priorities). From these informal conversations, the director became aware of those staff attitudes that impeded staff and service expansion to reach the Hispanic segment of the community.

The agency-community interface. Here administrators seek to find out staff attitudes about the community and the community's attitudes about the agency. Administrators have to formulate those questions to be posed to staff members and those to be posed to community members.

Staff questions might include: How do staff members define multicultural community practice? Is there really a need for this kind of practice? What types of skills are needed for this practice? What can the agency do to better support this practice? What kinds of staff members

are needed for this practice? How should staff be evaluated in this area? Some staff questions can be included in the agency fact-finding discussed above.

In the agency-community interface, several areas stand out as requiring information and feedback from the community. One area addresses the agency's image and reputation in the community. Another area is the community's definitions of its needs and priorities. Community questions might include: What are community perceptions of the agency? What kind of reputation does the agency have in the community? When the agency's name is mentioned, what comes to mind? What are the community's pressing needs and priorities? What can the agency do to respond to these needs and priorities? Who are the leaders in the community? Where do residents typically go for assistance? What are the community's agency-service utilization patterns? What are the barriers or obstacles to using the agency's services? Data-gathering methods include: community surveys and questionnaires, surveys of present and former clients from the community, interviews with community individuals knowledgeable about the community (key informants), and focus groups. The review of secondary data about the community (for example, community surveys conducted by other agencies) can also provide useful data about the community.

Any fact-finding mission should not be limited by the resources the agency has available. Clearly, the resource-rich agency may be in a better position to use paid consultants and more sophisticated methods; however, other agencies can benefit from the use of volunteer consultants and students who serve as social work interns. Administrators have to be creative in maximizing all the possibilities for data-gathering resources.

Formulation of an Intervention Plan

In the formulation of any intervention plan, objectives should be clear, precise, and tied to the agency's bottom line. For some human service agencies, the bottom line may be values and agency mission. For others, it may be contract and funding mandates. All diversity objectives should have a clear relevance to what the agency and its members deem to be important. These objectives then become embodied in the interventions that are formulated.

Administrators must consider how the plan will affect the agency's relationship with its environment. Plans that are consonant with the values, ideologies, and technologies in the prevailing environment may have the endorsement of agency constituencies. Plans that are out of step with the stakeholders in the task environment, particularly those who control agency resources, may have to be reformulated, or new sources of inputs may have to be tapped.

With the policy review and the information from staff and the community, administrators are ready to embark on the formulation of strategies for promoting diversity and empowerment. Although the content of the plan is crucial, the process of the plan's formulation is of equal significance.

In the agency. Worker participation in the formulation of a plan and in the decision making about its implementation is imperative for the plan's success. The participation of workers in the strategic planning activities can lead to insights about issues facing the agency (Armenakis et al., 1993). This participation and

involvement can further help administrators understand the agency's culture (Zamanou & Glaser, 1994). According to Pine et al. (1998, p. 20), participatory management is a commitment to carrying out a set of strategies that involve workers in organizational decisions. This participation fosters a collaboration between members of the agency that encourages all parties to cooperate in the plan's implementation. Participation leads to worker commitment and ownership of the proposed interventions.

For administrators seeking to increase diversity in the agency, strategic plans could emphasize the recruitment and hiring of workers from diverse groups through the placement of job advertisements in ethnic newspapers and on ethnic radio stations and the restructuring of the application and interview process to make it more user-friendly. In the absence of professionally qualified applicants who are members of diverse groups, the plan may consist of reviewing the role of paraprofessionals in the agency. Although slots for paraprofessionals may be more likely to be filled by racial/ethnic minority group members, administrators should be careful to avoid creating a two-tier staff system with racial/ethnic group members occupying the lower tier.

For agencies with a diverse workforce, strategic plans may target governance procedures and staff-conflict issues. Agencies with diverse staff often use hidden approaches to intergroup conflict because of management discomfort in addressing this tension. These hidden approaches may include ignoring the problem (remaining silent in the face of conflict), using the confidential manager-employee conference, and writing letters of reprimand for employee files. Administrators may want to move some issues (those that appear to be recurring or patterned) to a more open agenda through, for example, staff meeting discussions, the creation of a cross-cultural peer-complaint board, the use of a diversity task force as part of a pre-formal complaint review, the appointment of an ombudsman, or the establishment of a multistep complaint-resolution process. With this approach, structures and processes are designed to specifically mediate and resolve multicultural conflict issues.

If the intervention is a rewriting of the personnel manual and the agency's goals and objectives to include statements about diversity, a task force, ad hoc committee, or other work group with staff representation may be convened to tackle the issue. In addition, a process for communicating group deliberations and outcomes should be developed so that all members of the agency have an opportunity to review and comment on the proposals. Again, the intent here is to maintain an open and fair process that values feedback, collaboration, and cooperation.

If the intervention identifies training as the agency need, the success of the training depends on a work environment that nurtures and supports new skills. Top-down directed mandatory training may be met with resistance (Gregoire, Propp, & Poertner, 1998). Workers should participate in identifying their training needs, and the training should be tailored to meet those needs. In addition, training may be needed for all levels of staff including management if the new learning is to be diffused throughout the agency.

Because of the sensitivity surrounding diversity issues, administrators must strive to put forth an open agenda that encourages the discussion of sensitive topics and the participation of workers in this discussion. A veil of silence may be perpetuating suspicion and cynicism, which can be combated by these frank, direct discussions. Administrators become role models for conducting and participating in these discussions, using their oral persuasive communication ability to influence others. Oral persuasive communication involves the transmitting of explicit, direct messages through meetings and other personal presentations (Armenakis et al., 1993).

Case Study

In the historically African American agency situated in a community with a growing Hispanic population, the director used the agency's goal of increasing its funding base as an opportunity to initiate discussions of increasing agency staff and client diversity. Staff members enthusiastically encouraged the director to pursue obtaining a sizable contract with a county agency to provide welfare-to-work supportive services for its community welfare recipients. The application required a detailed description of the community, its welfare recipients, and the agency's capacity to respond to the needs of these recipients. The director formed a task force to assist with the completion of the application and used a portion of several staff meetings to engage workers in discussions of the application and its implications for the agency. The need to expand the staff to include bilingual, bicultural members was integrally linked with the agency's bottom line of survival and growth. The agency outlined the strategies it would use to recruit, screen, hire, and retain the additional staff it needed. Some of these strategies included using Spanish-language media (newspapers and radio stations) to advertise job openings and meeting with Hispanic community groups to recruit applicants and to publicize the program. Other strategies focused on the training of existing staff to enable them to work more effectively with Hispanic individuals and families. The agency was successful in signing a multiyear contract with the county.

The agency-community interface. The principle of participation is also operative as administrators begin to outline tentative interventions at the agency-community level. Community task forces, key informants, and previously identified community leaders can offer administrators feedback and input about interventions under consideration. Through these interventions, administrators seek to support the community's diversity by providing services and programs that advance community empowerment.

If the intervention is staff training, community input may help to focus and guide the training agenda to better meet the community's needs. If the intervention is community training, the community can also help outline training priorities, appropriate training times, possible training sites in the community, and methods of recruiting training participants. If particular services and programs are under consideration, community feedback can help structure these programs and services. If the community's needs and priorities are beyond the mandates of the agency, community observations may help channel agency attention to developing and providing a referral list, engaging in advocacy activities on behalf of the agency, and/or forging partnerships and collaborations with other community-based agencies.

Implementation

The formulated diversity plan is put into action and should have a schedule and set of benchmarks to monitor its progress. All roles should be carefully described so that all active parties in the implementation phase are aware of the expectations and demands facing them. The plan's clarity is essential for its success. Ambiguity can result when workers are allowed to use their discretion in interpreting the meaning and intent of the plan. The use of discretion may jeopardize consistency and uniformity in implementation in critical areas of the plan. Those areas that are flexible and open for workers to use their discretion should be discussed and identified. If there are particular areas that must be uniformly and consistently implemented across all workers, then, they should also be discussed and identified. Although no plan can cover all contingencies, some general rules may be developed to serve as guidelines for making decisions. Because agencies are dynamic entities that do change, the plan should be periodically reviewed and, when necessary, modified and updated.

A reward structure should also accompany the implementation of the plan, so that staff members know the value the agency attaches to the plan. In addition to money, agency reward systems may also include promotions, status changes, recognition, and appreciation (Sager, 1995). Sanctions should also be imposed when staff members fail in implementing their part of the plan. Rewards and sanctions communicate to workers that specific behaviors are now being rewarded whereas others will no longer be overlooked. Whatever the reward structure, it should be equitably applied and include procedures for grievance.

In the agency. Despite all the steps preceding it, the plan may still be met with staff resistance. Administrators must search out the sources of this resistance and attempt to counter it with forces that support the change. It may be necessary to hold special meetings (open forum) to address employee concerns, to meet with some staff members as a group, to approach individual employees directly, and/or to enlist the active assistance of employee leaders to overcome the resistance.

Plan monitoring with feedback to the staff helps to keep the plan and its goals in the forefront of employee attention. This agency goal is presented and treated as a priority. Administrators' public and open support of the plan and the accompanying reward structure further stress the centrality of the plan to the agency's mission. Thus, monitoring becomes a norm for making sure the plan remains on track and meets identified benchmarks.

With the implementation of new techniques, resources may have to be redistributed to support the change effort. Those workers with the skills and expertise required to implement will rise in status and importance whereas those who cannot develop appropriate skills may suffer a loss of power. In the implementation of the plan, new factions and power alliances may be created that alter the agency's usual way of doing business. This alteration may represent a temporary disruption of the agency's equilibrium, and it is expected that, over time, the new plan will establish a new agency homeostasis.

Case Study

Although everyone at the African American agency was excited about being awarded the welfare-to-work contract, that excitement was not as widespread during staff training sessions and during the new worker recruitment period. Whereas some staff members embraced the new learning as a way of moving the agency forward, other workers saw the training as an unnecessary imposition and inconvenience. To help overcome this resistance, the director solicited worker input about the training topics to be covered, scheduling of the training sessions, length of the sessions, and names of potential trainers. Each session was evaluated, and worker feedback was shared with trainers in preparation for the subsequent sessions. The director also attended the first series of training sessions as a participant to convey her need for this new knowledge. Although some resistance remained, the director was able to garner a significant level of worker support so that the disgruntled faction represented only a small part of the staff.

The agency-community interface. Here, too, a schedule, benchmarks, and reward structure are necessary to the plan's success. Monitoring entails feedback from both the staff and the community. Staff resistance to the agency's community practice plan has to be overcome with some of the same strategies that were noted above.

The importance of the plan can be communicated to the community through administrator presentations at community meetings, worker presentations, media coverage, key informants, community leaders, and other community residents. The collaborative planning process should enable the agency to receive support for its community-focused intervention.

Evaluation

Following the implementation phase, the effectiveness of the plan has to be evaluated. The clearly articulated objectives serve to guide the focus of the evaluation. The objectives define the criteria for success so that expected outcomes can be measured.

In the agency. Evaluation typically highlights agency changes that were caused by or related to the intervention. Evaluation questions may include: Does the agency have a more diverse workforce at Time 2 in comparison to Time 1? Has agency conflict and tension been reduced? How many times did the Diversity Task Force meet to resolve conflict, and what were the conflicts? Has more staff integration occurred? Do the perceptions of the culturally diverse staff (continue to) differ from those of the majority staff? Has the number of grievances been reduced? Has the agency been able to retain a higher percentage of its staff? Has worker morale and satisfaction improved?

Evaluation methods may include surveys, questionnaires, or content analysis of records/documents, and these may be administered at specific points in the implementation process. Surveys of current staff, exiting staff, and former staff may also reveal aspects of the plan's effectiveness. Document analysis can pinpoint changes in the applicant pool and the workforce.

The evaluation methods used are dependent on the agency resources, and, again, volunteer consultants and student interns may be used by agencies with limited resources. Administrators may also use their observations of the agency to inform them about changes, but these observations should be augmented with data from more objective sources.

Case Study

In the African American agency used as an example, evaluation was based on worker feedback about the training, the size and diversity of the

new applicant pool, and the actual hiring of bicultural, bilingual staff.

The agency-community interface. Evaluation of the agency's community-empowerment practice plan calls for measures taken on both the staff and the community. Staff members have their views about the effectiveness of the intervention, but these views may not be the same as those held by community residents. Observations from both sources provide a more comprehensive overview of the plan's effects.

The evaluation methodology employed is dependent on the intervention, the intervention objectives, the evaluation questions, and available agency resources.

Formalization of the Plan

Good ideas often leave the agency with the good administrator who had them. These good ideas may have been captured in particular agency activities and patterns that were established during the tenure of that administrator. With the exodus of this person, those patterns may become eroded or replaced by the activities of the next administrator. The administrator's authority of position and the control of resources are powerful enough for staff members to abide by that person's wishes, suggestions, and gentle proddings. Such compliance may lull administrators into thinking that this compliance negates the need for policy. In the absence of sound policy, discretion continues to dominate.

In the agency. After the implementation has been evaluated, decisions have to be made. Should the be plan be modified and then implemented again? Should all or part of the plan become permanent agency structure? If the plan proves to be effective, steps should be taken to institutionalize it through formalized policy mandates. With policy, discretion is circumscribed, and all agency personnel are mandated to follow the policy guidelines. A revised personnel manual that includes statements about the value of diversity-practice skills and the evaluation of staff diversity-practice skills communicates loudly that the agency is serious about this type of practice. Policies that authorize the use of ethnic media for advertising job vacancies also let the staff and the community know that the recruitment of members from diverse groups is an agency priority. Policies that dictate the manner in which grievances and conflict will be handled also minimize the role of discretion in resolving these conflicts. Task forces, staff work groups, and mediation groups may become institutionalized as part of the agency structure through the establishment of policy. In this manner, all the good ideas do not have to leave the agency when the innovative administrator leaves.

Case Study

For the African American agency under discussion, personnel policies were modified to include the recruitment of workers knowledgeable in African American and/or Hispanic culture, and staff performance reviews included an area focusing on the provision of culturally relevant and culturally sensitive service. Client exit interviews were instituted as one of several factors used to assess worker performance.

The agency-community interface. Although community practice that supports empowerment practice can vary according to the changing needs and demands of the community,

mechanisms for community input in the agency planning and decision-making process can be institutionalized through policy. Board diversity can be mandated by policy, and this diversity can boost organizational responsiveness by granting the community a voice in the agency. The community's voice can also be heard through the creation of special community advisory boards or task forces that are formalized in agency policy. The resources that community residents bring to the board, advisory group, or task force are perceived as just as valuable as the resources brought by affluent board members. In this view, community representation becomes associated with the agency's bottom line.

Structures and patterns that are vital to the agency's diversity mission should not be left to chance or the good intentions of administrators. Those activities and patterns that are valued by the agency find expression in agency policy that identifies the rewards/sanctions associated with those defined organizational behaviors. Agencies that profess a commitment to management practices that support diversity and empowerment but have not formalized this commitment are giving their workers and the community mixed messages. Policies are an agency's attempt to formally perpetuate a value, ideology, or structure. Policies then become crucial in holding agencies accountable for behaviors and outcomes.

CONCLUSIONS

Agencies must take care of business in-house before they can effectively intervene with the communities they serve. For agencies to empower disenfranchised communities, they must first empower workers and value the diversity they bring to the agency. Diversity carries with it a number of meanings, reactions, and perspectives. In addition, the systems and institutional frameworks show that social services operate in an environment that shapes the ideologies within agencies.

Change in management for diversity and empowerment is difficult to accomplish. Numerous barriers in society, in the profession, and in the agency exist to mute candid diversity discourse and, consequently, hinder attempts at organizational change. If this change is tied to the agency's bottom line, whatever it may be, then efforts to embrace techniques for the management of diversity and empowerment can be tested.

A framework was offered that bridged the agency and the community because empowered workers can then work to empower the community. To support the empowerment of the community, an agency must first support the empowerment of its workers. In this framework, leader orientation, information gathering, plan formulation, plan implementation, evaluation, and formalization shaped a process through which administrators could begin to apply the tenets of empowerment in their agency and in the agency-community interface. This framework advocated an orientation that valued diversity and supported empowerment through an inclusive, participatory management style that sought feedback from all levels in the agency and, when appropriate, from the community as well.

Diversity is a reality; yet, empowerment still seems to be an ideal. Agencies continue to face the challenge of developing organizational structures and management techniques that reflect the values the professions hold for individuals. These values do not just apply to individual clients—they apply to service providers and communities as well.

REFERENCES

Adams, P., & Nelson, K. (1997). Reclaiming community: An integrative approach to human services. *Administration in Social Work, 21,* 67-81.

Armenakis, A., Harris, S., & Mossholder, K. (1993). Creating readiness for organizational change. *Human Relations, 46,* 681-702.

Axinn, J., & Levin, H. (1982). *Social welfare: A history of the American response to need.* New York: Harper & Row.

Barnett, W., & Carroll, G. (1995). Modeling internal organizational change. *Annual Review of Sociology, 21,* 217-236.

Bertalanffy, L. (1974). General systems theory and psychiatry. In S. Arieti (Ed.), *American handbook of psychiatry* (2nd ed., Vol. 1). New York: Basic Books.

Brager, G., & Holloway, S. (1978). *Changing human service organizations.* New York: Free Press.

Charlton, A., & Huey, J. (1992). Breaking cultural barriers. *Quality Progress, 25,* 47-49.

Chen, C., & Eastman, W. (1997). Toward a civic culture for multicultural organizations. *Journal of Applied Behavioral Science, 33,* 454-471.

Donnellon, A., & Kolb, D. (1994). Constructive for whom? The fate of diversity disputes in organizations. *Journal of Social Issues, 50,* 139-155.

Garcia, M. (1995). An anthropological approach to multicultural diversity training. *Journal of Applied Behavioral Science, 31,* 490-504.

Gardenswartz, L., & Rowe, A. (1998). Why diversity matters. *HR Focus, 75,* S1-3.

Gil, D. (1990). Implications of conservative tendencies for practice and education in social welfare. *Journal of Sociology and Social Welfare, 17,* 5-27.

Glisson, C. (1989). The effect of leadership on workers in human service organizations. *Administration in Social Work, 13,* 99-116.

Gregoire, T., Propp, J., & Poertner, J. (1998). The supervisor's role in the transfer of training. *Administration in Social Work, 22,* 1-18.

Hasenfeld, Y. (1983). *Human services organizations.* Englewood Cliffs, NJ: Prentice Hall.

Hasenfeld, Y. (1987). Power in social work practice. *Social Service Review, 61,* 467-483.

Hasenfeld, Y. (1992). *Human services as complex organizations.* Newbury Park, CA: Sage.

Herman, R. (1998). You've got to change to retain. *HR Focus, 75,* S1.

Iglehart, A., & Becerra, R. (1995). *Social services and the ethnic community.* Boston: Allyn & Bacon.

Jansson, B. (1997). *The reluctant welfare state* (3rd ed.). Pacific Grove, CA: Brooks/Cole.

Katz, D., & Kahn, R. (1978). *The social psychology of organizations* (2nd ed.). New York: John Wiley.

Leiby, J. (1978). *A history of social welfare and social work in the United States.* New York: Columbia University Press.

Martin, G., Jr. (1990). *Social policy in the welfare state.* Englewood Cliffs, NJ: Prentice Hall.

Mor-Barak, M., & Cherin, D. (1998). A tool to expand organizational understanding of workforce diversity: Exploring a measure of inclusion-exclusion. *Administration in Social Work, 22,* 47-64.

Nicolini, D., Meznar, M., Stewart, G., & Manz, C. (1995). The social construction of organizational learning: Conceptual and practical issues in the field. *Human Relations, 48,* 727-746.

Parsons, R. (1988). Empowerment for alternatives for low income minority girls: A group work approach. *Social Work With Groups, 11,* 27-45.

Pearlmutter, S. (1998). Self-efficacy and organizational change leadership. *Administration in Social Work, 22,* 23-38.

Pine, B., Warsh, R., & Maluccio, A. (1998). Participatory management in a public child welfare agency: A key to effective change. *Administration in Social Work, 22,* 19-32.

Posner, B. (1992). Person-organizational values congruence: No support for individual differences as a moderating influence. *Human Relations, 45,* 351-361.

Resnick, H. (1978). Tasks in changing the organization from within (COFW). *Administration in Social Work, 2,* 29-44.

Riger, S. (1993). What's wrong with empowerment. *American Journal of Community Psychology, 21,* 279-292.

Ringer, B., & Lawless, E. (1989). *Race-ethnicity and society.* New York: Routledge.

Rothman, J., & Tropman, J. (1987). Models of community organization and macro practice perspectives: Their mixing and phasing. In F. Cox, J. Erlich, J. Rothman, & J. Tropman (Eds.), *Strategies of community organization* (4th ed.). Itasca, IL: F. E. Peacock.

Sager, J. (1995). Change levers for improving organizational performance and staff morale. In J. Rothman, J. Erlich, & J. Tropman (Eds.). *Strategies of community intervention* (5th ed.). Itasca, IL: F. E. Peacock.

Schein, E. (1992). *Organizational culture and leadership* (2nd ed.). San Francisco: Jossey-Bass.

Schein, E. (1996). Culture: The missing concept in organizational studies. *Administrative Science Quarterly, 41,* 229-240.

Schilling, R., Schinke, S., & Weatherly, R. (1988). Service trends in a conservative era: Social workers rediscover their past. *Social Work, 33,* 5-9.

Solomon, B. (1976). *Black empowerment.* New York: Columbia University Press.

Zamanou, S., & Glaser, S. (1994). Moving toward participation and involvement: Managing and measuring organizational culture. *Group & Organizational Management, 19,* 475-502.

Zimmerman, M. (1995). Psychological empowerment: Issues and illustrations. *American Journal of Community Psychology, 23,* 581-599.

CHAPTER TWENTY-TWO

Initiating and Implementing Change

FELICE DAVIDSON PERLMUTTER

The profession of social work is unique in its commitment to social change. This commitment is exemplified by the Code of Ethics of the National Association of Social Workers (1996, p. 9), which provides an important framework for the administrator's role in the initiation and implementation of change as it emphasizes the pursuit of justice and the shaping of social policies and institutions.

Levy (1979) focuses on administrators' role in regard to social change as he makes two central points. First, social administrators should support employees who seek to change agency practices and/or policies. Second, administrators throughout the organization should play a central role in creating a climate that supports the initiation and implementation of change.

There are several underlying assumptions in this chapter. A first assumption is that there must be a partnership among all levels of administration in a social agency in working for social change. Thus, middle managers must have the support of central administrators to be actors in the change process and vice versa. A second assumption of this discussion is that change is ongoing and continuous in every social agency, which must be responsive to an ever-changing social, economic, and political context. The role of administrators is to be sensitive to the need for change and to manage the process to produce better outcomes for consumers of services. A third assumption is that a commitment to social change may be necessary, but it is certainly not sufficient. Careful analysis and strategic planning must precede the process if any change effort is to be successful.

This chapter seeks to address these assumptions. We begin the discussion with a focus on the environmental context of social agencies. This is followed by a working definition of social change. We then discuss the dilemmas inherent in the change process and describe a model that can be helpful in organizing the change process. We conclude the chapter by suggesting some strategies for administrative action. The intent of this discussion is not to provide answers but rather to stimulate each administrator to determine an appropriate response that fits the specific people in the specific organization within its particular environment.

THE ENVIRONMENTAL CONTEXT

Because organizational change does not occur in a vacuum, it is essential to understand the context that stimulates change before we begin our exploration of the nature of this change and how to manage the process.

The external reality for the past three decades in our American society is one of continuously accelerating pressures imposed on the work environment. As early as the 1970s, this phenomenon was noted by an executive of a family service agency who came into his administrative position

> when there was still the usual rhythm of going on year to year, and changes, if they occurred, took about two to four years and you had a lot of time to get used to them. I don't believe that there is any place in the country that such a rhythm is possible today, at least if one is going to survive. (Perlmutter, 1980, p. 62)

Clearly, the pace of social, political, and economic change has become so intense in recent decades that commentators have difficulty finding language that adequately describes these dizzying phenomena. Emery and Trist's (1969) early discussion of "turbulent fields" identifies the rapidly shifting and uncertain environments that affect organizations.

In the human services, a number of turbulent trends present challenges to social service administrators. Traditionally, social service organizations have concentrated on providing quality professional services to well-defined and well-understood groups of clients, such as children and the aging, among others. However, major contemporary developments require new responses as the new client populations of social agencies reflect societal complexities in the social, psychological, legal, medical, and economic aspects of society. This can be illustrated by the increasing number of clients with AIDS, unmarried pregnant teenagers, abused women and children, chronically mentally ill, the frail and poor elderly, and immigrant populations (Hasenfeld, 1989). The need to broaden the repertoire of professional responses to serve these new populations effectively within social service agencies is clear.

Other dramatic changes relate to the changing structure of the nonprofit field. Many for-profit organizations have entered domains, such as child care and services for the aging, that have traditionally been under the aegis of nonprofit agencies. Not only are social service organizations competing with for-profits to stay in business, but the for-profit sector is attracting social workers from the nonprofit arena because of its higher salaries. And the advent of managed care has increased the turbulence in the field. The investors, and not the professionals, are calling the shots in regard to the provision of service, creating great stress on the professional community and the consumers it serves.

Another critical external impact on social agencies is their dependence on government contracts to support many of their services. The effect is complex, but of concern is the fact that the autonomy of social service agencies in the nonprofit sector has been threatened as all too often, agency policy has been overridden by the requirements specified in agency contracts with the public sector (Chisolm, 1995). Furthermore, as fewer public dollars have been available in recent times, many of these agencies have undergone dramatic change. These changes include downsizing, mergers, and, occasionally, even going out of business.

The stressors created by all these environmental elements make it clear that it is no longer business as usual. What may become usual is the necessity for social service administrators to initiate and implement meaningful change at an increasingly rapid pace.

A WORKING DEFINITION OF ORGANIZATIONAL CHANGE

There are many types of organizational change, ranging from small to large, from short-term to long-term. Big change is fundamental in nature and can transform the organization's "core form" (Haveman, 1992) and "distinctive character" (Selznick, 1957). Although big change is often linked to external changes in the agency's policy or task environment, change can also be linked to internal stimuli. For example, the development of computer technology, an external scientific development, has certainly brought change to social agencies. Examples of internal stimuli are the unionization of the agency staff or the decision to use BSWs in addition to MSWs to provide services to the clientele.

Complementary to large-scale change, illustrated above, is the importance of small change in organizational life, change that challenges management at all levels. These are changes that concern the organization's ability to be flexible and responsive to various elements in the system, including the consumers and the staff, as the organization continuously seeks to be more effective and more efficient. Thus, for example, the use of answering machines by the social work staff must be considered as it affects the consumers of the agency's service.

Although big change is usually seen as primarily the province of upper-level administration (Perlmutter & Gummer, 1995), this chapter examines the implications and possibilities for administrators throughout the organization. Thus, whereas chief executive officers (CEOs) are usually the major actors in the external system, middle managers are in a central position of having information concerning the effect of public policy on the consumers of service. CEOs are usually too far removed from the front line and too involved at the policy level and the external boundaries of the organization to have this information.

Two examples describe the role of different levels of administration in the initiation of change, both big and small. In the first example, administrators at all levels in a county welfare agency failed to recognize the opportunity to be involved in initiating a big change that would affect their organization. The administrators could have made an important contribution to a portion of their clients who were welfare recipients and for whom the 5-year welfare clock was ticking. Most of these clients were seeking employment in their local community where few jobs were available. The jobs that were available to them were in a plant that was located in a remote rural area and did not have accessible public transportation. The administrators at all levels of this welfare agency lost an opportunity that could have significantly met the needs of the clients being served. The executive could have played a role in the external environment by going to the County Commissioners to request van or jitney service for these people. She could have used the information provided by her middle managers regarding the numbers of people who could be served by a jitney service and thereby helped to move them from the welfare rolls into jobs. Instead, it was business as usual as caseworkers referred the recipients to outside employment agencies or told them to seek work on their own.

The second example illustrates how small change can be brought about within the social agency. A social work student intern who was placed in a hospital social work department became aware of the long wait for service in the lab where clients went for medical tests. Her supervisor, the unit director, encouraged her to document her observations. The student went to observe the situation and found that the technicians were often oblivious to the problem, frequently chatted among themselves, and were not responsive to the patients in the waiting room. She observed the laboratory for a 2-week period and systematically recorded the data. At the suggestion of the unit director, she reported her findings at a staff meeting of the social work staff. The director of the social work unit exemplified the administrative role discussed in the introductory section of this chapter. She not only supported the student's effort, thus initiating the change process, but she took the information to the appropriate channels to implement the change.

These two examples illustrate the central role of administrators in initiating change, both big and small. In the first example, the executive director did not recognize, or make possible, the involvement of all of her staff in the process, and an important opportunity was lost to serve agency clients. In the second example, the effectiveness of the middle manager was clear as she helped the student worker initiate the change and involved upper management in effecting the change.

Organizational change, as discussed above, can be large or small, depending on the problem being addressed. Other situations provide an opportunity for either the initiation or implementation of change (Perlmutter & Gummer, 1995). It is not unusual for an organization to change its status from being an informal self-help group, such as an AIDS support program, to becoming a formal social agency serving AIDS patients. This shift entails a basic change in the agency's grounds for legitimacy, and major administrative adjustments must be made in the shift from being an informal group with broad-based member involvement to becoming a formal bureaucratic structure. Similarly, when an organization shifts from a small nonprofit to a for-profit agency (e.g., a preschool nursery is incorporated into a for-profit child care corporation), major changes occur not only in the policy arena but also in the professional one. And when an organization merges with another agency to survive and to protect its services (e.g., two small mental health clinics become one entity), the consequences of this shift must be addressed. These are changes that begin at the upper administrative levels but certainly involve all the administrative levels in the organizations.

Smaller changes similarly create administrative challenges. When a client group brings a new set of problems to the agency, a change in the professional repertoire may be needed: Mental health professionals working with individual clients may be faced with families requiring family interventions. When the agency, because of budget problems, closes its neighborhood-based services and centralization occurs, new caseloads and work arrangements may be required. When new technology is introduced into the agency, and the staff is extremely resistant, new staff development approaches are necessary.

In all of these examples, it is essential that administrators analyze and understand the potential consequences for the organization and the consumers of the service. All the relevant actors throughout the organization must be involved so that the change is handled successfully.

DILEMMAS INHERENT IN ORGANIZATIONAL CHANGE

Because initiating and implementing organizational change are not simple or obvious processes, it is useful to understand some of the possible dilemmas and constraints inherent in the situation, which can help develop a clearer understanding and analysis as the basis for action (Handy, 1994).

A major dilemma, always present, and one that shapes all the other dilemmas, is the reality of the status quo pressures in organizational life, pressures that create inertia in all systems. The known is always safer than the unknown; risk taking carries potential benefits but also potential liabilities. Consequently, changes needed in the professional arena are usually viewed as a threat to practitioners' identity and competency and are rarely seen as opportunities to broaden their repertoire of professional competencies and to grow in professional stature. Similarly, technological changes, such as the use of e-mail, are usually resisted by social workers who are less comfortable in the technical arena and who often argue that the changes will interfere with the worker-client relationship.

And perhaps most fundamental is the conflict in values often experienced by social workers in human service organizations vis-à-vis the broader society. As Western societies in general, and the United States in particular, have become more conservative, most of the values that underpin the profession of social work are being threatened. As a profession committed to working with the poor, the disenfranchised, the disabled, and the elderly, among others, social work is often at odds with the larger society, which is increasingly less willing to support social programs that serve these vulnerable populations.

Social work administrators can too easily become co-opted by and assume the values of the larger society that create these conflicts. For example, a highly respected social work executive reported that his nonprofit mental health agency had dramatically cut the numbers of Medicaid clients they served. When asked where these clients would now go for service, his response was, "I don't know, but we can't carry them on our backs." This was an abdication of leadership from an administrator who should have helped his board of directors take some risks to continue to meet the needs of this client group as well as to ensure that the mission of the organization was being fulfilled.

Perhaps the biggest test of all is the dilemma created by whistle-blowers in the organization. A whistle-blower is one who not only sees wrongdoings in an agency but also initiates attempts to correct them. During the past few decades, as society has become more consumer-conscious, not only have consumers been mobilized on their own behalf, but professionals have become whistle-blowers, concerned with protecting their clients who were victims of poor professional practice or poorly produced products. Increasing numbers of workers in organizations have begun to make public those problems they witness in the workplace, often with dire and unexpected consequences to themselves. The protection of whistle-blowers is not a foregone conclusion, and the courts have created narrow exceptions to the "at will doctrine," where the employer (Halbert, 1997) can arbitrarily dismiss the worker. Consequently, the response to whistle-blowing is far from clear or consistent.

This is illustrated by the case of a physician who worked for Ortho Pharmaceutical Corporation. She was the only team member to protest clinical tests of a product that was a "slow carcinogen." Ortho dismissed the physician arguing that "as an employee at will, . . . she could be fired for good cause, or bad cause, or no cause at all" (Halbert, 1985, p. 2). The New Jersey Supreme Court ruled in favor of the employer, contending that the Food and Drug Administration had not disapproved the drug, that it was still in the testing phase, and that this was a "difference of medical opinion." The one dissenting opinion stated that the professional autonomy of the physician should have been respected and, in line with her professional ethics, she should not have been discharged (Halbert, 1985).

The issue of loyalty to the employing organization is often raised in relation to whistle-blowing: Should employees have a basic responsibility to the organization that employs them? In our view, the professional is bound by professional ethics irrespective of workplace, and the consequence for the consumer should be the focus; the concept of loyalty is not appropriate for an employing organization that is governed either by the profit-making motive or a balanced budget, for there is an inherent conflict in the situation.

It may be that whistle-blowers in the human services face a different situation than those in industry. In theory, this role is one that should be welcomed by professional social workers, whose priority should be meeting the needs of the population being served by the particular social agency. Nevertheless, it is not at all clear that social service agencies know how to deal with whistle-blowers, in spite of all the rhetoric to the contrary (Perlmutter, Bailey, & Netting, in press). The dilemma of meeting client needs while protecting agency stability is a difficult one.

The final dilemma concerns the issue of advocacy, directly related to the administrators' role in social change. Social workers as advocates have long been viewed as central to the profession (Ad Hoc Committee, 1969). And yet, maintaining the advocacy role within human service organizations is never simple to achieve (Ostrander, 1989). A major problem is that of "never biting the hand that feeds you." Because nonprofits are often dependent on external grants and contracts that support their programs, they feel that they are in a compromised position if they become advocates. This certainly puts administrators into a bind.

Goldman (personal communication, 1997), Executive Vice President of the Philadelphia Jewish Family and Children's Service, provocatively argues that agencies providing services to clients not only should not but cannot be effective advocates because of this dependency on external funding. Instead, he suggests that the advocacy function should be lodged in advocacy organizations or professional associations, which can freely identify the problems and bring the issues to the public. This is in contrast to the strong view taken by Gibelman and Kraft (1996), who argue that advocacy must be part of the ongoing leadership role in all human service organizations, a long-held and clearly articulated position in relation to the social work profession (Kramer, 1981; Richan, 1980).

Unfortunately, in reality, the many pressures for survival faced by human service organizations often put advocacy at the bottom of the list of roles played by their executives (Perlmutter & Adams, 1994). Both arguments merit examination because all social agencies are affected by and can affect social policy. Thus, a dilemma exists for social work administrators, who must take a position in regard to advocacy that requires careful analysis and consideration in relation to the particular agency circumstance.

This discussion identifies some of the dilemmas faced by social work administrators as they seek to initiate and/or implement change within their agencies. The more clearly understood the dilemmas inherent in the problem situation to be addressed, the better the possibility of developing an effective approach for the management of change.

MODELS FOR IMPLEMENTING CHANGE

An exploration of some theoretical models of change is provided in the literature. These articles (Gray & Ariss, 1985; Hasenfeld & Schmid, 1989; Perlmutter, 1969; Quinn & Cameron, 1983; Whetten, 1987), which approach the stages of organizational development from a theoretical vantage point (Patti, 1983), can be linked to Selznick's (1957) view of leadership, which is based on a developmental notion of organizational life: "To the extent that similar situations summon like responses . . . we may expect to find organizational evolutionary patterns . . . whose uniformity . . . provide[s] tools for more . . . perceptive diagnosis" (p. 103).

Specific models have been proposed that focus primarily on the administrative role in managing change. The models of Patti and Resnick (1985) and Kotter (1996) will be highlighted in this discussion.

Patti and Resnick (1985) explore two dimensions of the change process: One relates to the phases to be considered; the second relates to the type of leadership needed. The authors make the following assumptions.

> Although the administrator . . . is responsible for initiating the change, he or she can share much of the responsibility for change goals and processes with the staff. A second assumption is that management-initiated change can be a guided and directed process. (p. 270)

We will first address the phases of change; in a later section, we will discuss the leadership element.

The first phase, the planning phase, includes four steps. The first step is to identify the problem situation that should be addressed; it should be carefully defined and specified. Second, this should be followed by an analysis of the problem, determining whether it is internally or externally induced. The clarification of the objective of the change is a necessary third step, which keeps the participants focused throughout the process. This is followed by the "selection of a course of action," which must be tailored to fit the particular agency setting. Thus, the planning phase is completed, and we now move into the implementation phase.

The start-up phase also consists of several elements: communication, allocation of roles, and provision of resources (Patti & Resnick, 1985, p. 273). These are essential if the implementation of the change is to be successful as "the organization begins the process of consolidating new modes of operation" (p. 274). Of course, there will be a trial and error period with the opportunity for refinements and adjustments. The final phase, the evaluation phase, will allow for feedback "to determine whether the change strategy will be maintained, modified, or abandoned" (p. 275).

Kotter (1996) frames his discussion around unsuccessful change efforts as he focuses on the errors that are often made. Some errors he cites relate to problems of complacency, premature assumption of victory, and insufficient vision. He presents a focused eight-step framework that has a sharp public relations thrust and attempts to deal with the errors he describes. His eight stages consist of

> (1) establishing a sense of urgency, (2) creating the guiding coalition, (3) developing a vision and strategy, (4) communicating the change vision, (5) empowering broad-based action, (6) generating short-term wins, (7) consolidating gains and producing more change, and (8) anchoring new approaches in the culture. (Kerson, 1998, p. 96)

Although the two approaches have much in common, Patti and Resnick's (1985) model appears to be more participative in its approach in contrast to Kotter's (1996) more directive one. Both models should be examined because they can provide useful tools to those involved in change.

Both approaches must take into account internal factors. What is the organizational climate? How acknowledged, supported, and encouraged are all staff members of the organization? Is there merely lip service given or is it in fact a hospitable setting? The receptiveness to new ideas and to innovation is directly related to the comfort level of the staff members. In fact, in the early discussions of the benefits of unionization for social workers, there was a focus not only on issues related to the improvement of working conditions (Galper, 1980) but also on the benefits to the worker and the organizational climate when workers participate in agency decision making (Aronson, 1985; DiBarri, 1985). Designing a change strategy certainly is an opportunity for broad involvement, whichever approach is selected.

STRATEGIES FOR MANAGING CHANGE

As discussed earlier, one of the underlying assumptions of this discussion is that administrators at all levels of the social agency bear responsibility for the innovation and implementation of change. We will now examine some strategies that can be useful in this process. The discussion is organized around two dimensions, political and professional. Whereas in reality they are interrelated, for the purposes of this analysis, it is useful to explore each dimension on its own. Greater elaboration of specific executive-level strategies (Perlmutter, 1980) and specific middle management strategies (Perlmutter, 1983) demonstrate both the differences and similarities between these roles in dealing with change.

Political Strategies

Political strategies are usually viewed as applying to the broader political system in the agency environment as it affects the organization; these are usually seen as the major responsibility of the agency executive (Gardner, 1990). However, political strategies are not only important externally but equally important in the internal system. Furthermore, they play an important role in providing data necessary to support the external political positions taken by the agency.

As early as 1980, Gummer focused on the "power-politics model" as critical in viewing the internal organization as a political arena.

> The power-politics approach stems from the assumption of the ubiquity of self-interest as the motivating force in all human behavior, including behavior in organizations. Individuals in organizations will act to secure and promote their interests, these being determined by one's location in the structure. Action directed toward the interests of the organization as a whole . . . will occur only if there is some force operating to constrain self-interest behavior. (p. 46)

This perspective is important for administrative understanding as it makes explicit the self-interests of the actors within the organization and links them with the organizational interests of the total agency.

The reluctance of social work professionals to view power as part of their repertoire of skills is a long-standing problem and, indeed, a constraint. However, it is not unique to our profession. Pfeffer (1992), concerned with all professions, persuasively argues that "unless and until we are willing to come to terms with organizational power and influence, and admit that the skills of getting things done are as important as the skills of figuring out what to do, our organizations will fall further and further behind" (p. 32). It is important to recognize that power is an implicit part of the professional agenda, both internally and externally.

The ability of middle management to influence the political process is illustrated by the frustrations experienced by social workers in a child care setting, who observed that the ever-escalating fees for service, and the ever-diminishing state funds, were pushing many low-income families out of the system. After documenting this pattern, the workers gave the data to the executive director, who in turn brought it to the regional coalition of nonprofit child care agencies. A broad system of documentation among all the agencies was implemented and served an important function in the advocacy efforts of the coalition at the state level. This example also illustrates several points made above. First, it demonstrates a direct relationship between the internal actors of organizations, who can use their frontline experience to affect external social policies. Second, it illustrates the decision to have the advocacy role handled by the coalition of child care agencies, thus not putting any single agency at risk with their major contractor, in this case, the state agency.

Another external constraint relates to the very nature of the agency and its purpose. Social agencies are usually organized to deal with the most complex social problems in society; consequently, the very mission of the agency creates tensions and pressures on the professional staff. This is particularly true as the external environment is changing and the agency is under constant political pressure to change its mission or to broaden its goals. A central managerial approach to this constraint is to educate the professional staff about these pressures and to assure them that the tensions being experienced are a result of changing needs and not their own inadequacies. The involvement of staff in the change process is critical as they are key informants about the match between the agency's services and the potential changing needs. Their expertise cannot be overestimated, nor can the value of the empowerment this brings to the staff in its role in the change process.

Internally, the political process is equally important. In a social agency with an excellent and long-standing reputation in providing long-term clinical counseling services, a conflict arose between part of the social work staff that was committed to maintaining the clinical focus and part of the social work staff that was aware of a new client group with a different set of needs, needs more appropriately met by short-term, reality-based approaches. The political process that ensued over a 3-year period was a sophisticated and sensitive one, as arguments were made, data were presented, and viewpoints were influenced.

The executive director was actively involved in providing staff development and training over this period to give all staff members expertise in possible new approaches that could be taken because she recognized the role of self-interest in the situation. She thus played an effective role in initiating, facilitating, and making possible the implementation of change. Although there were conflicts and problems, in the long run, the agency was strengthened.

Another example of an internal political constraint grows out of the tendency for upper-level management to impose unrealistic expectations and demands on middle management as a result of its own administrative pressures. "Too often there is a weak relationship between the two groups, leading to little communication as well as a great deal of frustration and hostility" (Perlmutter, 1990, p. 96). Both administrative levels have the opportunity to create better channels of communication, on a formal as well as an informal level. For example, a formal monthly structured meeting can provide an opportunity for central administrators to share with other team members the new external policies that are affecting the agency. At the same time, middle managers can suggest lunch meetings with central administrators to allow for informal give and take.

The other side of this picture relates to the pressures of subordinates on their supervisors. The expectations created by the social work values of equality, collegiality, and participatory management add tensions in a formal agency system that has a bureaucratic structure. One strategy is to have a clear interpretation of agency structure and the role staff can play in the change process. In addition, a climate must be created that supports input and involvement in the initiation and implementation of change throughout the agency. Methods for empowering staff should be explored and can include, for example, creating the possibility for administrators at all levels to be responsible for setting the agendas, for chairing staff meetings, for leading staff training and development sessions, and also for initiating policy discussions. Shera and Page (1995) present a trenchant discussion of this subject.

Professional Strategies

It is clear that the changing world around us creates constant need for professional flexibility in the utilization and expansion of the approaches to delivering services. This is probably the major arena for internal agency change, the area that requires the most constant collection of information about new professional approaches and methodologies along with the ongoing collection of data concerning changing client needs.

The example discussed earlier, involving the agency in which social workers who were trained to provide long-term clinical mental health counseling were helped to expand their repertoire of skills, illustrates the professional challenge. In initiating the change process, the executive director hired a consultant who worked with the staff to think through the possibilities of new, more relevant approaches that would give them more skills while at the same time using staff experience and expertise to analyze the needs of a shifting client population. The possible professional approaches were not decreed by administrative fiat but were generated by the social workers themselves. As a result of this process, the consultant proceeded to design and implement a staff training program in which new modalities were taught without the usual resistance to change.

The design of strategies to address the political and professional issues is essential if all levels of administration are to be effective in the initiation and implementation of change. Patti and Resnick's (1985) focus on the type of leadership needed to be effective in a broad array of agency settings is most instructive, as they emphasize the need for flexibility in the leadership style to be used.

> For purposes of our model, we shall refer to leadership which falls on one end of the continuum as *directive* and that at the other end as *delegative*. The middle of the continuum we will call *participative* leadership. . . . The manager who uses a type of leadership at one point in the change process need not use that same style in successive steps. . . . While leadership may vary in each stage, it is probably true that it is easier to move from directive to more employee-centered styles, than vice versa. (pp. 275-276)

The bottom line for the effective initiation and implementation of change is that it requires careful planning before implementation is attempted. The more information that is available to inform the process, the more familiarity with different models and methods of operation, the greater the chance for success.

SUMMARY AND CONCLUSIONS

This chapter has presented some material designed to help social work administrators in their analysis and planning for the initiation and implementation of change. The discussion of the context of change, the types of change, the dilemmas inherent in change, and the models for action all form the basis for the development of intelligent strategies and approaches to the problem.

The problems are complex, and there are no clear-cut right or wrong answers. Administrators must be ready to take risks, try new things, work with new networks, and adjust or even abandon earlier approaches. The bottom line is that social work administrators must be flexible, ready to consider new ideas and new approaches to their work. And social work administrators must remember that the involvement of all levels in the organization in the process is not only appropriate but also necessary for change to be effectively implemented. Pfeffer (1992) emphasizes the importance of team effort when he states that "if you know your organization's strategy but your colleagues do not, you will have difficulty accomplishing anything" (p. 36).

REFERENCES

Ad Hoc Committee on Advocacy. (1969). The social worker as advocate: Champion of social victims. *Social Work, 14*(2), 16-22.

Aronson, R. L. (1985). Unionism among professional employees in the private sector. *Industrial and Labor Relations Review, 38,* 352-362.

Chisolm, L. B. (1995). Accountability of nonprofit organizations and those who control them: The legal framework. *Nonprofit Management and Leadership, 6*(2), 141-156.

DiBarri, E. (1985). Organizing in the Massachusetts purchase of service system. *Catalyst, 5,* 45-50.

Emery, F. E., & Trist, E. L. (1969). The causal texture of organizational environments. In F. E. Emery (Ed.), *Systems thinking* (pp. 241-257). New York: Penguin.

Galper, J. (1980). *Social work: A radical perspective.* Englewood Cliffs, NJ: Prentice Hall.

Gardner, J. W. (1990). *On leadership.* New York: Free Press.

Gibelman, M., & Kraft, S. (1996). Advocacy as a core agency program: Planning considerations for voluntary human service agencies. *Administration in Social Work, 20,* 43-59.

Gray, B., & Ariss, S. S. (1985). Politics and strategic change across organizational life cycles. *Academy of Management Review, 10,* 707-723.

Gummer, B. (1980). Organization theory. In F. D. Perlmutter & S. Slavin (Eds.), *Leadership in social administration* (pp. 22-49). Philadephia: Temple University Press.

Halbert, T. A. (1985). The cost of scruples: A call for common law protection for the professional whistleblower. *Nova Law Journal, 10,* 1-27.

Halbert, T. A. (1997). *Law and ethics in the business environment.* Minneapolis/St.Paul, MN: West.

Handy, C. (1994). *The age of paradox.* Boston: Harvard Business School Press.

Hasenfeld, Y. (1989). The challenge to administrative leadership in the social services: A prefatory essay. *Administration in Social Work, 13,* 1-11.

Hasenfeld, Y., & Schmid, H. (1989). The life cycle of human service organizations: An administrative perspective. *Administration in Social Work, 13,* 243-269.

Haveman, H. A. (1992). Between a rock and a hard place: Organizational change and performance under conditions of fundamental environmental transformation. *Administrative Science Quarterly, 37,* 48-75.

Kerson, T. S. (1998). Book review. *Administration in Social Work, 22,* 95-98.

Kotter, J. (1996). *Leading change.* Boston: Harvard Business School Press.

Kramer, R. M. (1981). *Voluntary agencies in the welfare state.* Los Angeles: University of California Press.

Levy, C. (1979). The ethics of management. *Administration in Social Work, 3,* 277-288.

National Association of Social Workers. (1996). *Code of ethics.* Washington, DC: Author.

Ostrander, S. A. (1989). Private social services: Obstacles to the welfare state? *Nonprofit and Voluntary Sector Quarterly, 18*(1), 25-45.

Patti, R. (1983). *Social welfare administration.* Englewood Cliffs, NJ: Prentice Hall.

Patti, R., & Resnick, H. (1985). Leadership and change in child welfare organizations. In H. Laird & C. Hartman (Eds.), *Handbook of child welfare* (pp. 269-288). Glencoe, IL: Free Press.

Perlmutter, F. D. (1969). A theoretical model of social agency development. *Social Casework, 50,* 467-473.

Perlmutter, F. D. (1980). The executive bind: Constraints upon leadership. In F. D. Perlmutter & S. Slavin (Eds.), *Leadership in social administration* (pp. 53-71). Philadephia: Temple University Press.

Perlmutter, F. D. (1983). Caught in between: The middle management bind. *Administration in Social Work, 8,* 147-161.

Perlmutter, F. D. (1990). *Changing hats: From social work practice to administration.* Silver Spring, MD: NASW Press.

Perlmutter, F. D., & Adams, C. T. (1994). Family service executives in a hostile environment. *Families in Society, 75,* 439-446.

Perlmutter, F. D., Bailey, D., & Netting, F. E. (in press). *Managerial supervision of the human services.* New York: Oxford University Press.

Perlmutter, F. D., & Gummer, B. (1995). Managing organizational transformation. In R. Herman and Associates (Eds.), *The Jossey-Bass handbook of nonprofit leadership and management* (pp. 227-246). San Francisco: Jossey-Bass.

Pfeffer, J. (1992). Understanding power in organizations. *California Management Review, 34,* 29-50.

Quinn, R. E., & Cameron, K. S. (1983). Organizational life cycles and shifting criteria of effectiveness: Some preliminary evidence. *Management Science, 29,* 33-51.

Richan, W. C. (1980). The administrator as advocate. In F. D. Perlmutter & S. Slavin (Eds.), *Leadership in social administration* (pp. 72-85). Philadelphia: Temple University Press.

Selznick, P. (1957). *Leadership in administration.* Evanston, IL: Row.

Shera, W., & Page, J. (1995). Creating more effective human service organizations through strategies of empowerment. *Administration in Social Work, 19,* 1-15.

Whetten, D. A. (1987). Organizational growth and decline processes. *Annual Review of Sociology, 13,* 335-358.

PART IV

Managing in Fields of Service: Issues and Challenges

Although there are universal features of social welfare administration, variations occur in specific fields of service. Differences in policy, financing, history, culture, and technology may require different management priorities. We have chosen four fields of service in which large numbers of social workers have management responsibilities. The reader will note that many of the same trends are occurring in each of these fields, although the trends are in different stages of development and implementation. For each field, the chapters set forth recent and likely future policy changes and discuss the major challenges, strategic and technical, facing managers. Exemplars and best practices are discussed in each of the chapters.

Friesen's Chapter 23, on mental health, deals with current trends in mental health policy, organization, and financing with particular emphasis on the pervasive influence of managed care on services for both children and adults. She examines tensions that are occurring in the mental health sector as managers seek to reconcile the demands of managed care with the traditional aims of mental health agencies.

As with metal health, agencies in the family and children's field are also experiencing new demands and dilemmas. These agencies confront the difficult dilemma of protecting children and, at the same time, preserving families and ensuring permanence for children. In Chapter 24, Weil argues for an integrated approach to a continuum of services for children and families, which will require more deliberate collaboration between public and private sectors and new patterns of leadership by agency directors.

No field is more rife with change and dislocation than health care. The emphasis on managed primary care, shorter hospital stays, and the growth of home-based care for the chronically ill, have forced social workers in health care to redefine their roles and functions. In Chapter 25, Weissman and Rosenberg detail these changes in the health care environment and argue that the survival of social work will hinge largely on finding new roles in health prevention and community care.

In Chapter 26, Wilber describes the field of services for older people as one in rapid transition. Faced with a burgeoning aged population, such agencies are pressed to develop a continuum of services that enable independent living, provide least restrictive care alternatives, support informal caregivers, and maximize consumer choice. Accomplishing these objectives, as she points out, will require administrators to be both collaborative and entrepreneurial.

CHAPTER TWENTY-THREE

Points of Tension:
Mental Health Administration
in a Managed Care Environment

BARBARA J. FRIESEN

The multiple and often conflicting demands historically faced by mental health administrators have recently been amplified by the implementation of managed care principles and practices. It is not possible to say that managed care has made things either better or worse. In some areas, managed care principles are compatible with the complex forces affecting mental health organizations, but in others, progress in the mental health field has been retarded or reversed by the implementation of managed care. For example, attempts to achieve more comprehensive and integrated services in response to calls for consumer- and family-centered care may be directly at odds with managed care plans' promotion of a short-term, "just enough" approach to service delivery (Institute of Medicine, 1997). In contrast, some authors argue that managed care can be a vehicle for achieving the kind of service integration that is sorely needed to most effectively serve consumers and families with the most complex needs (Ogles, Trout, Gillespie, & Penkert, 1998).

After a short history of mental health services and mental health administration, this chapter addresses current trends in mental health policy, organization, and financing of services in relation to managed care principles. Implications for administration that flow from this comparison are highlighted.

Mental health administration takes place across a wide variety of settings. These include public or private organizations where mental health services are primary, as well as mental health programs or units within larger host organizations. Increasingly, mental health administration also occurs through other arrangements: Work is accomplished primarily through contracting with providers, as in Christianson, Wholey, and Peterson's (1997) description of the health maintenance organization (HMO) manager. As Feldman and Gopelrud (1994) point out, people with mental disorders are more likely to receive treatment within the general health care sector than in the mental sector. Because much of this treatment, however, is not administratively distinguished from general medical care, this chapter is written from the perspective of administrators responsible for entire organizations or units whose focus is on services to people with mental health problems.

RECENT HISTORY AND CURRENT CONTEXT

Certainly, mental health agencies and institutions existed long before the 1960s, but that decade ushered in changes in mental health policy, treatment, and the organization and financing of services that foreshadowed many of the complex issues that challenge today's mental health administrators. Although community treatment of people with mental illness has periodically been in vogue across the last two centuries, in the 25 years before Congress passed the 1963 Comprehensive Community Mental Health Centers Act (P.L. 88-164), mental health services were largely delivered by state mental hospitals, specialized private or public mental

health agencies, and psychiatrists, psychologists, or other service providers in private practice. The focus of mental health services was almost entirely on the individual patient's treatment (and hoped-for "cure"), with little attention to services needed or received by other family members. Beginning in the 1950s, but accelerating in the 1960s and 1970s, the introduction of improved psychotropic medications was associated with a deinstitutionalization effort that moved thousands of people with mental illness out of state hospitals into a variety of community settings. A desire on the part of states to reduce the cost of state-funded mental health services was also an important factor in the reduction of the number of state hospital beds and the large-scale shift of people with mental illness to community settings, some of which provided appropriate care and treatment, whereas others were merely smaller institutional settings supported by federal rather than state funds.

The Community Mental Health Centers Act of 1963 and its amendments in 1965 introduced major changes in philosophy, funding, and organization of mental health services. First, community mental health centers were designed to serve specific geographic catchment areas, with federal funding flowing directly to communities. Central to the new approach was an emphasis on community-based rather than institutional treatment. The act also mandated attention to community education and prevention, reflecting a largely unsupported assumption that rates of mental illness could be affected by global community activities (Scull, 1992). Mental health services were to be provided to all in the catchment area that needed them, and continuity of care was to be assured across settings and across time, throughout the life span, if needed. Attention to issues such as access, availability, and appropriateness of services—and special attention to "under-served populations" (e.g., minority groups and the elderly)—was also a part of the vision for community-based services.

Much has been written about the legacy of the community mental health centers program and its failure to serve the most seriously ill (Gruenberg & Archer, 1979), although there is disagreement about the reasons for the direction taken by community mental health centers. Ahr (1991) asserts that channeling federal grants directly to communities bypassed state hospitals and other existing services, adding to the difficulty of developing coordinated services for people with serious psychiatric disorders. Other authors (e.g., Scull, 1992) maintain that there was deliberate discrimination against the seriously mentally ill by administrators of community programs, pointing to coinciding federal funding mechanisms that reinforced the pattern. Regardless of motivation, there is now little disagreement that the result of massive deinstitutionalization beginning in the 1950s, accelerating in the 1960s, and continuing to the present time is that many people with mental illness are poorly served, or not served at all, by either community or institutional programs. This is not to say that there are not excellent individual programs serving those with the most serious disabilities, but program resources cannot serve all who need help. Greenblatt and Rodenhauser (1993) note a particular problem for some adults with serious mental illness in the community: "A most distressing contradiction is now noted in our society—namely, the number of seriously ill mental patients who are homeless is now far greater than the number of such in public hospitals" (p. 98).

In the early 1970s, the negative impact of deinstitutionalization without adequate services was increasingly recognized, and new forms of community programs were developed. Although they varied widely in scope and objectives, these new community-based programs emphasized the need to replace the services received in the total institution (at least food, shelter, and psychiatric and basic medical care) with comprehensive community-based services, along with a number of new technologies such as case management and psychosocial rehabilitation (Bloom, 1984).

The 1970s also witnessed the development of an important grassroots family movement concerned with conditions both within state hospitals and in communities, with the stigma and blame often attached to people with mental illness and their families, and with development of new knowledge and treatment for mental illness. Scores of state and local grassroots organizations came together in 1979 to form the National Alliance for the Mentally Ill, which has exerted a powerful influence on national and state-level mental health policy since its inception. New knowledge about the biological basis of some mental disorders, advances in medications and other treatments, and the family advocacy movement created an environment that radically altered the direction of public services in the early 1980s.

With the passage of the federal Omnibus Budget Reconciliation Act of 1981, a newly created block grant system ended direct federal funding to community mental health centers, and mental health funds began to flow through state mental health authorities to communities. As a result of state concerns about controlling the costs associated with assuming virtually all responsibility for publicly funded mental health services, as well as successful advocacy by state and national family and consumer advocacy organizations, many states passed legislation focusing public funds on adults with the most serious mental disorders. There was a visible shift in goals regarding serious mental illness from cure to rehabilitation and management. At the same time, biomedical research into the causes and treatment of mental disorders was receiving increased financial and policy support within the National Institute of Mental Health, enthusiastically supported by the National Alliance for the Mentally Ill and other advocacy groups.

Health care costs continued to rise and spiral out of control during the decade of the 1980s, with sharp increases in inpatient care for adolescents and people needing treatment for substance abuse. This care, often inappropriate and certainly costly, contributed to a 50% increase in spending by employers for mental health and substance abuse treatment between 1986 and 1990 (England & Goff, 1993). Additional attempts to control medical costs, such as Diagnostically Related Groups (DRGs), were introduced during this period as one way of regularizing mental health practice, particularly in psychiatric hospitals.

Another federally stimulated reform, this time aimed at improving mental health services for children and adolescents, began in the 1980s. In 1984, Congress authorized the Child and Adolescent Service System Program (CASSP), embodying a community-based philosophy of systems of care that was in concert with much of the service philosophy for adults with mental illness (e.g., adequate community-based services, service coordination, comprehensive services) and of family and consumer advocacy movements in other childhood disability areas

(e.g., full family participation in decision making, individualization of services; Stroul & Friedman, 1986).

Stimulated at least in part by CASSP, a national family organization focusing exclusively on children's mental health issues, the Federation of Families for Children's Mental Health, was formed in 1989 (Friesen & Koroloff, 1990). This family organization has gained increasing membership and influence on local, state, and national policy since that time (Bryant-Comstock, Huff, & VanDenBerg, 1996).

After a decade of CASSP, during which small planning and development grants to the states laid the foundation for further development, federal dollars for expanded services (integrated systems of care) were authorized by Congress in 1993. This program, called Comprehensive Community Mental Health Services for Children with Serious Emotional Disturbances (ADAMHA Reorganization Act—P.L. 102-321, July 10, 1992), provides grants to states or local communities to build interagency systems of service. The grants are competitive; more than 40 were awarded as of October 1998, and many incorporated managed care principles.

Other notable developments that have become more visible in the 1990s include the growth of the consumer movement in adult mental health, which is challenging family control and the idea that cure is unlikely. This movement has introduced terms such as *psychiatric survivor* and *recovery* into the vocabulary of the mental health field. The consumer movement also has had considerable political influence, as noted by Elias and Navon (1996), who observe that a state restructuring process necessary to implement managed mental health care could not have been successful without the "support achieved through the active empowerment of consumers and advocates" (p. 275).

One of the most far-reaching developments of the 1990s has been the widespread application of various forms of managed care to publicly and privately funded mental health services. In response to calls from employers and government alike to control the costs of health care, this approach has been widely adopted in the mental health field. The term *managed care* is applied to organizational, fiscal, and practice arrangements that are so diverse in form and outcome as to defy description except either at a very abstract level or with regard to specific situations. Croze (1995) provides a definition that points to three specific aims. He defines managed care as "an arrangement or system in which there are financial, administrative, organization, and monitoring constructs whose end is to minimize resource allocation and maximize efficiency and quality" (p. 326).

It is important to note how applications of these principles (cost control, efficiency, and quality) may vary depending on the financing arrangements for different types of organizations. For-profit managed care companies are likely to emphasize cost containment and efficiency, with attention to quality seen as an issue related to maintaining competitiveness. Nonprofit or public managed-care entities may place more emphasis on quality, viewing efficiency and cost containment as means to enlarging the number of people who can be served. The tensions among these aims become even more apparent in mixed models, that is, when public agencies contract with for-profit companies to manage mental health services. In this case, the contracting agencies often attempt to ensure access and quality through contract stipulations and oversight (Chang et al., 1998;

Okunade & Chang, 1998). In the following section, these aims of managed care (cost control, efficiency, and quality), along with some of the predominant strategies used to achieve them, are examined in relation to current trends in the mental health field.

The remainder of this chapter addresses the profound impact that the various approaches to managing costs and care are having on the landscape of mental health services and administration. This impact was foreseen by Cummings (1995), who predicted seven paradigm shifts that would characterize the way in which mental health services would be transformed by managed care (Geller, 1996). These changes include the following shifts: (a) from seeing fewer patients for lengthy courses of treatment to seeing many clients for brief episodes of treatment; (b) from continuous treatment to brief and intermittent treatment throughout the life cycle; (c) from an emphasis on the therapist as the vehicle for change and treatment of psychopathology to the therapist as a catalyst for change, with an emphasis on growth; (d) from therapy as the most important event in the patient's life to therapy as an artificial situation (like an operating room), with significant changes occurring after scheduled therapy is finished; (e) from a view of therapy as the context for healing, with an emphasis on cure, to treatment as only the foundation for growth and change; (f) from the use of office-based individual and group psychotherapy as the main modalities to emphasis on the use of community resources; and (g) from fee-for-service as the economic basis for practice, which means the patient and therapist must constantly fight against limitations on benefits, to a situation where prospective benefits and capitation free the therapist to provide whatever services are needed.

CURRENT TRENDS, MANAGED CARE AIMS, AND MENTAL HEALTH ADMINISTRATION

This section focuses on three broad arenas that substantially influence current mental health services and administration: (a) conflicting forces regarding the appropriate definition, scope, and "territory" of mental health-related activity; (b) differences in philosophy and vision about how mental health services should be organized, financed, and delivered, especially to those with the most serious and complex needs; and (c) differing expectations about the results of mental health services. After exploring some of the major issues in each of these arenas, the three managed care aims of cost containment, efficiency, and quality are examined in light of the degree to which they are compatible or at odds with them. Implications for administrative practice are also suggested.

Definition and Scope of Mental Health Services

The conservative political climate that has characterized much of federal politics during recent years has been associated with efforts to limit the definition and scope of mental illness or disability as a qualification either for services or legal protections. Emphasis on "personal responsibility" has resulted in specific congressional action to limit support for mental health-related benefits and services. These include actions by Congress to

- severely restrict the eligibility definition for mental health-related disabilities under Supplemental Security Income (SSI) (Bazelon Center for Mental Health Law, 1998), a

move that has resulted in many children and adolescents losing benefits
- remove protections in the Individuals with Disabilities Education Act for children with disabilities, including mental or emotional disorders, with regard to behavior and discipline in the schools so that children could be segregated or expelled based on behavior that may be related to their disabilities (Association for Retarded Citizens, 1998)
- increase the extent to which juveniles can be prosecuted as adults (lower age limits, increased number of crimes for which juveniles can be prosecuted), applying adult standards for mitigating circumstances associated with mental health problems (Children's Defense Fund, 1998)

At the same time, a number of provisions explicitly designed to increase access to mental health services have increased opportunities and funding for mental health services:

- new federal funding for the Children's Health Insurance Program, or CHIP (Health Care Financing Administration, 1997)
- the Mental Health Parity Act or MHPA (Health Care Financing Administration, 1998) increased access and/or rights of people with mental or emotional disabilities through the Americans with Disabilities Act (U.S. Department of Justice, 1998)

Thus, the mental health policy climate has been dynamic in the past few years, at times posing challenges that demand incompatible organizational responses.

Compatibility of managed care aims with recent trends. Because cost containment is a core principle of managed care, the incentives within managed care plans to limit eligibility and services are compatible with the political and economic forces operating to limit eligibility for mental health services. Cost savings can be accomplished either by outright denial or limitation of benefits to individuals or by cost shifting to other systems. An Institute of Medicine report (1997) identifies cost shifting as a serious concern. Cost shifting may occur from one system or field to another (e.g., from mental health to child welfare or juvenile justice), or from private managed care plans to the public system. Cost shifting is accomplished largely by "skimming," that is, "screening out all but the healthiest enrollees" (p. 3).

With regard to the aims of efficiency and quality, managed care has also been discussed as a way to increase the number of people served through a strategy of releasing resources formerly concentrated on a few to be spread over more people within a population (increase "covered lives"). The assertion that more efficient use of resources will result in access for more people while simultaneously increasing quality has so far received mixed empirical support. For example, Chang and colleagues (1998) describe problems associated with TennCare, a managed mental health and substance abuse program in Tennessee, which spread resources previously earmarked for severely mentally ill people across the entire Medicaid population. The results were inadequate services for many TennCare enrollees, with losses in coverage and services especially pronounced for people with the most severe psychiatric disabilities. Conversely, Beinecke and Perlman (1997) found that access, appropriate utilization, quality of care, and the severity of clientele all were increased for outpatient providers in Massachusetts under managed care.

Implications for administrative practice. The rapidly changing and often contradictory policy environment creates the need for accurate and timely policy information; both the need for rapid access and the ability to digest the information will challenge the skills and the available time of many administrators. Some mental health organizations and consortia have created staff positions with responsibility for staying current with policy information and analysis through direct Internet access to government and nonprofit sources of policy documents and analysis, as well as other means.

Another central analytic task that mental health administrators must accomplish is to estimate the cost of services and accurately predict likely patterns of utilization. This analysis interacts with the controversy about the definition and scope of mental health services. Definitions of mental health that include a wider range of either people or services complicate the forecasting task and increase the probability of error and risk to the agency.

The complex and changing environment also calls for a high degree of organizational and administrative adaptability, which has outstripped the capacity of many leaders and organizations. Especially when organizations are large and complex, they may "resemble buses more than sports cars—they function best when not required to turn quickly" (Elias & Navon, 1996). The need to respond quickly has been complicated by the rapid changes in organizational relationships and structure that characterize much of today's mental health field. As noted by Elias and Navon (1996), "The industry is replete with acquisitions, mergers, buyouts, take-overs, restructuring, downsizing, and consolidation" (p. 270). Community agencies with long traditions of providing mental health services have disappeared because of either mergers or the inability to compete.

Much of this activity (i.e., consolidations, mergers, and other changes) has been in direct response to the fierce competition among mental health providers stimulated by the implementation of managed care. Mergers are often undertaken by two or more mental health organizations in response to changing from a fee-for-service to a capitated system of financing. Combining two or more organizations creates a larger client pool, may yield economies associated with consolidating administrative functions, and is intended to increase the ability of nonprofit organizations to compete with for-profit entities, an ability that has only been necessary in recent years.

In addition to the attention given to the survival and external relationships of the organization, administrative attention must also be turned to new challenges within. Watt and Kallman (1998) observe that managed care makes the work of direct service practitioners both more complex and less autonomous. Additional complexity is associated with an additional decision-making layer when the agency has a contract with a managed care company. Gatekeepers, often called case managers (Geller, 1996; Shore & Beigel, 1996), may have responsibility for pre-authorizing services, a function formerly exclusively the domain of practitioners. Munson (1996), expressing concern about the reduced autonomy of practitioners under managed care, also notes that practice arrangements that require pre-authorization mean that practitioners no longer discuss fees with clients, a transaction often believed to be a part of the therapeutic process.

In some cases, rather than contracting with an outside managed care company, the mental health organization serves as the managed care entity. In this instance, practitioners may be asked to assume considerable responsibility for managing the cost of service by working to minimize expenses on each of their cases and/or across their caseloads. In addition to monitoring the type and range of services authorized, managed care contracts may also set limits on the length of service, further reducing the autonomy of individual practitioners and requiring additional administrative monitoring.

These changes that increase complexity and reduce autonomy are likely to pose serious challenges to employee morale and may engender rebelliousness on the part of professional staff, who see conflicts between the demands of managed care and guidelines for professional ethics (Elpers & Abbot, 1992; Shore & Beigel, 1996; Watt & Kallman, 1998). In addition, responding to managed care guidelines for short-term intervention may require additional staff training or personnel changes.

Differences in Philosophy and Vision

The major contrast in philosophy and vision can be characterized by the terms *general* versus *specialized*. The more general, comprehensive vision has received considerable policy and financial support from the federal government, beginning with the Community Mental Health Centers Act of 1963. There is now broad agreement among many families, advocates, and mental health providers that adults and children with serious mental disorders should receive necessary supports and services to allow them to live in community (versus institutional) settings, integrated into their families, schools, neighborhoods, and workplaces. This more comprehensive view addresses the need to treat the "whole person," assuming that there is an interaction between emotional, physical, cognitive, and other processes. This view also recognizes the need to replace the broad array of services and supports formerly provided by institutions with similar functions in the community. However, these functions encompass a broad array of services, many of which are more commonly provided by social service than by mental health organizations.

In the area of children's mental health, this approach is associated with the term *system of care* (Stroul & Friedman, 1986), which refers to a coordinated set of services and supports to address the complex needs (physical, emotional, social, and educational) of children with mental or emotional disorders. This framework emphasizes individualized, integrated, culturally competent services that are coordinated across agencies, with full family participation in planning, decision making, and evaluation. Services should be provided in the least restrictive setting possible, avoiding out-of-home placement if possible, and emphasizing smaller, family-like settings and short-term hospitalization when necessary.

Mental health services for adults who have serious mental illness are designed within a similar framework, which acknowledges the need to address the physical and social as well as mental health treatment needs of people with mental illness. An intensive case management approach, Assertive Community Treatment (ACT), has been shown to prevent relapse and promote quality of life among this population, although it can be quite costly (Drake et al., 1998; Lehman, 1998).

The more specialized view of mental health services may also include a view of the whole person, but it concentrates resources and change efforts primarily at or within the person with the identified mental health problem. This focus and activity may exist regardless of beliefs about the etiology(ies) of mental disorders, although as Johnson, Cournoyer, and Fisher (1994) and others have demonstrated, theoretical perspectives and choices of intervention tend to be closely linked. Powerful constituencies who represent this position include operators and staff of specialized, out-of-home, out-of-community facilities (e.g., residential treatment programs, psychiatric hospitals) and individual practitioners across the mental health professions whose focus is primarily on individual treatment. The mental health professions (e.g., psychology, psychiatry, social work, psychiatric nursing) and professional schools are often highly invested in this view of mental health services, when it matches the knowledge and skills that characterize their pre-professional training programs. Traditional professional training has been severely criticized by proponents of the system of care view as constituting inadequate preparation for practice (Hanley & Wright, 1995).

Compatibility of managed care aims with recent trends. Certain consequences of managed care's emphasis on cost containment dovetail very well with aspects of the comprehensive systems of care perspective on mental health services. The preference for less expensive services, which puts limits on access to and length of stay in inpatient and residential programs, is congruent with principles of community-based and least restrictive care. Managed care also promotes a form of individualization through an emphasis on closely matching needs with the amount and duration of service. At least nominal family and consumer input is featured in many managed care plans, although participation by consumers in core decision making of managed care plans does not represent usual practice. Managed care organizations are also increasingly emphasizing consumer satisfaction, especially in competitive environments, and it is largely through this mechanism, operating more through the competitive market than through consumer satisfaction surveys, that quality is expected to improve (Cummings, 1996). Findings such of those of Lambert and colleagues (Lambert, Salzer, & Bickman, 1998) that consumer satisfaction may be unrelated to changes in pathology, however, indicate that much more attention must be paid to the definition and measurement of service effectiveness in relation to satisfaction.

Many features of managed care are consonant with a more traditional, specialized view of mental health services, which may be at odds with state-of-the-art definitions of quality. Specifically, managed care plans are often heavily biased toward a medical, acute care model, which may increase efficiency but also interrupt service continuity and be inappropriate for those with complex, ongoing needs. As Lynn (1996) points out,

> Concepts of continuity of care and assertive community treatment are not fully consistent with the theory of service delivery underlying managed care/competition. The former presumes flexible, discretionary, and distinctly non-standardized responses to individual clients. The latter depends on efficiency gains originating in a substantial degree of codification and standardization of responses to individual clients. (pp. 309-310)

In addition, many managed care programs funded with public monies are concentrating almost exclusively on Medicaid-eligible populations, which may have the effect of reducing services to those who are not Medicaid eligible (Stroul et al., 1996). On the other hand, some managed care approaches have used cost savings generated by blended funding to expand the pool of eligible recipients under the managed care plan (Cole, 1996).

Implications for administrative practice. The first reality that administrators face is that of operating in a field of opposing forces. Incentives and pressures to provide more comprehensive, continuous services resulting from federal policies such as the Comprehensive Community Mental Health Services for Children with Serious Emotional Disturbances (ADAMHA Reorganization Act—P.L. 102-321, July 10, 1992; Carpinello, Felton, Pease, DeMasi, & Donahue, 1998) are real, and funding is often contingent on demonstrating adherence to principles of comprehensive service. In addition, families and other advocates are also demanding not only that the needs of children with emotional disorders be comprehensively addressed, but that needs of the entire family be taken into account. In clear counterpoint to these pressures, managed care contracts provide incentives for short-term, specialized services provided to more clients. A number of agencies are now attempting to provide comprehensive services within a managed care system.

These conflicting pressures may make hiring, training, and supervising staff more challenging. For agencies that elect to provide comprehensive approaches, finding appropriately trained personnel may be difficult, unless candidates have received on-the-job experience in a comparable setting (Hanley & Wright, 1995). Recognizing the discrepancy between the staff skills needed within the system of care approach and the training received in many professional schools, various consultants, academics, and agency consortia have developed specialized training and certification programs for workers and supervisors (Jivanjee & Friesen, 1997).

A second important implication of a comprehensive approach to service delivery involves the agency's relationships with other organizations. Faced with the demand for more comprehensive services, few agencies can expand their array of services to meet the wide variety of needs presented by clients and families. So, for many agencies, comprehensive practice entails entering into interagency agreements both at the organizational level and at the level of direct practice. Examples of interagency agreements undertaken for the purpose of providing comprehensive services include contracts between mental health agencies and public schools to address the mental health and educational needs of children in a more integrated fashion, contracts between mental health and developmental disability programs to allow children with emotional disorders access to specialized respite care, and arrangements to out-station mental health staff within child welfare agencies. (See Chapter 14, this volume, for a further discussion of collaborative practice in administration.)

For some clients with complex needs, even the most complicated arrangements with other organizations may not result in an acceptable service package. When the needs of a client and/or family cannot be met with "off-the-shelf" services, it may be necessary to create and/or purchase a service or set of resources tailored specifically to the situation (VanDenBerg, 1993). The ability to develop highly individualized (wrap-around) services requires funds that can be used flexibly, which Burchard and Clarke (1990) define as the "linchpin" of individualized services. One of the most common approaches to achieving funding flexibility is the creation of a pool of funds contributed by several organizations (Burchard & Clarke, 1990; Cole, 1996). Working out pooled funding arrangements is an intensive, complicated process that requires much interpersonal as well as technical expertise (Stark County Family Council, 1998).

At the case level, another approach to providing comprehensive services is reflected in the development of interagency teams (Friesen & Briggs, 1995). These teams often review the most complex and vexing cases, with the dual goals of providing the most appropriate services possible and avoiding costly out-of-home care. In addition to responsibility for crafting the most clinically appropriate service package, such teams are also often responsible for management of service dollars (Cole, 1996). Many staff will need extra training, support, and supervision to function effectively on interagency teams. Although these teams can be effective in meeting their goals, staff involvement in such deliberations is costly in terms of the time devoted to such team meetings, time that is often not reimbursed either under fee-for-service or managed care arrangements.

Another major component in the comprehensive approach to providing services is extensive consumer and family involvement with mental health and other service organizations (Friesen & Koroloff, 1990; Geller, Brown, Fisher, Grudzinskas, & Manning, 1998). At the case level, many organizations now routinely involve consumers and/or family members in all deliberations about the planning, implementation, and evaluation of services. This emphasis, the result of consumer and family advocacy mounted in reaction to feelings of exclusion and blame, is represented by the phrase, "Nothing about me without me," which one mental health administrator made into lapel pins and distributed to all (Stark County Family Council, 1998). In addition to reflecting a more inclusive philosophy, there is also evidence that family participation in service planning results in better service coordination, higher satisfaction with services, and caregivers' perception that their children's needs were adequately met (Koren et al., 1997).

Many agencies have established a policy that consumers and/or family members are invited to be present in all instances when decisions are made about service planning or implementation. Translating this policy into practice, however, requires considerable administrative direction and support. Important areas of attention include reviewing intake practices and procedures to reduce the likelihood that families are discouraged by their initial interactions with the agency (Friesen & Koroloff, 1990; Koroloff, Hunter, & Gordon, 1995) and attending to the practical aspects of family participation (e.g., transportation, child care, timing and location of meetings). In addition, staff may need training and supervision regarding more inclusive practices, if this approach represents a change for them.

Recent years have also seen an increase in consumer and family involvement at the orga-

nizational and system level in such bodies as advisory committees, task forces, and boards of directors (Koroloff, Friesen, Reilly, & Rinkin, 1996). The advantages to such involvement include the design of more appropriate and consumer-friendly services and increased cultural competence of programs (Mason, Benjamin, & Lewis, 1996). There are many challenges to developing the effective involvement of consumers and/or family members in organizational and system-level decision making. These include the negative attitudes of professional staff, family challenges such as lack of transportation and child care, difficult work schedules, and lack of knowledge about how the organization/system works, along with lack of experience in serving on decision-making bodies (Koroloff et al., 1995).

Most barriers to consumer and family participation can be overcome, but this requires resources and administrative attention. In Sonoma County, California, the mental health agency has made a high commitment to the involvement of families at all levels. Family members serve on hiring committees, participate in decision making about contract preparation and renewal with partners from other systems (e.g., child welfare, juvenile justice), and serve on a Parent Advisory Council that provides advice and feedback to administrative staff (Simpson, Koroloff, Friesen, & Gac, 1998). In Stark County, Ohio, family members serve on the Policy Council of the Stark County Family Council, the coordinating body for the interagency system of care. The number of family members on the Policy Council was increased when council members, including agency directors, saw the value of family input and insisted that they should model the behavior they were promoting in their system (Stark County Family Council, 1998).

A third area where consumers and family members are much more active than in the past is evaluation. Both at the case and program level, individuals (family members and consumers) and organizations are becoming involved in the evaluation process. At the case level, involvement in evaluation is a routine function in agencies and systems that have developed a high level of consumer and family involvement. For example, in Missouri, the state mental health authority collaborated with the Missouri Coalition of Alliances for the Mentally Ill to develop and implement a system to monitor the results of the downsizing of state psychiatric hospitals (Evans & McGee, 1998). Currently, the Federation of Families for Children's Mental Health, a national support and advocacy organization, is developing a three-tiered evaluation training system for family members. The curriculum is designed to prepare family members to be consumers of research and evaluation, to participate in evaluation efforts in a variety of roles, and to assume leadership in research and evaluation activities.

Perhaps the biggest change in mental health practice and procedure during the last 10 years has been the proliferation of paid service-delivery roles for consumers and family members (Koroloff et al., 1996; Mowbray, Moxley, & Collins, 1998; Osher, 1998; Turner, Korman, Lumpkin, & Hughes, 1998). In adult mental health services, Mowbray et al. (1998) describe a peer support specialist role in which consumers supplement professionals in a case management/vocational program for individuals with severe mental illness. Participants in this program reported a number of benefits specific to the consumer-designated roles but also described a number of problems related to needs for structure, supervision, and training. The au-

thors suggest that mental health administrators provide anticipatory socialization throughout the agency (for consumers and staff alike) and provide ongoing supports for consumers in service-delivery roles.

In the children's mental health field, family members serve in a variety of capacities, including advocate (in schools, hospitals, juvenile justice system, and mental health planning meetings), case manager (with and without professional partners), member of interagency teams, and family support worker (Koroloff et al., 1996; Osher, deFur, Nava, Spencer, & Toth-Dennis, 1998). The addition of family members to agency staff rosters has proved to be beneficial in increasing access and acceptability of services and in raising awareness about the unintended impact of receiving services on children and families. Concerns associated with family members in service-delivery roles include issues such as confidentiality, questions about dual relationships (can a family member who is hired by a mental health agency still attend a support group?), role confusion and overlap, training, salary, and supervision. These issues are currently being worked out in a number of community sites around the country (Koroloff et al., 1996; Osher et al., 1998) but will continue to demand administrative attention in the near future.

Differing Expectations About the Results of Mental Health Services

The definition of *success*, that is, desired outcomes, in mental health is both value laden and highly political. A first step in designing an evaluation strategy is understanding the perspectives of various mental health constituencies with regard to results. At a minimum, the con-

	Consumer	Family	Service-Delivery System	Funders	Policymakers	Society at Large
Clinical symptoms	+	+	+	0	0	0
Functional status	+	+	+	+	+	+
Quality of life	+	+	+	0	0	0
Cost	+ 0	+ 0	+	+	+	+

Figure 23.1. Constituents' Orientation to Mental Health Outcomes

NOTE: + = Has positive investment in this outcome. 0 = does not have positive investment in this outcome.

stituencies of the mental health agency include the consumer (adult or child), the family, professional or organizational peers, funders, policymakers, and society at large. Each of these groups may have a different vision of how services should be delivered and different expectations about the results of services.

Outcomes of interest in mental health can be classified into a small number of clusters that include (a) clinical symptoms, (b) functional status, (c) quality of life, and (d) cost and cost-effectiveness. The following discussion addresses how various constituencies view these outcomes (it is summarized in Figure 23.1).

As suggested in Figure 23.1, consumers, families, and mental health organizations and their partners share many of the same values about the expected outcomes of mental health treatment. In general, these three groups all value a reduction in clinical symptoms. Consumers want relief from internal discomfort or embarrassing social relations, and families are likely to be concerned about both the subjective state of the person affected by mental disorders and possible annoying, upsetting, and/or dangerous

behavior on the part of the person with mental illness. Mental health organizations, as represented by clinicians and other treatment staff, will also be oriented toward symptom relief, as that is a central aspect of their training and focus. Funders, policymakers, and society at large are less likely to be concerned with symptoms, unless they translate into behavior that is annoying, threatening, or politically sensitive (Swanson et al., 1998).

Functional status is likely to be valued by all constituencies, although perhaps for different reasons. The concept of functioning generally includes cognitive, emotional, behavioral, and social dimensions. It involves the ability to learn and reason, to regulate emotions, to get along with family and friends, and to perform in socially acknowledged and valued roles (e.g., as student, employee, parent, friend, or neighbor). For the consumer and family, functional status is extremely important because it involves crucial issues such as the person's ability to stay in school or find and keep a job. Improved functioning is part of the raison d'être for the service-delivery system. For funders, policymakers, and society at large, interest in functioning is likely to be tied to concerns about cost, both the direct cost of services and supports and costs related to lost wages and productivity.

Interest in the quality of life as an outcome in mental health first arose in relation to adults who were being released from state hospitals and into the community, sometimes without adequate arrangements. Critics of deinstitutionalization rightly complained that moving people out of state hospitals and into group or nursing homes with deplorable physical conditions and little social life was not an improvement. The need to address the many domains of life that were attended to in the state hospital prompted the development of quality of life measures that address many aspects of a consumer's life in the community (Holcomb, Beitman, Hemme, Josylin, & Prindiville, 1998; Revicki, Simon, Chan, Katon, & Heiligenstein, 1998). For example, the Oregon Quality of Life Questionnaire (Bigelow, Gareau, & Young, 1991) addresses needs such as housing, safety, food and nutrition, employment, education, physical and mental health services, transportation, and social and recreational opportunities. A focus on the person's ability to meet the demands of society includes self and home maintenance, financial management, and use of time. A third broad dimension addresses the consumer's satisfaction with many aspects of life. The measurement of quality of life for youth with emotional or mental disorders and their families is less well developed than the method in the adult field.

Different concerns about the cost of services are also likely to be seen across constituencies. Consumers and families will be more focused on the cost of services to themselves, both because the inability to pay may reduce or block access to needed services and because of the extreme financial hardship experienced by many consumers and families related to the costs of services and medications. Service providers will be concerned about costs to families and consumers, about their own ability to manage costs within their budgets, and about costs in relation to service effectiveness. The interests of funders, policymakers, and society at large are also likely to focus on cost and effectiveness together.

The discussion of differing values and perspectives with regard to mental health outcomes thus far has focused at a rather global level, addressing broad categories of outcomes. It is important to note that when each of these areas is examined in greater depth, even greater differences emerge. For example, families whose children have serious emotional disorders may be pleased with a child's placement in a regular public school classroom with extensive social and behavioral supports, whereas some policymakers and members of the general public will question the value and/or cost-effectiveness of such an arrangement. Similarly, consumers and family members may consider the cost of expensive psychotropic medications much less relevant than their promise of symptom relief and improved functioning, but system/cost gatekeepers often deny such access (Institute of Medicine, 1997). Families and consumers are also likely to be highly interested in process issues such as access and availability of services and the extent to which services are consumer- or family-centered (Allen & Petr, 1998; Friesen & Koroloff, 1990; Koroloff & Friesen, 1997).

Compatibility of managed care principles with recent trends. Although disparities across constituencies with regard to valued outcomes are long-standing, managed care has brought these differences into sharp relief. The current behavioral health emphasis on short-term, episodic treatment (Cummings, 1995) may be appropriate for some groups, but it can be a poor fit for others. Several studies demonstrate that managed care programs undertaken by state mental health authorities reduced both access and quality of care for people with more complex and long-standing conditions, at least initially (Chang et al., 1998; Frank & Gaynor, 1994; Rohland, 1998). This is not to suggest that managed care principles cannot be successfully applied to populations with long-term requirements, but models that assume responsiveness to brief treatment and little need for ongoing monitoring and service may be inappropriate for those with the most serious mental illnesses (Glazer & Rosenbaum, 1998; Shore & Beigel, 1996; Watt & Kallmann, 1998).

In addition to the strain between a policy of brief treatment and the reality of long-term need, an emphasis on measurement of short-term results runs the risk of asking the wrong questions, obfuscating results that would be of great concern to all constituencies if they were understood. Osher (1998) asserts that all aspects of children's lives and the systems serving them are interconnected and that evaluation must take this fact into account. For example, she points out that shorter hospital stays have no meaning if children end up on the street or in juvenile detention. In this same vein, Usher (1998) enjoins managed care organizations to expand their conception of accountability of the mental health agency to include outcomes experienced by families, neighborhoods, and the community as a whole.

Implications for administrative practice. With more emphasis than ever on the formal measurement of service-delivery processes and their outcomes, it is also imperative for administrators to be clear about what outcomes are reasonable to expect from the mental health and other services provided by their organizations. Without such clarity, service programs and providers run the risk of being declared ineffective because of misunderstanding about the purposes of service or because of the application of inappropriate outcome measures. There is now a broad call for the specification of the theory on which programs are based (Savas, Fleming, & Bolig, 1998). Lynn (1996) provides an interesting example of implementation failure when such a foundation is absent.

As suggested earlier, a crucial step in preparing to assess the outcomes of service involves understanding and managing the multiple perspectives of the organization's constituencies. Once a set of outcomes is identified, the administrator and evaluation specialists can proceed to design a data collection, analysis, and feedback process that is useful to the organization and provides necessary data for external reporting requirements. The current evaluation literature is replete with strategies for obtaining a comprehensive picture of the outcomes of mental health services (Essock, 1998; Koch, Lewis, & McCall, 1998; Lunnen & Ogles, 1998; Rosenheck & Cicchetti, 1998).

The increased emphasis on data collection and service outcomes also poses challenges for the internal operation of the agency. Increased reporting requirements are likely to be seen as detracting from the "real work" of providing services to clients. When this is the case, the quality of information, as well as staff morale, can suffer. Hernandez, Hodges, and Cascardi (1998) suggest an approach that involves all stakeholders, including staff, in identifying outcomes and designing a feedback system that provides information for mid-course correction and service improvement. Rouse, Toprac, and MacCabe (1998) describe the implementation of a similar approach at the statewide level. Overall, the challenge for administrators is to build an organizational culture that encourages the use of data in service planning and delivery.

maker. They also face continuing and sometimes painful change, as new information about etiology and effective treatments makes some cherished programs (and perhaps staff) obsolete. To capitalize on rather than succumb to these changes, mental health managers will need skills in creating goal-oriented, highly adaptive organizations that have in place mechanisms for continual staff and organizational development. The ability to gather, distill, and use information from new as well as traditional sources is central to accomplishing these aims.

CONCLUSION

This chapter addresses some of the historical and recent trends in mental health that may affect the ability of administrators to effectively manage their organizations and/or systems. In particular, the realities of managed care and its interaction with competitive, dynamic policy and interorganizational environments pose significant challenges for today's mental health administrators. Now more than ever, it seems that balancing attention to external issues with appropriate attention to internal needs requires a wide range of skills. This suggests that successful administrators may need to be adept at obtaining the services of people with specialized skills (e.g., policy and fiscal analysis, evaluation, personnel management, and marketing) to meet changing and sometimes highly technical needs.

Mental health organizations are also changing from relatively predictable, somewhat protected systems to organizations with permeable boundaries, both in relation to other organizations and virtual organizations and with regard to the lines between staff, client, and policy-

REFERENCES

ADAMHA Reorganization Act—P.L. 102-321. (July 10, 1992).

Ahr, P. R. (1991). Administering state mental health programs: The evolution of the contemporary state agency. In C. Hudson & A. J. Cox (Eds.), *Dimensions of state mental health policy* (pp. 230-241). New York: Praeger.

Allen, R. I., & Petr, C. G. (1998). Rethinking family-centered practice. *American Journal of Orthopsychiatry, 68*(1), 4-15.

Association for Retarded Citizens. (1998, August 24). *Summary and background of the current issues regarding IDEA* [On-line]. Available: http://thearc.org/ga/summary_idea.htm

Bazelon Center for Mental Health Law. (1998, November 5). *Children's SSI program* [On-line]. Available: http://www.bazelong.org/kidsssi.html

Beinecke, R. H., & Perlman, S. B. (1997). The impact of the Massachusetts Managed Mental Health/Substance Abuse program on outpatient mental health clinics. *Community Mental Health Journal, 33*(5), 377-385.

Bigelow, D. A., Gareau, M. J., & Young, D. J. (1991). *Quality of Life Questionnaire.* Portland: Oregon Health Sciences University.

Bloom, B. L. (1984). *Community mental health: A general introduction.* Monterey, CA: Brookes-Cole.

Bryant-Comstock, S., Huff, B., & VanDenBerg, J. (1996). The evolution of the family advocacy movement. In B. A. Stroul (Ed.), *Children's mental health: Creating systems of care in a changing society* (pp. 359-374). Baltimore: Paul H. Brookes.

Burchard, J. D., & Clarke, R. T. (1990). The role of individualized care in a service delivery system for children and adolescents with severely maladjusted behavior. *The Journal of Mental Health Administration, 17,* 48-60.

Carpinello, S., Felton, C. J., Pease, E. A., DeMasi, M., & Donahue, S. (1998). Designing a system for managing the performance of mental health managed care: An example from New York State's Prepaid Mental Health Plan. *Journal of Behavioral Health Services Research, 25*(3), 269-278.

Chang, C. F., Kiser, L. J., Bailey, J. E., Martins, M., Gibson, W. C., Schaberg, K. A., Mirvis, D. M., & Applegate, W. B. (1998). Tennessee's failed managed care program for mental health and substance abuse services. *Journal of the American Medical Association, 279*(11), 864-869.

Children's Defense Fund. (1998, January 12). *Myths about S.10 and the truth about youth violence and juvenile justice* [On-line]. Available: http://www.childrensdefense.org/s10_myths.html

Christianson, J. B., Wholey, D., & Peterson, M. S. (1997). Strategies for managing service delivery in HMOs: An application to mental health care. *Medical Care Research and Review, 54*(2), 200-222.

Cole, R. F. (1996). The Robert Wood Johnson Foundation's mental health services program for youth. In B. A. Stroul (Ed.), *Children's mental health: Creating systems of care in a changing society.* Baltimore: Paul H. Brookes.

Croze, C. (1995). *Medicaid waivers: The shape of things to come.* Paper presented at the Fifth Annual National Conference on State Mental Health Agency Services Research and Program Evaluation, Alexandria, VA.

Cummings, N. A. (1995). Impact of managed care on employment and training: A primer for survival. *Professional Psychology: Research and Practice, 26,* 5-9.

Cummings, N. A. (1996). Behavioral health after managed care: The next golden opportunity for mental health practitioners. In N. A. Cummings, M. S. Pallak, & J. L. Cummings (Eds.), *Surviving the demise of solo practice: Mental health practitioners prospering in the era of managed care* (pp. 27-40). Madison, CT: Psychosocial Press.

Drake, R. E., McHugo, G. J., Clark, R. E., Teague, G. B., Xie, H., Miles, K., & Ackerson, T. H. (1998). Assertive community treatment for patients with co-occurring severe mental illness and substance use disorder: A clinical trial. *American Journal of Orthopsychiatry, 68*(2), 201-215.

Elias, E., & Navon, M. (1996). Implementing managed care in a state mental health authority: Implications for organizational change. *Smith College Studies in Social Work, 66*(3), 269-292.

Elpers, J. R., & Abbot, B. K. (1992). Public policy, ethical issues, and mental health administration. *Administration & Policy in Mental Health, 19*(6), 437-447.

England, M. J., & Goff, V. V. (1993). Health reform and organized systems of care. *New Directions for Mental Health, 59,* 5-12.

Essock, S. M. (1998). Management approaches for mental health program report cards [comment]. *Community Mental Health Journal, 34*(1), 107-109.

Evans, C. J., & McGee, C. (1998). Collaboration between a state alliance for the mentally ill and a state mental health authority in monitoring the consequences of downsizing. *Journal of Behavioral Health Services Research, 25*(1), 43-50.

Feldman, S., & Gopelrud, E. N. (1994). Mental health services. In R. J. Taylor & S. B. Taylor (Eds.), *The AUPHA manual of health services management* (pp. 611-622). Gaithersburg, MD: Aspen.

Frank, R. G., & Gaynor, M. (1994). Organizational failure and transfers in the public sector: Evidence from an experiment in the financing of mental health care. *Journal of Human Resources, 29*(1), 108-125.

Friesen, B. J., & Briggs, H. E. (1995). The organization and structure of service coordination mechanisms. In B. J. Friesen & J. Poertner (Eds.), *From case management to service coordination for children with emotional, behavioral, or mental disorders: Building on family strengths* (pp. 63-94). Baltimore: Paul H. Brookes.

Friesen, B. J., & Koroloff, N. M. (1990). Family-centered services: Implications for mental health administration and research. *Journal of Mental Health Administration, 17*(1), 13-25.

Geller, J. L. (1996). Mental health services of the future: Managed care, unmanaged care, mismanaged care. *Smith College Studies in Social Work, 66*(3), 223-239.

Geller, J. L., Brown, J. M., Fisher, W. H., Grudzinskas, A. J., Jr., & Manning, T. D. (1998). A national survey of "consumer empowerment" at the state level. *Psychiatric Services, 49*(4), 498-503.

Glazer, W. M., & Rosenbaum, J. F. (1998). Managed care versus managed money. *Journal of Clinical Psychiatry, 59*(Suppl. 2), 62-66.

Greenblatt, M., & Rodenhauser, P. (1993). Mental health administration: Changes and challenges. *Administration & Policy in Mental Health, 21*(2), 97-100.

Gruenberg, E., & Archer, J. (1979). Abandonment of responsibility for the seriously mentally ill. *Millbank Memorial Fund Quarterly/Health and Society, 57,* 485-506.

Hanley, J. H., & Wright, H. (1995). Child mental health professionals: The missing link in child mental health reform. *Journal of Child and Family Studies, 4*(4), 383-388.

Health Care Financing Administration. (1997, September 17). *Children's health insurance program* [On-line]. Available: http://www.hcfa.gov/init/kidssum.htm

Health Care Financing Administration. (1998, March 24). *HIPAA: The Health Insurance Portability and Accountability Act of 1996* [On-line]. Available: http://hcfa.gov/hipaa/mhpqsnas.htm

Hernandez, M., Hodges, S., & Cascardi, M. (1998). The ecology of outcomes: System accountability in children's mental health. *Journal of Behavioral Health Services Research, 25*(2), 136-150.

Holcomb, W. R., Beitman, B. D., Hemme, C. A., Josylin, A., & Prindiville, S. (1998). Use of a new outcome scale to determine best practices. *Psychiatric Services, 49*(5), 583-585, 595.

Institute of Medicine. (1997). *Managing managed care: Quality improvement in behavioral health.* Washington, DC: National Academy Press.

Jivanjee, P. R., & Friesen, B. J. (1997). Shared expertise: Family participation in interprofessional training. *Journal of Emotional and Behavioral Disorders, 5*(4), 211-215.

Johnson, H. C., Cournoyer, D. E., & Fisher, G. A. (1994). Measuring worker cognitions about parents of children with mental and emotional disabilities. *Journal of Emotional and Behavioral Disorders, 2*(2), 99-108.

Koch, J. R., Lewis, A., & McCall, D. (1998). A multistakeholder-driven model for developing an outcome management system. *Journal of Behavioral Health Services Research, 25*(2), 151-162.

Koren, P. E., Paulson, R. I., Kinney, R., Yatchmenoff, D., Gordon, L. J., & DeChillo, N. (1997). Service coordination in children's mental health: An empirical study from the caregiver's perspective. *Journal of Emotional and Behavioral Disorders, 5*(3), 130-137.

Koroloff, N. M., & Friesen, B. J. (1997). Challenges in conducting family-centered mental health services research. *Journal of Emotional and Behavioral Disorders, 5*(3), 130-137.

Koroloff, N. M., Friesen, B. J., Reilly, L. L., & Rinkin, J. (1996). The role of family members in systems of care. In B. A. Stroul (Ed.), *Children's mental health: Creating systems of care in a changing society* (pp. 409-426). Baltimore: Paul H. Brookes.

Koroloff, N. M., Hunter, R., & Gordon, L. J. (1995). *Family involvement in policy-making: A final report on the Families in Action project.* Portland, OR: Research and Training Center on Family Support and Children's Mental Health.

Lambert, W., Salzer, M. S., & Bickman, L. (1998). Clinical outcome, consumer satisfaction, and ad hoc ratings of improvement in children's mental health. *Journal of Consulting Clinical Psychology, 66*(2), 270-279.

Lehman, A. F. (1998). Public health policy, community services, and outcomes for patients with schizophrenia. *Psychiatric Clinics of North America, 21*(1), 221-231.

Lunnen, K. M., & Ogles, B. M. (1998). A multiperspective, multivariable evaluation of reliable change. *Journal of Consulting and Clinical Psychology, 66*(2), 400-410.

Lynn, L. E., Jr. (1996). Assume a network: Reforming mental health services in Illinois. *Journal of Public Administration Research Theory, 6*(2), 297-314.

Mason, J. L., Benjamin, M. P., & Lewis, S. A. (1996). The cultural competence model: Implications for child and family mental health services. In C. A. Heflinger & C. T. Nixon (Eds.), *Families and the mental health system for children and adolescents: Policy, services, and research* (pp. 165-190). Thousand Oaks, CA: Sage.

Mowbray, C. T., Moxley, D. P., & Collins, M. E. (1998). Consumers as mental health providers: First-person accounts of benefits and limitations. *The Journal of Behavioral Health Services Research, 25*(4), 397-411.

Munson, C. E. (1996). Autonomy and managed care in clinical social work practice. *Smith College Studies in Social Work, 66*(3), 241-260.

Ogles, B. M., Trout, S. C., Gillespie, D. K., & Penkert, K. S. (1998). Managed care as a platform for cross-system integration. *The Journal of Behavioral Health Services Research, 25*(3), 252-268.

Okunade, A. A., & Chang, C. F. (1998). Relative success of state-managed behavioral health care: Does the financing structure play any role? *Journal of Health Care Finance, 24*(3), 27-40.

Osher, T. W. (1998). Outcomes and accountability from a family perspective. *The Journal of Behavioral Health Services Research, 25*(2), 230-232.

Osher, T. W., deFur, E., Nava, C., Spencer, S., & Toth-Dennis, D. (1998). *New roles for families in systems of care* (Vol. 1). Washington, DC: American Institutes for Research, Center for Effective Collaboration and Practice.

Revicki, D. A., Simon, G. E., Chan, K., Katon, W., & Heiligenstein, J. (1998). Depression, health-related quality of life, and medical cost outcomes of receiving recommended levels of antidepressant treatment. *Journal of Family Practice, 47*(6), 446-452.

Rohland, B. M. (1998). Implementation of Medicaid-managed mental health care in Iowa: Problems and solutions. *Journal of Behavioral Health Services Research, 25*(3), 293-299.

Rosenheck, R., & Cicchetti, D. (1998). A mental health program report card: A multidimensional approach to performance monitoring in public sector programs. *Community Mental Health Journal, 34*(1), 85-106.

Rouse, L. W., Toprac, M. G., & MacCabe, N. A. (1998). The development of a statewide continuous evaluation system for the Texas Children's Mental Health Plan: A total quality management approach. *Journal of Behavioral Health Services Research, 25*(2), 194-207.

Savas, S. A., Fleming, W. M., & Bolig, E. E. (1998). Program specification: A precursor to program monitoring and quality improvement. A case study from Boysville of Michigan. *Journal of Behavioral Health Services Research, 25*(2), 208-216.

Scull, A. (1992). From asylum to community: Mental health policy in modern America [Book review]. *Milbank Quarterly, 70*(3), 557-579.

Shore, M. F., & Beigel, A. (1996). The challenges posed by managed behavioral health care [Sounding Board]. *The New England Journal of Medicine, 334*(2), 116.

Simpson, J. S., Koroloff, N. M., Friesen, B. J., & Gac, J. (1998). *Promising practices in family-provider collaboration* (Vol. 2). Washington, DC: American Institutes for Research, Center for Effective Collaboration and Practice.

Stark County Family Council. (1998). *The seamless system of care manual* [On-line]. Available: http://www.starkfamilycouncil.org/manual/contents.html

Stroul, B. A., & Friedman, R. M. (1986). *A system of care for children and youth with severe emotional disturbances* (Rev. ed.). Washington, DC: Georgetown University Child Development Center.

Stroul, B. A., Friedman, R. M., Hernandez, M., Roebuck, L., Lourie, I. S., & Koyanagi, C. (1996). System of care in the future. In B. A. Stroul (Ed.), *Children's mental health: Creating systems of care in a changing society* (pp. 591-612). Baltimore: Paul H. Brookes.

Swanson, J., Swartz, M., Estroff, S., Borum, R., Wagner, R., & Hiday, V. (1998). Psychiatric impairment, social contact, and violent behavior: Evidence from a study of outpatient-committed persons with severe mental disorder. *Social Psychiatry and Psychiatric Epidemiology, 33*(Suppl. 1), S86-94.

Turner, M., Korman, M., Lumpkin, M., & Hughes, C. (1998). Mental health consumers as transitional aides: A bridge from the hospital to the community. *The Journal of Rehabilitation, 64*(4), 35-44.

U.S. Department of Justice. (1998, February 15). *Enforcing the ADA* [On-line]. Available: http://www.usdoj.gov/crt/ada/octdec98.htm

Usher, C. L. (1998). Managing care across systems to improve outcomes for families and communities. *Journal of Behavioral Health Services Research, 25*(2), 217-229.

VanDenBerg, J. (1993). Integration of individualized services into the system of care for children and adolescents with emotional disabilities. *Administration and Policy in Mental Health, 20*(4), 247-258.

Watt, J. W., & Kallman, G. L. (1998). Managing professional obligations under managed care: A social work perspective. *Family and Community Health, 21*(2), 40-50.

CHAPTER TWENTY-FOUR

Services for Families and Children: The Changing Context and New Challenges

MARIE WEIL

This chapter focuses on current and emerging trends in the field of services for families and children, and it explicates major issues that will face administrators and planners in the next few decades as they promote better outcomes for America's children and families and seek to use resources to maximum effect. Rapid change is taking place in this field, and the arrangements of services are expected to continue to shift more toward preventive, home-based, and community-oriented services. Refinements and reorganizations are expected in the longer-established services related to authoritative intervention in families and planning for perma-

nency through reunification, kinship care, foster care, or adoption.

One of the difficulties frequently encountered when discussing this broad field is that terminology changes depending on where people work or what service areas they study. In an effort to clarify terminology relating to this field of practice, this chapter will use the following definitions, which are expected to become more common as the balance of services shifts in the new millennium. A single continuum of services for the entire field is envisioned moving from the least to most intrusive interventions in family life. *Family support,* the voluntary side of the continuum, denotes the range of developmental, preventive, home- and community-based services that are designed to help families function more effectively—and particularly to help parents successfully nurture, protect, and support their children and prepare them for roles in society. In this broad continuum, *family preservation* and *intensive family preservation* are seen as services that are the fulcrum, or balance point, between broad efforts to nurture and support families and state-sanctioned interventions to protect endangered children. *Child welfare* denotes the set of interventions that begin when a child is reported to public child welfare as being at risk of abuse and neglect; these interventions protect children when family functioning has broken down and assure permanency for children to promote their safety and continued development.

Administrators in this field have the particular challenge of responding to these diverse expectations, mediating these forces, and supporting workers who face difficult practice issues and decisions. They also face complex personnel, financing/resource allocation, planning, and evaluation issues. Boundary-spanning skills are critical in responding to issues of cross-system management, community connections, and outcome-focused service delivery. Creating and maintaining organizational cultures congruent with new expectations—for staff roles, for family-centered practice, and for collaboration—is a tall order. Leadership and strategies for strengthening services and improving organizational and interorganizational decision making will be critical to improving outcomes for America's children and families. This chapter looks first at the policy and political context, then considers the issues and directions in the service system, and concludes

with strategic choices administrators face in their efforts to strengthen their organizations, strengthen the child and family service system, and improve outcomes for America's children (Usher, 1998; Usher, Gibbs, & Wildfire, 1995).

THE POLICY CONTEXT

Roots of current controversies. Current value, policy, and political conflicts in the field of services for children and families parallel earlier divergences in policies and perspectives on intervention in family life (Costin, Karger, & Stoesz, 1996; McGowan, 1983). The weakening not only of the reluctant welfare state but also of the safety net for families and children now places many families at risk and may expose children and youth to the types of risks that early social work reformers sought to curtail (Blank, 1997; Courtney, 1998; Janssen, 1997; McGowan, 1983; Pelton, 1989). Early social workers were leaders in the development of both public child welfare and neighborhood-based services for children. They were also major leaders in forming the Federal Children's Bureau and in establishing Juvenile Courts. Women of Chicago's Hull-House—most particularly Jane Addams (1910, 1930), Grace Abbott (1938), and Sophonisba Breckinridge (1934)—worked intensively on these efforts, along with numerous other social workers and activists (Deegan, 1990).

Early service development trends illustrate tensions that still operate in the field related to society's view of children and of the rights of parents (Downs, Costin, & McFadden, 1996). Many leaders and organizations committed to protecting children promulgated a movement to "rescue" children from unworthy families—

who were members of the "dangerous classes"—by placing them with farm families in the Midwest and southern Midwest, away from their families in major northern U.S. cities (Brace, 1872; Brown & Weil, 1992). As a result of this approach, large numbers of poor children were separated from their parents and either placed in institutions or indentured to other families (Schene, 1998).

In 1874, the Society for the Prevention of Cruelty to Children was organized to protect children from maltreatment (Wells, 1995). During this same period, states developed legislation to protect children; these laws, with some variation, focused on abuse or physical cruelty (Giovannoni & Becerra, 1979; Wells, 1995). At this time, the Charity Organization Societies were also developed, the earliest efforts to coordinate service, eliminate overlaps, and develop cost-efficiency (Betten & Austin, 1990).

Another approach fostered by the Settlement Movement helped poor immigrant children by teaching their parents how to support and educate their children, speak English, obtain jobs, and become citizens and engaged members of their communities (Addams, 1960; Deegan, 1990). These different approaches, one focused on rescuing children from dangerous situations and the other on helping families perform their basic functions, thus have been and remain tensions in America's service system for families and children.

As the service system has grown, the child-rescue approach and community-based service approach have coexisted, and in some periods, the pendulum of social policy has swung forcefully one way or the other, with the child rescue approach usually prevailing (de Lone, 1979). Titles IV and V of The Social Security Act of 1935 (U.S. Statutes at Large 1935-1936) established Aid to Dependent Children to maintain poor children in their own homes and provided some limited funding to encourage states to develop child welfare services. The mid-20th century White House Conference on Children defined goals for America's children and helped to set the service development agenda of the 1960s (Brown & Weil, 1992). Orshanky's (1963) research indicated that one fourth to one third of American children lived in families with incomes below the poverty line. With the efforts of the Great Society programs and increased funding, the poverty rate for children dropped to 13.8% by 1969 (Children's Defense Fund, 1990). The political winds shifted in the 1970s with conservative political leadership, but some progressive policies were still instituted. However, in the 1980s, the neo-conservative movement reached gale force: Program funding was reduced, and programs were dismantled. As noted by Iatridis (1988), these reactionary policies "instituted a broad . . . destructive national policy of underdevelopment that affects all Americans" (p. 11). Once again, however, those most directly affected by this disinvestment are children of color, who are disproportionately investigated, taken into care, and placed—often still not attaining the desired permanency with a family or foster caretakers. Billingsley and Giovannoni (1972) wrote about "children of the storm," noting that African American children particularly are overrepresented in and underserved by the system.

Recent policy directions. In 1978, a landmark policy reestablished some rights of federally recognized American Indian groups to determine the care, protection, and adoption of their children. The Indian Child Welfare Act, Public Law 95-608 (1978 and since revised) gave tribal governments more rights in determining custody of Indian children. Under this act, placement preferences are to be considered first with extended kin or with Indian foster parents. A more preventive approach to services for Indian communities was outlined in the legislation but not funded, and tribes throughout the nation are still struggling to offer more appropriate, tribal-based preventive and supportive services (Pecora, Whittaker, & Maluccio, 1992; Sanders, 1998; vander Straeten & Sanders, 1998).

In 1974, The Child Abuse Prevention and Treatment Act (since amended) was passed. It provided definitions of abuse and neglect and laid out provisions for investigation, intervention, and treatment (Wells, 1995). The Adoption Assistance and Child Welfare Act, Public Law 96-272 (1980) specified that the purpose of services was "to protect and promote the welfare of all children and to prevent the separation of children from their families wherever family maintenance is desirable and possible"—and where not possible to provide safety and make a timely plan for permanency (Brown & Weil, 1992, p. 184; Conte, 1983; Magazino, 1983; Schorr, 1989). It introduced the concept of "reasonable efforts" to prevent placement. The act also specified reforms for home-based services, placement prevention, and reunification and established foster care funding in Title IV-E of The Social Security Act. However, child protective services (CPS) per se remained the predominant mode of service (Kamerman & Kahn, 1989; Shyne & Schroeder, 1978), and the resources to refocus on supportive and preventive services were not forthcoming. Despite program development and growing research results indicating the need for and success of services designed to strengthen families—particu-

larly parents' abilities to nurture and support their children (Bronfenbrenner, 1987; Schorr, 1989, 1997; Weissbourd & Kagan, 1989)—a backlash has continued against family-centered services (Besharov, 1998; Gelles, 1996; Jones, Neuman, & Shyne, 1976; Maluccio & Sinanoglu, 1981).

In the 1990s, the general economic climate and policies of social disinvestment have continued. The rate of child poverty rose to 22.3% in 1983. In 1996, at least one in five American children lived in poverty (O'Hare, 1996); In 1998, 40% of all Americans who were poor were children, while the poverty rate for African American children was 37% and for Hispanic/Latino children 34% (U.S. Census Bureau, 1999). These percentages of child poverty are higher than any other industrialized nation (Blank, 1997). Currently, the move from Aid to Families With Dependent Children (AFDC) to Temporary Assistance to Needy Families (TANF) is being evaluated; early evaluations indicate that although more parents are entering the workforce under TANF, their families are not getting out of poverty (Burtless, 1997; Institute for Wisconsin's Future, 1999a; Rooney, 1998). As TANF policies continue over time, families sanctioned off or no longer eligible for the program are likely to greatly increase the number of referrals to child welfare services (Center for Urban Economic Development, 1998; Courtney, 1998; Sherman, Amey, Duffield, Ebb, & Weinstein, 1998; Shook, 1999). Economic policies that further disadvantage low-income families affect child abuse and neglect, as child abuse statistics typically vary with unemployment rates (Blank, 1997).

Public Law 103-66, The Family Preservation and Support Initiative (1993) provided funding to states to plan and develop family support and family preservation services. This was a major move to build the preventive side of the service continuum and to promote means to keep children safe at home where possible. It was also an advance in community-oriented legislation, with its aim "to help communities build a system of family support services to assist vulnerable children and families prior to maltreatment" (Schene, 1998, p. 28). It was also an advance because it provided preservation services to families facing risk of placement who are able to mobilize their resources, learn new skills, and demonstrate commitment to safeguarding their children. Intensive and less intensive models of family preservation have since developed in most states (Hodges, 1994; Kinney, Haapala, & Booth, 1990; Whittaker, Kinney, Tracy, & Booth, 1990). P.L. 103-66 is one of the strongest supports for family and neighborhood-centered services since the ascendance of the settlements and the progressive movement. It has created a backlash among those who advocate for child rescue philosophy and seriously question the ability of adults to learn and use more supportive parenting skills; critics also question the ability of staff to accurately determine risk and select families appropriate for intensive intervention (Besharov, 1998; Gelles, 1996).

Reflecting the growing interest in intervention research, many family preservation programs and other family-based services have been evaluated. The results indicate considerable success, suggest means of program improvement, and identify problems in service targeting, model clarity, and measurement (Pecora, Fraser, Nelson, McCroskey, & Meezan, 1995; Whittaker et al., 1990). In a study of effectiveness of broadly defined family preservation and related services with control or comparison conditions, Fraser, Nelson, and Rivard (1997)

estimated effect sizes to compare programs. Their findings in this sample of rather diverse programs indicated that family preservation services "may be useful in preventing youth violence" and that family-focused psychoeducation in mental health "may prevent or delay relapse and hospitalization" (p. 138). Fairly promising findings were noted in the small number of reunification programs studied, and results in family preservation in child welfare were quite varied (as were the interventions). This careful study provides guidance for further research and indicates the need for both clarity of intervention model and appropriateness of instrumentation.

Although considerably more research is needed to test effects with subpopulations, it should be recognized that preventing placement is not the single outcome sought and that refined instrumentation is one key to improved research. In North Carolina, a 5-year evaluation study by Kirk (1994) using the North Carolina Family Assessment Scale indicated statistically significant relationships between strengths on the five domains and placement prevention, and between problems on the five domains and out-of-home placement (see also North Carolina Division of Social Services, 1999). The study findings show convincingly that "interventions are capable of improving family functioning across all the measured domains, albeit incrementally, and that these improvements in family functioning are statistically associated with placement prevention" (North Carolina Division of Social Services, 1999, p. 3). In sum, the 5-year North Carolina evaluation study indicates that

significant shifts in family functioning . . . occur during [services] that are associated with positive treatment outcomes; placement prevention rates have been very steady, ranging between 88% and 93% each year since 1994; [this] is a very cost-effective program and yields a favorable cost/benefit ratio; and benefits appear to accrue for families that have received the service (measured by living arrangements of families, service use, by families and their apparent abilities to handle family stress). (North Carolina Division of Social Services, 1999, p. 4)

Behind the positive findings over this period may be careful efforts to avoid model drift, to remain focused on the safety of children, and to operate from a clear strengths perspective in delivery of services.

Despite backlash (Myers, 1994), The Adoption and Safe Families Act, Public Law 105-89 (1997) was re-authorized. It increased family preservation and support program funding and responded to concerns for a front-burner stance on protection by renaming the effort "Promoting Safe and Stable Families." This act seeks to speed decision making and permanency by moving children more quickly from foster homes to permanent ones, terminating parental rights and promoting adoption. These goals echo those of P.L. 96-272 to promote permanency and speedy decision making. The move from economic assistance through AFDC to TANF will also greatly affect the lives of vulnerable children (Knitzer & Bernard, 1997). As Courtney (1998) has pointed out, "the goals of welfare reform, which is focused on adult self-sufficiency, compete with the goals of the child welfare system, which focuses on safe, nurturant child rearing" (p. 101).

These policy conflicts give evidence of the lack of an integrated family policy approach in the U.S. (Kamerman & Kahn, 1978, 1989). Research is being conducted to determine the effects of TANF (Burtless, 1997; Institute for

Wisconsin's Future, 1999b). In the future, longer-term research is needed to track labor force participation, family economic status, child welfare statistics, and child and family well-being for the working and nonworking poor (Rooney, 1998). The full impact of the devolution of funds to the states and the incongruence between TANF-oriented programs and family-centered programs remains to be seen. The United States also lacks the social development approach adopted by many nations in the global south, which emphasizes education and human development as the way to strengthen both the economy and civil society (Friedmann, 1996; Midgley, 1995). Despite the promise of the U.N. Declaration on the Rights of the Child adopted by hundreds of nations, the United States has never become a signatory (United Nations, 1949).

A coherent family policy would articulate support for and investment in families and children, especially in healthy child development, adult development, education, and skills. It would specify connective, preventive, supportive, treatment, preservation, and child welfare services. It would connect child well-being and family economic status. A comprehensive social development-focused family policy would cover at least the following nine sectors: (a) equal protections and fair access to opportunity, (b) economic security, (c) housing, (d) health care, (e) child care, (f) education, (g) supportive preservation and protective social services, (h) supports for community-based systems of care and community-building strategies, and (i) community-based economic and social development (Brown, 1992; Midgley, 1995; Mulroy & Shay, 1998; Weil, 1997).

Many of the problems that overwhelm the child welfare system are caused by the cumulative effect of the lack of sound policies to nurture and protect families in each of these areas. Social services, therefore, are left to take on the additional burdens related to major social problems, such as lack of affordable housing and lack of income security, as well as the complex service issues such as treatment and appropriate placement for children with dual diagnoses who are in care of the child welfare system.

Other nations have done significantly better in this regard. The United Kingdom and several other nations have adopted the "Looking After Children" assessment and outcome tracking system for children in care, which focuses on child well-being across a number of developmental domains (Jackson & Kilroe, 1995; Ward, 1995), whereas many U.S. programs are still problem-centered. For more than a decade, programs in Sweden have provided foster care for whole families; such efforts are beginning to be tested here. Family Group Conferencing (FGC), which was developed in New Zealand as a means of helping extended families and their support systems plan for the safety and well-being of abused or neglected children, has been tested in Newfoundland and Labrador. Early research indicates that FGC has demonstrated effectiveness in (a) placing the family at the center of planning; (b) integrating efforts of family, community, and government; (c) facilitating concurrent planning; and (d) ensuring the safety of child and adult family members while strengthening family unity (Burford & Pennell, 1996, pp. 45-46). FGC is now being tested in several U.S. sites (Pennell & Burford, in press). Both family preservation and FGC offer useful models for helping families come to grips with abuse and neglect. Where these efforts cannot succeed because of severity of problems, placement and long-term planning for children should begin immediately to increase the chances of children attaining stability

and consistent nurture in permanent homes. Sound economic policies for the underclass, the long-term poor, and the working poor, as well as investment in social development, would be major parts of a comprehensive family policy approach (Friedmann, 1996; Midgley, 1995; Wilson, 1987). Globalization of the economy and growing forces for privatization make such investments even more critical (Fisher & Karger, 1997). Poverty is not supposed to be a sufficient reason to remove a child from home; however, lacking other options and resources, it happens (Brown, Finch, Northen, Taylor, & Weil, 1982; Pelton, 1989).

A comprehensive family policy would integrate the sectors noted above; if that seems politically improbable, it should still be a major goal to develop and amend policies in each sector so that they are complementary with an investment in the health, social development, and economic security of families. Many of the problems encountered in efforts to coordinate services at local and state levels are caused by the conflicting policies across major agencies at federal and state levels (Center for the Study of Social Policy & Children's Defense Fund, 1994). A coordinated even if not comprehensive policy could pave the way for service coordination, interagency collaboration, and holistic approaches to increase child and family well-being. A coordinated approach could also promote positive outcomes for children when the various systems that affect families and children are in conflict.

Despite the problems cited, recent child welfare policies are moving to shore up both sides of the service continuum—family support and child protection and permanency. Indeed, although there are risks in the devolution of funding to states and increased local decision making with regard to equity and access, devolution may also provide states with the means to adopt outcome-oriented services and develop self-evaluation to guide policies and practice toward positive outcomes (Usher, 1995, 1998).

P.L. 99-457, later amended and incorporated into IDEA, P.L. 102-119, points the way to family-centered policies and practice in providing early intervention services to families with an infant experiencing developmental delays or disabilities. Part H of IDEA provides flexibility to states in structure of implementation, and it is family-centered in its assessment and service provision. In addition, it emphasizes parent/professional and interprofessional collaboration for service delivery and family involvement in all aspects of the case management process (Harbin & McNulty, 1990; Zipper, Rounds, & Weil, 1993). The recent public health-based in-home service programs also offer support and preventive services to families and child health services, giving another impetus to family-centered, holistically oriented services. Coordinated, family-focused policy would weave together and encourage collaboration among supportive services for families and the complex public sector systems for child welfare, child mental health, juvenile, and health services.

In several ways, P.L. 105-89 reframes the permanency planning intended but never adequately funded under P.L. 96-272, while the family preservation/family support legislation gives long-overdue recognition of the need to help families before total breakdown has occurred. In combination, The Family Preservation and Support Initiative, P.L. 103-66, and The Adoption and Safe Families Act, P.L. 105-89, offer legislation and funding (a) to build parts of the preventive side of the continuum and (b) to increase focus on timely decision making to promote permanency for children in a time frame more congruent with children's developmental needs. However, although newer policies do get closer to a family focus, the policies and funding are still inadequate to support the range of services that promote the welfare of children and their families across the continuum.

THE CONTEXT OF SERVICES: ISSUES AND IMPLICATIONS

Administrators of services for America's families and children now face increasing demands for higher standards of accountability and improved service quality, often without commensurate resources. They also face professional and public recognition that the typically fragmented system (or nonsystem) of services requires focused development and integration to address the reality that most troubled families need multiple services (Barth, Courtney, Berrick, & Albert, 1994; Weil, 1985; Young, Gardner, & Coley, 1994). There is growing recognition that families need developmental and supportive services, resources, and learning opportunities, well before they are at real risk of being drawn into the authoritative system of child protection (Allen, Brown, & Finley, 1992; Brown & Weil, 1992; Kagan, Powell, Weissbourd, & Zigler, 1987). Administrators and researchers recognize that families need intensive and mediating services such as family preservation and/or FGC to resolve issues of abuse and neglect of children, unless the seriousness of maltreatment necessitates placement and termination of parental rights (Brown & Weil, 1992; Burford & Pennell, 1998; McCroskey & Meezan, 1998). When placement is needed, it should be swift to provide for long-term protection and permanency (Barth et al., 1994; Waldfogel, 1998b).

In much of the continuum, service components may be offered by public or nonprofit agencies and, increasingly, for-profit organizations. Although the pressures for fiscal accountability and outcome-focused services are frequently expressed as positive goals, intra- and interagency conflict may emerge when funding is insufficient to provide for the services needed or when the multiple services needed to intervene in complex family problems cannot be effectively mobilized and orchestrated across the service system because of policy and program constraints. Funding streams and structures, in fact, may greatly impede cross-system service integration (Center for the Study of Social Policy & Children's Defense Fund, 1994).

Both public and nonprofit sectors are also affected by the challenges of developing sound working partnerships with each other and with the families they serve (Adams, Alter, & Krauth, 1995; Hodges, Weil, & Jenkins, 1995, 1996; Marsh & Crow, 1998). The impact of devolution of decision making for some programs and funding streams from the federal government to state and local governments has added further complexity to the service environment and brings opportunities as well as challenges (Usher, 1998).

Public sector. The public sector in child and family services faces external challenges to its domain and its mission to safeguard children. In some areas of the nation, it is pressured to "contract out" increasing numbers of even the most traditional child welfare services, including protective services (Underwood, Buncombe County, North Carolina, Department of Social Services,

personal communication, 1998). Some advocates urge the transfer of investigative and protective services to the court system (Pelton, 1998). Already faced with raised bars of accountability for funding and results, public child and family agencies (both state and county) now face the prospect of maintaining high standards of legal and financial accountability and, simultaneously, have more program tasks handled through external service contracts. With this trend, monitoring becomes even more complex (Schene, 1998). If this trend continues, public agency managers and their staff may find themselves serving more often as accountability case managers of contracts with nonprofit and for-profit service programs. All the proposed directions of change for public child welfare services challenge the current mission and would call for significant changes in focus, demand new skills, and require strategic management of change (Edwards & Eadie, 1994). This trend toward privatization of long-established child welfare services makes the information-management and service-monitoring functions of the public sector much more critical and more complex, from direct service to administrative levels. The possible realignment of public child welfare and court-offered services would cause major agency reorganizations and shifts in goals and management priorities. The public sector is continually challenged in terms of mission and mandate and is, of course, highly vulnerable to public and political criticism when things go wrong, most tragically in the event of the death of a child who is in state custody.

Nonprofit sector. The nonprofit sector in services for families and children faces increasing competition for funding (Herman & Heimovics, 1991). Often, the closer to the grassroots a program is, the more difficult it becomes to maintain basic operating costs. The number of nonprofits is increasing as competition for funding escalates (Edwards & Benefield, 1997). The nonprofit sector, long lauded as the arena for innovation and intervention model testing, could well find its intervention-planning options further restricted if it receives primary support from the public sector to carry out protective and permanency functions. If innovative services in family problem prevention and treatment are further curtailed, troubled families could lose their opportunity to solve problems and learn new skills in voluntary settings. Alternatively, if investments are made in the voluntary sector to fund developmental, preventive, and support services, some of the strain on the public sector would be relieved (Schene, 1998; Usher, 1998; Waldfogel, 1998a). If local communities and states take seriously the proposals for developing community-based partnerships and collaboratives that would focus on support and prevention services to obviate the need for formal child protection services in many families, the nonprofit sector could take on much of this development (Adams & Nelson, 1997; Armstrong, 1997; Minicucci, 1997). Public CPS could then focus only on high-risk families (Waldfogel, 1998b). Nonprofits could build collaborative community networks to serve lower-risk families and coordinate with the public sector agencies when risks to children increase. Substantial funding for such preventive system development might come from the public sector, but it would also require major resource development in the voluntary sector.

Finally, as nonprofits face increased competition for funding, they also encounter pressures to develop not only executive leaders but also strong boards that can effectively advocate for funds and the organization's mission (Taylor Chait, & Holland., 1999). In a contested funding environment, boards and executive staff will be called on more frequently to represent the organizations' added value to funders, local political/economic elites, families, the service system, and society (Edwards & Austin, 1998; Heifetz & Laurie, 1999; Kotter, 1998a).

Major organizational tensions will continue to affect services for families and children. Stronger partnerships between the public and nonprofit sector have long been sought to strengthen the field (Waldfogel, 1998b). However, at this time, factors in the political/economic environment, particularly fiscal pressures on the service system arising from the implementation of TANF, "may hasten the creation of comprehensive systems of service by compelling state and local officials in different service areas to work together" (Usher, 1998, p. 219). Over time, these pressures and the professional impetus to develop comprehensive service systems may lead to a reallocation of the roles and balance of responsibility between the nonprofit and public sectors.

THE SERVICE CONTINUUM

What is called for in system reform is a comprehensive continuum of services, from informal community supports to local systems of care for children. A community-based continuum of services responds to the reality that families have distinct strengths, needs, and problems. The current debate pitting child protection against family preservation ignores the more complex reality of multiple needs within families and different needs across families. An expanded range of support services will aid specific responses to issues presented by families. Figure 24.1 presents a modified version of the Family-Centered Service Continuum developed to assist counties in North Carolina in local planning to implement family preservation and/or family support services (Weil & Luckey, 1995).

This continuum is family centered and community based; it begins with the informal systems, which are or should be the first supports for families or children in need: family, extended family, networks of friends, coworkers, and so on. A serious challenge to human service and child-serving agencies is learning to work more effectively with these natural support systems to prevent problems and to move families into prevention programs when needed (Weil, 2000; Whittaker & Garbarino, 1983). The second line of prevention for families should be community supports such as neighbors, religious communities, civic organizations, settlement house programs, youth centers, and so on, which can provide socialization, recreation, and support for children and their families (Brown et al., 1982). Broadening the service network to include and work effectively with these important civic institutions offers another challenge to service providers. Building a responsive, community-based system also calls for programs at all points on the continuum to engage family members and community members/leaders in planning, governance, and evaluation of services (Adams & Nelson, 1997; Marsh & Crow, 1998).

FAMILY SUPPORT

Although there have been supportive services since the settlement and progressive move-

ments, the last 15 years have seen massive growth in programs whose primary goal is to provide support, education, and skills development for parents and children (Weissbourd, 1987). Bronfenbrenner (1987) has called this the "quiet revolution"—a grassroots movement to develop locally based programs to support families. Numerous studies indicate a pattern of results establishing that family

> to a greater extent than any other context, influenced the capacity of individuals at all ages to learn and to succeed in other settings—in preschool and school, in the peer group, in higher education, and in the workplace, the community, and the nation as a whole. (Bronfenbrenner, 1987, p. xiii)

Equally important, a broad set of studies document that the viability of family processes is greatly affected by the family's larger social environment. Indeed, studies show that "the capacity of families to function effectively, particularly under stress, depended to a significant degree on the availability and provision of social support from persons outside the immediate family, such as kin, friends, neighbors and coworkers" (Bronfenbrenner, 1987, p. xiii). It was a natural conceptual step, then, to recognize that preventive and developmental services could nurture positive family life and forestall family breakdown and dysfunction. As family resource centers and family support programs emerged in the 1970s, programs were designed to develop and mobilize support and to help families learn to cope more effectively with basic development issues as well as crises. Programs burgeoned in the 1980s and 1990s (some using funding from the Family Support Act); there is a wide range of programs and different focuses; however, all family support programs

492

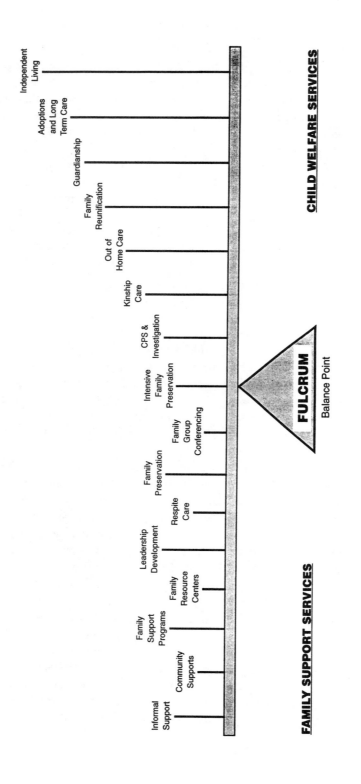

Figure 24.1. Family and Children's Service Continuum © Weil, 1999.

support a central goal: "increasing the capacities of all families to nurture their children and of all communities to nurture families" (Goetz & Peck, 1994, p. 1). A hallmark of family support programs has been the involvement of parents in planning, monitoring, and governing programs (Mulroy & Shay, 1998).

The family support movement is now firmly established and encompasses programs, supports, and services ranging from parenting classes to full-scale comprehensive family resource centers (Goetz & Peck, 1994; Kagan et al., 1987; McCroskey & Meezan, 1998). If more widely available, these services could be a great boon to families facing developmental crises and could provide the means to render supportive services in a voluntary setting. There are many program types such as Head Start, parent support and education programs, parent leadership development programs, adolescent parenting programs, parents as teachers programs, and family resource centers (Comer, Fraser, & Weil, 1994). All share basic principles: commitments to equality and respect; involvement of parents as resources for each other and partners in program governance; employment of a community-based, culturally responsive style that includes a bridge to other services; parent education and skills building; and a style that is strengths-based and voluntary (Goetz & Peck, 1994). Family support programs could well serve families who have the types of problems that are reported to CPS but screened out; such children may well not be subject to abuse or endangering neglect, but they still face risks in terms of development and family functioning. It seems logical and perhaps necessary for these services to remain voluntary and to be lodged in community-based, easily accessible settings.

For family support programs and family resource centers to become full partners in the service continuum, they need clear purposes and goals. Often, purpose is stated in a way that implies the program can "serve everyone" when in fact it can serve a small geographic area or a specific population. If family support programs are to be evaluated, program objectives should indicate the population to be served, program components, desired outcomes, and ways to measure those outcomes. Administrators in this growing field should work to develop a culture that creates a learning organization that is culturally competent, responsive to changes in families' needs and perceptions, and open to modification to fit local community needs.

As part of normal development, many families across social class lines need information and referral services and links to resources; likewise, many different types of families need family education and skill training to learn more about child and adolescent development, family development, crisis management, and peer support groups. Support groups can be diversely focused on very young parents, on grandmothers raising their grandchildren, or on circles of friends for children with emotional problems or developmental delays. Group-based services are often not viewed as a critical component of the service system for families and children. Administrators in the public and nonprofit sectors should consider expanding support groups and multifamily problem-solving groups—both for children and parents and as a means to build informal supports for families that are often isolated.

Leadership development is typically not considered an element in the service continuum, but as consumers become more engaged in planning and evaluation of services, it is very important to provide leadership development experiences so that participation is not reduced to tokenism (see Friesen, Chapter 23, this volume). Many family support programs are governed by boards that are at least one third parents and community leaders. The lack of development, prevention, and support programs are still often the major gaps in service networks or have not expanded beyond demonstration sites. Program development in this area is a critical need to support families in community-based settings. For example, in one city (Asheville, North Carolina), part of the local family preservation/family support grant was used to train potential clients and representatives from low-income communities to participate in program planning, governance, and evaluation. These representatives have become full participants in governance of the city-wide collaborative for all services for children and families (Weil & Hodges, 1995).

Respite care services need to be expanded and to have greater emphasis in the system. They are of vital importance to parents who have children with serious developmental disabilities or serious emotional/behavioral disorders. Respite services may be the community-based service most helpful in enabling parents to maintain children with such problems at home. In this way, they can be seen as both family support and a form of family preservation.

FAMILY PRESERVATION

Family support programs need to be closely connected to other community-based and civic organizations. Building credibility in the community is an important task for administrators and staff, and developing good collaborative relations is an element of program development (Mulroy & Shay, 1998). Collaboration not only helps programs find their niche in the community ecology, but critically can connect participating families to other needed resources. In family support programs, it is important that all staff are trained to recognize signs of abuse and neglect and to assure that they understand their obligation to report if needed. Families exiting family preservation might be encouraged to engage with a family support program, and safety issues could emerge with these or other families.

Intensive Family Preservation Services (IFPS) can be seen as the fulcrum between the support and protection sides of the service continuum. This relatively new form of service is a catalyst for an intensive intervention with families when children are at imminent risk of out-of-home placement. Its purpose is to protect children and to prevent unnecessary out-of-home placements (Hodges, 1994; Kinney et al., 1990). IFPS are "brief, time-limited, home-based, and family-centered services" designed to help families in crisis to "maintain children safely in their home while remaining together as a family unit" (Hodges, 1994, p. 1). The major goals of IFPS are "(1) to protect children, (2) to maintain and strengthen family bonds, (3) to stabilize the crisis situation, (4) to increase the family's skills and competencies, and (5) to facilitate the family's use of a variety of formal and informal helping resources" (Whittaker & Tracy, 1990, p. 2). Although projects differ considerably with regard to public or private auspice, program structure, and intervention emphasis (Pecora, 1990; Whittaker et al., 1990), common elements include (a) imminent risk as the criteria for program entry; (b) crisis-oriented services; (c) accessibility of staff; (d) intake and assessment processes designed to ascertain if children can remain at home safely during the intervention; (e) focus on the family as a unit; (f) home-based and community-based services; (g) services focused on teaching skills, obtaining resources, and counseling focused on family interaction patterns; (h) provision of services identified by the family as major needs; (i) small caseloads and intensive involvement of the worker with the family; and (j) time-limited engagement with the family (Whittaker et al., 1990).

Nonintensive Family Preservation is similar; however, the 1993 Family Support Act legislation broadened the definition to include at-risk families in services before they reach the crisis of imminent placement (Hodges, 1994). These services typically extend for a longer period of time—perhaps up to 5 months—with less weekly face-to-face time with families than the intensive model. Indeed, given the range of designs, it can be difficult to distinguish between such family preservation programs and family-centered casework (Fraser et al., 1997). This model drift and variation poses problems in comparative program evaluations. Both models focus on family-centered, strengths-based practice and efforts to reduce family isolation by connecting family members to extended family, neighborhood supports, and community resources.

FAMILY GROUP CONFERENCING

FGC is another service offered when placement is likely. FGC is designed specifically to bring together extended family and supportive friends with the professionals working with the family. Careful work is done to prepare all participants for the conference. At a family group meeting, often for the first time, the family group and its supporters hear the full story of issues and problems that need to be addressed to ensure child safety (Hudson, Morris, Maxwell, & Galaway, 1996; Marsh & Crow, 1998). After professionals present the facts and respond to questions, the professionals leave the conference room, and the family develops a plan for securing the safety of the children and for remedying other related problems. The local authority staff representative from child protective or juvenile services reviews the plan and decides if it adequately ensures safety. If so, it is put in place, and both family members and local authority staff monitor the situation. This service is designed to empower, to engage the family in problem solving, and to broaden responsibility for child safety (Pennell & Burford, in press). If the initial plan fails, another conference can be held, after which the family can enact another plan, or the children may be placed with kin or in formal foster care. FGC then can also be seen as a service to sustain and support families through increasing extended family responsibility for the safety of children.

Family Preservation as the Fulcrum of the Continuum

Family preservation, IFPS, and FGC mark the transition from developmental/prevention/problem solving services to state-sanctioned intervention because serious risk to children is evident. IFPS were not intended to be a panacea for all troubled families but rather to provide a new service at the point of a major crisis—imminent risk of placement—to provide motivated families with an opportunity to do intensive work to assure that children are safeguarded and then to connect to additional supportive services (Whittaker et al., 1990). IFPS is discussed as voluntary; however, it is presented as the alternative to placement, and parents must agree to work intensively to make major family life changes. If families make major strides and safety is assured, families may enter step-down or supportive community services.

CHILD WELFARE

Child protective investigation may take place before or following family preservation and FGC efforts. If children are endangered and if family preservation does not or cannot work to provide safety, there may be a family group conference to ascertain if relatives can and should care for the children for the long term, perhaps seeking guardianship. Alternately, the children would be taken into care by the public child welfare agency. Kinship care is increasingly used to enable a child to remain in a familiar environment with relatives with whom a relationship is already established (Berrick, 1998). If kinship care is not an appropriate option, the logical step is nonrelative foster care or placement in a group home or residential treatment center. If the mental health or juvenile justice system is the public authority involved, either a psychiatric hospital or training school may be the placement.

System reform efforts have focused largely on moving children from placement to a permanent home. Options include family reunification, if children can be safe at home, or adoption—the creation of a new family—as preferred choices, with long-term placement when that offers the best chance for permanency. Adolescents who have been in care need to be prepared for independent living; this service is all too often missing from community systems.

Many system reform efforts have sought to reduce the time that children are in temporary foster care and to assure that the child welfare system moves with deliberate speed to assure permanency. The W. K. Kellogg initiative, Families for Kids, works to assure that a child has one worker, one placement, and one year to permanency (Usher, 1998). New research and service-monitoring efforts are being developed that can track an individual child's placement and outcomes and provide program staff and administrators with means to internally evaluate processes and outcomes and take corrective action as needed to hasten permanency (Usher, 1995; Usher et al., 1995).

The merits of family reunification are debated. These efforts may well be more successful when families have had the opportunity to participate in step-down services related to family preservation or in specifically designed reunification services that engage the family in problem solving and preparation for the child's return. Fraser and colleagues (1997) note promising data from family reunification evaluations. Such services typically focus on building needed supports for the predictable crises of reunification. A child might be placed with a relative on a long-term basis if the possibility of return home is remote or inappropriate. Adoption, if feasible, is typically the preferred course of action to assure permanency (Barth, 1992; Downs et al., 1996). Otherwise, long-term foster care or foster-adopt placements may be the optimal route for some children (Downs et al., 1996). Independent living and preparation for emancipation may be the only choice. The high rate of former foster children who "age out" at 18 and end up homeless and jobless within a year indicates the need for ongoing supportive services. These services might include remaining connected to foster families or using group-based living arrangements with some supports.

Because many children who have been physically or sexually abused have emotional or behavioral problems, support services are needed for adoptive parents, foster parents, and families engaged in kinship care. Specialized foster care parents are more likely to receive training, but there is usually little ongoing support for new families created by adoption or families undertaking kinship care. Figure 24.2 is a schematic illustration of a community-based and family-centered system of care in which families can connect to informal support systems and to voluntary family support programs as needed. Community-based services, family preservation, and IFPS programs are the outer, protective circles in the community-based system.

At the point of major crisis, the formal systems are engaged in child welfare to provide crisis intervention, out-of-home care if needed, and reunification where possible. With reunification or adoption, families should be reconnected to family support programs and to peer-support and advocacy groups and encouraged to build a substantial informal support system.

Child welfare challenges. Several quite different strategies are being promulgated currently that would change the nature of public child welfare services and its relation to the courts and the nonprofit sector. As Waldfogel (1998b) notes,

> The problems facing CPS have led a number of individuals and groups to rethink child protection in recent years. One stream of reform proposals focuses on the concerns about overinclusion, capacity, and service orientation, and suggests that the mandate of CPS should be more narrowly defined and more vigorously pursued. A second reform stream emphasizes the additional need to broaden access to services that protect children and strengthen families, and recommends building partnerships between CPS agencies and a variety of community partners as a way of remedying the problems related to underinclusion and service delivery. (p. 109)

A third proposal recommends moving the investigation and protective functions from public child welfare agencies and lodging them in the court system (Pelton, 1998). Advocates for moving protective services in toto to the jurisdiction of the courts hold that the change would enable public child welfare to do what it does better—develop and implement plans for permanency (Pelton, 1998).

There is likely to be local and state experimentation with all three of these options in the near future. Each would require major administrative commitments to orchestrate changes in the service system, demanding increased emphasis on interagency boundary spanning and collaboration (Eadie, 1998). If such changes occur, agencies will need not only to work more effectively together but also to engage in public education about changes and develop strategies to increase public trust (Herzlinger, 1999). With some of the proposed directions for system change, the nonprofit sector could maintain its ability to innovate and test new ideas, using its flexibility to respond rapidly to changing service needs or new populations and offering a wide array of voluntary, relatively informal services to support families. This change would free the public sector to concentrate on innovative ways of serving the most at-risk children and providing protective and permanency ser-

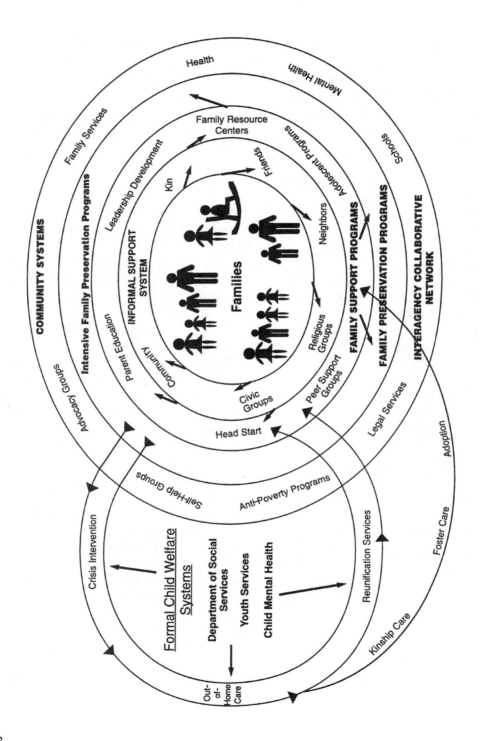

Figure 24.2. Community-Based, Family-Centered System of Services for Families and Children ©Weil, 2000.

vices (Schene, 1998; Waldfogel, 1998a). Efforts for preservation and treatment might be lodged in either or both systems. It seems likely that the major pressures on protective services will require some system changes to cope with the high degree of organizational tension and to respond to growing demand for outcome-oriented service delivery. These pressures are:

1. Overinclusion: Some families are referred to CPS who should not be.
2. Capacity: The number of families referred to the system exceeds the system's ability to respond effectively.
3. Underinclusion: Some families who should be referred to CPS are not.
4. Service orientation: The authoritative approach of CPS is not appropriate for many of the families referred to it.
5. Service delivery: Many families do not receive the services they need. (Waldfogel, 1998a, with the Harvard Executive Session on Child Protection)

These sets of issues pose important challenges for administrators in public and nonprofit sectors alike.

A central problem facing public child welfare agencies is shifting political whims that tout a single operating principle for services—most recently either a press for family preservation or a single-minded focus on child protection and child rescue (Lowry, 1998).

> A crucial problem is the fact that child welfare systems have for decades operated under a changing series of single operating principles. Because these systems lack the capacity to do what is, after all, a difficult job that calls for subtle, sophisticated judgments, they have redefined that job into a far simpler one in which staff apply only the single operating principle current at the time. Every so

often, in response to either changing fashion or public reaction, the tide turns and the operating principle changes. (Lowry, 1998, p. 124)

Often, agencies do not choose this strategy; rather, they are propelled in one direction or the other in response to shifting local or state political tides. This problem also is likely to be related to the deprofessionalization of child welfare and high caseloads.

Perhaps the greatest strategic challenge to administrators, particularly in the public sector, is to press for and build community and political support for public/nonprofit partnerships that together can provide the full range of services needed.

LEADERSHIP/ADMINISTRATIVE CHALLENGES AND STRATEGIC CHOICES

Child Welfare Reform

System reform. The central administrative challenge is to lead the process of system reform in child welfare. With competing visions of how child welfare services should evolve focusing on investigation, protective services, and permanency (Harvard Executive Session on Child Protection, 1997; Schene, 1998; Waldfogel, 1998b) or transferring all investigation and protective services to the courts (Pelton, 1998), administrators have major strategic choices to make about the direction of services. Both these views are responses to the decade-long concerns about the system's inability to handle the ever-increasing number of reports and investigations, its inability to serve large numbers of families who are at risk, and negative outcomes for children who are in the system for the long term (Schene, 1998; Schorr, 1989; Waldfogel, 1998a). Either of these systemic change proposals raises political, policy, practice, and value questions. Leaders in system reform favor the option of the public sector working collaboratively with nonprofits to develop a comprehensive community-based system (Harvard Executive Session on Child Protection, 1997; Schene, 1998; Usher, 1998; Waldfogel, 1998a), and experiments are under way testing shared investigations by CPS and law enforcement.

Generally, it is now recognized that "there is an acute need to mobilize additional resources from the community to partner with CPS in protecting children . . . a portion of the families who now come to CPS could effectively be served on a voluntary basis by other community agencies" (Schene, 1998, p. 36). The Harvard Executive Session on Child Protection, a meeting of reform-minded administrators and analysts, in a series of position papers, proposes a new partnership paradigm

> in which the public CPS agency shares responsibility for child protection with a wide range of partners in the community to provide a more differentiated response to children at risk of abuse or neglect. This new paradigm sees reform proceeding along two tracks: one track is to improve the capacity of CPS to respond effectively to the high-risk cases that need authoritative intervention; the other track is to enhance the capacity of community partners to provide services to help protect children in both high- and low-risk families. (Waldfogel, 1998b, p. 110)

The states of Iowa, Missouri, and Florida have pioneered efforts to develop stronger community-based systems. Preliminary findings in all three experiments show promise:

1. The Iowa Patch Project began in 1991 and "seeks to resolve the problems of service orientation and service delivery by using a neighborhood-based interagency team to deliver CPS to families at risk of abuse or neglect." The evaluation indicates that CPS workers have developed "closer working relationships with both colleagues and clients" and that they now look more closely at "underlying problems [such as] poverty, inadequate housing, mental illness, unemployment, and substance abuse."

2. Missouri is experimenting with differential response. Where commission of a crime is likely, CPS and law enforcement conducts a mandatory investigation; for others family assessment and service delivery are handled in a "nonauthoritative" structure. Since 1994, only 20% of cases in reform sites have been referred to the investigation track; and work is under way to refine screening decision processes.

3. Florida has also strengthened the involvement of law enforcement in investigations, and CPS has focused on developing an "assessment- and service-oriented response for *all* families reported." Florida demonstration sites have also sought "to enhance cooperation between the CPS agency and community partners" including development of "community safety agreements" with persons willing to help with support (Waldfogel, 1998b, pp. 112-117).

The overburden in the system is evident, and the pressures for change are inexorable. Administrators must prepare to lead such local system reform efforts, building collaborations in accord with particular community issues. Preparation is also needed to respond to the concerns of workers and of community agencies about such proposed changes. It is not unusual for public sector workers to view any shifts in priority as temporary—education and shared vision building with staff and community partners is needed to move reform forward (Argyris, 1998; Kotter, 1998a, 1998b). Child welfare staff and community agencies are likely to fear that they will be held responsible if a child being served in a reform project dies (Waldfogel, 1998b). Indeed, dealing with mandated responsibility and legal risks is the most serious concern in developing community partnerships. Shared accountability is a serious issue. Although there are obvious risks in experimenting with reform strategies, the status quo is unacceptable. The challenges may be great, but the opportunities to serve families better make the risks worth taking. To implement system reform in CPS, other changes are needed.

Practice and data. In child welfare, it is critically important to build on current demonstrations and expand the use of monitoring and case data systems that not only track services and outcomes for individual children but also reveal agency patterns in service delivery, particularly in time elapsed between system entry and permanency (Usher et al., 1995). Building systems for self-evaluation not only provides needed information for taking corrective action but also moves CPS into a "learning organization" approach (Garvin, 1998; Usher, 1995).

Technology. To develop and use service-monitoring systems, child welfare agencies need resources for appropriate hardware and software to handle case data reporting as well as large data-system management. Workers, planners, and managers need computer access and consultation to set up self-evaluation systems. The feedback from self-evaluation reports on all children can provide agencies with a powerful tool for service-quality management and goal-attainment assessment. As child welfare agencies broaden community partnerships, the ability to provide information to each other will become increasingly important.

Case management/service provision issues. Many children in foster care and other out-of-home placements are also involved with the child mental health system. As mental health programs come under stricter case management regulations and consequent service limitations, serious questions are raised about the system's ability to help children with severe emotional and behavioral disorders heal (see Friesen, Chapter 23, this volume). Even family preservation programs lodged in mental health settings are feeling these constraints, along with the pressures caused by internal policies that will not count interagency case conferences and planning meetings as billable case management services (vander Straeten & Weil, 1999). Children who are involved in mental health and child welfare or juvenile justice systems are often severely troubled and underserved in relation to their mental health needs. As service sessions are limited under managed care, leaders in the full child and family system must advocate for these most vulnerable children.

Workforce development. The turnover rates for work in public child welfare are high. Agencies need to count the costs of staff turnover and work for higher salaries and more reasonable job responsiblities for frontline workers (Underwood, Buncombe County, North Carolina, Department of Social Services, personal communication, 1998). With proposed system changes, it may finally be the time to reprofessionalize CPS services and provide highly skilled workers for children facing the greatest risks. More feasible caseloads, more teamwork, more collaborative work with community partners, and a better balance of job requirements are needed. Taking a lead from IFPS practice, CPS workers need more support and mentoring for the high-demand, high-stress responsiblilities they carry. In addition, the workforce as well as families served is becomming more diverse, and leaders need to build culturally responsive organizations (Daly, 1998).

Other issues for child welfare. Many other areas in child welfare services need strengthening. Kinship care needs to be expanded and evaluated; adoption options for older children of color and for children with disabilities need to be strengthened through specialized recruitment; adolescents need increased support as they become adults and live independently; and public sector programs need to strengthen public/private partnerships in all these areas. If the excessive burden of the CPS system can be shared through community partnerships, the practice improvements noted here can happen. The knowledge is available, but opportunities to strengthen "deep end" services are requisite.

OVERALL SYSTEM DEVELOPMENT AND REFORM

Partnership building across the continuum. New kinds of partnerships are needed that can create community-based and family-centered services focused on smaller geographic areas (Adams et al., 1995; Waldfogel, 1998a). These should increase decentralization of public services (Brown et al., 1982; Waldfogel, 1998b)

and engage nonprofits and community organizations in community-based systems of care (Burrell, 1995; Mulroy & Shay, 1998; Weil, 1997). Such changes can transform child and family services if interorganizational collaboration becomes a closely woven network of easy-to-access services on the preventive side of the continuum and if the public sector can focus more closely on interventions with families at most serious risk for child abuse and neglect (American Public Welfare Association, 1991; Schene, 1998). Shared accountability and public sector liability are serious issues to be worked out, but this strategy could restore the opportunities for both sectors to work at their optimal level—specializing in outcome-focused interventions—one for prevention and preservation, the other for protection and permanency (Schene, 1998).

Community partnerships. Equally important is the need to transform services so that new partnerships are carried forward not only among agencies participating in the formal service system but also through partnership building with community-based programs, community organizations, and informal systems (Adams & Nelson, 1997; Armstrong, 1997; Kretzmann & McKnight, 1994; Pennell & Burford, in press; Usher, 1998; Waldfogel, 1998b; Weil, 2000). The Ford, A. E. Casey, E. M. Clark, and W. K. Kellogg foundations have all recently supported partnership-building efforts. Most critical, and perhaps most challenging, is the need for public and nonprofit agencies to test empowerment and strengths-oriented models and to work mutually with the families they serve (Saleebey, 1997; Simon, 1994). Now and in the future, agencies will need to develop partnerships with clients, former clients, and community leaders to participate in planning, governance, and evaluation of services and the operation of service networks (Lee, 1994; Weil, 2000; Weil & Hodges, 1995). When children are adopted or taken into care, the corollary in partnership building will be to move the new family or caretaking constellation into supportive services or networks.

Dueling initiatives and service integration. As a variety of types of system reform initiatives occur in many parts of the nation, efforts to build collaboration can become even more complex. If a community is participating in several initiatives, each of which is sponsored by a particular agency or system, each agency may seem to be competing with all the others to create collaboration on its terms (Usher, 1996). This phenomenon has been called dueling initiatives, resulting in a process that can be confusing to service providers and families (Usher, 1996).

The impetus for creating comprehensive systems of family and children's services is similar to that which drives managed care in mental health—a desire to achieve the best possible outcomes within explicit resource constraints. Yet, the challenges of building a system in which that principle can be achieved are substantial, and their complexity grows in direct proportion to the number of systems involved. As a result, such ventures involve inherent conflicts related to the pooling and allocation of resources, to differences in professional perspectives and approaches to service, and to the willingness of state and local governments to delegate some of their authority to new collaborative entities (Usher, 1998, p. 217).

This challenge becomes greater when broadbased community partnerships are sought to alter the frequently fragmented service network.

If partnerships are to develop fully and the domination of any single system is to be diminished, a growing number of scholars and administrators are urging the creation of neighborhood- or community-based systems to coordinate development of comprehensive services (Adams & Nelson, 1997; Harbert, Finnegan, & Tyler, 1997; Usher, 1998; Waldfogel, 1998a). Service-integration perspectives have evolved from earlier assumptions about coordination among public sector agencies to the broad community perspective (Adams & Nelson, 1997; Hassett & Austin, 1997; Kamermann & Kahn, 1992). Indeed, there is growing momentum in practice and the literature to connect service-system development to community development, which may encompass economic development as well as service integration (Adams & Nelson, 1997; Kretzmann & McKnight, 1994; Mulroy & Shay, 1998; Weil, 1997).

In these efforts, it will be important for leaders to use effective boundary-spanning strategies and to develop experimental service networks in which some services are closely linked and others more loosely coupled (Halley, 1997; Harbert et al., 1997; Hassett & Austin, 1997). Austin (1997) cites three clusters of principles that can guide this development:

Principles of Resource Distribution
    Fairness and equity
    Adequacy of income/economic support
    Equality of access and opportunity
Principles of Decision Making and Authority
    A community approach to problem solving
    Consumer ownership
    A decentralized neighborhood-based service
        delivery system
Principles of Service Design and Delivery
    Proactive prevention-oriented services

A deep commitment to racial and cultural diversity

Comprehensive and noncategorical services

Universal federal family investment policies (Austin, 1997, pp. 6-7)

To accomplish this kind of system development, social service leaders can use the following processes to manage change in the neighborhood context: (a) employing organizational self-assessments and community needs assessments; (b) engaging collaborative partners in developing vision, mission, and goals; (c) assuring that all stakeholders are represented including clients, potential clients, and community members/leaders; (d) planning together for priority setting and system development; (e) analyzing existing and needed services; (f) developing strategies for strengthening collaboration and promoting service integration; (g) developing strategies for managing change; and (h) engaging visionary risk-taking leadership (Austin, 1997; Weil & Dunlop, 1998). To succeed at these complex processes, a community-based program will need a capacity-oriented approach: the capacity to lead, the capacity to innovate, and the capacity to implement (Eadie, 1998).

CHALLENGES AND STRATEGIC CHOICES AT THE FULCRUM OF FAMILY PRESERVATION

Model variation. In the field of family preservation, several generally successful models of IFPS have been designed and tested in multiple states. That is, there is a knowledge base, a theory base, and now a research base to use in designing and operating IFPS programs. However, with nonintensive family preservation

services, there are a variety of different approaches and considerable model drift. This creates increased responsibility for administrators not only to articulate what their program does but to clearly specify the intervention and desired outcomes and to measure program effectiveness.

CONCLUSION

The task before leaders in services to families and children is to transform the system so that it operates effectively to support families and to protect children. What is called for is (a) a shared new way of thinking about the whole continuum of services, (b) ways of connecting families to the full range of services that they need, and (c) community-based partnerships to weave together informal and formal supports in the nonprofit and public sector so that families get the type and level of service that they need along with resource management to solve problems.

Leaders in services for families and children need skills and supports in two major areas to meet current demands: (a) abilities and approaches to analyze and deal with internal and external challenges to outcome-oriented service provision, and (b) abilities and approaches to make strategic choices in relation to risks and opportunities in developing community-based, family-centered systems of care. In the next decade, leadership needs to be collaborative, entrepreneurial, and transformative. In both nonprofit and public sectors, administrators need to creatively combine values, vision, and mission with entrepreneurial, marketing, and advocacy strategies. Values and vision should focus on positive outcomes for children, youth, and families, and mission should state the means to do so. Common themes of dynamic/innovative leaders include developing a vision, engendering commitment and trust, and facilitating organizational learning (Bennis & Nanus, 1985; Garvin, 1998). In services for families and children, additional themes will be critical: boundary spanning, collaborating within and across public and nonprofit sectors, learning from successes and failures of reform initiatives, and taking a community-centered approach. That will mean engaging in reform and service integration, "taking the community rather than the service system" as the starting point (Adams & Nelson, 1997, p. 67). Outreach to neighborhoods and collaboration at all levels will be needed.

Although all staff will deal with these issues, leaders have the particular challenge of responding to these diverse expectations, mediating these forces, and supporting workers who face difficult practice issues and decisions. In this field, managers face complex personnel, financing/resource allocation, planning, and evaluation issues. Creating and maintaining organizational cultures congruent with new expectations—for staff roles, for family-centered practice, and for collaboration—is a tall order. Leadership and strategies for building partnerships, strengthening services, and improving organizational and interorganizational decision making will be critical to improving outcomes for America's children and families.

REFERENCES

Abbott, G. (1938). *The child and the state* (Vols. 1 and 2). Chicago: University of Chicago Press.

Adams, P., Alter, C., & Krauth, K. (1995). *Strengthening families and neighborhoods: A community-centered approach. Final report on the Iowa Patch Project* [Mimeo]. Iowa City: University of Iowa.

Adams, P., & Nelson, K. (1997). Reclaiming community: An integrative approach to human services. *Administration in Social Work, 21*(3/4), 67-82.

Addams, J. (1910). *Twenty years at Hull-House.* New York: Macmillan.

Addams, J. (1930). *The second twenty years at Hull-House.* New York: Macmillan.

Addams, J. (1960). *A centennial reader.* New York: Macmillan.

Allen, M. L., Brown, P., & Finley, B. (1992). *Helping children by strengthening families: A look at family support programs.* Washington, DC: Children's Defense Fund.

American Public Welfare Association. (1991). *A commitment to change: Report of the National Commission on Child Welfare and Family Preservation.* Washington, DC: Author.

Argyris, C. (1998). Teaching smart people how to learn. In *Harvard Business Review on knowledge management* (pp. 81-108). Boston: Harvard Business School Press.

Armstrong, K. L. (1997). Launching a family-centered, neighborhood-based human services system: Lessons from working the hallways and street corners. *Administration in Social Work, 21*(3/4), 109-126.

Austin, M. J. (1997). Service integration: Introduction. *Administration in Social Work, 21*(3/4), 1-8.

Barth, R. (1992). Adoption. In P. Pecorra, J. K. Whittaker, & A. N. Maluccio (Eds.), *The child welfare challenge: Policy, practice, and research.* New York: Aldine De Gruyter.

Barth R. P., Courtney, M., Berrick, J. D., & Albert, V. (1994). *From child abuse to permanency planning: Child welfare services, pathways, and placements.* New York: Aldine De Gruyter.

Bennis, W., & Nanus, B. (1985). *Leaders: The strategies for taking charge.* New York: Harper & Row.

Berrick, J. D. (1998, Spring). When children cannot remain home: Foster family care and kinship care. *The Future of Children, 8*(1), 72-87.

Besharov, D. J. (1998, Spring). Four commentaries: How we can better protect children from abuse and neglect. *The Future of Children, 8*(1), 120-132.

Betten, N., & Austin, M. J. (Eds.). (1990). *The roots of community organizing, 1917-1939.* Philadelphia: Temple University Press.

Billingsley, A., & Giovannoni, J. (1972). *Children of the storm: Black children and American child welfare.* New York: Harcourt Brace Jovanovich.

Blank, R. M. (1997). *It takes a nation: A new agenda for fighting poverty.* Princeton, NJ: Princeton University Press/Russell Sage Foundation.

Brace, C. L. (1872). *The dangerous classes of New York and twenty years' work among them.* New York: Wynkoop & Hallenbeck.

Breckenridge, S. (1934). *Social work and the courts.* Chicago: University of Chicago Press.

Bronfenbrenner, U. (1987). Foreword: Family support: The quiet revolution. In S. L. Kagan, D. R. Powell, B. Weissbourd, & E. F. Zigler (Eds.), *America's family support programs.* New Haven, CT: Yale University Press.

Brown, J. (1992). Social policy: Families and children. In J. Brown & M. Weil (Eds.), *Family practice.* Washington, DC: Child Welfare League of America.

Brown, J., Finch, W. A., Northen, H., Taylor, S. H., & Weil, M. (1982). *Child, family, neighborhood: A master plan for social service delivery.* New York: Child Welfare League of America.

Brown, J., & Weil, M. (Eds.). (1992). *Family practice.* Washington, DC: Child Welfare League of America.

Burford, G., & Pennell, J. (1996). *Family group decision-making project implementation report summary.* St. Johns, Newfoundland: Memorial University of Newfoundland, Institute for Social and Economic Research.

Burford, G., & Pennell, J. (1998). *Family group decision-making project: Outcome report, Vol. 1.* St. Johns, Newfoundland: Memorial University Press.

Burrell, K. (1995). *Missouri's child protection services system and current differential reponse demonstration project: Case study prepared for the Executive Session on Child Protection, Kennedy School of Government.* Available from the Malcolm Weiner Center for Social Policy, Kennedy School of Government, Harvard University, 79 John F. Kennedy Street, Cambridge, MA 02138.

Burtless, G. T. (1997, Spring). Welfare recipients' job skills and employment prospects. *The Future of Children, 7*(1), 39-51.

Center for the Study of Social Policy & Children's Defense Fund. (1994). *A guide for planning: Making strategic use of the family preservation and support services program.* Washington, DC: Center for the Study of Social Policy.

Center for Urban Economic Development. (1998, June). *Welfare reform at age one: Early indicators of impact on courts and agencies based on reports from community-based service providers.* Chicago: University of Illinois at Chicago.

Children's Defense Fund. (1990). *A children's defense budget.* Washington, DC: Author.

Comer, E., Fraser, M., & Weil, M. (1994). *Conceptual framework for viewing family support.* Chapel Hill: University of North Carolina, School of Social Work.

Conte, J. (1983). Service provision to enhance family functioning. In B. McGowan & W. Meezan (Eds.), *Child welfare: Current dilemmas—future directions.* Itasca, IL: F. E. Peacock.

Costin, L. B., Karger, H. J., & Stoesz, D. (1996). *The politics of child abuse and neglect in America.* New York: Oxford University Press.

Courtney, M. (1998, Spring). The costs of child protection in the context of welfare reform. *The Future of Children, 8*(1), 88-103.

Daly, A. (1998). *Workplace diversity: Issues & perspectives.* Washington, DC: NASW Press.

Deegan, M. J. (1990). *Jane Addams and the men of the Chicago school, 1892-1918.* New Brunswick, NJ: Transaction Books.

de Lone, R. (1979). *Small futures: Children, inequality, and the limits of liberal reform.* New York: Harcourt Brace Jovanovich.

Downs, S. W., Costin, L. B., & McFadden, E. J. (1996). *Child welfare and family services: Policies and practice.* White Plains, NY: Longman.

Eadie, D. C. (1998). Building the capacity to lead innovation. In R. L. Edwards, J. A. Yankey, & M. A. Altpeter (Eds.), *Skills for effective management of nonprofit organizations* (pp. 27-44). Washington, DC: NASW Press.

Edwards, R. L., & Austin, M. J. (1998). Managing effectively in an environment of competing values. In R. L. Edwards, J. A. Yankey, & M. A. Altpeter (Eds.), *Skills for effective management of nonprofit organizations.* Washington, DC: NASW Press.

Edwards, R. L., & Benefield, E. A. S. (1997). *Building a strong foundation: Fund-raising for nonprofits.* Washington, DC: NASW Press.

Edwards, R. L., & Eadie, D. C. (1994). Meeting the change challenge, managing the growth in the nonprofit and public human service sectors. *Administration in Social Work, 18*(2), 107-123.

Edwards, R. L., Yankey, J. A., & Altpeter, M. A. (Eds.). (1998). *Skills for effective management of nonprofit organizations.* Washington, DC: NASW Press.

Fisher, R., & Karger, H. (1997). *Social work and community in a private world: Getting out in public.* New York: Longman.

Fraser, M. W., Nelson, K. E., & Rivard, J. C. (1997). Effectiveness of family preservation services. *Social Work Research, 21*(3), 138-153.

Friedmann, J. (1996). *Empowerment: The politics of alternative development.* Cambridge, MA: Blackwell.

Garvin, D. A. (1998). Building a learning organization. In *Harvard Business Review on knowledge management* (pp. 47-80). Boston: Harvard Business School Press.

Gelles, R. J. (1996). *The Book of David: How preserving families can cost children's lives.* New York: Basic Books.

Giovannoni, J. M., & Becerra, R. M. (1979). *Defining child abuse.* New York: Free Press.

Goetz, K., & Peck, S. (Eds.). (1994). *The basics of family support.* Chicago: Family Resource Coalition.

Halley, A. A. (1997). Applications of boundary spanning theory to the concept of service integration in the human services. *Administration in Social Work, 21*(3/4), 145-168.

Harbert, A. S., Finnegan, D., & Tyler, N. (1997). Collaboration: A study of a children's initiative. *Administration in Social Work, 21*(3/4). 83-108.

Harbin, G. L., & McNulty, B. A. (1990). Policy implementation: Perspectives on service coordination and interagency cooperation. In S. J. Meisels & J. P. Shonkoff (Eds.), *Handbook of early childhood education.* New York: Cambridge University Press.

Harvard Executive Session on Child Protection, Kennedy School of Government. (1997). Position papers available from the Malcolm Weiner Center for Social Policy, Kennedy School of Government. Harvard University, 79 John F. Kennedy Street, Cambridge, MA 02138.

Hassett, S., & Austin, M. J. (1997). Service integration: Something old and something new. *Administration in Social Work, 21*(3/4), 9-30.

Heifetz, R. A., & Laurie, D. L. (1999). The work of leadership. In *Harvard Business Review on leadership.* Boston: Harvard Business School Press.

Herman, R. D., & Heimovics, R. D. (1991). *Executive leadership in nonprofit organizations.* San Francisco: Jossey-Bass.

Herzlinger, R. E. (1999). Can public trust in nonprofits and government be restored? In *Harvard Business School Review on nonprofits* (pp. 1-28). Boston: Harvard Business School Press.

Hodges, V. G. (1994). *Family preservation concept paper.* Chapel Hill: University of North Carolina, School of Social Work.

Hodges, V. G., Weil, M., & Jenkins, R. (1995, October). *Collaboration for implementation of family preservation and family support services.* Paper presented at NASW Meeting of the Profession, Philadelphia, PA.

Hodges, V. G., Weil, M., & Jenkins, R. (1996, October). *Implementing family preservation and family support services: Interagency collaboration and self-evaluation.* Paper presented at NASW Meeting of the Profession, Cleveland, OH.

Hudson, J., Morris, A., Maxwell, G., & Galaway, B. (Eds.). (1996). *Family group conferences: Perspectives on policy and practice.* Monsey, NY: Willow Tree Press.

Iatridis, D. (1988). New social deficit: Neoconservatism's policy of social underdevelopment. *Social Work, 33*(1), 11-15.

Institute for Wisconsin's Future. (1999a). Life after welfare: Just barely making it. *W-2 Connection, 2*(1).

Institute for Wisconsin's Future. (1999b). W-2 problems reach across Wisconsin, frustration in communities is growing. *W-2 Connection, 2*(2).

Jackson, S., & Kilroe, S. (1995). *Looking after children: Good parenting, good outcomes* [Training guide]. London: Her Majesty's Stationery Office.

Janssen, B. S. (1997). *The reluctant welfare state* (3rd ed.). Pacific Grove, CA: Brooks/Cole.

Jones, M., Neuman, R., & Shyne, A. A. (1976). *A second chance for families: Evaluation of a program to reduce foster care.* New York: Child Welfare League of America Research Center.

Kagan, S. L., Powell, D. R., Weissbourd, B., & Zigler, E. F. (Eds.). (1987). *America's family support programs.* New Haven, CT: Yale University Press.

Kamerman, S., & Kahn, A. (1978). *Family policy: Government and families in fourteen countries.* New York: Columbia University Press.

Kamerman, S., & Kahn, A. (1989). *Social services for children, youth, and families in the United States.* New York: Columbia University Press/Annie E. Casey Foundation.

Kamerman, S., & Kahn, A. (1992). *Integrating services integration: An overview of initiatives, issues, and possibiities.* New York: National Center for Children in Poverty.

Kinney, J., Haapala, D., & Booth, C. (1990). *Keeping families together: The Homebuilders Model.* New York: Aldine De Gruyter.

Kirk, R. (1994). *North Carolina Family Assessment Scale.* Chapel Hill: University of North Carolina School of Social Work.

Knitzer, J., & Bernard, S. (1997). *The new welfare law and vulnerable families: Implications for chid welfare/child protection systems.* New York: National Center for children in Poverty.

Kotter, J. P. (1998a). Leading change: Why transformation efforts fail. In *Harvard Business Review on leadership* (pp. 1-20). Boston: Harvard Business School Press.

Kotter, J. P. (1998b). What leaders really do. In *Harvard Business Review on leadership* (pp. 37-60). Boston: Harvard Business School Press.

Kretzmann, J., & McKnight, J. (1994). *Building communities from the inside out: A path toward finding and mobilizing a community's assets.* Chicago: ACTA.

Lee, J. A. B. (1994). *The empowerment approach to social work practice.* New York: Columbia University Press.

Lowry, M. R. (1998, Spring). Four commentaries: How we can better protect children from abuse and neglect. *The Future of Children, 8*(1), 120-132.

Magazino, C. J. (1983). Services to children and families at risk of separation. In B. McGowan & W. Meezan (Eds.),

Child welfare: Current dilemmas—future directions.
Itasca, IL: F. E. Peacock.

Maluccio, A., & Sinanoglu, P. (Eds.). (1981). *The challenge
of partnership: Working with parents of children in foster
care.* New York: Child Welfare League of America.

Marsh, P., & Crow, G. (1998). *Family group conferencing in
child welfare.* Oxford, UK: Blackwell Science.

McCroskey, J., & Meezan, W. (1998, Spring). Family-centered services: Approaches and effectiveness. *The Future of Children, 8*(1), 54-71.

McGowan, B. (1983). Historical evolution of child welfare
services: An examination of the sources of current problems and dilemmas. In B. McGowan & W. Meezan
(Eds.), *Child welfare: Current dilemmas—future directions.* Itasca, IL: F. E. Peacock.

Midgley, J. (1995). *Social development: The development
perspective in social welfare.* Thousand Oaks, CA: Sage.

Minicucci, C. M. (1997). Assessing a family-oriented neighborhood service agency: The Del Paso Heights Model.
Administration in Social Work, 21(3/4), 127-143.

Mulroy, E. A., & Shay, S. (1998). Nonprofit organizations
and innovation: A model of neighborhood-based collaboration to prevent child maltreatment. In P. A. Ewalt,
E. M. Freeman, & D. L. Poole (Ed.), *Community building: Renewal, well-being, and shared responsibility* (pp.
95-106). Washington DC: NASW Press.

Myers, J. B. (Ed.). (1994). *The backlash: Child protection
under fire.* Thousand Oaks, CA: Sage.

North Carolina Division of Social Services. (1999, January). *Annual report 1988: North Carolina Department
of Health and Human Services, Intensive Family Preservation Services.* Raleigh, NC: Author.

O'Hare, W. P. (1996). *Kids Count data book: State profiles
of child well-being.* Baltimore: Annie E. Casey Foundation.

Orshanky, M. (1963, July). Children of the poor. *Social Security Bulletin, 26*(7), 3-13.

Pecora, P. J. (1990). Designing and managing family preser-
vation services: Implications for human services admin-
istration curricula. In J. K. Whittaker, J. Kinney, E. M.
Tracy, & C. Booth (Eds.), *Reaching high-risk families:
Intensive family preservation in human services.* New
York: Aldine de Gruyter.

Pecora, P., Fraser, M. W., Nelson, K. E., McCroskey, J., &
Meezan, W. (1995). *Evaluating family-based services.*
New York: Aldine De Gruyter.

Pecora, P., Whittaker, J. K., & Maluccio, A. N. (1992). *The
child welfare challenge: Policy, practice, and research.*
New York: Aldine De Gruyter.

Pelton, L. (1989). *For reasons of poverty: A critical analysis
of the public child welfare system in the United States.*
New York: Praeger.

Pelton, L. (1998). Four commentaries: How we can better
protect children from abuse and neglect. *The Future of
Children, 8*(1), 120-132.

Pennell, J., & Burford, G. (in press). Family group decision
making: Protecting children and women. *Child Welfare.*

Rooney, B. J. (1998). *Reconceptualizing poverty as quality
of life: Implications for theory, measurement, and intervention.* Unpublished paper, University of North
Carolina, Chapel Hill.

Saleebey, D. (Ed.). (1997). *The strengths perspective in social work practice* (2nd ed.). New York: Longman.

Sanders, T. I. (1998). *Strategic thinking and the new science.*
New York: Free Press.

Schene, A. (1998, Spring). Past, present, and future roles of
child protective services. *The Future of Children, 8*(1),
23-38.

Schorr, L. B. (1989). *Within our reach: Breaking the cycle of
disadvantage.* New York: Doubleday/Anchor Books.

Schorr, L. B. (1997). *Common purpose: Strengthening families and neighborhoods to rebuild America.* New York:
Anchor Books/Doubleday.

Sherman, A., Amey, C., Duffield, B., Ebb, N., & Weinstein,
D. (1998, December). *Welfare to what? Early findings
on family hardship and well-being.* Washington, DC:
Children's Defense Fund/National Coalition for the
Homeless.

Shook, K. (1999, February). *Does the loss of welfare income
increase the risk of involvement with the child welfare
system?* Paper presented at the Society for Social Work
and Research Conference, Austin, TX.

Shyne, A., & Schroeder, A. (1978). *A national study of social services to children and their families* (OHDS No.
78-30150). Washington, DC: U.S. Department of
Health, Education, and Welfare.

Simon, B. L. (1994). *The empowerment tradition in American social work: A history.* New York: Columbia University Press.

Taylor, B. E., Chait, R. P., & Holland, T. P. (1999). The new
work of the nonprofit board. In *Harvard Business Review on nonprofits* (pp. 53-76). Boston: Harvard Business School Press.

United Nations. (1949). *United Nations declaration of
the rights of the child* (Doc A/C.3/50/L.28). New York:
Author.

United States Census Bureau. Data for 1998, released 1999.

Usher, C. L. (1995). Improving evaluability through self-
evaluation. *Evaluation Practice, 16*(1), 59-68.

Usher, C. L. (1996, August). *Accountability and local governance: Devolution and dueling initiatives—issues in services for families and children.* Conference presentation,
North Carolina Family Preservation and Family Support Project, East Carolina University, Greenville, NC.

Usher, C. L. (1998, May). Managing care across systems to improve outcomes for families and communities. *The Journal of Behavioral Health Services & Research, 25*(2), 217-229.

Usher, C. L., Gibbs, D. A., & Wildfire, J. B. (1995). A framework for planning, implementing, and evaluating child welfare reforms. *Child Welfare, 74*(4), 859-876.

vander Straeten, S., & Sanders, J. (1998, July). *Developing a regional family preservation/family support system: A strategy to strengthen and preserve rural communities.* The 23rd Annual National Institute on Social Work and Human Services in Rural Areas, Chapel Hill, NC.

vander Straeten, S., & Weil, M. (1999, August). *Final report: Best practices in family preservation in children's mental health.* Unpublished paper, University of North Carolina, Chapel Hill.

Waldfogel, J. (1998a). *The future of child protection.* Cambridge, MA: Harvard University Press.

Waldfogel, J. (1998b). Rethinking the paradigm for child protection. *The Future of Children, 8*(1), 104-119.

Ward, H. (Ed.). (1995). *Looking after children: Research into practice* (Second report to the Department of Health). London: Her Majesty's Stationery Office.

Weil, M. (1985). Key components in providing efficient and effective services. In M. Weil & J. M. Karls (Eds.), *Case management in human service practice: A systematic approach to mobilizing resources for clients* (pp. 29-71). San Francisco: Jossey-Bass.

Weil, M. (1997). Community building: Building community practice. In P. L. Ewalt, E. M. Freeman, S. A. Kirk, & D. L. Poole (Eds.), *Social policy: Reform, research, and practice* (pp. 35-61). Washington, DC: NASW Press.

Weil, M. (2000). Social work practice in the social environment: Integrated practice—An empowerment/structural approach. In P. Allen-Meares & C. Garvin (Eds.), *The handbook of social work direct practice.* Thousand Oaks, CA: Sage.

Weil, M., & Dunlop, M. (1998). *Family-centered services: Community planning manual.* Chapel Hill: University of North Carolina.

Weil, M., & Hodges, V. G. (1995). *North Carolina family preservation and family support programs: Annual evaluation report* (Report of planning and implementation in 40 counties). Chapel Hill: University of North Carolina, School of Social Work.

Weil, M., & Luckey, H. (1995). *North Carolina state plan for family preservation and family support.* Chapel Hill: University of North Carolina, Chapel Hill.

Weissbourd, B. (1987). A brief history of family support programs. In S. L. Kagan, D. R. Powell, B. Weissbourd, & E. F. Zigler (Eds.), *America's family support programs.* New Haven, CT: Yale University Press.

Weissbourd, B., & Kagan, A. (1989, January). Family support programs: Catalysts for change. *American Journal of Orthopsychiatry, 59*(1), 20-31.

Wells, S. J. (1995). Child abuse and neglect overview. In R. L. Edwards (Ed.), *Encyclopedia of social work* (19th ed., pp. 346-353). Washington, DC: NASW Press.

Whittaker, J. K., & Garbarino, J. (Eds.). (1983). *Social support networks: Informal helping in the human services.* New York: Aldine De Gruyter.

Whittaker, J. K., Kinney, J., Tracy, E. M., & Booth, C. (1990). *Reaching high-risk families: Intensive family preservation in human services.* New York: Aldine De Gruyter.

Whittaker, J. K., & Tracy, E. M. (1990). Family preservation services and education for social work practice: Stimulus and response. In J. K. Whittaker, J. Kinney, E. M. Tracy, & C. Booth (Eds.), *Reaching high-risk families: Intensive family preservation services.* New York: Aldine de Gruyter.

Wilson, W. J. (1987). *The truly disadvantged: The inner city, the underclass, and public policy.* Chicago: University of Chicago Press.

Young, N., Gardner, S., & Coley, S. (1994). *Making a difference: Moving to outcome-based accountability for comprehensive service reforms* (Resource brief No. 7). Falls Church, VA: National Center for Service Integration.

Zipper, I. N., Rounds, K. A., & Weil, M. O. (1993). *Service coordination for early intervention programs: Parents and professionals.* Cambridge, MA: Brookline Books.

CHAPTER TWENTY-FIVE

Health Care and Social Work: Dilemmas and Opportunities

ANDREW WEISSMAN

GARY ROSENBERG

This chapter will focus on the changing political philosophy affecting the delivery of health and social services, the changing nature of not-for-profit institutions with special attention to health care, and the implications of these transformations for social work functions in health care organizations.

The present focus on hospital reorganization, as well as the resulting changes in current social work department structures and staffing levels, may not be the most advantageous way for social work functions to be delivered (Berger, Jensen, Mizrahi, Scesny, & Trachtenberg, 1996; Globerman, 1999; Michalski, Creighton, & Jackson, in press; Neuman, in press). Instead, social work's role in health care may change significantly if the profession focuses less on the hospital and acute episodes of illness and more on the continuity of care and aspects of health that include prevention, wellness, health promotion, and primary care as well as our more traditional roles in chronic illness.

In addition, the future viability of social work will require that health care systems provide for the management, training, and supervision of social work by social workers, through whatever arrangements. When this is not provided, organized social work staff tend to be replaced with other multiservice staff including social work, but with social workers working in isolation from each other.

POLITICAL AND IDEOLOGICAL SHIFTS: IMPLICATIONS FOR HEALTH CARE

The conservative political changes that have taken place in our federal and state governments have reduced the scope and size of all government programs. "Devolution, from the federal government to the states, and from the states to the localities, is the order of the day" (Schuerman, 1999, p. 1).

Programs have been cut, functions have been slashed, and the remaining tasks—reduced by budget cuts—have been outsourced to the marketplace. The remaining obligations have been re-engineered to conform to the standards of the private sector. These actions have been applied to such programs as the national park system and the Coast Guard as well as to the nonprofit human service fields.

These alterations are based on a central political notion that less government is better, that government program intervention is inefficient when compared to the private sector and market forces. Government activities are thought to be enhanced by injecting competitive market pressures into the public and voluntary sectors.

The ideological shift has changed the role of the individual from citizen to consumer. In an important result, those unable to purchase services in the market as consumers are reduced to an underclass of recipients. "Citizens have rights. Consumers have choices. Recipients get only what they are allocated" (O'Connor, 1998, p. 7).

These trends have been observed in the nonprofit world and the health care sector in particular.

Additionally, nonprofit and/or voluntary sector agencies are transforming themselves into market players who increasingly target services to the well-off and seek to expand their role as service providers on market terms to those who can pay for services. A radical, historic shift in society's health care process took place driven totally by market forces and entirely outside regulatory management. (Nieves, 1998, p. xiii)

The U.S. is witnessing the most drastic industry reorganization since the 19th century—the corporate takeover of American health care. Giant health systems have been created, formed not by their own desires, but in the crucible of employer and insurer for lower costs and by a government unable to legislate health care reform. (The Governance Committee, 1993, p. 2)

The failed effort to reshape the financing of medical care and to make it universally available has allowed the increasing domination of managed medical care. This change in medical care has allowed managed care and privatization to begin engulfing other social health realms, such as mental health services and child welfare, by mandating restricted choice in care to those served by social agencies and by privatizing these services. Managed care can be seen, it has been noted, as an "insurmountable opportunity."

Although the process of market-driven health care is still evolving, some clear trends do emerge. Costs of health care are being lowered by reducing the time a person spends in the hospital; by ending apparent overutilization of tests and procedures that provide little added quality or value; by shifting from more expensive hospital-based treatment to less expensive outpatient treatment; and by the negotiation of lower payments for hospitals and physicians by both insurance companies and the federal and state governments.

Managed care has shifted the priorities of care providers and focused on elements of the health care system that were previously neglected. More specifically, a major shift has occurred by moving from a tertiary-based acute care structure of hospital treatment to a health care system with incentives for prevention, health education, and primary care (Kotelchuck, 1994; Rosenberg, 1994). Managed care has also created a system that emphasizes efficiency and cost reduction. In some instances, this trend brought needed business practices to health care providers and institutions. In other instances, the emphasis on profit has totally overwhelmed the original missions of health care organizations. For example, in the quest for profit and competition for market share, for-profit and not-for-profit health care organizations alike have cut costs and minimized psychosocial services that enhance coping adaptation and compliance. The inexorable movement to achieve efficiency in hospitals has resulted in "many discipline-specific departments . . . being dismantled and the resulting losses and anger are enormous" (Globerman, 1999, p. 14). Institutions striving mightily to adjust to these new reimbursement parameters tend not to deal with their personnel in the most sensitive and caring manner. An organization

fighting to survive tends to ignore human resource and program quality issues until a later time.

RE-ENGINEERING HEALTH CARE SERVICES

The health care management literature reflects contradictory results for re-engineering and restructuring. On one hand, these activities have resulted in efficiency improvements such as shorter admissions processes, decreasing incident reports, fewer delays in obtaining lab and other tests, streamlining of long and complex interactions such as getting an inpatient an X-ray, a reduced number of individuals a patient/family has to deal with in the hospital, increased communication among staff members, more time for staff to spend with a patient, and less time allotted to administrative chores (Globerman, 1999; Neuman, 2000).

On the other hand, re-engineering efforts, which have paraded under banners such as total quality management, mergers and acquisitions, and turnarounds, have not accomplished their goals, according to most assessments. Kotter (1995) notes that fewer than 15 of the 100 or more companies he has studied have successfully transformed themselves. The Health Care Advisory Board characterized the results of re-engineering as "a disappointment all around" (Neuman, in press). Re-engineering of work processes, however, has been shown to be effective, whereas many restructuring efforts made without the rigor of process re-engineering have been less effective. Furthermore, when implementation is complete, a re-engineered organization has enabled people to work together differently: Many employees find that being allowed to think, to create, and to change the way work is done as a team is quite rewarding and adds significantly to the bottom line of the hospital program.

However, the speed with which health care organizations and hospitals adopted major institutional restructuring points to the hard financial realities facing health care providers. The years of cost-plus budgeting had led to extremely inefficient health care delivery systems, which allowed for-profit health care organizations, with a limited focus on profit maximization, to compete quite successfully with nonprofit and public counterparts. The for-profit sector had one master, profit. The community hospital and voluntary hospital, the academic health scene centers and neighborhood health care organizations, have many missions and customers, including those who cannot pay for the full cost of care.

Three focal issues still seem to face health care institutions: access, resources, and quality. Access issues and the allocation of resources have been discussed elsewhere (Rosenberg, 1998). The management of quality care is important for health care organizations. Quality is likely to be an important factor in determining market share and the allocation of resources to programs and departments. Quality in health care is the degree to which services to individuals and populations increase the likelihood of desired health outcomes, consistent with professional knowledge. We must always be prepared to change our notion of what constitutes quality as knowledge increases and we know more about what works and does not work. Quality is linked to the process of care delivery and to the outcomes of that care. Outcomes must be linked to a process that can change;

otherwise, they are not worth measuring. Overuse, underuse, and misuse of health services are the three categories frequently discussed under the rubric of quality (Chassin & Sui, 1996).

The changes occurring in hospitals are couched in various languages: re-engineering, restructuring, downsizing, mergers, product line management, and program management. However, all seek to change the health care institutions from conventional, hierarchical bureaucratic organizations—structured for the benefit of physician practice and the teaching of house staff, with some emphasis on research—to organizations that are structured for the most expeditious and efficient care of patients. Where traditional models valued order and centralized control, these newer flatter organizations value innovation and the flexibility to respond to changing financial and patient care conditions. For example, when surgical units are underused, they are closed temporarily, and other patients use the facilities they occupied. Or floors are converted permanently or temporarily to step-down units requiring less intensive use of resources, to nursing home status, or even to emergency department areas. Social work departments that were typically structured with a director, associate directors, assistant directors, supervisors, and line staff workers have changed dramatically as staff are assigned to working patient care teams with a loose affiliation to a centralized department, if it still exists.

THE ROLE OF SOCIAL WORK IN THE "NEW HEALTH CARE ORGANIZATION"

What, then, is the role of social work and its scope of activity in this new organizational environment? Do social work staff in health care become foot soldiers in the production of care, or will their future as care managers or care entrepreneurs involve purchasing or producing packages of care on behalf of government, citizens, consumers, or corporate welfare providers (O'Connor, 1998)? Will social work focus on vulnerable people and populations and those who do not access services? Can we convert a predominantly hospital-focused practice to a community practice addressing health in its broadest context?

It is clear that the usual functions and ways of organizing social work do not work as effectively as they did in the past. Doing nothing is not an option for social work managers and departments. Departments cannot ignore the realities of this new operational environment. Social work managers must have contingency plans and strategies for initiating change. To ignore the environment is to doom the department and the role of the professional social worker in health care.

An important aspect of this proactive stance is the newly emerging importance of information management: Social work service data and financial data are integral parts of a managed care system. If social work managers cannot use data effectively, they are at the mercy of third-party administrators and contracting agents who have business data systems that can be used to restrict rather than enhance services. Social work managers will develop competencies in information technology applications, such as

- Business aspects of care delivery such as cost, business planning for new programs, and return on investment
- Useful/relevant clinical information systems that capture inputs and outcomes and provide standards of good practice
- Community health information networks providing linkages among cooperating health and social agencies and between them and the main campus hospitals
- Provision of the appropriate security, privacy, and confidentiality safeguards to information system usage

It is just as clear that social work managers within health care organizations must be flexible, thoughtful, and attuned to the unique forces at work in their particular environments. They must be sensitive to tensions within the health care system and be able to understand the strengths and weaknesses of the systems in which they operate. Most clearly, as large health care systems emerge from local hospitals, community clinics, groups of physicians, and clusters of service providers, it is imperative that social work managers join with other departments and managers to create new systems of social health care delivery rather than attempt to survive alone as separate departments.

The burden of keeping the social work profession in health care alive through the work of staff social workers assigned, hired, and managed by non-social workers, as suggested by some authors, cannot work without supporting social work management structures (Globerman, 1999; Neuman, 2000). Staff who are hired, paid for, supervised, and promoted by separate departments will, quite logically, see their loyalty to that department or unit and not to a "profession." In the past, this has led to distinct social work specialties: psychiatric social work, pediatric social work, medical social work—at odds with each other and vying for status.

Hospital social work departments have to evolve into health system departments of social work designed, as the new payment structures develop, to keep capitated patients and families healthy and well. When patients and families become ill, the function of social work is to help create a seamless continuity of coordinated and high-quality health care services, capable of returning people to the least restrictive environments possible and with the highest level of functioning our services can provide. This also means developing health education programs that help patients understand and carry out their treatment plans.

As previously stated, the authors contend,

> Our central role should be to the community to provide services to the under-served, the disenfranchised, the chronically ill, those who out of ignorance, and where our current systems foster abuse, utilize the most expensive care in an inappropriate manner. We need to design and implement programs that provide the right mix of health care services at the right time. These include programs that aim at prevention, health promotion, wellness, and continuity. Programs that encompass community outreach to vulnerable populations need to be further developed and implemented. (Rosenberg & Weissman, 1995, p. 113; see also Rosenberg, 1994; Rosenberg & Holden, 1999; Simmons, 1994)

These activities should be tied to the primary care health care systems developing in all large health care organizations. Accomplishing these goals also means mobilizing community resources that are available for both health promotion and for the support of patients and families in a much more formal way than most social work departments do now (Rehr, Rosenberg, & Blumenfield, 1998).

There are successful examples of these types of innovations seen in practice today:

- Social workers and nurses formed a case management department that reduced the number of days for which their hospital was de-

nied payment by managed care companies. The number of denied days was reduced by 75%. (Hammer & Kerson, 1998)

- Telephone outreach services were provided to elderly patients recently released from the hospital in an effort to coordinate their care by home care teams. (Berkman, Heinik, Rosenthal, & Burke, 1999)

- A screening tool was developed by Berkman et al. (1996) for elderly patients in primary care, providing a needed inroad and early indicator for social work intervention; an outpatient geriatric assessment tool helps identify people at high risk. (Saltz, Schaefer, & Weinreich, 1998)

- Better linkages were developed between hospitals and community agencies to provide for the bio-psycho-social needs of the poor receiving mental health care. (Francoeur, Copley, & Miller, 1997)

- A preadmission psychosocial screening program was created for older orthopedic surgery patients that helped organize community and family resources for the patient and family after surgery. (Epstein et al., 1998)

- Those practice interventions and innovations that help re-establish the previous lifestyles of people suffering traumatic brain injury have been explicated. (Brzuzy & Speziale, 1997)

- Hospital-based programs were developed for community teenagers who are pregnant, helping them to become effective parents and begin to lead more productive lives. (Rothenberg & Weissman, in press)

As these examples illustrate, the opportunities for innovative social work services to contribute to the overall mission of the health care system are numerous. Social workers will need to replicate and expand on these and other innovations if they are to consolidate their place in the new health care environment. To take advantage of these openings may mean writing grants and more closely collaborating with community agencies as we seek to create exciting new programs and improve the standards of practice.

CURRENT AND FUTURE PERSPECTIVES ON THE ROLE OF THE SOCIAL WORKER

What do social workers need to know as they see more acutely ill people and are asked to serve them with fewer resources and in shorter periods of time? In the past, there was time to engage patients and families, some more willing than others, and feel a sense of accomplishment when they were helped to overcome obstacles to better functioning or improved care in the community.

Now, the social worker has to address quickly the immediate problems of patients and families who often do not want to hear what we have to say. Workers have to choose from a daunting array of problems and focus on the one that will help patients leave the hospital the soonest, often leaving other issues to be addressed by other agencies or by families themselves.

The active involvement of patients and families in the selection of problems to be addressed is a useful intervention in itself, and maintaining it is a hallmark of good practice. In the past, a rapid but thorough assessment of a patient family's problems and strengths was a bare minimum before planning an intervention. Now, the focus is on family strengths and mobilization of supporting resources in the patient's network. Progressive practice often begins by mobilizing these supports and resources before a patient enters the hospital.

In outpatient settings, in primary care settings, or in the provision of social work services to the chronically ill, as in the acute care setting, workers need to find out what the patient family wants, what the demands of the care system are on them, and how to reach agreement on the next steps to be taken. This strikes many social workers as less than an ideal approach to helping people, but under the current systems of reimbursement, managed care, and/or capitation, important parameters of care are defined by the structure of the financial payments and not by treatment needs, as social work practitioners define them.

Limits to health care treatment and social work treatment in particular have been established in a way that seems almost random to social workers, but these limits can also be seen as a response to social work's lack of data supporting our cost-effectiveness, a lack of demonstrable outcome data to support best practice interventions, and a weak effort at accepted quality management processes (Rehr, Rosenberg, & Blumenfield, 1998).

Social workers and other health professionals are acquiring a broad range of skills and are being called on to accept multiple roles and tasks that are shared with others as well as specific to social work practice. We are witnessing the emergence of a multipurpose health care team member who performs a large number of functions. It is clear that rigid boundaries between occupations are not sustainable. It may be that the traditional concept of professions is a bit outdated and that professions such as social work are best conceptualized as having permeable boundaries, both encompassing and being encompassed by other occupations.

Hence, social workers will be competing for employment with a wider range of health care and human services workers. Of course, the reverse is also true: Numerous new positions in health care are open to social workers. For example, the decrease in management positions in general and in social work in particular has meant that social workers sometimes report to non-social work managers, and some social workers run large departments of quality assurance, government relations, and community relations or hold other significant leadership positions where they are employed as managers of non-social work functions in health care. Multifunctional management is in the tradition of the settlement houses, and the settlement model is a useful one in thinking about future social work management in health care (Harkavy & Puckett, 1994). The opportunities to lead and manage programs to improve the human condition, integrate health and social services, and enable people to solve community problems that enhance health and well-being is the challenge for the future health care manager.

REFERENCES

Ai, A., Dunkle, R. E., Peterson, C., Saunders, D., Bolling, G., & Steven, F. (1998). Self-care and psychosocial adjustment of patients following cardiac surgery. *Social Work in Health Care, 27*(3), 75-95.

Berger, C. S., Jensen, J., Mizrahi, T., Scesny, A., & Trachtenberg, J. (1996). The changing scene of social work in hospitals: A report of a national study by the Society for Social Work Administration in Health Care and NASW. *Health and Social Work, 21*, 167-177.

Berkman, B., Shearer, S., Simmons, W. J., White, M., Robinson, M., Sampson, S., Holmes, W., Alison, D., & Thomson, J. A. (1996). Ambulatory elderly patients of primary care physicians: Functional, psychosocial, and environmental predictors of need for social work case management. *Social Work in Health Care, 22*(3), 1-20.

Berkman, P., Heinik, J., Rosenthal, M., & Burke, M. (1999). Supportive telephone outreach as an international strategy for elderly patients in a period of crisis. *Social Work in Health Care, 28*(4), 63-76.

Brzuzy, S., & Speziale, B. A. (1997). Persons with traumatic brain injuries and their families: Living arrangements and well-being postinjury. *Social Work in Health Care, 26*(1), 77-88.

Chassin, M., & Sui, A. L. (1996). Academic quality improvement: New medicine in old bottles. *Quality Management in Health Care, 4*(4), 40-46.

Epstein, J., Turgerman, A., Rotstein, Z., Horoszowski, H., Honig, P., Baurch, L., & Noy, S. (1998). Preadmission psychosocial screening of older orthopedic surgery patients: Evaluation of a social work service. *Social Work in Health Care, 27*(2), 1-25.

Francoeur, R. B., Copley, C. K., & Miller, P. J. (1997). The challenge to meet the mental health and biopsychosocial needs of the poor: Expanded roles for hospital social workers in a changing healthcare environment. *Social Work in Health Care, 26*(2), 1-13.

Globerman, J. (1999). Hospital restructuring: Positioning social work to manage change. *Social Work in Health Care, 28*(4), 13-30.

The Governance Committee. (1993). *Vision of the future.* Washington, DC: The Advisory Board.

Hammer, D., & Kerson, T. S. (1998). Reducing the number of days for which insurers deny payment to the hospital: One primary objective for a newly configured department of case management. *Social Work in Health Care, 28*(2), 31-49.

Harkavy, I., & Puckett, J. L. (1994). Lessons from Hull House for the contemporary urban university. *Social Service Review, 68*(3), 299-321.

Kotelchuck, R. (1994). The New York City health system: A paradigm under siege. *Social Work in Health Care, 20*(1), 21-34.

Kotter, J. P. (1995, March/April). Leading change: Why transformation efforts fail. *Harvard Business Review,* pp. 59-66.

Michalski, J., Creighton, E., & Jackson, L. (in press). The impact of hospital restructuring on social work services: A case study of a larage university-affiliated hospital in Canada. *Social Work in Health Care.*

Neuman, K. (2000). Understanding organizational reengineering in health care: Strategies for social work survival. *Social Work in Heatlh Care, 31*(2).

Nieves, J. (1998). Foreword. In *Humane managed care?* (p. xiii). New York: NASW Press.

O'Connor, I. (1998, August). *Rethinking social work and the human services in Australia: An introduction.* Paper presented at the Academy of Social Services in Australia.

Rehr, H., Rosenberg, G., & Blumenfield, S. (1998). Prescription for social and health care: Responding to the client, the community, and the organization. In H. Rehr,

G. Rosenberg, & S. Blumenfield (Eds.), *Creative social work in health care* (pp. 153-181). New York: Springer.

Rosenberg, G. (1994). Social work, the family, and the community. *Social Work in Health Care, 20*(1), 7-20.

Rosenberg, G. (1998). Preparing social workers for a managed care environment. In G. Schamess & A. Lightburn (Eds.), *Humane managed care?* Washington, DC: NASW Press.

Rosenberg, G., & Holden, G. (1999). Prevention, A few thoughts. *Social Work in Health Care, 28*(4), 1-11.

Rosenberg, G., & Weissman, A. (1995). Preliminary thoughts on sustaining a central social work department. *Social Work in Health Care, 20*(4), 111-116.

Rothenberg, A., & Weissman, A. (in press). The development of hospital-based programs for pregnant and parenting teens. *Social Work in Health Care.*

Saltz, C. C., Schaefer, T., & Weinreich, D. M. (1998). Streamlining outpatient geriatric assessment: Essential social, environmental, and economic variables. *Social Work in Health Care, 27*(1), 1-14.

Schuerman, J. R. (1999). Editorial. *Social Service Review, 73,* 1-2.

Simmons, J. (1994). Community-based care: The new health social work paradigm. *Social Work in Health Care, 20*(1), 35-46.

CHAPTER TWENTY-SIX

Aging

KATHLEEN H. WILBER

Mrs. C. is a recent widow in her early 80s. Besides being physically frail, she is unable to accurately answer questions about her age, birth date, or place of residence. Since the death of her husband, she has been unable to pay her bills, keep her apartment clean, or adequately prepare food. Although she appears to have little in the way of assets, she believes that she is related to the King of England and had a grandfather in Montana who has willed her money. She alleges that this money, which she kept in a suitcase, has been stolen from her by the manager of her building, along with her furniture, dishes, and personal belongings. Mrs. C. does not have a working phone; her refrigerator has been disconnected; there is no food in her house, and she remembers eating little in recent days. Her companions are two uncaged birds and a small dog.

Mrs. C.'s case illustrates the complexities and organizational independencies inherent in serving the subset of older people who require assistance from human service organizations (HSOs). Although she managed adequately throughout her adult life, failing health, loss of social support, and cognitive impairment have jeopardized Mrs. C.'s ability to care for herself and to provide for her basic needs. In addition to low income and functional problems, she is eligible for a variety of services on the basis of her age, which serves as a proxy for need.

Mrs. C.'s case raises a number of important questions: What does she need, and which providers can best help? How can providers work effectively across their various specializations to provide continuity? What is the unique role of the manager in developing, administering, and coordinating programs and services for multiproblem older adults in contrast to other populations? What are new emerging models designed to serve individuals such as Mrs. C., and how do these models affect the management of services for older people. To address these issues, I begin this chapter with a discussion of unique characteristics of older adults and the intra-organizational and contextual issues that result from the special needs of the older population. This is followed by a discussion of the varied and eclectic roles of managers in organizations that serve older adults. I focus on the context of diversity, the meaning of work, the importance of interacting with the broader service-delivery network, the new roles of information systems in service delivery, and the function that outcome measures, particularly consumer satisfaction, are beginning to serve in the field of aging. I conclude with a discussion of managers as advocates and entrepreneurs in a rapidly evolving and increasingly important field.

THE UNITED STATES AS AN AGING SOCIETY

Like most other developed and developing countries, the United States is an aging society. During the 20th century, average life expectancy increased dramatically, from slightly less than 50 years in 1900 to more than 75 years in 1990. This impressive achievement combined with a decreasing birthrate has resulted in the "graying of America." Currently, the age 65+ group is the fastest-growing segment of the population, increasing at more than twice the rate of the under 65 population. Within the 65+ population, the oldest old (age 85+) group is showing the most dramatic growth. Increases in the senior population will accelerate even more dramatically starting in 2011, when members of the largest generation in history, the baby boomers, begin to turn 65, creating both a need and an opportunity for social work. Schneider (1997) notes that those age 65 and older currently compose about 12% of the population but account for one third of health care costs. Without dramatic improvement in the health of this population, the demand for services and the costs of care are expected to increase substantially in the coming decades.

Because HSOs are people-processing organizations (Hasenfeld, 1983) designed to assist and transform clients, it is important for managers to understand the unique characteristics and needs of the client group, the core competencies essential to serving this population, and the organizational and policy environment in which organizations function. Although we tend to talk about "senior citizens" as a homogeneous group, the population of adults age 65+ is exceedingly diverse. Older adults encompass an age span of over 40 years and a wide range of health and mental health conditions, ranging from individuals who are healthy, high-functioning, and productive to those who are cognitively and functionally dependent. Contrary to stereotypes, the vast majority of older adults fall into the category of healthy aging, with less than 5% living in institutional settings such as nursing homes. Nevertheless, older adults are more likely than younger people to have chronic health conditions that impair functioning, and consequently, they are more likely to turn to formal organizations for assistance. Similarly, although most older adults are economically secure, some subgroups, particularly the oldest old, women, minorities, and those who live alone, have high rates of poverty. Most older adults retain their cognitive abilities. Yet, cognitive impairment from dementing illnesses, such as Alzheimer's disease and stroke, increases

TABLE 26.1 Types of Organizations That Serve Older Adults

- Assisted living facilities
- Area agencies on aging
- Adult day care
- Alzheimer's associations
- Case management organizations (includes public, voluntary, and proprietary)
- Disability/rehabilitation services
- Departments of public social services (including adult protective service programs and in-home supportive services)
- Health clinics
- Health departments
- Home health agencies
- Hospice
- Hospitals
- Housing
- Information and referral services
- Mental health
- Money management
- Meals programs
- Ombudsman
- Private charities
- Guardianship/conservatorship
- Retired Senior Volunteer Programs/Senior companions
- Senior centers
- Skilled nursing facilities
- Social Security Offices
- Transportation

NOTE: This list, originally developed for California, has been modified somewhat to represent programs and services found throughout the country.

with advanced age from less than 3% at age 65 to more than 25% at age 85+ (Schneider, 1997), resulting in a subset of older adults who have compromised decision-making capacity.

Older people are served by a variety of organizations, including those that target them specifically, such as senior centers, and others that serve clients of all ages, such as hospitals. Services are provided in diverse settings including the client's home, community-based day services, group homes, skilled nursing facilities, rehabilitation centers, and comprehensive medical centers. Services are offered in public, voluntary, and corporate settings to individuals referred to as consumers, patients, residents, clients, participants, and customers.

Torres-Gil (1992) has identified over 80 programs at the federal level directed toward older people. When state and locally funded services are added, the result is an intricate web of agencies that fund and regulate a diverse array of services. Some examples of programs available to older adults are listed in Table 26.1. Because many organizations that serve older adults are funded by different entities, managers must be aware of mandates, requirements, and regulations from a variety of government departments and agencies. For example, skilled nursing facilities (SNF) are regulated by the Health Care Financing Administration at the federal level. At the state level, using California as an example, the Department of Health Services regulates SNFs, the Department of Aging monitors adult day care, and the Department of Social Services is charged with overseeing assisted living facilities, called Residential Care Facilities for the Elderly. Given this diverse regulatory environment, organizations that provide a variety of services may need different licenses, staffing requirements, and certification.

CORE VALUES GUIDE
SERVICE DELIVERY

Despite the great variety of aging services, several core values have emerged to guide service delivery. These include facilitating the older person's ability to age in place (Callahan, 1992a), striving to offer the least restrictive appropriate alternative (Wilber & Reynolds, 1995), centering decisions to the greatest extent possible around the older adult's preferences and expressed needs (Kaufman & Becker, 1996; Wetle & Walker, 1996), supporting informal caregivers (Doty, 1986), and clinically integrating services to provide a seamless continuum (Evashwick, 1996). *Aging in place* recognizes that individuals should not be forced to relocate to different settings because they require higher levels of care. Rather, to the extent possible, services should be designed to serve the consumers in the setting of their choice, typically the home, and should be flexible enough to address changing needs. *The least restrictive appropriate alternative* is a term that originated with a court case, *Lake v. Cameron* (1966), in which the District of Columbia Court of Appeals ruled that less restrictive alternatives must be sought before an individual may be held in an institution. Over the years, this ruling has resulted in the value that consumers are served with as few constraints placed on them as possible. It also suggests that individuals are served in the least restrictive care setting, and their rights and liberties are recognized and respected. *Consumer-directed care* is the notion that, to the extent feasible, decisions about care are made by the recipient of service rather than dictated by the provider. To support informed decisions, providers need to listen to recipients' concerns and questions, inform them of available choices,

and discuss the consequences of using available options.

In contrast to the myth that families abandon older adults, over 80% of the care for older people not in skilled nursing facilities is provided by unpaid informal caregivers (Doty, Stone, Jackson, & Adler, 1996; Wiener, Illson, & Hanley, 1994). Because of the high demands of caring for a frail older person, high stress, burnout, and caregiver burden may become problems. Formal services that value, support, and complement informal care, including counseling, support groups, and respite services, offer effective means to ensure continuity and service effectiveness. Finally, clinical integration of services seeks to overcome the fragmentation that results from multiple providers and caregivers. The goal is to provide services that consumers perceive to be seamless when it is necessary to weave together services of multiple providers.

SERVICES FOR OLDER ADULTS
ARE EVOLVING IN A
HYPER-TURBULENT ENVIRONMENT

The environment of aging organizations can be characterized as dynamic, rapidly changing, and even hyper-turbulent. Reduced public funding, the dramatic changes in health care discussed in Chapter 25, increased private sector product development, and questions of whether public dollars should fund services to all older Americans or target those in greatest need have changed the context of aging services. Recently, the role of the federal government in such traditionally sacrosanct programs as Social Security and Medicare has been questioned. Media portrayals have characterized older people as "greedy geezers" enjoying benefits at the expense of other needy groups, particularly children. And some groups have complained of inequity among the generations in the allocation of public dollars (Hewitt & Howe, 1988).

As with social welfare programs for other groups, a number of programs for older adults have come under increased scrutiny. Yet, to some extent, programs targeting aging have been protected from those seeking to reduce the government's role in social services by public opinion polls that demonstrate persistent and widespread support for such programs across all age groups. For example, a recent survey found that about 90% of Americans of all ages believe that spending on Social Security is "about right" or "too little" (Munnell, 1998). One explanation for this support is that older adults have traditionally been viewed as "the deserving poor" (Achenbaum, 1983). This portrayal is based, in part, on ageist stereotypes that view older people as frail, forgetful, and unable to earn money by working. A second perspective is that because of life-long contributions to family, community, and the Social Security program, older people have earned the right to publicly funded retirement. A third view is that the economic support for older people from social insurance programs such as Social Security increases financial independence and reduces reliance on their adult children. Widespread support also relates to the reality that aging is a condition that affects everyone including public officials who make policy decisions and their families (Callahan, 1992b).

Changes in policy priorities and funding streams are changing how services are organized. As Mrs. C's case illustrates, older adults who require assistance often need services from multiple providers with functional specializa-tions in areas such as health, mental health, personal care, transportation, and housing. Traditionally, these services have been offered by different organizations paid for by different delivery streams, requiring efforts to link and coordinate services to address the needs of the whole person. Increasingly, efforts to consolidate services for older people are driven by health care organizations. Expansion of Medicare and Medicaid coupled with reductions in social service funding have led to concerns about the "medicalization" of services for older people (Cox & Parsons, 1994; Estes, Swan, & Associates, 1993). As part of this trend, health care organizations are expanding their missions, merging with competitors, or vertically integrating to develop comprehensive services within a single setting. In addition to increased reliance on biomedical solutions, the move toward large-scale complex organizations to deliver services to older adults is being driven by several trends. These include (a) recognition by private sector health care and housing developers of an emerging market of affluent older people, (b) efforts to contain public costs through managed care and consolidation, and (c) the need for investment capital to develop and launch new innovative service models. These models include assisted living facilities that provide housing and supportive services, managed care health plans that offer preventive services and benefits such as prescription drugs not offered by Medicare fee-for-services, and community-based long-term care programs that provide a wide array of services for older people who wish to remain in their homes.

After the Medicare program, with a budget of over $200 billion in 1997, the two major payment sources for older adults services are (a) older individuals themselves and their families and (b) state Medicaid programs, with Medicaid second only to education as the largest budget item for most states. Although older adults and people with disabilities make up about one quarter of Medicaid beneficiaries, they account for two thirds of Medicaid expenditures (Wiener, 1996). Because about 80% of long-term care Medicaid dollars are directed to institutional care, there is increasing interest in reducing the "nursing home bias" as well as using managed care to contain costs. As more services move to capitated arrangements, however, organizations require increased capital for providers to assume the risk of paying for and providing care.

MANAGERS OF PROGRAMS FOR OLDER ADULTS HAVE ECLECTIC ROLES

Given a context of diverse mandates and service missions, what is it that managers of aging organizations do? To what extent are their activities similar or different from each other? To what extent are they similar or different from managers in other HSOs, or even in other product-oriented services? What are the core competencies of knowledge and skill areas required to manage aging services?

Chapter 12 describes the tasks and functions performed by managers of HSOs. To replicate Mintzberg's (1975) study of executives in complex organizations, Masunaga (1998) analyzed data from 34 managers of aging services, each of whom had been shadowed for 16 hours. Like Mintzberg's managers, managers in aging engaged in activities characterized by brevity, interruption, fragmentation, and variety, with diversity of activities reflected in the work of individual managers. Although managers per-

formed many of the same core functions (e.g., gathering and conveying information, supervising, planning, problem solving), no typical pattern emerged. Although they were similar to Mintzberg's managers, managers in aging services spent more time on activities categorized as interpersonal, which includes roles as figurehead, leader, and liaison. Much of this time was spent directly with client-related issues, as well as supervision and "tours," or "management by walking around" (Peters & Waterman, 1982). The focus on client issues was most prevalent for managers of long-term care facilities. Information gathering and disseminating also was a prominent activity for managers in aging settings.

Traditionally, managers in aging have worked in organizations that are relatively small, offering them the opportunity to get to know the individuals their organizations serve. Some managers, either from necessity or interest serve as substitute operators for staff who provide direct service. For example, a director in adult day care not only knows the attendees but pitches in to provide service when extra caregiving help is needed. A nursing home administrator spends his lunch hour feeding dependent residents to model teamwork, emphasize the priority of patient care, and assess quality. Because the clients, staff, and managers are "under the same roof," tours offer a practical means to monitor performance, supervise diverse staff, and create a culture of accountability and participation.

MANAGING PROFESSIONAL AND ETHNIC DIVERSITY

As Mrs. C.'s case shows, older adults who need help from HSOs may have multiple, complex problems that require treatment from a variety of professionals and paraprofessionals. Yet, professionals often have different agendas and values, and at times, they work at cross-purposes with each other. Organizing and clinically integrating services requires coordination between disciplines and often across organizational boundaries. (For further discussion, see Chapter 14.) Several recently implemented programs offer examples of efforts to clinically integrate diverse services. For example, the Program of All Inclusive Care for the Elderly (PACE), modeled on the successful On Lok program in San Francisco, integrates the financing and service delivery of all medical and long-term care services for its enrollees. Currently expanding to a number of sites across the country, PACE is an interdisciplinary program: In addition to social workers, it includes nurses, physicians, therapists, van drivers, and nursing and therapy assistants in client conferences and treatment decision making. Staff meets daily in nonhierarchical team meetings to discuss problems and track progress. One of the important roles of managers is to facilitate input and interaction based on familiarity with the issues rather than on professional status to ensure that van drivers as well as physicians actively contribute (On Lok, Inc., 1995).

Because not all organizations offer services under one roof, other vehicles, such as case conferences, are used to coordinate care across organizations. For example, to battle elder abuse, the Los Angeles-based fiduciary abuse specialists team (FAST) regularly brings together attorneys, adult protective services workers, case managers, law enforcement officers, and health care professionals, who share ideas, explore resources, and examine problems from different perspectives.

In addition to professional diversity, managers of aging services need skills to manage an increasingly ethnically diverse workforce. For example, a skilled nursing facility might employ a white male administrator and a predominantly Filipino and female skilled nursing staff, an African-American therapy team, and Latino nurses aides, resulting in different languages, cultures, and approaches to care. In addition to miscues from language differences, misunderstandings can occur as a result of different values and norms of behavior. For example, out of respect for authority, a Latina aide does not express her disagreement with an administrator who asks for her feedback on a controversial matter. The manager, who values open communication, fails to recognize that, for some of his staff, respect is valued over complete candor. Thus, he misinterprets the aide's communication.

Whereas the workforce is increasingly diverse, the older population is predominately white. Dementing illnesses that affect cognition and judgment, as well as prejudices that developed in an era that was less accepting of differences, may regrettably result in bigoted behavior and offensive comments. This creates a climate that managers must address through staff in-service sessions, counseling, support, and, where appropriate, client counseling. In addition, managers must balance the rights and responsibilities of staff with recognition of the culturally based preferences of their clients. Because many services for older adults are low tech/high touch, culture is an important determinant of satisfaction with care (Markides & Wallace, 1996). Older adults of color are underrepresented in institutional care because of norms of family responsibility and filial piety and perhaps because facilities too often fail to address language and cultural preferences. The experience of providers suggests that adult children who have acculturated to the United States are increasingly willing to place their parents in health facilities and community-based day programs, suggesting the need for enhanced language capacity, culturally sensitive programming, and outreach to ethnic minorities.

Managers should also recognize that staff, because of their close contact and interactions with consumers, might be most sensitive to individual needs and preferences. One study indicated that staff were sometimes caught between their awareness of skilled nursing facility residents' desire for quality of care and the legitimate limitations of the facility (Cohn & Sugar, 1991). Managers can play an important role in enhancing both the quality of care and staff satisfaction by facilitating ongoing communication among consumers, their families, staff, and management.

THE MEANING OF WORK IN AGING SERVICES

Human capital is the major resource in organizations that serve older adults. In that much of the direct service work in aging entails low-skilled, hands-on, personal care, such as assistance with activities of daily living, it is extremely important for managers to recognize the inherent dignity and significance of such work and to convey that it is socially respected, meaningful, and appreciated. For example, Wilber and Specht (1994) found that, although workers in adult day care were at risk of burnout because of high stress on the job and at home, they reported less burnout than other so-

cial and health-related positions, in part because of the value they attached to their work. Workers also rated characteristics of their environment, including autonomy, support, and control, more favorably than standardized norms. Respondents identified direct work with clients as the most rewarding aspect of their job, whereas organizational factors such as paperwork and lack of adequate resources were the most bothersome. Managers can reduce staff burnout by minimizing paperwork and staying out of the way of appropriate staff-level decision making (Perrow, 1986). For example, the "Eden Alternative," a model of institutional care, offers a natural habitat of birds, dogs, cats, and rabbits; indoor and outdoor plants; vegetable gardens; intergenerational programs; and staff-level decision making. As part of this model, staff are responsible for scheduling their own work, which Thomas (1996) suggests has increased satisfaction and reduced absenteeism. Program implications are that managers should hire competent staff, train them well, give them the autonomy and support to design flexible work roles and engage in client-centered problem solving, and minimize excessive documentation, oversight, and paperwork.

Despite such efforts, an ongoing problem in aging services, particularly those that serve the most vulnerable clients, is excessively high caseloads. For example, adult protective services and public guardians often have many times the recommended caseload of 30 to 50 clients. In such circumstances, managers must serve as advocates for their employees while simultaneously striving to make the work environment as productive as possible. Efforts to enhance productivity such as strategic planning, team building, and motivation become both more difficult and more important under such circumstances.

MANAGERS WORK IN A NETWORK OF INFORMAL RELATIONSHIPS

Because few organizations have the capacity to provide the needed range of services, organizing and delivering diverse services is an ongoing problem. Managers must identify their niche, their specific mission, and role and analyze the interdependencies they have with other providers to maintain strategic alliances and relations. Currently, most service-delivery systems for older adults lack a formal organizing structure; rather, coordination is built on informal interorganizational relationships and client-referral networks. As Evashwick (1996) points out, individual services for older adults are better developed than the mechanisms to integrate these services. Care coordination, or case management, is one mechanism to bundle services for consumers like Mrs. C., who need help from several programs. As a means to clinically integrate services, care coordination is preferred by many managers because, unlike interventions, such as consolidation, that alter the way services are fundamentally organized, care coordination does not change structural relationships between organizations (Austin, 1983).

Despite provider preference for autonomy, a number of states are beginning to experiment with reorganizing their service-delivery structures for older people. Building from state Medicaid programs, which fund about half of long-term care costs, many states are experimenting with systems that link acute and long-term health care with in-home and community-based social services. Although no single model has emerged, several states, most notably Oregon, Washington, and Colorado, have been identified as examples of innovative systems (Coleman, 1996; U.S. General Accounting Office, 1994). In addition, promising new approaches to organize and deliver services to older people may be found in the application of technology to develop effective information systems. (See Chapter 16 for further discussion of information systems.)

VIRTUAL ORGANIZATIONS: MANAGING AND USING INFORMATION SYSTEMS

HSOs are by nature information intensive (Zawadski, 1996). For example, organizations serving Mrs. C. may need and collect a variety of data yet remain unaware that other organizations are involved. As the information revolution changes how age-based HSOs relate to each other, there is increasing interest and opportunity to develop integrated information systems (IIS). Although the development of tools such as shared assessments and client-tracking mechanisms is in its infancy, such approaches hold the promise of more efficient and effective delivery. According to Zawadski (1996), an IIS is "an array of multiple information sets linked together in an organized way" (p. 180). Such a system can track Mrs. C. across service settings (e.g., from the hospital to a board and care, to day care), document her service utilization, and manage billing, while simultaneously providing aggregate data about service use and cost. Ultimately, an IIS should result in better information to assess client outcomes.

Unfortunately, many organizations that serve older people have failed to keep pace with the demands for information. Computer-literate staff and up-to-date hardware and software are too often in short supply and relegated to a low priority. As we evolve to an information economy, the development of effective internally and externally linked IIS will be essential. Managers must be prepared to convince both funders and staff that this is a priority area. In facility-based SNF care, federal requirements mandate an assessment using a nationally standardized minimum data set (MDS) within 2 weeks of an individual's admission. This information is increasing knowledge about the characteristics of individuals served in SNFs. In addition, to help track individuals across settings and build an integrated information system, efforts are under way to apply the MDS to in-home and community services (Morris et al., 1997). Such efforts are likely to transform the way services are delivered and the way information is used to evaluate programs and measure outcomes in the coming years.

MEASURING CONSUMER OUTCOMES

One of the primary approaches to measuring outcomes is to assess consumer satisfaction, which, by relying on the subjective evaluation of the client (Maciejewski, Kawiecki, & Rockwood, 1997), is linked to the value of consumer-directed care. Consumer satisfaction is also of increasing interest as more HSOs seek to implement total quality management and focus on continuous quality improvement (Martin, 1993).

A study by Cohn and Sugar (1991) found differences in how older consumers, their families, staff, and management defined the quality of life and quality of care. In addition to differing assumptions about quality, information asymmetry is a problem for consumers trying to evaluate the technical quality of professional services. For example, consumers such as Mrs. C. may lack the ability to evaluate the technical quality of their care. In such instances, family members may provide a second option of consumer input. Some services, for very frail older people, actually regard the family, generally the adult children, as the client. Because family members may be the legal guardians or the informally acknowledged decision makers for adults with dementia, they may well be the consumer's proxy. Nevertheless, to the greatest extent feasible, it is important to include the opinion of the older adult client in decisions.

In addition to consumer satisfaction, a number of generic and specific instruments have been developed to measure service quality and outcomes (e.g., see Kane, 1997; Kazis, Skinner, Miller, Clark, & Lee, 1996). One of the greatest challenges of outcome studies for vulnerable older adults is unrealistic goals and expectations. For example, for a frail older adult, a successful intervention may be one that slows decline rather than restores or improves functioning. Yet, although prognoses in chronic care are often unclear, making it difficult to predict treatment effects, mandates for services tend to focus on restoring functioning. In the future, improved IIS coupled with efforts to better measure outcomes offer the promise of increasing the manager's capacity to evaluate the extent to which goals are achieved and services are effective. The ability to assess outcomes will also serve managers who are increasingly called on to demonstrate that they deliver cost-effective services with proven value to both clients and funding organizations.

MANAGERS MUST BE ADVOCATES AND ENTREPRENEURS

Traditionally, aging services have been dominated by small, community-based organizations. Currently, however, several trends are changing this landscape. The first is the prospective payment system (PPS), under which the provider is paid a fixed payment in advance rather than reimbursed for costs after they have been incurred. In 1984, Medicare hospital payment moved from cost reimbursement to PPS, based on categories of illnesses called diagnostic related groups (DRGs). Payment for physicians came under prospective payment in the early 1990s, with the resource-based relative value system (RBRVS). The Balanced Budget Act of 1997 included prospective payment for nursing homes and home health organizations receiving Medicare payment beginning in January 1999. Under this system, SNFs are reimbursed using an acuity-based approach called resource utilization groups (RUGs), which is similar to DRGs in that higher reimbursement is tied to higher patient-acuity categories.

The second trend is capitated managed care, under which the provider is paid a fixed amount whether or not a service is provided and is financially at risk for all required care. Several models of community-based care, developed from national demonstrations such as the PACE program discussed earlier, use capitated delivery systems. Increasingly, managers can expect to receive capitated reimbursement and to be financially at risk for services.

Another trend is the "corporatization" of aging services. Because many innovations require large amounts of capital, smaller programs are merging into larger, more resource-rich organizations, particularly in health care, housing, and assisted living. Organizations in these sectors are increasingly run by managers with skills in financial management and cost accounting. In addition to mergers between nonprofit organizations, some nonprofits have been purchased by proprietary corporations evolving into publicly traded companies. Sometimes, these organizations compete with nonprofits; other times they focus on high-income elderly.

A consequence of a market approach to services for elders is that the client population remaining for traditional HSOs may be composed of the most vulnerable and difficult-to-serve older adults. Increasingly, for those HSOs who serve vulnerable older people, mission matters. Managers must work with key stakeholders to clearly identify their organization's mission, target population, and strategic goals. And increasingly, as more needs chase fewer public dollars, managers will need to develop fundraising capacity within their organizations to address unmet needs. This means that managers should assess their needs for development staff who can build and enhance their organization's endowment and discretionary funding capacity. To the extent that such a strategy is effective, managers will have a stronger base from which to develop innovative programs, support underfunded areas, help the organization weather funding uncertainties, or provide a cushion when cash flow is tight.

THE FUTURE

It is both an exciting and a challenging time to manage HSOs for older adults. Population aging is transforming society, affecting areas as diverse as family relationships; work and retirement; and the management, organization, and delivery of health care and social services. Important questions for the 21st century include: How much will we as a society benefit from medical breakthroughs to overcome the burdens of disease and disability linked with the aging process? To what extent will an emphasis on wellness and successful aging affect the individual social and economic costs associated with the later decades of life? How will we respond to the individual needs and problems not conquered by technology or healthier lifestyles?

Social service organizations, threatened by reduction in publicly funded social welfare programs on the one hand, may find competition from large health care providers developing comprehensive health and social service delivery models on the other. It is unclear how small, traditional social services organizations will fare in an increasingly competitive environment of larger well-funded providers. However, it is clear that managers of programs that serve elders will need sophisticated managerial skills to ensure that their organizations survive and thrive in a highly competitive marketplace.

Currently, the field of aging is undergoing a rapid transition. Increasing numbers of older adults and an expanded variety of services offer greater opportunities to work in the field of aging than ever before. New providers and services are entering the field at a breathtaking rate, creating exciting opportunities to address the needs and preferences of older people. Those responsible for HSOs for older people need to balance mission and management to ensure that their organizations flourish in a future that promises to be the most challenging, competitive, and promising period ever for HSOs for older people.

REFERENCES

Achenbaum, A. W. (1983). *Shades of gray: Old age, American values, and federal policies since 1920*. Boston: Little, Brown.

Austin, C. (1983). Case management in long-term care: Options and opportunities. *Health and Social Work, 8*(1), 16-30.

Callahan, J. J. (1992a). Aging in place. *Generations, 16*(2).

Callahan, J. J. (1992b). Foreword. In W. N. Leutz, J. A. Captiman, M. MacAdam, & R. Abrahams (Eds.), *Care for frail elders: Developing community solutions*. Westport, CT: Auburn House.

Cohn, J., & Sugar, J. A. (1991). Determinants of quality of life in institutions: Perceptions of frail older residents, staff, and families. In J. E. Birren, J. E. Lubben, J. Cichowlas Rowe, & D. E. Deutchman (Eds.), *The concept of measurement of quality of life in the frail elderly*. New York: Academic Press.

Coleman, B. (1996). *New directions for state long-term care systems: Vol. 1. A review*. Washington, DC: American Association of Retired Persons.

Cox, E. O., & Parsons, R. J. (1994). *Empowerment-oriented social work practice with the elderly*. Pacific Grove, CA: Brooks/Cole.

Doty, P. (1986). Family care of the elderly: The role of public policy. *Milbank Memorial Fund Quarterly, 64*, 34-75.

Doty, P., Stone, R., Jackson, M. E., & Adler, M. (1996). Informal caregiving. In C. J. Evashwick (Ed.), *The continuum of long-term care: An integrated systems approach* (pp. 125-141). Albany, NY: Delmar.

Estes, C. L., Swan, J. H., & Associates. (1993). *The long-term care crisis: Elders trapped in the no-care zone*. Newbury Park, CA: Sage.

Evashwick, C. J. (1996). *The continuum of long-term care: An integrated systems approach*. Albany, NY: Delmar.

Hasenfeld, Y. (1983). *Human service organizations*. Englewood Cliffs, NJ: Prentice Hall.

Hewitt, P. S., & Howe, N. (1988). Future of generational politics. *Generations, 7*(3), 10-13.

Kane, R. L. (1997). Approaching the outcome questions. In R. L. Kane (Ed.), *Understanding health outcomes research* (pp. 1-15). Gaithersburg, MD: Aspen.

Kaufman, S. R., & Becker, G. (1996). Frailty, risk, and choice: Cultural discourses and the question of responsibility. In M. Smyer, K. W. Schaie, & M. B. Kapp (Eds.), *Older adults' decision making and the law.* New York: Springer.

Kazis, L. E., Skinner, K., Miller, D., Clark, J., & Lee, A. (1996). Quality of life with chronically ill elderly. In J. C. Romeis, R. M. Cle, & J. E. Whorle (Eds.), *Applying health services research to long-term care.* New York: Springer.

Lake v. Cameron, 364 F.2d 657 (124 U.S. App. D.C. 1966).

Maciejewski, M., Kawiecki, J., & Rockwood, T. (1997). Satisfaction. In R. L. Kane (Ed.), *Understanding health outcomes research* (pp. 67-89). Gaithersburg, MD: Aspen.

Markides, K. S., & Wallace, S. P. (1996). Health and long-term care needs of ethnic minority elders. In J. C. Romeis, R. M. Coe, & J. E. Morley (Eds.), *Applying health services research to long-term care.* New York: Springer.

Martin, L. (1993). *Total quality management in human service organizations.* Newbury Park, CA: Sage.

Masunaga, H. (1998). *Managers in aging-related organizations: Are their managerial activities similar?* Unpublished manuscript, Andrus Gerontology Center, Los Angeles.

Mintzberg, H. (1975). A manager's job: Folklore and fact. *Harvard Business Review, 53,* 49-61.

Morris, J. N., Fries, B. E., Steel, K., Ikegami, N., Bernabei, R., Carpernter, G. I., Gilgan, R., Hirdes, J. P., & Topinkova, E. (1997). Comprehensive clinical assessment in community settings: Applicability of the MDS-HC. *Journal of the American Geriatric Society, 45*(8), 1017-1024.

Munnell, A. M. (1998). *Public support Social Security despite weak confidence.* Available: http://www.nasi.org/Update/May98/support.htm

On Lok, Inc. (1995). *PACE fact book: Information about the program of all-inclusive care for the elderly.* San Francisco: Author.

Perrow, C. (1986). *Complex organizations: A critical essay* (3rd ed.). New York: Random House.

Peters, T. J., & Waterman, R. H. (1982). *In search of excellence.* New York: Free Press.

Peterson, D. A. (1990). Personnel to serve the aging in the field of social work: Implications for educating professionals. *Social Work, 35,* 412-418.

Schneider, E. L. (1997). Population aging: Consequences for long-term care financing. In K. H. Wilber, E. L. Schneider, & D. Polisar (Eds.), *A secure old aging: Approaches to long-term care financing.* New York: Springer.

Thomas, W. (1996). *Life worth living: How someone you love can still live in a nursing home: The Eden alternative in action.* Acton, MA: Vanderwyk & Burnham.

Torres-Gil, F. M. (1992). *The new aging: Politics and change in America.* New York: Auburn House.

U.S. General Accounting Office. (1994). *Long-term care issues* (GAO/HRD-109). Washington, DC: Government Printing Office.

Wetle, T., & Walker, L. (1996). Ethical issues across the long-term care continuum. In C. J. Evashwick (Ed.), *The continuum of long-term care: An integrated systems approach* (pp. 253-264). Albany, NY: Delmar.

Wiener, J. M. (1996). *Can Medicaid long-term care expenditures for the elderly be reduced?* New York: The Commonwealth Fund.

Wiener, J. M., Illson, L. H., & Hanley, R. J. (1994). *Sharing the burden: Strategies for public and private long-term care insurance.* Washington, DC: The Brookings Institution.

Wilber, K. H., & Reynolds, S. L. (1995). Rethinking alternatives to guardianship. *The Gerontologist, 35,* 39-56.

Wilber, K. H., & Specht, C. V. (1994). Prevalence and predictors of burnout among adult day care providers. *The Journal of Applied Gerontology, 13,* 282-298.

Zawadski, R. (1996). Integrated information systems for chronic care: A model linking acute and long-term care. In C. J. Evashwick (Ed.), *The continuum of long-term care: An integrated systems approach* (pp. 179-191). Albany, NY: Delmar.

Author Index

Abbott, G., 482
Abels, P., 90, 93
Abraham, L. M., 206
Abramson, M., 70
Aburdene, P., 61
Abush, R., 234
Achenbaum, A. W., 525
Acker, J., 107
Ackerman, J., 118
Adams, C. T., 373, 451
Adams, J., 177, 182, 254
Adams, J. S., 226
Adams, P., 60, 427, 489, 490, 491, 502, 503, 505
Adams, S. M., 278
Addams, J., 482, 483
Aditya, R., 306, 315
Adler, M., 524
Agosta, J., 365
Agranoff, R., 288, 300
Aguinis, H., 231
Ahr, P. R., 463
Aiken, M., 157
Akabas, S. H., 40
Albert, V., 488
Alderfer, C. P., 176, 179, 180
Aldrich, H. E., 141, 142
Alexander, J., 285, 298
Allen, M. L., 488
Allen, P., 309

Allen, R. I., 475
Allison, M., 345, 353
Almeder, R., 73
Alperin, D. E., 40
Alter, C., 10, 283, 284, 285, 286, 289, 291, 293, 294, 298, 489
Alter, J., 289
Altpeter, M. A., 4, 42
Alvesson, M., 102, 103, 105, 106
Amey, C., 484
Anderson, D., 164
Andrews, F. E., 32
Andrews, K. R., 72
Andron, S., 253
Anerson, P., 98
Anspach, R. R., 13, 270
Anthony, R. N., 4, 253
Aponte, J., 363
Archer, J., 463
Arches, J., 175, 229
Arguello, D. F., 258
Argyris, C., 92, 122, 199, 283, 501
Ariss, S. S., 451
Armenakis, A., 431, 432, 436, 437
Armstrong, K. L., 490, 502
Arndt, E. M., 252
Aronson, E., 225, 232
Aronson, R. L., 452
Arvey, R. D., 171, 172, 206

Ashford, S. J., 278, 279
Ashforth, B. E., 220
Ashkenas, R., 292
Aske, D. K., 197
Astley, W. G., 96, 284
Atherton, C. R., 258
Atwater, P., 4
Au, C., 22, 249, 261
Au, C.-F., 89
Auluck, R., 257
Austin, C., 529
Austin, D., x, 5, 7, 8, 9, 14, 21, 22, 355
Austin, D. M., 42, 43, 47, 48
Austin, K. M., 82
Austin, M., 59
Austin, M. J., 247, 256, 284, 288, 290, 300, 395(n),
     399, 406, 407, 412, 415, 483, 490, 503, 504
Austin, N., 268
Avolio, B., 308, 316
Axelrod, N. R., 117
Axinn, J., 429

Baetz, M., 306
Bailey, D., 450
Baker, G., 297
Bales, F., 306
Bandura, A., 177, 181, 182, 186, 229
Banergee, M. M., 158
Bargal, D., 22, 93, 256, 305, 307, 310, 312, 314,
     315
Barker, R., 115, 116
Barker, R. A., 199, 200, 208, 210
Barker, W. F., 274
Barnet, R., 363
Barnett, W., 146, 431
Barney, J. B., 157
Baron, R. L., 256
Barr, S., 125
Barry, V., 74
Barth, R., 488, 489, 496
Bartlett, H. M., 77
Bartlett, J., 199
Bass, B., 256, 304, 307, 308, 311, 312, 314, 315,
     316
Baum, J., 97, 98
Baum, J. A. C., 42, 98, 135, 141, 142, 144, 146, 248
Baxter, E. H., 254
Bayles, M. D., 71
Beach, D. S., 410
Beadles, N. A., 196
Beauchamp, T. L., 77

Becerra, R., 426, 483
Beck, D., 225
Becker, G., 524
Beder, H., 289
Beinecke, R. H., 467
Beitman, B. D., 475
Bell, G. H., 287, 290
Benefield, E. A. S., 490
Benjamin, M. P., 472
Bennett, P., 252
Bennis, W., 122, 305, 307, 311, 312, 313, 315, 505
Benotsch, E. G., 235
Benson, J., 96, 140, 147, 287, 289, 290
Benson, R. A., 254
Berger, C. S., 511
Bergquist, W., 285, 287, 289, 295, 296, 297
Berkman, P., 516
Berman, E. M., 343
Berman, R. I., 253, 256
Bernard, S., 486
Bernardin, H. J., 414
Bernstein, S. R., 190
Berrick, J. D., 488, 496
Berry, P. A., 253
Bertalanffy, L., 427
Besharov, D. J., 484, 485
Besharov, D. S., 82
Bess, G., 49
Betten, N., 483
Betwee, J., 285, 289
Beyer, J., 100, 101, 102, 208, 209, 210, 211
Bickman, L., 470
Biegel, D., 363
Bielawski, B., 254
Biestek, F. P., 77
Bigelow, D. A., 475
Bilbrey, P., 253
Billings, A. G., 232
Billingsley, A., 483
Billitteri, T. J., 127
Birleson, P., 207
Bixby, N. B., 251
Black, R. B., 257
Blades, S. D., 367
Blanchard, K., 306
Blanchare, A., 256
Blank, R. M., 482, 484
Blankertz, L. E., 226
Blau, P. M., 141, 157, 201, 210
Blazek, J., 374
Bleeke, M. A., 251
Blodgett, T. B., 419

Bloom, B. L., 463
Blum, A., 363
Blumenfield, S., 311, 516, 517
Blumenthal, J. A., 235
Boehm, W., 44
Boettcher, R. E., 260
Bogin, D., 12, 14, 22, 406
Bok, S., 70, 74
Bolig, E. E., 476
Bolman, L. E., 122
Booth, C., 485
Borgatti, S. P., 158
Borman, W. C., 171
Bouchard, T. J., 206
Bowen, D. E., 183
Bowers, D., 306
Bowman, J. S., 71, 72
Brace, C. L., 483
Brager, G., 431
Brand, R., 57
Brandt, L., 32
Brannon, D., 412
Brass, D. J., 157
Braverman, H., 105
Brawley, E. A., 253
Bray, D., 310
Breckinridge, S., 34, 35, 482
Bremner, R. H., 34, 36
Brief, A. P., 235
Briggs, H. E., 471
Brill, N. I., 173
Brillant, E. L., 39
Bristow, N., 395(n), 396, 407, 410
Brittain, J. W., 148
Broadhurst, B. P., 29, 31
Brodkin, E. Z., 96
Brodsky, A., 227
Brody, R., 4, 5, 12, 102, 396, 412, 413, 417
Bronfenbrenner, U., 484, 491
Brown, D. W., 298
Brown, F., 119
Brown, J., 472, 483, 484, 486, 487, 488, 491, 502
Brown, P., 488
Brown, S. H., 404
Brown, S. P., 196, 197, 202, 205
Brownstein, C. D., 222
Bruni, J. R., 199
Bruno, F. J., 28, 29, 30, 34, 35
Brush, D. H., 171
Bryant-Comstock, S., 464
Bryman, A., 208, 307
Bryson, J. M., 55, 252, 343, 345

Brzuzy, S., 516
Buckley, W., 158
Buford, B., 60
Burbridge, J., 62
Burchard, J. D., 471
Burford, G., 487, 488, 495, 502
Burghardt, S., 190
Burke, A. C., 365, 369
Burke, M., 235, 516
Burke, R. J., 220, 227, 233, 234
Burkhead, E. J., 234
Burns, J., 304, 307, 308, 311, 316
Burns, T., 139
Burrell, G., 102
Burrell, K., 502
Burt, R. S., 157, 158
Burtless, G. T., 484
Busky, R., 257
Butler, R. J., 148
Buunk, B. P., 226, 227
Byington, D., 107

Calas, M., 106, 107, 170, 309
Caldwell, D., 211
Callahan, D., 70
Callahan, J. J., 524, 525
Cameron, K. S., 101, 451
Campbell, A., 410
Campbell, D., 40
Campbell, M., 309, 310
Campbell, P., 310
Capaiuolo, A., 16
Caputo, R. K., 253, 254
Carlson, J. E., 255
Carpinello, S., 470
Carrillo, D. F., 252
Carroll, G., 142, 146, 211, 431
Carson, M. J., 30
Cascardi, M., 477
Cascio, W. F., 399, 414
Cashman, J. F., 250
Cassell, P., 104
Cavanagh, J., 363
Chakravarthy, B. S., 138
Chambers, C. A., 34
Champy, J., 64
Chan, K., 475
Chang, C. F., 465, 467, 476
Chapman, D. F., 196
Charlton, A., 427
Chassin, M., 514

Chatman, J., 92, 201, 210, 211
Chau, K. L., 254
Chen, B., 61
Chen, C., 427
Cherin, D., 427
Chernesky, R., 96, 316
Cherniss, C., 173, 174, 227, 229, 232, 236
Chess, W., 16, 169, 170, 185, 186, 187, 220, 223, 224, 225, 272, 314, 316
Chestnut, D. E., 231
Cheung, K. F. M., 254
Cheung, P., 96
Chia, R., 103
Child, J., 140, 141, 143
Chisolm, L. B., 447
Christensen, A. J., 235
Christian, W. P., 4, 247
Christianson, J. B., 462
Cicchetti, D., 476
Clark, J., 530
Clark, L. A., 235
Clarke, R. T., 471
Clegg, S., 105
Clinton, W., 125
Cloward, R., 105
Cnaan, R. A., 255
Cohen, J., 285
Cohen, S., 57, 232
Cohn, J., 528, 530
Colby, I. C., 254
Cole, R. F., 470, 471
Coleman, B., 529
Coleman, J., 157
Coley, S., 488
Colignon, R. A., 158
Collins, E. G., 419
Collins, J., 315
Collins, M. E., 473
Collins, R. C., 253
Comer, E., 493
Conger, J., 312, 316
Connell, D. W., 196
Considine, M., 283, 297
Conte, J., 484
Cooke, P., 57
Cooke, R. A., 201
Coons, A., 306
Cooper, C. L., 234
Cooper, R., 102, 103
Cooper, T. L., 73, 74, 83
Copeland, V. C., 255
Copley, C. K., 516

Cordes, C. L., 220, 225, 227, 234
Corfman, S., 379
Cornelius, D. S., 365
Costin, L. B., 482
Coulson, R., 418
Cournoyer, D. E., 469
Courtney, M., 253, 482, 484, 486, 488
Cox, E. O., 525
Cox, F. M., 397(n)
Cox, T., 220, 227
Crawford-Mason, C., 57
Creed, W. E., 92
Creighton, A., 145
Creighton, E., 511
Cress, D., 96
Crimando, W., 253
Cronkite, R. C., 232
Cropanzano, R., 220
Crouch, R., 363
Crow, G., 489, 491, 495
Crow, R. T., 4, 5
Crowell, J., 15
Croze, C., 465
Crull, P., 419
Cummings, L. L., 278, 413
Cummings, N. A., 465, 470, 476
Curphy, G., 304
Curtner-Smith, M. E., 254
Cutlip, S. M., 33
Cyert, R. M., 4
Czarniawska-Joerges, B., 101
Czirr, R., 257

Daguio, D., 82
Daley, J., 355
Dalton, G., 407
Daly, A., 502
Damanpour, F., 251
Dansereau, F., 93
D'Aunno, T., 95, 145, 310
Davidowitz, R. G., 374
Davis, K. E., 177, 182
Davis-Sacks, M. L., 185, 186
Deal, R., 164
Deal, T., 101, 122, 200, 201, 256
Dean, J. W., 183
deCharms, R., 230
Deci, E. L., 177, 183
Deegan, M. J., 482, 483
Deetz, S., 102, 103, 105, 106
deFur, E., 473

Delbecq, A., 207
DeLois, K., 256
de Lone, R., 483
Demaree, R. G., 205
DeMasi, M., 470
Dembroski, T. M., 235
Deming, W. E., 156, 178, 183-184
Demone, H. W., 5
Demone, H. W., Jr., 119, 124, 125, 126(n)
Denhardt, K. G., 75
DeNisi, A., 170, 183
Denison, D. R., 196, 198, 199, 201, 203
Dennis, S., 287, 290
Denton, P., 96
Dessler, G., 179, 180, 183
Devana, M., 307
DiBarri, E., 452
Diddams, M., 279
Diedrick, E., 15, 24
Dill, W. R., 135
DiMaggio, P. D., 145
DiMaggio, P. J., 207, 211
Dinerman, M., 44
DiNitto, D., 107, 254
Dinkmeyer, D., 412
Dipboye, R. L., 406, 413, 414
DiTomaso, N., 196
Dobbin, F., 146
Dobyns, L., 57
Doeff, A. M., 274
Doelker, R. E., 256
Dolgoff, R., 72, 75
Dollard, J., 177, 181
Donahue, S., 470
Donaldson, L., 94, 139
Donnellon, A., 428, 431, 432, 434
Dorwart, R., 368
Doty, P., 524
Doub, N. H., 257
Doueck, H. J., 256
Dougherty, T. W., 220, 225, 227, 234
Downs, S. W., 482, 496
Doz, Y. L., 285
Drake, R. E., 469
Dressel, P. L., 222
Drucker, P., x, 4, 20, 42, 47, 57, 58, 64, 89, 249, 250, 267, 269, 270
Druckman, D., 268, 269
Dryfoos, J. D., 286
Duffield, B., 484
Dukes, D., 201
Duncan, R. B., 134

Dunham, A., 33
Dunkerley, D., 105
Dunlop, M., 504
Dunnette, M., 170, 309
Durham, C. C., 228
Durick, M., 95, 188, 203, 209, 220, 223, 225, 226

Eadie, D., 344, 345, 489, 497, 504
Eagly, A., 316
Eastman, K., 308, 315
Eastman, W., 427
Ebb, N., 484
Echikson, W., 56, 57
Eckstein, D., 412
Edelman, B. L., 136, 141
Edelman, L., 146
Edelwich, J., 227
Eder, R. W., 410
Edward, R., 105
Edwards, R., x, 4, 21, 22, 39, 42, 48, 57, 395(n), 489, 490
Egan, M., 294
Eisenberg, P., 115
Elazar, D. J., 58
Eldridge, W., 344, 352
Elias, E., 464, 467
Elliott, M., 56
Elpers, J. R., 468
Else, J. F., 388
Emerson, P. M., 141
Emery, F. E., 137, 446
England, M. J., 464
English, R. A., 123, 212
Ephross, P. H., 257
Epstein, I., 254
Epstein, J., 516
Erwin, P. J., 235
Essock, S. M., 476
Estes, C. L., 525
Etzioni, A., 12, 123
Evan, W. M., 135, 251
Evans, C. J., 473
Evans, R., 252
Evashwick, C. J., 524, 529
Everett, M. G., 158
Evers, A., 64
Ewing, D. W., 418
Ezell, M., 255, 257, 258, 260, 312, 313, 316, 380, 386

Fabricant, M. B., 190
Faherty, V. E., 17
Falcione, R. L., 211
Faletti, M., 355
Fan, P., 222
Fargerhaugh, S., 101
Fedor, D. B., 278
Feild, H. J., 414
Feild, H. S., 404
Feinauer, D., 252
Feldman, S., 462
Felton, C. J., 470
Fenzel, L., 62
Ferlauto, R. C., 257
Ferris, G. R., 410
Ferris, N., 344
Fiedler, F., 306
Files, L. A., 250, 259
Finch, W. A., 487
Finley, B., 488
Finnegan, D., 63, 503
Finney, J. W., 232
Fisher, G. A., 469
Fisher, R., 57, 60, 487
Fisher, W. H., 472
Fishman, D. B., 173, 174
Fleenor, J., 237
Fleishman, E. A., 199
Fleishman, J. L., 74
Fleming, W. M., 476
Fletcher, J., 81
Fletcher, K., 21
Folkman, S., 231, 232
Follett, M. P., 42, 47
Fombrun, C. J., 284
Forrester, J. W., 159, 160, 163, 166
Fortune, A. E., 222
Fost, D., 363
Foucault, M., 103
Fox, R., 233
Fralicx, R. D., 213
Francoeur, R. B., 516
Frank, R. G., 476
Frankel, M. S., 76
Frankena, W. K., 77
Fraser, M., 256, 485, 493, 495, 496
Freeman, E., 344, 345, 349
Freeman, H. E., 254
Freeman, J., 141, 142, 146, 148, 149, 207
Freidson, E., 123
Freudenberger, H. J., 225
Friedman, M., 234

Friedman, R. M., 464, 469
Friedmann, J., 486, 487
Friesen, B. J., 464, 471, 472, 475, 494, 501
Friesen, P., 140
Frost, P., 101, 200

Gac, J., 472
Gaebler, T. A., 196, 213
Galaskiewicz, J., 141
Galaskiewicz, Y., 141
Galaway, B., 495
Galbraith, J. R., 94
Gallagher, J. G., 114
Galper, J., 105, 452
Gant, L. M., 187, 224
Garbarino, J., 491
Garbarro, J., 312
Garcia, J., 306
Garcia, M., 425
Gardenswartz, L., 426, 427
Gardner, J. W., 453
Gardner, S., 488
Gareau, M. J., 475
Garet, M., 164
Gargiulo, M., 288
Garland, S. B., 56
Garnett, D., 62
Garvin, D. A., 501, 505
Gauthier, T. P., 404
Gavin, M. B., 235
Geismar, L. L., 44
Geller, J. L., 465, 468, 472
Gellerman, W., 76
Gelles, R. J., 484, 485
Gent, M. J., 199
Gentry, M. E., 257
George, J., 235
Gerbino, K., 420
Gerdes, K. E., 254
Gergen, K. J., 102, 103
Gewirth, A., 79
Gibbs, D. A., 482
Gibelman, M., 16, 20, 114, 116, 119, 123, 124, 125, 126, 126(n), 127, 128, 256, 257, 362, 451
Gibson, J., 61, 412
Giddens, A., 104
Gidron, B., 146
Gil, D., 429
Gilbert, N., 294
Gillespie, D. F., 12, 14, 22, 156, 158
Gillespie, D. K., 461

Gingerich, W. J., 365
Ginsberg, L., 4, 123, 247, 311
Giovannoni, J., 483
Glaser, S., 196, 436
Glass, D. C., 231, 234
Glazer, W. M., 476
GlenMaye, L., 256
Glenn, J. M., 32, 33
Glisson, C., 12, 14, 22, 93, 95, 121, 122, 126, 188,
    196, 201, 202, 203, 204, 205, 206, 207, 209,
    220, 223, 225, 226, 238, 260, 272, 310, 313,
    315, 432
Globerman, J., 511, 513, 515
Goetz, K., 493
Goff, V. V., 464
Goldstein, H., 127, 380
Goodale, J. G., 410
Gordon, G., 196, 211
Gordon, L., 35, 36, 472
Gordon, W. E., 77
Gore, A., 58
Gorovitz, S., 79
Gortner, H. F., 78
Gottesman, E. W., 107, 252
Gouldner, A., 200, 289
Gowdy, E., 312, 314, 344, 345, 349
Graham, P., 42, 47
Granof, M. H., 384
Grant, D., 310
Grant-Griffin, L., 363, 364
Grasso, A. J., 254
Grasso, J., 314, 315
Gray, B., 285, 289, 290, 292, 293, 297, 451
Green, R. K., 40
Greenblatt, M, 463
Greene, R. R., 256
Gregiore, T., 4, 437
Gresov, C. G., 207, 211
Grob, G. N., 99
Gronbjerg, K. A., 40, 96, 362, 363, 368, 372
Gross, G., 252, 313, 344
Grossman, B., 96
Groze, V., 388
Grudzinskas, A. J., Jr., 472
Gruenberg, E., 463
Gryski, G. S., 254
Guard, M., 64
Gummer, B., x, 7, 9, 16, 22, 42, 48, 57, 59, 97, 169,
    184, 185, 189, 257, 258, 363, 447, 448, 453
Gundry, L., 208
Gunnarson, S. K., 199
Gunther, J., 57

Gurwitt, R., 62
Guterman, N., 93, 186, 228, 229, 256, 310, 314,
    315
Gutierrez, L., 15, 256
Guy, M. E., 73, 75

Haapala, D., 485
Habermas, J., 105
Hackman, J. R., 177, 183
Hadley, T. R., 253, 364
Hage, J., 157, 283, 284, 285, 286, 291, 298
Hagerty, J. E., 33
Hahn, A. P., 285
Halbert, T. A., 450
Hall, H., 127
Hall, P. D., 249
Hall, R. H., 114, 157
Halley, A. A., 503
Hamel, G., 285
Hammer, D., 516
Hammer, M., 64
Hamstra, B. W., 404
Hanbery, G. W., 253
Handler, J. F., 96, 105, 106
Handy, C., 200, 449
Haney, T. L., 235
Hanks, L. L., 222
Hanley, J. H., 469, 471
Hanley, R. J., 524
Hannah, G. T., 4, 247
Hannan, M. T., 98, 141, 142, 146, 207
Harbert, A., 63, 503
Harbin, G. L., 488
Hardcastle, D. A., 222, 260
Hardiman, P. F., 379
Hardina, D., 373
Hardy, C., 134
Harkavy, I., 518
Harris, R. G., 251
Harris, S., 431
Harris, W., 62
Harrison, D. F., 220
Harrison, J. R., 211
Harshbarger, D., 5, 7
Hart, S. L., 92
Harter, J. J., 199
Hartman, E. A., 252
Hartmann, H. I., 107
Hasenfeld, Y., x, 5, 7, 8, 13, 15, 21, 22, 40, 90, 96,
    101, 118, 123, 135, 137, 146, 149, 212, 247,

248, 250, 253, 310, 426, 429, 431, 446, 451, 522
Hassett, S., 284, 288, 290, 300, 503
Haveman, H. A., 447
Haverines, R., 64
Hawkins, F., 57
Hawley, A., 133
Hay, T., 289
Haynes, K., 48, 316
Hays, S. W., 412
Healey, J. H., 157
Healy, J., 251
Healy, L. M., 18
Hebden, J. E., 211
Hechter, M., 295
Hedberg, B., 138
Heggestad, E. C., 170, 173, 180, 181
Heider, F., 177, 182
Heifetz, R. A., 490
Heiligenstein, J., 475
Heimerdinger, J. F., 374
Heimovics, R. D., 489
Heinik, J., 516
Hellriegel, D., 199
Helms, L. B., 255
Hemme, C. A., 475
Hemmelgarn, A., 93, 188, 196, 201, 202, 203, 205, 209, 210, 272
Henkin, A. B., 255
Henneman, E., 285
Heraclitus, 56
Herman, R., x, 426, 489
Hernandez, M., 477
Herriot, S. R., 138
Herron, D., 64
Hersey, P., 306
Herzberg, F., 176, 179, 180, 182, 185
Herzlinger, R. E., 497
Heshizer, B., 418
Hessels, M., 196
Hewitt, P. S., 525
Hicks, D. T., 254
Hickson, D. J., 134
Higgs, C., 404
Hile, M., 62, 336
Himle, D., 185, 314, 406
Hirsch, P., 197
Hodges, S., 477
Hodges, V. G., 485, 489, 494, 495, 503
Hodge-Williams, J., 257
Hodgkinson, V. A., 114, 125
Hoefer, R., 7, 16, 258

Hoeltke, G., 404
Hofstede, G., 201, 207, 208, 211
Hogan, J., 304
Hogan, R., 304
Holahan, C. J., 232
Holcomb, W. R., 475
Holden, G., 516
Holley, W. H., 414
Hollis, E. V., 44
Holloway, S., 431
Holmes, J., 253
Homans, G., 156
Hornby, H., 388
Hoskisson, R. E., 157
Hosmer, L. T., 75
Hough, L., 170
House, R., 306, 315
Houston-Vega, M., 82
Howe, N., 525
Howell, W. C., 406, 413, 414
Hoy, W. K., 199, 200, 201, 203
Huber, G. P., 134
Hudak, J., 344
Hudson, B., 291
Hudson, J., 495
Hudson, W. W., 274
Huelsman, T. J., 235
Huey, J., 427
Huff, B., 464
Hughes, C., 473
Hulin, C. L., 276
Hull, C. L., 175, 176
Humber, J., 73
Hunter, C., 379
Hunter, R., 472
Hunzeker, J. M., 255
Hutchinson,, G. E., 142
Huxham, C., 146
Hyde, A. C., 404
Hyde, C., 41, 96, 107
Hylton, L. F., 289, 290, 291

Iannello, K. P., 107
Iatridis, D., 483
Iglehart, A., 14, 15, 426
Iles, P., 257
Illson, L. H., 524
Ingraham, P. W., 125
Itzhaky, H., 251
Ivancevich, J. M., 412
Iverson, R. D., 235

Jackall, R., 73
Jackson, L., 511
Jackson, M. E., 524
Jackson, P. R., 229
Jackson, S., 220, 225, 227, 228, 487
Jacobs, H., 344
Jacobs, J., 316
Jacobsen, M., 257
Jaffe, E. D., 253
Jaffe, R., 253
Jahoda, M., 179
James, L., 156
James, L. A., 197, 205
James, L. R., 196, 197, 199, 203, 205, 206, 207, 211
Janicki, M., 364
Janssen, B. S., 482
Jansson, B., 429
Jansson, B. S., 17, 371
Janz, T., 410
Jaraytne, S., 406
Jayaratne, S., 16, 92, 169, 170, 185, 186, 187, 220,
    223, 224, 225, 228, 229, 272, 314, 316
Jelinek, M., 197
Jenkins, R., 489
Jennings, B., 75, 78, 80, 83
Jensen, J., 401(n), 413, 415, 418, 511
Jensen, M., 309
Jette, A., 363
Jick, T., 292
Jivanjee, P. R., 471
Johns, R., 34, 47
Johnson, H. C., 469
Johnson, I. C., 213
Johnson, J. J., 200, 201, 203
Johnson, P. J., 254
Johnston, W., 316
Jones, A., 156
Jones, A. P., 197, 199
Jones, E. E., 177, 182
Jones, G. R., 198
Jones, M., 484
Jones, S. A., 40
Jones-McClintic, S., 364
Jonsen, A. R., 81
Jordan, D., 197
Joseph, M. V., 72
Josylin, A., 475
Joyce, P. G., 379
Joyce, W. F., 197, 203
Judge, T. A., 228
Julia, M., 254
Julian, D., 344, 345

Kadushin, A., 255, 412, 413, 415
Kafry, D., 225, 232
Kagan, A., 484
Kagan, S. L., 488, 493
Kahn, A., 38, 286, 484, 486, 488, 503
Kahn, E. M., 253
Kahn, R., 169, 169(n), 174, 427
Kalin, D. H., 379
Kallmann, G. L., 468, 476
Kamerman, S., 38, 286, 484, 486, 488, 503
Kane, R. L., 530
Kanfer, R., 170, 173, 180, 181
Kanter, R., 42, 47, 107, 146, 297
Kanungo, R., 312
Kaplan, B. J., 30
Karau, S., 316
Karger, H., 57, 60, 63, 482, 487
Katon, W., 475
Katz, D., 427
Kaufman, J., 344
Kaufman, S. R., 524
Kawiecki, J., 530
Kaye, J., 345, 353
Kaye, L. W., 253
Kazanjian, R. K., 94
Kazis, L. E., 530
Kazmarski, K., 45
Kearney, R. C., 412
Kearns, K., 169, 374
Keller, T., 93
Kelley, H. H., 177, 182
Kelly, K., 336
Kelly, T., 233
Kemp, S. P., 412
Kendall, L. M., 276
Kennedy, A., 101, 200, 256
Kenney, J. J., 251
Kerr, S., 292
Kerson, T. S., 452, 516
Ketchen, D. J., 155, 157
Kettner, P., 12, 13, 23, 39, 49, 64, 91, 254, 270, 271,
    272, 273, 355, 361, 363, 364, 372, 379
Keys, P., 4, 16, 247, 311
Kieser, A., 143
Kilroe, S., 487
Kim, D. H., 164
Kim, H., 268
Kim, Y. W., 251
Kimberly, J. R., 156
Kingsley, G., 61
Kinlaw, D. C., 254
Kinney, J., 485, 494

Kirk, R., 485
Kirk, S. A., 185, 227, 228, 230, 232
Kirk, S. S., 234
Kirschner, D. S., 32
Kish, R. K., 378, 384, 386, 388
Klein, A. R., 255
Kligman, D., 58
Klingner, D. E., 398
Kluger, A. N., 170, 183, 228
Knitzer, J., 486
Koch, J. R., 476
Koeske, G. F., 12, 22, 185, 187, 220, 227, 228, 230, 231, 232, 233, 234, 255
Koeske, R. D., 12, 22, 187, 220, 227, 231, 232
Kolb, D., 428, 431, 432, 434
Komaki, J., 309
Konold, T. R., 235
Konrad, A. M., 298
Koontz, H., 344
Koren, P. E., 472
Korman, M., 473
Koroloff, N. M., 472, 473, 475
Korsgaard, M. A., 279
Koshel, J. J., 379
Kotelchuck, R., 513
Kotler, P., 4
Kotter, J., 312, 313, 451, 452, 490, 501, 513
Koury, N., 253
Krackhardt, D., 157
Kraft, S., 451
Kramer, R., 40, 96, 122, 127, 169, 367, 451
Kraus, A., 253
Krauth, K., 489
Krepcho, M., 62
Kreps, G. L., 134
Kretzmann, J., 502, 503
Kucic, A. R., 253
Kuhl, J., 180, 181
Kuk, G., 220
Kuland, R., 256
Kultgen, J., 81
Kurke, L. B., 135
Kurzman, P., 35, 40
Kuttner, R., 57

Lachman, R., 96
Ladd, R. T., 205
Ladenson, R. F., 76
Lake, D., 310
Laliberte, L., 225
Lambert, W., 470

Lammers, C. J., 134
Lammers, W., 58
Landrigan, P. J., 255
Langwell, K. M., 129
Lao Tse, 357
La Puma, J., 81
Latham, G. P., 407, 410
Latting, J. K., 256
Lauffer, A., 63, 253
Launier, R., 231
Laurie, D. L., 490
Lawler, E., 180, 267, 269, 309
Lawless, E., 428
Lawrence, P. F., 298
Lawrence, P. R., 139, 149
Lazarus, R. S., 231, 232
Leavitt, S. E., 256
LeBlang, T. R., 257
Leblibei, H., 149
Lebold, D. A., 39
Lee, A., 530
Lee, J. A. B., 503
Lee, J. L., 285
Lee, L. J., 256
Lee, R. T., 220
Leeichsenring, K., 64
Lefton, M., 286
Lehman, A. F., 469
Leiby, J., 28, 29, 30, 429
Leifer, R., 134
Leigh, T. W., 196, 197, 202, 205
Leighninger, L., 35, 43, 44
Leiter, M., 220, 227, 229, 231, 232
Lens, S., 28, 34, 35
Lester, R. E., 211
Levin, H., 429
Levine, C. H., 252
Levine, S., 134
Levinthal, D., 138
Levy, C., 72, 73, 74, 412, 445
Lewin, K., 178
Lewis, A., 476
Lewis, H., 9
Lewis, J. A., 91, 179, 247
Lewis, M. D., 91, 179, 247
Lewis, S. A., 472
Lewontin, R. C., 138
Lief, H. O., 233
Light, D. W., 291
Likert, R., 122, 306
Linder, B., 62
Lipsky, M., 94, 127

Litwak, E., 289, 290, 291
Litwin, G. H., 199
Locke, E., 179, 228, 268, 310, 313, 407
Loewenberg, F., 72, 75
Lohmann, R., 377
Lomi, A., 146
Lopatka, K. T., 418
Loring, M. T., 253
Lorsch, J. W., 139, 149, 298
Louis, M. R., 200, 209, 210, 211
Lovell, E., 398, 410
Lowell, J. S., 29
Lowenstein, S., 114
Lowery, C. M., 196
Lowndes, V., 145
Lowry, M. R., 499
Lubove, R., 28, 29, 30, 32
Lucas, R., 210, 211
Luckey, H., 491
Lumpkin, M., 473
Lumsden, C. J., 142
Lundberg, C. C., 200
Lunnen, K. M., 476
Luthans, F., 170, 182
Lutz, C., 253
Lynett, P. A., 256
Lynn, L. E., Jr., 470, 476
Lyons, T., 344, 345

Macarov, D., 45
MacCabe, N. A., 477
MacDougall, J. M., 235
Maciejewski, M., 530
MacLeod, G. K., 365
Madzar, S., 278
Magazino, C. J., 484
Mager, R. F., 413
Magnabosco, J. L., 64
Maher, K. J., 257
Makhijani, M., 316
Malka, S., 310, 315
Maluccio, A., 426, 484
Mancoske, R. J., 255
Manning, T. D., 472
Mansfield, R., 199
Manz, C., 431
March, J. G., 138
Marini, M. M., 222
Markides, K. S., 527
Marks, B., 62
Marley, M., 258

Marsden, P. V., 158
Marsh, P., 489, 491, 495
Martin, G., Jr., 429
Martin, J., 101, 200
Martin, L., 254, 530
Martin, L. L., 5, 7, 12, 13, 22, 23, 39, 49, 57, 59,
    63, 64, 91, 178, 183, 189, 270, 271, 272,
    273, 361, 363, 364, 372, 379
Martin, L. M., 202
Martin, M. E., 18
Martin, P., 207, 316
Martin, P. Y., 93, 95, 96, 100, 107, 206, 270
Martinko, M., 310
Marty, M. E., 29
Maslach, C., 93, 220, 225, 227
Maslow, A., 176, 179, 180, 182
Mason, J. L., 472
Masunaga, H., 526
Mathiesen, T., 284, 290
Matthews, K. A., 234
Mausner, B., 176, 179
Maxwell, G., 495
Maxwell, M. S., 107
Mayers, R. S., 324(n), 325(n), 383, 388
Mayfield, E. C., 404
McCall, D., 476
McCallion, P., 22, 57, 184, 185, 189, 363, 364
McCann, J. E., 290
McClomb, G., 260, 313
McConkie, S. S., 69, 71, 72
McCord, L., 285
McCormick, E. J., 404, 406, 407
McCready, D. J., 276, 388
McCroskey, J., 485, 488, 493
McEwen, W. J., 146
McFadden, E. J., 482
McGee, C., 473
McGee, J., 157
McGowan, B., 482
McGregor, D., 178
McIntyre, C. L., 200, 201, 203
McIntyre, M. D., 197, 199, 205, 206
McKay, A., 254
McKelvey, L., 235
McKinney, J. B., 387
McKinney, J. J., 235
McKnight, J., 231, 502, 503
McLaughlin, C. P., 48
McLean, F. H., 32
McLennan, R., 358
McMurtry, S. L., 364
McNeece, C. A., 254

McNeeley, J., 61
McNeely, R. L., 222, 223, 224, 253
McNulty, B. A., 488
McNutt, J. G., 18, 45
Meenaghan, T., 60
Meezan, W., 485, 488, 493
Meier, E., 31
Meinert, R., 75, 311, 312
Meinhard, A. G., 144, 146
Melda, K., 365
Melia, R., 62
Melkers, J., 61
Menefee, D., 22, 248, 249, 251, 252, 253, 254, 255,
    256, 257, 258, 260, 284, 312, 313, 362, 363
Menzel, D. C., 71
Meritt-Haston, R., 399
Metcalf, H. C., 42, 47
Meuel, D., 285, 289
Meyer, A. D., 157
Meyer, D. R., 379
Meyer, J., 97, 99, 123, 145, 146
Meyerson, D., 101
Meznar, M., 431
Michalski, J., 511
Middleman, R., 412
Midgley, J., 486, 487
Miles, R., 92, 134, 149
Mileti, D. S., 156
Miller, D., 140, 530
Miller, D. B., 253
Miller, L., 79, 272, 276
Miller, N. E., 177, 181
Miller, P. J., 516
Miller-Spellman, M., 419
Milofsky, C., 367
Miner, E. J., 257
Minicucci, C. M., 490
Mintzberg, H., 42, 90, 94, 137, 140, 155, 307, 357,
    526
Mirabella, R. M., 20, 46
Miringoff, M., 22
Mirr, R. K., 388
Mirvis, P. H., 174
Mishra, A. K., 196, 201, 203
Mitchell, T., 170, 306
Mizrahi, T., 511
Mizruchi, M. S., 141
Moline, M. E., 82
Moore, J., 125, 128, 129
Moore, L. F., 200
Moore, S., 251
Moos, R. H., 232

Mor, V., 225
Morales, A. T., 116
Moran, L., 256
Mor-Barak, M., 427
Morch, H., 231
Morgan, G., 91, 252
Morin, R., 125
Morin, W. J., 418
Moroney, R. M., 91
Morris, A., 495
Morris, J. N., 530
Morrison, T., 285
Morrow, P. C., 183
Morton, M. J., 41
Mossholder, K., 431
Motamedi, K. K., 138
Motowidlo, S. J., 171, 172
Mottaz, C. J., 223, 225
Mowbray, C. T., 473
Mowday, R., 188
Moxley, D. P., 473
Moyer, D., 330
Mufson, D. W., 404
Mulaik, S. A., 205
Mullarkey, S., 229
Mullen, E., 64
Mulroy, E. A., 486, 493, 494, 502, 503
Mumby, D. K., 103
Munnell, A. M., 525
Munson, C. E., 412, 468
Munz, D. C., 235
Murphy, K. R., 171, 172
Murphy, M. J., 90, 93
Murray, J., 252, 313, 344
Murty, S. A., 158
Musselwhite, E., 256
Musser-Granski, J., 252
Mutschler, E., 253
Myers, J. B., 486

Nadler, D. A., 267
Nadler, M. B., 267
Nagda, B. A., 187
Nagel, S., 63
Naisbitt, J., 59, 61
Nalbandian, J., 398
Nanus, B., 305, 307, 311, 312, 313, 315, 505
Nava, C., 473
Navon, M., 464, 467
Neilson, R., 322
Nelson, K., 60, 427, 485, 490, 491, 502, 503, 505

Nelson, R. R., 138
Netting, F. E., 251, 364, 365, 367, 369, 450
Neugarten, D. A., 419
Neugeboren, B., 100
Neuijen, B., 201
Neuman, K., 511, 513, 515
Neuman, R., 484
Newcombe, T., 62
Nicolini, D., 431
Nieves, J., 512
Niles-Jolly, K., 199
Norlin, J., 16, 185, 316
Northcraft, G. B., 278, 279
Northen, H., 487
Nuehring, E. M., 82
Nurius, P. S., 412

O'Connell, B. J., 230, 234, 235
O'Connor, G. G., 285
O'Connor, I., 512, 515
Odewahn, C. A., 4, 5
Odiorne, G. S., 411, 413, 414, 417
Ogles, B. M., 461, 476
O'Hare, W. P., 484
Ohayv, D. D., 201
Okunade, A. A., 465
Oldham, G. R., 177, 183
Olekalns, M., 235
Oliver, C., 98, 135, 144, 146
O'Looney, J., 251, 285
Olson, E., 15
Olson, L., 62
O'Neill, M., 21, 46
O'Reilly, C. A., 157, 201, 210, 211
Orlikowski, W. J., 104
Orsburn, J. D., 256
Orshanky, M., 483
Osborne, D., 196, 213
Osher, T. W., 473, 476
Oster, S. M., 122, 146, 391
Ostrander, S. A., 450
Ostroff, C., 237
O'Toole, J., 163
O'toole, J., 358
Ott, J. S., 200
Ouchi, W., 197, 200, 201, 203, 206, 308
Owens, J., 287

Packard, T., 314
Packer, A., 316

Page, J., 256, 314, 455
Page, W. J., 114, 115, 122, 123, 126
Paine, W. S., 225
Palmer, A., 251
Parker, S. K., 229
Parsons, R., 430, 525
Parsons, T., 156
Passell, P., 125
Pasternak, R. E., 253
Pattakos, A. N., 288, 300
Patterson, I., 252, 344, 352
Patti, R., 4, 5, 6, 7, 8, 12, 15, 16, 17, 22, 33, 46, 71,
    79, 90, 95, 169(n), 247, 250, 251, 254, 259,
    260, 261, 310, 312, 313, 315, 378, 396, 420,
    451, 452, 455
Paul, M. C., 203
Pavilon, M. D., 257
Pawar, S., 308, 315
Payne, B. L., 74
Payne, R. L., 199
Pearlin, L. I., 232
Pearlmutter, S., 93, 432
Pease, E. A., 470
Peck, S., 493
Pecora, P., 13, 14, 254, 399, 405(n), 412, 420, 484,
    485, 494
Pedigo, S. L., 396
Pelton, L., 482, 487, 489, 497, 499
Penkert, K. S., 461
Pennell, J., 487, 488, 495, 502
Pennings, J., 140, 143, 207, 211
Pepper, N. G., 255
Perkins, A. L., 201
Perlman, B., 252
Perlman, R., 286
Perlman, S. B., 467
Perlmutter, F., 4, 6, 17, 38, 107, 252, 253, 373, 446,
    447, 448, 450, 451, 453, 454
Perloff, J. D., 255
Perrin, E. B., 379
Perrone, G., 328
Perrow, C., 94, 95, 140, 142, 145, 528
Perry, P., 355, 402
Peters, C. L., 202
Peters, T., 42, 101, 195, 196, 208, 213, 268, 315,
    526
Peterson, M. S., 462
Peterson, S., 159, 166
Petr, C. G., 213, 475
Pettiford, E. K., 256
Pettigrew, A., 200
Petty, M. M., 196, 203

Peyrot, M., 62
Pfeffer, J., 92, 94, 95, 96, 101, 134, 140, 141, 142, 144, 149, 155, 210, 453, 456
Phares, E. J., 230
Pierce, S., 276, 388
Pillsbury, J. B., 253
Pine, B., 426, 427, 436
Pines, A. M., 225, 232
Pines, B. A., 18
Pipe, P., 413
Piskora, B., 56
Pittman-Munke, P., 32
Piven, F. F., 105
Plant, R., 77
Poertner, J., 4, 6, 7, 12, 13, 14, 15, 79, 90, 100, 102, 251, 253, 260, 270, 273, 274, 310, 312, 419, 437
Pondy, L., 307
Pops, G. M., 73
Porras, J., 315
Porter, L., 188
Posner, B., 432
Poulin, J. E., 185, 186, 187, 188, 228, 260
Poulos, C., 62
Powell, D. M., 38
Powell, D. R., 488
Powell, G. N., 107
Powell, W., 145, 207, 211
Powers, C., 286
Preston, A. E., 174
Price, R., 95, 145, 179
Prindiville, S., 475
Printz, T., 61
Propp, J., 437
Provan, K. G., 286, 289
Pruger, R., 79, 272, 276
Puckett, J. L., 518
Pugh, A. L., III, 164, 166
Pugh, D. L., 74, 80
Pulice, R., 368
Pumphrey, M. W., 77
Putnam, L. L., 103

Quadagno, J., 105
Quinn, R. E., 22, 42, 92, 101, 451
Quist, N., 81

Rabin, C., 229
Rabinovitz, J., 128
Radley, S., 395(n)

Rafferty, J. A., 365, 369
Rahn, S. L., 276, 388
Ramsdell, P., 187, 314
Randolph, W. A., 285, 298
Rapp, C., 4, 6, 7, 12, 15, 79, 90, 100, 102, 251, 253, 260, 270, 273, 310, 312, 419
Rappaport, M., 257
Rauch, R., 16, 313
Rauktis, M. E., 255
Raymond, G. T., 17, 258
Reamer, F. G., 8, 70, 72, 75, 77, 81, 82
Reed, M., 92
Rees, D., 234
Rehr, H., 516, 517
Reichers, A. E., 199
Reicken, G., 253
Reid, N., 57
Reilly, L. L., 472
Reitan, T. C., 141, 145
Rendon, G., 395(n)
Rensvold, R. B., 278
Rentsch, J. R., 199, 200, 201, 207, 210
Rescher, N., 75
Reskin, B. F., 107
Resnick, H., 420, 432, 451, 452, 455
Revicki, D. A., 475
Reynolds, S. L., 524
Rhodes, G., 412
Rhodes, M. L., 72
Richan, W. C., 451
Richardsen, A. M., 220, 227, 233, 234
Richardson, G. P., 164, 166
Richmond, B., 159, 166
Richmond, M. E., 31
Riger, S., 429
Rimer, E., 7, 15, 17, 46
Ringer, B., 428
Rinkin, J., 472
Ritchie, J. B., 72, 73
Rivard, J. C., 485
Roberts, D. M., 257
Roberts, K. H., 157
Roberts, N., 164, 166
Roberts-DeGennaro, M., 257
Robertson, M. A., 404
Robinson, B. S., 235
Robinson, S. E., 226
Rockwood, T., 530
Rodenhauser, P., 463
Roe, R. A., 169(n), 170, 171, 172, 181, 185, 189
Rogge, M., 158
Rohland, B. M., 476

Romanelli, E., 148
Ronen, S., 174, 180
Rooney, B. J., 484, 486
Rooney, R. H., 256
Rosario, M., 231
Roseman, E., 418
Rosenbaum, J. F., 476
Rosenberg, G., 253, 513, 514, 516, 517
Rosenbloom, D. H., 404
Rosengren, W., 286
Rosenheck, R., 476
Rosenman, R. H., 234
Rosenthal, D. M., 71
Rosenthal, M., 516
Rosenzweig, J., 260
Ross, A. I., 226
Ross, A. R., 404
Ross, J., 206
Ross, W. D., 73
Rossi, P. H., 254
Rothausen, T. J., 237
Rothenberg, A., 516
Rothman, J., 425
Rothschild, J., 107
Rotter, J. B., 230
Rounds, K. A., 488
Rouse, L. W., 477
Rousseau, D. M., 197, 198, 201, 208
Rowan, B., 99, 123, 145
Rowe, A., 426, 427
Rubinow, I. M., 34
Ruffolo, M., 252, 313, 344
Ryan, W. P., 169

Sachdeva, P. S., 96
Safran, C., 419
Sager, J., 438
Salamon, L. M., 11, 39, 89, 169, 249
Salancik, G. R., 96, 140, 141, 210
Salazar, C. S., 251
Saleebey, D., 502
Salmon, R., 256
Saltz, C. C., 516
Salzer, M. S., 470
Sanders, G., 201
Sanders, J., 484
Sanders, R. P., 125
Sanders, T. I., 484
Sandfort, J. R., 104
Sarason, S. B., 173
Sarason, Y., 104

Sarri, R. C., 15
Sashkin, M., 307
Sathe, V., 200
Savage, A., 95
Savas, S. A., 476
Sawyer, H. W., 253
Sayles, L., 42
Scesny, A., 511
Schaefer, C., 232
Schaefer, T., 516
Schatz, H. A., 47
Schaufeli, W. B., 93, 226, 227
Schein, E., 197, 200, 201, 207, 208, 209, 307, 315, 431
Schene, A., 483, 485, 489, 490, 499, 500, 502
Schervish, P., 16, 20, 114, 116
Schiedermayer, D. L., 81
Schilling, R., 429
Schinke, S., 429
Schkade, L. L., 324(n), 325(n)
Schlesinger, M., 368
Schmid, H., 9, 21, 135, 138, 140, 146, 149, 252, 305, 307, 314, 451
Schneider, B., 196, 199, 200, 203, 211, 237
Schneider, E. L., 523
Schneider, R. L., 253
Schoech, D., 13, 14, 321(n), 324(n), 325(n), 328
Schoenherr, R. A., 157
Schon, D., 314
Schooler, C., 232
Schoonhoven, C. B., 95
Schorr, L. B., 196, 213, 214, 484, 500
Schrage, M., 163
Schram, S. F., 103
Schroeder, A., 484
Schuerman, J. R., 512
Schuler, R. S., 220, 228
Schwab, D. P., 413
Schwab, R. L., 220, 228
Schwartz, A. Y., 107, 252
Schwartz, E. E., 6, 7
Scott, R., 97
Scott, R. W., 97, 123
Scott, W. R., 92, 99, 134, 144, 145, 146
Scull, A., 462, 463
Scurfield, R., 17
Seashore, S., 306
Segal, N. L., 206
Segal, U. A., 253
Selber, K., 47
Self, D. J., 81
Seligman, M. E., 228

Sells, S. B., 197
Selznick, P., 200, 447, 451
Senge, P., 159, 161, 162, 358
Shaffer, W., 164
Shafritz, J. M., 404
Sharon, N., 253
Shaw, R. B., 201
Shay, S., 486, 493, 494, 502, 503
Sheafor, B. R., 116
Shehadi, F., 71
Sheinfeld Gorin, S. N., 96
Shera, W., 256, 314, 454
Sheridan, J., 209, 211, 314
Sherman, A., 484
Sherraden, M. W., 379
Sherwood, J. J., 210
Shields, G., 254
Shin, J., 260, 313
Shinn, M., 231, 232
Shook, K., 484
Shore, M. F., 468, 476
Shulman, L., 415
Shyne, A., 484
Siciliano, J., 344
Siefert, K., 185
Simmons, J., 516
Simon, B. L., 502
Simon, G. E., 475
Simon, H. A., 205
Simpson, J. S., 472
Sinanoglu, P., 484
Singer, J. E., 268
Singer, M., 40, 49
Singh, J., 42, 97, 141, 142, 144, 146, 248
Singleton, C. A., 255
Sink, D. W., 257
Skeel, J. D., 81
Skidmore, R., 6, 93, 114, 122, 247
Skinner, B. F., 175, 176
Skinner, K., 530
Slavin, S., x, 4, 6, 247, 396
Slocum, J. W., 197, 199, 203
Sluyter, G., 420
Smart, J. J. C., 78
Smircich, L., 106, 107, 170, 197, 207, 309
Smith, D. B., 237
Smith, P. C., 276
Smith, S. R., 127
Snell, L., 62
Snoeyenbos, M., 73
Snow, C., 134, 149, 157
Snow, D. A., 96

Snyder, N. M., 102
Snyderman, B., 176, 179
Soderfeldt, B., 169(n)
Soderfeldt, M., 169(n)
Solomon, B., 426
Solomon, E. E., 212, 213
Solomon, J., 355
Solomon, R. C., 76, 77, 78, 79
Sorensen, J. E., 253
Sorkin, D., 344
Sosin, M., 289
Souflee, F., 91, 247
Souflee, F., Jr., 179
Sparks, K., 189
Specht, C. V., 528
Specht, H., 294
Spector, P. E., 230, 234, 235, 272, 275, 276
Spencer, S., 4, 6, 44, 473
Speziale, B. A., 516
Spitzer, W., 312
Spreier, S. W., 213
Sprinthall, N. A., 75
Stacey, R. D., 353
Stagner, R., 309
Stajkovic, A. D., 170, 182
Stalker, G. M., 139
Stamm, A. J., 16
Standley, A. P., 364
Staples, L. H., 256
Starbuck, W. H., 134
Starr, P., 99
Staw, B. M., 180, 206
Steers, L., 188
Stehle, V., 128
Stein, H., 5
Steiner, J., 252, 313, 344, 345
Stern, L. W., 362
Stewart, D. W., 75
Stewart, G., 431
Stoesz, D., 57, 63, 482
Stogdill, R., 304, 306
Stone, R., 524
Stone-Romero, E. F., 231
Stowers, G., 257, 373
Strachan, J. L., 40
Strang, D., 145
Strauss, A., 101
Streepy, J., 225
Street, E., 4, 36, 47
Stringer, R. A., 199
Strom, K., 365
Stroul, B. A., 464, 469, 470

Suchman, M. C., 136, 141
Suczek, B., 101
Sugar, J. A., 528, 530
Sui, A. L., 514
Sundel, H. H., 253
Sung, K. T., 254
Sutton, J., 146
Sutton, R., 95, 145, 201
Swan, J. H., 525
Swanson, J., 474
Swartz, M., 197
Swope, C., 63
Szapocnik, J., 355

Taber, M., 274
Tagiuri, R., 199
Tambor, M., 188, 396
Tattersall, A., 252
Taylor, A. L., 44
Taylor, B. E., 490
Taylor, F. W., 122
Taylor, M. S., 276, 277
Taylor, S., 237
Taylor, S. E., 234
Taylor, S. H., 487
Taylor, V., 107
Tead, O., 47
Teare, R. J., 17, 258, 404
Teather, E. C., 420
Teel, K., 80
Teicher, M., 77
Tetrick, L. E., 203, 207
Thatchenkery, T. J., 102, 103
Thomas, H., 157
Thomas, J. B., 157
Thomas, W., 134, 528
Thompson, J. D., 7, 134, 135, 139, 140, 146, 149,
    209
Thompson, J. J., 248, 251, 252, 253, 254, 255, 256,
    257, 258, 284, 313
Thompson, J. R., 125
Thompson, P., 407
Thurow, L., 57
Thyness, P., 314, 406
Tichy, N., 157, 307
Timms, N., 77
Tjosvold, D., 290, 296
Tobin, S. S., 364
Tolbert, L. G., 100
Tolbert, P. M., 145
Tolman, E. C., 178

Tolsdorf, C. C., 158
Toprac, M. G., 477
Torres-Gil, F. M., 523
Toseland, R. W., 257
Toth-Dennis, D., 473
Trachtenberg, J., 511
Tracy, E. M., 485, 494
Trecker, H. B., 4, 47
Trice, H., 100, 101, 102, 208, 209, 210, 211
Tripodi, T., 185, 187, 314
Trist, E., 137, 300, 446
Tropman, J., 257, 425
Trout, S. C., 461
Tucker, D., 42, 97, 98, 142, 144, 146, 248
Turner, M., 473
Tushman, M. L., 98, 267
Tyler, N., 63, 503

Ulrich, D., 135, 292
Um, M., 220
Urwick, L. F., 42, 47
Usher, C. L., 254, 476, 482, 488, 489, 490, 496,
    500, 501, 502, 503

Valdez, T. A., 396
Van Cott, H., 268
VanDenBerg, J., 464, 471
vander Straeten, S., 484, 501
VandeWalle, D., 278
van Dierendonck, D., 226, 227
Vangen, S., 146
van Gorp, K., 227
Van Maanen, J., 197
van Ryn, M., 187
Van Scotter, J. R., 172
Vassil, T. V., 257
Venkatraman, N., 157
Verbeke, W., 196, 199, 200
Vestal, K. W., 213
Vigilante, J. L., 77
Vinokur, A. D., 179, 187
Vinokur-Kaplan, D., 12, 14, 22, 170, 173, 185, 186,
    187, 223, 224, 406
Vinter, R. D., 378, 384, 386, 388
Vogel, L., 252, 344, 352
Volgering, M., 196
Von der Embse, T. J., 396
Vroom, V., 178, 306

Waddock, A., 146
Wageman, R., 297
Wagner, M., 13, 14
Waite, F. T., 30, 32, 36
Waldfogel, J., 489, 490, 497, 499, 500, 501, 502, 503
Walker, L., 524
Wall, T. D., 229, 230
Wallace, S. P., 527
Walsh, J. A., 255
Walters, J., 59
Walton, M., 178, 183, 184
Wamseley, G. L., 140
Wamsley, G. L., 95
Ward, H., 487
Warg, L.-E., 169(n)
Warner, A. G., 31
Warsh, R., 426
Waterman, J. R. H., 101
Waterman, R., 42, 196, 208, 213, 315, 526
Waters, J., 307
Watson, D., 235, 256
Watt, J. W., 468, 476
Way, I. F., 251
Weatherley, R., 94, 429
Weaver, C. N., 253
Weber, M., 91, 118, 122, 156, 312
Webster, J., 235
Webster, S., 252, 344
Weganast, D., 257
Weick, K., 92, 100, 101, 108, 134, 149, 309
Weil, M., 61, 93, 483, 484, 486, 487, 488, 489, 491, 492, 493, 494, 501, 502, 503, 504
Weinbach, R., 4, 5, 6, 63, 95, 118, 119, 362, 367, 396, 404, 411, 412, 413, 418
Weiner, M. E., 4, 5, 7, 47, 173, 247, 396
Weinreich, D. M., 516
Weinstein, D., 484
Weirich, T. W., 96
Weisbrod, B. A., 39, 89
Weisner, S., 257
Weiss, J., 207
Weiss, J. O., 257
Weiss, R. M., 95, 126
Weissbourd, B., 484, 488, 491
Weissman, A., 516
Weitzman, M. S., 114, 125
Wellford, W. H., 114
Wells, S. J., 483, 484
Were, K., 276, 388
Wernet, S. P., 40

Wester, B., 40
Westley, S., 307
Wetle, T., 524
Wexler, S., 255
Weyley, K. N., 399
Wheatley, M. J., 163
Wheelock, J., 388
Whetten, D. A., 451
Whiddon, B., 93
White, P. E., 134
White, S. S., 203
Whiting, L. A., 257
Whitt, A. J., 107
Whittaker, J. K., 484, 485, 491, 494, 495, 496
Whittington, R., 141
Wholey, D., 462
Wiener, C., 101
Wiener, J. M., 524, 526
Wiener, Y., 206, 209
Wiggs, M., 380
Wilber, K. H., 524, 528
Wildfire, J. B., 482
Wilkins, A., 308
Wilkins, A. L., 200, 201
Wilkins, H. L., 203, 206
Williams, C. A., 233
Williams, E., 309
Williams, F. G., 251
Williams, G. T., 82
Williams, L. J., 235
Williams, M. L., 235
Williams, R. B., 235
Williamson, G. M., 232
Willmott, H., 106
Willoughby, K., 61
Wilson, C. E., 211
Wilson, D. C., 148
Wilson, W., 41
Wilson, W. J., 487
Wimberley, E. T., 253
Winbush, G., 363
Winter, S. G., 138
Wish, N. B., 20, 46
Wistow, G., 64
Wodarski, J. S., 251
Wolf, T., 380, 384, 385, 391
Wolfe, T., 397(n)
Wolk, J. L., 251
Woodward, J., 139
Wright, H., 469, 471
Wright, N. D., 69, 71, 72

Wright, T. A., 220
Wright, W. S., 256
Wyers, N. L., 255
Wylie, M., 252, 344

Yamatani, H., 222
Yankey, J., 4, 39, 40, 42, 48, 49, 146, 253, 395(n)
Yasai-Ardekani, M., 134
Yates, B. T., 273
Yetton, P., 306
York, A., 146
York, R. O., 257
Yorks, L., 418
Young, D. J., 475
Young, D. R., 39
Young, D. W., 4, 253
Young, N., 488
Young, R. C., 142
Yourdon, E., 328
Yuen, F., 287
Yukl, G., 268, 304, 305, 306, 307, 309, 313, 314, 315

Zald, M. N., 96, 140, 145
Zaleznik, A., 305
Zamanou, S., 196, 436
Zawadski, R., 529
Zedeck, S., 399
Zefran, J., 323
Zeller, D., 229
Zelman, W. N., 253
Zenger, J. H., 256
Ziegenfuss, J., 344, 352
Zigler, E. F., 488
Zimmerman, M., 429
Zipper, I. N., 488
Zlotnik, S., 309
Zuboff, S., 91
Zucker, L., 99, 100, 145, 146
Zunz, S. J., 258, 259, 406
Zychlinski, E., 146

Subject Index

AASSW. *See* American Association of Schools of Social Work

Abbott, Edith, 35

Abbott, Grace, 35

Academy of Certified Social Work Managers, 43

Accommodations, reasonable, 402-403

Accountability, 61-62, 489
    financial management and, 378, 380, 381
    in management paradigm, 14-15
    resources and, 253-254, 363-364, 369

Accrediting bodies, 9, 44

ACOSA. *See* Association for Community Organization and Social Administration

Acquisitions and mergers, 467-468, 513

ACT. *See* Assertive Community Treatment

Active management by exception, 308

Act utilitarianism, 79

ADA. *See* Americans with Disabilities Act

Adaptation, and task environment, 138-141, 146-148

ADC. *See* Aid to Dependent Children

Addams, Jane, 30

Administration in Social Work, 43

Administration, terminology of, 4-6. *See also* Social welfare management

Adoption and Safe Families Act, 270, 486, 488

Adoption Assistance Act, 270

Adoption Assistance and Child Welfare Act, 484

Adoptive parents, 496, 497

Advanced Practice licensing examination, 46

Advocacy:
    aging services and, 531
    change and, 450-451
    disvalued groups and, 10
    in management model, 255
    trends in, 65

AFDC. *See* Aid to Families With Dependent Children

Affirmative action, 396, 398-399

African Americans. *See* Race and ethnicity

Age:
    burnout and, 225, 226
    job satisfaction and, 224-225

Age Discrimination in Employment Act, 396

Aging, 521-532
    baby-boomer generation and, 49
    core values and, 524
    demographics of, 11, 59-60, 522-523, 532
    environment of services in, 523, 524-526
    in an aging society, 522-523

Aging in place, 524

AIDS-HIV, 38, 362

Aid to Dependent Children (ADC), 35, 36, 483

Aid to Families With Dependent Children (AFDC), 35, 37, 38, 39, 287, 484, 486. *See also* Temporary Assistance to Needy Families

Aligning, 252-253

Alternative service organizations, 38

American Association of Schools of Social Work (AASSW), 44, 46
American Public Welfare Association (APWA), 36, 38, 42
American Social Science Association, 29
American Social Security Association, 34
Americans with Disabilities Act (ADA), 399, 402-403, 404
Annual Program Meetings (APM) structure, 43
Anxiety, and job response, 235-236
APM. *See* Annual Program Meetings structure
Appraisal, performance, 412-416
APWA. *See* American Public Welfare Association
Archetypes, 162-163
ASA. *See* Attraction-selection-attrition framework
Asian Americans. *See* Race and ethnicity
Assertive Community Treatment (ACT), 469
Assessment:
    aging services and, 530
    budget process and, 387-388
    families, children, and, 485-486
    strategic planning and, 349-350
Association for Community Organization and Social Administration (ACOSA), 43
Associations, in historical perspective, 42-43. *See also names of specific associations*
Attitudes, and job response, 226-231
Attraction-selection-attrition (ASA) framework, 237
Attributes:
    of leaders, research on, 305-306, 310-312
    of workers, and job response, 226-237
Attribution theories, 177(table), 182
Attrition, 237. *See also* Job response
Audits, and financial management, 379, 387-388
Auspices of practice, 114-121, 259
Autonomy:
    aging services and, 529
    collaboration and, 291, 298
    managed care and, 468
    position descriptions and, 406
    worker, 186-187, 229, 230

Baby boom generation, 49, 60
Balancing loops, 160-162
Bargaining, and task environment, 146
Barnett, James, 30, 32
BARS. *See* Behaviorally anchored rating scales
Behavior:
    human relations perspective and, 92-94
    of leaders, research on, 306
    See also Tasks and functions; Work performance

Behaviorally anchored rating scales (BARS), 414
Behaviorist orientation to motivation, 175
Behavior-over-time (BOT) graphs, 159, 163-166
Beliefs, 226-227. *See also* Values
Benevolence, as core value, 75
Bentham, Jeremy, 79
Bidding, 378-379. *See also* Contracting
Bioethics, 70
Blacks. *See* Race and ethnicity
Block grant system, 463
Boards of directors:
    financial management and, 380-381
    governance structure and, 120, 121
    historical perspective on, 30, 32, 33, 34, 37, 40-41
    resource development and, 371
BOT graphs. *See* Behavior-over-time graphs
Bottom-up approach, in IT strategy, 329
Boundaries, environmental, 134-135
Boundary blurring, 125-129
Boundary issues, and ethics, 73, 82
Boundary spanning, 251, 503
Breadth and depth, and ecology theory, 142
Breckinridge, Sophrenisba, 35
Budgets:
    cycle of, stages in, 381-388
    planning and, 356, 383-386
    responsibilities for, 378, 381-388
    staff diversity and, 392
    See also Financial affairs
Bureaucracies:
    boundary blurring and, 126, 127
    organization type and, 117-118
    substructure and, 122
Bureaucratic ethos, 74, 80
Burnout, 185, 187
    aging services and, 528
    demographics and, 225-226
    leadership and, 314, 315
    morale and, 272
    worker attributes and, 220-221, 226-228, 231-238
    See also Job satisfaction
Business administration paradigm, 7
Business organizations, 118-119
Bylaws, 119

Capital, human, 410, 528
Capitalism, 7, 30, 36, 56-57
Capitated delivery systems, 531. *See also* Managed care

Case management, in historical perspective, 38
Casework model, 44
Cash flow management, 391
Cash reserves, 380
CASSP. *See* Child and Adolescent Service System Program
Caucasians. *See* Race and ethnicity
Causal loop diagrams (CLDs), 160-162, 163-166
CEOs. *See* Chief executive officers
Certainty, need for, 209
Change, 445-456
    big and small, 447-449
    client outcomes and, 273
    collaboration and, 285-289
    dilemmas in, 449-451
    diversity, empowerment, and, 430-432
    environmental context for, 446-447
    family and children's services and, 502-504
    health care services and, 511-518
    implementation models for, 451-452
    information and, 269-270, 322, 323
    organizational theory and, 105-108
    planning for, 357-358
    resource development and, 362-370
    strategies for, 452-455
    See also Innovation
Chaplin, Charlie, 173
Charisma, 312
Charitable giving, 127-128
Charitable organizations, in historical perspective, 29, 30-32. *See also* Nonprofit organizations
Charity Organization Societies (COSs), 29-32, 38
Chief executive officers (CEOs), 120-121. *See also* Executives
Chief information officers (CIOs), 326
Child Abuse Prevention and Treatment Act, 484
Child and Adolescent Service System Program (CASSP), 464
Child protective services (CPS), 484, 496-502. *See also* Family and children's services
Children's services. *See* Family and children's services
Child welfare, 482-484, 496-502. *See also* Family and children's services
Church organizations, 28, 29. *See also* Religious organizations
CIOs. *See* Chief information officers
Circular A-133, 379
Circular processes, 158-162
Civil Rights Act of 1964, 396
Civil War, 28
CLDs. *See* Causal loop diagrams
Cleveland Associated Charities, 32

Client outcomes, and information, 270-271, 273-274. *See also* Consumers/clients; Information; Outcomes; Performance
Climate, organizational. *See* Organizational climate
Cliques, 158
CLOC. *See* Counselor Locus of Control scale
Closed-loop structure. *See* Feedback
Coalition, and task environment, 147
Codes of ethics, 72, 77, 81-82, 170, 391, 445
Cognitive structure, and collaboration, 293-294
Cognitive theory, 306
Cohesion, social, 100-102
Collaboration, 283-301
    advice on, 300-301
    competition and, 63
    costs/benefits of, 284, 288-290
    forms of, 284, 290-291, 298
    importance of, 283, 285-289
    in aging services, 527, 529
    in education for management, 21
    in family and children's services, 500-501, 502-505
    in health care services, 515
    in management paradigm, 10-12
    in mental health sector, 471
    levels of, 298-300
    phases and tasks in, 292-300
    prerequisites of, 283-284, 291-292
    restructuring and, 64
    terminology of, 284-285
    See also Partnerships; Task environment
Colleges and universities. *See* Education for social welfare management
Commitment, in management paradigm, 13-14
Communication:
    collaboration and, 292-293
    importance of, 251
    information and, 328
Communism, collapse of, 56-57
Community:
    diversity, empowerment, and, 425-442
    family and children's services and, 497-505
    health care services and, 516
    historical perspective on, 37-38
    mental health sector and, 462-463, 468-469
    rediscovery of, 60-61
Community Chest, 33, 34
Community Mental Health Centers Act, 462, 468
Community Practice in Social Work, 43
Competencies, in personnel management, 407-410
Competing values theory, 22
Competition, 63, 146

assessment of, 348-349
boundary blurring and, 128-129
collaboration and, 288
environment forces and, 248
in aging services, 532
in family and children's services, 503
in mental health sector, 468, 470
resource development and, 364, 365, 369
Complaints, risk, and ethics, 82
Complexity, and structure, 156, 157
Comprehensive approach, in mental health sector, 470-472
Comprehensive Community Mental Health Centers/ Services Acts, 462, 470
Computer technology. *See* Information technology
Confidentiality, 72, 73, 335-336
Configuration, and structure, 156-157
Conflict resolution, 292-293, 314-315
Connectivity, and information technology, 336-337
Consideration, in leadership, 306, 308, 314
Constituencies:
    expectations of, 9-10
    financial affairs and, 371, 378-379
    information and, 270
    political economy and, 96-97
    textbook attention to, 48
Constitution of organization, 119
Consultation, ethics, 80-82
Consumer choice initiatives, 364-365
Consumer-directed care, 524
Consumers/clients:
    aging services and, 524, 530-531
    as constituencies, 9
    emphasis on, 65, 100, 102
    health care services and, 512-513, 515-516, 517
    in management paradigm, 9, 15
    mental health sector and, 464-465, 472-476
    participation of, 15, 472, 515-516, 517, 524
    satisfaction in, 315. *See also* Quality
Contingency approach to leadership, 306-307
Contingency planning, 355-356
Contingency theory, 94-95, 139-140, 145, 306
Contingent reward, in leadership, 308
Continuous improvement, 336
Continuous quality management. *See* Total quality management
Continuum of services, 481-482, 490-491, 502, 516
Contracting, 362, 372, 374, 378, 462
    boundary blurring and, 126-129
    change and, 447, 489
    ethics and, 73
    information and, 270, 321-322, 327-328

in historical perspective, 39-40, 49, 51
trends in, 63
See also Resource development
Control:
    fiscal, 386-387
    in management paradigm, 14-15
    job response and, 229-231, 238
    motivation and, 186-187
    organizational theory and, 102-104
    structure and, 157, 158
Convergence of organization types. *See* Boundary blurring
Cooperation, and task environment, 146-147. *See also* Collaboration
Co-optation, 146-147
Copability, 138
Coping strategies, 231-232
Core technology, 203-205
Core values, 75-77, 524
Corporatization, 531
COSs. *See* Charity Organization Societies
Cost accounting, 4
Cost analysis, 388
Costs:
    health care and, 512-513. *See also* Managed care
    mental health sector and, 464, 467, 469-470
    perceived, 278
    shifting of, 467
Council on Social Work Administration, 43
Council on Social Work Education (CSWE):
    Annual Program Meetings of, 43
    curricula data from, 18
    historical perspective on, 43, 44, 45, 47
Counselor Locus of Control (CLOC) scale, 230
CPS. *See* Child protective services
Creaming (skimming), 13, 74, 467
Critical theory, 105-106
Crosby, Philip, 183
CSWE. *See* Council on Social Work Education
Cultural competence, 392, 425. *See also* Diversity
Culture, organizational. *See* Organizational culture
Curricular issues, 17-19, 43-47. *See also* Education for social welfare management

Darwinian approach, 141
Data administration, 326. *See also* Information; Information technology
Death, organizational, 98, 142-143
Decision making:
    ethical, 74-82
    family members and, 472

information management and, 321-339
   leadership and, 314
   moral dilemmas and, 8-9
   motivation and, 187
   perceived cost and, 278
Decision process theory, 306
Declaration on the Rights of the Child, 486
Deconstruction, 102-104
Decremental budget process, 383
Deficiency needs, 176(table), 179
Deinstitutionalization, 364, 462, 463, 475
Delayed effects, in feedback loops, 161-162
Delegating, by managers, 120-121, 252, 314
Deming, W. Edwards, 183, 184
Democratic ethos, 74-75, 80
Demographics:
   aging and, 11, 59-60, 522-523, 532
   collaboration and, 11
   diversity, empowerment, and, 426
   environment and, 136
   job response and, 222-226
   politics and, 58
   resource development and, 362-363
Density dependence, 98
Deontological versus teleological theories, 78-80
Depth and breadth, and ecology theory, 142
Deterministic versus voluntaristic theory, 41-42
Development:
   in budget cycle, 383-386
   in IT applications. See Information technology
   in resources. See Resource development
   in staff training, 411-412
Devine, Edward T., 31
Devolution of policy, 58-59, 512
Diagnostically related groups (DRGs), 464, 531
Direct case conferences, in historical perspective, 38
Disabilities, people with:
   ADA and. See Americans with Disabilities Act
   aging services and, 532
   demographics of, 11
   family services and, 488
   See also Mental health sector
Discrimination, 396, 398, 403, 463
Disruption, and task environment, 147
Distributive justice, 72
Disvalued groups, 10
Diversity, 425-442
   aging services and, 526-528
   barriers to, 428-430
   competencies and, 408
   framework for, 430-441
   importance of, 426-427

organizational, 98
   personnel management and, 392
   systems theory and, 427-428
Divine right of rulers, 71
Doctoral education, 31, 45
Domain, and environment, 134-135
Domination, and social change, 105-106, 107
Donors, as constituents, 9
Downsizing, 268, 270, 514
DRGs. See Diagnostically related groups
Drive, in leadership, 310-311
Dual degree option, 19. See also Education for social
   welfare management
Dual structure, in public welfare sector, 36-37
Duties:
   ethics and, 73, 75-77
   See also Tasks and functions

Ecological perspective, 97-99, 141-144. See also
   Environmental context; Environments
Economics:
   environment and, 136
   free-market mechanisms and, 56-57
   globalization and, 57-58
   planning and, 341-342
   See also Financial affairs; Political-economy
   theory
Economies of scale, 288
Eden Alternative, 528
Education for social welfare management:
   future of, 50, 261
   historical perspective on, ix, 30-33, 43-47, 48
   management practice variations and, 258
   quality of, 17-19, 261
   strategic choices for, 19-21
EEOC. See Equal Employment Opportunity
   Commission
Effectiveness:
   climate, culture, and, 214
   diversity and, 425
   financial management and, 392
   leadership and, 305, 306, 307, 309-315
   manager behavior and, 259-260
   organizational theory and, 91, 94
   personnel selection and, 403-404
   theory of practice and, 23
   worker expectation of, 227-228
   See also Efficiency; Performance
Efficiency:
   contingency theory and, 94-95
   health care services and, 513

information and, 272, 276
mental health sector and, 467, 470, 476
See also Effectiveness; Performance
80/20 rule, 325
Elderly adults. *See* Aging
Emergency assistance programs, 35-36
Employees. *See* Personnel management; Workers
Empowerment, 425-442
    barriers to, 428-430
    change and, 453
    definition of, 426
    dimensions of, 429-430
    framework for, 430-441
    human relations perspective and, 93
    importance of, 426-427
    information and, 337
    in management paradigm, 13-14
    leadership and, 314
    systems theory and, 427-428
Enacted environment, 134
Endowments, 380-381
End users of IT applications, 330-332, 333
Engels, Friedrich, 28
Engineering, and scientific management, 47
Entitlement programs, 36, 59
Entrepreneurial management, 64, 531
Environmental context, 55-65, 133-137
    change and, 274, 446-447
    financial affairs and, 362-370, 378-381
    forces in, 248-249
    resource development and, 362-370
    worker motivation and, 177-178(table), 183-184, 188-189
    See also Ecological perspective; Managers; Organizational climate; Organizational culture; Tasks and functions
Environmental scanning, 348-349
Environments:
    climate and culture imported from, 206-207
    general, 135-136
    objective versus subjective, 134
    task. *See* Task environment; Tasks and functions
Equal employment opportunity, 396, 398-399, 402
Equal Employment Opportunity Commission (EEOC), 396, 399, 404, 420(n)
Equal Pay Act, 398
Equity belief, 226-227
Equity theory, 177(table), 182-183
Ethical egoism, 78
Ethics, 69-83
    administrative dilemmas and, 72-74
    codes of, 72, 77, 81-82, 170, 391, 445

committees on, 80-82
decision making and, 74-82
financial management and, 391-392
historical perspective on, 70-72
in management paradigm, 8-9
job response and, 238
moral and ethical theory and, 77-80
risk management and, 82-83
work performance and, 170
Ethics consultation, 80-82
Ethnicity. *See* Race and ethnicity
Evaluation:
    in diversity and empowerment management, 439-440
    in family and children's services, 485-486, 501
    in mental health sector, 473-476
    of collaboration, 300
    of personnel, 412-416
    of programs, in planning, 354-355
Evaluators, managers as, 254
Exception, management by, 308
Executives:
    governance and, 120-121
    historical perspective on, 30, 32-33, 37, 41
    pay of, 129
    See also Managers
Expansion to new markets, 287
Expectancy theory, 175, 178
Expectations:
    in mental health sector, 473-477
    job response and, 227-228
    of constituencies, 9-10
Expenditures. *See* Budgets; Costs; Financial affairs
Experience level, and management practice variations, 259
Experimental designs, on climate and culture, 215
Expertise, and information technology, 330
Externality, and job response, 230

Facilitation, by managers, 256
Failures, organizational, 98, 142-143
Families for Kids, 496
Family and children's services, 481-505
    challenges in, 504-505
    child welfare in, 482-484, 496-502
    context for, in policies, 482-488
    context for, in services, 488-490
    definitions in, 481-482
    development and reform in, 502-504
    family group conferencing in, 487, 495-496

family preservation in, 482, 484-486, 494-496,
    502, 504
family reunification in, 496
family support in, 481-482, 491-494
mental health sector and, 463, 464, 469-476
resource development and, 362-363
service continuum in, 481-482, 490-491 502
Family Preservation and Support Initiative, 484-485,
    488
Family Support Act, 495
FAST. *See* Fiduciary abuse specialist team
Federation of Families for Children's Mental Health,
    464
Feedback:
    child welfare agencies and, 501
    motivation and, 183, 276-279
    personnel management and, 406, 414, 415-416
    system dynamics and, 158, 159-166
Feigenbaum, Armand V., 183
Females. *See* Gender; Women
Feminist perspective, 91(table), 103, 106-108, 309.
    See also Gender; Women
FGC (family group conferencing). *See* Family and
    children's services
Fiduciary abuse specialist team (FAST), 527
Financial affairs, 113, 124-129, 377-392
    boundary blurring and, 125-129
    budgetary planning and, 356
    cash flow management in, 391
    challenges in, 388-391
    community rediscovery and, 60
    constituencies and, 9
    ethics and, 391-392
    flexibility in, 471
    funding sources and, 124-125, 378
    funding sources and, alternative, 372-373
    funding sources and, diversified, 368-369
    future trends in, 49-50
    historical perspective on, 33, 39-40
    importance of, 377-378
    monitoring of, 390-391
    organization type and, 124-125
    reports in, 390-391
    resource administration and, 253
    resource development and, 361-374
    responsibilities in, 381-388
    revenue forecasting in, 385, 389-390
    See also Resources
First movers, 148
Fiscal characteristics, 113, 124-129. *See also*
    Financial affairs
Fiscal year, 381

Flexibility, in leadership, 312
Follett, Mary Parker, 47
Ford, Henry, 91
Fordism, 91
Forecasting:
    of cash flow, 391
    of revenues, 385, 389-390
Form 990, 380
Formalization, and structure, 156, 157
Formal systems, in organizational structure, 121,
    122, 123
For-profit organizations:
    as organization type, 115, 116
    as subsidiaries of nonprofits, 380
    boundary blurring and, 128
    climate, culture, and, 212-213
    contracting and, 128
    funding sources for, 124, 125
    governance of, 120, 121
    mission of, 118
    resource development and, 365
Foster care, 496-497
Founding, organizational, 97-99
Free-market mechanisms, 56-57
Functional budgeting, 384
Functions and tasks. *See* Tasks and functions
Fund raising, 361, 371-373. *See also* Financial affairs;
    Resource development
Futuring, 252

Gender:
    burnout and, 225-226
    job satisfaction and, 223-224
    management practice variations and, 257-258
    personnel management and, 398, 399
    resource development and, 363
    salary and, 222-223
    See also Diversity
General environment, 135-136
Generalism, and task environment, 147-148
Genetic variations, 141
Gifts, charitable, 127-128
Glass ceiling, 223-224
Global economy, 57-58
Global village, 150
Goals:
    contracting and, 127
    feedback loops and, 161
    funder and agency, 367
    innovation and, 252
    linking of, 173-174

organizational theory and, 91-92
planning and, 345
worker motivation and, 176(table), 179
worker performance and, 173-174
God's order, and ethics, 71
Good-aggregative utilitarianism, 79
Goodnow, Frank, 71, 72, 74
Governance, 11-12, 119-123, 296-298, 300. *See also* Organizational structure
Government Performance and Results Act (GPRA), 13, 61, 321, 379
Government role:
  as constituency, 9
  boundary blurring and, 126, 127
  collaboration and, 11-12
  future trends for, 49
  historical perspective on, 28, 29, 34-39, 41
  in family and children's services, 482-488
  in health care services, 512
  in mental health sector, 462, 463-464
  policy devolution and, 58-59, 512
  resource development and, 363-364
  See also Contracting; Public organizations
GPRA. *See* Government Performance and Results Act
Grants, 361, 362, 371, 373, 379, 463. *See also* Financial affairs; Resource development
Grassroots movements, 463, 491
Graying of America, 59-60, 522
Grievances, in personnel management, 417, 418-419
Growth needs, 176(table), 179

Hadassah, 349, 350(figure)
Health care services, 511-518
  historical perspective on, 40, 51
  politics, ideology, and, 512-513
  re-engineering of, 513-514
  role of social work in, 514-518
  See also Managed care
Health of workers, 233-234, 235
Hierarchy of needs, 176(table), 179
Hiring, 398, 399, 402-404, 405(table), 471
Hispanics. *See* Race and ethnicity
Historical perspectives, 27-51
  and the future, 48-51
  on associations, 42-43
  on education, ix, 30-33, 43-47, 48
  on ethics, 70-72
  on family and children's services, 482-483
  on mental health sector, 462-465
  on organizational climate and culture, 199-201
  on planning, 341-342

on social work literature, 47-48
on theory, 40-42
Historical perspectives, chronological:
  beginnings, 27-28
  19th century, 28-31
  20th century, 31-48
  21st century, 48-50
Historical perspectives, forces in:
  limited liability stock corporation, 29
  public social welfare sector, emergence of, 34-37
  public social welfare sector, recent developments in, 37-39
  voluntary sector, emergence of, 30-32
HIV-AIDS, 38, 362
Hollis/Taylor Report, 44
Honor, as core value, 75
Hoover, Herbert, 34
Hopkins, Harry, 35
HSR. *See* Human Services Referral case
Hull House, 35, 482
Human capital, 410, 528
Human relations perspective, 92-94
Human relations theory, 22
Human resources, 396. *See also* Personnel management
Human service organizations:
  comparisons for, 212
  terminology of, 5-6
  See also Social welfare management
Human Services Referral (HSR) case, 163-165

IDEA family services, 488
Idealized influence, 308
Ideologies:
  critical theory and, 106
  health care services and, 512-513
  integration, cohesion, and, 100
  leadership and, 307
  terminology and, 4-6
IFPS. *See* Intensive family preservation services
Immigrants, 11
Implementation:
  in budget cycle, 386-387
  in change, 449-455
  in diversity and empowerment management, 438-439
  in IT, 325(table). *See also* Information technology
  in strategic planning, 344-345, 352, 353-354
Income taxes, 379-380. *See also* Taxes
Incorporation, articles of, 119
Incremental budget process, 383

Indian Child Welfare Act, 483-484

Indicators, 12. *See also* Measurement

Individual consideration, 308, 314

Individually focused approaches to motivation, 175, 176(table), 178-181, 185

Individual merit, ideology of, 428

Induction process, for personnel, 410-411

Industrial Revolution, 28

Inequity, and equity theory, 182-183

Inequity belief, 226-227

Informal systems, in organizational structure, 121, 122, 123

Information:
    adaptation and, 138-139
    aging services and, 529-530
    decision making and, 321-339
    diversity, empowerment, and, 276-279, 434-436
    health care services and, 515
    in management paradigm, 14-15
    management of, 321-339, 515
    measuring results and, 273-276
    right, 269-272
    service outcomes and, 267-280
    See also Measurement

Information technology (IT):
    budget process and, 384
    change and, 322, 323
    decision making and, 321-339
    definitions for, 322, 338-339
    environment of, 62-63, 64
    health care services and, 515

Information technology (IT) application development:
    change and, 336-337
    end users and, 330-332, 333
    expertise and, 330, 334
    guidelines for success in, 332-336
    organizational structure and, 326-327, 330, 331(figure), 332
    stages in, 323-325
    tools and techniques in, 327-328

Initiating structure, in leadership style, 306

Innovation, 203, 251-252, 516-517, 529. *See also* Change

Inspirational motivation, 308

Institutionalization, and organizational theory, 99-100

Institutional theory, 22, 144-145, 146

Institutional versus technical organizations, 99

Integration, and organizational culture, 100-102

Intellectual stimulation, 308, 314

Intensive family preservation services (IFPS), 482, 494-495, 496, 502, 504. *See also* Family and children's services

Interactionally focused approaches to motivation, 177(table), 181-183, 186-188. *See also* Job response

Interdependence. *See* Boundary blurring; Collaboration; Networks; Partnerships

Internality, and job response, 230

Internal Revenue Service (IRS), 378, 379, 387, 388

International issues, 150, 486-487

Internet, 328, 335, 336-337

Interviews, employment, 399, 400-401(table), 404, 405(table)

IRS. *See* Internal Revenue Service

IT. *See* Information technology

Jackson, James F., 32

Job performance. *See* Work performance

Job redesign, 183

Job response, and worker attributes, 219-238

Job satisfaction, 176(table), 179-180, 185-188
    aging services and, 528
    demographics and, 223-225
    leadership and, 314, 315
    morale and, 272, 275-276
    position descriptions and, 406
    worker attributes and, 228-230, 232-238
    See also Burnout

Job Satisfaction Survey (JSS), 276

JOBS program, 39

Job tasks, 404, 406-407. *See also* Tasks and functions

Johnson, Lyndon, 37

JSS. *See* Job Satisfaction Survey

Juran, Joseph M., 183

Justice:
    as core value, 75-76
    distributive, 72

Kant, Immanuel, 78

Kinship care, 496, 497

Knowledge:
    adaptation and, 140
    collaboration and, 286
    leadership and, 312
    organizational theory and, 103, 105

Knowledge work, levels of, 409-410

Labor markets, 57, 59

La Follette, Robert, 34
Laissez-faire leadership, 308
Lake v. Cameron, 524
Language:
    integration, cohesion, and, 100-101
    of management and administration, 4-5
    organization type and, 116
    social control and, 103
Lathrop, Julia, 35
Lawsuits, 82
Leadership, 303-316
    change and, 451, 455
    climate, culture, and, 208-209
    collaboration and, 297
    compared to management, 304-305
    components of, 310-315
    definitions of, 304, 305
    diversity, empowerment, and, 432-433
    effectiveness and, 305-307, 309-315
    families, children, and, 493-494, 499-505
    feminine theories on, 309
    human relations perspective and, 92, 93, 94
    importance of, 303
    information and, 268-269
    manager behavior and, 256-257, 260
    research approaches to, 305-309
    teamwork and, 256-257
    theories on, 42, 305-309
    theories on, and effectiveness, 305-307, 309-315
    theories on, and implications, 315-316
    transactional, 304, 308
    transformational, 304, 308-309
    See also Motivation
Learning, organizational, 138-139
Least restrictive appropriate alternative, 524
Legal issues:
    environment and, 136
    families, children, and, 482-483
    financial management and, 379, 380
    goal attainment and, 91
    personnel management and, 396, 398-403
    public agency mission and, 117, 118
    risk, ethics, and, 82-83
Legitimation, and environment, 135, 137, 145
Levels of knowledge work, 409-410
Liability, 82
Licensing examination, 46
Life-cycle theory, 306
Limited liability stock corporation, 29
Limits to Growth archetype, 162
Line-item budget, 384
Lockheed-Martin, 56-57

Locus-aggregative utilitarianism, 79
Locus of control, 230-231, 238
Long-range funding sources, 372-373
Long-range planning, 341, 342

Males. *See* Gender
Malpractice, 82
Managed care, 40, 51, 270
    accountability and, 61, 378
    aging services and, 526, 531
    financial affairs and, 365, 378
    information technology and, 321-322
    mental health sector and, 465, 466-477
    politics, ideology, and, 512-513
    strategic planning and, 342
    See also Health care services
Management:
    compared to leadership, 304-305
    essential elements of, 7
    helping role of, 5
    level of, 259
    social welfare management as variant of, 6-8
    terminology of, 4-6
    See also Social welfare management
Management by objectives (MBO), 4, 414
Management environment, 248-249. *See also*
        Environmental context; Environments
Management information system (MIS), 326. *See also*
        Information; Information technology
Managers:
    as advocators, 255, 531
    as boundary spanners, 251
    as communicators, 251
    as entrepreneurs, 64, 531
    as evaluators, 254
    as facilitators, 256
    as futurist-innovators, 251-252
    as leaders. *See* Leadership
    as organizers, 252-253
    as policy practitioners, 254-255
    as resource administrators, 253-254
    as resource developers, 361-374
    as supervisors, 255-256
    as team builders-leaders, 256-257
    eclectic roles of, 526-532
    See also Behavior; Tasks and functions
Marketing, 4, 64
Marx, Karl, 28
Marxist theory, 105
Marxist theory, Neo-, 91(table)
Maslach-Pines burnout scale, 185

MBA degree and programs, 46, 50, 51, 258
MBO. *See* Management by objectives
MDS. *See* Minimum data set
Measurement:
  accountability and, 61
  climate, culture, and, 199, 201
  financial management and, 379
  in aging services, 530-531
  information and, 273-276
  in management paradigm, 12-13
  in mental health sector, 474-476
  structure and, 156
  work performance and, 170-173
  See also Performance
Medicaid, 40, 127, 470, 525, 526, 529
Medicare, 49, 127, 524, 525, 531
Men. *See* Gender
Mental health of workers, 233-234
Mental health sector, 461-477
  current trends in, 466-477
  definition and scope in, 465, 466-468
  demographics of, 11
  expectations of results in, 473-477
  historical perspective on, 462-465
  managed care and, 465, 466-477
  paradigm shifts in, 465
  philosophy and vision in, 468-473
  variety of settings for, 462
Mentoring, 314
Mergers and acquisitions, 467-468, 513
Merit, individual, 428
Meta-ethics, 77-78. *See also* Ethics
Milford Conference Report, 33
Milieus, and environment, 135
Mill, John Stuart, 79
Mimicry, 207
Minimum data set (MDS), 530
MIS. *See* Management information system
Mission:
  operating authority and, 117-119
  planning and, 345-348
  resource development and, 362, 370-371
Monitoring, and financial management, 390-391
Morale, staff, 272, 275-276, 468, 476-477
Moral issues:
  ethics and, 69, 72, 75, 77-80
  in management paradigm, 8-9, 12
  job response and, 238
  organizational theory and, 90, 100, 104-105
  See also Ethics
Motivation, 93, 276-278, 308
Motivation and work performance, 169-190

  definitions and approaches to, 170-173
  environmental focus and, 177-178(table), 183-184, 188-189
  importance of, 169-170, 189-190
  individual focus and, 175, 176(table), 178-181, 185
  interactional focus and, 177(table), 181-183, 186-188
  linking of goals in, 173-174
  process, outcome, and, 171, 189
  studies on, 184-189
  theoretical approaches to, 174-184
Motives of leaders, 310-312. *See also* Attributes
MPA degree and programs, 46, 258
MPH degree, 46
MSW degree and programs, 45, 258. *See also* Education for social welfare management
Multicultural diversity competence, 425. *See also* Diversity
Multifunctional management, 518

NA. *See* Negative affectivity
Narratives, 101
NASW. *See* National Association of Social Workers
National Association of Public Child Welfare Administrators, 42
National Association of Social Workers (NASW):
  Code of Ethics of, 72, 77, 82, 170, 391, 445
  historical perspective on, 43
  job surveys by, 16, 222-225, 233
National Conference of Charities and Correction, 29, 34
National Conference of Social Work, 34, 36
Natural selection, 142
Needs, climate, and culture, 209-211
Needs theories, 176(table), 179-180
Negative affectivity (NA), 235-236
Negligence, 82
Negotiation, 292-293, 386
Neo-institutionalism, 99-100
Neo-Marxist theory, 91(table)
Network for Social Work Managers, 43
Networks:
  advice on, 300-301
  aging services and, 529
  costs/benefits of, 284, 288-290
  forms of, 290, 298
  importance of, 285-289
  levels of, 298-300
  phases and tasks in, 292-300
  prerequisites of, 291-292

structure and, 157-158
terminology of, 284
New leadership approach, 307-309, 315
Niches, and environment, 135, 142
Nonintensive family preservation services, 495. *See also* Family and children's services
Nonprofit organizations (NPOs):
    as organization type, 115-116
    boundary blurring and, 127-128
    business sector and, 4-5
    climate, culture, and, 212-213
    contracting and, 127-128
    education for management of, 20-21
    family and children's services in, 489-490
    for-profit subsidiaries of, 380
    funding sources for, 124, 125
    future trends for, 49-50
    governance of, 120, 121
    historical perspective on, 28-34, 36-38, 39-40, 46
    management challenges in, 249-250
    mission of, 117
    resource development and, 361-374
    trends since 1970s in, x
Nonsectarian agencies, 115
Normative ethics, 77, 78. *See also* Ethics
Norms:
    culture and, 201-209, 214, 269
    leadership and, 307
    See also Ethics; Organizational culture; Standards; Values
North Carolina Family Assessment Scale, 485
NPOs. *See* Nonprofit organizations
Nursing homes, 523, 526. *See also* Skilled nursing facilities

Objective environment, 134
Obligational partnerships, 290, 298, 299(table)
Older adults. *See* Aging
Omnibus Budget Reconciliation Act of 1981, 463
Operating authoring, 114-121, 259
Operational planning, 353-357
Oppression, and social change, 105-106, 107
Organization adaptation theories, 138-141
Organizational chart, 121
Organizational climate:
    change and, 445, 452
    compared to culture, 198-199, 200
    definition of, 198
    development of, 206-209
    historical perspective on, 199-201
    importance of, 201-205, 215-216

interorganizational differences in, 205-206, 211-214
job response and, 228, 237
maintenance of, 209-211
nature of, 195-199
worker motivation and, 188-189
See also Organizational culture; Worker attributes
Organizational culture:
    compared to climate, 198-199, 200
    critical theory and, 106
    definitions of, 197-198
    development of, 206-209
    historical perspective on, 199-201
    importance of, 201-205, 215-216
    information and, 269, 278
    integration, cohesion, and, 100-102
    interorganizational differences in, 205-206, 211-214
    leadership and, 307, 314
    maintenance of, 209-211
    nature of, 195-199
    See also Organizational climate; Worker attributes
Organizational design, 94-95, 207-209
Organizational environments:
    definition of, 133-135
    general, 135-136
    See also Environmental context; Environments; Task environment
Organizational mimicry, 207
Organizational structure, 113-123
    aging services and, 529-530
    boundary blurring in, 125-129
    business and, 118-119
    changes of, 118, 129, 145
    climate, culture, and, 207-209
    collaboration and, 296-298
    definition of, 113
    financial characteristics and, 113, 124-129. *See also* Financial affairs
    governance and, 119-123
    information technology and, 326-327, 330, 331(figure), 332
    mission and, 117-119
    operating authoring and, 114-121, 259
    performance and, 155-167
    positional approach to, 156-157, 166, 167(table)
    professionals and, 123
    relational approach to, 157-158, 166, 167(table)
    substructures in, 121-123
    systems approach to, 155-156, 158-167
    task environment and, 145, 148-149
    trends in, 63-64

Organizational theory, 89-108
    administrative tasks and, 90, 91(table)
    deterministic versus voluntaristic, 41-42
    historical perspective on, 40-42
    importance of, 89-90, 108
    on founding and survival, 97-99
    on goal attainment, 91-92
    on institutionalization, 99-100
    on integration and social cohesion, 100-102
    on knowledge, power, and control, 102-105
    on management of people, 92-94
    on proficiency and efficiency, 94-95
    on resource mobilization, 95-97
Organizations, basic mission of, 22-23. *See also*
    Mission
Organizations, types of, 114-117, 117(table)
    boundary blurring and, 126(table)
    climate, culture, and, 211-214
    funding sources and, 124(table)
    mission and, 117-119
    See also Organizational structure
Organizing, 252-253, 322-323
Orientation of personnel, 410-411
Outcomes:
    aging services and, 530-531
    health care services and, 514. *See also* Managed
        care
    information and, 267-280
    manager behavior and, 259-260
    stresses, strains, and, 220-238
    See also Measurement; Performance
Output, cost per unit of, 388
Overinvolvement of workers, 233, 238
Ownership:
    in management paradigm, 13-14
    in organizational culture, 102

PA. *See* Positive affectivity
PACE. *See* Program and All Inclusive Care for the
    Elderly
Participatory management, 93
Partnerships:
    advice on, 300-301
    costs/benefits of, 284, 288-290
    financial management and, 379
    forms of, 290-291, 298
    importance of, 283, 285-289
    in family and children's services, 502-503
    information technology and, 62-63, 64
    levels of, 298-300
    phases and tasks in, 292-300

    prerequisites of, 291-292
    terminology of, 284
    See also Collaboration
Passive management by exception, 308
Path-goal theory, 306
Patient involvement, 515-516, 517, 524
Pay. *See* Salaries
People systems, 396. *See also* Personnel management
Perceived environment, 134
Perceptions, worker:
    climate and, 202-210, 214
    decision making and, 278
    job response and, 226-227, 228-230
    See also Organizational climate
Per-client program cost, 388
Performance:
    accountability and, 61-62
    categories of, 270-276
    effectiveness and. *See* Effectiveness
    financial management and, 379
    human relations perspective and, 92-93
    information and, 268-280
    in management paradigm, 12-13
    in mental health sector, 473-476
    organizational structure and, 155-167
    personnel management and, 406-407, 412-419
    worker motivation and, 169-190
    See also Job response; Measurement
Performance appraisal of personnel, 412-416
Performance budgeting, 384
Performance Partnership Grants (PPG), 379
Personality traits:
    job response and, 234-236
    motivation and, 180-181
    See also Worker attributes
Personal Responsibility and Work Opportunity
    Reconciliation Act (PRWORA), 39, 41, 59
Person-environment interactions, 236-237. *See also*
    Environments; Job response
Personnel management, 395-420
    affirmative action and, 396, 398-399
    competencies in, 407-410
    diversity and, 392
    equal employment opportunity and, 396, 398-
        399, 402
    financial management and, 391-392
    importance of, 395-396
    in aging services, 528-529
    in family and children's services, 501-502
    in mental health sector, 468, 471
    interviews in, 399, 400-401(table), 404,
        405(table)

key functions of, 395-396, 419-420
management model and, 252-253
orientation in, 410-411
performance appraisal and, 412-416
performance problems and, 416-419
policies in, 417-418
position descriptions in, 404, 406-407
recruitment in, 398, 399, 403-404, 405(table),
    407, 408(table)
resource development and, 371-372
selection in, 398, 399, 402-404, 405(table), 471
staff development in, 411-412
training and, 411-412
See also Workers
Personnel manual, 396, 397(table)
Person-process-product model, 309, 310, 311(table)
Ph.D. programs, 31, 45
Philanthropic organizations, in historical perspective,
    28-32. *See also* Nonprofit organizations
Planning, 341-358
budgets and, 356, 383-386
characteristics of, 342
contingency, 355-356
diversity, empowerment, and, 436-441
importance of, 341-342, 357-358
IT implementation and, 332
long-range, 341, 342
operational, 353-357
program, 353, 354-355
strategic. *See* Strategic planning
Planning programming budgeting system (PPBS), 383
Policy practice, 254-255
Political-economy theory, 95-97, 140-141
Politics:
change and, 453-455
child welfare agencies and, 499
environment and, 58, 136
health care services and, 512-513
historical perspective on, 41
job response and, 238
mental health sector and, 466, 473
program implementation and, 97
theory on, 22
Population dynamics, 98
Population ecology, 97-99, 141-144, 145, 146
Positional approach to organizational structure, 156-
    157, 166, 167(table)
Position announcements, 407, 408(table)
Position descriptions, 404, 406-407
Positive affectivity (PA), 235-236
Postmodernism, 102-104
Poverty, 11

Power:
change and, 453
climate, culture, and, 210
organizational theory and, 103-104
political, 58, 453
task environment and, 141, 147
Power-politics model, 453
PPBS. *See* Planning programming budgeting system
PPS. *See* Prospective payment system
Privacy, 335-336. *See also* Confidentiality
Private good, 9
Private organizations, 115, 213-214, 259. *See also*
    Nonprofit organizations
Private/public structures, dual, 36-37
Privatization, 63, 321, 489
boundary blurring and, 125, 128
definition of, 125
historical perspective on, 39-40, 49
resource development and, 365
Productivity, 57-58, 102, 272
Professional culture, 314. *See also* Organizational
    culture
Professional ethics, 70-71. *See also* Ethics
Professional paternalism, 73
Professional worldview, 312
Proficiency, and contingency theory, 94-95. *See also*
    Effectiveness
Profit organizations. *See* For-profit organizations
Program and All Inclusive Care for the Elderly
    (PACE), 527, 531
Program planning, 353, 354-355, 386
Project budgeting, 384
Projections:
of cash flow, 391
of revenues, 385, 389-390
Promotional partnerships, 290, 298, 299(table)
Proprietary organizations. *See* For-profit
    organizations
Prospective payment system (PPS), 531
Prototyping, in IT strategy, 329-330
PRWORA. *See* Personal Responsibility and Work
    Opportunity Reconciliation Act
Psychological climate, 196-197
Public administration, and ethics, 71-72
Public good, 9
Public organizations:
as organization type, 115
climate, culture, and, 213-214
funding sources for, 124, 125
governance of, 120, 121
management practice variations and, 259
mission of, 117-118, 489

resource development and, 365-366
Public/private structures, dual, 36-37
Public social welfare sector, in historical perspective,
        34-39
Purchase-of-service contracts, 49, 126-129. *See also*
        Contracting

Quality:
        aging services and, 530-531
        climate, culture, and, 102, 213
        financial affairs and, 381
        health care services and, 514
        leadership and, 315
        mental health sector and, 467, 468, 470, 476
        See also Total quality management
Quality management, trends in, 64
Quality of life, 177(table), 183, 475
Quasi-private organizations, 126(table)
Quasi-public organizations, 126(table)
Quinlan, Karen Anne, 80

Race and ethnicity:
        aging services and, 526-528
        burnout and, 225, 226
        job satisfaction and, 224
        management practice variations and, 258
        personnel management and, 398, 399
        resource development and, 363
        salary and, 222-223
        See also Diversity; Empowerment
Radical feminism, 106. *See also* Feminist perspective
Rational model of organizations, 91-92
RBRVS. *See* Resource-based relative value system
Reasonable accommodations, 402-403
Recruitment, of personnel, 398, 399, 403-404,
        405(table), 407, 408(table)
Re-engineering, 64, 268, 270, 513-514
Reference modes, 159
Regulations, 379, 380. *See also* Legal issues
Rehabilitation Act, 398
Reinforcement theory, 175, 176(table)
Reinforcing loops, 160, 162
Relational approach to organizational structure, 157-
        158, 166, 167(table)
Relations-oriented activities, in leadership, 314-315
Religious organizations, 28, 29, 115
Religiosity, 136, 238. *See also* Spirituality
Reports, in financial affairs, 390-391
Request for proposal (RFP), 327-328, 361
Resource-based relative value system (RBRVS), 531

Resource dependence theory, 141, 143-144, 145,
        146
Resource development, 361-374
        dilemma resolution and, 367-370
        environment changes and, 362-370
        management skills for, 370-374
        resource allocation and, 367-368
Resources:
        administration of, 253-254
        collaboration and, 287
        health care services and, 514
        information and, 271, 275
        long- and short-term needs for, 368
        political economy perspective on, 95-97
        scarcity of, 248, 364
        stewardship of, 373-374
        task environment and, 138-146
        See also Financial affairs
Resource utilization groups (RUGs), 531
Respite care services, 494
Results:
        emphasis on, 64
        expectations and, 473-477
        information and, 273-276
        See also Outcomes; Performance
Revenue forecasting, 385, 389-390. *See also*
        Financial affairs
Rewards, and leadership, 308, 311(table)
RFP. *See* Request for proposal
Richmond, Mary, 31-32
Rights of the Child, U.N. Declaration on the, 486
Risk:
        change and, 449
        climate, culture, and, 207-208
        collaboration and, 289-290, 292
        ethics and, 82-83
        resource development and, 365-366
Roles, and structure, 156, 157. *See also* Tasks and
        functions
Roosevelt, Franklin D., 35
RUGs. *See* Resource utilization groups
Rules, institutional, 99-100
Rule utilitarianism, 79
Russell Sage Foundation, 32, 33

Salaries, 129, 222-223
San Mateo County Human Services Agency,
        351(figure)
Scientific management, 47, 74, 91, 174
Scientific method, 71
Screening of job applicants, 403-404, 405(table)

Sectarian agencies, 115
Security, and information technology, 335-336
Selection of personnel, 398, 399, 402-404, 405(table)
Self-confidence, 311-312
Self-efficacy:
    job response and, 228, 229, 230, 232, 238
    motivation and, 181-182, 186-187
Self-esteem, 228, 229, 277, 278
Self-regulation mechanisms, 172-173, 180-181
Sense-making, 100-102
Service continuum, 481-482, 490-491, 502, 516
Service events, and information, 271, 274-275
Settlement houses, 30, 518
Settlement Movement, 483
Sexual harassment, 418-419
Simulations, for performance investigations, 166
SITO evaluation, 300
Skilled nursing facilities (SNFs), 523, 527-531
Skills, 312-313, 328. See also Attributes
Skimming. See Creaming
Slow movers, and task environment, 148
SNFs. See Skilled nursing facilities
Social change, 105-108. See also Change
Social cohesion, 100-102
Social control, 102-104. See also Control
Social diagnosis, 31
Social exchange theory, 141, 226
Social learning theory, 177(table), 181
Social Security, 35, 36, 38, 45, 127, 483, 524-525
Social structures, and resource development, 362-363
Social support, for workers, 187-188
Social welfare management:
    as variant of general management, 6-8
    dual models of, 37
    environmental context of, 55-65
    essential characteristics of, 6-15, 90, 250
    historical perspective on, 27-51
    importance of, 3, 259
    integrated treatment needed for, ix-x
    paradigm of, 8-15
    purpose of, 259
    social worker careers and, 15-17, 517-518
    terminology of, 5-6
    theory of practice and, 21-23
    trends and, 48-51, 63-65
Social welfare society, 61
Social work:
    as calling versus profession, 184
    education for. See Education for social welfare management
    ethical context for, 72, 77. See also Ethics

    historical perspective on, 43-47, 48, 50
    management careers in, 15-17, 45-46
    terminology of, 6
    trends since 1970s in, ix-x
Society for Organizing Charity, 31. See also Charity Organization Societies
Society for the Prevention of Cruelty to Children, 483
Software and hardware selection, 334-335. See also Information technology
Span of control, 157, 158
Specialism, 147-148
Specialization, 468-469, 470
Spirituality, 61, 238. See also Religiosity
SSI. See Supplementary Security Income program
SSO. See Stresses, strains, outcomes
Stabilizing loops, 160-161
Staff morale, 272, 275-276, 468, 476-477. See also Personnel management; Workers
Standardized minimum data set, 530
Standards, in management paradigm, 12-13. See also Norms; Values
Status change measures, 274
Stereotypes, 10
Stigmatized consumers, 10
Stories, integration, and cohesion, 101
Strain, 220-221. See also Stresses, strains, outcomes
Strategic planning, 4, 446
    definitions of, 343, 344
    elements of, 343-345
    guide for, 346(figure)
    implementation in, 344-345, 352, 353-354
    innovation and, 252
    need for, 341-342, 357-358
    operational planning and, 356-357
    steps in, 345-353
    strategy formulation in, 350-353
    trends in, 64-65
Strategies:
    change and, 452-455
    job response and, 231-233
    leadership and, 307
    task environment and, 146-149
Strategy building, 307
Stress, 14, 220-221
Stresses, strains, outcomes (SSO), 220-238
Structural contingency theory, 139. See also Contingency theory
Structural equivalence, 158
Structurally focused approaches to motivation, 177-178(table)
Structuration theory, 104-105

Structure, organizational. *See* Organizational
    structure
Structured methodology, 328
Style approach to leadership, 306, 315
Subcultures, 101. *See also* Organizational culture
Subjective environment, 134
Substructures, 121-123
Supervision:
    change and, 453
    management model and, 255-256
    personnel management and, 406-407, 412
Supplementary Security Income (SSI) program, 38,
    49
Survival:
    organizational theory and, 95-96, 97-99
    task environment and, 138-145
Systemic partnerships, 290-291, 298, 299(table). *See
    also* Partnerships
Systems, 22, 121-123, 469
    diversity, empowerment, and, 427-428
    information management and, 326-328
    structure, performance, and, 155-156, 158-167

TANF. *See* Temporary Assistance to Needy Families
Task environment, 135-151
    characteristics of, 137-138
    collaboration in, 283-301
    ecological theories and, 141-144
    institutional theory and, 144-145, 146
    organization adaptation theories and, 138-141
    strategies of adaptation to, 146-148
    strategy, structure, and, 148-149
    typology and, 135-137
Task-oriented activities, 313-314
Tasks and functions:
    agency outcomes and, 259-260
    early studies of, 250-251
    fiscal responsibilities and, 381-388
    future research and, 260-261
    model of, 251-257
    personnel management and, 395-396, 419-420
    variation in, 257-259
Tasks, in position descriptions, 404, 406-407
Taxes:
    boundary blurring and, 127-128, 129
    financial management and, 379-380
    gifts and, 127-128
Taxpayer Bill of Rights 2, 129
Taylor, F. W., 74, 91, 122, 174
Team building, 256-257
Team work:
    in change strategies, 456
    in IT applications, 334

in mental health sector, 471
Technical versus institutional organizations, 99
Technologies:
    change and, 449
    child welfare agencies and, 501
    climate, culture, and, 203-204, 208
    core, 203-205
    dissemination and, 4
    environment and, 136
    hard and soft, 204
    importance and ambiguity of, 90
    information and. *See* Information technology
    knowledge and, 286
    pressure to use, 321-322
    structuration theory and, 104
Teleological versus deontological theories, 78-80
Temporary Assistance to Needy Families (TANF), 39,
    268, 484, 486, 490. *See also* Aid to Families
    With Dependent Children
Termination, in personnel management, 418
Textbooks, 47-48
Theoretical issues:
    historical perspective on, 40-42
    in change, 451-452
    in collaboration, 285-291
    in diversity and empowerment management, 427-
        428
    in leadership, 42, 305-316
    in morals and ethics, 77-80
    in motivation and work performance, 174-184
    in structure and performance, 156-165
    in task environment, 138-146
    organizational. *See* Organizational theory
    practice and, 21-23
Theory Y, 178(table)
Thermostat analogy, 277. *See also* Feedback
Third-party governance, 11-12
360-degree performance measures, 172
Top-down approach, in IT strategy, 329, 330
Total quality management (TQM), 4, 22
    information and, 268, 270
    manager behavior and, 260
    worker motivation and, 178(table), 183-184, 189
    See also Quality
TQM. *See* Total quality management
Training:
    for leadership, 316
    historical perspective on, 30-31, 32-33
    information technology and, 333, 334
    personnel management and, 411-412
    See also Education for social welfare management
Trait-focused approaches, 305-306, 310-312, 315.
        See also Individually focused approaches;
        Personality traits

Transactional leadership, 304, 308
Transformational leadership, 304, 308-309
Trust, and collaboration, 294-295
Turnover, 237, 315. *See also* Burnout; Job response;
     Job satisfaction
Type A behavior pattern, 234-235

U.N. Declaration on the Rights of the Child, 486
United Jewish Appeal-Federation, 347(figure)
United Way, 39, 124, 269, 344
Universities and colleges. *See* Education for social
     welfare management
Utilitarianism, 78-80

Values:
     aging and, 524
     change and, 449-450
     climate, culture, and, 101, 102, 197-198, 201,
          206, 209-210, 214
     core, 75-77, 524
     environment and, 136
     ethics and, 75-77
     information and, 269
     in management paradigm, 12
     leadership and, 307
     organizational structure and, 123
     political economy and, 97
     worker motivation and, 180
     See also Beliefs; Ethics
Vietnam Era Veterans' Readjustment Assistance Act,
     398
Virtual organizations, 529-530
Virtual therapy, 336-337
Vision:
     collaboration and, 293-294
     diversity, empowerment, and, 432
     information and, 268
     in mental health sector, 468-473
     leadership and, 307, 313
     planning and, 345-348
     shared, 293-294
Vocabulary. *See* Language
Voluntaristic versus deterministic theory, 41-42
Voluntary organizations, in historical perspective, 29,
     30-32, 39, 40-41. *See also* Nonprofit
     organizations

Wages. *See* Salaries
Warner, Amos, 31

War on Poverty, 37
Wealth, disparity in, 11
Weber, Max, 74, 118
Web sites, 328. *See also* Internet
Welfare capitalism, 30, 36
Well-worn paths of service, 202
Whistle-blowing, 74, 450
Whites. *See* Race and ethnicity
Wilson, Woodrow, 71, 72, 74
Women:
     future trends for, 50
     goals, performance, and, 174
     leadership and, 309, 316
     See also Feminist perspective; Gender
Work characteristics:
     job response and, 236-237, 238
     See also Organizational climate; Organizational
          culture
Worker attributes, 226-237
Workers:
     as valuable resource, 169
     attributes of, 226-237
     climate, culture, and, 188-189, 195-215
     empowerment of, 276-279
     ethics and, 73, 74, 82
     in management paradigm, 12, 13-14
     morale of, 272, 275-276
     motivation and, 169-190
     multifaceted conceptualization of, 189
     organizational theory and, 92-94
     perceptions of, 202-210, 214, 226-230, 278
     See also Personnel management
Workers, and job response:
     demographics and, 222-226
     recommendations on, 237-238
     worker attributes and, 226-237
Work performance:
     climate, culture, and, 188-189, 201-214
     empowerment and, 276-279
     motivation and, 169-190
     personnel management and, 406-407, 412-419
     See also Job response; Organizational climate; Or-
          ganizational culture
Worldview, professional, 312

YMCA, 30, 33-34, 47, 96, 344
YWCA, 30, 33-34

ZBB. *See* Zero-based budgeting
Zero-based budgeting (ZBB), 383

About the Authors

Catherine Foster Alter is Dean and Professor at the Graduate School of Social Work, University of Denver. She is co-author with Jerald Hage of *Organizations Working Together* and has worked extensively in the area of interorganizational relations.

David M. Austin is the Bert Kruger Smith Centennial Professor at the University of Texas, Austin, School of Social Work. He has written extensively on the organization and administration of human services. Among his books is the *Political Economy of Human Service Programs.*

Michael J. Austin is Professor of Management and Planning at the University of California, School of Social Welfare. He is formerly the dean at the University of Pennsylvania School of Social Work and has contributed numerous articles and books to macro practice over the past thirty years, including the recently edited, *Human Services Interpretation.*

David Bargal is a social worker and social psychologist and currently Professor on the faculty of the Paul Baerwald School of Social Work, the Hebrew University. He is an internationally known expert in industrial social work and writes extensively on leadership and organization groups and intergroup conflict.

Daniel Bogin is currently employed as an analyst at Andersen Consulting in New York City.

Mark Ezell is Associate Professor at the University of Kansas, School of Social Welfare. He consults widely on program and policy development in the children and youth services field and is currently completing his book *Advocacy in the Human Services.*

Barbara J. Friesen is Director of the Research and Training Center on Family Support and Children's Mental Health at Portland State University and Professor of Social Work at the

572

Graduate School of Social Work there. She has conducted several federally funded national projects on partnering with families and communities to better serve children with emotional disorders.

Margaret Gibelman is Professor and Director of the Doctoral Program at Yeshiva University, Wurzweiler School of Social Work. She has published widely in the area of nonprofit organizations, including her most recent book, *The Privatization of Human Services* (with Harold Demone).

David F. Gillespie is a sociologist and Professor at the George Warren Brown School of Social Work. He is the editor of the *Journal of Social Service Research* and a nationally known expert on community response to disasters. His most recent book is *Quantitative Methods in Social Work: State of the Art,* co-edited with Charles Glisson.

Charles Glisson is Professor and Director of the Children's Mental Health Services Research Center at the University of Tennessee, Knoxville. Long a prolific contributor to research and scholarship on human service organizations, he is currently studying the relationship between service-delivery system characteristics and outcomes for dependent children in care.

Yeheskel Hasenfeld is Professor of Social Welfare at the University of California, Los Angeles, School of Public Policy and Social Research. He conducts research on welfare policy and has contributed extensively to the literature on human service organizations, including the recent books *Human Services as Complex Organizations* and *Human Service Organizations*.

Alfreda P. Iglehart is Associate Professor, Department of Social Welfare, School of Public Policy and Social Research. She is co-author of *Social Services and the Ethnic Community* with Dr. Rosina M. Becerra.

Gary F. Koeske is Professor in the School of Social Work, University of Pittsburgh. He has published extensively on the individual attributes, interpersonal processes, and organizational conditions associated with worker job response and performance.

Randi Koeske is Associate Professor, Department of Psychology, University of Pittsburgh-Greensburg. Her research interests include work and student stress, women's health, and the relationship between spirituality and women's coping with trauma experience, about which she is currently writing a book.

Lawrence L. Martin is Associate Professor at the School of Social Work, Columbia University. He has written extensively on human service management, including such recent books as *Measuring the Performance of Human Service Programs* (with Peter Kettner) and *Designing and Managing Programs* (with Robert Moroney and Peter Kettner).

Philip McCallion is an Assistant Professor in the School of Social Welfare at the University at Albany. He practiced as an administrator and had extensive experience with development and fund-raising prior to becoming an academic. In recent years, his scholarly interests have focused on management in the human services.

David Menefee is Associate Professor in the School of Social Work, Columbia University.

He consults widely with human services organizations on building better management systems. In recent years, he has conducted research and written extensively on the nature of management practice in human service organizations.

Rino J. Patti is Professor and Director of the Doctoral Program at the University of Southern California, School of Social Work. He was formerly dean of the school for 9 years and, prior to that, Professor at the University of Washington in Seattle. Throughout his career, his teaching and scholarly interests have focused on the organization and administration of social welfare services, with particular emphasis on the processes and conditions in organizations that produce high-quality, effective social services. Since 1993, he has been the editor of *Administration in Social Work*. He is the author of nearly 50 articles and book chapters and several books, including *Managing for Service Effectiveness in Social Welfare* (with John Poertner and Charles Rapp), *Social Welfare Administration: Managing in a Developmental Context,* and *Change From Within* (with Herman Resnick).

Peter J. Pecora is Manager of Research Services at the Casey Family Program and Professor in the School of Social Work, University of Washington. He is widely known for his work on the evaluation of children's services programs, including *Evaluating Family-Based Services* (with others), and is a leading expert in personnel management in social service agencies. His book with Michael Austin, *Managing Human Services Personnel,* is a well-known reference.

Felice Davidson Perlmutter is Professor, School of Social Administration, Temple University.

She is a frequent contributor to the literature on the management of social welfare organizations. Among recent books are *From Welfare to Work: Corporate Initiatives and Welfare Reform* and *Changing Hats.*

John Poertner is Associate Dean and Professor at the School of Social Work, University of Illinois-Urbana, and an expert in the design and evaluation of children's services. His book, *Social Administration* (with Charles Rapp), is a standard text for management courses in schools of social work around the nation.

Frederic G. Reamer is Professor in the School of Social Work, Rhode Island College. He is widely known for his seminal work on ethics in the professional literature and has recently led the effort by the National Association of Social Workers to revise the profession's code of ethics.

Gary Rosenberg is the Edith J. Baerwald Professor of Community and Preventitive Medicine at the Mount Sinai School of Medicine and Senior Vice President of Mount Sinai NYU Health in New York City. He is editor of the journal *Social Work in Health Care,* and a frequent contributor to the literature on management and evaluation of health care services.

Hillel Schmid is Associate Professor and former Director of the Graduate Program in Management of Community and Nonprofit Organizations and Public Policy at the School of Social Work, the Hebrew University of Jerusalem. He has been a frequent contributor to the literature on the management and organization of human services programs, and nonprofit organizations.

Dick Schoech is Professor at the University of Texas at Arlington, School of Social Work. He has long been a leader in the field of information technology and is currently under contract with the Texas Department of Protective and Regulatory Services to develop employee-performance support systems. He recently published the book *Human Services Technology.*

Jeffrey R. Solomon is President of Andrea and Charles Bronfman Philanthropies and a consultant on strategic management in the nonprofit sector.

Diane Vinokur-Kaplan is Associate Professor at the School of Social Work, University of Michigan. She and her colleagues have analyzed several large studies on predictors of job satisfaction and burnout among human service workers, the results of which have been widely published in the professional literature.

Michael Wagner is the Director of Personnel for the Casey Family Program in Seattle, Washington.

Marie Weil is Berg-Beach Distinguised Professor of Community Practice and Associate Director of the Jordan Institute for Families at the School of Social Work, University of North Carolina, Chapel Hill. She is editor of the *Journal of Community Practice* and has contributed extensively to the literature in the area of management, community organization, and services for families and children.

Andrew Weissman is Clinical Associate Professor in the Department of Community and Preventative Medicine at Mount Sinai School of Medicine and Administator in the Office of the Senior Vice President at Mount Sinai NYU Health in New York City. He is the managing editor of "Social work in Health Care" and has written widely on health care including, recently, "Social Work Leadership in Health Care" (with Gary Rosenberg).

Kathleen H. Wilber is Associate Professor of Gerontology and Public Administration at the University of Southern California. She does research on the organization and management of services for older people and is a frequent contributor to the management literature.